Key to 1:250 000 Maps, atlas pages 86-205

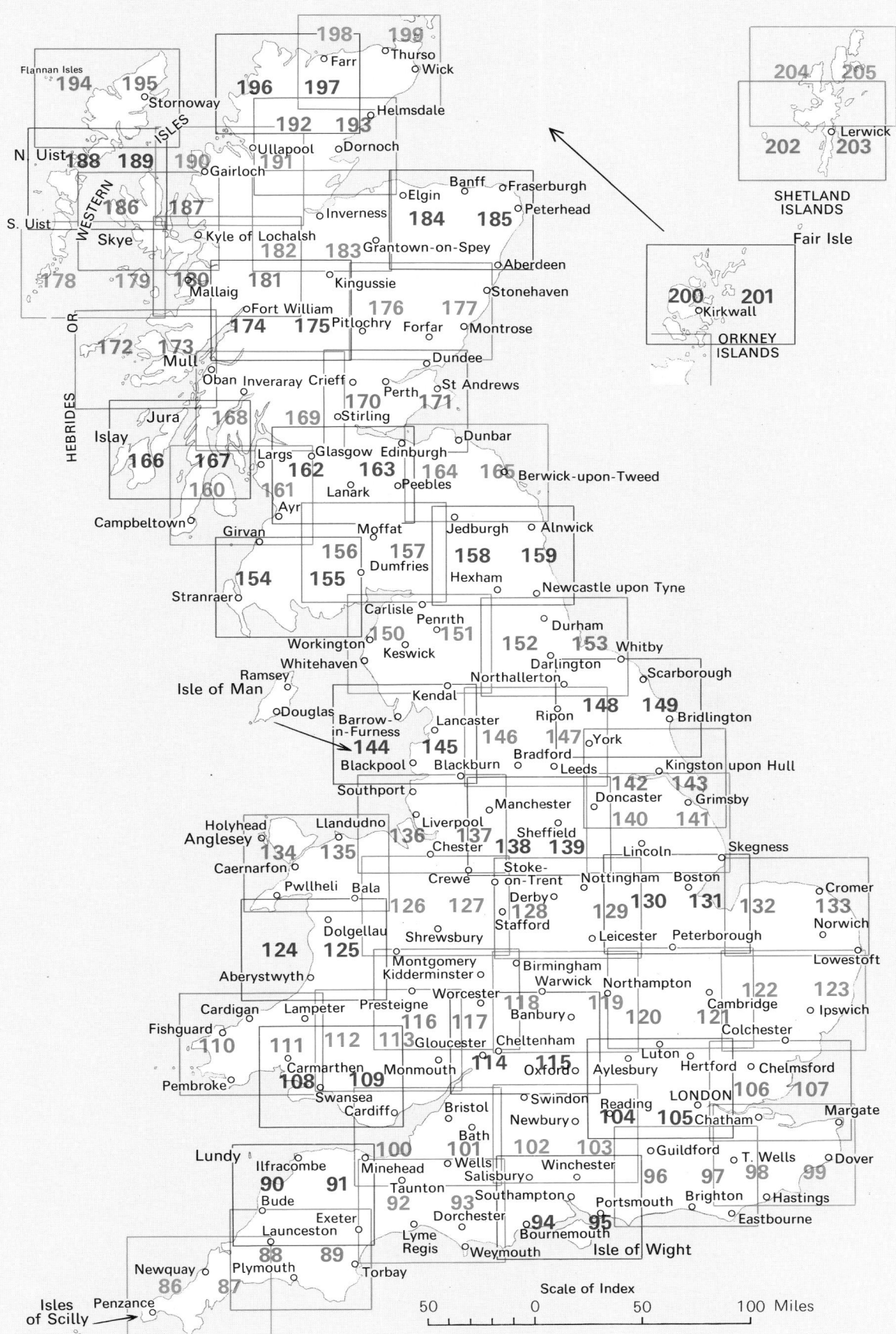

Scale of Index

50   0   50   100 Miles

THE ORDNANCE SURVEY

NATIONAL

ATLAS

OF GREAT BRITAIN

THE ORDNANCE SURVEY

NATIONAL ATLAS

OF GREAT BRITAIN

GUILD PUBLISHING
LONDON

This edition published 1986 by Book Club Associates
by arrangement with
Ordnance Survey   and   Country Life Books
an imprint of
The Hamlyn Publishing Group Limited

1:250 000 maps (pages 86–205), index and endpapers by
Ordnance Survey, Southampton © Crown Copyright 1986

Arrangement and all other material, including national maps
(pages 8–83) © The Hamlyn Publishing Group Limited 1986

Reference section pages 8–83 created by Lionheart Books

Printed and bound by Jarrold and Sons Ltd, Norwich

CONTENTS

A SHORT HISTORY OF THE ORDNANCE SURVEY
The National Mapping Organisation

A contemporary sketch of William Roy's Survey of Scotland.

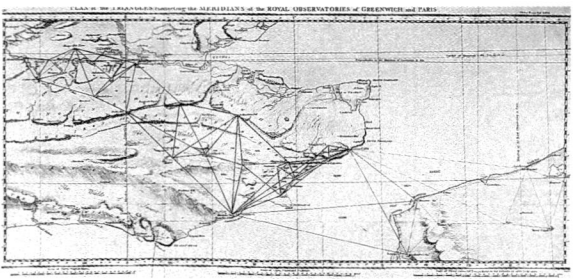

Triangulation connection between the Royal Observatories of Greenwich and Paris – a contemporary map showing the triangulation scheme connecting the Greenwich and Paris meridians; the connection took six years to complete.

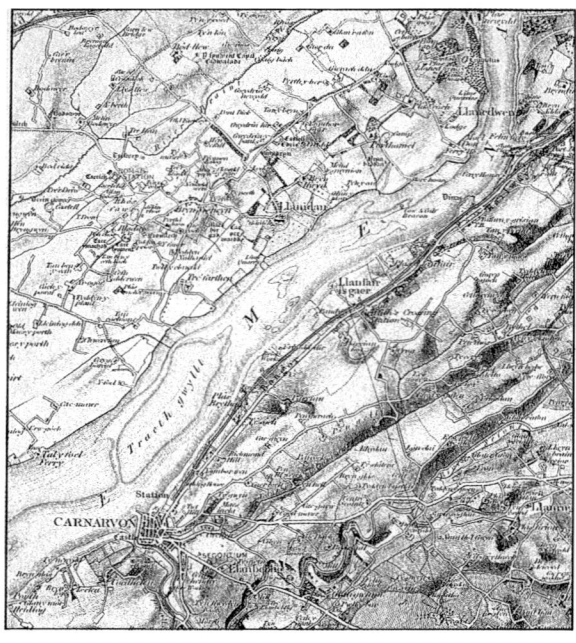

Extract from One-Inch map first published in 1841 – an interesting comparison can be made with the same area shown in the Landranger 2nd Series extract on the next page.

The formation of the Ordnance Survey owes much to the advocacy of General William Roy, a renowned surveyor engineer and archaeologist of the 18th century. As a young man he was responsible for the production of a military map of Scotland following the 1745 Rebellion. Later he directed the first scientific survey operation carried out in Britain; the precise measurement of a survey base line at Hounslow Heath (now London Airport) and the triangulation connection with France. The establishment of a national organisation to be responsible for survey and mapping of the country was not to take shape, however, until after his death in 1790.

In 1791, Britain found itself under threat of invasion from France. The British Army required accurate mapping of the south coast of England for military purposes at 1 inch to 1 mile scale. The survey was carried out by the Board of Ordnance, a Crown organisation, responsible for army engineering, artillery and other armaments at that time. The name Ordnance Survey stems from this time; their first offices in the Tower of London are commemorated today in the Ordnance Survey coat of arms.

As the threat of invasion receded, civilian applications for the mapping were identified. The industrial revolution was under way, with the associated rapid expansion of towns and road and rail networks, and politicians, administrators, civil engineers and others were quick to recognise the value of accurate maps. The survey was gradually extended to cover other areas of the country and Ordnance Survey was given the task of carrying out the work. Moreover, surveys were undertaken to produce maps at much larger scales to give even more detailed and accurate information. There were scientific applications, too, including the mapping of archaeological sites so that by the mid 19th century, Ordnance Survey had assumed its modern role of providing a national survey for scientific, military, government and public use. The authority for many of its activities is the Ordnance Survey Act of 1841.

As urban and industrial development continued, the demand for more detailed large scale maps increased. The original 1 inch to 1 mile series was retained as a general map but in 1840 the scale of 1:10 560 (6 inches to 1 mile) was authorised for the survey of northern England and Scotland which at that time had not been covered by 1 inch to 1 mile scale mapping. It was found, however, that even this scale was inadequate for all purposes, and there then followed a long controversy surrounding the choice of a suitable base scale for maps of Great Britain. This was resolved in 1863 when it was decided to adopt a scale of 1:2500 (25 inches to 1 mile) for cultivated areas, 1:10 560 (6 inches to 1 mile) for uncultivated areas of mountain and moorland and 1:500 (10 feet to 1 mile) for towns of more than 4000 population. Smaller scale maps including the one-inch map were to be derived from these large-scale surveys.

The first 1:2500 scale survey of cultivated areas was completed in 1893 and by 1914 the first revision had been completed. During the period of the 1:2500 survey there were considerable advances in map production, including the introduction of zincography (a process of etching the map image onto zinc plates for printing; previously the image had been transferred to or hand drawn on special smooth limestone blocks), photography and colour printing. The design and content of the mapping also developed in response to technical advances, user demand and economic pressures to stem the rising cost of the national survey. The latter led in 1893 to the abandonment of the 1:500 series of town plans unless locally funded.

Economies were intensified by World War I, and Ordnance Survey, in line with other government organisations suffered considerable cutbacks in manpower and resources, so much so that only revision of large scale maps covering areas of rapid change could be continued. It was unfortunate that these restrictions coincided with government legislation on land registration (1925), town planning (1925), land drainage (1926), slum clearance (1930) and land valuation (1931), all of which in one way or another required accurate mapping for implementation. By the early 1930s it became clear that Ordnance Survey had been left ill-equipped to supply sufficiently accurate maps. A Departmental Committee under the chairmanship of Sir

J C (later Lord) Davidson was set up in 1935 to consider how to restore the effectiveness of the national survey.

Its report, although published in 1938, could not be implemented until after World War II, but it formed the framework on which the present Ordnance Survey was developed. The major recommendations of the Davidson Report included: the introduction of a metric National Grid as a reference system for all large and small scale maps; the recasting of the 1:2500 series on national instead of county lines using a national projection (the method of depicting the earth's surface as a flat plane) rather than separate county projections which had caused problems of fit and accuracy along county borders; the introduction of a system of continuous revision for large scale maps; the testing of a larger 1:1250 (50 inches to 1 mile) scale of survey for densely population urban areas; the trial of a 1:25 000 (2½ inches to 1 mile) medium scale map which, if successful, was to be extended to cover the whole country.

After the war, these recommendations were implemented, with large scale surveys, metric conversion and revision proceeding at 1:1250, 1:2500 and 1:10 000 (6 inches to 1 mile) scales. Smaller scale maps of one inch to one mile, 1:25 000 (2½ inches to 1 mile), 1:250 000 (1 inch to 4 miles) and 1:625 000 (10 miles to 1 inch) were all published as derivations from the large scale surveys. The one-inch national series was converted to 1:50 000 scale in the early 1970s.

Today, Ordnance Survey is a civilian government department with headquarters in Southampton and a network of small local survey offices throughout the country. The resurvey task initiated after World War II in response to the Davidson Report has been completed and the emphasis now is on the revision of this huge archive of survey information, to keep it up-to-date and meet user demand. New technology has been used to aid the surveyors and draughtsmen in their task. An increasing number of Ordnance Survey 1:1250 and 1:2500 maps are being produced using automated cartographic techniques. Information collected and recorded by the surveyor in graphic form is converted by electronic means into digital form and stored in a computer databank. The graphic information is recorded as a series of numerical co-ordinates which identify the precise location of the feature on the ground. Once the information is stored on the computer it can be recalled to produce an exact scale map copy, or a larger scale or smaller scale copy as required. Furthermore, selected detail can be recalled rather than the whole map.

While the techniques of survey and mapping have developed and improved dramatically since the early years of the Ordnance Survey, and are still developing, the customers for accurate detailed maps remain basically the same. Computer generated maps are very much in demand from local government, coal, gas, electricity, water and construction industries and others concerned with the maintenance and development of the infrastructure of Great Britain. Ordnance Survey's objective is to continue to meet this demand as well as satisfying the general public's need for small scale derived mapping for educational, leisure and many other purposes.

Editor's Note
The reference section of this atlas has been compiled with the aim of providing comprehensive and up-to-date information on many aspects of Great Britain in the 1980s, from geology to government, climate to culture. Facts and figures have come from a wide variety of sources and have been interpreted in as objective a manner as possible. The most recent available statistics have been included but since there is often a lapse of some years before figures are published, the year of the latest information will frequently vary from subject to subject and exact comparisons have not always been feasible. The most recent census, for example, was in 1981 so demographic statistics are limited to that date. Metric units have been used throughout for consistency.

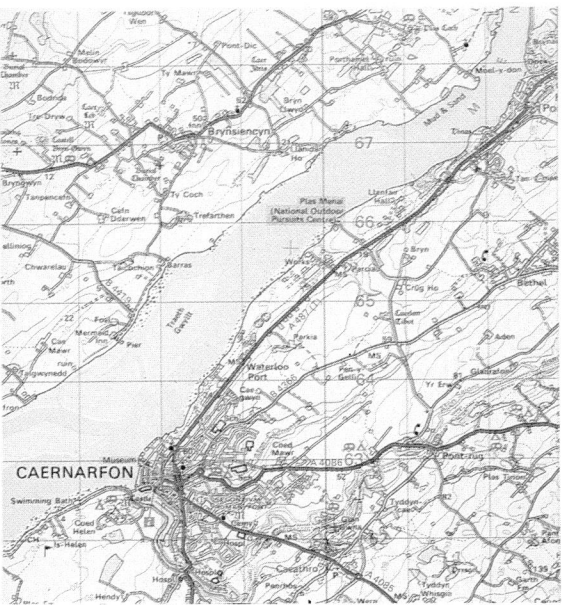

Extract from modern Landranger (1:50 000 scale) map – the dramatic hill shading of the early version shown on the previous page has been softened, towns and villages have grown in size and the spelling of some of the place names has changed.

Modern surveying – using an electromagnetic distance and angle measuring instrument (EDM Geodometer).

EVOLUTION

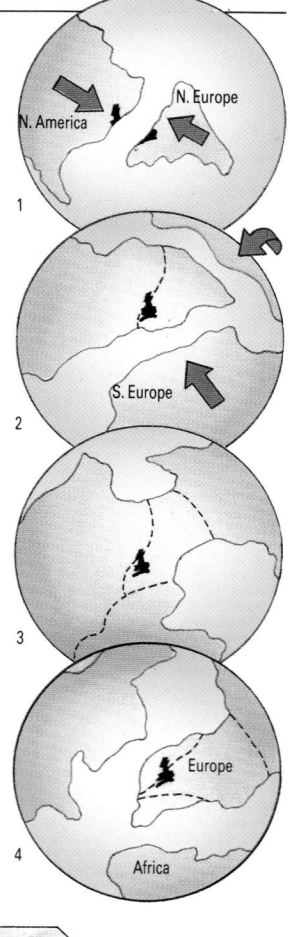

At any time in the geological past, the Britain of today would have been quite unrecognizable. High mountains, deserts, tropical swamps, shallow seas, deep ocean basins, freezing ice-caps – these have all occupied the area where the British Isles now lie. This bewildering array of landscapes supported populations of equally bizarre animals and plants. The proof of all this lies in the rocks all around. In the contorted rocks of Scotland and Wales, the roots of ancient mountain chains are to be found. The same regions also display vast thicknesses of shales, made from mud that once lay at the bottom of former oceans. Coal-measures mark the sites of ancient forests. In the Midlands, sandstones that carry the structures of ancient dunes

[For the complete geological timescale see the map key on page 11.]

show where deserts covered the land 370 million years ago. The shallow-water limestones of England's south coast show trails of footprints where, more than 130 million years ago, dinosaurs walked across limy mudflats looking for forage. The clay of the London basin contains fossils of crocodiles and palm kernels, showing that it was laid down at the mouths of muddy sub-tropical rivers. Throughout Britain, mountains are scarred with U-shaped valleys cut by Ice Age glaciers, and the adjoining lowlands are piled with glacial debris.

Geographical and biological studies of present-day Britain indicate that the land is still evolving and that the climate, landscape, flora and fauna will, in only a few million years, be quite different.

Geography of the past

The drifting of continents has had a profound effect on Britain's geological history. During the Ordovician (1), part of Britain lay on the North American landmass and part on the North European. An ocean lay between. In early Devonian times (2) these two continents collided, forcing up along the join the Caledonian Mountains. By the Permian (3), this combined landmass had fused with that of South Europe. The 'supercontinent' so formed then broke up, and by the Tertiary period (4) Britain was part of what we now call Europe.

Ordovician – 450 million years ago
During the lower Palaeozoic – the Cambrian, Ordovician and Silurian periods – the region that was to become Britain was split in two. The Iapetus Ocean, probably as great in size as the modern Atlantic, lay between them. Gradually the two continental masses moved together, with a great deal of volcanic activity between. Rocks formed in the lower Palaeozoic consist largely of shales.

Devonian – 370 million years ago
In Devonian times the two continents collided, obliterating the Iapetus Ocean and crushing up the vast range of the Caledonian Mountains in between. The northern part of Scotland was then forced into its present position. It was a time of deserts, and most Devonian rocks are desert sandstones. Fossils include, from northern Scotland, the first land-plants and freshwater lake fish, and, in the south, marine creatures.

Carboniferous – 300 million years ago
As the Caledonian Mountains eroded away, shallow seas spread over the area. The eroded debris from the mountains encroached on the seas and produced vast delta swamps, clothed in exotic forests. Mountain-building in northern Europe threw up the Variscan Mountains in the south of the region. The Carboniferous rocks include limestones from the shallow seas and coal deposits from the swamps.

Iapetus Ocean

Caledonian Mountains

Variscan Mountains

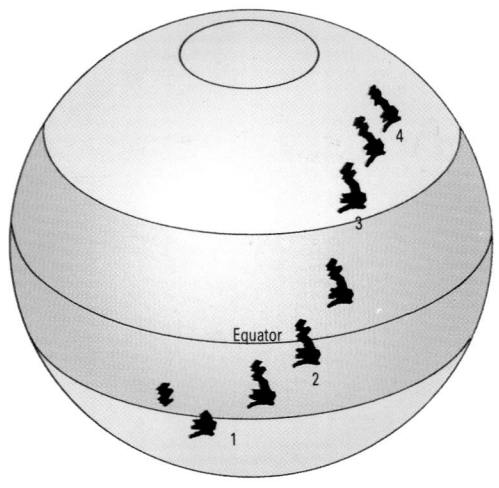

Shifting landmass, changing climate

Britain's climatic history is partly due to the movement of its landmass area across the globe over the past 400 million years. During the Devonian period (1), Britain lay in the southern desert belt of the Earth. By the Carboniferous (2), it lay across the equator, and rain forests flourished. The next period, the Permian (3), found Britain in the northern desert belt, and hot, dry conditions again prevailed. Since then the steady northward movement (4) has produced progressively cooler and moister conditions. (Steps 1 and 3 above correlate with steps 2 and 3 in diagram left.)

Ice Age – 400,000 years ago

The final stamp on the British landscape was placed during the Pleistocene period when, for reasons still unclear, world climate cooled, producing the Ice Age. Ice caps formed on the highlands, and these spread as glaciers into the lowlands, meeting up with ice sheets that reached across the North Sea from Scandinavia. The moving ice sheets modified the scenery significantly. But during the Ice Age there were several glacial phases, separated from one another by interglacial phases with a warmer climate than at present; each phase lasted tens of thousands of years. The map shows the extent of the ice sheet during the most extensive glaciation phase 430,000 to 375,000 years ago.

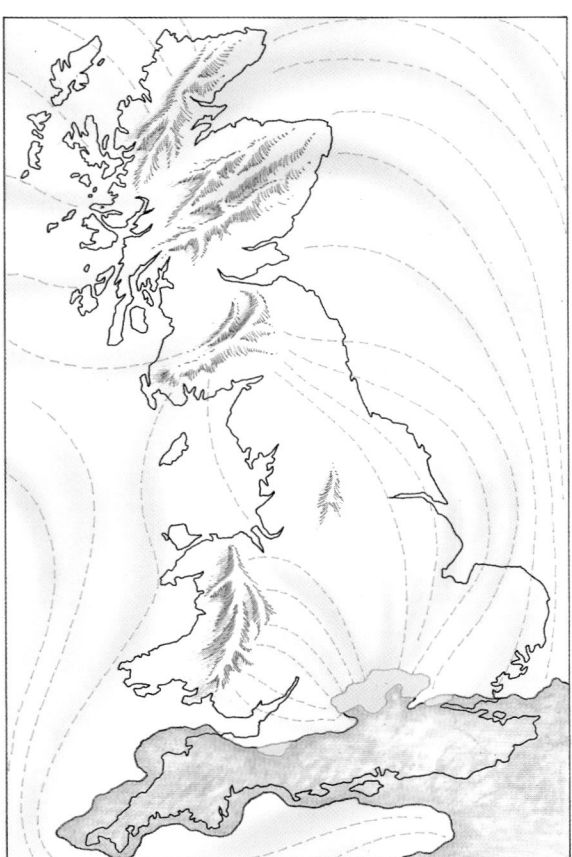

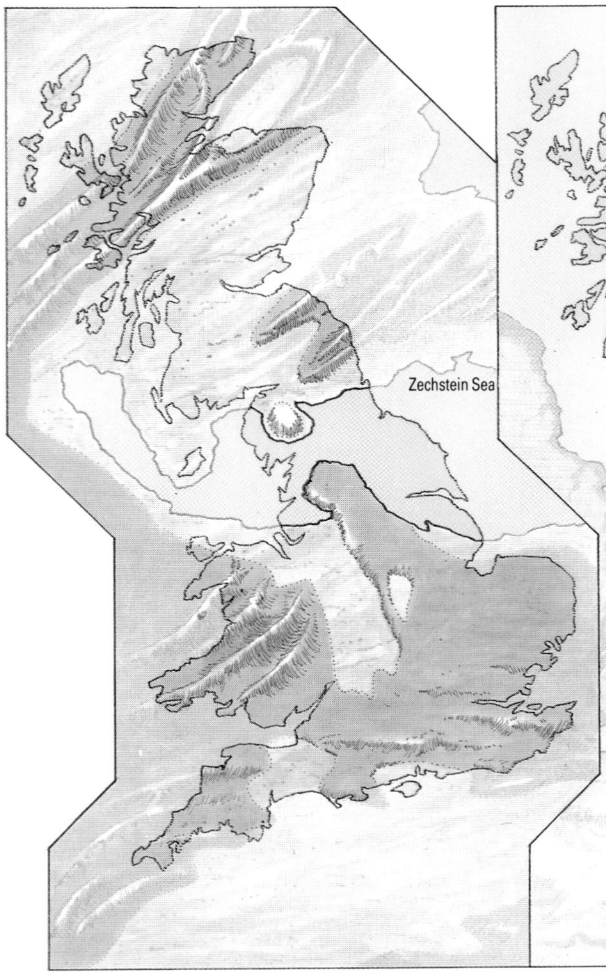

Permian – 250 million years ago

In Permian and Triassic times, another desert period followed. The Variscan Mountains continued to rise and the area of Britain consisted of mountains and desert basins. A shallow inland sea, the Zechstein, spread across from Germany. Gradually the Permian mountains were eroded to Triassic hills. Typical rocks of the time are desert sandstones. The land animals were mostly desert reptiles.

Jurassic – 150 million years ago

The Jurassic and Cretaceous periods had more equable climates. There were few hills now, and the area consisted largely of shallow seas and low wooded islands. The vegetation of conifers and ferns was browsed by dinosaurs. The marine shales and limestones of the time contain fossils of sea reptiles and molluscs. By the end of the Cretaceous the sea covered almost the whole area; deposits of chalk were created.

Lower Tertiary – 60 million years ago

By the Tertiary, the modern distribution of highlands and lowlands had been established. The shallow sea in south-east England was filling up with mud and clay washed in by rivers from the northern and western highlands. There was volcanic activity in Scotland as the newly created Atlantic Ocean continued to widen. Crocodiles and large mammals roamed the subtropical swamps and forests.

GEOLOGY

Probably no area in the world of similar size displays so great a richness and diversity of geological features as does Britain. Examples of most types of rocks, minerals, soils and land forms that exist in the world are to be found somewhere within the landmass of the British Isles.

Old fold mountains stretch south-west to north-east across northern and southern Scotland and Wales. Four hundred million years ago these formed a vast, almost continuous, mountain chain similar in size and form to the modern Himalayas. Now only isolated highland areas remain. Millions of years of weathering and erosion have cut deeply into the contorted sedimentary rocks and exposed the cores. Here the rocks have been subjected to great pressure and heat, creating new, metamorphic rocks, and the molten material forced up in the mountain-building process has solidified into the intrusive igneous rocks.

Evidence of later mountain-building some 280 million years ago lies in the Pennine chain and in the highland areas of Cornwall and Devon that form the heart of the south-west peninsula.

Relatively undisturbed sedimentary rocks form the rest of the country, and stretch out under the North Sea, where they contain great oil reserves. Being laid down in a gradual, sequential manner, the sedimentary rock layers give an unbroken record of events in Britain's geological history from the Carboniferous period onwards.

Although there is no modern volcanic activity in the area, large lava flows that formed less than 50 million years ago lie on the Scottish islands. Fingal's Cave on the Isle of Staffa is a fine example. And the remains of volcanic islands dating from 450 million years ago appear in Wales and in the Lake District. Notable examples are Cader Idris and Snowdon, which are both in Wales.

Igneous rocks are formed from hot molten material – magma – that has cooled and hardened. Sedimentary rocks are formed as fragments of rocks – pebbles, sand and mud particles – are deposited by rivers and seas then cemented together; the pressure of the upper layers forms rock material in the lower layers.

Sedimentary

Igneous

Main geological units
The bedrock of the British Isles, right, can be divided into several major structural units. Large-scale faults and thrusts in the rock layers, representing cracks and shears in the Earth's crust produced by mountain-building activity, can be traced over tens of kilometres.

	Young rock cover – post-Permian period
	Old rock cover – Old Red Sandstone and Carboniferous
	Variscan belt – Devonian and Carboniferous
	Caledonian belt
	Precambrian basement

Sections through the landmass
Contorted and metamorphosed rocks of Scotland (section A) are cut by numerous faults. From North Wales across

to northern England (B), the twisted rocks, more than 400 million years old, give way to gently folded sediments laid down 200 million years later. A section from the

Midlands of England to the Isle of Wight (C) shows rocks gently folded by the same Earth movements that built the Alps far away to the south.

Section A Length of Scotland

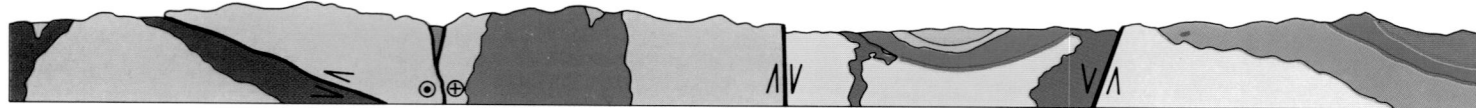

Section B North Wales–Northern England

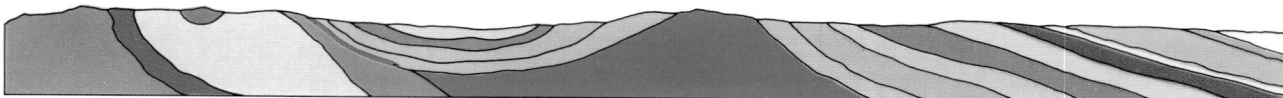

Section C Midlands–Isle of Wight

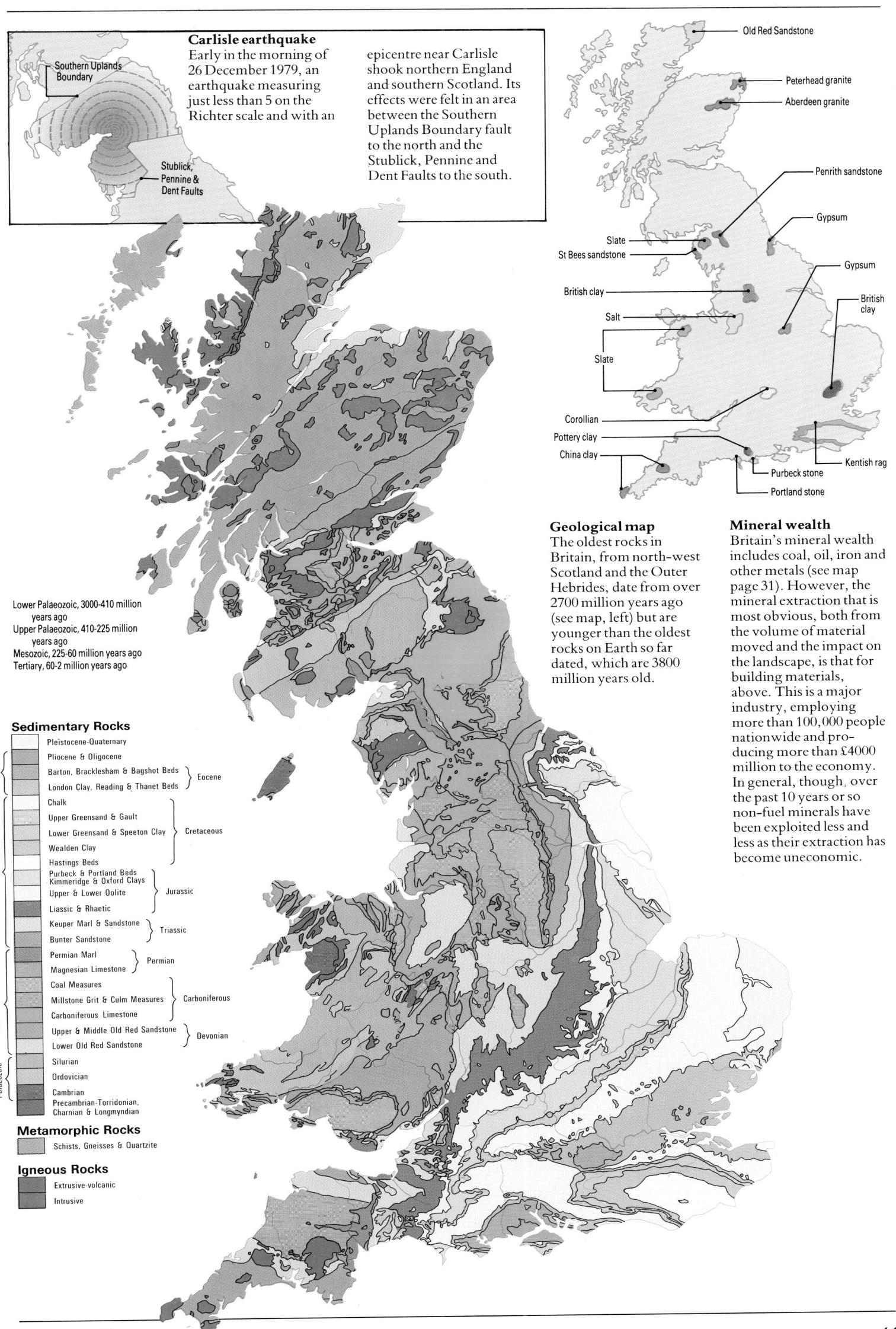

Southern Uplands
Boundary

Stublick,
Pennine &
Dent Faults

Old Red Sandstone

Peterhead granite

Aberdeen granite

Penrith sandstone

Gypsum

Slate
St Bees sandstone

Gypsum

British clay

British
clay

Salt

Slate

Corollian

Pottery clay

China clay

Kentish rag

Purbeck stone

Portland stone

Geological map
The oldest rocks in
Britain, from north-west
Scotland and the Outer
Hebrides, date from over
2700 million years ago
(see map, left) but are
younger than the oldest
rocks on Earth so far
dated, which are 3800
million years old.

Mineral wealth
Britain's mineral wealth
includes coal, oil, iron and
other metals (see map
page 31). However, the
mineral extraction that is
most obvious, both from
the volume of material
moved and the impact on
the landscape, is that for
building materials,
above. This is a major
industry, employing
more than 100,000 people
nationwide and pro-
ducing more than £4000
million to the economy.
In general, though, over
the past 10 years or so
non-fuel minerals have
been exploited less and
less as their extraction has
become uneconomic.

Lower Palaeozoic, 3000-410 million
      years ago
Upper Palaeozoic, 410-225 million
      years ago
Mesozoic, 225-60 million years ago
Tertiary, 60-2 million years ago

Sedimentary Rocks

Tertiary	Pleistocene-Quaternary
	Pliocene & Oligocene
	Barton, Bracklesham & Bagshot Beds — Eocene
	London Clay, Reading & Thanet Beds
Mesozoic	Chalk
	Upper Greensand & Gault
	Lower Greensand & Speeton Clay — Cretaceous
	Wealden Clay
	Hastings Beds
	Purbeck & Portland Beds
	Kimmeridge & Oxford Clays
	Upper & Lower Oolite — Jurassic
	Liassic & Rhaetic
	Keuper Marl & Sandstone — Triassic
	Bunter Sandstone
Upper Palaeozoic	Permian Marl — Permian
	Magnesian Limestone
	Coal Measures
	Millstone Grit & Culm Measures — Carboniferous
	Carboniferous Limestone
	Upper & Middle Old Red Sandstone — Devonian
	Lower Old Red Sandstone
Lower Palaeozoic	Silurian
	Ordovician
	Cambrian
	Precambrian-Torridonian, Charnian & Longmyndian

Metamorphic Rocks

Schists, Gneisses & Quartzite

Igneous Rocks

Extrusive-volcanic

Intrusive

11

PHYSICAL GEOGRAPHY

The landscape of Britain is determined primarily by the geology of the area. The different types of underlying rock, laid down during the great Earth movements of the past, produce different kinds of countryside. Hard granites form high moorland dotted with crumbling castle-like tors, as in Exmoor and Dartmoor. Chalk gives rise to undulating downs cut by dry valleys, scenery so typical of Hampshire, Sussex and Kent. Clay produces flat poorly drained grassland, for which East Anglia is renowned.

Some Earth movements and their effects on Britain's physical geography are still going on today. For example, it is only about 10,000 years ago that the glaciers of the last Ice Age retreated. Once a great weight, such as that of ice, is removed, the Earth's crust springs up again. This rebound is still happening in the north of the country, lifting Scotland slowly out of the ocean, and is balanced by a general subsidence in the south, where flooded river valleys along England's south coast are becoming inlets of the sea.

Superimposed on all this are the effects on the landscape of the weather and the ocean. Rain, wind and frost are gradually breaking down all exposed rocks, especially in hilly and mountainous areas, and the rivers are transporting the debris down towards the lowland plains and the sea. The waves and winds of the ocean are attacking and breaking up the rocks and headlands, and transporting the broken material away to form new beaches. The landscape is constantly changing.

The work of rivers

In its youthful stage, near its source in the mountains, a river erodes the underlying rock, forming a V-shaped valley. In its mature stage, it is moving fast enough to transport rock debris and gently erode its bed. It cuts a winding valley across the land. Where river bends get silted up, it changes course. In its old age, the river deposits the material it has carried from the uplands. Round Britain, most rivers eventually enter estuaries with strong tides that carry the debris seawards.

The scenery of glaciation

For most of the past two million years Britain was subjected to the effects of an Ice Age. At times, the average annual temperature fell to −9°C and ice sheets more than 1000 m thick extended southwards as far as London in the east and to the Channel in the south. Movements of the ice sheets and the valley glaciers ripped great volumes of rocky material from the uplands, producing scoured surfaces and deep U-shaped valleys, as in the Welsh and Cumbrian mountains. When the glaciers melted all this transported material was left as sandy mounds, gravelly banks and thick layers of boulder clay on the lower land. Huge boulders torn from their outcrops were left stranded tens of kilometres away.

At Ingleborough in the Pennines a large block of rock lies stranded in a curious position. Such 'erratics' indicate glacial action – wind and water cannot move such large masses.

Highest, largest, longest

In Britain, the term mountain is used only for land which rises above 600 m. The rugged topography of the Grampians, Welsh and Cumbrian mountains produces not only the highest peaks – the diagram, right, shows the four or five highest for Scotland, Wales and England – but also the largest lakes and the sources of the longest rivers.

BEN NEVIS 1343
BEN MACDUI 1311
BRAERIACH 1294
CAIRN TOUL 1292
CAIRN GORM 1244
SNOWDON 1085
CARNEDD LLEWELYN 1062
CARNEDD DAFYDD 1066
GLYDER FAWR 999
GLYDER FÂCH 994
SCAFELL PIKES 969
SCA FELL 963
HELVELLYN 950
SKIDDAW 930
BOW FELL 902

MOUNTAINS (HEIGHT m)

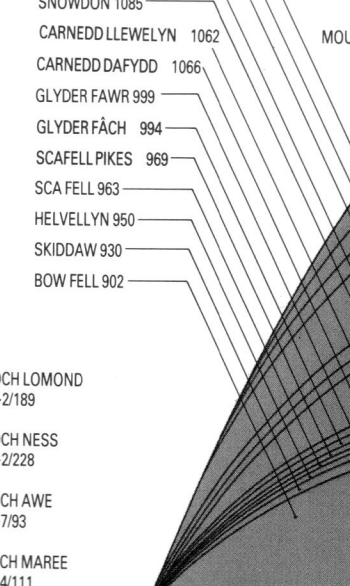

LAKES (AREA km²/DEPTH m)

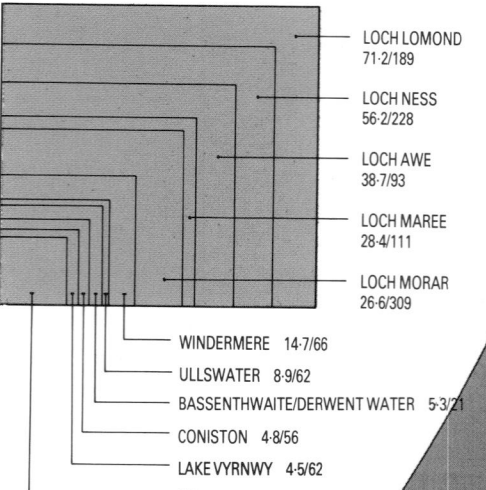

LOCH LOMOND 71·2/189
LOCH NESS 56·2/228
LOCH AWE 38·7/93
LOCH MAREE 28·4/111
LOCH MORAR 26·6/309
WINDERMERE 14·7/66
ULLSWATER 8·9/62
BASSENTHWAITE/DERWENT WATER 5·3/21
CONISTON 4·8/56
LAKE VYRNWY 4·5/62
BALA LAKE 4·3/38

SPEY 157
CLYDE 158
NENE 161
TAY 188
WYE 215
GREAT OUSE 230
AIRE-HUMBER 260
TRENT 300
THAMES 346
SEVERN 354

RIVERS (LENGTH km)

Highland and lowland zones

A section N-S through Britain, below (see main map for position of the section line), shows that the older deformed rocks in the centre of the ancient Caledonian mountain chain have survived as rugged uplands and the younger relatively undisturbed rocks of south-east England have produced flat plains or, at most, gentle downlands.

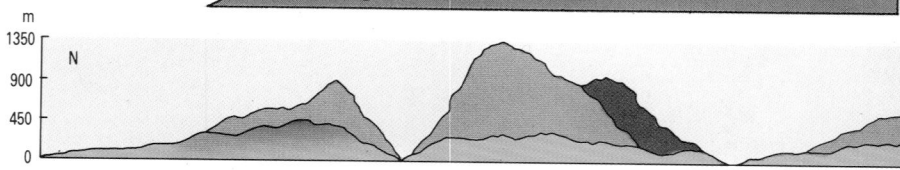

m
1350
900
450
0

N

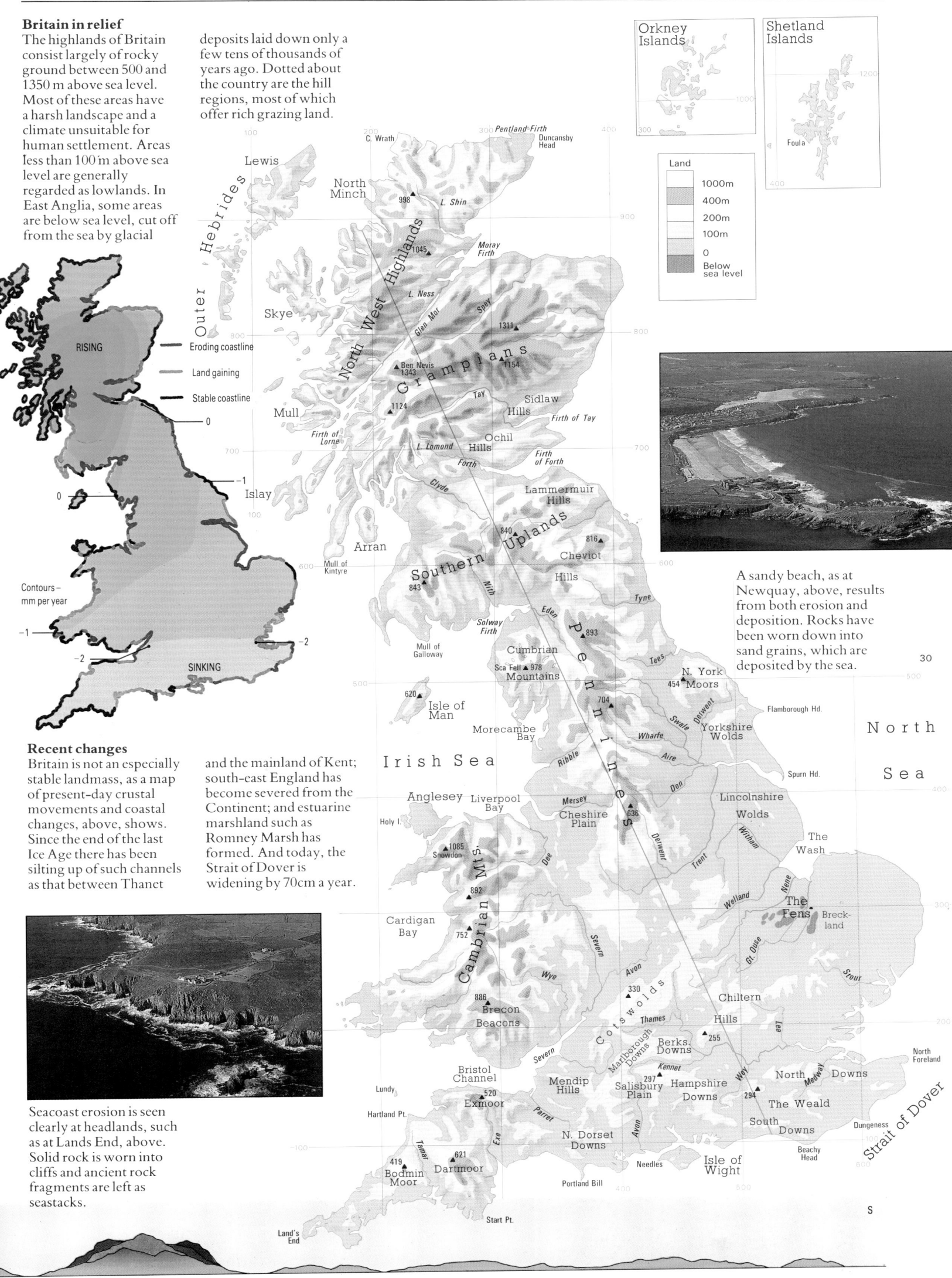

Britain in relief

The highlands of Britain consist largely of rocky ground between 500 and 1350 m above sea level. Most of these areas have a harsh landscape and a climate unsuitable for human settlement. Areas less than 100 m above sea level are generally regarded as lowlands. In East Anglia, some areas are below sea level, cut off from the sea by glacial deposits laid down only a few tens of thousands of years ago. Dotted about the country are the hill regions, most of which offer rich grazing land.

RISING

Eroding coastline
Land gaining
Stable coastline

0

−1

0

−2

Contours −
mm per year

−1

−2

SINKING

Recent changes

Britain is not an especially stable landmass, as a map of present-day crustal movements and coastal changes, above, shows. Since the end of the last Ice Age there has been silting up of such channels as that between Thanet and the mainland of Kent; south-east England has become severed from the Continent; and estuarine marshland such as Romney Marsh has formed. And today, the Strait of Dover is widening by 70cm a year.

Seacoast erosion is seen clearly at headlands, such as at Lands End, above. Solid rock is worn into cliffs and ancient rock fragments are left as seastacks.

Orkney Islands

Shetland Islands

Foula

Land
1000m
400m
200m
100m
0
Below sea level

A sandy beach, as at Newquay, above, results from both erosion and deposition. Rocks have been worn down into sand grains, which are deposited by the sea.

Outer Hebrides
Lewis
C. Wrath
North Minch
Pentland Firth
Duncansby Head
998
L. Shin
1045
Moray Firth
Skye
L. Ness
Spey
Glen. Mor
1311
North West Highlands
Grampians
Ben Nevis 1343
1154
1124
Tay
Sidlaw Hills
Firth of Tay
Mull
Firth of Lorne
Ochil Hills
L. Lomond
Forth
Firth of Forth
Arran
Clyde
Lammermuir Hills
Southern Uplands
840
816
Cheviot Hills
Mull of Kintyre
843
Nith
Solway Firth
Eden
Tyne
Mull of Galloway
Cumbrian Mountains
893
Sca Fell 978
Tees
Pennines
N. York Moors
454
620
Isle of Man
704
Swale
Derwent
Yorkshire Wolds
Flamborough Hd.
Morecambe Bay
Wharfe
Aire
Spurn Hd.
Irish Sea
Ribble
Anglesey
Liverpool Bay
Mersey
636
Don
Lincolnshire Wolds
Holy I.
Cheshire Plain
Derwent
The Wash
1085
Snowdon
Trent
Witham
892
Dee
Welland
Nene
The Fens
Breckland
Cambrian Mts.
Cardigan Bay
752
Severn
Avon
Gt. Ouse
Stour
886
Wye
330
Cotswolds
Chiltern Hills
255
Brecon Beacons
Thames
Marlborough Downs
Berks. Downs
Kennet
North Downs
Medway
Severn
297
Hampshire Downs
294
The Weald
Lundy
Bristol Channel
520
Mendip Hills
Salisbury Plain
Avon
South Downs
Dungeness
Hartland Pt.
Exmoor
Parret
N. Dorset Downs
Beachy Head
Exe
Needles
Isle of Wight
North Foreland
Tamar
621
Portland Bill
Strait of Dover
419
Bodmin Moor
Dartmoor
Start Pt.
Land's End

North Sea

30

S

CLIMATE

Britain has a temperate climate. The reason for this is twofold. First, the surrounding sea acts as a temperature buffer. Water tends to take longer to heat up and to cool down than does both land and air so that in general the sea is cooler than the land in summer and warmer in winter, and coastal areas can experience cool conditions when inland it is warm and vice versa. Second, Britain lies in the latitudes that come under the influences of both the warm air moving northwards from the tropics and the cold air sweeping down from the North Pole. The prevailing winds resulting from the inter-action of these two air masses are either warm south-westerlies or cold north-easterlies. The Gulf Stream, which carries warm water from the tropics to the Arctic, has a moderating effect along Britain's west coast but its overall influence is minor.

The turbulence between the polar and tropical air masses produces 'frontal systems'. A front is a boundary between two distinct and opposing masses of air. As a front passes over a particular place it brings with it constantly changing conditions of temperature, cloud cover and rainfall. These fluctuating conditions, so typical in Britain, constitute 'the weather'.

In general terms, in winter the west of Britain is warmer than the east, and in summer the south is warmer than the north. The south-east shows the greatest contrasts in temperature. The west has more rainfall than the south, while in some parts of the east most of the annual rainfall occurs during the summer months.

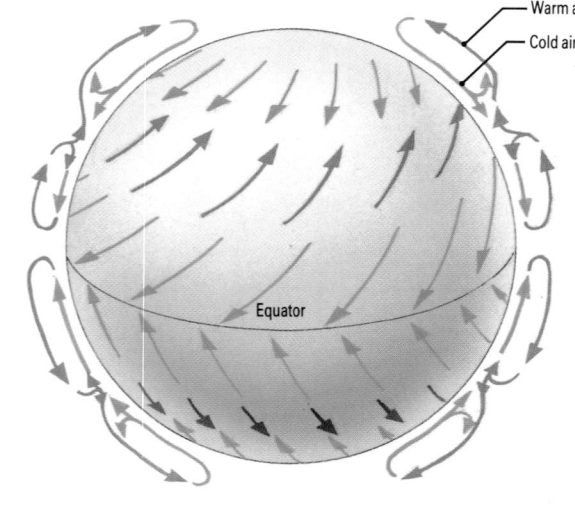

Warm air
Cold air

Equator

Global air circulation
Warm air is constantly rising at the equator. It then moves north and south at high altitudes. When this air becomes cool, it descends. This is near the tropics. In the Northern Hemisphere, some of the air then spreads southwards and some moves further northwards. Cold air from the North Pole is spreading outwards, and the two air masses meet over Britain. However, the turning of the Earth deflects northerly and southerly winds east and west respectively.

▲▲▲ Cold front
◖◖◖ Occluded front
◗◗◗ Warm front

Frontal systems
Cold and warm air masses do not mix but slide past each other, producing fronts. The friction between the air masses creates eddies, with the opposing fronts swirling around and competing against each other. As each eddy develops (see diagram), successive cold and warm fronts pass over the land.

Depressions or rain areas
Frontal systems passing over Britain tend to have a common history. The cold north-east and warm south-west winds meet over the Atlantic Ocean. As they slide past one another they begin to curl round, the north-easterlies turning southwards forming a cold front and the south-westerlies turning northwards forming a warm front. The winds spiral inwards towards a low-pressure area at the apex of the two fronts. This whole system drifts eastwards over Britain as the Earth turns on its axis. From the ground, the approach of a warm front can be seen by a sequence of high-, medium-, then low-altitude clouds coming from the west. As the warm front itself passes over, there is usually rainfall. This is followed by a settled warm spell as the warm air mass moves over. The cold front then passes, bringing with it rain and a drop in temperature.

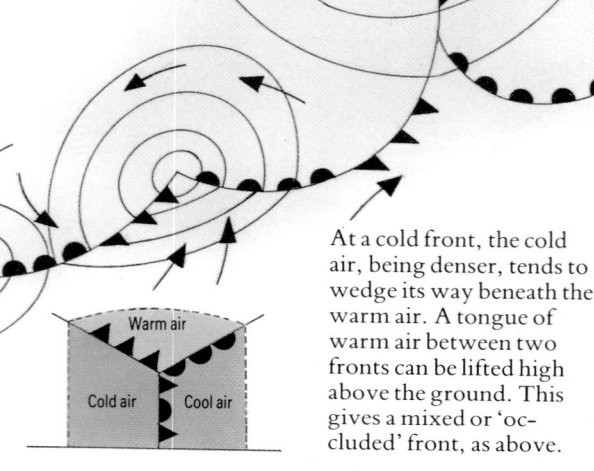

Warm air

Cold air   Cool air

At a cold front, the cold air, being denser, tends to wedge its way beneath the warm air. A tongue of warm air between two fronts can be lifted high above the ground. This gives a mixed or 'oc-cluded' front, as above.

Frontal systems approach Britain from the south-west. The winds within a system, however, always spiral into its centre and so they blow from different points of the compass depending on where in the system they are. Hence, as a frontal system passes, the winds blow, in succession, from the south, the west and finally the north.

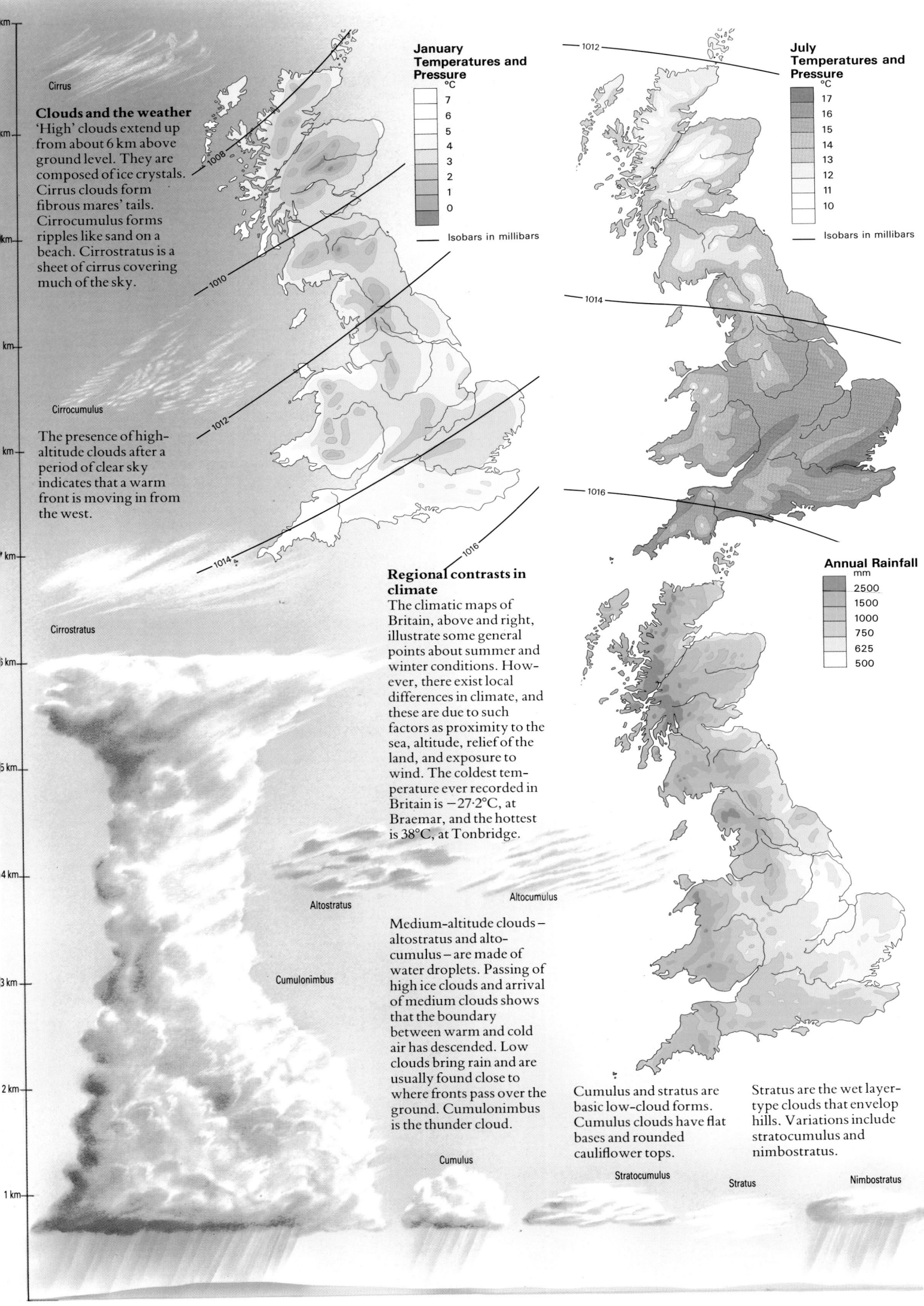

Clouds and the weather
'High' clouds extend up from about 6 km above ground level. They are composed of ice crystals. Cirrus clouds form fibrous mares' tails. Cirrocumulus forms ripples like sand on a beach. Cirrostratus is a sheet of cirrus covering much of the sky.

The presence of high-altitude clouds after a period of clear sky indicates that a warm front is moving in from the west.

Cirrus

Cirrocumulus

Cirrostratus

Altostratus

Cumulonimbus

Altocumulus

Cumulus

Stratocumulus

Stratus

Nimbostratus

January Temperatures and Pressure
°C
7
6
5
4
3
2
1
0

——— Isobars in millibars

July Temperatures and Pressure
°C
17
16
15
14
13
12
11
10

——— Isobars in millibars

Annual Rainfall
mm
2500
1500
1000
750
625
500

Regional contrasts in climate
The climatic maps of Britain, above and right, illustrate some general points about summer and winter conditions. However, there exist local differences in climate, and these are due to such factors as proximity to the sea, altitude, relief of the land, and exposure to wind. The coldest temperature ever recorded in Britain is −27·2°C, at Braemar, and the hottest is 38°C, at Tonbridge.

Medium-altitude clouds – altostratus and alto-cumulus – are made of water droplets. Passing of high ice clouds and arrival of medium clouds shows that the boundary between warm and cold air has descended. Low clouds bring rain and are usually found close to where fronts pass over the ground. Cumulonimbus is the thunder cloud.

Cumulus and stratus are basic low-cloud forms. Cumulus clouds have flat bases and rounded cauliflower tops.

Stratus are the wet layer-type clouds that envelop hills. Variations include stratocumulus and nimbostratus.

NATURAL HABITATS

The geological evolution of Britain, its rock structure, physical geography and climate have all worked together to produce its natural habitats. Soils have been formed by breakdown of the rocks by ice, water and wind and the addition of organic material from living creatures. The nature of the soil and the climate determine which plants can grow in a particular area. The vegetation then gives rise to the animal life.

In every habitat, each living creature depends upon another. The plants use the energy of sunlight to build up foodstuffs from carbon dioxide in the air and water and nutrients drawn up from the soil. A plant's food is for its own use, but inevitably plant-eating animals come and take it. These animals are chased and eaten by predators which may, in turn, be eaten by other predators. Every plant that is not grazed and animal that is not hunted to death eventually dies. When it does, its remains are eaten by scavenging creatures and broken down by decomposing organisms such as fungi and bacteria. This results in carbon dioxide being returned to the atmosphere and nutrients to the soil, and so the cycle of life continues.

Although not a stable condition, as animals and plants struggle for survival, it is the natural one. However, human beings disrupt the simple cycle. Ever since large-scale farming started in Britain, some 4500 years ago, the natural vegetation of the land has been gradually transformed. Today, open landscape continues to be turned into farmland or given over to urban development.

Dominant layer

Shrub layer

Under-growth

Humus layer

Topsoil

Subsoil

Weathered rock

Bedrock

Habitat composition
Taking as an example a forest, trees form the dominant layer. Then come varying amounts of lower shrub and under-growth. Humus, on the surface of the soil, consists of organic material. Plant roots and soil animals lie in the topsoil layer. Pebbles and stones lie on the bedrock.

Sun

Nutrients in the soil

Plants

Primary consumers (herbivores)

Secondary consumers (1st order predators)

Tertiary consumers (2nd order predators)

Scavengers and decomposers

Mixed habitats
Britain has a very wide variety of natural environments. In many places, such as here at Wicken Fen, different habitats can be found close to one another.

Food chains
Food chains – living systems in which energy is passed around by one creature eating another – are found in every habitat. In each example of habitat shown opposite some of the representative creatures are illustrated, colour-coded to indicate their position on the generalized food chain shown left.

Soil types
Soil – the loose substance that covers rocks – consists of a complex mixture of rocky and biological materials, worked on by weather and burrowing organisms. In Britain many different types are to be found. Cambisol is little altered from the original rock. Rendzina is a thin soil found over limestone. Gleysol is a grey, wet muddy soil formed from unconsolidated sediments. Fluvisol is found in river valleys and has an organic-rich surface. Luvisol is wet and clayey. Histosol is mostly peat. Podsol has a cemented layer and is found on hills. Arenosol is pale and sandy. Ranker is a dark soil on hard rocky slopes. The names are mostly Russian in origin, a legacy of where most pioneering soil study was done.

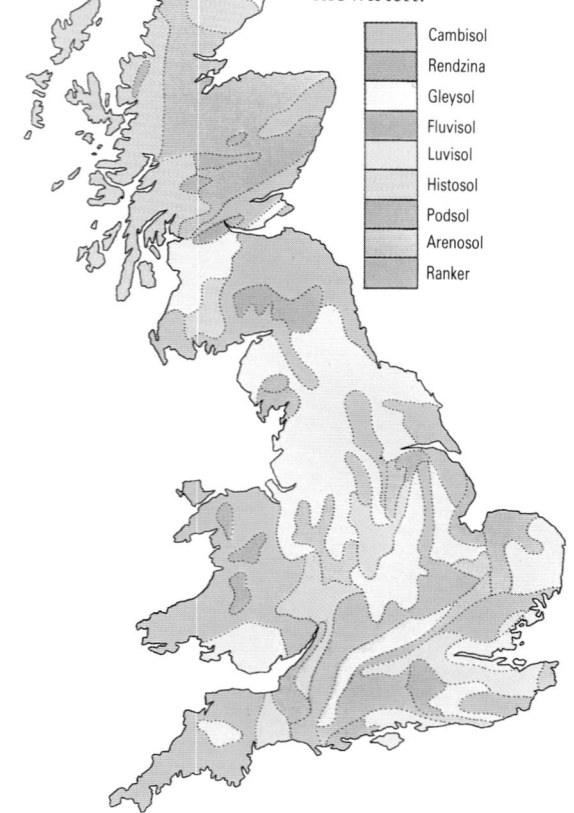

Cambisol
Rendzina
Gleysol
Fluvisol
Luvisol
Histosol
Podsol
Arenosol
Ranker

Birch scrub

The rocky northern isles of Scotland support only scrubby woodlands of birch and mountain ash, with an undergrowth of bracken and heather. The open nature of the habitat encourages birds of prey, giving them a clear view of the ground and its inhabitants.

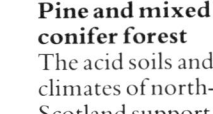
Kestrel

Wood mouse

Ground beetle

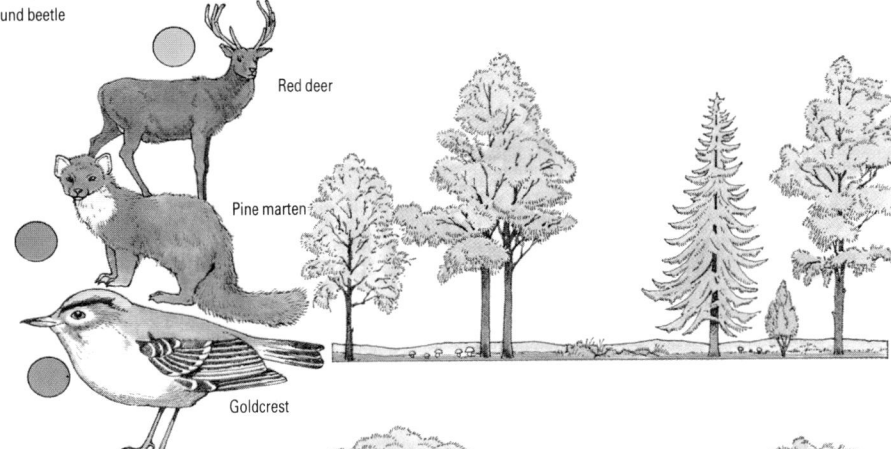
Red deer

Pine marten

Goldcrest

Potential vegetation

The map below gives an idea of the type of vegetation expected across Britain if the land was relatively free of human interference. This is very theoretical since all natural habitats have been broken up and in places completely destroyed; they are now impossible to map accurately.

Pine and mixed conifer forest

The acid soils and the cool climates of north-east Scotland support hardy coniferous trees. The fall of needles from such trees produces a deep ground-litter that decomposes only slowly; the lack of humus sometimes yields little undergrowth.

Deciduous forest

The traditional woodland of most of Britain consists of oak, ash and, in the south, beech. Such forests produce a vigorous shrub layer and undergrowth. The rich variety of plants supports many different animals.

Tawny owl

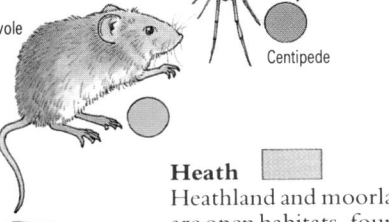
Bank vole

Centipede

Buzzard

Heath

Heathland and moorland are open habitats, found on sandy and peaty soil respectively. Heather and bracken are typical large plants, with mosses and lichens providing the undergrowth. The sunny aspect of these open lands encourages reptiles.

Common lizard

Bumble bee

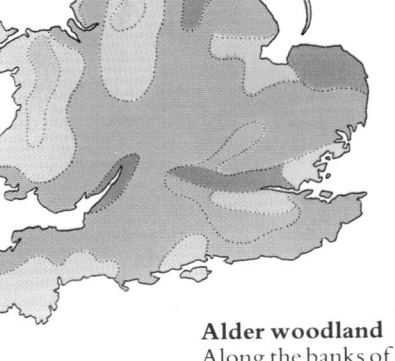

Oak & beech forest

Mountain vegetation (not illustrated)

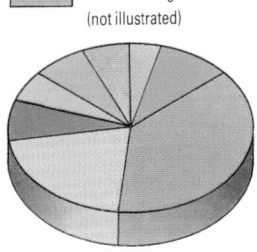

Proportion of each natural habitat type

In the Middle Ages, forests occupied more than 35% of the land. Today they account for less than 10% and only a few isolated ancient forest areas remain; Epping Forest, Essex, is a good example.

Alder woodland

Along the banks of rivers the main trees are water-loving types such as alder and willow. Rushes and sedges grow in wet areas. Aquatic birds, like herons and ducks, feed on the animals and plants that are found in still and flowing water.

Dragonfly

Heron

Mallard

Salt marshes

Tidal areas support hardy plants that can survive immersion both in salt water and fresh, and also frequent drying. Tough grasses colonize salty mudbanks, and wading birds probe for burrowing invertebrates in the open mudflats.

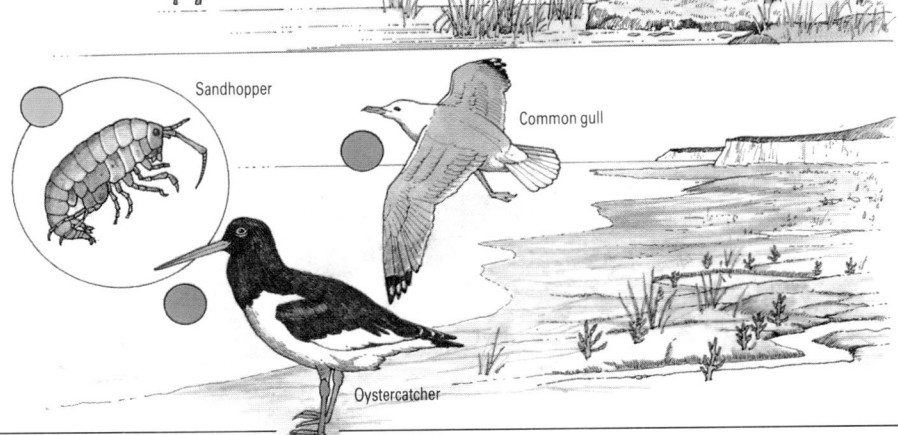
Sandhopper

Common gull

Oystercatcher

BRITAIN IN THE MID-18TH CENTURY

In 1750 Britain was still a traditional, agrarian society, as yet untouched by the upheavals of industrialisation. The great majority of people were poor and lived and worked on the land, like their ancestors before them. Only about one-tenth of the population lived in towns or cities, of which London with its 750,000 or so inhabitants was by far the largest. Since the Civil War of the 17th century, power rested no longer with the monarchy, but with a government dominated by aristocratic landowners, whose interests determined policy at home and abroad.

Aggressive imperial expansion abroad gave Britain a lead in international trade, opened up new markets and stimulated the growth of the navy. In the New World, sugar and cotton plantations worked by slaves yielded huge profits for their British owners, as did the slave trade itself.

At home, where slavery was illegal, the number of impoverished rural labourers increased as larger, more productive, landholdings were created, backed by the force of law. The Enclosure Acts cleared wasteland, common pasture and woodland, and deprived villagers of their traditional rights to collect wood, graze animals and set traps. Severe trespass and game laws were passed to protect private property. Slowly, the British peasantry began to disappear as the smaller landowners were squeezed out of the market.

This was a period that saw the traditional self-sufficiency and barter of rural life replaced by a cash economy and widespread distribution of basic commodities. Artisans and traders of all kinds found an expanding market for their goods, and the growth of transportation gradually led to improvements in the roads and waterways.

At home and abroad, the pursuit of profit brought with it a steady accumulation of capital. In trade and commerce a new middle class was developing, while changes on the land created a labour surplus. These were the preconditions for the industrial revolution that was soon to transform British society.

Parliament

Parliament consisted of a small, powerful House of Lords and a House of Commons elected by a tiny fraction of the adult male population. As members were not paid, both chambers were run by rich merchants, bankers and landowners, whose interests predominated. Many towns, including Birmingham, Manchester, Sheffield and Leeds, were not represented at all. Scotland had only one more MP than Cornwall. Some of the rural boroughs represented had only a handful of voters. They became known as rotten boroughs. Each county returned two MPs, irrespective of size. Voting was not secret, and bribery and intimidation were rife.

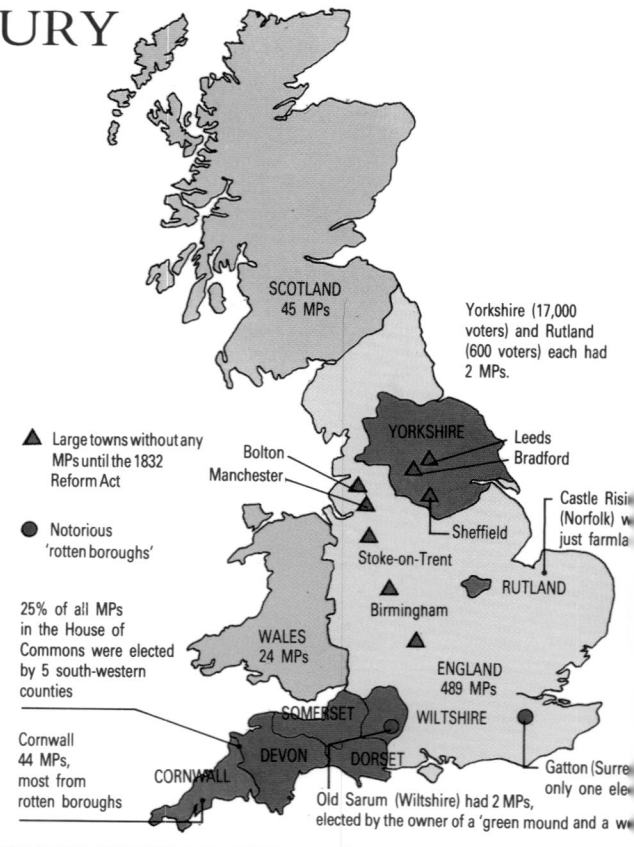

SCOTLAND 45 MPs

Yorkshire (17,000 voters) and Rutland (600 voters) each had 2 MPs.

▲ Large towns without any MPs until the 1832 Reform Act

● Notorious 'rotten boroughs'

25% of all MPs in the House of Commons were elected by 5 south-western counties

YORKSHIRE — Leeds, Bradford
Bolton
Manchester
Sheffield
Stoke-on-Trent
Castle Risi (Norfolk) w just farmla
RUTLAND
Birmingham
WALES 24 MPs
ENGLAND 489 MPs
SOMERSET WILTSHIRE
DEVON DORSET
Gatton (Surre only one ele
Cornwall 44 MPs, most from rotten boroughs
CORNWALL
Old Sarum (Wiltshire) had 2 MPs, elected by the owner of a 'green mound and a w

The urban and rural poor

Food, mainly cereals, absorbed much of the income of the poor. They hardly ever ate meat, and their clothes were home-made or cast offs from the local gentry. When bad harvests pushed up the price of bread, people took to the streets (left).

A third of the population lived in villages or small market towns in the agricultural belt across the middle of Britain. For landless labourers (below) the seasonal nature of the work kept them and their families in great poverty.

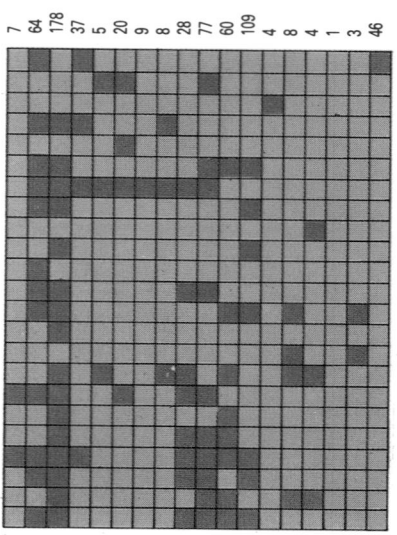

Overseas trade

The Navigation Acts of the 17th century ensured that all trade between Britain and its colonies was carried on by British ships. The colonies could buy their manufactured goods only from Britain, and they were forbidden to sell outside the Empire. Consequently, goods that arrived at British ports from the colonies were often re-exported to Europe at a great profit. Newcastle, like other small ports, also imported a variety of goods from Europe, in return exporting cloth and sometimes coal. Complicated trade regulations and high customs duties led to widespread smuggling.

Imports to Newcastle upon Tyne 1744

	Belgium	Holland	Germany	France	Jersey	Italy	Spain	Portugal	Sweden	Norway	Russia	Denmark	Turkey	Africa	East Indies	USA	S. America	Canada
No. ships	7	64	178	37	5	20	9	8	28	77	60	109	4	8	4	1	3	46

Apples and pears
Oranges
Currants, grapes
Onions
Nuts
Grain
Wine
Spirits
Sugar
Beef, pork
Cheese
Bones
Hides, horses, hoofs
Sealskins
Guano
Timber
Bark
Flax, hemp
Rope
Mats
Oil cake
Linseed
Grease

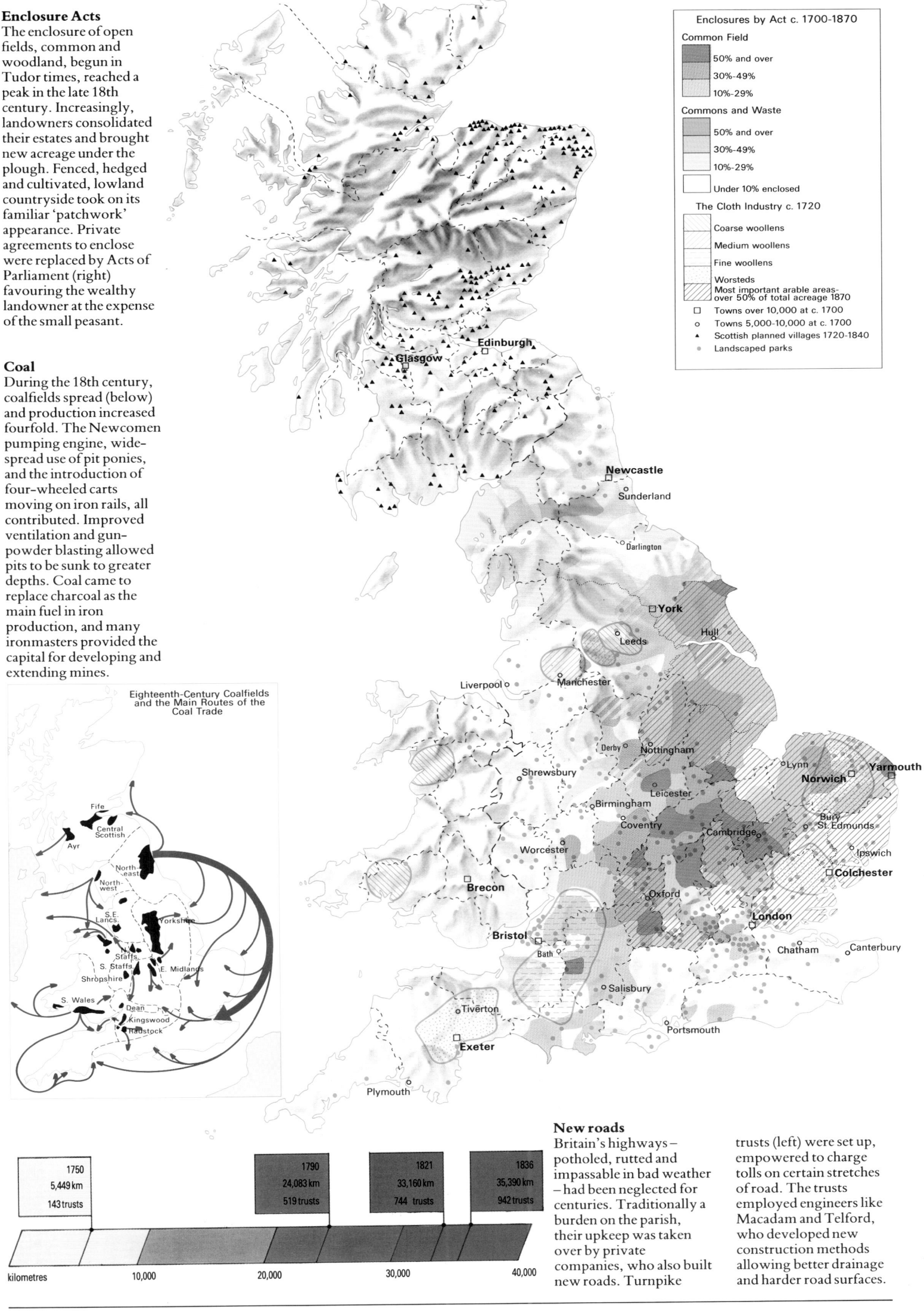

Enclosure Acts

The enclosure of open fields, common and woodland, begun in Tudor times, reached a peak in the late 18th century. Increasingly, landowners consolidated their estates and brought new acreage under the plough. Fenced, hedged and cultivated, lowland countryside took on its familiar 'patchwork' appearance. Private agreements to enclose were replaced by Acts of Parliament (right) favouring the wealthy landowner at the expense of the small peasant.

Coal

During the 18th century, coalfields spread (below) and production increased fourfold. The Newcomen pumping engine, widespread use of pit ponies, and the introduction of four-wheeled carts moving on iron rails, all contributed. Improved ventilation and gunpowder blasting allowed pits to be sunk to greater depths. Coal came to replace charcoal as the main fuel in iron production, and many ironmasters provided the capital for developing and extending mines.

Eighteenth-Century Coalfields and the Main Routes of the Coal Trade

Fife
Central Scottish
Ayr
North-east
North-west
S.E. Lancs.
Yorkshire
N. Staffs.
S. Staffs.
Shropshire
E. Midlands
S. Wales
Dean
Kingswood
Radstock

Enclosures by Act c. 1700-1870

Common Field
- 50% and over
- 30%-49%
- 10%-29%

Commons and Waste
- 50% and over
- 30%-49%
- 10%-29%

- Under 10% enclosed

The Cloth Industry c. 1720
- Coarse woollens
- Medium woollens
- Fine woollens
- Worsteds
- Most important arable areas— over 50% of total acreage 1870
- □ Towns over 10,000 at c. 1700
- o Towns 5,000-10,000 at c. 1700
- ▲ Scottish planned villages 1720-1840
- • Landscaped parks

Glasgow
Edinburgh
Newcastle
Sunderland
Darlington
York
Leeds
Hull
Liverpool
Manchester
Derby
Nottingham
Lynn
Norwich
Yarmouth
Shrewsbury
Leicester
Bury St. Edmunds
Birmingham
Coventry
Cambridge
Ipswich
Worcester
Colchester
Brecon
Oxford
London
Bristol
Chatham
Canterbury
Bath
Salisbury
Tiverton
Portsmouth
Exeter
Plymouth

New roads

Britain's highways – potholed, rutted and impassable in bad weather – had been neglected for centuries. Traditionally a burden on the parish, their upkeep was taken over by private companies, who also built new roads. Turnpike trusts (left) were set up, empowered to charge tolls on certain stretches of road. The trusts employed engineers like Macadam and Telford, who developed new construction methods allowing better drainage and harder road surfaces.

	1750 5,449 km 143 trusts		1790 24,083 km 519 trusts	1821 33,160 km 744 trusts	1836 35,390 km 942 trusts

kilometres   10,000   20,000   30,000   40,000

THE INDUSTRIAL REVOLUTION

In 1829 Thomas Carlyle characterised his age as 'the Age of Machinery'. He was describing the world's first industrial revolution. From the 1780s Britain was transformed by mechanical innovation, multiplying the productive power of human society. Economic growth was accompanied by a population explosion, providing labour and domestic markets for finished goods. The dramatic rise in supply and demand, imports and exports, investment and profit, set in motion forces that continued to accelerate the process of change.

Initially the Industrial Revolution was based on cotton, coal and steam power, but from the 1830s the railway boom stimulated iron and steel production. Industrial landscapes mushroomed across the coalfields and textile regions: factories, mines, workshops, blast furnaces, railways and steam engines surrounded by the cramped terraces that housed the first generation of industrial workers – and their successors.

The power to make things, and to move goods and people faster than ever before instilled confidence in those who turned 'muck into brass'.

'Progress' became a byword for the men who made fortunes from commerce and industry – the new middle class – and they were quick to claim political power. The 1832 Reform Act enfranchised the £10-householder and ended the old regime of landed wealth. Industrial society would henceforth be directed by the beliefs, values and aspirations of the middle class, not the aristocracy.

For the men, women and children who were driven in search of work to the new factory towns, industrialisation brought new levels of exploitation and hardship. The upheaval, and the bitterness and misery it caused, found expression in Luddite machine-breaking and, more positively, in early trade unionism.

After the 1830s, new forms of social control evolved – the Poor Law, factory legislation and improvements in urban conditions. The old moral and economic order of rural society had gone for ever, replaced by the political economy of industrial capitalism and the spectacle, in William Blake's words, of 'dark satanic mills' in 'England's green and pleasant land'.

The cotton trade
Between 1800 and 1840 the mechanisation of the textile industry brought about a huge rise in cotton imports and exports and revenue increased fourfold. Inventions such as the spinning jenny, flying shuttle and, later, power loom, revolutionised production in the Lancashire cotton mills – Britain's first factories.

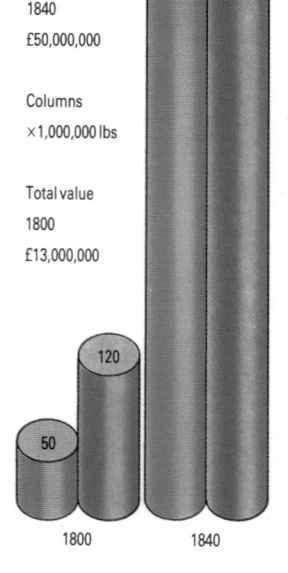

Imports
Exports

Parliamentary reform
The 1832 Reform Act had two main objectives: a more just and rational distribution of seats, and the extension of voting rights to the new middle classes. New urban seats were created to even out major discrepancies in constituency size. Most of the rotten boroughs, controlled by local landowners, were abolished. After 1832, a man qualified to vote who owned or rented a house worth £10 or more a year. This added about 300,000 new voters to the previous half-million – altogether, about 7% of the adult population. Later reforms (1867 and 1884) enfranchised male ratepayers, but even by 1914 only one third of the adult population could vote, with women still excluded.

New boroughs with 2 seats
1. Manchester
2. Birmingham
3. Leeds
4. Greenwich
5. Sheffield
6. Sunderland
7. Devonport
8. Wolverhampton
9. Finsbury
10. Marylebone
11. Lambeth
12. Bolton
13. Bradford
14. Blackburn
15. Oldham
16. Brighton
17. Halifax
18. Stockport
19. Stoke-on-Trent
20. Stroud

New boroughs with 1 seat
21. Ashton-under-Lyne
22. Bury
23. Chatham
24. Cheltenham
25. Dudley
26. Frome
27. Gateshead
28. Huddersfield
29. Kidderminster
30. Kendal
31. Rochdale
32. Salford
33. South Shields
34. Tynemouth
35. Wakefield
36. Walsall
37. Warrington
38. Whitby
39. Whitehaven
40. Merthyr Tydfil

▲ Boroughs abolished

● New boroughs with 1 seat

• New boroughs with 2 seats

Percentage adults entitled to vote:

Year	%
1831	5%
1832	7%
1867	16%
1884	23·5%

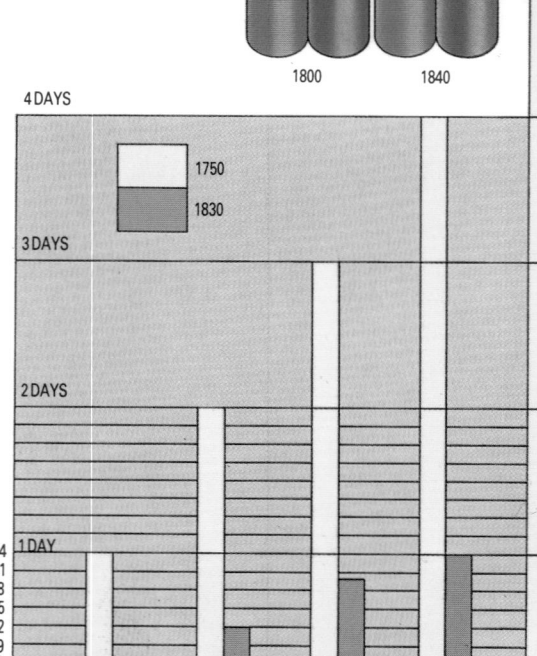

Faster travel
Even before the railways, great progress was made in reducing travelling time and costs. Between 1750 and 1830, journey times between some major cities were cut by 80% (above). A network of canals linking industrial centres was built, to speed up the movement of freight. The harder, more durable road surfaces developed by the turnpike trusts encouraged the building of faster, more comfortable carriages. During the great coaching age, speeds of 20 km/h were maintained, with stops at coaching stations for fresh horses and for passengers. Daily newspapers were delivered by stagecoach, and the Royal Mail developed as a regular national postal service.

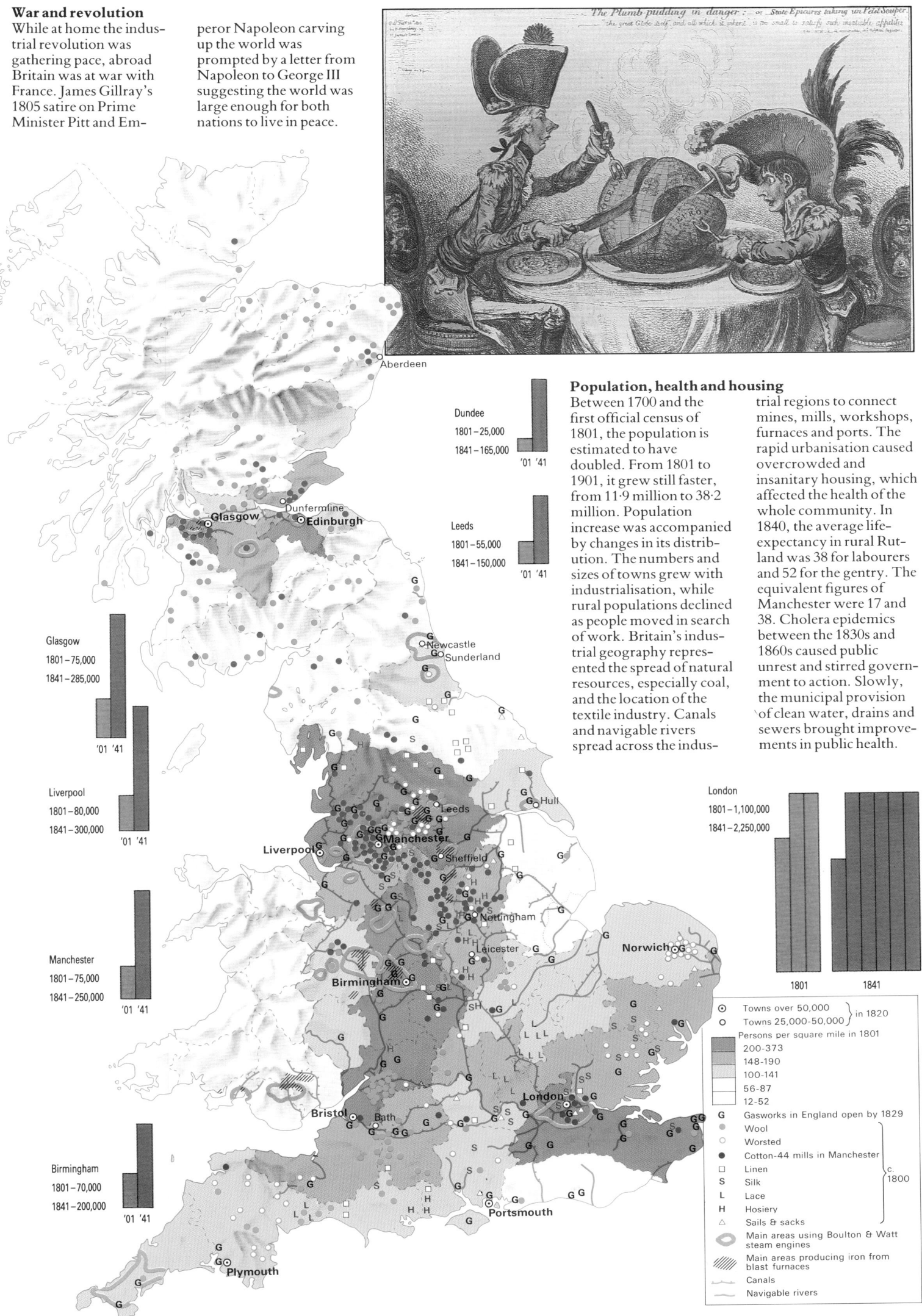

War and revolution

While at home the industrial revolution was gathering pace, abroad Britain was at war with France. James Gillray's 1805 satire on Prime Minister Pitt and Emperor Napoleon carving up the world was prompted by a letter from Napoleon to George III suggesting the world was large enough for both nations to live in peace.

The Plumb-pudding in danger :– or State Epicures taking un Petit Souper.

"the great Globe itself, and all which it inherit" is too small to satisfy such insatiable appetites.

Population, health and housing

Between 1700 and the first official census of 1801, the population is estimated to have doubled. From 1801 to 1901, it grew still faster, from 11·9 million to 38·2 million. Population increase was accompanied by changes in its distribution. The numbers and sizes of towns grew with industrialisation, while rural populations declined as people moved in search of work. Britain's industrial geography represented the spread of natural resources, especially coal, and the location of the textile industry. Canals and navigable rivers spread across the industrial regions to connect mines, mills, workshops, furnaces and ports. The rapid urbanisation caused overcrowded and insanitary housing, which affected the health of the whole community. In 1840, the average life-expectancy in rural Rutland was 38 for labourers and 52 for the gentry. The equivalent figures of Manchester were 17 and 38. Cholera epidemics between the 1830s and 1860s caused public unrest and stirred government to action. Slowly, the municipal provision of clean water, drains and sewers brought improvements in public health.

Dundee
1801 – 25,000
1841 – 165,000
'01 '41

Leeds
1801 – 55,000
1841 – 150,000
'01 '41

Glasgow
1801 – 75,000
1841 – 285,000
'01 '41

Liverpool
1801 – 80,000
1841 – 300,000
'01 '41

Manchester
1801 – 75,000
1841 – 250,000
'01 '41

Birmingham
1801 – 70,000
1841 – 200,000
'01 '41

London
1801 – 1,100,000
1841 – 2,250,000
1801 1841

Legend

⊙ Towns over 50,000 } in 1820
○ Towns 25,000-50,000

Persons per square mile in 1801
- 200-373
- 148-190
- 100-141
- 56-87
- 12-52

G Gasworks in England open by 1829
- Wool
○ Worsted
● Cotton-44 mills in Manchester
□ Linen
S Silk   } c. 1800
L Lace
H Hosiery
△ Sails & sacks

Main areas using Boulton & Watt steam engines

Main areas producing iron from blast furnaces

Canals

Navigable rivers

21

WORKSHOP OF THE WORLD

The Great Exhibition of 1851 announced to the world that Britain was an industrial nation second to none. Although German and North American competitors were later to take the lead, for the time being Britain's world dominance was assured. The Victorian and Edwardian eras were years of peace, stability and prosperity, which laid the foundations of modern urban society. 'Of all decades in our history', wrote the contemporary historian G.M. Young, 'a wise man would choose the 1850s to be young in.'

But 19th-century Britain was also a very divided society, and many did not share in the prosperity. While skilled workers who were in regular employment benefited from rising wages and 'self-help' forms of association such as co-operative stores and friendly societies, millions of unskilled and casual labourers led a precarious existence, with only the punitive deterrent of the workhouse to underwrite the risks of near-starvation wages, bad food, overcrowding and disease. To make matters worse, the vast reserves of cheap labour upon whom the new 'free-market' economy depended were constantly swollen by immigrants from Ireland and eastern Europe. One in four of the population lived below a very meagre poverty line.

As well as class differences, society was also divided very rigidly according to gender. In an age that upheld the virtues of family life, married women could expect to see their health ruined by excessive child-bearing and inadequate medical care. Working-class women were especially disadvantaged, poorly paid in the labour market and overburdened – and without means – in the home.

The extremes of wealth and want generated great Victorian social movements for improvement and reform. Philanthropists, radicals and socialists all devoted their energies to making a less needy, more democratic, more egalitarian society. By the end of this period, the government had accepted, at least in principle, that the state had some duty to care for the well-being of its people.

A powerful unifying force in Britain at this time, which lasted up to World War I and beyond, was the Empire and all that it stood for. Jubilee celebrations for the Queen Empress, Boer War jingoism and popular music-hall songs invited the humblest subject to identify with nationhood and take pride in a empire on which 'the sun never set'.

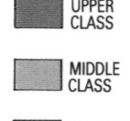

£6079 (0·5%)

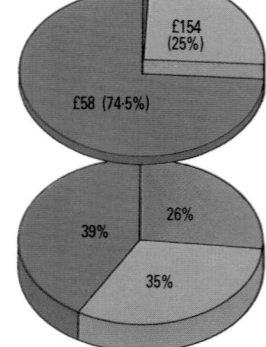

■ UPPER CLASS

▨ MIDDLE CLASS

■ WORKING CLASS

(1867 figures)

£154 (25%)

£58 (74·5%)

39%   26%   35%

Income and wealth
The upper class, whose annual income of £6000 plus was 26% of the national income, was still very rich compared with the much larger middle class (above). The working-class masses were by far the poorest.

Victorian women
The Victorian middle classes perfected an ideal of separate spheres for men and women. The public world of trade and commerce was essentially a male preserve. Women were confined to the home – 'the angel of the hearth' (right) and guardian of the family's moral well-being. A woman was always expected to place her family's needs above her own. Lower down the social scale, the National Federation of Women Workers (below), formed in 1906, unionised many thousands of unskilled women workers.

Domestic service
By 1914, there were about 1·5 million domestic servants in Britain, men and women of all ages (right). Life was hard and the hours were long. Some families had just one servant, while the wealthier ones had as many as 30.

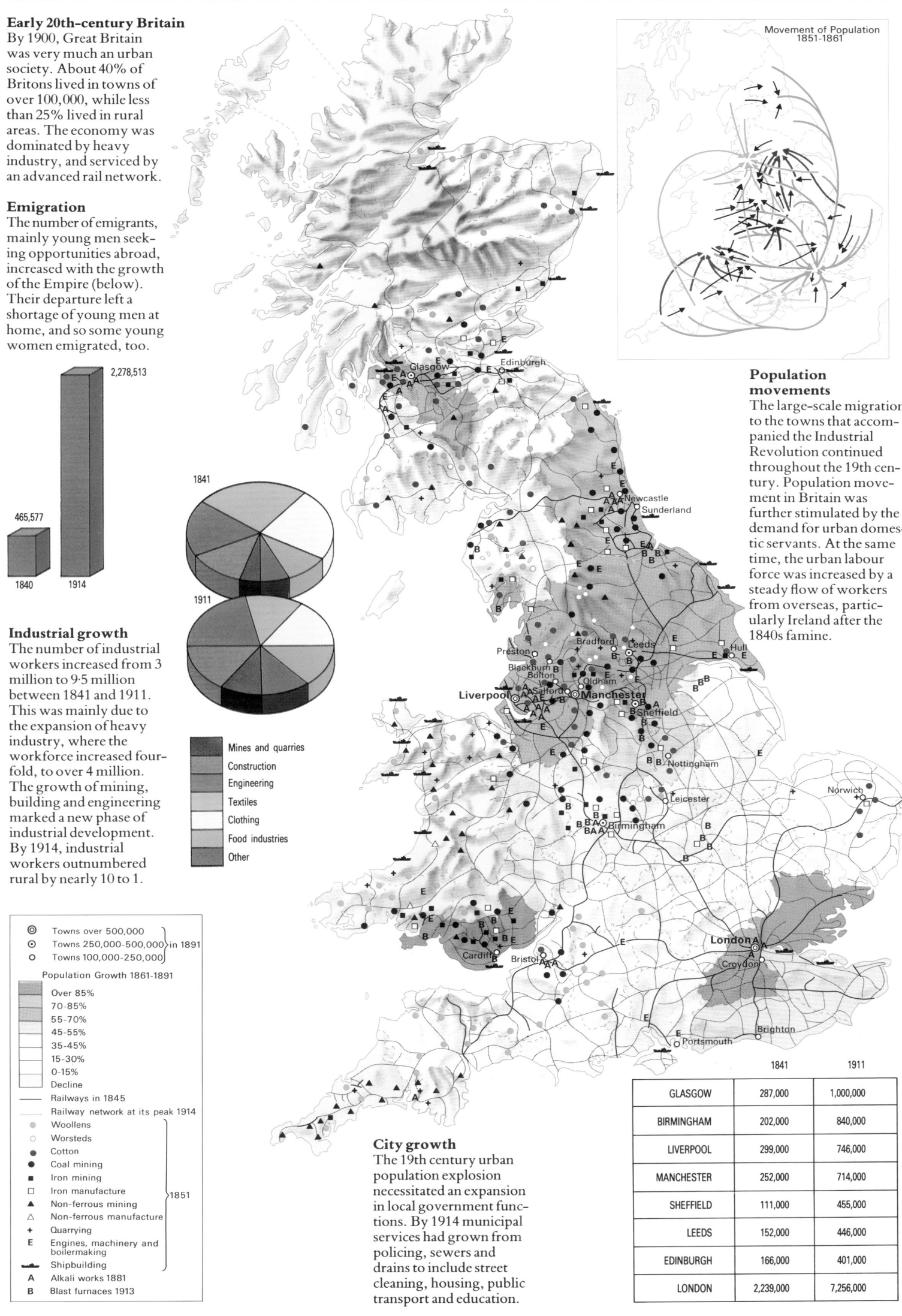

Early 20th-century Britain

By 1900, Great Britain was very much an urban society. About 40% of Britons lived in towns of over 100,000, while less than 25% lived in rural areas. The economy was dominated by heavy industry, and serviced by an advanced rail network.

Emigration

The number of emigrants, mainly young men seeking opportunities abroad, increased with the growth of the Empire (below). Their departure left a shortage of young men at home, and so some young women emigrated, too.

2,278,513

465,577

1840   1914

1841

1911

Industrial growth

The number of industrial workers increased from 3 million to 9·5 million between 1841 and 1911. This was mainly due to the expansion of heavy industry, where the workforce increased four-fold, to over 4 million. The growth of mining, building and engineering marked a new phase of industrial development. By 1914, industrial workers outnumbered rural by nearly 10 to 1.

Mines and quarries
Construction
Engineering
Textiles
Clothing
Food industries
Other

Movement of Population 1851-1861

Population movements

The large-scale migration to the towns that accompanied the Industrial Revolution continued throughout the 19th century. Population movement in Britain was further stimulated by the demand for urban domestic servants. At the same time, the urban labour force was increased by a steady flow of workers from overseas, particularly Ireland after the 1840s famine.

Glasgow
Edinburgh
Newcastle
Sunderland
Preston
Bradford   Leeds   Hull
Blackburn
Bolton   Oldham
Liverpool   Salford   Manchester
Sheffield
Nottingham
Norwich
Leicester
Birmingham
Cardiff
Bristol
London
Croydon
Brighton
Portsmouth

	Towns over 500,000	
	Towns 250,000-500,000	in 1891
	Towns 100,000-250,000	

Population Growth 1861-1891

Over 85%
70-85%
55-70%
45-55%
35-45%
15-30%
0-15%
Decline

Railways in 1845
Railway network at its peak 1914

Woollens	
Worsteds	
Cotton	
Coal mining	
Iron mining	
Iron manufacture	1851
Non-ferrous mining	
Non-ferrous manufacture	
Quarrying	
E Engines, machinery and boilermaking	
Shipbuilding	
A Alkali works 1881	
B Blast furnaces 1913	

City growth

The 19th century urban population explosion necessitated an expansion in local government functions. By 1914 municipal services had grown from policing, sewers and drains to include street cleaning, housing, public transport and education.

	1841	1911
GLASGOW	287,000	1,000,000
BIRMINGHAM	202,000	840,000
LIVERPOOL	299,000	746,000
MANCHESTER	252,000	714,000
SHEFFIELD	111,000	455,000
LEEDS	152,000	446,000
EDINBURGH	166,000	401,000
LONDON	2,239,000	7,256,000

TWO WORLD WARS

World War I (1914–18) brought with it the dislocation of British society. The loss of life on a hitherto unprecedented scale shattered Edwardian complacency, while the accumulated war debts strained Britain's economy and hastened its decline relative to the USA. Overseas, British imperial supremacy was rocked by Irish republicanism and Indian nationalism, and at home labour discontent once again raised its head. The bitter defeat of the General Strike of 1926 represented a major setback for the labour movement.

Soon after the war, in 1918, women gained the vote after half a century of campaigning: first, just those over 30, together with all men over 21 years of age, and later, in 1928, women over 21, too. Labour replaced the Liberals as the party of opposition, while outside Parliament disillusion with old values gave expression to the growth of the new ideologies of communism and fascism. However, they neither achieved mass support nor took root as they did in Continental Europe.

The collapse of the New York stockmarket, the 'Wall Street crash' of 1929, signalled world wide economic slump. In Britain, where successive Conservative and Labour governments had been struggling to restore the balance of payments, a coalition National government was formed to deal with the crisis. It cut back public expenditure and began to run down the traditional heavy industries, with fearful consequences for employment.

There were now two Britains: in the north and north-west whole communities lost their livelihoods and had to rely on means-tested poor relief for subsistence; in the south-east and the midlands new light manufacturing and consumer goods industries flourished and living standards improved.

There was gradual economic improvement in the late 1930s, but it was war, which had been feared for some time, that eventually brought about full employment and formed the basis of a new social consensus. World War II (1939–45) was fought as a 'just war': democracy and freedom against fascism and tyranny. The war effort rested on the morale of the whole nation, as aerial bombardment directly involved the civilian population. Winston Churchill emerged as the popular wartime leader whose rhetoric reinforced the collective will to win and left the people of post-war Britain determined never to return to the poverty and waste of the 1930s.

War and class-war
When World War I broke out in August 1914, nationalist fervour swung the Labour party and the TUC behind the government's recruitment drive. Unions co-operated with employers in a war that claimed the lives of 750,000 Britons, with more than 1·5 million injured or missing (below). After the 1918 armistice, prices rose steeply and labour disputes returned. Unemployment soared, and in 1921 miners, railway and transport workers formed an ill-fated triple alliance in an unsuccessful bid to prevent their wages being cut. The *Punch* cartoon (centre) shows what the employers thought of it.

Government spending
After the Liberals introduced pensions and national insurance in 1909–11, government spending rose steeply to nearly £70 million by 1920. Almost half the government's revenue was from duties on sugar, beer and tobacco. The 1920s saw government attempting to reduce its expenditure, with cutbacks in civil service pay following in 1931. During the 1930s the government spent more on encouraging business than on welfare provision. By 1939, the government's largest source of revenue, about 40%, came from direct taxes.

——— Education
– – – – Unemployment
· · · · · Health
–·–·– Old age pensions

PUNCH, OR THE LONDON CHARIVARI.—April 20, 1921.

THE PROBLEM-PICTURE OF 1921.
HOW TO MAKE THE TAIL WAG.

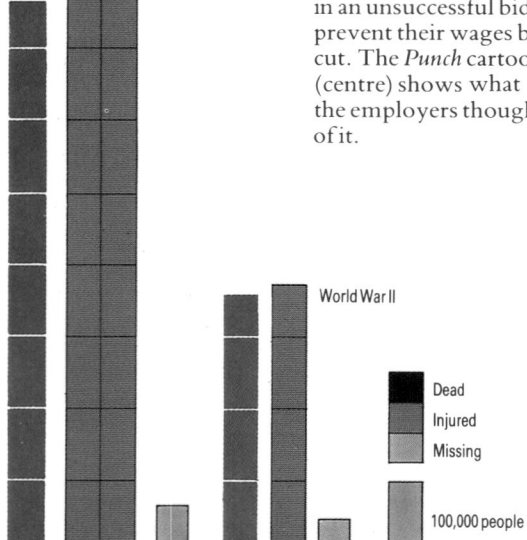

World War I

World War II

■ Dead
■ Injured
□ Missing

□ 100,000 people

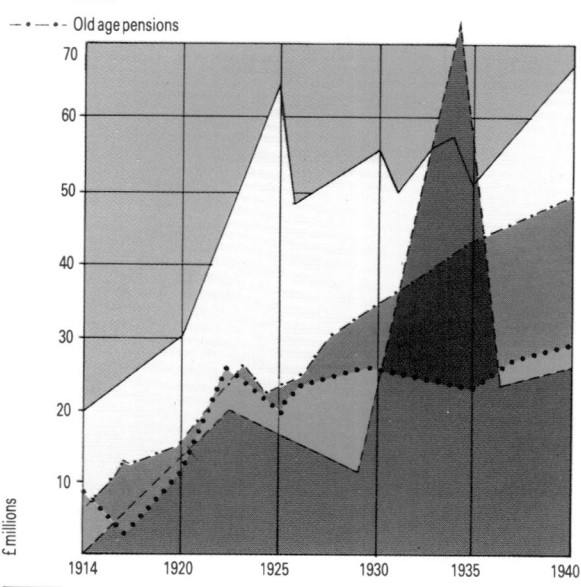

Crisis in the 1930s

The depression of the 1930s was exacerbated by the dependence of many towns on a single industry. When, in 1930, unemployment first reached 3 million and the Labour government failed to balance its budget, foreign creditors, fearful of an economic collapse, began to withdraw their gold from the Bank of England. That autumn, the gold standard was abandoned, and a National government, made up of all parties, was elected to solve the crisis. Under this government, unemployment fell to 1·7 million by 1937, but was rising again when war intervened in 1939.

Smaller families

The average number of children in a family fell from 6·16 in the 1860s to as low as 2·07 in the 1930s. This resulted from better education and understanding of family economics, the rise of the status of women from that of mere child-bearer, and the use of contraception. Also, a modicum of social welfare reduced the need for large, self-supporting families.

1861	1899	1915	1934

■ Individual in family

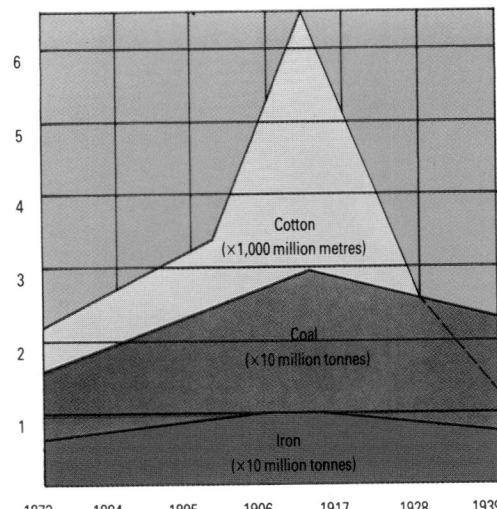

Industries in decline

The neglect of foreign markets at the expense of military requirements during World War I accelerated Britain's already declining share of world trade in the inter-war period. The older industries – cotton, coal, and iron and steel – suffered most. By the mid-1930s Japan had replaced Britain as the world's major supplier of cotton. Demand for coal fell and coal exporters faced stiff competition from Germany and Poland. In the iron and steel industries, imports began to outstrip exports.

Changes in Population 1931-1938

- ☐ Decrease
- ☐ 0-10% increase
- ▨ 10-20% increase
- ▧ Over 20% increase
- ⚓ Major ports
- ⚓ Other ports

Ill-balanced Industry (more than 30% of workers in a single industry)

- —M— Mining
- —I— Iron ore
- —W— Wool
- —C— Cotton
- – – – Pottery
- Q Quarrying
- S Iron & steel
- T Steel & tinplate
- E Engineering
- Sh Shipbuilding
- R Railway works
- Ru Rubber
- Ch Chemicals
- D Naval dockyards
- X Other textiles & clothing
- F Footwear
- B Bricks
- Pa Paper
- G Glass
- Fu Furniture
- Fo Food

Major areas of unemployment
- ▨ Over 15%
- ▧ Under 15%

New industries

During the 1930s industries based on car-making (opposite) and other mass-production consumer goods thrived on the edge of towns such as Oxford, Luton, Coventry and London.

RECONSTRUCTION AND GROWTH

Post-war Britain promised a better deal for everyone, based on consensus politics and full employment. The 1942 Beveridge Report had outlined measures to eliminate the five evil giants – Want, Disease, Ignorance, Idleness and Squalor – and in the first post-war general election of 1945, the Labour party, with its commitment to wholesale social reform, won a landslide victory. The new government founded the welfare state, based on the universal provision of health, education and social insurance. For the next 30 years, Labour and Conservative governments pledged to maintain it, but failed to achieve the standards found elsewhere in Europe.

The 1945 Labour government's immediate problem was to stabilise an economy crippled by war debts to the United States. Rationing of foodstuffs and other essentials was introduced, but the measure proved unpopular and, in 1951, was ended by the Conservatives. By the late 1950s the austerity was past, and a huge expansion in the production of consumer goods ushered in the 'affluent society'.

A new youth market emerged. 'Pop' music – epitomised by the Beatles – became a major industry, and youth culture – from 'mods and rockers' to 'hippies' and, later, 'punks' – was seized on by advertising and the media. The all-round boom economy created labour shortages and attracted immigrant workers from Asia, the Caribbean and southern Europe, who took many of the least-inviting and worst-paid jobs.

Despite this apparent prosperity, Britain's position was in decline as the USA and USSR emerged as 'superpowers' and the nuclear age dawned. In the wake of colonial conflicts, from Cyprus to Malaya, Britain lost an empire but emerged as the leader of a pluralistic, multi-racial commonwealth. This and French opposition deflected Britain from an early involvement in the European Economic Community, which it eventually joined in 1973 as a lesser European power.

During the post-war boom, living standards improved as never before. Consumer expenditure in the 1950s nearly doubled, as a new range of electrical and other durable goods, such as those shown here, became commonplace in British homes.

Inflation and unemployment

Post-war reconstruction of industry and transport, with expanding world trade, helped government to keep down unemployment. In the 1950s and 1960s, with inflation at 3–4%, jobs were plentiful, especially in the public services. However, in the next 10 years, the value of the £ fell first by half, and then again by a third. In 1973, the price of oil trebled, and in 1975 inflation reached 27%, as production slowed and unemployment levels not seen since the 1930s became widespread. Since 1980, inflation has fallen, but there has been a steep rise in unemployment.

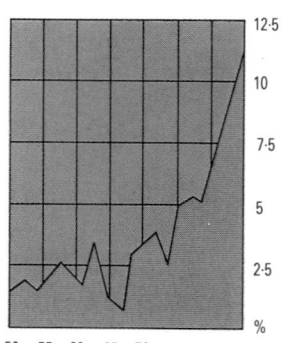

Unemployment

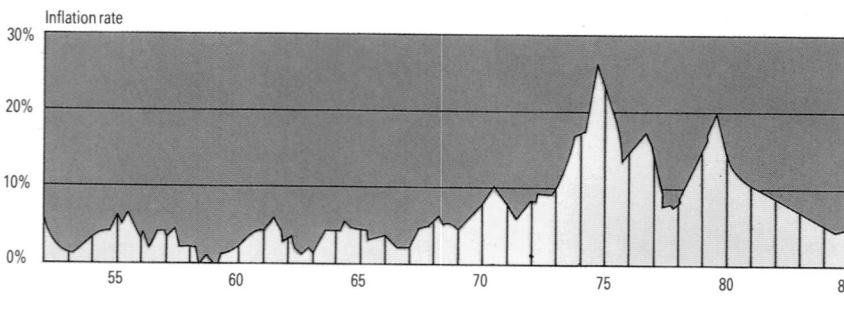

Occupational change

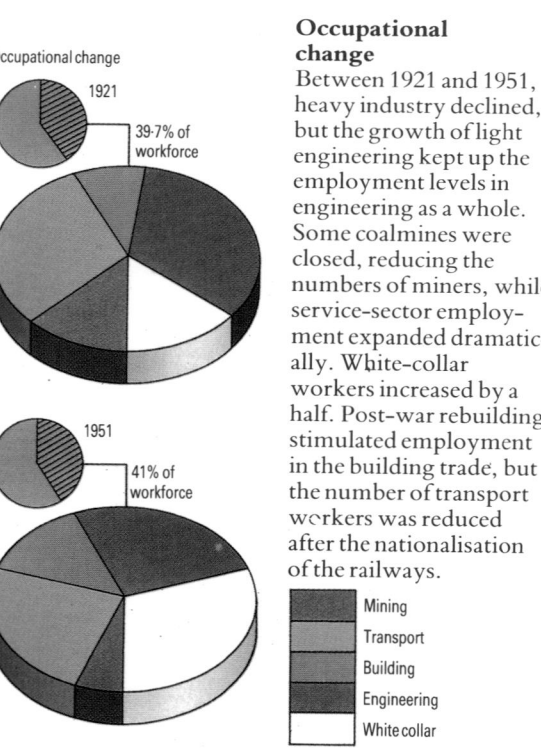

Between 1921 and 1951, heavy industry declined, but the growth of light engineering kept up the employment levels in engineering as a whole. Some coalmines were closed, reducing the numbers of miners, while service-sector employment expanded dramatically. White-collar workers increased by a half. Post-war rebuilding stimulated employment in the building trade, but the number of transport workers was reduced after the nationalisation of the railways.

- Mining
- Transport
- Building
- Engineering
- White collar

Working population

Since the war, traditional opposition to women working outside the home has declined. The share of the workforce accounted for by women has grown steadily, with a sharp increase in 1964–79. By 1974, immigrant workers, male and female, made up 7·5% of Britain's workforce, many of whom have settled and made their home in Britain.

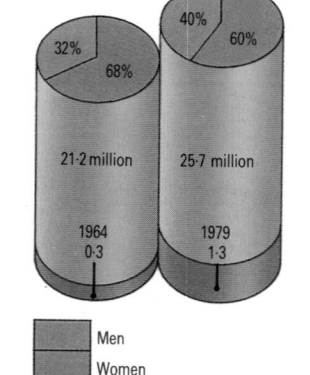

- Men
- Women

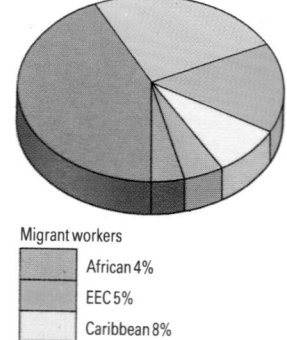

Migrant workers
- African 4%
- EEC 5%
- Caribbean 8%
- Indian/Paki 14%
- Irish 27%
- Others 42%

Britain's post-war economic miracle could not last, for successive governments had failed to establish the economy on a sound footing. As early as 1967, Harold Wilson's Labour government was forced to devalue the pound. Ten years later, another Labour government was reduced to borrowing money from the International Monetary Fund. The conditions of the loan included major cuts in public spending, which took place against a background of rising unemployment.

Growing disillusion with the welfare state, and the apparent failure of consensus politics, strengthened the appeal of the new right. In the general election of 1979, Margaret Thatcher, who exemplified this break with the post-war tradition, led the Tories to victory. She introduced 'monetarism' as the solution to Britain's economic ills, and invoked the 'Victorian values' of self-help and a free market economy. Under her government, inflation was brought under control. Unemployment, on the other hand, fuelled by a world recession, continued to rise.

Mortality patterns

From 1950 to 1975 life expectancy in Great Britain increased by about three years for men, to 70, and by over four years for women, to 75. Today, people die less from water- and food-borne diseases than from diseases of the heart and circulation and cancers. The major causes of death for Britons aged between 1 and 24, and for men up to 44, are accidents, poisoning and violence. For women 24-64, cancers are the main cause, and for men over 45 and women over 65, circulatory diseases.

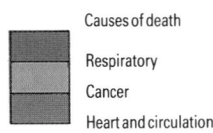

Causes of death
- Respiratory
- Cancer
- Heart and circulation

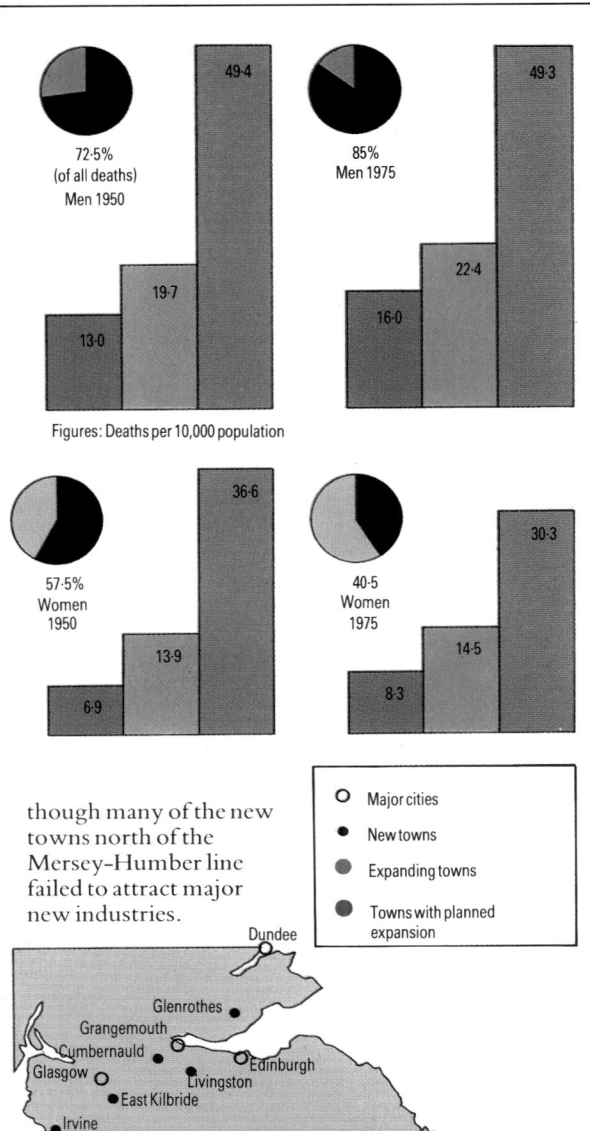

Figures: Deaths per 10,000 population

Black Britons

Between 1966 and 1978 Britain's black population almost doubled, to about 3·5% of the total population. About 40% were Afro-Caribbean, the others mainly Asian. Most settled in low-paid jobs in the inner-city areas of Greater London, the West Midlands and Yorkshire. In the late 1970s, as the economy declined, a relatively high proportion of them became unemployed. Tighter immigration controls have since reduced the number of immigrants.

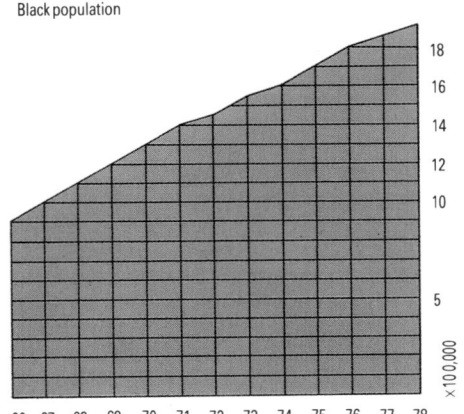

Black population

New towns

After the war, the government took control of building, directing labour and materials into solving the desperate housing shortage. By 1952, 1,200,000 new flats and houses had been built, mostly by local councils. The New Towns Act of 1946 was aimed chiefly at reducing overcrowding in the main cities. By 1950, work had begun on the first 12 new towns: 7 were to take population from London, 4 were to serve the densely populated coalmining communities of Durham, South Wales and Scotland, and one was for the Corby steel industry. The government also passed legislation concerning the location of industry, though many of the new towns north of the Mersey-Humber line failed to attract major new industries.

Population trends

Up to the 1960s Great Britain's population grew quite quickly, with a high birth rate and falling death rate. By the mid-1970s the growth rate had slowed almost to a stop. In 1977 there were 35% fewer births per year than in 1964. Couples were marrying later and having smaller families. Regional population changes in the 1970s and early 1980s reflected not so much the falling birth rate as the decline of the older industrial cities relative to the new industries and new towns.

Type of area	Population 1981 × 1,000,000	% Growth 1978-81
Inner London	2·5	−17·7
Outer London	4·2	−5·0
Large cities	2·2	−5·1
New towns	2·2	+15·1
Resorts	3·3	+4·9

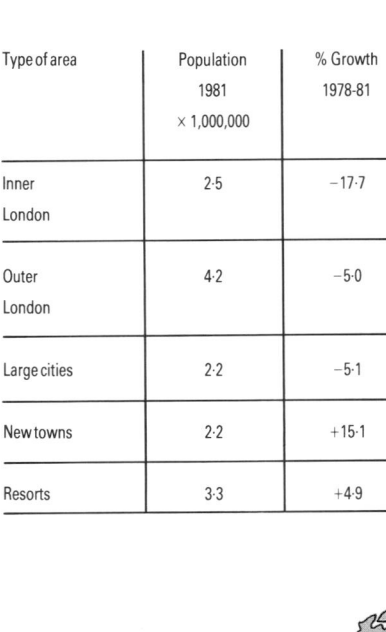

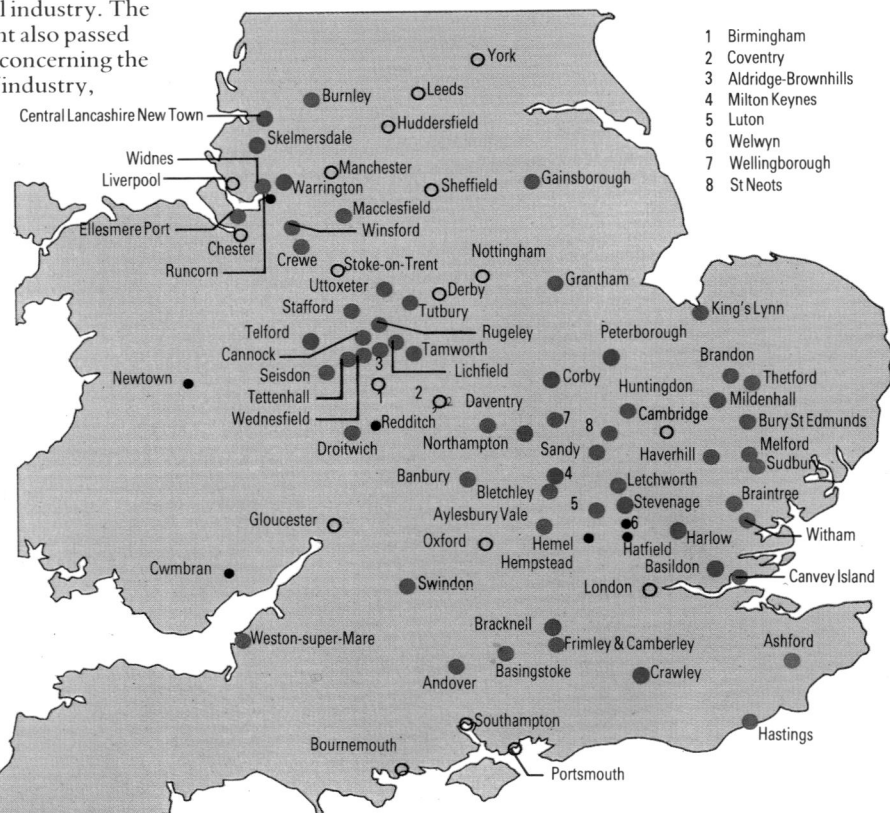

- ○ Major cities
- ● New towns
- ● Expanding towns
- ● Towns with planned expansion

1 Birmingham
2 Coventry
3 Aldridge-Brownhills
4 Milton Keynes
5 Luton
6 Welwyn
7 Wellingborough
8 St Neots

BRITAIN IN THE 1980s

Britain in the 1980s has its share of social contradictions, with widening gaps between rich and poor, employed and unemployed, and prospering and depressed regions. The impact of the economic recession and cuts in public spending have been uneven, affecting some groups much more than others. Living standards, education and work opportunities today very much depend on where people live and on their class, gender, and ethnic background.

New affluence

For many in work the 1980s have brought affluence, especially in the southern shires where the sunrise industries – particularly computers and electronics – have grown up. Technological innovation has created a new range of consumer goods and opened up new cultural possibilities. Home computers, video-tape recorders, personal cassette-radios and cable TV are becoming increasingly common in the British home.

Consumer spending has also reflected a growing public concern with diet and health and fitness in general. In particular, the interest in jogging, aerobics and health foods has expanded consumer markets. So too has youth culture, with its emphasis on new styles mixed with nostalgia, seen in many of today's hair styles and clothes designs.

Population

In 1951 the population of Great Britain was 48,854,000. It grew by 5% between 1951 and 1961, and then by another 5%, to 53,979,000, over the next decade. By 1981 the rate of increase had fallen to about 0·5%. The population figure itself fell slightly between 1982 and 1983 despite an increase in life expectancy and fall in infant mortality over the previous decade.

	1973	1983
Live births (×1,000)	779	721
Deaths (×1,000)	669	662
Life expectancy (years)		
Men	69	71
Women	75	77
Infant mortality (per 1,000)	17	10

Standard of living

Though average earnings rose between 1973 and 1983, nearly 5 million households continued to live in overcrowded conditions. Moreover, 5% of households, mostly in privately rented property, still shared the basic amenities of hot water, a bath and outside wc. The proportion of households having the use of a car rose, but access was not evenly distributed: 70% in the south-west and East Anglia, compared with 51% in the north and 52% in Scotland.

(1975=100)	1973	1983
Average weekly earnings	35·9	146·1
Retail price index (1980=100)	69·4	248·6
Households having use of:	%	%
Car	53·9	62·1
TV set	93·4	96·9
Telephone	43·4	77·3
Central heating	38·5	63·9
Refrigerator	77·6	97·0
Deep freeze	NA	34·2
Washing machine	66·6	81·3

Education

Between 1973 and 1983 the proportion of pupils and students in full-time education increased. There was also a slight drop in the pupil-to-teacher ratios, as the number of children of school age fell faster than the number of teachers. In Scotland, more than 40% of children stay on at school after 16, compared with Devon, Norfolk and Lancashire, where the figure is less than 25%. Some inner cities spend up to twice as much per child on education as some rural boroughs.

	1973	1983
Pupils in state schools		
Primary (no. per teacher)	26	22
Secondary (no. per teacher)	17	16
% in comprehensives	50·7	91·1
Participation in full-time education (as % of age group)	%	%
2-4 school	15·7	29·2
16-17 school	28·9	26·3
further education	7·4	15·4
18-20 school	2·3	1·0
further education	4·8	7·9
Universities	5·5	6·2
No. in full-time higher education (×1,000)	482·2	568

Marriage

Between 1973 and 1983 there was an increase in the ratio of civil to religious marriages, occasioned partly by the proportional increase in second marriages. In 1984 the median age for a first marriage was 24·7 for men and 22·6 for women, in both cases the highest it had been for 30 years. The median age for remarriage of both divorced men and women has also increased in recent years, and the divorce rate has now slowed up considerably since 1980.

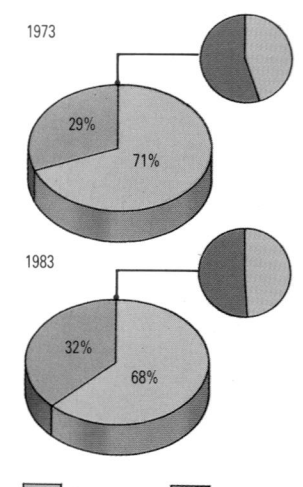

Young and old

Britain's pensioners (women aged 60 and over and men aged 65 and over) have increased in number since 1951. The 1960s saw a 17% rise over the previous decade, while in the 1970s the number rose by a further 10%. About 30% of today's pensioners live alone, with less than 5% looked after in old people's homes. From 1951 the number of children under 16 also grew. At the height of the 'bulge', in 1971, it reached 13 million, but since has fallen back to 1960s levels.

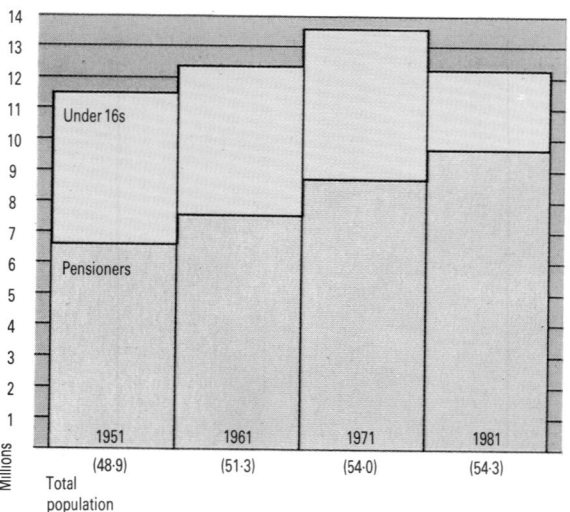

Smoking and health

In 1982, for the first time, smokers were a minority in every social group. The reduction has been greatest among professional men and women and least among manual workers, and overall greater among men than women. Still, smoking remains the largest single cause of preventable death. In 1985, 1 in 7 of deaths were from smoking-related diseases, and the death toll since 1945 is 3 million. A further 1½ million deaths from smoking are expected by the year 2000.

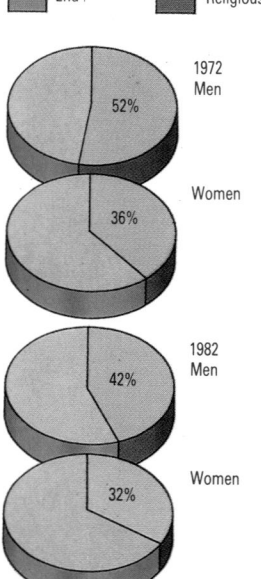

Population patterns

Social and economic planning depends on knowing how the population will change. Death rates are much easier to predict than birth rates, which fluctuate in response to short-term social and economic changes. Present projections suggest that Britain's population will increase by about 4% by the year 2000. There will also be an increase in the average age of the population, the group showing the fastest rate of growth being the over 60s, in particular the over-75s.

Positive and negative effects

At the opposite extreme, for those sections of Britain's population living in a marginal economy of dole queues or irregular – and sometimes undeclared – income, life is a struggle. Public spending cuts in social services, health care and housing have reduced the living standards, in particular, of many low-paid and casual workers, single parents, and the elderly and infirm. In the inner cities and those regions dependent on declining industries, hardship is increasing. The mounting frustration and discontent has sometimes expressed itself in emotional scenes on industrial picket lines, and in more extreme cases, in outbreaks of urban rioting.

However, alongside these conflicts, the 1980s have also seen the growth of constructive social movements, with an emphasis on peace, women's rights, and concern for the environment. While these movements and the methods they employ are not always supported by the public at large, they have succeeded in focusing attention on problems of crucial importance to the modern age. How those problems are resolved will play a large part in determining what Britain will be like in the 1990s and beyond.

Ethnic minorities

Since 1951 the proportion of non-whites resident in Britain but who were born overseas has increased from 2% to 6%. Their distribution has been uneven. By the 1980s the highest concentration (1 in 20) was in the south-east, followed by the West Midlands (just under 1 in 25), the East Midlands and Yorkshire and Humberside (both 1 in 50) and the north-west (just under 1 in 50). For all other regions – including Scotland – the figure is about 1 in 100.

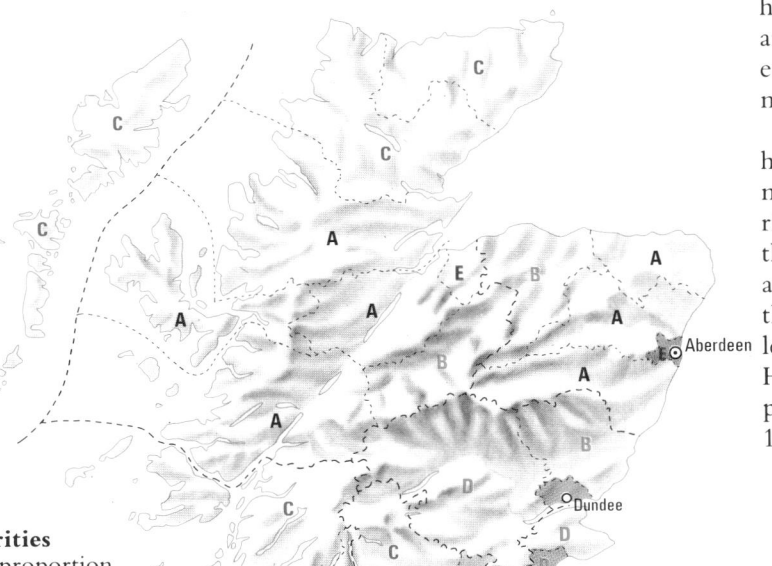

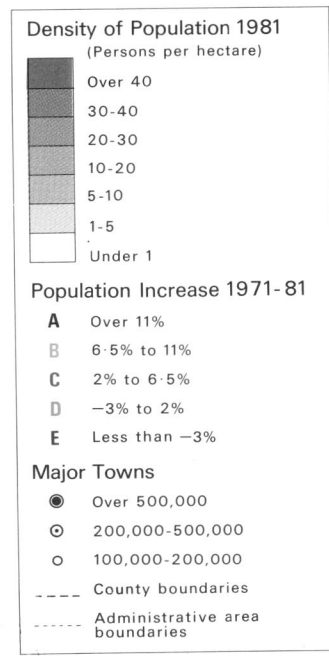

Density of Population 1981
(Persons per hectare)

- Over 40
- 30-40
- 20-30
- 10-20
- 5-10
- 1-5
- Under 1

Population Increase 1971-81

A	Over 11%
B	6·5% to 11%
C	2% to 6·5%
D	−3% to 2%
E	Less than −3%

Major Towns

- ◉ Over 500,000
- ⊙ 200,000-500,000
- ○ 100,000-200,000
- ---- County boundaries
- ⋯⋯ Administrative area boundaries

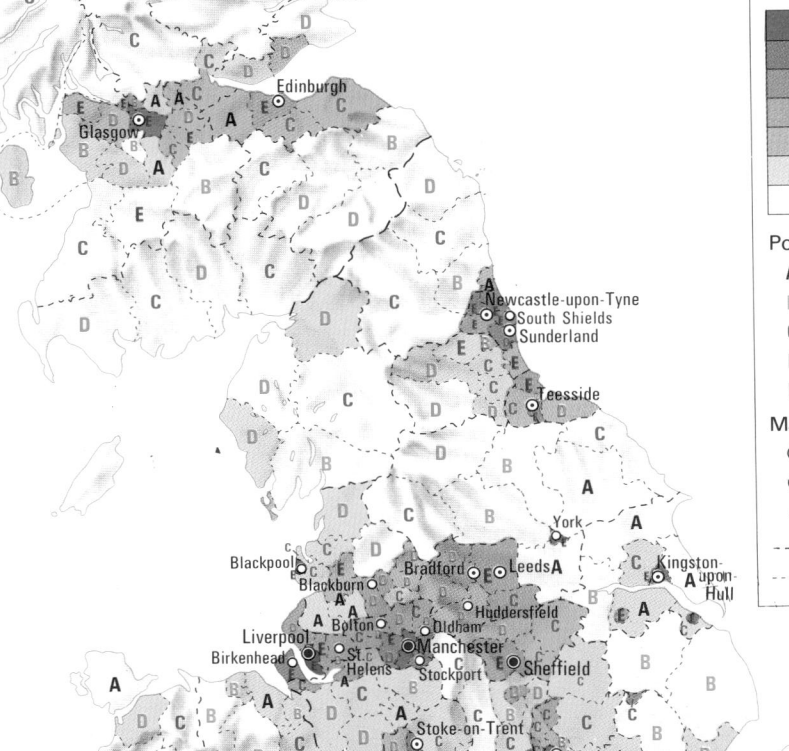

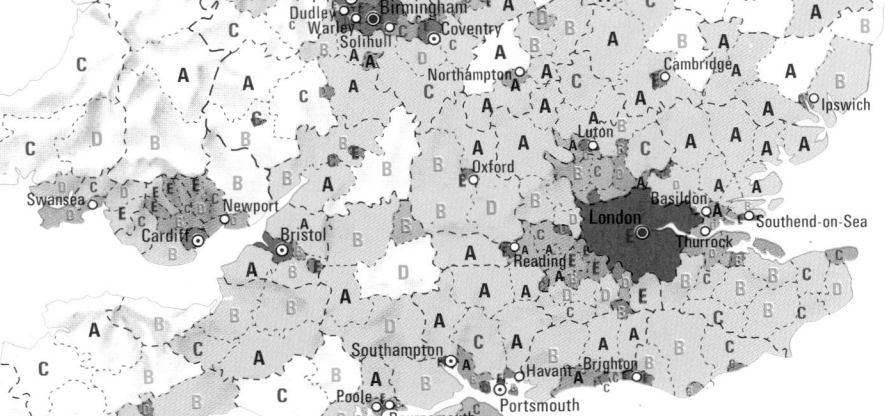

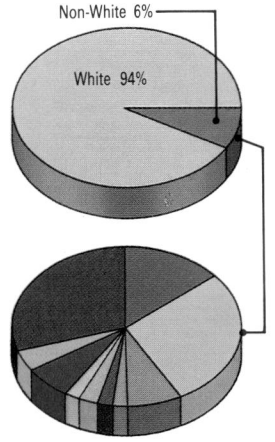

Non-White 6%

White 94%

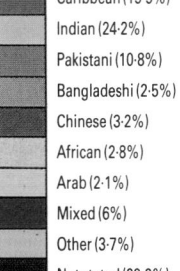

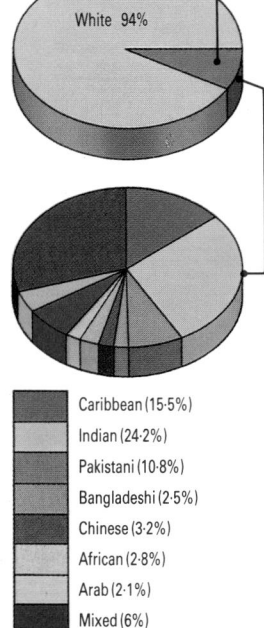

- Caribbean (15·5%)
- Indian (24·2%)
- Pakistani (10·8%)
- Bangladeshi (2·5%)
- Chinese (3·2%)
- African (2·8%)
- Arab (2·1%)
- Mixed (6%)
- Other (3·7%)
- Not stated (29·2%)

COAL, OIL AND GAS

Britain has the largest energy resources of any country in western Europe, and since 1980 it has been almost self-sufficient in national energy supply. Almost 95% of its energy needs are met by coal, oil and gas. The remainder comes from nuclear and hydroelectric power.

Britain accounts for 15% of total western European primary energy consumption (second only to West Germany), but national energy consumption has fallen by 10% in the past 10 years. This has been the result mainly of industrial recession. This period has also seen a continuing shift away from use of coal, which has been increasingly replaced by North Sea gas and oil, and to a lesser extent by nuclear power.

Coal

Coal is still Britain's richest natural energy resource. At current rates of consumption, there are sufficient reserves to last 300 years. Coalmining is the exclusive right of the National Coal Board (NCB), which was set up in 1947 to manage the industry as all coal mines passed into public ownership following the Coal Nationalisation Act 1946.

The bulk of the nation's coal (72%) is used to generate electricity. But demand for coal is falling steadily – by 19% since 1973 – and is expected to continue falling. A combination of plans by the government to expand nuclear power, the opening in 1986 of a cross-Channel electricity supply link providing cheap French electricity, and the loss of markets to imported coal during the 1984 miners' strike suggest that demand for home-produced coal will continue to fall. In the 20 months to September 1985, 34 (out of a total of more than 150) pits were closed or faced with closure for economic reasons.

Oil

In 1979 annual world oil consumption peaked at nearly 24 billion barrels. Since then it has fallen by 14%. No major industrial country has cut its consumption more dramatically than Britain. Since the peak year of 1973, British oil consumption has fallen by 27%, in line with the decline of industry. However, during the same period, the country's petrol consumption has increased by more than 20%. More than half the growth in national energy demand between 1959 and 1978 was due to increased needs of transport, and half of that from private transport. The number of private cars has grown by more than 400% since the early 1950s.

Currently, annual oil consumption is around 880 million barrels. Proven reserves of oil in the North Sea amount to over 3100 million barrels but total remaining reserves may be more than five times as much as this. Offshore oil production and oil refining are carried out almost exclusively by privately owned companies of which British Petroleum (BP) and Shell Transport and Trading are the two largest British companies.

Gas

Over the past 10 years natural gas production in Britain has remained fairly steady, while consumption has risen by 42%. The proportion contributed by gas to the national energy budget has almost doubled since the early 1970s. It now provides more than a third of British energy. At the current rates of consumption, natural gas resources in the North Sea are projected to run out in the next decade, when an increasing proportion will be piped in from Norwegian gas fields.

Privately owned companies predominate in gas production while the publically owned British Gas Corporation is responsible for gas distribution.

Sources of energy   1984-85

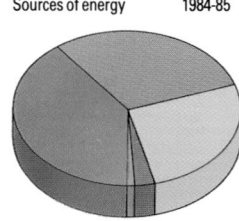

Energy supplied

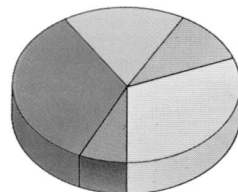

Consumers

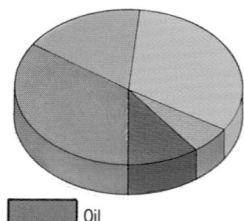

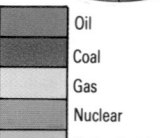
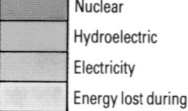
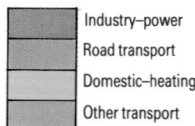

- Oil
- Coal
- Gas
- Nuclear
- Hydroelectric
- Electricity
- Energy lost during conversion

- Industry–power
- Road transport
- Domestic–heating
- Other transport
- Other (lighting, electrical appliances etc.)

Energy flow

The diagram, right, shows the energy flow pattern for Britain: the sources of energy, the proportion used in generating electricity, and the end uses. Conversion losses and low efficiency mean that, ultimately, more energy is wasted than is put to work.

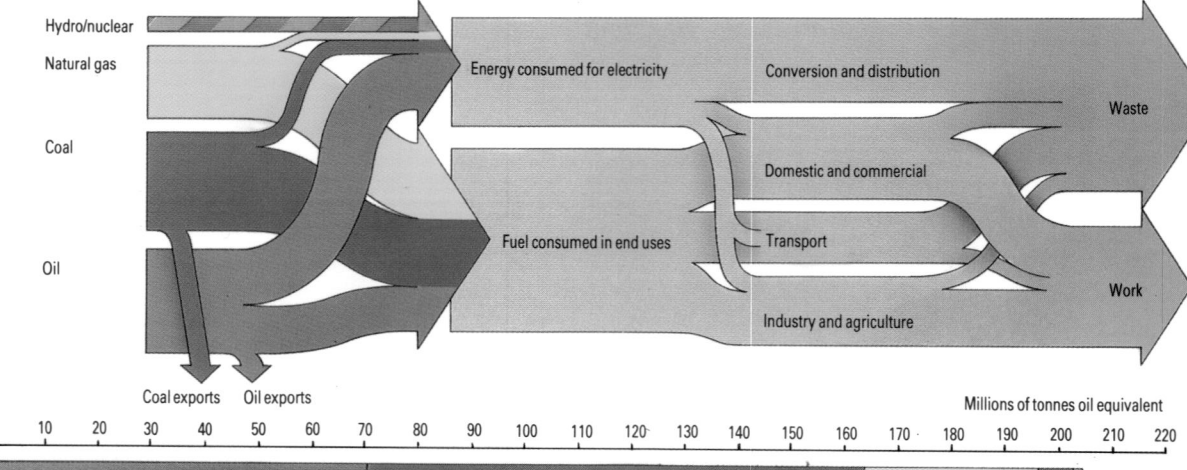

Energy use

Britain is better supplied with energy than many other industrialised countries. But a major change in fortune is likely in the next 30 years as oil and gas particularly become less available and more expensive. To date, there has been little investment in alternative sources of energy, other than nuclear power. In the short term, the Department of Energy is encouraging greater energy-use efficiency.

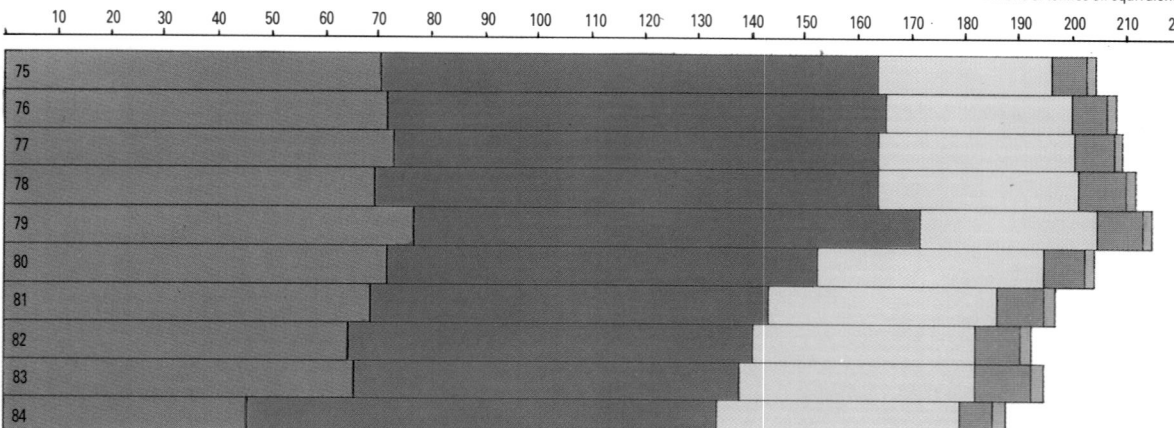

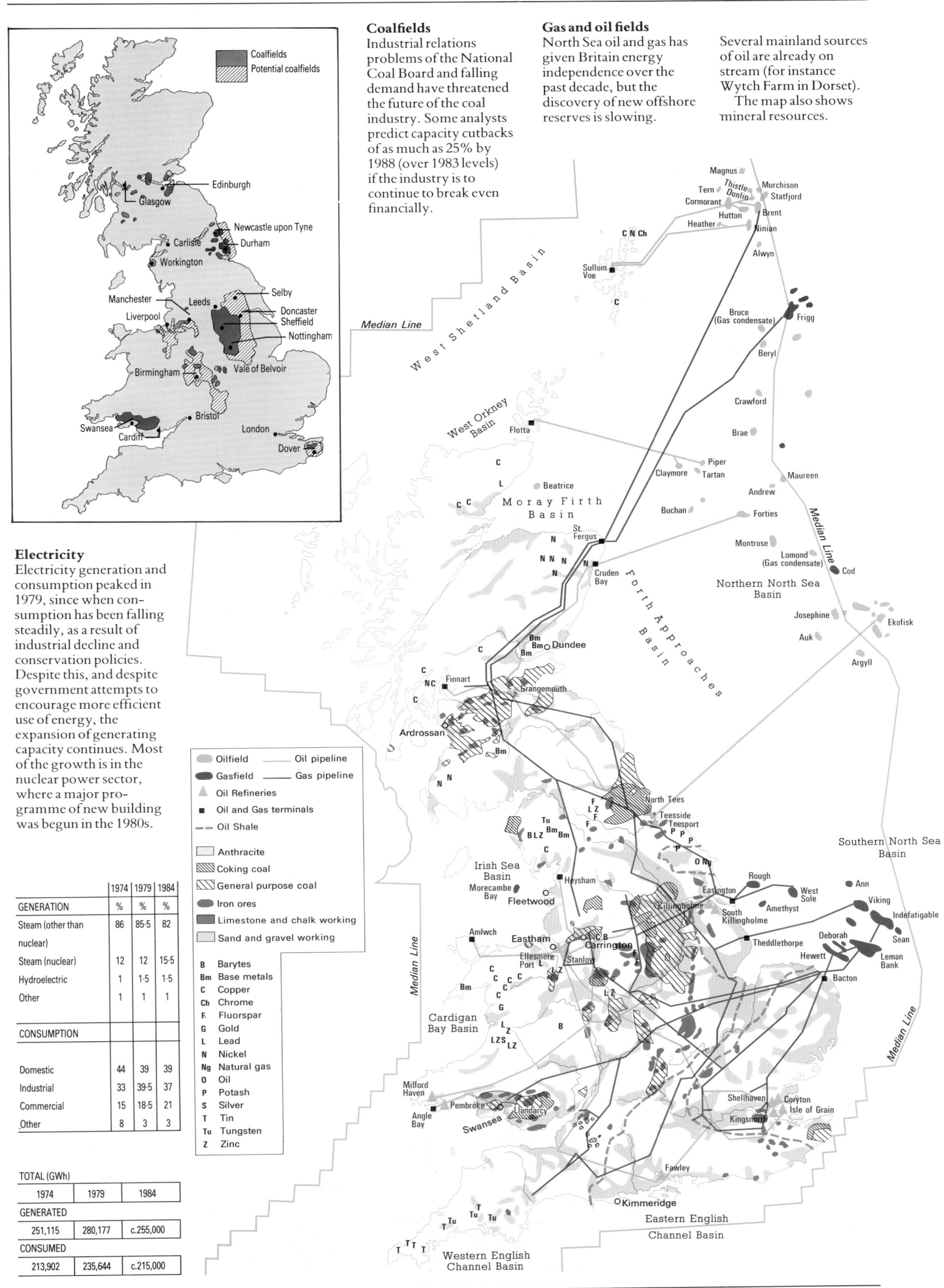

Coalfields

Industrial relations problems of the National Coal Board and falling demand have threatened the future of the coal industry. Some analysts predict capacity cutbacks of as much as 25% by 1988 (over 1983 levels) if the industry is to continue to break even financially.

Gas and oil fields

North Sea oil and gas has given Britain energy independence over the past decade, but the discovery of new offshore reserves is slowing.

Several mainland sources of oil are already on stream (for instance Wytch Farm in Dorset).
The map also shows mineral resources.

Electricity

Electricity generation and consumption peaked in 1979, since when consumption has been falling steadily, as a result of industrial decline and conservation policies. Despite this, and despite government attempts to encourage more efficient use of energy, the expansion of generating capacity continues. Most of the growth is in the nuclear power sector, where a major programme of new building was begun in the 1980s.

	1974	1979	1984
GENERATION	%	%	%
Steam (other than nuclear)	86	85·5	82
Steam (nuclear)	12	12	15·5
Hydroelectric	1	1·5	1·5
Other	1	1	1
CONSUMPTION			
Domestic	44	39	39
Industrial	33	39·5	37
Commercial	15	18·5	21
Other	8	3	3

TOTAL (GWh)

1974	1979	1984
GENERATED		
251,115	280,177	c.255,000
CONSUMED		
213,902	235,644	c.215,000

Legend

- Oilfield — Oil pipeline
- Gasfield — Gas pipeline
- Oil Refineries
- Oil and Gas terminals
- Oil Shale
- Anthracite
- Coking coal
- General purpose coal
- Iron ores
- Limestone and chalk working
- Sand and gravel working

- B Barytes
- Bm Base metals
- C Copper
- Ch Chrome
- F Fluorspar
- G Gold
- L Lead
- N Nickel
- Ng Natural gas
- O Oil
- P Potash
- S Silver
- T Tin
- Tu Tungsten
- Z Zinc

NUCLEAR AND HYDROELECTRIC POWER

Nuclear power

Nuclear power has not become the popular energy source once predicted. Its problems have been many and controversial: doubts about capital costs and productivity, about reactor safety, and about the safety of transporting nuclear fuel and depositing of nuclear waste. There is also concern about the generation of increasing amounts of plutonium, a product of uranium fission, and how this could lead to nuclear weapons proliferation.

Nuclear power currently supplies 16% of Britain's electricity, but the proportion is planned to rise to 25% by 1995. There are 10 nuclear power plants in operation, with 6 more planned or under construction. The Central Electricity Generating Board (CEGB) power stations are serviced by British Nuclear Fuels (BNFL), which in 1984 became a public limited company. The United Kingdom Atomic Energy Authority (UKAEA) is responsible for the economic, safety and environmental aspects of the nuclear power industry.

The future of the nuclear power building programme depends largely on the outcome of the lengthy public enquiry held in 1984–85 into the planned installation of a new station at Sizewell on the Suffolk coast. The Sizewell B station is to be an American-designed Pressurized Water Reactor (PWR).

Hydroelectric power

Hydroelectric power provides nearly a quarter of the world's electricity but makes only a fractional contribution to British energy needs – currently less than 1·5%.

There is thought to be limited potential for further substantial development of this natural energy resource in Britain, although Dinorwig power station in North Wales shows what is possible. Dinorwig – the biggest power station of its kind in Europe – can meet total Welsh needs.

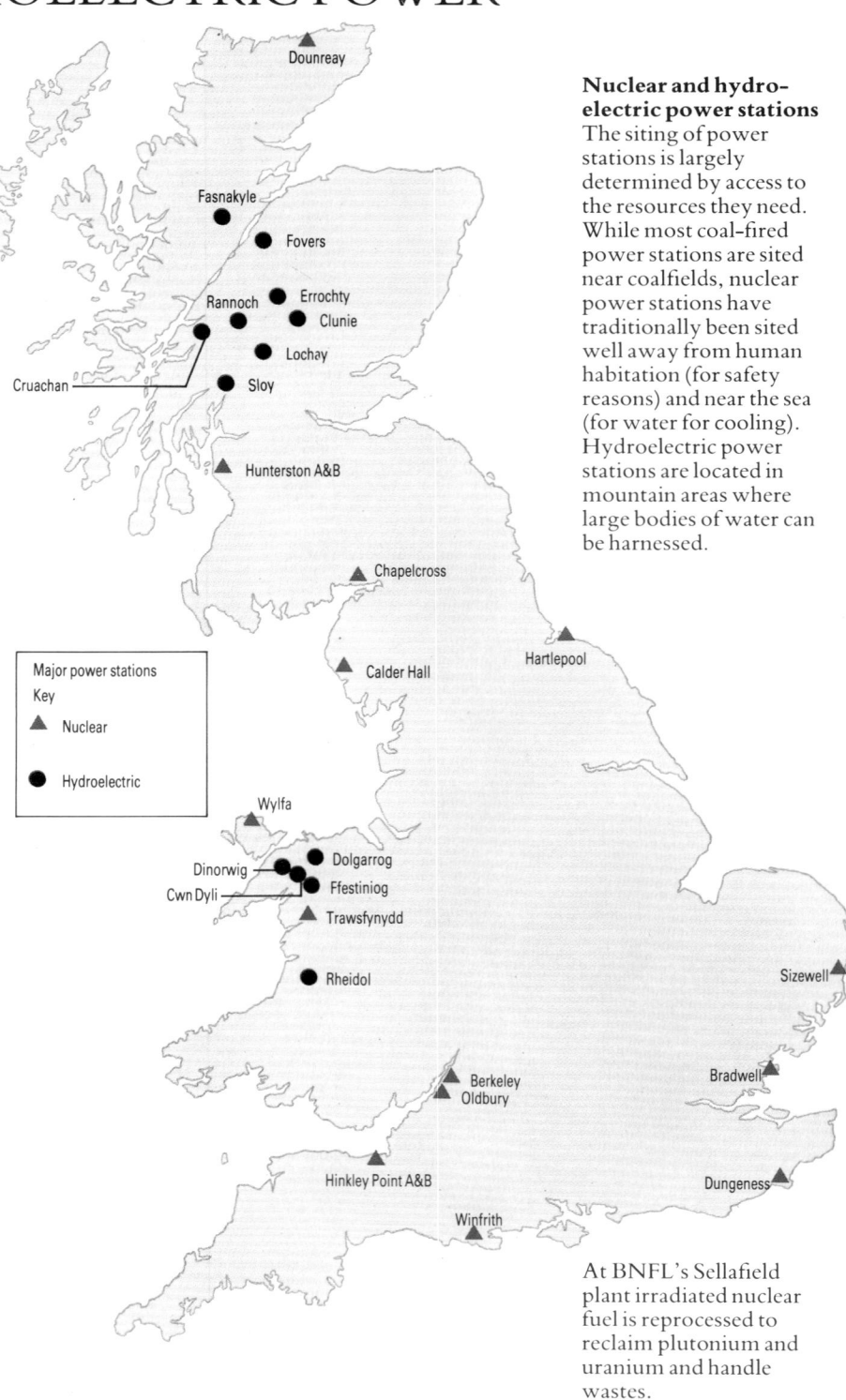

Nuclear and hydro-electric power stations
The siting of power stations is largely determined by access to the resources they need. While most coal-fired power stations are sited near coalfields, nuclear power stations have traditionally been sited well away from human habitation (for safety reasons) and near the sea (for water for cooling). Hydroelectric power stations are located in mountain areas where large bodies of water can be harnessed.

Major power stations
Key
▲ Nuclear
● Hydroelectric

At BNFL's Sellafield plant irradiated nuclear fuel is reprocessed to reclaim plutonium and uranium and handle wastes.

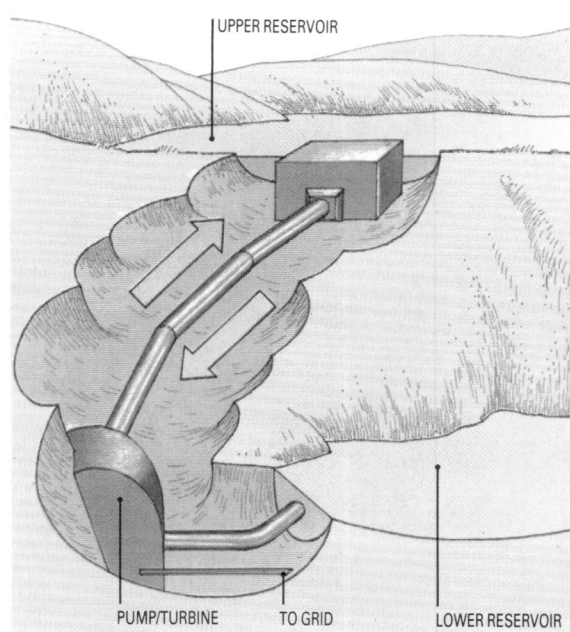

UPPER RESERVOIR

PUMP/TURBINE   TO GRID   LOWER RESERVOIR

Pumped storage schemes

Power stations like Dinorwig exploit the difference in water levels between two reservoirs. Water falling from an upper reservoir turns the turbines that produce the electricity. The water is pumped back using electricity generated in off-peak periods.

ALTERNATIVE ENERGY SOURCES

Coal, oil, gas and nuclear fuels are non-renewable resources. The government is now spending more than £10 million a year in support of its renewable, or alternative, energy programme. Alternative energy sources currently make a negligible contribution to national energy needs, but the prospect of increasingly expensive and scarce oil in particular has encouraged steady research into the possibilities of tapping the energy of solar radiation, tides and sea waves, wind, and heat from hot, dry rocks beneath the Earth's surface.

The potential of these different sources is still at an early stage of investigation, but there seem to be good prospects in Britain for harnessing wind, tidal and geothermal power.

The biggest 'alternative' source of energy (with current technology), however, is energy conservation, that is using the country's existing energy supply more efficiently.

Energy conservation

About 60% of the energy supplied in Britain is wasted – during conversion, distribution and consumption. Research has shown that with more efficient use, Britain could cut its energy needs by half at no cost to its standard of living. This could be achieved in several ways.

First, the heat produced by electricity generation at power stations is often treated as waste. In coal-fired stations, for example, two-thirds of the heat generated is lost through the cooling towers. This energy could instead be harnessed and used. Such 'combined heat and power' schemes could be used to provide district heating.

Second, many buildings lack adequate insulation. Heat dissipation through walls, windows and roofs can be greatly reduced with even simple 'do-it-yourself' measures.

Third, in a well-insulated home or office, 'free heat gain' – the heat given off by lights, machines and human bodies – can be exploited.

Fourth, motor vehicles could be made more fuel-efficient. As little as 12% of the petrol put into the least efficient cars is converted into useful motive power at the wheels; the rest is given off as heat or lost through drag.

The government, through the Department of Energy, is encouraging cost-effective energy conservation measures, investigating improved methods of energy utilisation, and discouraging wasteful use of energy. In 1983 it set up an Energy Efficiency Office which, as one of its functions, is developing home energy audits.

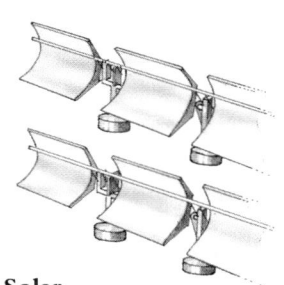

Solar
The price of solar systems has yet to fall enough to make them attractive for use on a large scale in Britain, although about 20,000 homes do have solar-heated water.

Tidal/wave
The Severn estuary provides a potential site for tidal power. Exploitation of energy generated by the waves is likely to be limited due to expense and complexity.

Wind
Some 10,000 windmills were used in Britain in the 19th century. Only a few hundred are now in use. Parts of Scotland and south-east England hold the greatest potential.

Geothermal
Geothermal energy uses the heat of rocks at great depth to heat water and uses the resultant steam to generate electricity. Experiments in Cornwall have been promising.

Domestic energy conservation
Many British homes use central heating without adequate insulation, so much of the heat is wasted and fuel bills are higher than they need be.

Homes can be made more energy efficient with double glazing, roof insulation, lagged pipes and hot water tanks, cavity wall insulation, and draught excluders. Together these can reduce heat losses by up to as much as 40%.

1 Lagged pipe work etc
2 Roof space insulation
3 Double glazing
4 Cavity wall insulation
5 Residual heat from occupants and cooker etc.
6 Efficient draft exclusion
7 Improved car design

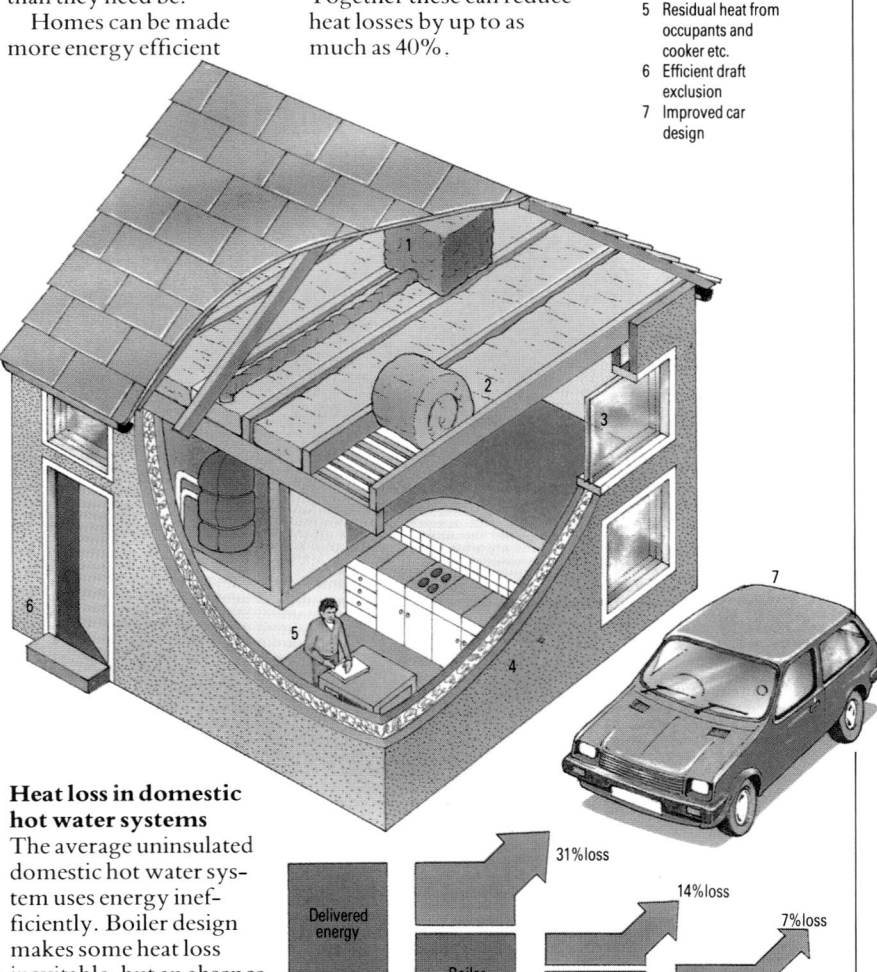

Heat loss in domestic hot water systems
The average uninsulated domestic hot water system uses energy inefficiently. Boiler design makes some heat loss inevitable, but an absence of lagging around tanks and pipes can result in up to a quarter of the heat generated being lost.

Delivered energy 100% — Boiler 69% — 31% loss — Tank 55% — 14% loss — Pipes 48% — 7% loss

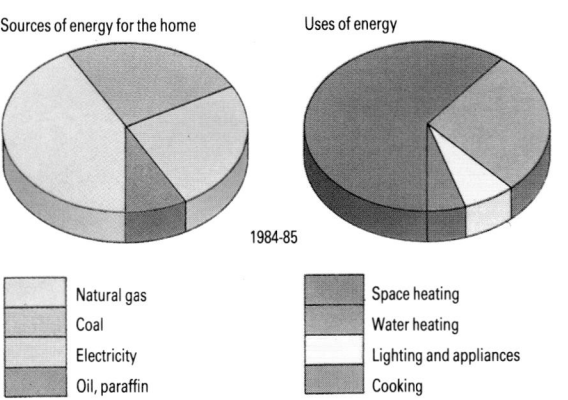

Sources of energy for the home

Uses of energy

1984-85

Natural gas
Coal
Electricity
Oil, paraffin

Space heating
Water heating
Lighting and appliances
Cooking

THE CONTROL OF POLLUTION

Pollution is not a new problem. Smoke from coal-burning was a health hazard in Britain as early as the 14th century. In 1952, an estimated 4000 Londoners died from the effects of a particularly virulent winter smog.

The attention given to pollution in the last 20 years has resulted in the imposition of increasingly strict controls on industry, with many positive results. But the problem is by no means solved. Acid pollution, contamination of air and water by heavy metals, and the disposal of nuclear waste remain major issues.

Acid pollution

Acid pollution is one of the most harmful and pervasive forms of air pollution. In the last decade it has become a major international political issue as the pollution produced by one country can be carried to others, where its full effects are felt.

When oil and coal are burned, they give off sulphur dioxide (SO_2) and nitrogen oxides (NO_x). Some of these chemicals are 'dry deposited' as gas and particles near the sources. Others react with moisture in the atmosphere, turning to acid and returning to Earth as 'wet deposited' pollution – acid rain, snow, fog and sleet.

Britain is the fourth largest source of SO_2 in the world, and a major source of NO_x. Most SO_2 and NO_x are by-products of electricity generation by coal-fired power stations. Petrol-driven road vehicles are also a major source of NO_x.

While the effects of acid pollution in Britain are not yet thoroughly researched, forest damage is suspected, lake and river acidification is reported, and building corrosion is common – £20 million is being spent on the restoration of Westminster Abbey alone.

Carbon dioxide

The burning of oil, coal and natural gas gives off carbon dioxide (CO_2), which accumulates in the atmosphere and reduces the amount of solar radiation reflected back into space from the Earth. This creates a 'greenhouse effect'. A doubling of CO_2 concentrations could increase global temperatures by 2–3°C, altering weather patterns, disrupting ecosystems and moving crop-growing regions further north. As a major coal consumer (accounting for 18% of the western European total), Britain is a major source of carbon dioxide.

Lead

One of the most controversial pollution issues of recent years has been that of the effects of lead on health. The toxic effects of lead are well known. Less certain is how harmful it is at the levels to which people are routinely exposed, from contaminated food and water, and from motor vehicle exhaust fumes. The effects of lead on the mental development of children have come under particular scrutiny. Several European countries are now following the example of the USA in introducing lead-free petrol.

Nuclear waste

Spent fuel from a nuclear power station contains uranium and plutonium that can be used again, and a small quantity of radioactive waste. Reprocessing (of the kind carried out at Sellafield, for example) separates the reusable material from the waste, which must then be disposed of safely. The disposal of radioactive waste has caused considerable public concern.

Until stopped by public opposition, Britain dumped liquid wastes of low radiation levels into the sea. Such dumping may eventually be permanently banned. High-level wastes present a different problem. Liquid wastes of this type are generally kept in special concrete storage tanks, which must be scrupulously maintained while the wastes are solidified for more permanent disposal. Solid high-level wastes will take thousands of years to de-activate; Britain is now researching the best rock formations in which to bury the waste.

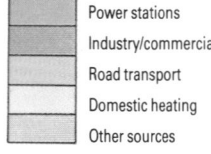

Didcot power station in Oxfordshire is one of the largest coal-fired power stations in Britain.

Acid in the atmosphere
The burning of fossil fuels for energy production and to drive industry is the largest source of acid pollution (and of carbon dioxide).

There are several ways of cleaning emissions. Coal can be washed before it is used to remove sulphurous deposits; sulphur can be removed from coal during burning; or exhaust gases – from power stations and cars alike – can be filtered. Many of these processes are expensive, but the repair of damage to soils, forests and lakes will be more expensive in the long term.

SO_2

NO_x

- Power stations
- Industry/commercial
- Road transport
- Domestic heating
- Other sources

Spread of air pollution
When the local effects of sulphur pollution were first noticed in Britain, the solution used was to build higher chimneys to disperse the pollutants to the winds; many existing coal- and oil-fired power stations, for example, bear chimneys that are 200m or more tall. But constructing tall outlet chimneys had the effect of carrying the pollutants further afield.

1   50% dry deposited

2   30% in local rain

3   20% forms acid in clouds that can travel over 1500km from the source

Water pollution

Despite recent progress, many British rivers and lakes are still polluted. The sources are both direct (industrial discharge and sewage) and indirect (the run-off from the soil of groundwater acidified by acid pollution).

Fertilisers washed off farmland can produce a massive overgrowth of algae and a reduction in oxygen levels in water, killing fish and plants. Nitrates from sewage and fertilisers could pose a particular health threat if they were to get into drinking water. Pesticide run-off can kill wildlife and in extreme cases could threaten public health. Heavy metals such as cadmium (from fertilisers and smelting) and mercury (from industrial effluent and sewage) can find their way into drinking and coastal water. The chemicals are highly poisonous and their ill-effects are cumulative. Cadmium levels in some especially heavily polluted estuaries have encouraged recommendations that no-one should regularly eat shellfish from the waters.

Polluted rivers and coasts

Parts of Britain's coast are subject to pollution from industrial waste and untreated domestic sewage and more than 2800 km of rivers are too polluted to support animal life. Organic pollution changes the oxygen content of river water and the sensitivity of different invertebrates to this change gives a relatively simple means of visually estimating the amount of pollution.

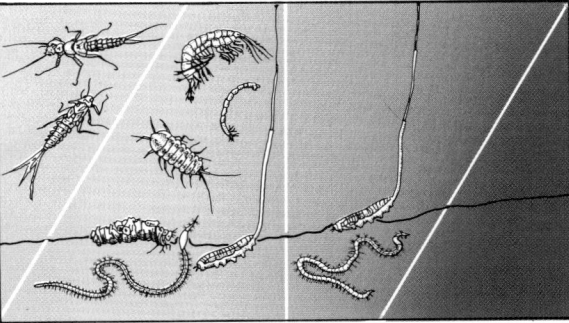

A Stonefly nymph	B Caddis fly larva	C Sludge worm	D No life
Mayfly nymph	Freshwater shrimp	Rat-tailed maggot	
	Sludge worm		
	Rat-tailed maggot		
	Water louse		
	Bloodworm		

Animals shown at A will only be found in clean water while those at B will indicate some pollution. If only animals shown at C are found, fairly serious pollution can be expected; these creatures are protected from the effects of pollution, the former by its ability to store oxygen in its bloodstream, the latter because it breathes oxygen from the surface of the water by means of its breathing tube. If no life is found, the water is obviously seriously polluted.

Control measures

Pollution control legislation in Britain is not yet wide-ranging and is often variable in effect. There is no national toxic waste management policy; controls on pesticides are voluntary; and only recently has the 1974 Control of Pollution Act started to become fully enforced on a nationwide basis. The only statutory obligations regarding water quality are contained in the 1973 Water Act, which calls for a general 'national policy' for maintaining inland water quality. Air pollution, though, has been markedly reduced since the 1956 Clean Air Act. Since 1960, the average concentration of smoke in the atmosphere has fallen by 80%.

In the mid-19th century, the lower Thames was an open sewer. Thousands of people died from recurring epidemics of Asiatic cholera. Attempts to clean up the river paid off in the 1970s, when mercury levels fell following controls on industrial discharges. Fish have now returned.

NATURE CONSERVATION

Unlike many other countries, Britain has little true wilderness left. The need to support a large population on a small land area has radically remodelled the British landscape, reducing the area left for wildlife and natural habitat. Agricultural intensification during and since World War II has wrought particularly marked changes. Wetland, moorland, heathland and downland have been 'reclaimed'; hedgerows and woodland have been cleared to make bigger fields that are easier to plough and crop; and increasing quantities of chemical fertilizer have been applied to the land. The resulting increase in yields has been remarkable, but the natural environment has suffered proportionately.

Two Countryside Commissions (one for England and Wales, one for Scotland) and the Nature Conservancy Council are primarily responsible for statutory nature conservation. Working in conjunction with local authorities, they are, under the Wildlife and Countryside Act of 1981, empowered to preserve and enhance the environment by, for example, restricting development, acquiring and reclaiming derelict land, and instigating amenity schemes. The Commissions are also responsible for maintaining the integrity of the country's 'green belts', the areas designated around large cities and towns where it is intended the land should be left open and free from further development of roads, industry or housing.

Britain's statutory protected areas offer great, but not complete, relief from development. Nearly three-quarters of national park land is privately owned, and much of it is actively farmed; a fifth of Exmoor's moorland was lost to farming between 1947 and 1976. Then there is confusion over what Areas of Outstanding Natural Beauty are supposed to achieve – they are not protected from development by farming, forestry or industry. And Sites of Special Scientific Interest are often maintained only through voluntary agreements between local authorities and farmers to keep the land out of intense agricultural production – farming using traditional methods is permitted.

Buttermere, a glacial valley lake in the heart of the Lake District National Park. Britain's national parks cover some 13,600 sq km, or 9% of the area of England and Wales. The public are encouraged to visit these areas while still protecting the environment by the provision of free car parks, camping and caravan areas, nature trails and information centres.

Urban spread

In the last 30 years, the population of Britain's big urban areas has been falling, and that of towns and rural areas growing. One result is that 15,000 hectares of land a year are being covered by new development. Inner city renewal has meanwhile not always taken place – millions of houses need major repairs, and 46,000 hectares of land have been left derelict in England alone.

Forestry

Deciduous woodland is the natural vegetation of Britain which was once almost entirely covered in forest. Today, Britain has less forest cover by proportion than any other European country except Ireland – a sparse 9%. Half of this is coniferous woodland planted since 1895. Ancient woodlands and broadleaf forests of oak, beech and other native species make up less than one-third of Britain's forest cover. The biggest changes have been wrought by clearance for agriculture or conversion to conifer plantations. Conifers are grown for timber and as raw material for the paper industry.

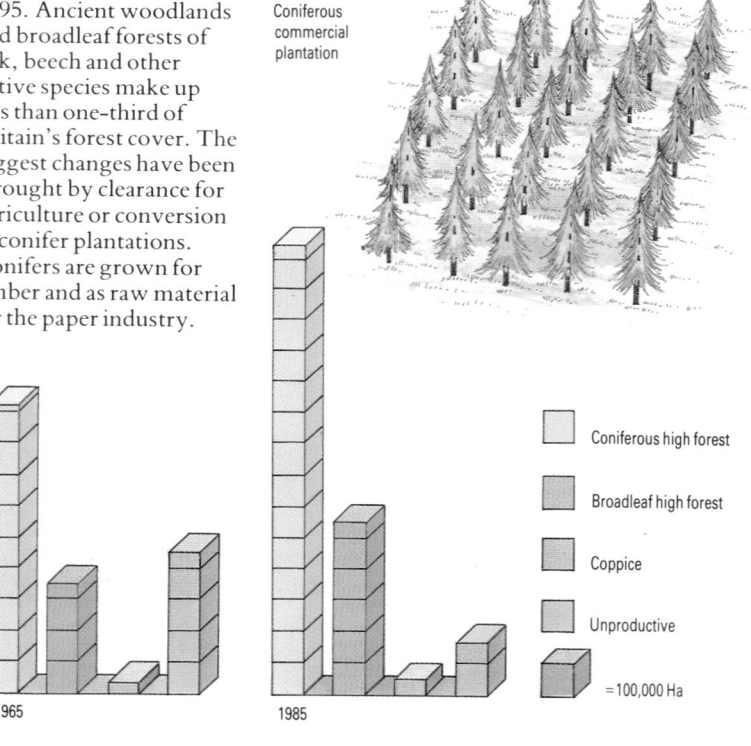

Natural mixed broadleaf

Coniferous commercial plantation

Coniferous high forest

Broadleaf high forest

Coppice

Unproductive

= 100,000 Ha

1965

1985

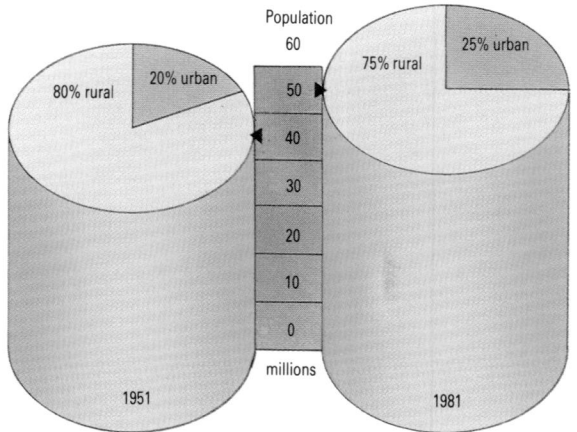

Population
60

80% rural   20% urban   50   75% rural   25% urban

40

30

20

10

0
millions

1951   1981

Habitat loss and threatened wildlife

Between 1945 and 1972, 80% of hedgerow trees – once one of Britain's richest reservoirs of flora and fauna – died through disease or were removed. Hedgerows were removed at a rate of 7250 km per year, and nearly a third of Britain's ancient woodlands were cleared. Since then removal of hedgerows has slowed but today wetlands, meadows, moorland and grassland are similarly at risk. Habitat loss such as this is the main threat to wildlife. Britain has about 1400 flowering plant species, 420 native mammal, bird, reptile, amphibian and fish species, and 50,000 species of insects and other invertebrates. But nearly one-fifth of the plants, and many of the mammals, birds and reptiles, are threatened.

WETLANDS About 100,000 hectares of wetland are drained every year, threatening the plants, birds and fish that depend on them.

OTTERS Throughout Europe otters are on the decline. Pesticides and the removal of river vegetation are the main causes.

ORCHIDS These are among the rarest of British plants. Many species have been pushed to the edge of extinction as a result of habitat loss from urban development.

BADGERS These woodland creatures are thought to spread tuberculosis to cattle. Thousands have been gassed in the past seven years.

THE NORFOLK BROADS Although man-made, these are an important site for wildlife and recreation. Yet all but three of the Broads are now seriously polluted.

Changing land use and conservation

With over 54 million people packed into a small area of land, conflict over differing land use priorities is hard to avoid. One result is that Britain's land use questions have an environmental dimension, and vice versa. But with more than four-fifths of the land area given over to farming, agriculture is the major factor. Unlike urban land, rural land is subject to little legislative control.

Urban
Forestry
Agriculture

80·3%
10·2%
9·5%

×1,000,000 Ha

National Parks
National Park Direction Areas (Scotland)
Areas of Outstanding Natural Beauty
National Scenic Areas (Scotland)
Heritage Coast and Coastal Conservation Zones (Scotland)
Green Belt
Proposed Green Belt
Areas of Special Scientific, Landscape or Historic Interest

Protected areas

Britain's protected areas range from the 10 national parks (the Lake District is the biggest) to the 3900 Sites of Special Scientific Interest (which can be as small as a copse or roadside verge). There are also 33 Areas of Outstanding Natural Beauty in all parts of the country, and 1195 km of heritage coast. Many of these areas are protected as much for recreation as for conservation.

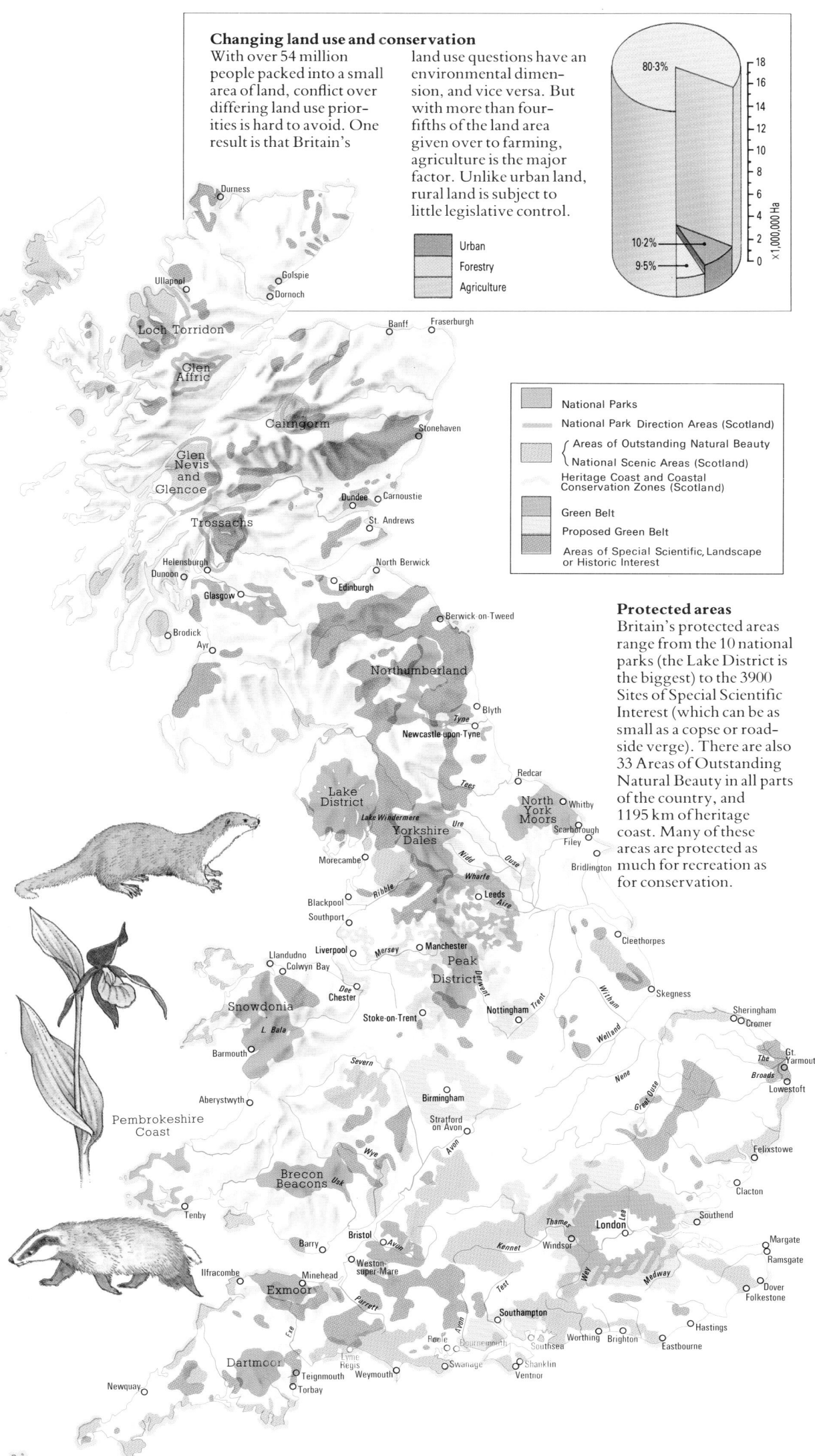

OLD AND NEW NETWORKS

Traditional means of communication such as the letter post, radio and newspapers are still with us, but in the last five years or so they have been joined by new computer-based methods of information transfer such as teletext and electronic mail.

In telecommunications, the trend is towards transmitting information in the form of a rapid series of electrical pulses, because these 'digital' signals are less vulnerable to electrical interference than the wavelike (analogue) signals they are replacing. Computers also process information in digital form. The convergence of computer and communication technologies gave rise to Information Technology (IT) and sparked off the communications explosion. Today, telephone calls, TV pictures and computer data can be transmitted in digital form via common links that include, nationwide, underground cables and microwave relays and, internationally, undersea cables and satellite systems.

Dish aerials at the London Teleport receive from satellites microwaves carrying TV signals. Microwaves are radio waves with wavelengths of less than 30 cm.

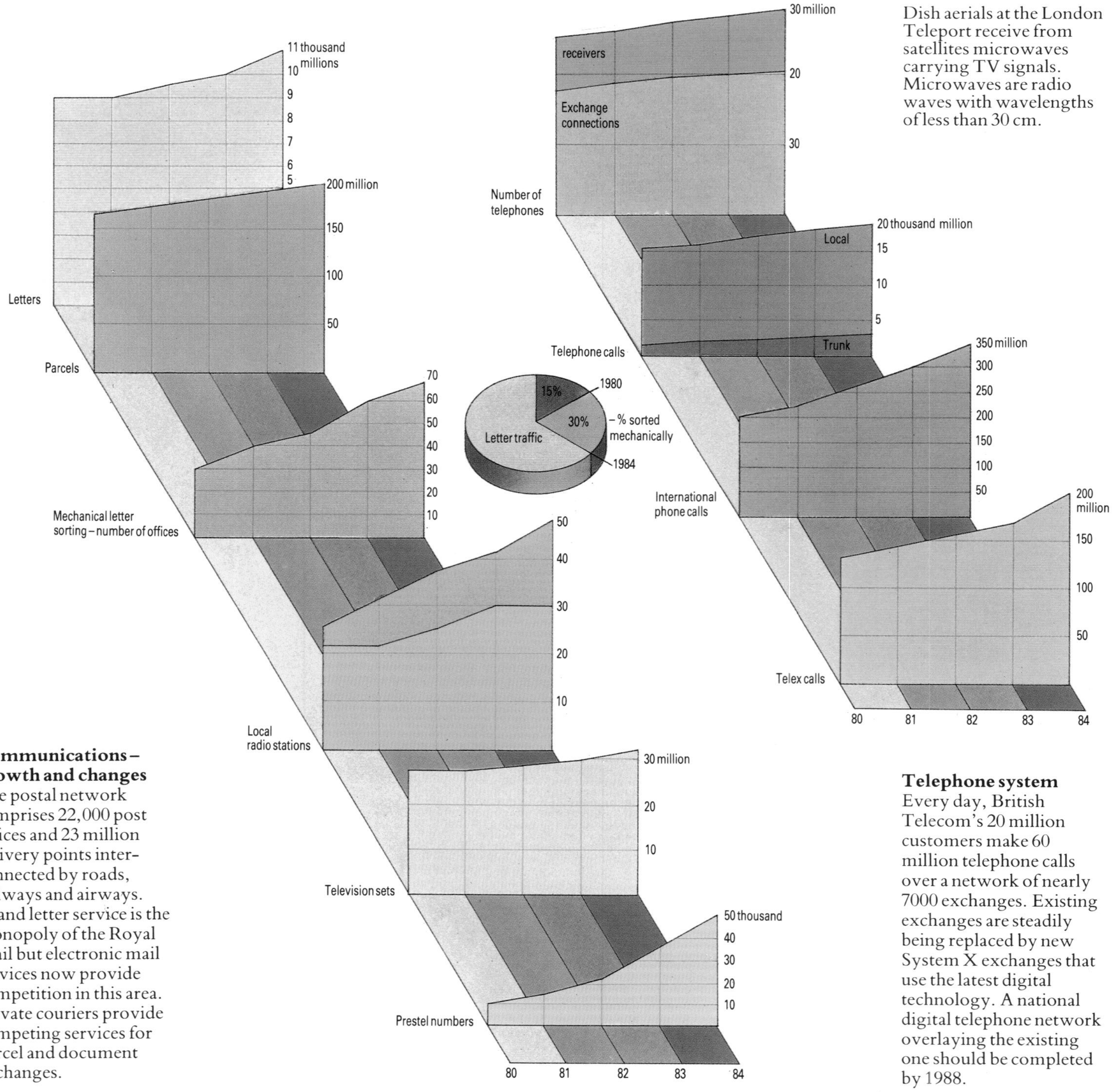

Letters — 11 thousand millions / 10 / 9 / 8 / 7 / 6 / 5

Parcels — 200 million / 150 / 100 / 50

Mechanical letter sorting – number of offices — 70 / 60 / 50 / 40 / 30 / 20 / 10

Letter traffic — 15% 1980 / 30% – % sorted mechanically / 1984

Local radio stations — 50 / 40 / 30 / 20 / 10

Television sets — 30 million / 20 / 10

Prestel numbers — 50 thousand / 40 / 30 / 20 / 10

80 81 82 83 84

Number of telephones — 30 million / 20 / 30 (receivers / Exchange connections)

Telephone calls — 20 thousand million / 15 / 10 / 5 (Local / Trunk)

International phone calls — 350 million / 300 / 250 / 200 / 150 / 100 / 50

Telex calls — 200 million / 150 / 100 / 50

80 81 82 83 84

Communications – growth and changes

The postal network comprises 22,000 post offices and 23 million delivery points interconnected by roads, railways and airways. Inland letter service is the monopoly of the Royal Mail but electronic mail services now provide competition in this area. Private couriers provide competing services for parcel and document exchanges.

Telephone system

Every day, British Telecom's 20 million customers make 60 million telephone calls over a network of nearly 7000 exchanges. Existing exchanges are steadily being replaced by new System X exchanges that use the latest digital technology. A national digital telephone network overlaying the existing one should be completed by 1988.

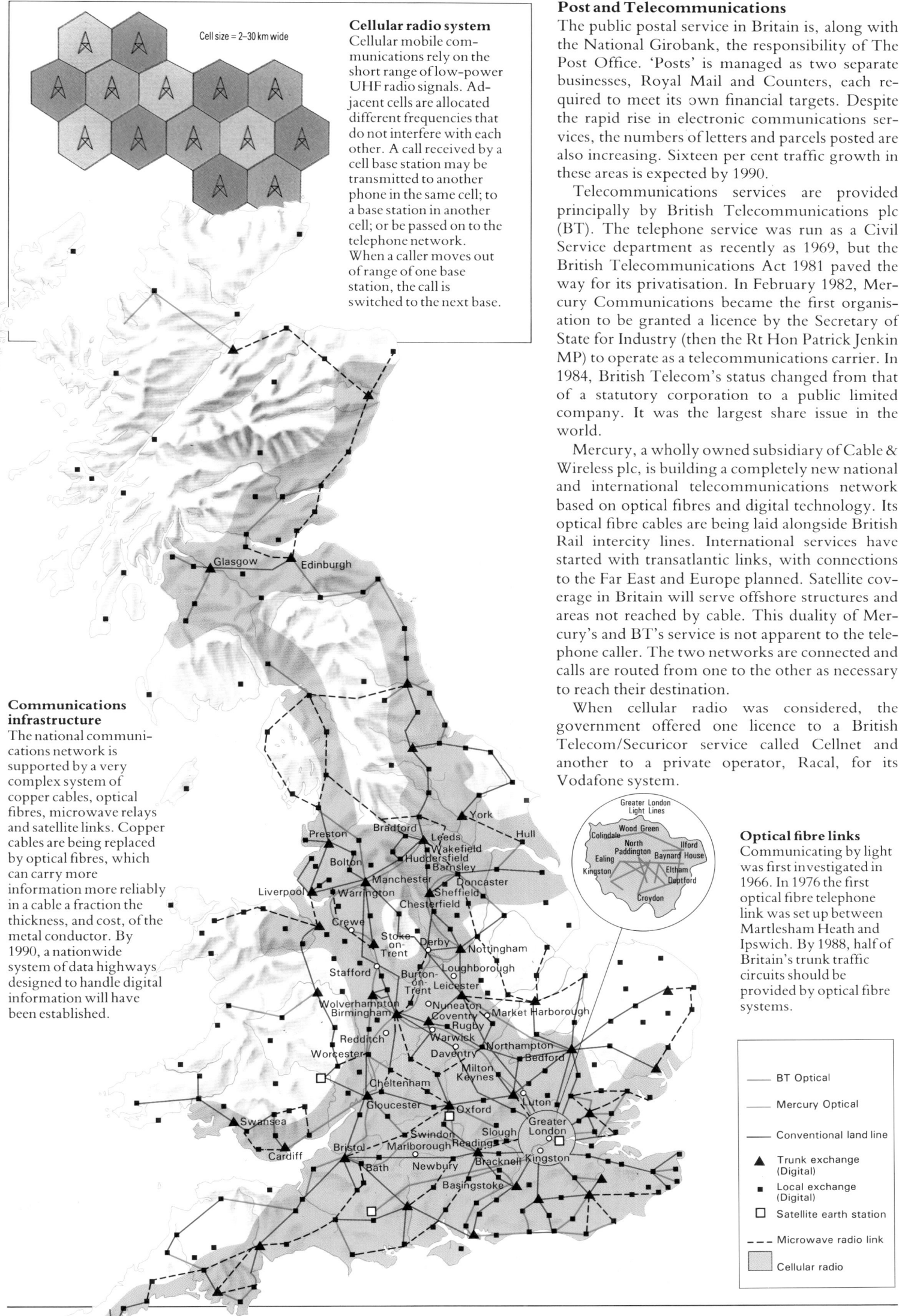

Cellular radio system

Cellular mobile communications rely on the short range of low-power UHF radio signals. Adjacent cells are allocated different frequencies that do not interfere with each other. A call received by a cell base station may be transmitted to another phone in the same cell; to a base station in another cell; or be passed on to the telephone network. When a caller moves out of range of one base station, the call is switched to the next base.

Cell size = 2–30 km wide

Post and Telecommunications

The public postal service in Britain is, along with the National Girobank, the responsibility of The Post Office. 'Posts' is managed as two separate businesses, Royal Mail and Counters, each required to meet its own financial targets. Despite the rapid rise in electronic communications services, the numbers of letters and parcels posted are also increasing. Sixteen per cent traffic growth in these areas is expected by 1990.

Telecommunications services are provided principally by British Telecommunications plc (BT). The telephone service was run as a Civil Service department as recently as 1969, but the British Telecommunications Act 1981 paved the way for its privatisation. In February 1982, Mercury Communications became the first organisation to be granted a licence by the Secretary of State for Industry (then the Rt Hon Patrick Jenkin MP) to operate as a telecommunications carrier. In 1984, British Telecom's status changed from that of a statutory corporation to a public limited company. It was the largest share issue in the world.

Mercury, a wholly owned subsidiary of Cable & Wireless plc, is building a completely new national and international telecommunications network based on optical fibres and digital technology. Its optical fibre cables are being laid alongside British Rail intercity lines. International services have started with transatlantic links, with connections to the Far East and Europe planned. Satellite coverage in Britain will serve offshore structures and areas not reached by cable. This duality of Mercury's and BT's service is not apparent to the telephone caller. The two networks are connected and calls are routed from one to the other as necessary to reach their destination.

When cellular radio was considered, the government offered one licence to a British Telecom/Securicor service called Cellnet and another to a private operator, Racal, for its Vodafone system.

Communications infrastructure

The national communications network is supported by a very complex system of copper cables, optical fibres, microwave relays and satellite links. Copper cables are being replaced by optical fibres, which can carry more information more reliably in a cable a fraction the thickness, and cost, of the metal conductor. By 1990, a nationwide system of data highways designed to handle digital information will have been established.

Optical fibre links

Communicating by light was first investigated in 1966. In 1976 the first optical fibre telephone link was set up between Martlesham Heath and Ipswich. By 1988, half of Britain's trunk traffic circuits should be provided by optical fibre systems.

Greater London Light Lines

Colindale · Wood Green · Ilford · North Paddington · Baynard House · Ealing · Eltham · Kingston · Deptford · Croydon

——	BT Optical
——	Mercury Optical
——	Conventional land line
▲	Trunk exchange (Digital)
■	Local exchange (Digital)
☐	Satellite earth station
- - -	Microwave radio link
▦	Cellular radio

BROADCASTING AND THE PRESS

Television

Two organisations are authorised by the government to provide national public television and radio broadcasts, the British Broadcasting Corporation (BBC) and the Independent Broadcasting Authority (IBA). The British Broadcasting Company began broadcasting in this country in 1922. In 1926 it became the British Broadcasting Corporation (BBC). The BBC, whose second television channel opened in 1964, operates under the terms of a licence from the Home Secretary. It derives most of its income from licence fee receipts.

The Television Act, 1954, created the Independent Television Authority (ITA) to select and take responsibility for the activities of the new independent television (ITV) companies that the Act made possible. The first ITV transmission was in September 1955. Now, 16 ITV companies (15 area contractors plus TV-am) provide 99% of the population with local and networked programmes. ITV's second channel, Channel 4, opened in 1982. The service is financed by subscriptions from the 15 ITV area contractors. ITV generates income from selling advertising time.

In January 1983, the BBC launched Britain's first early morning television programme, 'Breakfast Time'. This was followed a month later by independent television's early morning breakfast-time service, provided by TV-am.

British television viewers now watch about 30 million television sets, more than one per household. But today, the television set is a vehicle not only for watching broadcast and cable television programmes, but also for viewing videotape films and gaining access to computer-based information systems. These are the teletext and viewdata services.

Teletext

Television signals contain brief blank periods between frames, originally inserted to allow the receiver to 'recover' before the next picture began. Television receivers no longer need this recovery period, which is now used for the transmission of extra data. Pages of information are transmitted in digital code. When the page number selected by the viewer coincides with the page number transmitted, the page appears on the screen instead of, or superimposed on, the live picture. This is teletext. The BBC's teletext service is called CEEFAX and ITV's is called ORACLE.

TV systems

Television programming can now reach the home from transmitters fed by land-line, microwave or satellite; directly from satellites using roof-top dish aerials; or by underground cable from a central TV station.

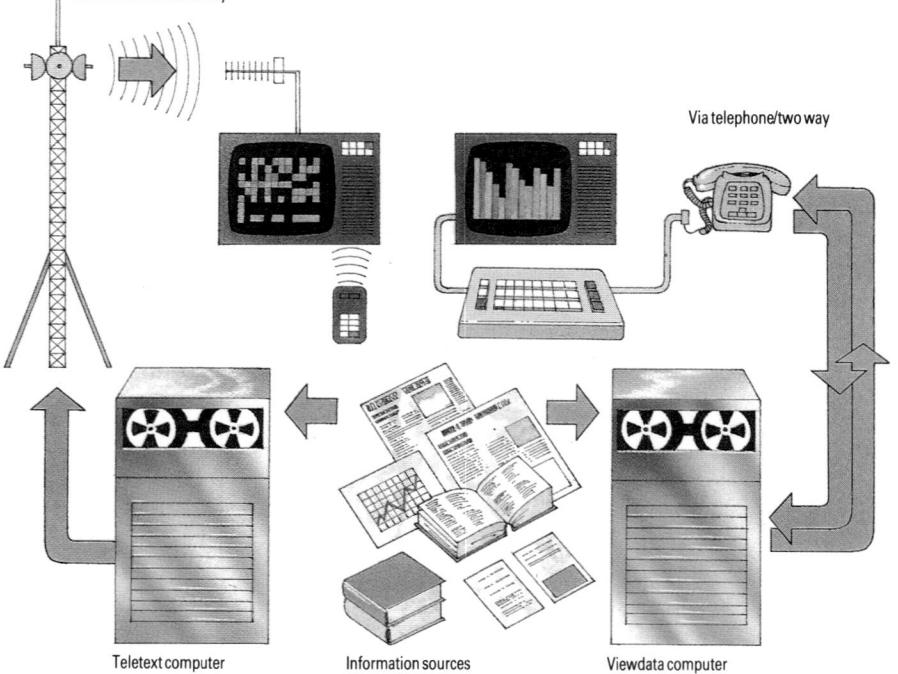

Domestic dish aerial
Ground station receiver
Transmitter Earth station
Cable TV station
Cable link
Cable link
Aerial broadcast
Conventional domestic receivers
Domestic receivers

A typical viewdata screen shot

Viewdata

British Telecom's Prestel, the world's first public viewdata service, was introduced to Britain in 1979. Users can access over 310,000 pages (screens) of information on their own computer terminals. Prestel is used by businesses to distribute information. Users are charged for the phone call and the use of each page.

Via TV broadcast/one way

Via telephone/two way

Teletext computer
Information sources
Viewdata computer

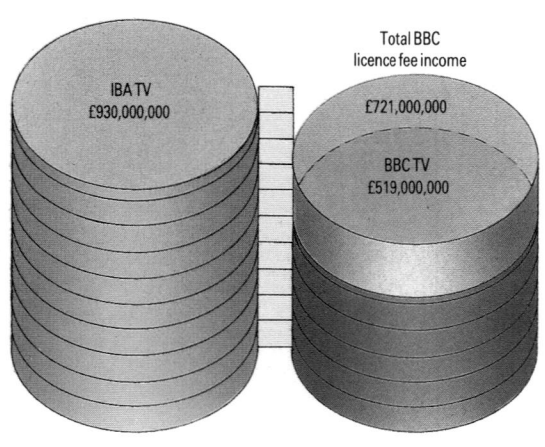

IBA TV
£930,000,000

Total BBC licence fee income

£721,000,000

BBC TV
£519,000,000

Radio

In 1971, the government transformed the ITA into the Independent *Broadcasting* Authority (IBA) and made it responsible for the establishment of Independent Local Radio (ILR). The first 3 stations opened in 1973 and now there are over 50. About 17·5 million people listen to their local ILR station every week. ILR has a 28% share of all radio listening. The BBC also operates local radio stations (currently 30) to complement its 4 network and national regional services. In 1985, the Home Secretary invited applications for licences to operate community radio stations. Twenty were selected to begin the experimental service in 1986. Stations must offer programming not offered by local radio.

The press

National and regional morning and national Sunday newspaper circulations have shown little change in recent years, but free newspapers have experienced rapid growth. Free papers began as classified advertising sheets with little or no editorial content. Their advertising revenue and economical production methods allow publishers to give them away and still show a profit. Editorial content has been increased and free papers now compete with established 'paid-for' newspapers.

Fleet Street, the centre of Britain's newspaper industry, continues to suffer from out-of-date production methods and poor management–union relations. There has been considerable resistance to the introduction of new technology, but the growth of the free press, the adoption of some new technology in the regional press, and the advent of News (UK), publishing a national daily newspaper, *Today*, by the most advanced production methods available, all challenge traditional production methods in the national press.

New technology

The production of newspapers (and magazines and books) was a labour-intensive and therefore costly task until the information-handling capacity of current computer and communications technology bypassed some of the traditional production stages. Trade unions have resisted new technology where it threatens the jobs of their members. However, one of its advantages is that editorial and printing centres need not be physically close to one another. They can be linked by telephone or satellite. Reduced production costs have also made 'free' newspapers possible.

Radio funding

BBC radio is funded from a proportion (28% in 1984–85) of licence fee receipts. Each ILR station is financed from its own sales of advertising time, which is limited to a maximum of 9 minutes per hour. Independent television and radio must be self-supporting.

Who owns the Press?

Press ownership is shifting away from wealthy individuals and companies towards smaller groups and businesses as new production methods make newspaper publishing more economical. However, the national press is still owned and controlled by relatively few people, who also have major interests in retail trades and television.

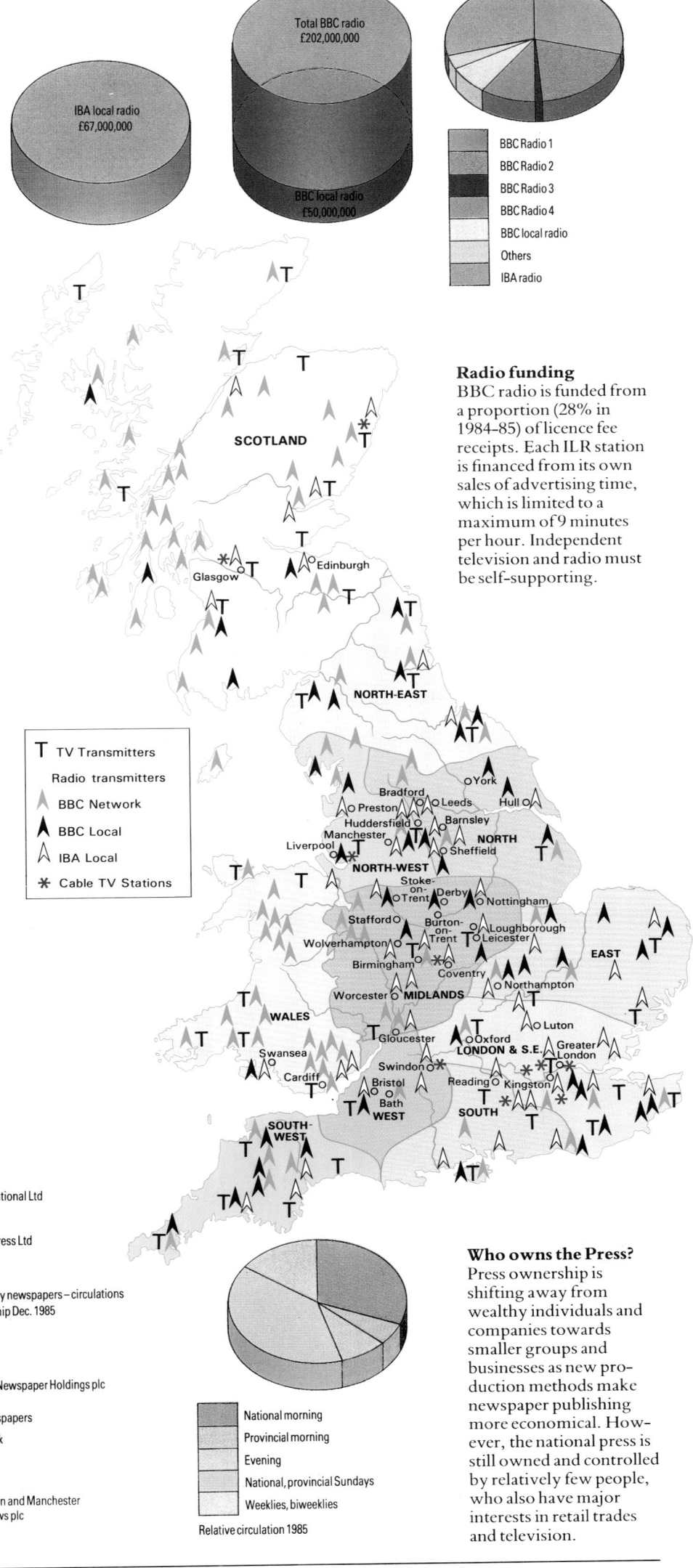

IBA local radio £67,000,000

Total BBC radio £202,000,000

BBC local radio £50,000,000

- BBC Radio 1
- BBC Radio 2
- BBC Radio 3
- BBC Radio 4
- BBC local radio
- Others
- IBA radio

TV Transmitters
Radio transmitters
BBC Network
BBC Local
IBA Local
Cable TV Stations

National daily newspapers – circulations and ownership Dec. 1985

The Sun — News International Ltd
Daily Mirror — Pergamon Press Ltd
Daily Express
Daily Mail — Associated Newspaper Holdings plc
Daily Star — United Newspapers
Daily Telegraph — Conrad Black
Guardian — The Guardian and Manchester Evening News plc
Times
Financial Times — Pearson plc

Millions

- National morning
- Provincial morning
- Evening
- National, provincial Sundays
- Weeklies, biweeklies

Relative circulation 1985

AGRICULTURE AND FISHING

Agriculture

With respect to climate and soil type, less than 20% of Britain's land is of high farming quality and more than 30% is of low quality. Furthermore, each year agriculture loses some 10,000 hectares of arable land to meet the needs of housing, industry and transport. However, farming is one of Britain's success stories in terms of output, efficiency and self-sufficiency. The agricultural industry produces over 60% of the country's food requirements with less than 3% of its working population. Currently, the number of agricultural workers represents less than a third of the post-war (1946) farming workforce and is the smallest proportion of the population engaged in agriculture of any western European country.

In general, farming patterns in Britain represent a sophisticated adjustment to physical conditions, to market demands, and to changing agricultural technology. Overall, Britain is a country of mixed farming. The main arable areas are mostly in the east and some parts of the Midlands and southern England. In the west, where rainfall and relief make arable cropping difficult, grassland for livestock production predominates.

Technology has made a considerable contribution to agricultural efficiency. Today there are more than 500,000 tractors and some 57,000 combine harvesters in use, and a million tonnes of nitrogen fertilisers are applied to the land each year. State support to farmers has also played a major part. Following the 1948 Agriculture Act, the Ministry of Agriculture provided farmers with deficiency payments, grants and subsidies of various kinds. Subsidy and support for agriculture was increased further when in 1973 Britain joined the European Economic Community (EEC) and became subject to its Common Agricultural Policy (CAP). The basis of the CAP is the intervention of guaranteed prices set for agricultural products and the levy of duties on agricultural imports from outside the EEC, together with other subsidies, payments and assistance to farmers. Britain's greater efficiency in agriculture, the small proportion of its resources devoted to it, and its high level of food imports relative to the Community member states, has put it at a disadvantage under the CAP. Farmers receive poor rewards for their high productivity, and imported foods carry particularly high prices. This has led to pressure for reform of the CAP, which commands nearly two-thirds of the total Community budget, and for increased reimbursement on Britain's membership contribution – in 1984-85 Britain contributed some £1700m to the EEC, of which just over £1000m was reimbursed.

Common Agricultural Policy

Support for Agriculture dominates the EEC Annual Budget. Levels of price support are determined annually by the Council of Ministers on the basis of proposals presented by the European Commission. They consist of a minimum price at which the member states are willing to purchase excess production which cannot be marketed profitably. It is this arrangement that has led to the surplus stocks, or mountains, of agricultural produce generated but not sold – except at below-cost prices to, for instance, the USSR.

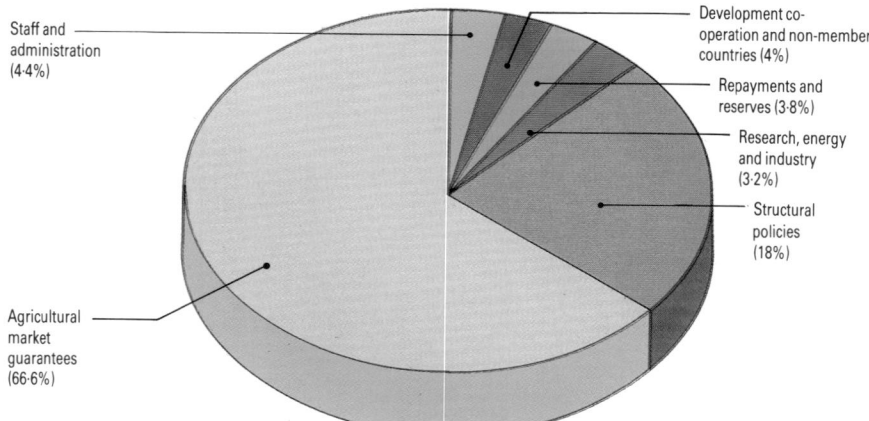

Staff and administration (4·4%)
Development co-operation and non-member countries (4%)
Repayments and reserves (3·8%)
Research, energy and industry (3·2%)
Structural policies (18%)
Agricultural market guarantees (66·6%)

Agricultural produce self-sufficiency

While the value of home-produced food related to total food consumed in Britain has increased over the years, so too has the cost of processing and distributing this food. However, home production of some principal foods has increased dramatically over the past 10 years (% by weight of total supplies): meat (78 to 89%), cheese (60 to 70%), butter (18 to 66%), wheat (59 to 100%).

■ Home production as % of total consumed
■ Home production as % of indigenous types
■ Food processing and distribution costs as % of total expenditure

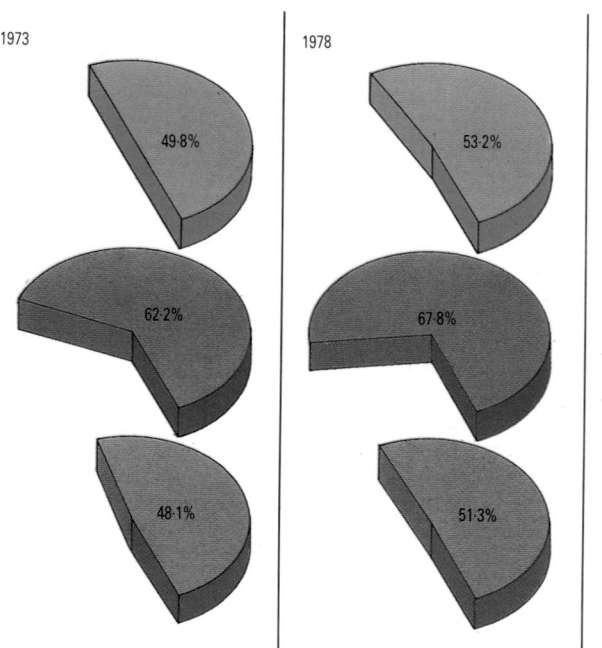

1973 — 49·8% / 62·2% / 48·1%
1978 — 53·2% / 67·8% / 51·3%

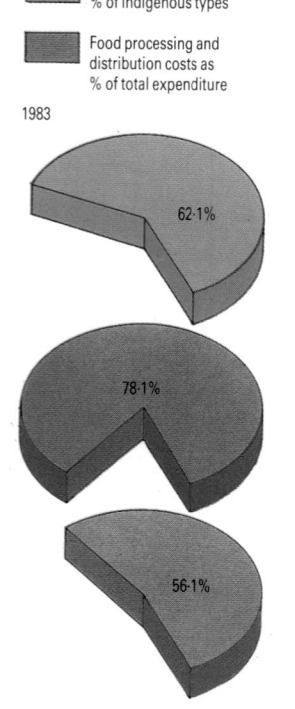

1983 — 62·1% / 78·1% / 56·1%

Size of farms, numbers of workers

The size of agricultural holdings in Britain ranges from less than 2 hectares to well over 200. The smallest employ only 1 or 2 people, and the largest rarely employ more than 10. The total agriculture workforce is around 700,000, of which 25% are women, 20% are part-time, and 30% are seasonal or casual workers. Of the total of 243,000 holdings, some 31,000 large farms account for about half of total output, and half of all farms account for some 90% of total output. Therefore the remaining half of all farms account for less than 10% of output. This unexpected situation (see graph) is a result primarily of the high mechanisation and productivity of many large farms but also of changes in working conditions of farm labourers and in the types of crops being cultivated.

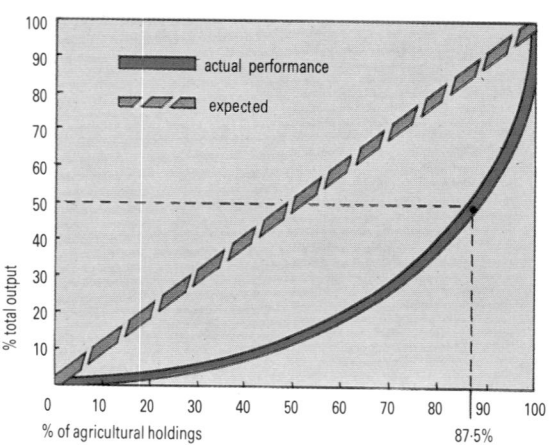

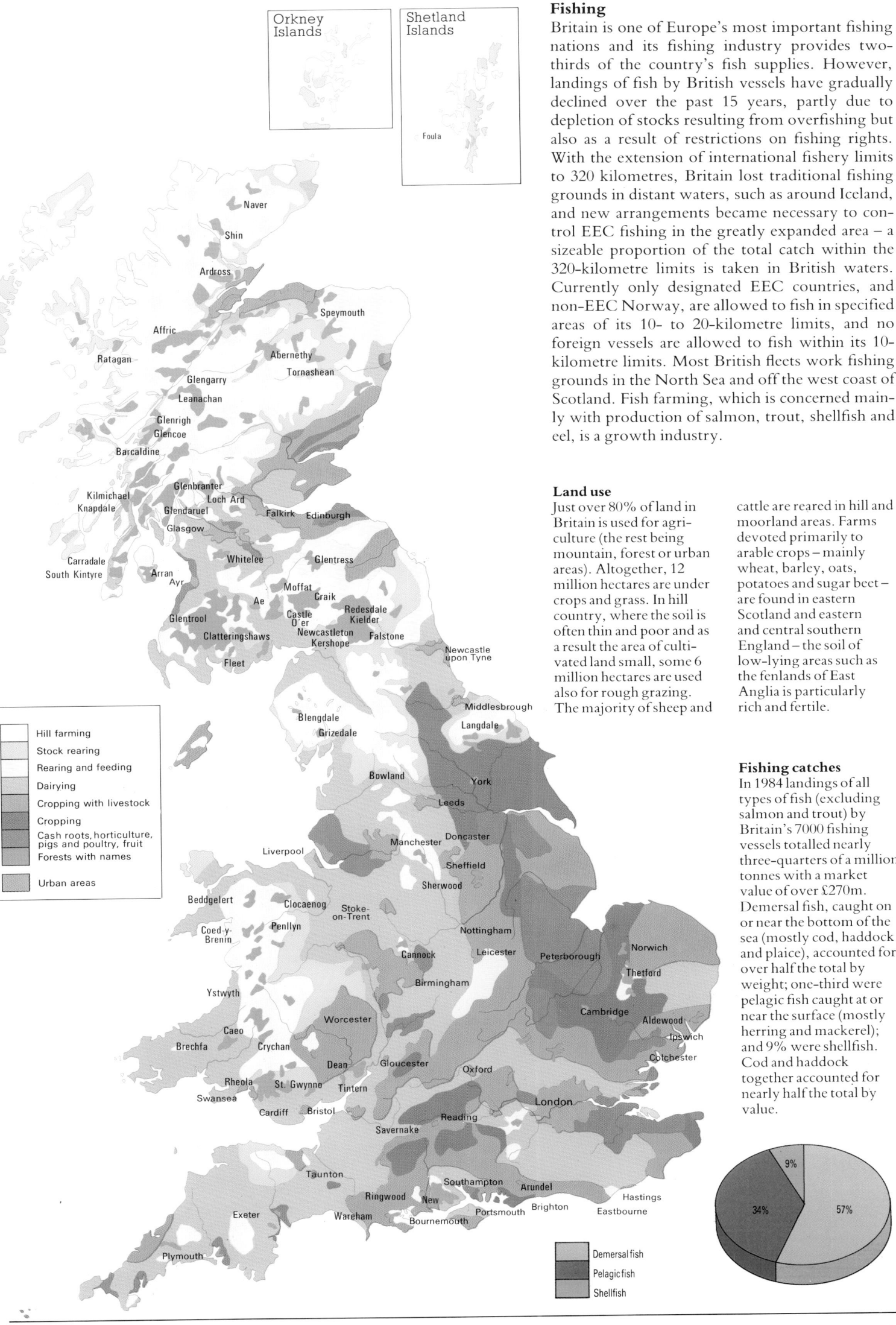

Orkney
Islands

Shetland
Islands

Foula

Naver

Shin

Ardross

Speymouth

Affric

Abernethy

Ratagan

Tornashean

Glengarry

Leanachan

Glenrigh
Glencoe

Barcaldine

Glenbranter

Kilmichael
Knapdale
Loch Ard

Glendaruel

Falkirk   Edinburgh

Glasgow

Carradale
South Kintyre

Arran
Ayr

Whitelee

Glentress

Moffat

Craik

Ae

Castle
O'er

Redesdale
Kielder

Glentrool

Clatteringshaws

Newcastleton
Kershope

Falstone

Fleet

Newcastle
upon Tyne

Blengdale

Middlesbrough

Grizedale

Langdale

Bowland

York

Leeds

Doncaster

Manchester

Liverpool

Sheffield

Sherwood

Beddgelert

Clocaenog

Stoke-
on-Trent

Nottingham

Coed-y-
Brenin

Penllyn

Norwich

Cannock

Leicester

Peterborough

Thetford

Birmingham

Ystwyth

Worcester

Cambridge

Aldewood

Caeo

Ipswich

Brechfa

Crychan

Colchester

Dean

Gloucester

Oxford

Rheola
St. Gwynno

Tintern

Swansea

Cardiff   Bristol

London

Reading

Savernake

Taunton

Southampton

Arundel

Ringwood

New

Hastings

Exeter

Wareham

Portsmouth

Brighton

Eastbourne

Bournemouth

Plymouth

Legend

- Hill farming
- Stock rearing
- Rearing and feeding
- Dairying
- Cropping with livestock
- Cropping
- Cash roots, horticulture, pigs and poultry, fruit
- Forests with names
- Urban areas

Fishing

Britain is one of Europe's most important fishing nations and its fishing industry provides two-thirds of the country's fish supplies. However, landings of fish by British vessels have gradually declined over the past 15 years, partly due to depletion of stocks resulting from overfishing but also as a result of restrictions on fishing rights. With the extension of international fishery limits to 320 kilometres, Britain lost traditional fishing grounds in distant waters, such as around Iceland, and new arrangements became necessary to control EEC fishing in the greatly expanded area – a sizeable proportion of the total catch within the 320-kilometre limits is taken in British waters. Currently only designated EEC countries, and non-EEC Norway, are allowed to fish in specified areas of its 10- to 20-kilometre limits, and no foreign vessels are allowed to fish within its 10-kilometre limits. Most British fleets work fishing grounds in the North Sea and off the west coast of Scotland. Fish farming, which is concerned mainly with production of salmon, trout, shellfish and eel, is a growth industry.

Land use

Just over 80% of land in Britain is used for agriculture (the rest being mountain, forest or urban areas). Altogether, 12 million hectares are under crops and grass. In hill country, where the soil is often thin and poor and as a result the area of cultivated land small, some 6 million hectares are used also for rough grazing. The majority of sheep and cattle are reared in hill and moorland areas. Farms devoted primarily to arable crops – mainly wheat, barley, oats, potatoes and sugar beet – are found in eastern Scotland and eastern and central southern England – the soil of low-lying areas such as the fenlands of East Anglia is particularly rich and fertile.

Fishing catches

In 1984 landings of all types of fish (excluding salmon and trout) by Britain's 7000 fishing vessels totalled nearly three-quarters of a million tonnes with a market value of over £270m. Demersal fish, caught on or near the bottom of the sea (mostly cod, haddock and plaice), accounted for over half the total by weight; one-third were pelagic fish caught at or near the surface (mostly herring and mackerel); and 9% were shellfish. Cod and haddock together accounted for nearly half the total by value.

9%

34%

57%

- Demersal fish
- Pelagic fish
- Shellfish

INDUSTRY AND INVESTMENT

The main characteristic of recent trends in Britain's industrial structure has been the decline in its manufacturing industries as producers, investors and employers. The nature of the decline is, on the one hand, competitive, on the other, technological.

Falling competitiveness

Britain's share of world trade in manufactures – a key measure of competitiveness – fell from over 20% of the total to less than 9% from 1939 to 1985. The decline may be attributed not only to price factors but also to poor quality, design, delivery dates, after-sales service and marketing. It has not merely been the result of entry into foreign markets of newly industrialised countries, such as Hong Kong and Taiwan, since Britain's recent performance has been well below that of its established industrial competitors, the United States, West Germany and Japan. At a time when patterns of international trade are increasingly influenced by the decisions of multinational companies on location, investment, choice of technology and products, a significant proportion of Britain's companies seem to have been wasting their energies on the wrong goods and trying to sell them in the wrong markets.

Investment and technology

Manufacturing is becoming an increasingly capital- as opposed to labour-intensive production activity. Its success depends on investment in technologies which reduce the requirement for labour. In Britain over the past decade, total investment in the industrial sector has increased, mainly as a result of oil exploration, retrieval and processing, but investment in manufacturing has

gradually declined and, like output, now stands at a level lower than in 1979 (currently some 10% of total investment). The country is faced with the problem of investing either in traditional manufacturing to enhance competitiveness by utilising the latest technologies, or in alternative industries that will form a new base of output, exports and employment. On a world basis, future economic activity in industrialised countries is likely to be in the fields of microelectronics, robotics and information technology.

After the oil runs out

Currently, Britain's North Sea oil revenues are sheltering it from its balance of payments problems arising from the decline of manufacturing. This will continue only for as long as the oil is accessible, recoverable and marketable at ruling prices – proven reserves indicate that this is no more than ten years. The service sector is providing alternative production and employment opportunities, but not at the same rate as manufacturing's decline and with much less contribution to exports. It is hoped that the microelectronics industry will prove a major growth area but to date Britain has experienced a net deficit in foreign trade in this field. Britain must seriously consider how far its traditional manufacturing can apply the latest technologies to win back lost export and domestic markets. Only by sacrificing employment opportunities in the short-term can long-term employment in manufacturing become more assured. With its manufacturing trade balance in the red for the first time since the Industrial Revolution, Britain needs robust long-term alternative industries before the oil runs out.

National employment

Dominating the picture is the increasing concentration of jobs in the South-east. There are two reasons for this. First, the decline in primary and manufacturing industries (top half of table below) has affected this region less than others. Second, the South-east benefits from a large presence of expanding service industries (bottom half of table). Population densities and movements, and membership of the European Economic Community, have reinforced these trends.

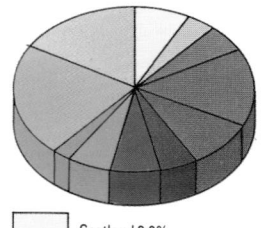

- Scotland 9·3%
- Wales 4·3%
- North 4·9%
- North-west 11·4%
- Yorks & Humber 8·4%
- E. Midlands 6·8%
- W. Midlands 9·3%
- South-west 7·4%
- East Anglia 3·4%
- Greater London 16·6%
- S. East (exc GL) 18·2%

Industries employing above national average

Industries employing highest regional proportion

Regional distribution of employees and employment (mid-1985)

Manufacturing accounts nationally for just over 25% of jobs, yet the West Midlands employs 36·2% of workers in its various manufacturing industries while in the South-east almost 50% of jobs are in the service sector. A study in 1979 by the National Economic Development Office (NEDO) found that the contribution of the fastest-growing industries (energy; chemicals; electrical engineering; finance; transport and communications) to both output and employment of a region meant that the South-east was highly favoured.

	TOTAL GB	S.E. (exc GL)	S.E. (GL only)	East Anglia	South-west	West Midlands	East Midlands	Yorks and Humber	North-west	North	Wales	Scotland
INDUSTRIAL SECTOR % of regional employment accounted for by each industrial sector: (rounded figures)												
Agriculture, forestry, fishing	1·6	1·8	0·1	4·8	2·9	1·5	2·2	1·5	0·7	1·3	2·6	2·1
Energy and water supply	2·9	1·7	1·3	1·6	1·7	2·4	5·1	5·4	2·5	5·1	5·3	4·0
Metal manufacturing and chemicals	3·7	2·8	1·8	2·7	2·9	5·5	4·1	5·9	4·5	6·7	6·3	2·4
Metal goods, engineering and vehicles	12·2	15·0	7·3	11·2	11·7	22·3	13·1	10·1	12·5	11·7	9·1	9·3
Other manufacturing	9·8	7·8	7·4	11·3	9·1	8·4	17·3	13·0	11·4	9·2	7·2	10·6
Construction	4·4	4·3	4·1	4·7	4·9	3·8	4·2	4·5	4·1	4·5	4·9	5·9
Wholesale distributors, hotels, catering	10·6	10·3	11·0	11·8	13·4	10·5	8·9	11·0	10·3	9·5	9·3	10·7
Retail distribution	10·3	11·3	9·4	11·3	10·1	9·8	9·2	10·1	10·7	10·7	10·3	11·0
Transport and communications	6·1	5·7	9·5	6·2	5·3	4·4	5·2	5·1	5·8	5·4	5·3	5·7
Banking, insurance and finance	9·3	8·5	18·1	7·4	8·2	7·4	6·3	6·9	8·1	6·0	5·9	7·4
Public administration and defence	8·7	7·8	10·8	7·1	7·7	8·2	7·3	7·3	9·4	8·1	11·9	8·0
Education, health and other services	20·3	22·9	19·4	19·9	22·2	15·8	17·0	19·3	20·1	21·6	22·0	22·0

Employment trends

In 19th century Britain, the agricultural industry declined in the wake of mechanisation, and manufacturing and energy industries grew. This century has seen a continuation of this trend, but increasingly the picture is one of manufacturing's own decline in favour of service sector employment. A hundred years ago it would have been hard to imagine the country producing half its temperate food needs with 3% of its labour force, and 40 years ago to picture an economy in which no more than 20% of workers are in manufacturing. Moreover, a sizeable proportion of these workers would be performing non-manual functions. Yet for Britain this is what present trends suggest by the end of the century.

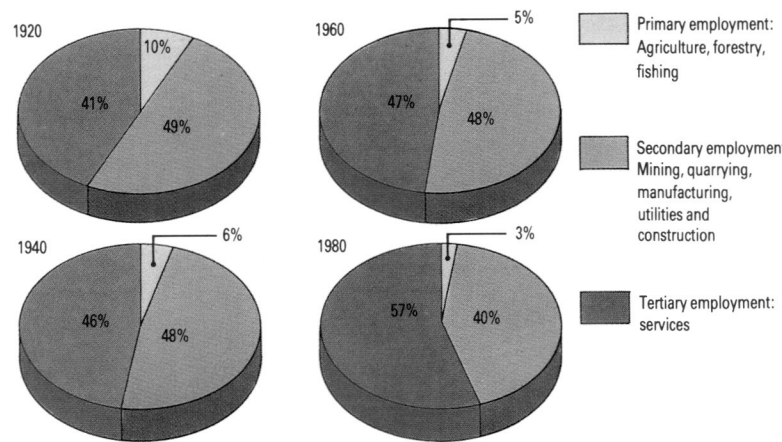

Primary employment: Agriculture, forestry, fishing

Secondary employment: Mining, quarrying, manufacturing, utilities and construction

Tertiary employment: services

Decline in manufacturing activity

The British economy has traditionally relied heavily upon manufacturing to provide jobs. However, the loss of nearly 3 million jobs in manufacturing since 1970 has been partly offset by a growth in other sectors of industry, such as in the service sector, where almost 500,000 jobs have been created. Yet employment growth outside manufacturing has been erratic; in some periods there have even been job losses in the service sector as a result of Britain's stagnant economy. Jobs disappearing in manufacturing are typically those of full-time, manual, male workers, while new jobs emerging in the service sector are typically part-time, non-manual, and filled by female workers.

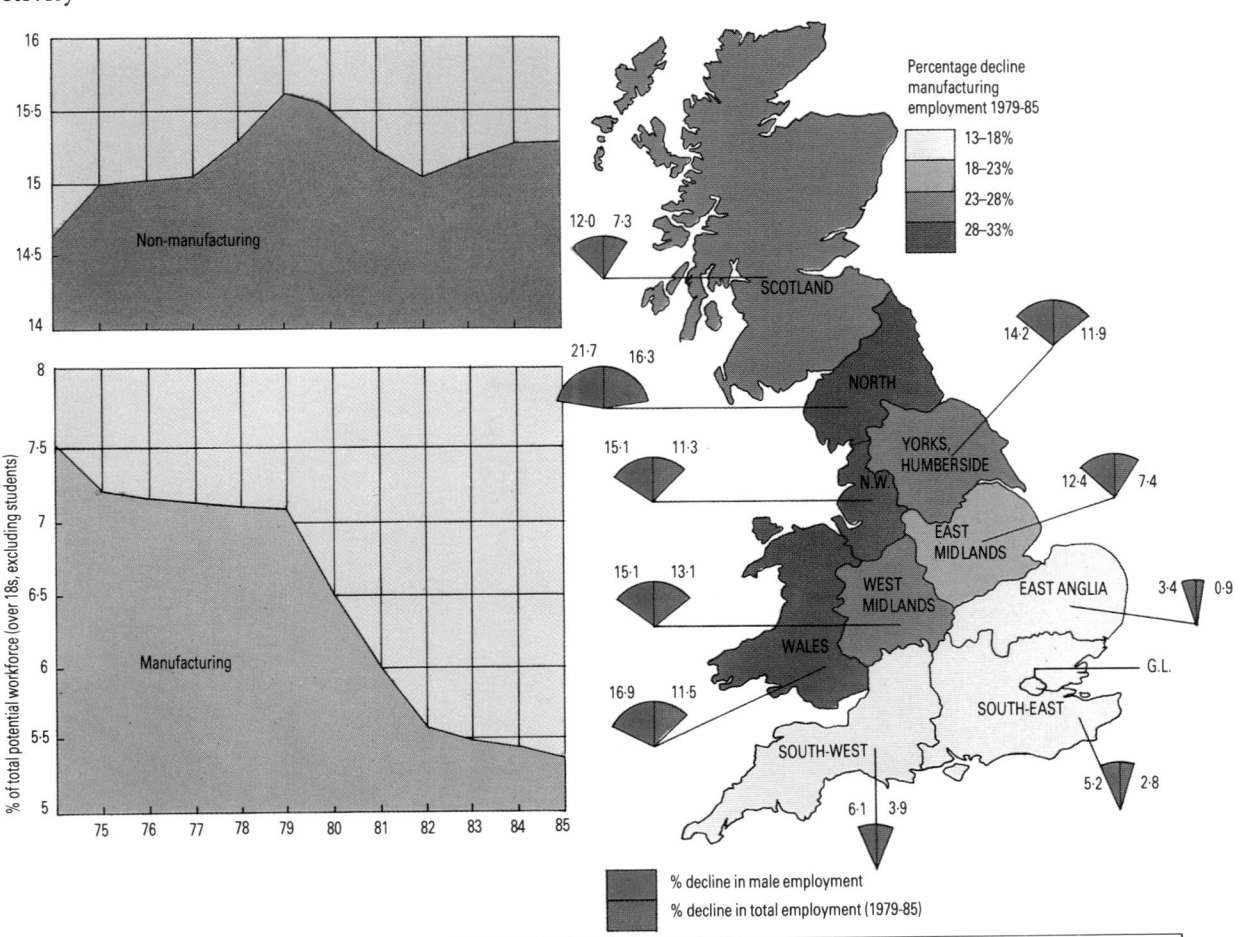

Percentage decline manufacturing employment 1979-85
13–18%
18–23%
23–28%
28–33%

% decline in male employment
% decline in total employment (1979-85)

The North: a case history

The North of England is currently experiencing the worst combined and cumulative problems of regional economic disadvantage. In the first half of 1984, the region had the highest redundancy rate (2·8%), and the highest unemployment rate (nearly 19%) of any region in 1984 and 1985. Alongside this, output in the North fell from 91·1% to 89·6% of the national average between 1974 and 1983, and government spending on social security and other state benefits has in recent years been higher than for any other region except Wales. Explanations are not hard to find. In 1974 manufacturing accounted for 35·6% of the region's output; by 1983 it had fallen to 28·6%. Also there was a decline in construction employment of 39%; a fall of 25% in jobs in the energy industries (mainly coal); and even a drop of 4·5% in service sector employment. Surprisingly, though, the NEDO report (see table caption opposite) showed the North is well placed for fast-growing industries.
Right: A new pharmaceutical plant near Newcastle. Large companies can receive from the state financial inducements to create employment in economically depressed areas.

EMPLOYMENT AND UNEMPLOYMENT

For some 20 years after World War II Britain's economy was run with no more than 2% of the workforce unemployed – less than half a million people. Throughout 1985 unemployment remained above the three million mark (13·5%). There are several reasons why the country has slipped so far away from full employment.

Deflationary policies

First, adjustments made since the early 1970s to meet fluctuations in the country's economy have all contributed to the rise in unemployment. Measures taken in budgets and public spending reviews have increasingly been responses to rises in inflation, balance of payments deficits, and oil price shocks. The adoption of a tight monetary policy has reduced inflation. However, associated increases in interest rates and the resulting higher exchange value for the pound have posed problems for the economy. Consumer spending has decreased, as has investment in plant and equipment, and the higher exchange rate has made exports less competitive. Thus demand for goods and sevices in the economy has been increasingly inadequate to support jobs.

The supply side

Apart from the management of demand, there is the quality of production. Here the two factors referred to on pages 44-45 are again significant. The competitive factor means that Britain's falling share of world trade in manufactures has reduced the ability of its manufacturing industries to offer jobs, while the technological factor has meant that fewer workers are required to produce the same level of output, let alone a lower one.

Finally, there is the 'structural' dimension. Industry's reduced ability to offer employment has coincided with a period in which the numbers seeking work – the labour supply – have risen. The rise is due to the sharp increase in both the number of young people entering the labour market – a legacy of the post-war birth bulge – and the number of women seeking work.

What can be done?

Economists have identified three main solutions to the problem. First, matters can be left to market forces and international competition. However, this puts manufacturing under more pressure, which might lead to increased unemployment. While special measures such as Youth Training Schemes can cushion the blow of unemployment for particular age groups, job losses in manufacturing fall most heavily on already disadvantaged regions and categories of workers. Second, economic demand can be boosted through internationally co-ordinated reflation. Increased public investment on, say, railways and roads, would run less risk of increasing imports than would tax reductions that left consumers free to buy British or not. Finally, consideration can be given to reducing hours of work, to earlier retirement, to training and study leave, and to job sharing, so that the work is spread among a larger number of people. The increased use of microelectronics technology may reinforce such policy redirection.

Working population and employed labour force

The rise in Britain's unemployment has not been a smooth one. From 1945 to 1967 unemployment was held at an average level of ⅓ million. It was not until 1971 that it crept above ¾ million. By 1980 it stood at 1½ million. The first half of the 1980s saw it pass the 3 million mark. There has been a progressively shorter period between each doubling. This is the result of the reduced capacity of the economy to provide and sustain jobs (the lower line on the graph), together with the increased numbers looking for work as the labour force increases (upper line).

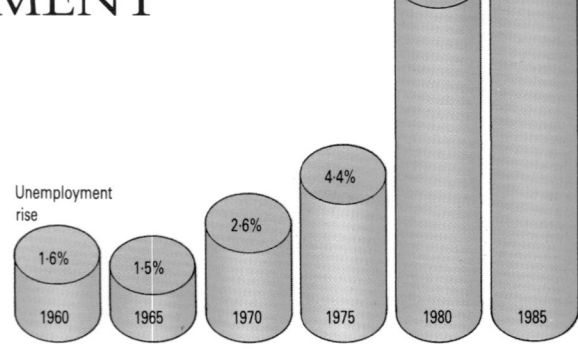

Unemployment rise

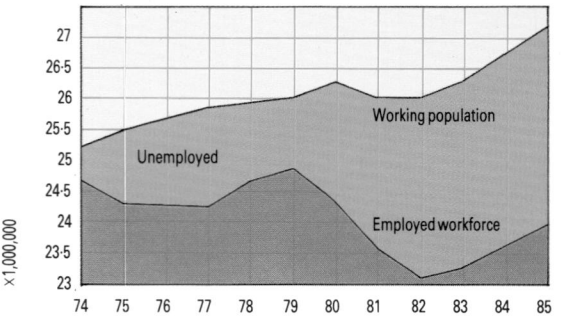

Regional unemployment

Such aggregate unemployment figures conceal the problems faced by certain regions of the country. The table, right, compares the South-east, the least affected region, with the five worst affected regions. In the latter, over half the male unemployment has occurred since 1979. Regional inequalities are even more marked for long-term unemployment (for more than one year).

Male unemployment (selected regions) 1984-85	% of total workforce	Additional % unempl. compared with '79	Long-term male unemployed as % rate of total unemployed	Long-term male unemployment rate
South-east	11·6	+7·3	38·31	4·4
Yorkshire and Humberside	17·2	+10·7	43·7	7·5
West Midlands	17·8	+11·7	50·9	9·2
North-west	19·7	+11·6	48·9	9·6
Wales	20·0	+11·5	44·6	8·9
North	22·4	+12·5	47·5	10·5

Total workforce = all over-18s excluding students

The flexible firm

Apart from any pressure from rising unemployment upon traditional employment and work-time patterns, many British employers are now looking to introduce more flexibility into the numbers they employ, the form of their employment contracts, the jobs workers do, and the way in which they are paid. They are seeking to achieve this by reorganising their labour force into a small core group of professional and skilled key workers, surrounded by groups of semi-skilled, part-time and contract employees – the end of the hierarchical structure of the firm.

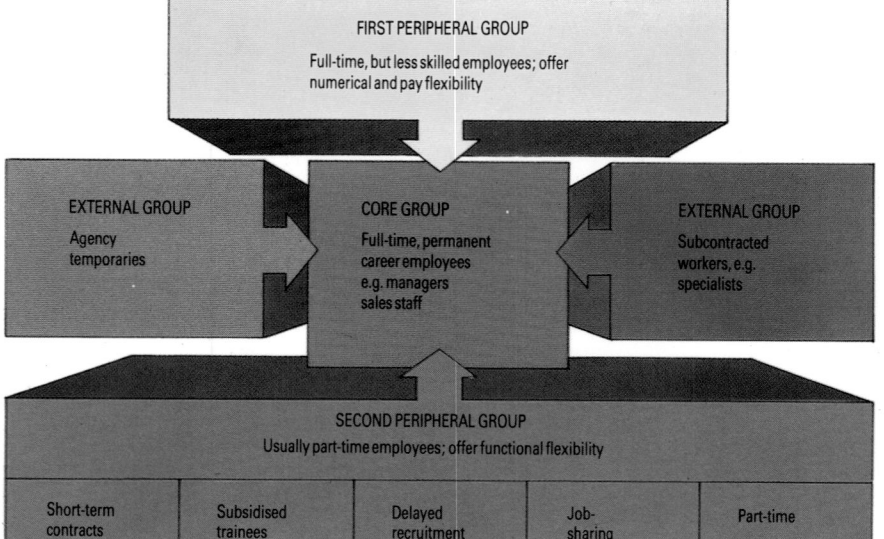

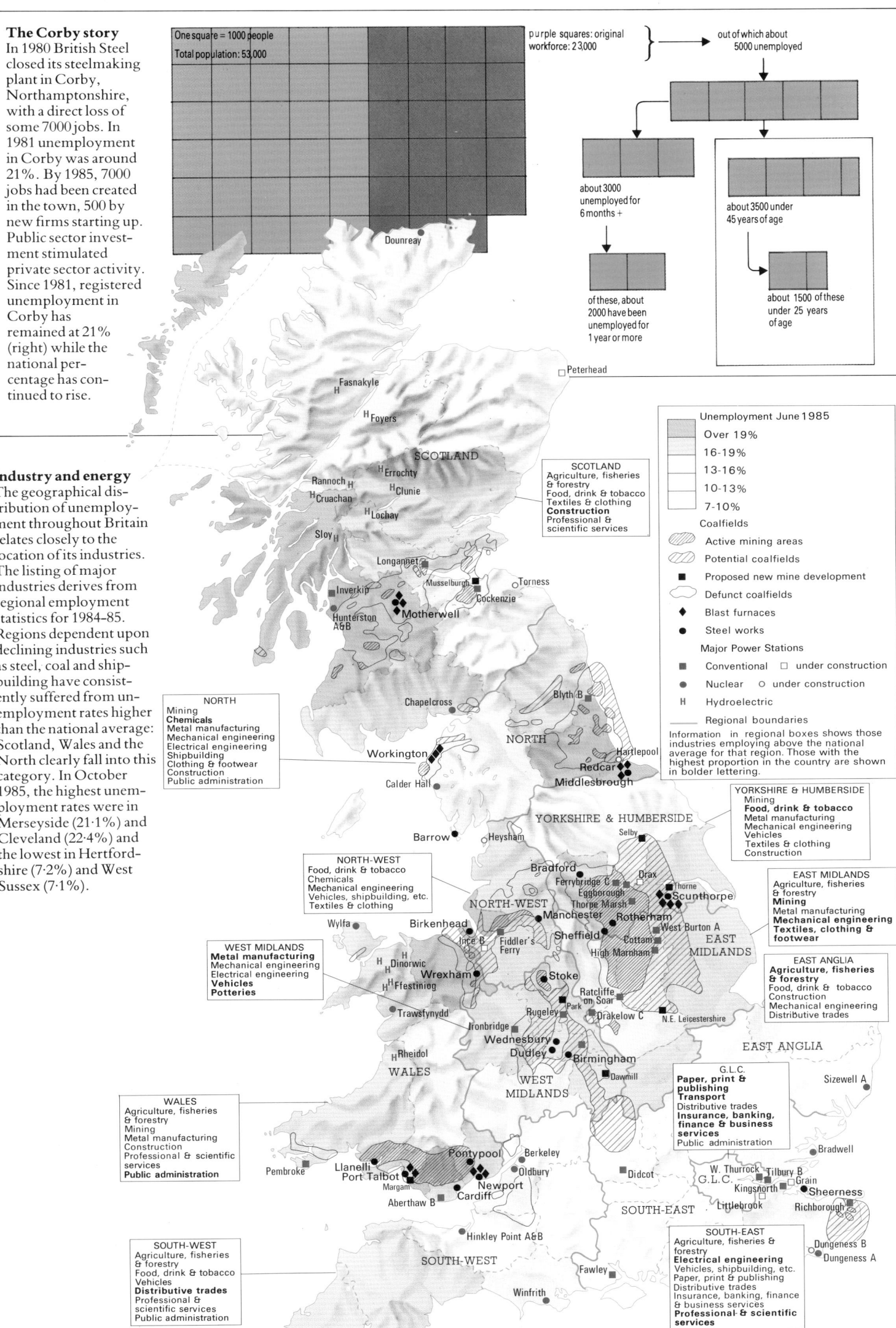

The Corby story

In 1980 British Steel closed its steelmaking plant in Corby, Northamptonshire, with a direct loss of some 7000 jobs. In 1981 unemployment in Corby was around 21%. By 1985, 7000 jobs had been created in the town, 500 by new firms starting up. Public sector investment stimulated private sector activity. Since 1981, registered unemployment in Corby has remained at 21% (right) while the national percentage has continued to rise.

One square = 1000 people
Total population: 53,000

purple squares: original workforce: 23,000

out of which about 5000 unemployed

about 3000 unemployed for 6 months +

of these, about 2000 have been unemployed for 1 year or more

about 3500 under 45 years of age

about 1500 of these under 25 years of age

Industry and energy

The geographical distribution of unemployment throughout Britain relates closely to the location of its industries. The listing of major industries derives from regional employment statistics for 1984–85. Regions dependent upon declining industries such as steel, coal and shipbuilding have consistently suffered from unemployment rates higher than the national average: Scotland, Wales and the North clearly fall into this category. In October 1985, the highest unemployment rates were in Merseyside (21·1%) and Cleveland (22·4%) and the lowest in Hertfordshire (7·2%) and West Sussex (7·1%).

SCOTLAND
Agriculture, fisheries & forestry
Food, drink & tobacco
Textiles & clothing
Construction
Professional & scientific services

NORTH
Mining
Chemicals
Metal manufacturing
Mechanical engineering
Electrical engineering
Shipbuilding
Clothing & footwear
Construction
Public administration

NORTH-WEST
Food, drink & tobacco
Chemicals
Mechanical engineering
Vehicles, shipbuilding, etc.
Textiles & clothing

WEST MIDLANDS
Metal manufacturing
Mechanical engineering
Electrical engineering
Vehicles
Potteries

WALES
Agriculture, fisheries & forestry
Mining
Metal manufacturing
Construction
Professional & scientific services
Public administration

SOUTH-WEST
Agriculture, fisheries & forestry
Food, drink & tobacco
Vehicles
Distributive trades
Professional & scientific services
Public administration

YORKSHIRE & HUMBERSIDE
Mining
Food, drink & tobacco
Metal manufacturing
Mechanical engineering
Vehicles
Textiles & clothing
Construction

EAST MIDLANDS
Agriculture, fisheries & forestry
Mining
Metal manufacturing
Mechanical engineering
Textiles, clothing & footwear

EAST ANGLIA
Agriculture, fisheries & forestry
Food, drink & tobacco
Construction
Mechanical engineering
Distributive trades

G.L.C.
Paper, print & publishing
Transport
Distributive trades
Insurance, banking, finance & business services
Public administration

SOUTH-EAST
Agriculture, fisheries & forestry
Electrical engineering
Vehicles, shipbuilding, etc.
Paper, print & publishing
Distributive trades
Insurance, banking, finance & business services
Professional & scientific services

Unemployment June 1985
Over 19%
16–19%
13–16%
10–13%
7–10%

Coalfields
Active mining areas
Potential coalfields
■ Proposed new mine development
Defunct coalfields
♦ Blast furnaces
● Steel works

Major Power Stations
■ Conventional □ under construction
● Nuclear ○ under construction
H Hydroelectric
—— Regional boundaries

Information in regional boxes shows those industries employing above the national average for that region. Those with the highest proportion in the country are shown in bold lettering.

Dounreay
Peterhead
Fasnakyle H
H Foyers
SCOTLAND
Rannoch H
H Errochty
H Clunie
H Cruachan
H Lochay
Sloy H
Longannet
Inverkip
Musselburgh
Torness
Cockenzie
Hunterston A&B
♦ Motherwell
Chapelcross
Blyth B
NORTH
Workington
Hartlepool
Calder Hall
Redcar
Middlesbrough
Barrow
Heysham
Selby
YORKSHIRE & HUMBERSIDE
Bradford
Ferrybridge C
Drax
Thorne
Eggborough
Scunthorpe
Thorpe Marsh
NORTH-WEST
Manchester
Rotherham
EAST MIDLANDS
Wylfa
Birkenhead
Sheffield
West Burton A
Ince B
Fiddler's Ferry
Cottam
High Marnham
EAST MIDLANDS
H Dinorwic
Wrexham
Stoke
H Ffestiniog
Ratcliffe on Soar
N.E. Leicestershire
EAST ANGLIA
H Trawsfynydd
Park
Drakelow C
Rugeley
Ironbridge
Sizewell A
H Rheidol
Wednesbury
Dudley
Birmingham
WALES
WEST MIDLANDS
Dawmill
Bradwell
Llanelli
Pontypool
Berkeley
W. Thurrock G.L.C.
Pembroke
Port Talbot
Oldbury
Tilbury B
Grain
Margam
Newport
Didcot
Kingsnorth
Sheerness
Aberthaw B
Cardiff
Littlebrook
Richborough
SOUTH-EAST
Hinkley Point A&B
Dungeness B
SOUTH-WEST
Fawley
Dungeness A
Winfrith

47

FOREIGN TRADE

Britain has traditionally been, and remains, a trading nation. Currently, it exports some 30% of production in order to cover the equally high percentage of expenditure on imports. However, the relationship between exports and imports has altered over the years, swinging from deficit to surplus and back again, and altering in relative composition, destinations and origins.

There are four main reasons for the country's trading role. First, Britain lacks certain raw materials and as a result of its climate is unable to produce certain foodstuffs, which it must import. Second, it is superior in producing certain goods and services, such as electronics and merchant banking, which other countries need. Third, Britain has to compete with other countries' products in its home market and abroad. Lastly, it has become an oil-producing nation.

Changes in trading patterns

Britain's Industrial Revolution made it the world leader in iron and steel, textiles and railways. Deposits of iron ore and coal, the development of spinning and weaving machinery, the exploitation of crude steelmaking technology, and steam-engine power, gave the country a head start. This advantage was lost soon after World War II. Japan developed a steel industry based on high-quality raw materials and exploiting large-scale production and advanced technology, while many foreign companies exploited the low wages, poor labour organisation and lack of social provision in developing countries in order to undercut prices for textile and clothing production. Furthermore, changing consumer tastes and greater affluence meant that the motor car and aeroplane superseded rail as a means of transport.

International trade shares

Britain's share of world trade in manufactures has fallen by over 50% since World War II and continues to fall. The prime cause is a long-term deep-rooted decline in its international competitiveness.

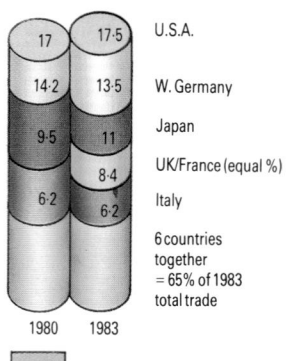

	1980	1983	
U.S.A.	17	17·5	
W. Germany	14·2	13·5	
Japan	9·5	11	
UK/France (equal %)		8·4	
Italy	6·2	6·2	

6 countries together = 65% of 1983 total trade

EEC (44·7%/45·5%)

Other Western Europe (12·4%/17·0%)

North America (16·3%/14%)

Other developed countries (5·2%/6·8%)

Oil exporting countries (8·2%/3·5%)

Rest of world (13·2%/13·2%)

Goods traded

The composition of Britain's visible exports and imports reflects both its natural advantages and disadvantages and, increasingly, its competitiveness. The need to import certain raw materials and foodstuffs remains unavoidable, but the change from surplus to deficit in foreign trade in manufactured and semi-manufactured goods has caused successive governments great alarm. The country is losing ground, both in terms of traditional specialisation and its domestic markets. Imports have reached very high levels: two-thirds of all vehicles and one-half and one-third respectively of electrical and mechanical engineering products are foreign. Some British industries have disappeared in the face of foreign competition.

Food, beverages, tobacco

Basic materials

Oil

Other mineral fuels and lubricants

Semi-manufactured goods

Finished manufactured goods

Commodities, transactions not classified by type

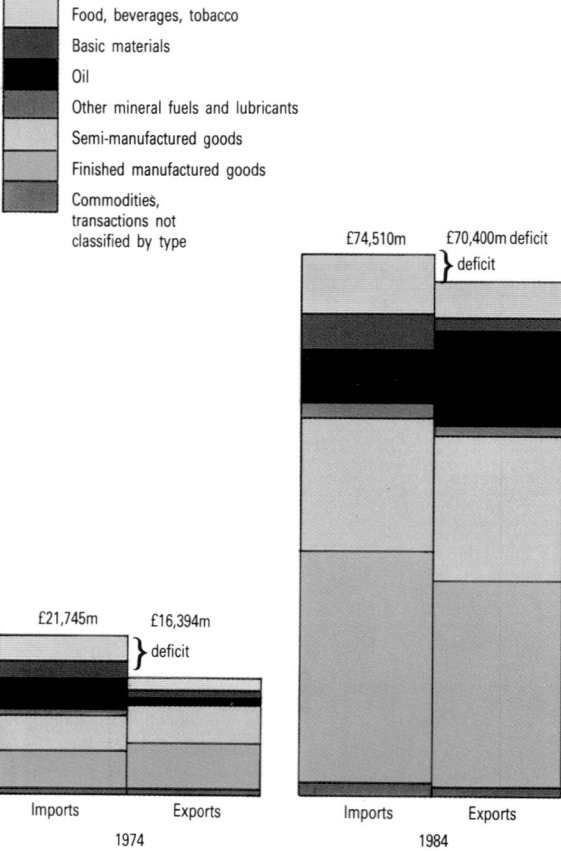

£21,745m £16,394m } deficit

Imports Exports 1974

£74,510m £70,400m deficit } deficit

Imports Exports 1984

Britain's trading partners

Nearly half the country's exports and imports are now accounted for by the European Economic Community (EEC). However, in the decade since Britain's entry, the trade deficit with the EEC has increased tenfold.

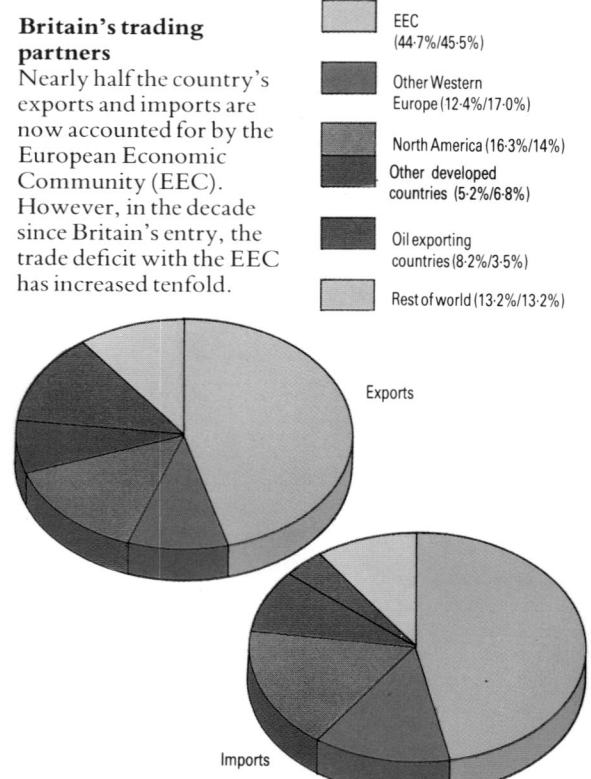

Exports

Imports

Invisible trade

Since 1974 Britain has earned a surplus from its invisible transactions. These fall into three main groups: receipts from payments arising from services, such as tourism, sea and air transport, and the commercial and financial activities of the City of London; interest, profits and dividends on past British investments overseas; and 'transfers', which are both government and private financial movements. Within transfers, the present net outflow of some £2 billion cancels out the surplus on interest, profits and dividends, partly as a result of government contribution to the EEC.

Current account

Combining visible and invisible trade figures provides the overall 'current account' of the balance of payments. This has improved from a deficit of £3 bn in 1974 to a surplus of £6·5 bn in 1981 but has since reduced to £0·9 bn.

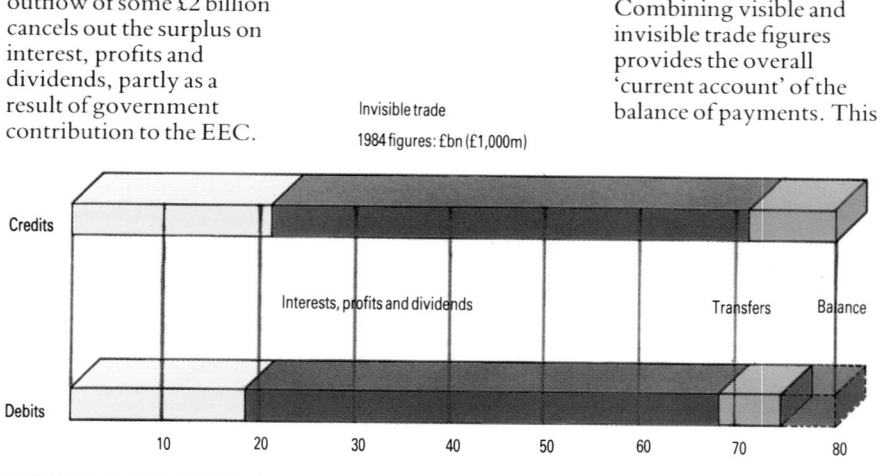

Invisible trade
1984 figures: £bn (£1,000m)

Credits

Interests, profits and dividends

Transfers Balance

Debits

10 20 30 40 50 60 70 80

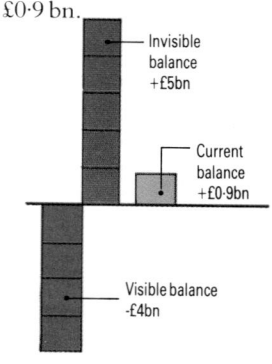

Invisible balance +£5bn

Current balance +£0·9bn

Visible balance -£4bn

Balance of payments

This has three components: visible trade, invisible trade and capital movements. Visible trade comprises raw materials, fuels, food and manufactured goods. Britain has traditionally covered its import bill for the first three items by exporting manufactures. In the past 15 years, though, there have been two key changes. First, after being faced with massive increases in its import bill as a result of oil price rises, North Sea oil production started and generated revenues that created a balance of payments surplus. Second, hidden by this change in oil fortunes, British manufacturing saw its balance of payments surplus turn to deficit in 1983.

Invisible trade is an additional source of foreign currency, and includes transport, tourism, insurance and the returns from investment abroad. 'Invisibles' have always made a positive contribution to the balance of payments but they amount to only a fraction of visible trade figures. The imbalance of payments will become greater still as North Sea oil production declines and if manufacturing continues to slide into deficit. Also, the main item of benefit on the invisibles account, interest, profits and dividends, is tied in with capital movements, the third component.

Capital movements represent the outflow and inflow of funds to set up production or purchase assets overseas. Since the abolition of exchange controls in 1979, there has been a large movement of British funds overseas by companies and by financial institutions. Without investing abroad, Britain's foreign currency income generated under 'invisibles' would not be realised. However, high levels of overseas investment deprive the country's manufacturing industry of much needed capital.

Britain as an oil-producing nation

Between 1974 and 1984 Britain experienced a complete turnaround from deficit to surplus on its oil account. But in the same period manufacturing moved from surplus to deficit. For oil to continue to support the balance of payments, either improved oil exploration techniques must lead to new resources being discovered, or new industrial products and processes must be developed to supplement oil and manufacturing's export contribution.

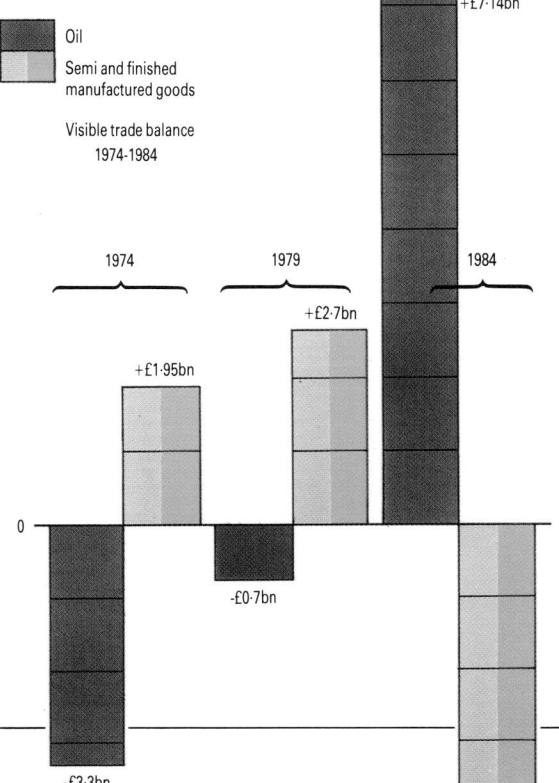

Oil

Semi and finished manufactured goods

Visible trade balance 1974-1984

1974   1979   1984

+£7·14bn

+£2·7bn

+£1·95bn

0

-£0·7bn

-£3·3bn

-£3·7bn

Influence of the multinationals

Multinational companies (MNCs) are characterised by having production facilities in more than one country. They can therefore influence patterns of foreign trade by their own strategic business decisions. So large proportions of a country's exports, while leaving the country physically, merely pass from one location of an MNC's production chain to another. In Britain, the influence of MNCs is illustrated by their contribution to the decline of manufacturing in the West Midlands. In 10 major companies within the region recent years have seen one-third of their workforce being made redundant and large-scale disinvestment in Britain. The con-

sequences for employment, production and exports for their British operations are illustrated below.

The companies: GEC, GKN, Cadbury, Dunlop, Lucas, Tube Investments, IMI, Delta, Glynwed and BSR

1 % of global workforce in Britain
2 % of world production in Britain
3 British exports as % of total overseas sales

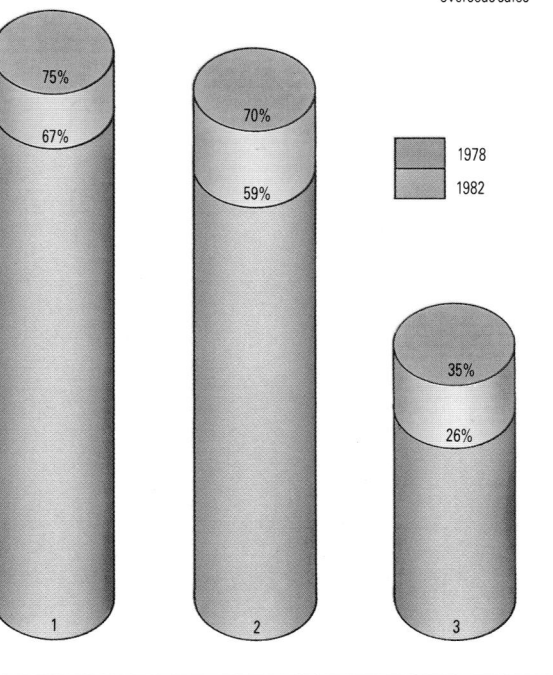

75%
67%

70%
59%

35%
26%

1978
1982

1   2   3

British Petroleum's Magnus oil production platform in the North Sea. In the 1970s, at the time of the Middle East oil crisis and anticipated North Sea oil bonanza, some politicians suggested using Britain's revenues and benefits from oil to finance the regeneration of industry through increased investment in the private and public sectors. Today part of oil revenues are used to cover the costs of unemployment.

THE PUBLIC SECTOR

The public sector is concerned with taxation, borrowing and expenditure by central and local government. The government reviews its expenditure plans each year in the Budget and from this sets taxation and borrowing levels.

As public expenditure in Britain approached 50% of all spending in the mid-1970s, economists and politicians became concerned with the prospects of the government spending more of the taxpayers' money than the taxpayers themselves. Yet the scale and use of public spending are inevitable responses to economic and social circumstances. Total public spending includes both direct spending on goods and services such as hospitals and teachers' pay, and 'transfer payments' such as unemployment benefit, social security, and retirement pensions. Currently, nearly half of all public spending is transfer payments, so that the government's direct command over economic resources is no more than a quarter of total spending in the economy. The rise in unemployment and the increased proportion of older people make increasing demands on the public purse. These changes in employment and population structures leave the government with less revenue from taxes on those in work to finance the increased expenditure.

Control of public expenditure

Arguments supporting the strict control and, if possible, reduction of public expenditure include the virtues of market forces, the inflationary consequences of a high rate of public spending, and the importance of a flourishing wealth-creating private sector. A high priority for the government recently has been to hold down the level of funding needed to run the state sector. By reducing the call on private sector resources, through tax cuts and other concessions, it has sought to provoke the private sector into creating services (such as health care) which were the traditional preserve of the state. It has also looked to greater profitability in manufacturing industry as the first step towards creating better long-term employment prospects.

There are, however, counter-arguments for financing certain economic activities, especially health and education, from government funds. Evidence is put forward that the free availability of these services at the point of consumption is good for the economy and not merely convenient for the recipient. Failure to spend on such provision creates disadvantages and costs for the community more generally. Similarly, reasons are advanced for taking advantage of the contribution that public spending can make to the level of demand – and therefore the level of economic activity and employment – in an economy. If demand is low, public spending can compensate for this, especially through public capital investment such as road building, in ways that need not lead to accelerated inflation or increase in imports. In addition, the contributions of government spending to the quality of housing, training and education, transport and so on in the economy can contribute to the effectiveness of the private sector.

Public expenditure and GDP

Currently, public expenditure represents some 40% of total national spending (the Gross Domestic Product or GDP). Governments have sought to reduce this amount by cuts in actual and planned spending and reductions in benefits. Recently, the figures have been kept down by the inclusion of revenue from sales of assets – privatisation of companies such as British Telecom – as 'negative' public spending.

Ratio of expenditure to GDP YEAR	Planning total plus net debt interest	Percentage of total expenditure on goods and services
80-81	42·5%	24%
81-82	44%	24%
82-83	43·5%	24%
83-84	42·5%	24%
84-85	42·5%	23%

Managing the economy

Public spending is a major component of demand in the economy, along with consumer spending, private investment and exports. Each component of demand can be lowered or raised by government economic measures and policies in order to either curb inflation or to boost demand and sustain a higher level of output and employment. Public expenditure can even be financed by borrowing, provided it boosts economic activity and leads to higher tax revenues. The diagram below shows four possible policies (lower taxes etc.) that together may create full use of all resources.

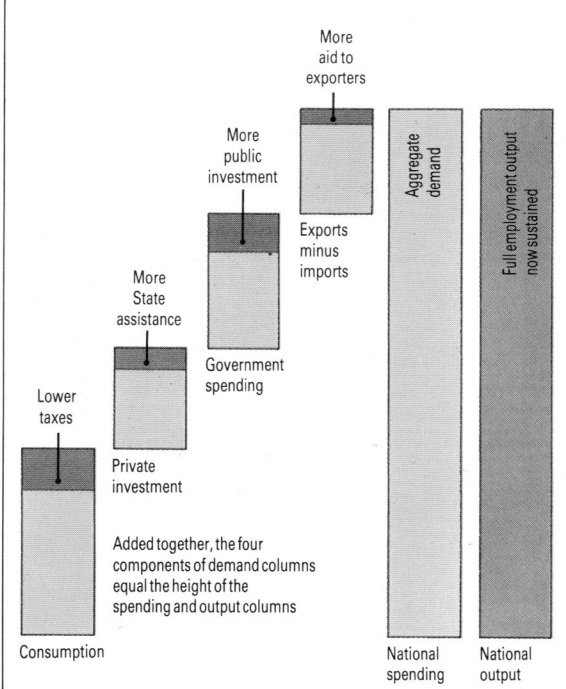

Planned public spending in real terms

There are three ways of looking at the composition of public expenditure: by programmes, by spending authorities, and by economic categories. Programmes broadly reflect government departments. They are dominated by social security (30% of total spending). Spending authorities are bodies that control actual expenditure. These are dominated by central government. Public corporations, or nationalised industries, make relatively minor demands on the public purse as they raise most of their own finance through pricing policies. Economic categories illustrate how the money is spent within the various departments.

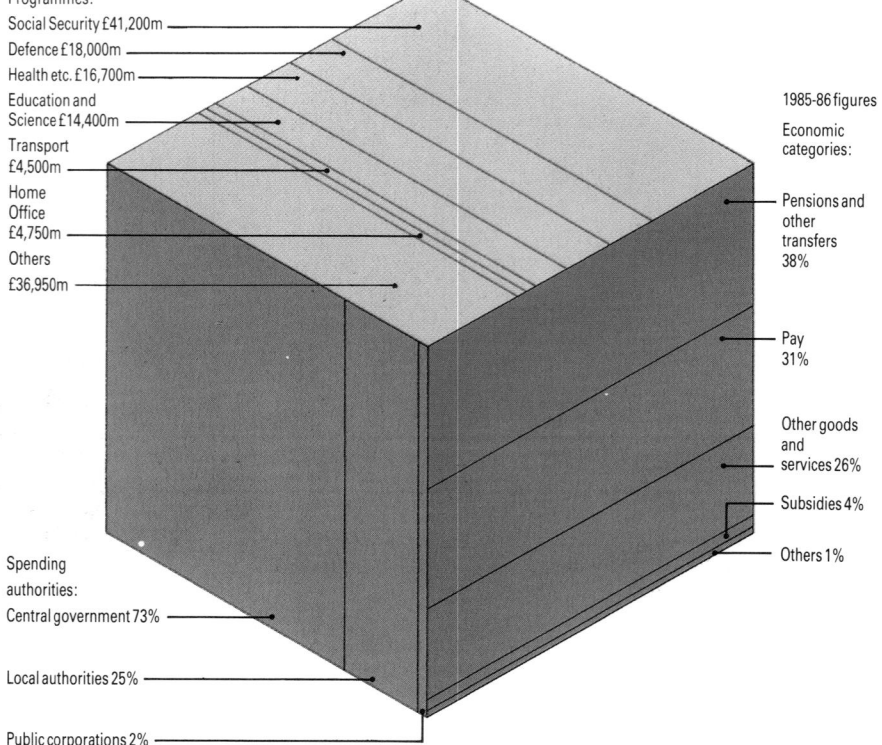

Government departments

Although Health and Social Security accounts for more public expenditure than any other government department, Defence (including Royal Ordnance Factories) has the greatest number of civil servants (over 200,000). The highest concentration of civil servants is in the South-east, with more than 1 in 3 of the total. However, the past 10 years have seen an increasing number of civil service departments being moved out of London to decentralise the system – Vehicle Licence to Swansea, Overseas Development to East Kilbride, Income Tax to Shipley, Customs and Excise to Southend. In the same period there has been a 20% reduction in staffing levels.

Public spending 1983-87

Changes in expenditure over recent years show social security (currently some £42 bn) top of the 'league table' of gains and losses and spending on trade and industry, employment and energy (£6 bn) at the bottom. Housing (£6·1 bn), which used to rank high in the table, has been the second biggest loser of funds. (In real terms, the planning total increased by less than 1%.)

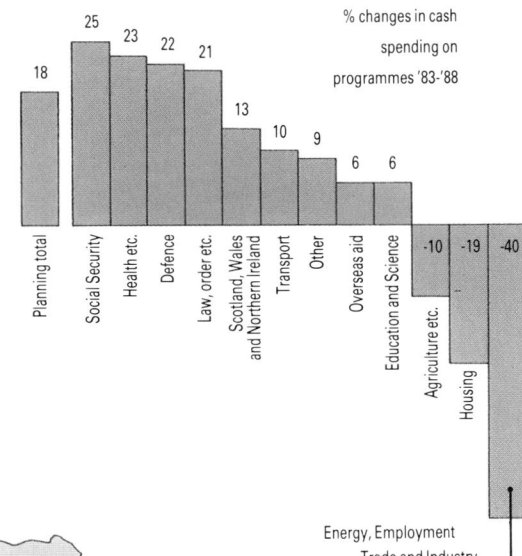

% changes in cash spending on programmes '83–'88

- Planning total — 18
- Social Security — 25
- Health etc. — 23
- Defence — 22
- Law, order etc. — 21
- Scotland, Wales and Northern Ireland — 13
- Transport — 10
- Other — 9
- Overseas aid — 6
- Education and Science — 6
- Agriculture etc. — −10
- Housing — −19
- Energy, Employment Trade and Industry — −40

Civil servants by departments

- Agriculture, fisheries and food 2%
- Customs and excise 4%
- Defence 31%
- Education and Science 0·5%
- Employment group 8%
- Environment/Transport 7·5%
- Health and Social Security 15·3%
- Home Office 5·5%
- HMSO 0·8%
- Treasury 0·8%
- Inland Revenue 11%
- National Savings 1·6%
- Scottish Office 2%
- Trade and Industry 2%
- Others 8%

Intermediate Areas 4·3%
Development Areas 40·2%
Special Development Areas 55·5%

Expenditure on assistance to industry 1984-85 – total £630m

Development areas

Government assistance to industry is concentrated in regions most in need of job-creation schemes – the development areas. Areas of very high unemployment are designated Special Development Areas and receive most support. Firms investing in such areas qualify for building grants, tax allowances for depreciation provision and other forms of preference.

Special Development / Intermediate Areas

Development Areas

(Map cities: Glasgow, Newcastle, Leeds, Manchester, Nottingham, Birmingham, Corby, Cardiff, Bristol, London, Bodmin, Plymouth)

Regional capital expenditure

Currently, the greatest item of capital expenditure (investment to create or maintain productivity and services for future output) is economic services, including employment, agriculture, trade and industry, road building and water supply. In 1982-83 this totalled nearly £2bn. Health and Social Services, and General Administration and Defence each accounted for just under £1bn investment, while Education, as well as Housing and Community Development accounted for some £½bn each. The South-east was the region attracting the greatest share of capital spending in each of the first three categories listed, while in the last category Scotland accounted for 50% of the total.

Education and Health

In recent years, total expenditure by health authorities and education authorities has been greatest in Scotland on a per head of population basis. Figures for selected regions, right, illustrate the wide range of expenditure levels.

Education 1984-85 — Annual figures

Region	£ per head
North	£220
Yorks & Humbs	£220
East Anglia	£185
South-east	£230
Wales	£265
Scotland	£330

Health

Region	£ per head
West Midlands	£225
Northern	£245
Yorkshire	£230
East Anglian	£230
N.E. Thames	£280
Oxford	£210
Wales	£270
Scotland	£310

INCOME AND WEALTH

Three main factors determine a family's standard of living: first, the number of individuals in the family that are actively working and earning an income; second, the individuals' jobs and levels of pay; and, third, any other sources of income available to the family. Other factors are government taxation on income; any benefits provided by the state; and any assets, either inherited or saved, owned by members of the family that bestow economic advantages.

Similar criteria are used to determine the levels of income and wealth of a locality, a region or the country as a whole. The general principles of how these factors influence the distribution of wealth are considered in the text below and opposite, while the British picture is highlighted in the diagrams and captions.

Consider two families living next door to each other. The first comprises two working parents and two older working children. The second consists of an unemployed father, a non-working mother, a school-leaver yet to find a job and a grandmother living in. In each case the family unit comprises four people, but the activity rates –

the balance between working population and dependents – are very different. The first family is putting more into the national economy in tax, the second is drawing more in state benefits. The influence of family structure upon the total incomes of the two households is considerable, even before actual levels of pay and income are considered. The income of the first family could be eight times greater than that of the second.

Pay levels are nevertheless important. Salaries of non-manual workers tend to be higher than those of their manual counterparts, while men's pay generally remains higher than women's. Industry, occupation and age also account for pay differences, as does the sector – private or public – and the mechanism for pay determination that applies. Unearned income from various sources – interest, dividends and rent – varies according to the nature of the family's investment and ownership of assets. Also, entitlements to certain state benefits are directly related to unearned income as well as earned income. Proportions of unemployed and retired members in the family are of particular significance in this respect.

Sources of household income

The main source of household income in Britain is wages and salaries (currently about 66%). The greatest regional dependence upon wages and salaries is in the East Midlands (70%). Social security benefits and pensions feature most prominently in the North (11% and 12·2% respectively), and self-employment in East Anglia (8·6%).

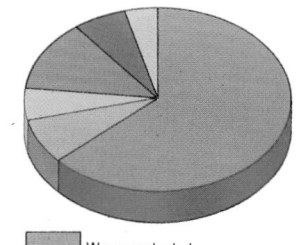

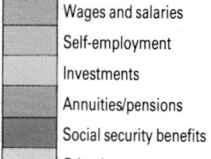

Wages and salaries
Self-employment
Investments
Annuities/pensions
Social security benefits
Other income

Activity rates

Activity rates are measured as the percentage of the adult population (aged 16 and over) in the civilian labour force – those in or seeking employment. They are an important factor reflecting population structure and the level of economic activity, and influencing overall income levels. Activity rates for men are considerably higher than for women, but they have been decreasing steadily while those for women increased in the 1970s and have been flattening out in

the 1980s. For both men and women, the highest regional activity rates are to be found in the South-east and the lowest in Wales.

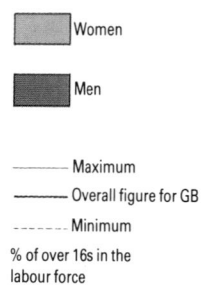

Women

Men

——— Maximum
——— Overall figure for GB
------ Minimum

% of over 16s in the labour force

84
81
75·2

46·6
43·9
36·7

1971

79·8
77·5
72·6

48·3
47·3
41·8

1979

76·1
74·7
69·8

49·1
47·6
41·8

1983

Personal income

The table below compares the 1982-83 average gross weekly income for currently the most well-off region of Britain (the South-east) with the four poorest. Comparison of the data with that for 1979-80 shows that in recent years the difference in per capita income between the South-east and the other regions has widened – 40% up in the South-east and only 31% up in Wales and the West Midlands, for example. With the retail price index (a measure of the cost of living) going up by 34·5% between 1980 and 1983, real income per capita rose by over 5% in the South-east but elsewhere in the country fell by an almost equal amount.

The map, right, reflects how this pattern of inequality is altered by taxation. It shows annual personal income after income tax and national insurance contributions deductions for the regions. Wales still has the lowest average income level (£3231),

with the West Midlands, the North, and Yorkshire and Humberside only slightly better placed. At the top, the South-east is ahead again (£4188, with Greater London £4567). In fact, the South-east is the only region with a figure higher than the national average (£3697).

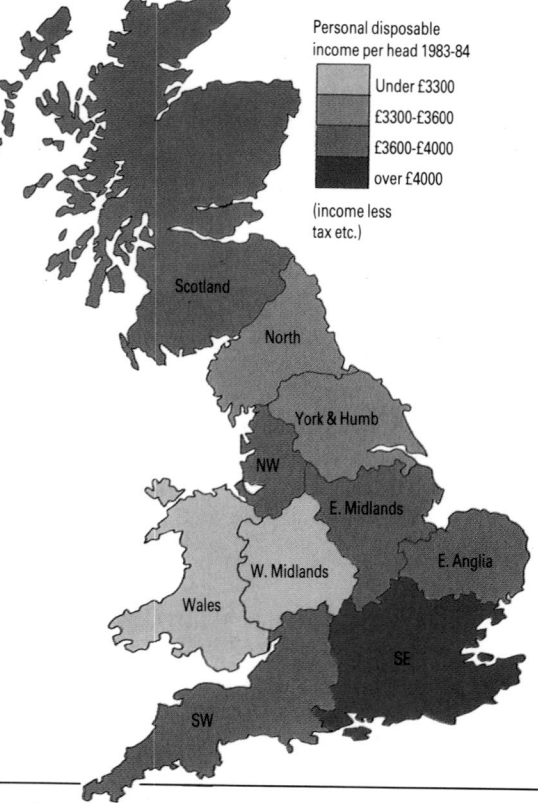

Personal disposable income per head 1983-84

Under £3300
£3300-£3600
£3600-£4000
over £4000

(income less tax etc.)

Scotland
North
York & Humb
NW
E. Midlands
W. Midlands
E. Anglia
Wales
SE
SW

Household income in £ – selected regions	Average income per week 1982-83		Income derived from social security benefits
	Per person	Per household	
North	66·8	158·5	17·3
Yorkshire, H'side	65·7	163·2	15·7
South-east	89·4	210·5	10·9
W. Midlands	69·5	174·1	15·3
Wales	64·6	166·4	17·6

Social wage, assets and non-financial factors

Standards of living are not determined by gross income levels alone, since these are subject to deductions for taxation and national insurance. Moreover, tax liability does not relate solely to income level; mortgage interest for the home owner-occupier is an important qualification for reduced liability at any income level. Personal disposable income (net take-home pay after stoppages) is therefore more important than gross income as a determinant of an individual's standard of living. Every individual also derives benefits from public expenditure (see pages 50-51). The benefit from the collective provision of services and facilities by the state, without a direct charge for such transactions, is known as the social wage.

The distribution of wealth is also determined by savings, by assets owned such as land, dwellings, stocks and shares, and by the economic advantages their ownership bestows beyond the income derived from them. Under the British tax system only the income yielded from wealth attracts taxation and not the ownership of the wealth itself, except where it is transferred at death. Finally, knowledge of rights, access to facilities and familiarity with entitlements and procedures are also important in the distribution of income and wealth.

The prosperity map

A prosperity index, developed by Newcastle University's Centre for Urban and Regional Development Studies, shows that prosperity in the south of England is 30% higher than that of Scotland or Wales. At the top is Winchester, Hampshire, with very low unemployment (5·3%), job expansion and many two-car families, while at the other extreme is Consett, Co. Durham, where a steelworks closure has pushed unemployment up to 25%.

Distribution of wealth

Variations in income are far less extreme than variations in wealth, which is concentrated in the hands of a tiny minority. For the very richest, stocks and shares represent a substantial element, while middle-class wealth is tied up more in property and savings. If occupational and state pension rights are classed as wealth, the concentrations become less pronounced – the shares of the richest 1% and 10% fall from that shown below to 12% and 35% respectively.

Earnings and working hours

The highest average earnings for men and women – both manual and non-manual workers – are to be found in the South-east. The lowest average earnings for men are those for workers in the South-west (manual) and East Midlands (non-manual), and for women in the East Midlands (manual) and Yorkshire and Humberside (non-manual). The average full-time working week, excluding overtime, is around 38 hours for men and 36 hours for women.

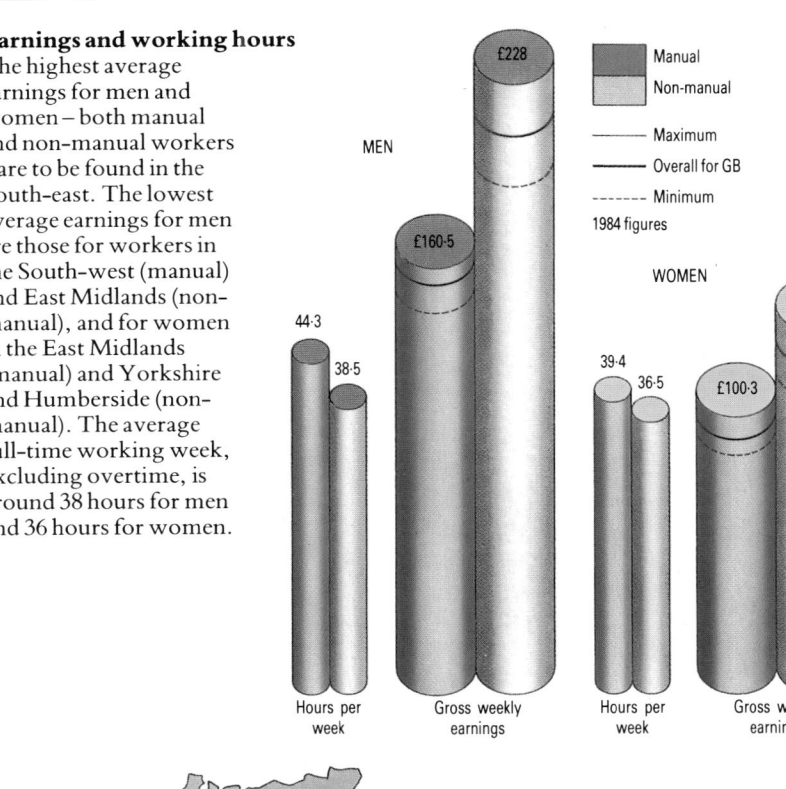

MEN

WOMEN

Manual
Non-manual
Maximum
Overall for GB
Minimum
1984 figures

44·3 38·5 £160·5 £228

39·4 36·5 £100·3 £136·9

Hours per week   Gross weekly earnings

Hours per week   Gross weekly earnings

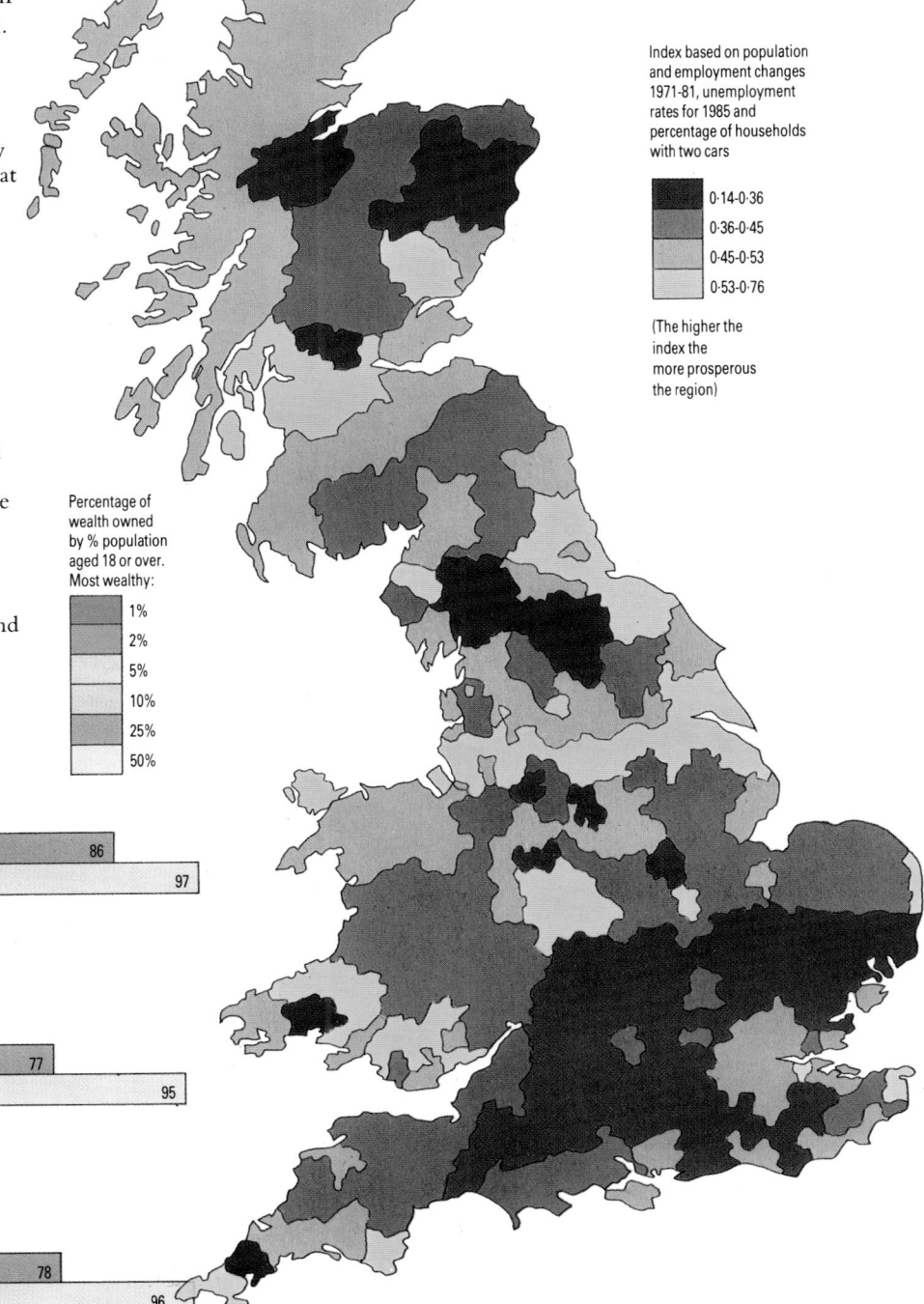

Index based on population and employment changes 1971-81, unemployment rates for 1985 and percentage of households with two cars

0·14-0·36
0·36-0·45
0·45-0·53
0·53-0·76

(The higher the index the more prosperous the region)

Percentage of wealth owned by % population aged 18 or over. Most wealthy:

1%
2%
5%
10%
25%
50%

1971
31
39
52
65
86
97

1979
22
28
40
54
77
95

1983
20
27
40
54
78
96

THE NATIONAL ECONOMY

An overview of the recent picture

As far as manufacturing is concerned, the last few years have been characterised by a contraction of economic activity. Jobs have been lost, output has fallen and, if North Sea oil exploration and retrieval are discounted, there has been a decrease in investment and a surplus in the balance of foreign trade has become a deficit. Britain's lack of competitiveness internationally is all the more serious given the unique, though temporary, advantages of the 'oil effect'. In this sense, the economy could only get better; it may be that the rates of growth and the productivity improvements achieved in the mid-1980s owe more to the low starting base of the economy created by recession than to the strength of subsequent performance.

Post-war Britain has suffered from an economic vicious circle. Arising from low output, low productivity and high unit costs have come low exports, high imports, low investment, inflation and low profits. Inevitably, this had led to continued low economic growth. This would have mattered less if Britain's key competitors had not been enjoying a contrasting economic virtuous circle, with investment, output and productivity leading to international competitiveness, profitability and growth. This contrast may not be solely an economic distinction. Social structures, political policies and the absence of an institutional machinery for directing investment and innovation contribute to the difference in effectiveness of the British economy compared to countries such as Sweden and West Germany.

Tackling the problem

Undoubtedly, the decline of manufacturing is the main cause of Britain's economic problems. With output falling and foreign trade in deficit for the first time, with investment reduced in real terms, and with more than three million unemployed as evidence of decline, the engine of the British economy is in need of overhaul. However, for the economy to grow, not only must manufacturing be boosted but disparities within the economy must also be resolved. Three of these are particularly significant. First, the private and public sectors are seen as competitors for limited government funds, yet they are interdependent and can benefit from economic encouragement. Second, regional fortunes have in recent years been allowed to diverge more and more although the economic problems of regions such as the North are to some extent a consequence of the increasing prosperity of the South-east. Third, a dual economy has started to emerge, with a thriving financial sector based in London co-existing with economic and social decline elsewhere, and this makes it difficult to achieve a nationwide democratic consensus.

Currently, the government is seeking to boost the economy by lowering income tax rates and public expenditure levels. It is also seeking to reduce inflation, create jobs by setting up training schemes, encourage investment in new technology and offering financial assistance to companies wishing to set up new plants. Furthermore, it is striving for better trading terms within the European Economic Community.

Circular flow of income

There are three key processes in an economy, which lead to the three approaches to measuring its value – the national income. Each process, with appropriate definitions and adjustments for foreign trade, leads to the same figure, but each has a different emphasis. All income is derived from economic activity: pay, profits or rent. This income is all spent on consumption, savings or investment. The proceeds of this expenditure go on the products and services generated by the economy. Income from output completes and restarts the economic cycle.

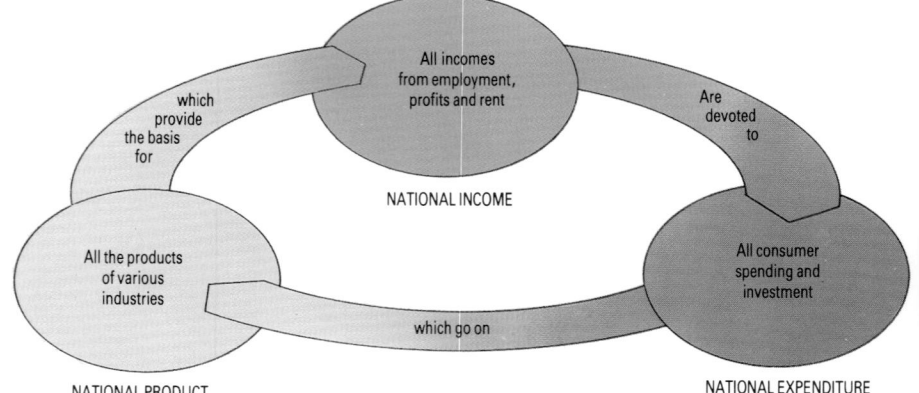

Britain's comparative performance

The overall level of activity in an economy can be defined as the total value added in the production of goods and services in a year – the annual Gross Domestic Product (GDP). A comparison of GDP per head of population between Britain and its major industrial competitors (below) shows that in recent years other countries have continued to do better. A comparison of the total sizes of GDPs (lower chart below), shows Britain had the slowest growth of all countries in all the periods, although recently its performance has matched that of other European countries.

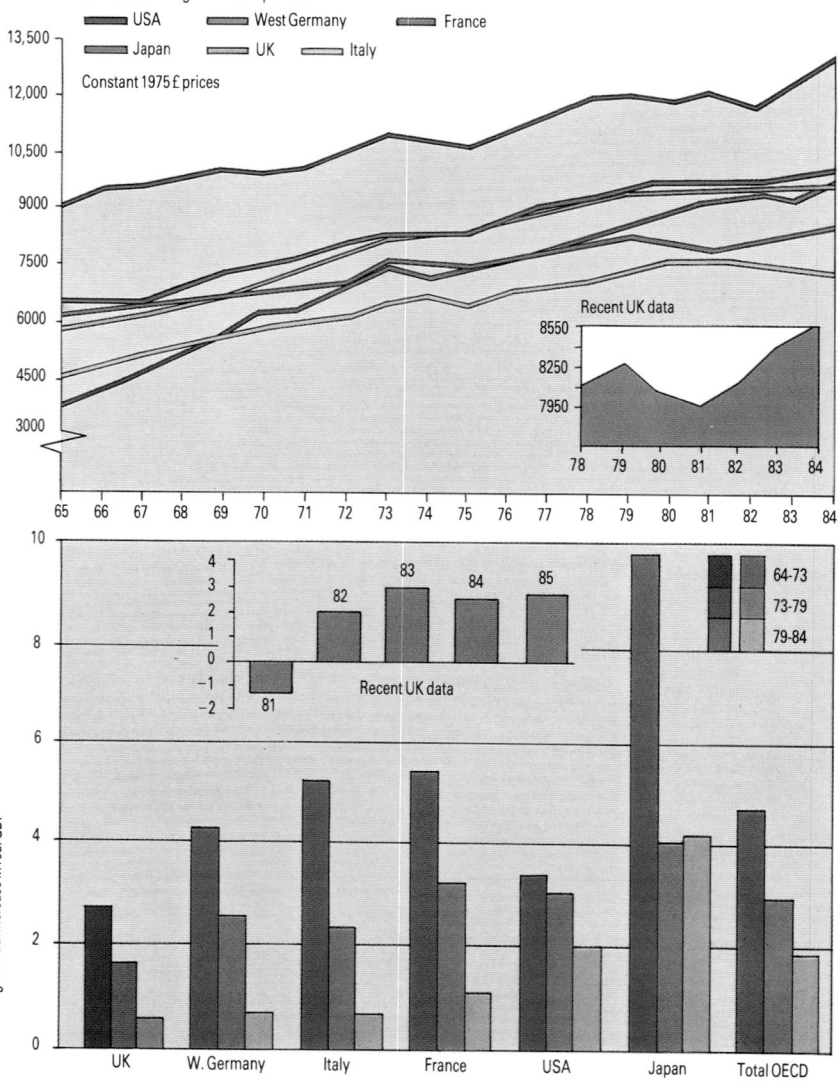

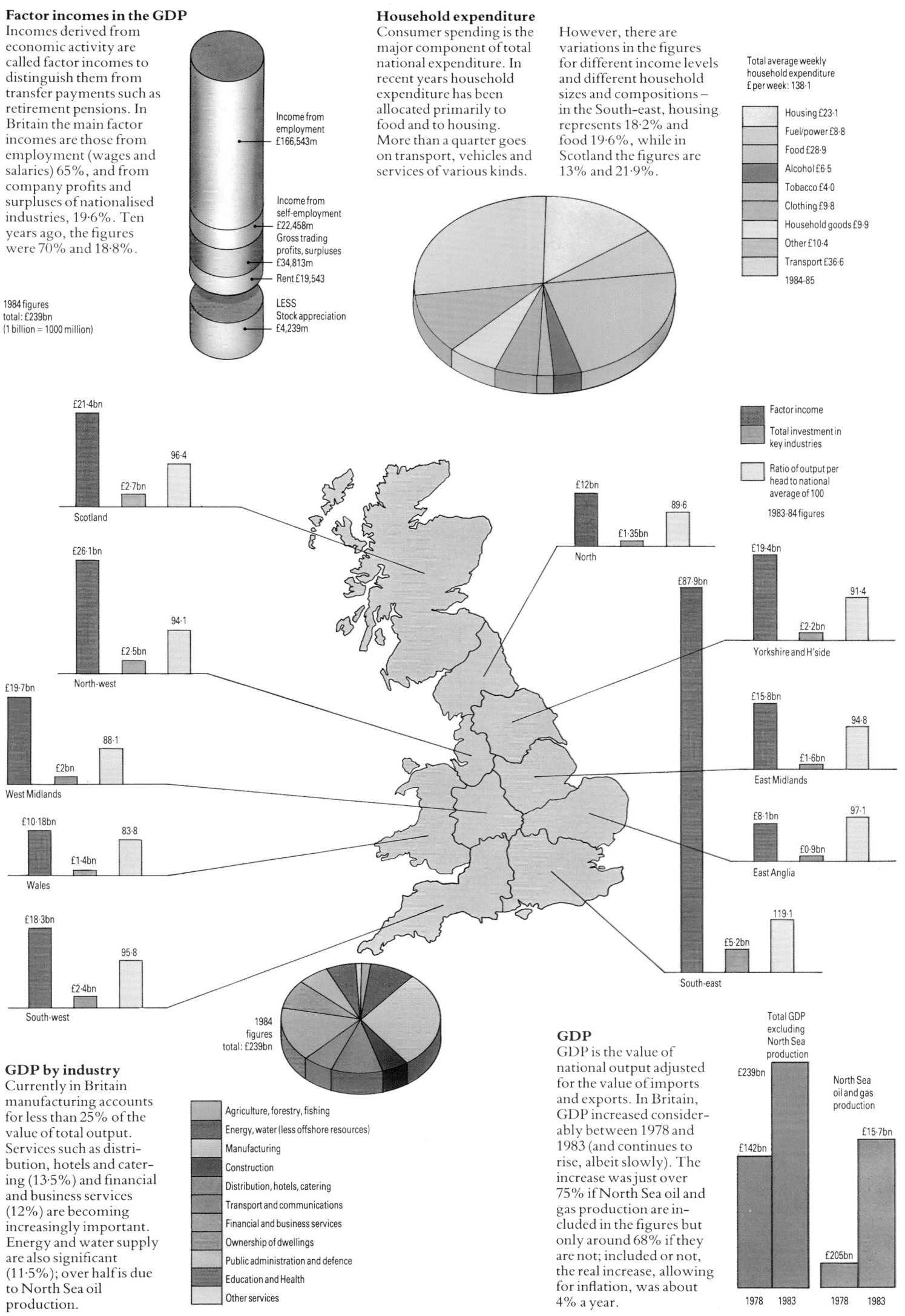

Factor incomes in the GDP

Incomes derived from economic activity are called factor incomes to distinguish them from transfer payments such as retirement pensions. In Britain the main factor incomes are those from employment (wages and salaries) 65%, and from company profits and surpluses of nationalised industries, 19·6%. Ten years ago, the figures were 70% and 18·8%.

1984 figures
total: £239bn
(1 billion = 1000 million)

Income from employment
£166,543m

Income from self-employment
£22,458m

Gross trading profits, surpluses
£34,813m

Rent £19,543

LESS
Stock appreciation
£4,239m

Household expenditure

Consumer spending is the major component of total national expenditure. In recent years household expenditure has been allocated primarily to food and to housing. More than a quarter goes on transport, vehicles and services of various kinds.

However, there are variations in the figures for different income levels and different household sizes and compositions – in the South-east, housing represents 18·2% and food 19·6%, while in Scotland the figures are 13% and 21·9%.

Total average weekly
household expenditure
£ per week: 138·1

Housing £23·1
Fuel/power £8·8
Food £28·9
Alcohol £6·5
Tobacco £4·0
Clothing £9·8
Household goods £9·9
Other £10·4
Transport £36·6

1984-85

Factor income

Total investment in key industries

Ratio of output per head to national average of 100

1983-84 figures

Scotland £21·4bn — £2·7bn — 96·4

North-west £26·1bn — £2·5bn — 94·1

West Midlands £19·7bn — £2bn — 88·1

Wales £10·18bn — £1·4bn — 83·8

South-west £18·3bn — £2·4bn — 95·8

North £12bn — £1·35bn — 89·6

Yorkshire and H'side £19·4bn — £2·2bn — 91·4

East Midlands £15·8bn — £1·6bn — 94·8

East Anglia £8·1bn — £0·9bn — 97·1

South-east £87·9bn — £5·2bn — 119·1

1984 figures
total: £239bn

Agriculture, forestry, fishing
Energy, water (less offshore resources)
Manufacturing
Construction
Distribution, hotels, catering
Transport and communications
Financial and business services
Ownership of dwellings
Public administration and defence
Education and Health
Other services

GDP by industry

Currently in Britain manufacturing accounts for less than 25% of the value of total output. Services such as distribution, hotels and catering (13·5%) and financial and business services (12%) are becoming increasingly important. Energy and water supply are also significant (11·5%); over half is due to North Sea oil production.

GDP

GDP is the value of national output adjusted for the value of imports and exports. In Britain, GDP increased considerably between 1978 and 1983 (and continues to rise, albeit slowly). The increase was just over 75% if North Sea oil and gas production are included in the figures but only around 68% if they are not; included or not, the real increase, allowing for inflation, was about 4% a year.

Total GDP excluding North Sea production

£239bn

£142bn

North Sea oil and gas production

£15·7bn

£205bn

1978   1983   1978   1983

ROAD AND RAIL

Over the last 25 years or so, the most spectacular change in Great Britain's transport system has been the building of motorways and the closure of many railway lines.

Between 1950 and 1959 the number of vehicles on British roads doubled, to 8·7 million, of which 5·2 million were cars. This was due partly to a rise in people's income, after a period of post-war austerity, but more importantly to the end of petrol rationing in 1953. The government responded by building new, faster roads. In December 1958, Britain's first motorway was opened, the 13-kilometre Preston bypass, followed in 1959 by the first stretch, 116 kilometres, of the M1. Since then, the motorway network has grown to over 2,700 kilometres and is still growing.

The boom in road traffic begun in the 1950s was bad for the newly nationalised railways, who, with worsening finances, were ill-equipped to face competition. A modernisation plan started in the late 1950s had to be scrapped because of mounting losses. By the early 1960s the railways were losing more than £100 million a year.

The government, unwilling to subsidise them further, responded with a plan to close one-third of the railway network and thereby make the railways more profitable. Of nearly 29,000 kilometres of track open in 1961, less than 17,000 kilometres survive today.

During the 1960s British Rail (BR) rose to the challenge of competition from roads and air travel by electrifying the London–Birmingham–Glasgow line to run faster trains and cut passengers' journey times. Since then, BR has introduced faster trains on other lines, including 'high-speed' trains, which, with a top speed of over 200km/h, are the fastest diesel trains in the world. The line from London's King's Cross to Edinburgh is being electrified and, by 1990, will carry passengers at speeds of up to 225km/h. Freight, too, is now being moved much faster by rail, with modern wagons capable of running at 145km/h.

Nearly two-thirds of all freight moved in Great Britain is transported by lorry. Lorries are now bigger and heavier (up to 38 tonnes including the load), with a maximum permitted speed limit of 80km/h (50 mph). There are more than 100,000 road haulage firms in Great Britain, most of them very small with only one or two lorries. The largest, the National Freight Company, passed from the public sector into private hands in 1982. Its counterpart in passenger transport, the National Bus Company, which runs a fleet of long-distance coaches, is also likely to be privatised.

Investment, public and private, has been concentrated on the major routes linking the big cities. The journey from London to Glasgow, whether by road or rail, is much faster today than it was 20 or 30 years ago. Yet, over the same period, local passenger services have declined steadily. Partly because of a lack of investment, partly because of an increase in car ownership, the number of local buses on Britain's roads went down from 42,000 in 1961 to 26,000 in 1984. The brunt of both bus and rail cuts has been borne by the rural areas, many of which are less accessible by public transport today than they were in the 1950s.

The interchange between the M6 and the M38 at Gravelly Hill near Birmingham, popularly known as 'Spaghetti junction', is the centrepiece of Britain's motorways. Each of its three arms carries more than 50,000 vehicles every day. However, the increase in traffic, particularly heavy lorries, has caused cracks to appear, and the junction is often closed for repairs.

How people travel
The results of a 1979 survey on forms of travel in Britain (below) show that the most common methods of making everyday journeys (any distance over 50m) are the car (including van or lorry) and walking. The importance of walking shows how short everyday journeys often are: many are less than 1km. It also shows that Britons, unlike Americans, find it quickest, and often most convenient, to cover short distances on foot.

Passenger transport
Since World War II, there has been a significant shift from public to private transport. Between 1959 and 1984 car and motorcycle travel, measured in passenger kilometres (number of travellers × distance they travel), increased threefold, from 13bn to 42bn, while bus travel nearly halved. Train travel, apparently, declined only slightly, but the figures conceal a substantial drop in the overall number of rail users.

Passenger km × 1 billion

Air | Bus | Train | Car | Air | Bus | Train
1959 | 1984

Car (43%)
Walking (39%)
Bus (11%)
Bicycle (3%)
Train (2%)
Motorcycle (1%)
Other (1%)

Freight transport
Between 1959 and 1984 the volume of freight moved by road, measured in tonne kilometres (weight × distance moved) more than doubled. So too did the volume of freight moved by coastal shipping. By contrast, the equivalent figure for rail more than halved.

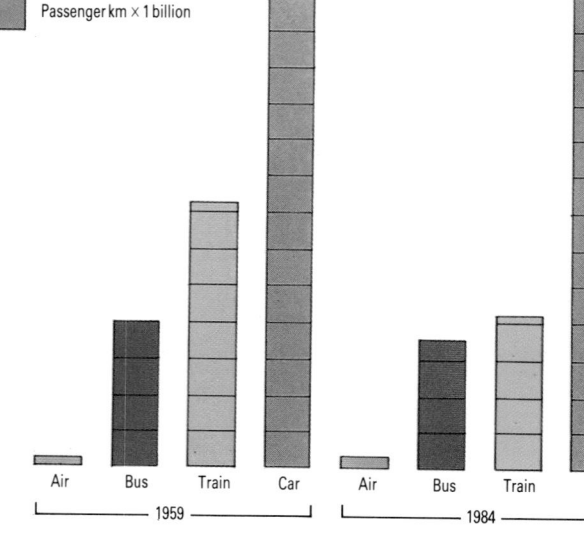

tonne km × 1 billion

Ship | Rail | Road | Ship | Rail | Road
1959 | 1984

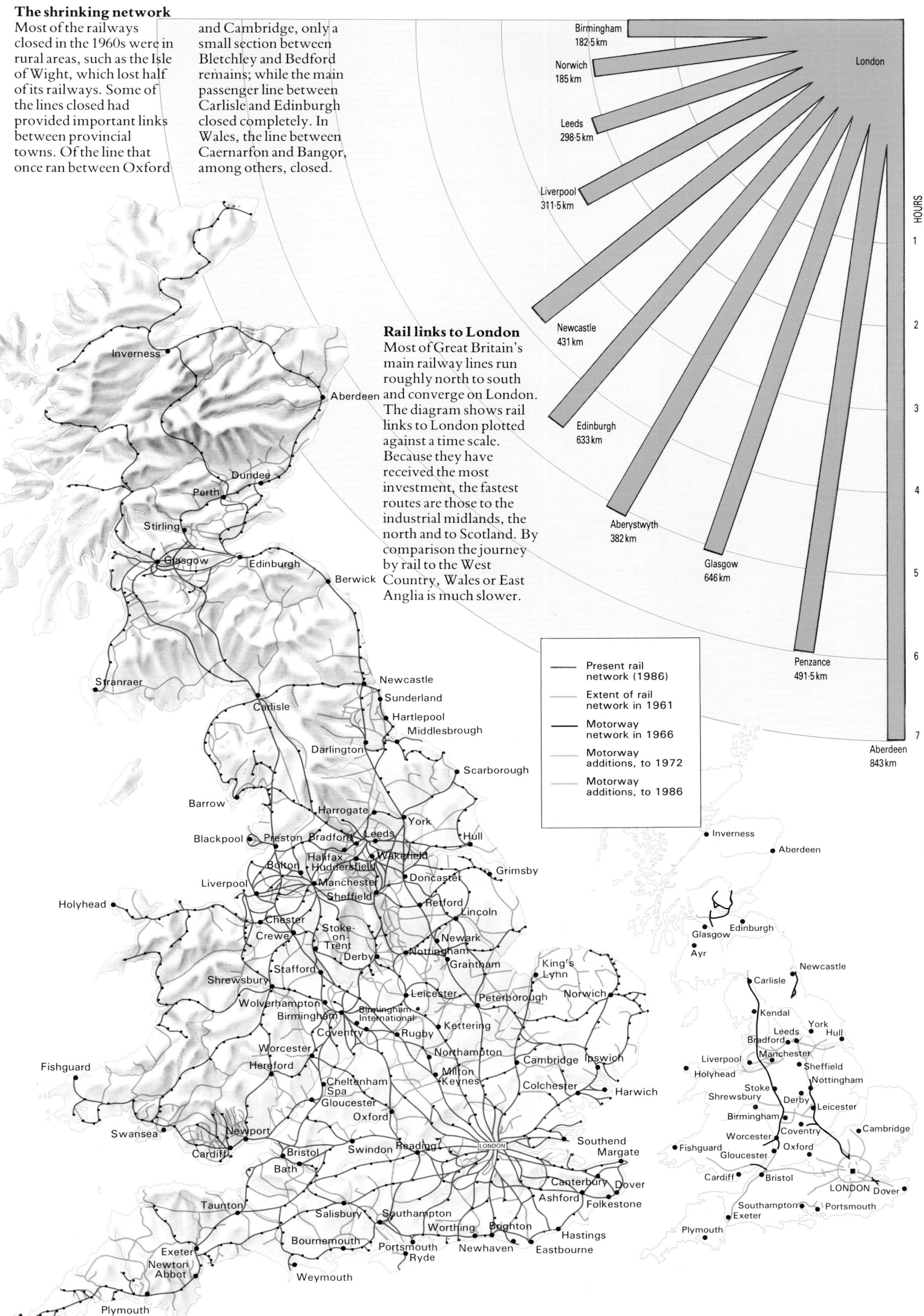

The shrinking network

Most of the railways closed in the 1960s were in rural areas, such as the Isle of Wight, which lost half of its railways. Some of the lines closed had provided important links between provincial towns. Of the line that once ran between Oxford and Cambridge, only a small section between Bletchley and Bedford remains; while the main passenger line between Carlisle and Edinburgh closed completely. In Wales, the line between Caernarfon and Bangor, among others, closed.

Rail links to London

Most of Great Britain's main railway lines run roughly north to south and converge on London. The diagram shows rail links to London plotted against a time scale. Because they have received the most investment, the fastest routes are those to the industrial midlands, the north and to Scotland. By comparison the journey by rail to the West Country, Wales or East Anglia is much slower.

HOURS

Birmingham
182·5 km

Norwich
185 km

Leeds
298·5 km

Liverpool
311·5 km

London

Newcastle
431 km

Edinburgh
633 km

Aberystwyth
382 km

Glasgow
646 km

Penzance
491·5 km

Aberdeen
843 km

Present rail
network (1986)

Extent of rail
network in 1961

Motorway
network in 1966

Motorway
additions, to 1972

Motorway
additions, to 1986

PORTS, AIRPORTS AND TRUNK ROADS

Just as travel within Great Britain has seen a shift from rail to road over the past quarter-century, so too patterns in travel to and from Great Britain have changed.

Once the great ocean-going liners, such as the *Queen Elizabeth* and *Queen Mary*, ran a weekly service from Southampton to New York. In 1961, around 250,000 passengers crossed the Atlantic to North America by sea. By 1983, the number had dropped to 30,000, and most of the liners were serving as pleasure-cruise ships or had been scrapped. Only the *QEII*, the last great liner to be built, still sails regularly across the Atlantic, catering for the richer package tourists.

By the early 1950s an airliner could cross the Atlantic, without refuelling, in 15 hours, compared with the fastest ocean liner, which took five days. In 1962, for the first time, more people flew into Britain than arrived by sea. That lead was increased during the 1960s by the widespread use of jet aircraft, with cruising speeds of 880 km/h, more than twice as fast as the old propeller planes they replaced. In the early 1970s the first widebodied jets were introduced, which, with their much greater carrying capacity, made long-distance flying far cheaper and brought about substantial reductions in air fares.

However, for short crossings to Europe, it is still cheaper and often more convenient to go by sea. Since the 1960s the volume of passenger and freight transport crossing the Channel by this route has increased considerably. There has been a large expansion in cross-Channel heavy lorry traffic, encouraged by the growth of Britain's motorways and the raising of the weight limit on British roads to accommodate the larger European lorries.

However, the future of the cross-Channel ferries is uncertain, now that Britain and France have agreed to build the Channel Tunnel. The tunnel is scheduled to open to the public in 1993, running shuttle trains from near Folkestone to carry cars and lorries to near Calais. There will also be passenger trains from London to Paris direct,

which will cut the average journey time by half, to about three hours.

Britain's improvements in international transport over the past few decades have not been altogether painless. Residents living near London's Heathrow airport, which already handles around 250,000 aircraft every year, are opposed to the building of a fifth terminal at Heathrow because of the extra noise it will create. Likewise, a longstanding proposal to expand Stansted to provide a third London airport is very much out of favour with the local townspeople. There has also been opposition to the increase in heavy lorries, which, protesters say, pollute the air with diesel fumes and noise, damage the roads and are a menace to other road users.

International passengers
Today, long-distance sea travel has been largely superseded by long-distance air travel. The sharp increase, between 1961 and 1984, in the number of passengers flying in or out of Britain was due partly to the introduction of widebodied jet airliners and cheap package holidays. Over the same period, passenger arrivals and departures at sea ports more than trebled, largely because of the increase in cross-Channel passengers to and from France and the Low Countries.

British Caledonian aircraft at Gatwick airport. With a fleet of 40 planes and 7 on order in 1986, 'B Cal' is Britain's largest private airline. State-owned British Airways operates 138 aircraft, 31 helicopters, and has another 7 planes on order.

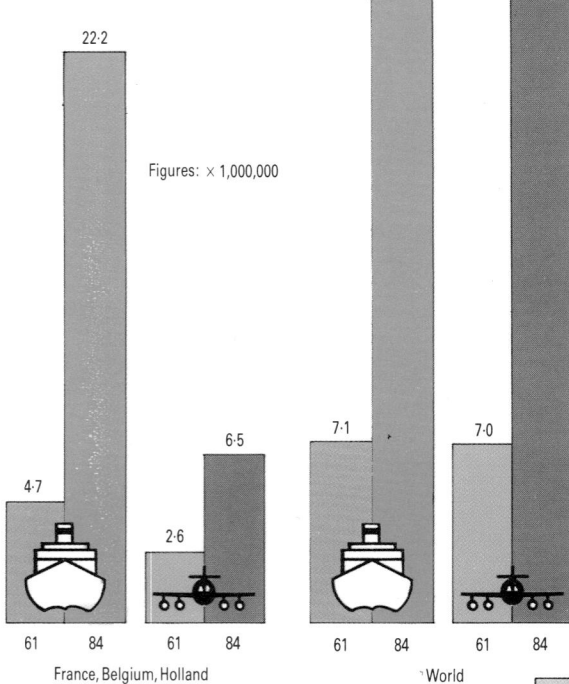

Figures: × 1,000,000

France, Belgium, Holland | World

Major ports
Sullom Voe, in the Shetland Islands, became Britain's busiest port, because of North Sea oil. Until 1977 it was insignificant, but in 1978 it first handled more than 1 million tonnes of oil, and in 1983 overtook London as Britain's busiest port. Most of Sullom Voe's cargo is oil destined for refineries at ports such as Milford Haven. The North Sea ports of Tees and Hartlepool also owe much of their importance to oil. The port of London declined as container ships became too large for the Thames.

= 2,000,000 tonnes

Dover | Felixstowe | Clyde | Manchester | Liverpool | Medway | Orkneys | Grimsby/Immingham | Southampton | Forth | Milford | Tees/Hartlepool | London | Sullom Voe

The transport system

The trunk roads are Great Britain's main traffic arteries. The government maintains the motorway system, which carries nearly 13% of the nation's traffic, and 12,000 km of other trunk roads. These roads are the responsibility of the Department of Transport, in England, or the Scottish and Welsh Offices. BR, with a turnover in 1983 of £3·2 bn, controls all the main railways. Sea ports are mostly in the hands of trusts, such as the Dover Harbour Board, or local councils.

Air passengers

Heathrow is Britain's busiest airport, handling 29 million passengers in 1984 (about half of all Britain's air passengers). The opening of a fourth terminal in 1986 increased its capacity to 38 million. Gatwick is the second busiest airport, with about 14 million a year. Heathrow and Gatwick are owned by the British Airways Authority. BAA also own Aberdeen and Glasgow airports. Many airports are in the hands of local councils, including Manchester airport, Britain's third largest.

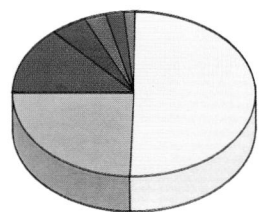

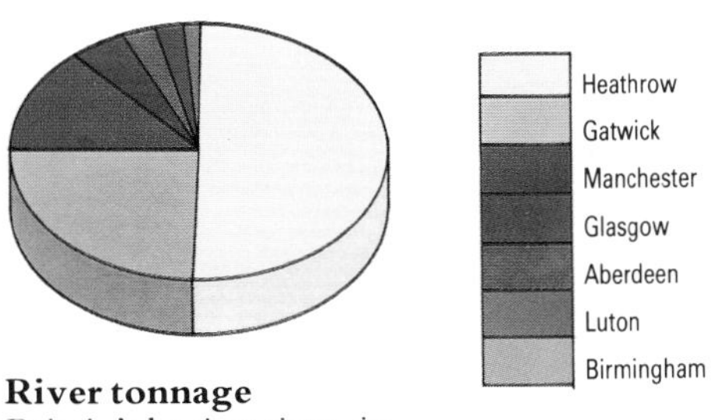

Heathrow
Gatwick
Manchester
Glasgow
Aberdeen
Luton
Birmingham

River tonnage

Britain's busiest river, in terms of its share of freight, is the Thames. Nearly 20 million tonnes of goods are picked up every year by sea-going ships from ports on the River Thames like Tilbury, while a further 4 million tonnes are internal to the river, such as oil carried from Canvey Island to distribution points upstream. The Humber, Britain's next busiest river, accounts for the movement of nearly 9 million tonnes of freight every year.

Thames
Humber
Mersey/ Manchester Ship Canal
Forth

Trent
Orwell
Clyde
Ouse
Medway
Severn

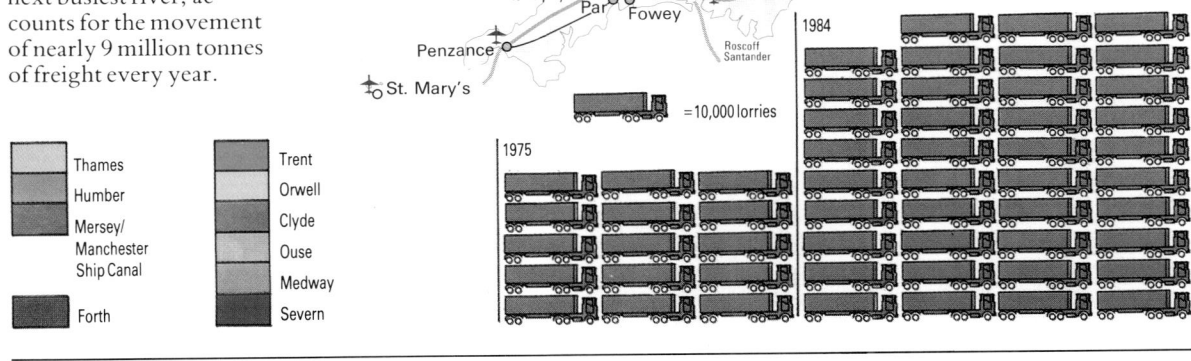

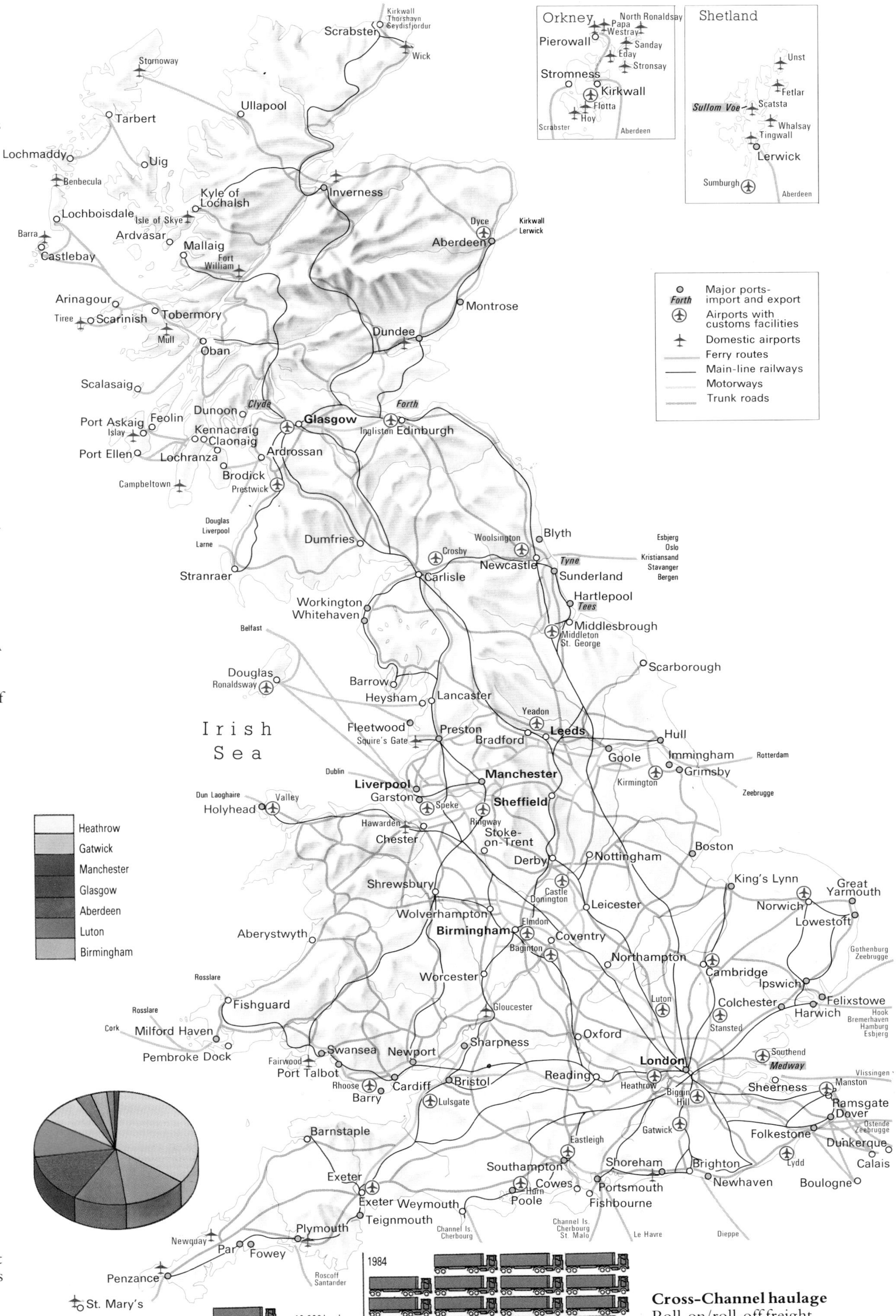

= 10,000 lorries

1975

1984

Cross-Channel haulage

Roll-on/roll-off freight traffic across the Dover Straits is growing fast. In nine years the number of heavy lorries (over 30 tonnes) crossing by ferry in either direction increased from around 151,000 to 392,000.

INNER CITIES

Today many of the great cities of the Industrial Revolution are in decline, with falling employment, rising crime, poor housing and movement of population away from the inner cities out to the suburbs, commuter belts or beyond.

Most of today's inner city areas were themselves once suburbs, built on the edges of cities in Victorian times. The Great Exhibition of 1851 was held in London's Hyde Park, then on the western edge of the city. By 1906 that edge had moved five kilometres further west, to White City, where the Imperial Exhibition of that year was held. As London's suburbs began to sprawl, encouraged by subsidised housing and the development of bus and tram routes into open country, they gradually enveloped villages such as Highgate and Chiswick. At the same time, the overcrowded City of London population started falling.

For the first time, in the 1950s, the population of many major cities started to fall. London's total population peaked at 8·5 million in 1939 and has been falling ever since. Nowadays, only towns of fewer than 200,000 inhabitants – mostly the newer towns – have static or increasing populations.

Often inner city depopulation was the result of an official policy to relieve overcrowding. Some London councils, for example, built 'overspill' estates, as far away as Bodmin in Cornwall. The development of new towns, such as Harlow and Milton Keynes, was also intended to attract people out of London and to encourage employers to relocate.

From the 1960s London, in common with other major cities, also began to lose jobs. The old industries around which the cities had grown up, and which supported the economy of the inner cities, were in decline, and the newer growth industries could not make up the job losses. They were, in any case, often developed in the new towns or on greenfield sites away from the city, where building and land were less expensive.

With most investment in building – whether homes, factories or offices – going outside the city, many inner city buildings fell into disrepair. To make matters worse, some of the investment that did go to the inner cities was misguided. The 1960s housing boom produced a rash of redevelopment schemes in which many a sound Victorian house was pulled down to make way for a modern tower block. Many of the tower blocks are themselves now being demolished, either because of structural problems or because councils recognise the failure of this vast social experiment.

The problems the inner cities face today pose a challenge to government now and in the future. If the more affluent continue to move away, and the inner cities fail to attract investment, the cost of basic amenities, such as street lighting, will increasingly be borne by fewer and fewer people. Moreover, those who remain will be the socially disadvantaged who cannot afford to move – the old, the one-parent families, the poorly paid and the unemployed. So far, attempts at reviving the inner cities by means of new housing, development schemes, and, in London, housing co-operatives, have generally failed to arrest the decline.

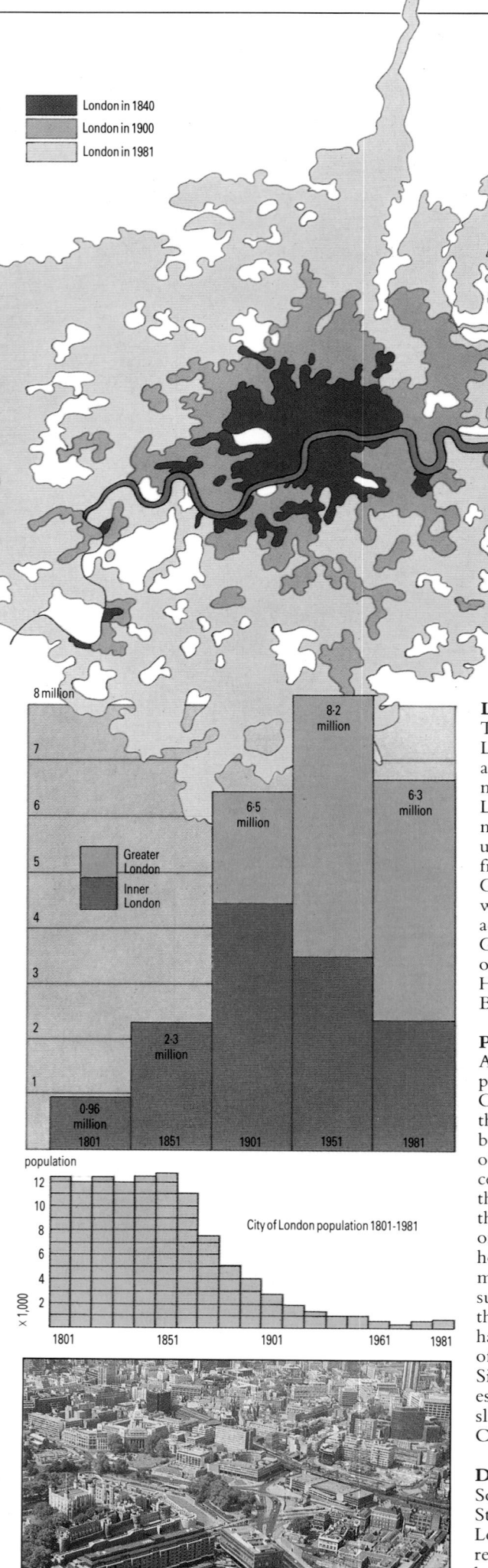

London in 1840
London in 1900
London in 1981

London's spread
The ancient core of London is the City, an area known as the 'square mile'. Since the 1800s London has spread, mostly to the west, upwind of the smells from the city. Today the Greater London area, which until 1986 was administered by the Greater London Council, occupies 1,600 km² from Hayes in the west to Bexley in the east.

Population losses
As London expanded, the population first of the City, and eventually of the whole of London, began to fall. From a peak of 128,000 on the 1851 census, the population of the City fell to 27,000 by the turn of the century, as offices began to replace homes, and people moved out to suburbs such as Hackney. By 1971 the resident population had fallen to 4,000, many of whom were caretakers. Since then, a new housing estate in the Barbican has slightly increased the City's population.

Dockland revival
Some disused docks, like St Katharine's, in London, are being redeveloped. New buildings such as Tower Hotel and a trade/conference centre stand alongside busy shops that have been converted from old warehouses.

City of London population 1801-1981

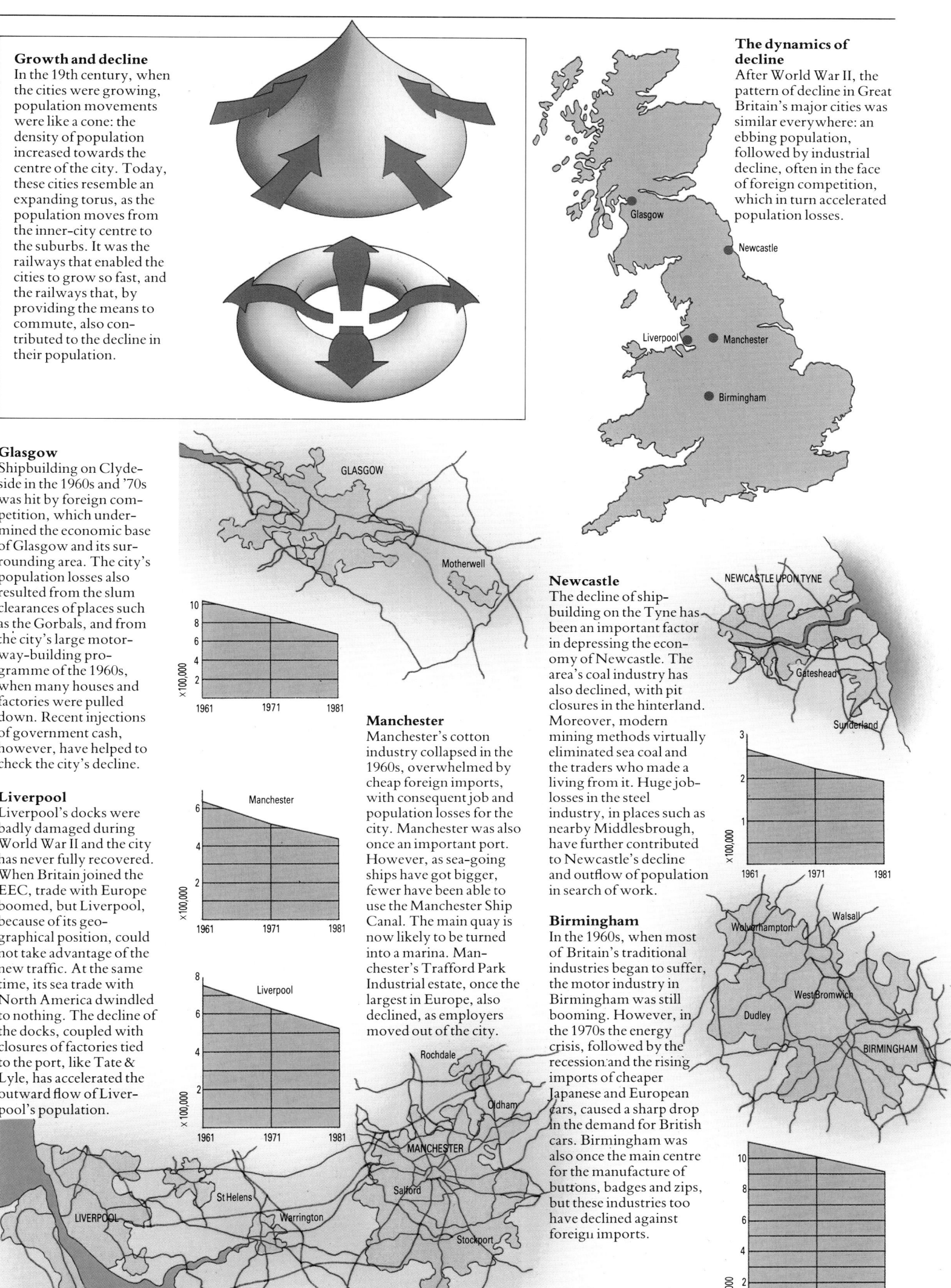

Growth and decline

In the 19th century, when the cities were growing, population movements were like a cone: the density of population increased towards the centre of the city. Today, these cities resemble an expanding torus, as the population moves from the inner-city centre to the suburbs. It was the railways that enabled the cities to grow so fast, and the railways that, by providing the means to commute, also contributed to the decline in their population.

The dynamics of decline

After World War II, the pattern of decline in Great Britain's major cities was similar everywhere: an ebbing population, followed by industrial decline, often in the face of foreign competition, which in turn accelerated population losses.

Glasgow

Shipbuilding on Clydeside in the 1960s and '70s was hit by foreign competition, which undermined the economic base of Glasgow and its surrounding area. The city's population losses also resulted from the slum clearances of places such as the Gorbals, and from the city's large motorway-building programme of the 1960s, when many houses and factories were pulled down. Recent injections of government cash, however, have helped to check the city's decline.

Liverpool

Liverpool's docks were badly damaged during World War II and the city has never fully recovered. When Britain joined the EEC, trade with Europe boomed, but Liverpool, because of its geographical position, could not take advantage of the new traffic. At the same time, its sea trade with North America dwindled to nothing. The decline of the docks, coupled with closures of factories tied to the port, like Tate & Lyle, has accelerated the outward flow of Liverpool's population.

Manchester

Manchester's cotton industry collapsed in the 1960s, overwhelmed by cheap foreign imports, with consequent job and population losses for the city. Manchester was also once an important port. However, as sea-going ships have got bigger, fewer have been able to use the Manchester Ship Canal. The main quay is now likely to be turned into a marina. Manchester's Trafford Park Industrial estate, once the largest in Europe, also declined, as employers moved out of the city.

Newcastle

The decline of shipbuilding on the Tyne has been an important factor in depressing the economy of Newcastle. The area's coal industry has also declined, with pit closures in the hinterland. Moreover, modern mining methods virtually eliminated sea coal and the traders who made a living from it. Huge job-losses in the steel industry, in places such as nearby Middlesbrough, have further contributed to Newcastle's decline and outflow of population in search of work.

Birmingham

In the 1960s, when most of Britain's traditional industries began to suffer, the motor industry in Birmingham was still booming. However, in the 1970s the energy crisis, followed by the recession and the rising imports of cheaper Japanese and European cars, caused a sharp drop in the demand for British cars. Birmingham was also once the main centre for the manufacture of buttons, badges and zips, but these industries too have declined against foreign imports.

STATE AND CONSTITUTION

The United Kingdom does not have a written constitution. Instead, formal and informal procedures and practices have become established, which determine how the government and Parliament operate together. The British constitution is thus a system of laws, customs and conventions which have developed between the Crown, Parliament and people over more than 500 years. These define the composition and powers of state organisations, and regulate them in their dealings with one another, and with the private citizen.

Power and legislation

In the British state, power flows from the monarchy – known constitutionally as the Crown. Members of the civil service, police forces and the armed sevices are all servants of the Crown. However, Parliament is the supreme legislative body. All legislation must have the assent of the two parliamentary chambers, the House of Commons and the House of Lords, and the Crown. The powers that government departments and other organisations have are normally delegated to them by Parliament. If Parliament has not legislated in a particular area, the Crown is held to have prerogative powers, and the Crown and its servants may do as they wish. If Parliament has legislated, then administrative and legal arrangements are controlled by statute law, expressed in Acts of Parliament or regulations made under statute.

The British constitution

The powers of Parliament and those of the Crown overlap as shown. Immediately below the Crown is the Privy Council, which includes the Prime Minister and members of past and present cabinets, the leader of the Opposition in Parliament, and important members of opposition parties, as well as a small number of senior serving or retired civil servants or diplomats. Members of the Privy Council take the title 'Right Honourable', and are addressed as such during debates in the House of Commons. The Privy Council is summoned to meet from time to time at Buckingham Palace. The Crown can rule directly, through the Privy Council, by making Orders-in-Council. An Order-in-Council using statutory powers has to be laid before both Houses of Parliament, who must give their consent if the Order is to become law. An Order that uses prerogative powers of the monarchy, for example in the interests of the defence of the realm, is not subject to Parliament's approval.

Public spending

Public expenditure includes spending by local authorities, as well as central government organisations and agencies. Most is spent by central government on social security, including pensions and other payments from the National Insurance system. The next biggest item is defence and the armed forces, which, as a share of public spending, rose by nearly 2% over seven years. In 1978/9 more was spent on education than on defence, but this has since been reversed.

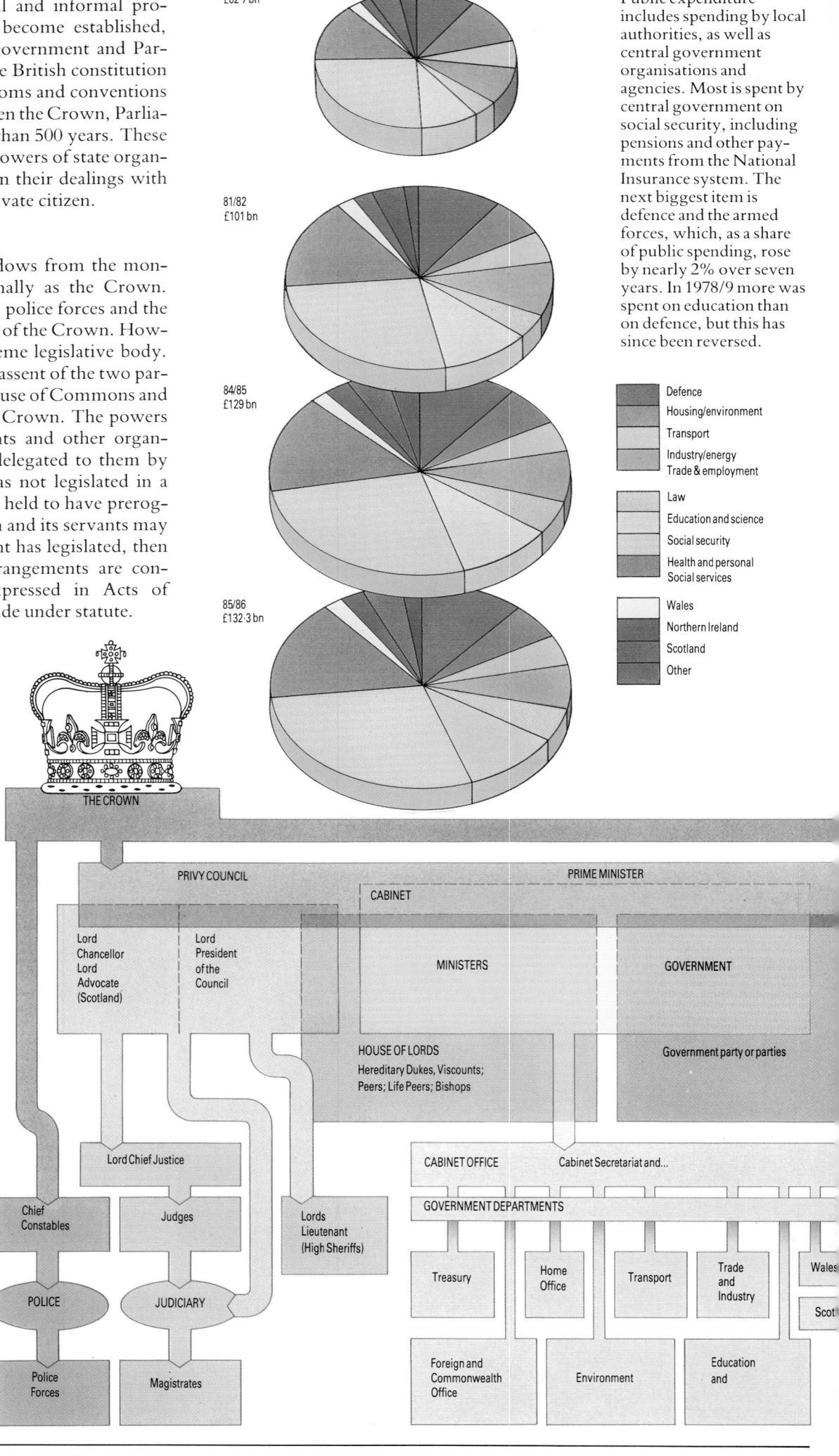

Government

The head of government is the Prime Minister, who is appointed and invited to form a government by the Crown. The Prime Minister is selected on the basis that he or she can command the support of a majority of Members of Parliament in the House of Commons. The constitutional convention is that the Prime Minister will be the leader of the majority party (the party holding most seats) in the Commons. There is no clear precedent for whom the Crown should choose if there is no one party in the House of Commons whose leader can command the support of a majority of MPs.

The Prime Minister appoints all the other members of the government from the ranks of the majority-party Members of Parliament or their supporters in the House of Lords. Up to 24 key ministers are appointed to be members of the Cabinet. Major government decisions are usually taken or endorsed by the Cabinet as a whole. The decisions of the Cabinet then become the formal decisions of Her (or His) Majesty's Government.

Members of the Cabinet always include the Chancellor of the Exchequer, and the Secretaries of State who head the larger government departments. Ministers in charge of smaller ministries, or working inside the larger departments, do not necessarily belong to the Cabinet. Junior members of the government are appointed as Parliamentary Under-Secretaries or Parliamentary Private Secretaries to Ministers and Secretaries of State. In all, about 100 MPs and peers (House of Lords members) are usually appointed to government posts.

The Queen at the Palace of Westminster for the State Opening of Parliament. Each year, on this occasion, members of both Houses go to the House of Lords to hear the Queen's Speech. This is a statement, read aloud by the Queen and written by the government, which announces its plans for legislation during the coming session of Parliament and its major policy objectives.

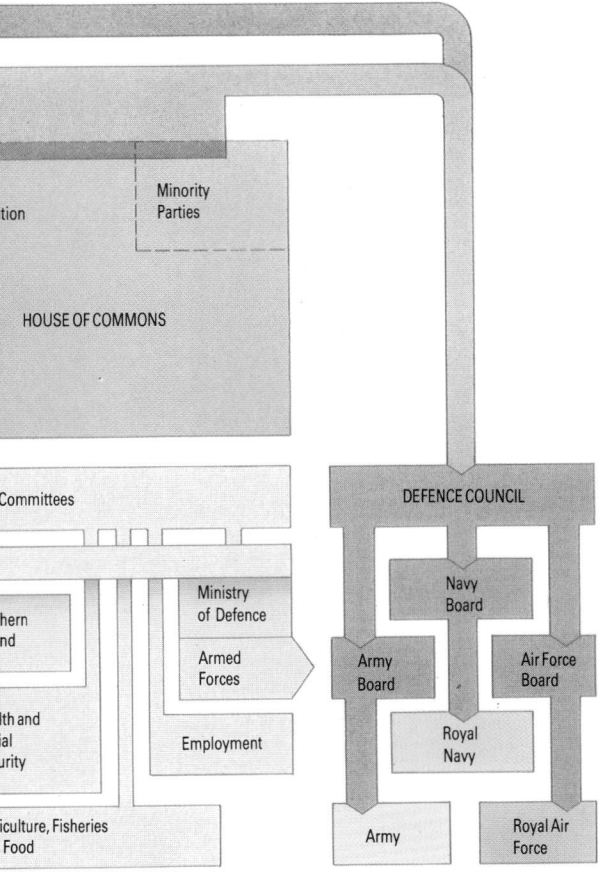

Cabinet committees
Cabinet government is central to the British government system. Important government decisions are taken, not by individual ministers and departments, but by cabinet committees of ministers, officials, or both. Some of the committees are permanent, while others may be brought together to consider a single issue, and are then dissolved. These are called MISC (for Miscellaneous) or GEN (for General) committees. The Cabinet is the highest administrative body in the elected executive system. The Prime Minister and other ministers are in charge of the executive departments of state, and are expected to account to Parliament for their expenditure and activities. Individual MPs do not have an absolute right to information from government ministers or departments, but may pursue inquiries by asking questions in Parliament or through the work of special parliamentary committees.

Major Cabinet Committees

Cabinet (C)
Run by Prime Minister

Overseas and Defence Affairs (OD)
Run by Prime Minister

European Economic Community (OD [E])
Run by the Foreign Secretary

Home Defence of Britain (OD [HD])
Run by the Home Secretary

South Atlantic (Falklands) (OD [SA])
Run by the Prime Minister

Economic affairs (E)
Run by the Prime Minister

Nationalised industries (E[NI])
Run by the Prime Minister

Civil Service (E[CS])
Run by the Minister for the Civil Service

Pay policy for public sector (E[PSP])
Run by the Chancellor of the Exchequer

Home affairs, education, social policy (H)
Run by the Home Secretary

Environmental affairs (EN)
Run by the Secretary of State for the Environment

Joint Intelligence Committee (JIC)
Run by the Cabinet Office Co-ordinator of Intelligence

British Security and Intelligence services (PSIS)
Run by the Cabinet Secretary

Government publicity plans (MIO)
Run by the Press Secretary to the Prime Minister

Public Records Policy (MISC 3)
Run by the Attorney General's Department

Nuclear weapons (Trident) (MISC 7)
Run by the Prime Minister

Grants to local authorities (MISC 21)
Run by the Home Secretary

The Queen's Speech and future legislation (QL)
Run by the Leader of the House

PARLIAMENT

Members of Parliament in the House of Commons are elected to their seats for the lifetime of a Parliament, normally a maximum of five years. Voting takes place at either a General Election (for all seats in the House of Commons) or a by-election (when a seat falls vacant). Election is by a simple majority vote of those eligible to vote in their constituency (electoral area). Since the enactment of the Representation of the People Acts (1918 and 1928), Britain has had universal adult suffrage.

The House of Commons has 650 seats, made up of 523 for England, 38 for Wales, 72 for Scotland and 17 for Northern Ireland. The other parliamentary chamber, the House of Lords, seats the Lords Spiritual (Archbishops and senior Bishops of the Church of England) and the Lords Temporal (hereditary and life peers). Members of the House of Lords are not elected.

All-party committees

Any draft law, or 'Bill', presented before Parliament must have the majority support of both Houses at each of its three readings before it can become an Act of Parliament. In the process, the Bill often undergoes amendments. Between the second and third readings, the Bill will normally be referred to an all-party committee, known as a standing committee, for closer scrutiny. The committee stage is followed by a report stage, when further amendments may be considered.

The House of Commons

The present chamber was designed and built in 1950, replacing an older chamber destroyed by German bombing in 1941. The Commons' business is directed and controlled by the Speaker or his or her deputy. While the Speaker is presiding, the Commons' mace, a symbol of parliamentary authority, is placed in the centre of the chamber. In Parliament, members of both Houses have certain unique privileges, including immunity from prosecution for anything they may say.

Sometimes a select committee will also consider the detailed terms of a Bill. The main work of the better-known select committees, however, is to hold major investigations into issues of public interest. In 1979, changes were made in the select committee system to enable MPs to conduct a closer examination of the expenditure, administration and policies of the major government departments.

The political parties

The major national political parties represented in the House of Commons since 1945 have been the Conservative Party and the Labour Party, with the Liberal Party in third place. For the 1983 election, the Liberal Party formed an electoral Alliance with the newly founded Social Democratic Party (SDP). Since 1970, nationalist parties in Scotland and Wales have also been permanently represented in the House of Commons.

Broadly, the Conservative Party favours reduced government regulation of economic and industrial activity, and diminished public expenditure. Its main sources of income are private donations, mostly from business. By contrast, the Labour Party is traditionally in favour of the redistribution of wealth and greater governmental control of economic affairs in order to create a more egalitarian society. Eighty per cent of Labour Party funds are provided by trade unions, and the balance by members' subscriptions.

The popular vote

In every General Election since 1945, more than 90% of parliamentary seats have been held by the Labour and Conservative parties. There has been one minority government, between February and October 1974, when Labour had only 301 out of 635 seats. In 1950, Labour polled the largest number of votes but held a minority of seats. In 1945, Labour under Clement Attlee gained an overall majority of 146 seats, the largest-ever postwar majority. In 1983, Conservative PM Margaret Thatcher held an overall majority of 144 (the second largest). The 1970s saw the arrival of new parties: the Scottish National Party (SNP) and the Welsh National Party (Plaid Cymru). The Social Democratic Party, led by disaffected former Labour ministers, made its electoral debut in 1983.

Taxation

Each year, the Chancellor of the Exchequer asks Parliament to approve his Budget, including the government plans for taxation. Taxes are collected by two government departments: the Inland Revenue and Customs and Excise.

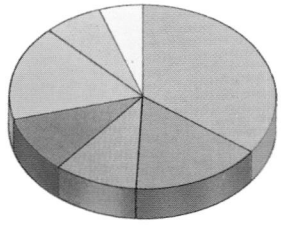

Key (£bn)
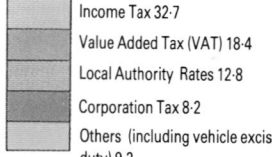
Income Tax 32·7
Value Added Tax (VAT) 18·4
Local Authority Rates 12·8
Corporation Tax 8·2
Others (including vehicle excise duty) 9·2
Oil duties/ Petroleum Revenue 13·3
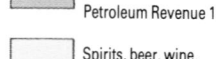
Spirits, beer, wine, tobacco duties 7·9

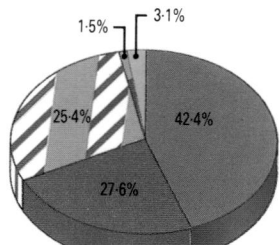

3·1%
1·5%
25·4%
42·4%
27·6%

Share of vote 1983 election

Conservative
Labour
Liberal
SDP } Alliance
Welsh/Scottish Nat.
Others

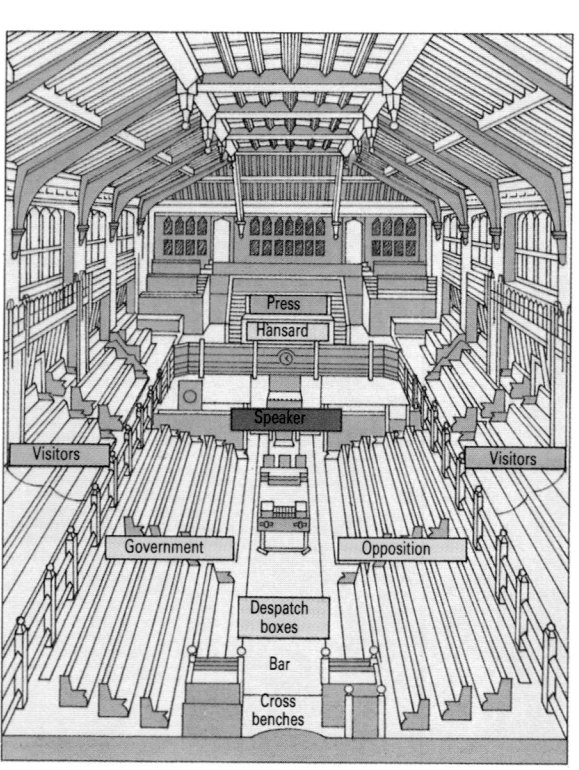

Press
Hansard
Speaker
Visitors
Visitors
Government
Opposition
Despatch boxes
Bar
Cross benches

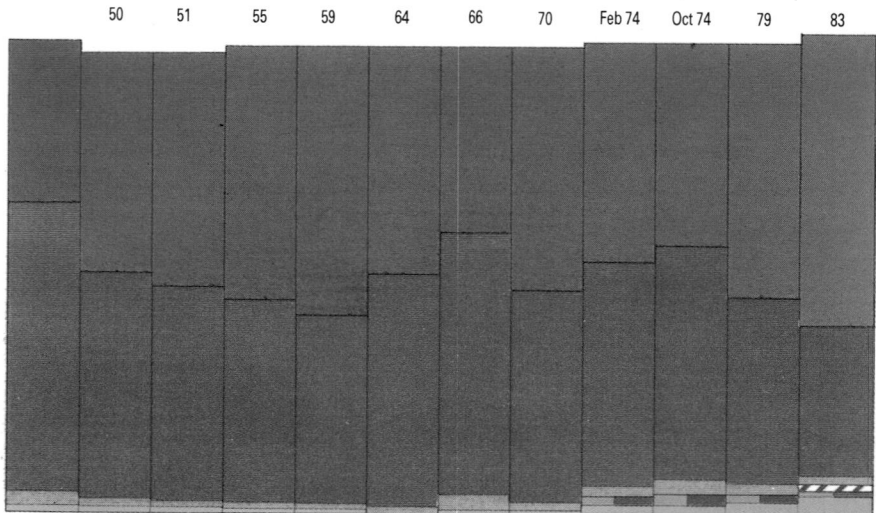

50   51   55   59   64   66   70   Feb 74   Oct 74   79   83

Constituencies

The 1983 General Election returned a Conservative government with an enhanced majority. The safest Conservative seats are in the country areas of England and the richer metropolitan districts. Labour draws its main support from inner-city industrial areas, the north of England, Scotland and Wales. Support for the Liberal/SDP Alliance is more evenly spread. As the 1983 election showed, the numbers of eligible voters can vary considerably between constituencies: 94,000 in the Isle of Wight, as compared with 22,000 in the Western Isles of Scotland. Most constituencies, however, have between 52,000 and 75,000 electors. The proportion of electors using their vote also varied, from about 50% to 90%. The highest turnouts were in rural areas, whereas low voter turnouts were recorded in the inner-city areas of London, Manchester, Birmingham and Glasgow. British constituencies are also grouped into larger 'Euro-constituencies', each of which elects a Member of the European Parliament (MEP).

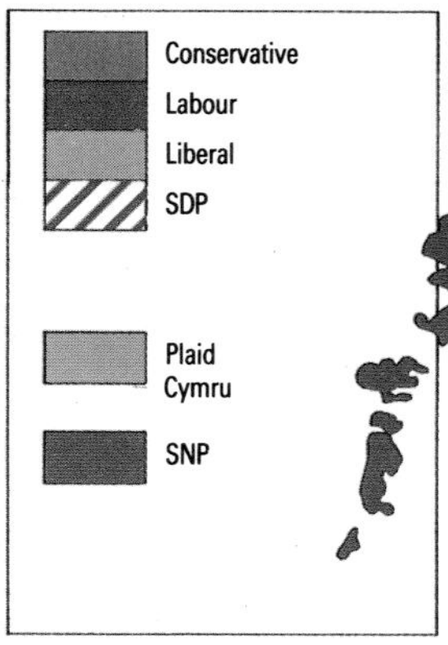

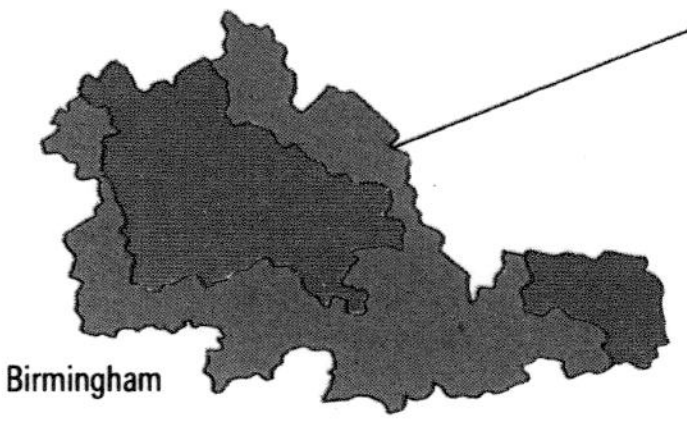

Conservative	
Labour	
Liberal	
SDP	
Plaid Cymru	
SNP	

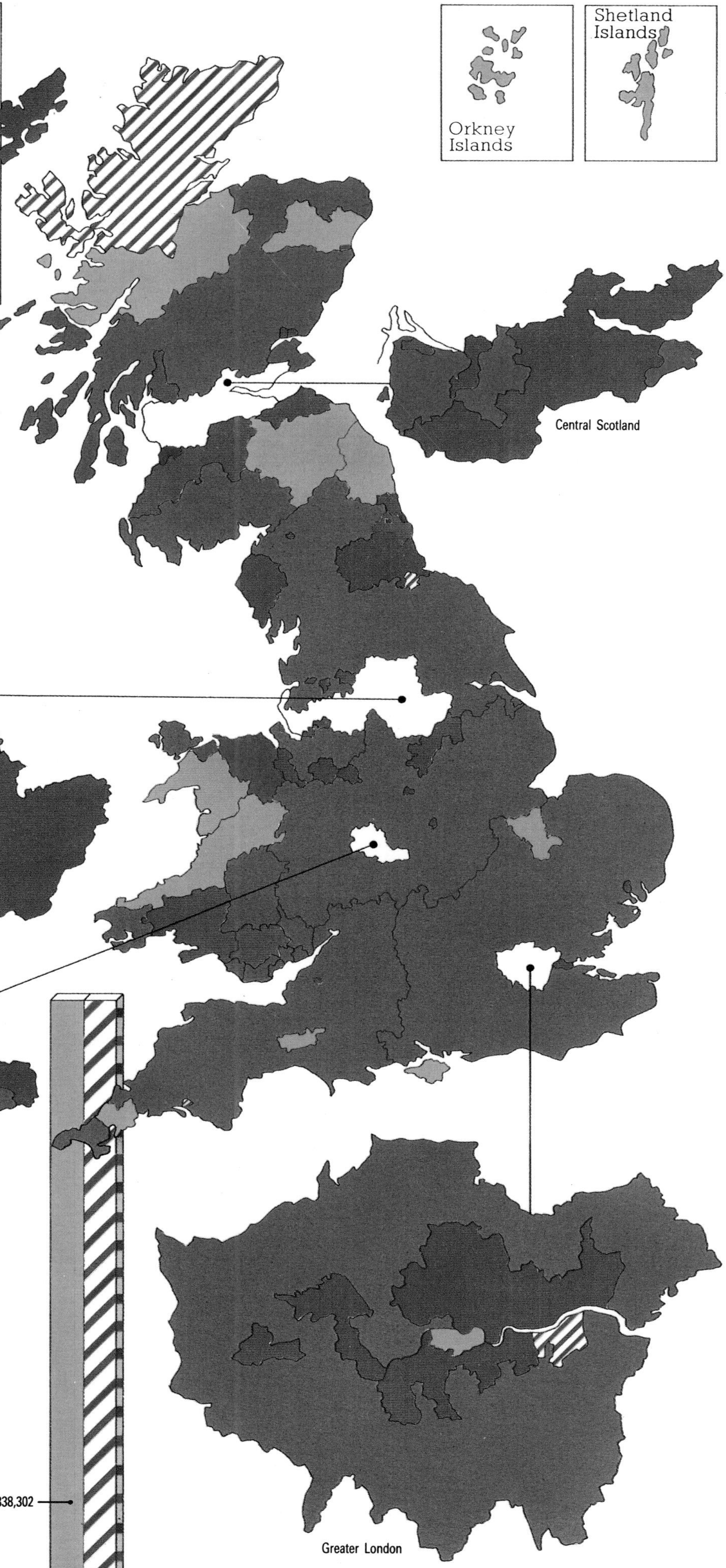

Orkney Islands

Shetland Islands

Central Scotland

Liverpool/Manchester

Birmingham

Greater London

Votes per MP

Under Britain's present electoral system the number of seats held by a party in Parliament does not reflect the total number of votes polled by that party in a General Election. On the basis of the 1983 General Election results the Conservatives benefited most from the system and the SDP/Liberal Alliance came off worst. The election results (right) showed that the Alliance needed, on average, more than 10 times as many votes per MP as the victorious Conservatives. Proportional representation (PR), a system used in other democratic countries, would have produced different results. With PR, the number of MPs elected is, as far as possible, proportional to the share of the national vote each party obtains. In Britain, however, some MPs are elected not so much because of their party but because they are considered to be good representatives of their constituents' interests.

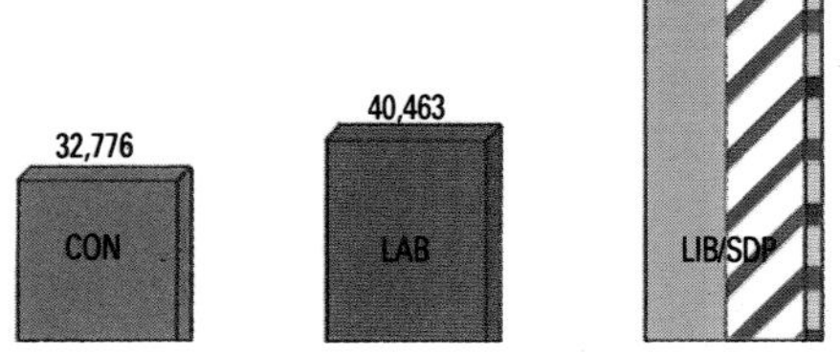

338,302

32,776
CON

40,463
LAB

LIB/SDP

LOCAL GOVERNMENT AND ADMINISTRATION

Compared to many western countries, the British government system is highly centralised. Central government appoints all members of many public bodies, including those responsible for health, water, sewerage, gas and electricity distribution. Local government authorities have only such functions and powers as have been granted them by Parliament, and even then they may have only minimal discretion as to how to carry out their duties within the context of central-government policy decisions. In matters of education, social services, housing, fire protection, planning policy and road maintenance, central government determines national policy, leaving local authorities responsible for its detailed execution.

All judiciary functions are centrally controlled, and elected local authorities have only limited powers in respect of local police forces. Many government activities, such as the provision of social security or employment services, or the regulation of trade and industry, have no local government component, elected or otherwise.

Local government reform

Since local government reform of the 1960s and 1970s, there has generally been in England and Wales a two-tiered system of district and county (or Metropolitan County) councils. In 1963 the London County Council was extended to become the Greater London Council (GLC) in the first of three major reforms. Complete restructuring of local authority functions, and the formation of further Metropolitan Counties, followed the Local Government Act of 1972, and similar reforms took place in Scotland two years later. Subsequently, the GLC and Metropolitan Counties were abolished, in 1986. Representatives of the government and district councils were appointed to joint boards and agencies to take over the responsibilities of the Metropolitan Councils.

The division between county and district council is much longer established in Scotland, having

begun when Royal Charters were first granted to independent 'burghs' during the early middle ages. Today, Scotland has 9 regional councils, 53 district councils and 3 islands councils. Regional and district councils work together on industrial development, local amenities and tourism.

Local authority elections

Throughout Britain, local authority elections are held every four years. Traditionally candidates have not always represented nationally-organised political parties, and many 'independent' members still sit on parish, district and county councils. However, by 1973, more than half of councils in England and Wales, and one-third of those in Scotland, were controlled by a single national political party. Five years later, four out of five English and Welsh councils, and three out of five councils in Scotland, were controlled by one party, including Scottish and Welsh national parties.

County councils

In England and Wales, county councils are responsible for education, fire, consumer protection, major roads, overall structure planning, passenger transport, and refuse disposal. District councils deal with housing, local roads, building and development control, local amenities (such as parks) and refuse collection. In Scotland, regional councils have functions akin to those of an English county though they usually cover larger geographical areas, with special arrangements for the Scottish Highlands and islands.

Local government income

Local authorities are financed primarily by rates – the tax levied each year on property owners, according to the value of the house or other premises they own. Evaluation of the property is made by the Inland Revenue. Rate income to local authorities is supplemented by direct grants from central government. Rate support grants can be used as a means of redistributing resources between wealthier and poorer areas, or to control local authority spending.

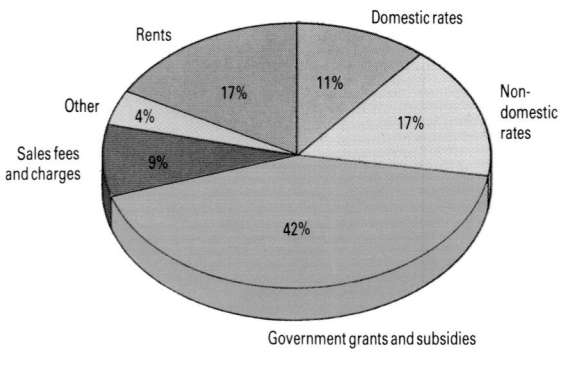

Domestic rates 11%
Non-domestic rates 17%
Government grants and subsidies 42%
Sales fees and charges 9%
Other 4%
Rents 17%

1 TYNE AND WEAR
2 CLEVELAND
3 WEST YORKSHIRE
4 SOUTH YORKSHIRE
5 GREATER MANCHESTER
6 MERSEYSIDE

7 WEST MIDLANDS
8 BEDFORDSHIRE
9 BERKSHIRE
10 WEST GLAMORGAN
11 MID GLAMORGAN
12 SOUTH GLAMORGAN

Local authority employees

In 1985, over 1·9 million people were employed by local authorities in Great Britain, including administrative, professional and technical staff, policemen, firemen, teachers and manual workers. Nearly half of all local government workers are employed in the education service. Pay and conditions for local authority staff are set by individual councils, but often within the framework of a wider trade union agreement.

Carving up the capital

Before it was abolished in 1986, along with five other Metropolitan County councils, the Greater London Council was responsible for strategic planning, large-scale housing provision, major roads and traffic management schemes, arts and recreation, London Transport, and many other public functions. A directly-related authority, ILEA (Inner London Education Authority) which runs schools and polytechnics in central London, continued to operate but is now a directly elected body. London boroughs continue to deal with local planning, housing, local roads and parks, libraries and amenities, social services and (in outer London boroughs) education. Further legislation introduced in the 1980s has reduced local authorities' powers to determine the level of rates they may levy, or the purposes for which they plan their expenditure, and replaced parts of the 'rate support' system with more stringent government controls.

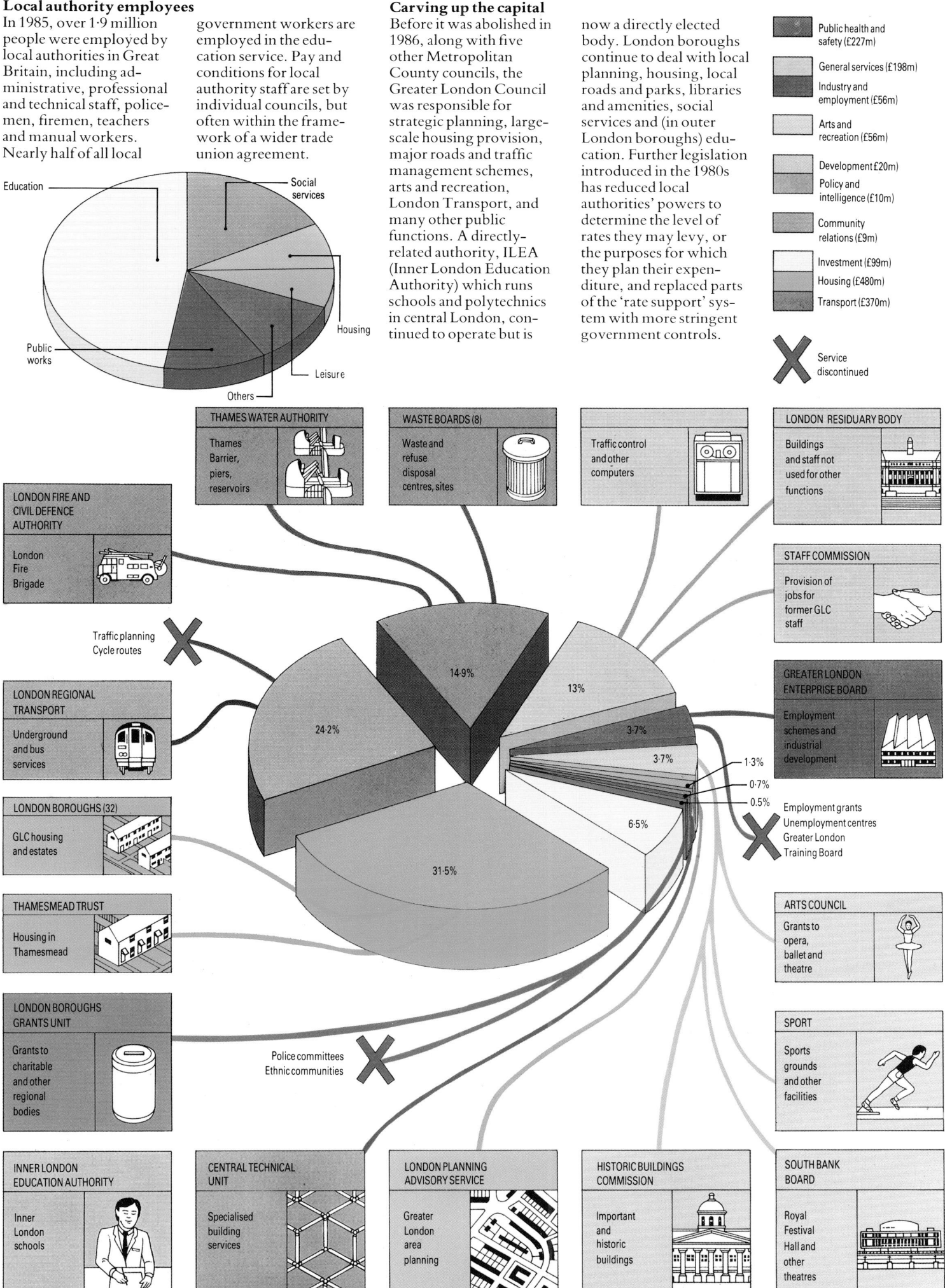

Public health and safety (£227m)
General services (£198m)
Industry and employment (£56m)
Arts and recreation (£56m)
Development £20m
Policy and intelligence (£10m)
Community relations (£9m)
Investment (£99m)
Housing (£480m)
Transport (£370m)

Service discontinued

THAMES WATER AUTHORITY — Thames Barrier, piers, reservoirs

WASTE BOARDS (8) — Waste and refuse disposal centres, sites

Traffic control and other computers

LONDON RESIDUARY BODY — Buildings and staff not used for other functions

LONDON FIRE AND CIVIL DEFENCE AUTHORITY — London Fire Brigade

STAFF COMMISSION — Provision of jobs for former GLC staff

Traffic planning Cycle routes

LONDON REGIONAL TRANSPORT — Underground and bus services

GREATER LONDON ENTERPRISE BOARD — Employment schemes and industrial development

LONDON BOROUGHS (32) — GLC housing and estates

Employment grants Unemployment centres Greater London Training Board

THAMESMEAD TRUST — Housing in Thamesmead

ARTS COUNCIL — Grants to opera, ballet and theatre

LONDON BOROUGHS GRANTS UNIT — Grants to charitable and other regional bodies

SPORT — Sports grounds and other facilities

Police committees Ethnic communities

INNER LONDON EDUCATION AUTHORITY — Inner London schools

CENTRAL TECHNICAL UNIT — Specialised building services

LONDON PLANNING ADVISORY SERVICE — Greater London area planning

HISTORIC BUILDINGS COMMISSION — Important and historic buildings

SOUTH BANK BOARD — Royal Festival Hall and other theatres

14·9% 13% 3·7% 3·7% 1·3% 0·7% 0·5% 6·5% 24·2% 31·5%

DEFENCE AND ARMED FORCES

Today, most British overseas commitments, except in Europe and the Falkland Islands, have been withdrawn, substantially altering both the pattern and extent of British military activity since World War II. Britain's military resources are now concentrated in the United Kingdom and West Germany, with the armed forces equipped and organised primarily for operations in central Europe.

Broadly, British defence forces are organised to carry out two long-established policies: participation in the North Atlantic Treaty Organisation (NATO) military alliance, and the maintenance and operation of strategic nuclear weapons.

Some full-time units in Britain form part of the special NATO Allied Mobile Force, and can operate in outlying NATO regions such as Turkey or Norway. Mobile and airborne troops could also be used in British 'rapid deployment force' operations outside the normal NATO area, in accordance with plans developed with the United States.

A large part of the British defence budget is spent on the research and development, operation and maintenance of nuclear weapons. These include both strategic long-range nuclear missiles carried by Polaris submarines, and nuclear bombs with which to arm Royal Air Force aircraft and Royal Navy helicopters. The Polaris system, which forms the basis of Britain's policy of nuclear deterrence, may in the future be replaced by the still more powerful Trident.

Britain in NATO

The NATO treaty was signed in Washington in April 1947. Britain, the United States, Canada and nine other European countries formed the NATO alliance to oppose the growing military might of the Soviet Union. Today 16 countries belong to NATO. The Eastern European defence treaty organisation, the Warsaw Pact, was set up in opposition to NATO in 1955.

NATO and the Warsaw Pact both operate collective security systems, in which the United States and the Soviet Union respectively take a leading role. NATO is controlled by the North Atlantic Council, which normally meets in Brussels. Britain participates through a Permanent Representative and a civil and military staff. NATO countries can be represented at meetings of the Council by their heads of state, or by foreign or defence ministers. Such meetings are usually held two or three times annually.

There are three major NATO Commanders, one of whom is always a British admiral based in Britain. He is known as Commander-in-Chief, Channel, and has his headquarters at Northwood in north-west London. The other two major NATO commanders, who are always US officers, are the Supreme Allied Commander, Atlantic (SACLANT), based in North Virginia, and the Supreme Allied Commander, Europe, based in Brussels.

Armed forces

From a defence budget of £17 billion (1985), £500 million was spent on Polaris submarines, and a further £2·5 billion on the Royal Navy as a whole. Most of the Army's expenditure of £2·8 billion went on maintaining British forces in West Germany; £800 million is spent on home land forces. At a cost of £3·7 billion, the Royal Air Force was the most expensive service, while the direct costs of the Territorial Army and other reserve forces were £300 million. Defence support functions are also costly, and include £2·3 billion on research and development, £1·3 billion on training and £3 billion on the administration and maintenance of headquarters and defence bases in Britain.

Polaris submarine HMS *Revenge* leaves the Clyde estuary on 'deterrent patrol'. *Revenge* is one of four Polaris submarines, each of which carries 16 missiles armed with nuclear warheads. One submarine leaves before the previous one has returned, so that the Polaris deterrent is present at sea at all times. Each patrol lasts two months.

Armed Forces (1985)		
Front line units	Unit	No.
Royal Navy		
Submarines	Vessels	24
Carriers and assault ships	Vessels	4
Other craft (Destroyers; frigates; anti-mine; patrol)	Vessels	107
Airborne	Squadrons	17
Royal Marines	Commandos	4
Regular Army		
Armoured corps	Regiments	9
Artillery	Regiments	22
Engineers	Regiments	13
Infantry	Battalions★	56
Special Air Services (SAS)	Regiments	1
Army Air Corps	Regiments	4
Territorial Army	Regiments	20
Infantry	Battalions	35
Royal Air Force		
Strike/attack	Squadrons	11
Offensive support	Squadrons	5
Air defence	Squadrons	9
Maritime patrol	Squadrons	4
Reconnaissance/early warning	Squadrons	4
Transport/tankers	Squadrons	14
Search and rescue	Squadrons	2
Surface to air missiles	Squadrons	8
Ground defence	Squadrons	5
Auxiliary Air Force	Squadrons	6

★A battalion is part of a regiment, the largest army unit.
Infantry figures are commonly given in battalions.

Intelligence-gathering is vital to Britain's defence. Radar stations such as the one shown, right, belong to a nation-wide radar network which monitors the movements of both civil and military aircraft.

Many military bases are linked to satellites, which are used for communication, navigation, and photographic and electronic reconaissance, and would warn of any missile strike against Britain.

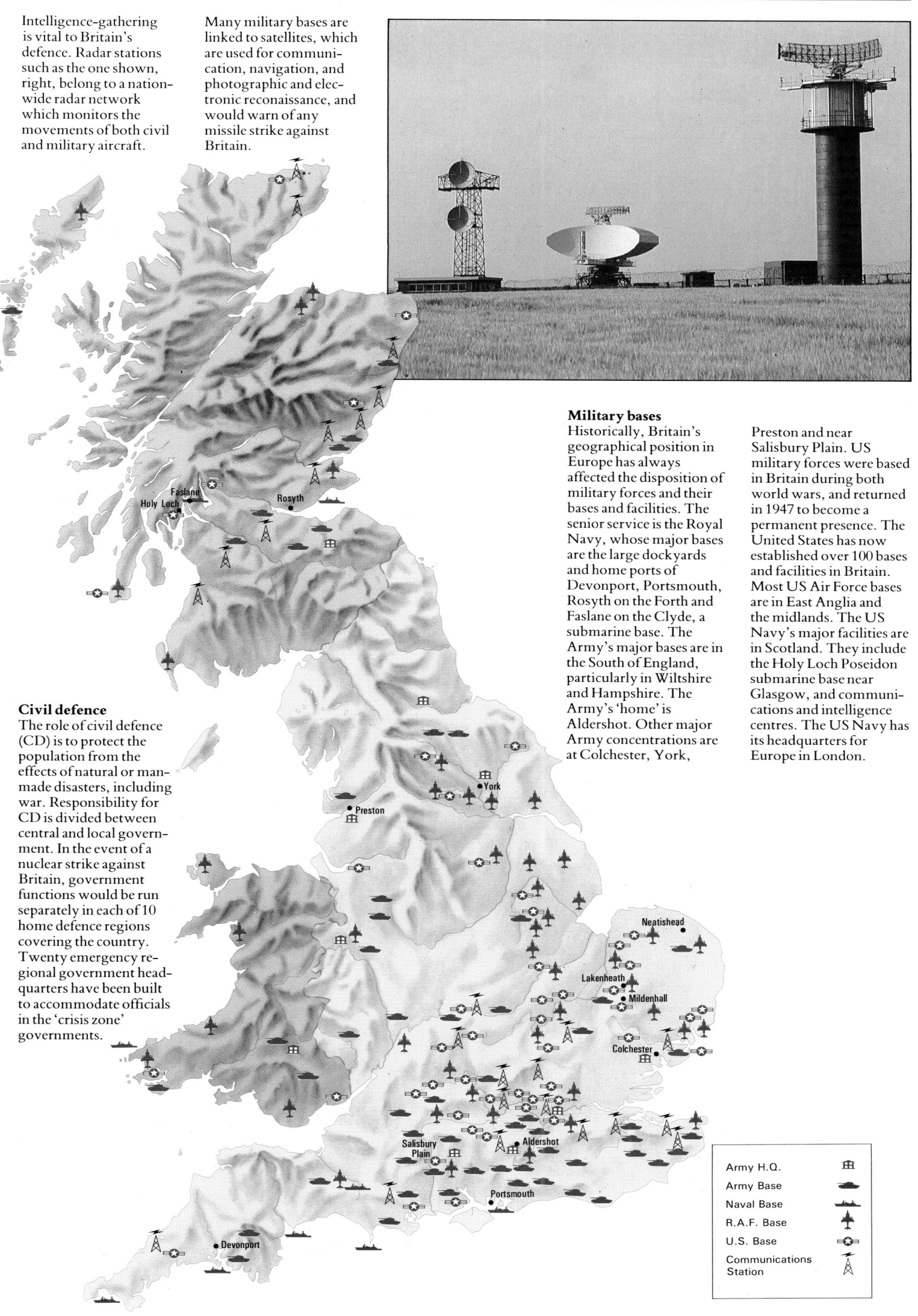

Military bases

Historically, Britain's geographical position in Europe has always affected the disposition of military forces and their bases and facilities. The senior service is the Royal Navy, whose major bases are the large dockyards and home ports of Devonport, Portsmouth, Rosyth on the Forth and Faslane on the Clyde, a submarine base. The Army's major bases are in the South of England, particularly in Wiltshire and Hampshire. The Army's 'home' is Aldershot. Other major Army concentrations are at Colchester, York, Preston and near Salisbury Plain. US military forces were based in Britain during both world wars, and returned in 1947 to become a permanent presence. The United States has now established over 100 bases and facilities in Britain. Most US Air Force bases are in East Anglia and the midlands. The US Navy's major facilities are in Scotland. They include the Holy Loch Poseidon submarine base near Glasgow, and communications and intelligence centres. The US Navy has its headquarters for Europe in London.

Civil defence

The role of civil defence (CD) is to protect the population from the effects of natural or man-made disasters, including war. Responsibility for CD is divided between central and local government. In the event of a nuclear strike against Britain, government functions would be run separately in each of 10 home defence regions covering the country. Twenty emergency regional government headquarters have been built to accommodate officials in the 'crisis zone' governments.

Army H.Q.	田
Army Base	
Naval Base	
R.A.F. Base	
U.S. Base	
Communications Station	

AIRSPACE AND SEASPACE

Every day, thousands of civil and military aircraft operate over Britain, at heights ranging from ground level to 10,000 metres and above. To enable them to do so safely, sophisticated rules, navigational arrangements and monitoring systems are necessary. The procedures used by civil aircraft are administered and controlled by the National Air Traffic Services (NATS) of the Civil Aviation Authority, who have established a series of airways. Major British and international airports are connected by these airways, which are known by such titles as Green One (Birmingham to Dublin) or Amber Two (London to Paris).

Royal Air Force units protect British airspace by detecting, investigating and, if need be, engaging with unidentified aerial activity in the NATO-agreed UK Air Defence Region. This region can extend as far as 320 kilometres from the coast, and as high as 25,000 metres. Information from radar stations and other surveillance systems is co-ordinated with aircraft and missile units by the control centres in the UK Air Defence Ground Environment (UKADGE) system.

The key components of Britain's UKADGE are a network of civil and military radar stations, whose information is shared between NATS and military radar controllers. NATS and the RAF co-ordinate the tracking of civil aircraft from two joint civil–military control centres: London Air Traffic Control Centre, at West Drayton, near Heathrow airport, and the Scottish Air Traffic Control Centre at Prestwick, near Ayr. Flight plans for civil aircraft are filed at these control centres and immediately become available for military air defence controllers to check. West Drayton and Prestwick also supervise search and rescue services provided by the RAF.

To co-ordinate transatlantic flights to and from Europe, a joint British–Irish civil air traffic control organisation, the Shanwick Oceanic Control, has been established. Information about civil aircraft movement is shared between its two control centres, at Prestwick and Shannon Airport, Eire.

Airspace

Besides operating the main airways, NATS also has an 'upper ATS (Air Traffic Services)' route system, used by aircraft flying at 27,500 metres and above. These routes are for longer-distance flights, and for international flights crossing Britain. When aircraft cross from one nationally controlled airspace to another, the flight is 'handed over' to the new country's control system. The first information on an unidentified flight crossing into British airspace would probably come from the NATO radar system NADGE (NATO Air Defence Ground Environment). The airspace above certain places in Britain may be designated as a 'danger area', or as 'prohibited' or 'restricted'. Civil aircraft are warned not to enter these areas at prescribed times, if at all. Danger areas are often declared above military firing ranges or exercise areas. Nuclear power plants are usually surrounded by prohibited airspace.

Fisheries
Oil/gas exploration

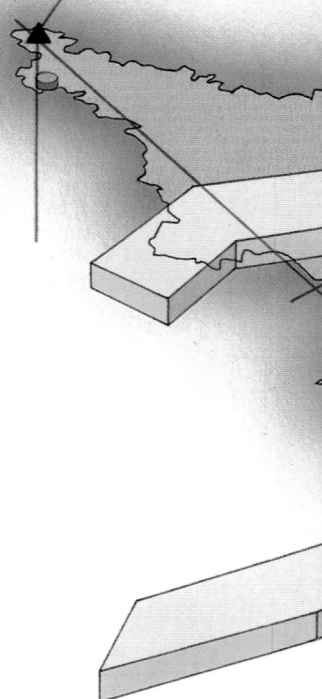

Boeing 747 over the houses at Heathrow. The United Kingdom low-flying system was reviewed in the 1970s after crashes between low-flying civil and military aircraft. Civil low flying is concentrated around major airports.

Military low flying is restricted near cities, but is more in evidence in remote countryside areas. A special low-flying zone, the Highlands Restricted Area, is used by RAF and US Air Force pilots to practise low-level flying at night.

North Sea tapestry
Policing Britain's 'offshore tapestry' of fisheries and energy resources (oil and gas fields in the North Sea) is undertaken by the Royal Navy's Fisheries Protection Squadron, and RAF Nimrod maritime aircraft. The air/sea patrols are also responsible for reporting oil spillages around the UK, or any infringement of British fishing limits. To counter any attack on an oil rig or other resources, a Royal Marine response force is based at Arbroath, Scotland.

Early warning

The Royal Air Force has nine air defence squadrons patrolling British airspace. These include both Phantom and Tornado aircraft. At selected airfields, such as Leuchars in Scotland, the service maintains an Interceptor Alert Force, with pairs of aircraft ready to take off at short notice to identify any unknown aircraft in the region.

Northern waters are patrolled by RAF Shackleton airborne early-warning aircraft, equipped with long-range radar. The Shackletons, whose design dates from World War II, are supplemented by AWACS, a more modern NATO and US Air Force early-warning aircraft. Maritime surveillance is carried out jointly by the RAF and the Royal Navy. The RAF provides Nimrod maritime surveillance aircraft which are normally based at St Mawgan, Cornwall, and at Kinloss, on the Moray Firth.

If Britain were ever attacked from the air, the RAF's principle task would be to defend major British and American airbases, using interceptor aircraft and missiles. Long-range surface-to-air Bloodhound missile batteries are already installed in the East Anglia and Lincolnshire areas, and shorter-range Rapier missile units could be positioned around some key military airfields. Civil and industrial targets would be less defensible and more vulnerable to attack.

RAF operators at a UKADGE long-range radar station. Each of four main radar control centres and six smaller reporting posts co-ordinate the activities of defending aircraft and missiles.

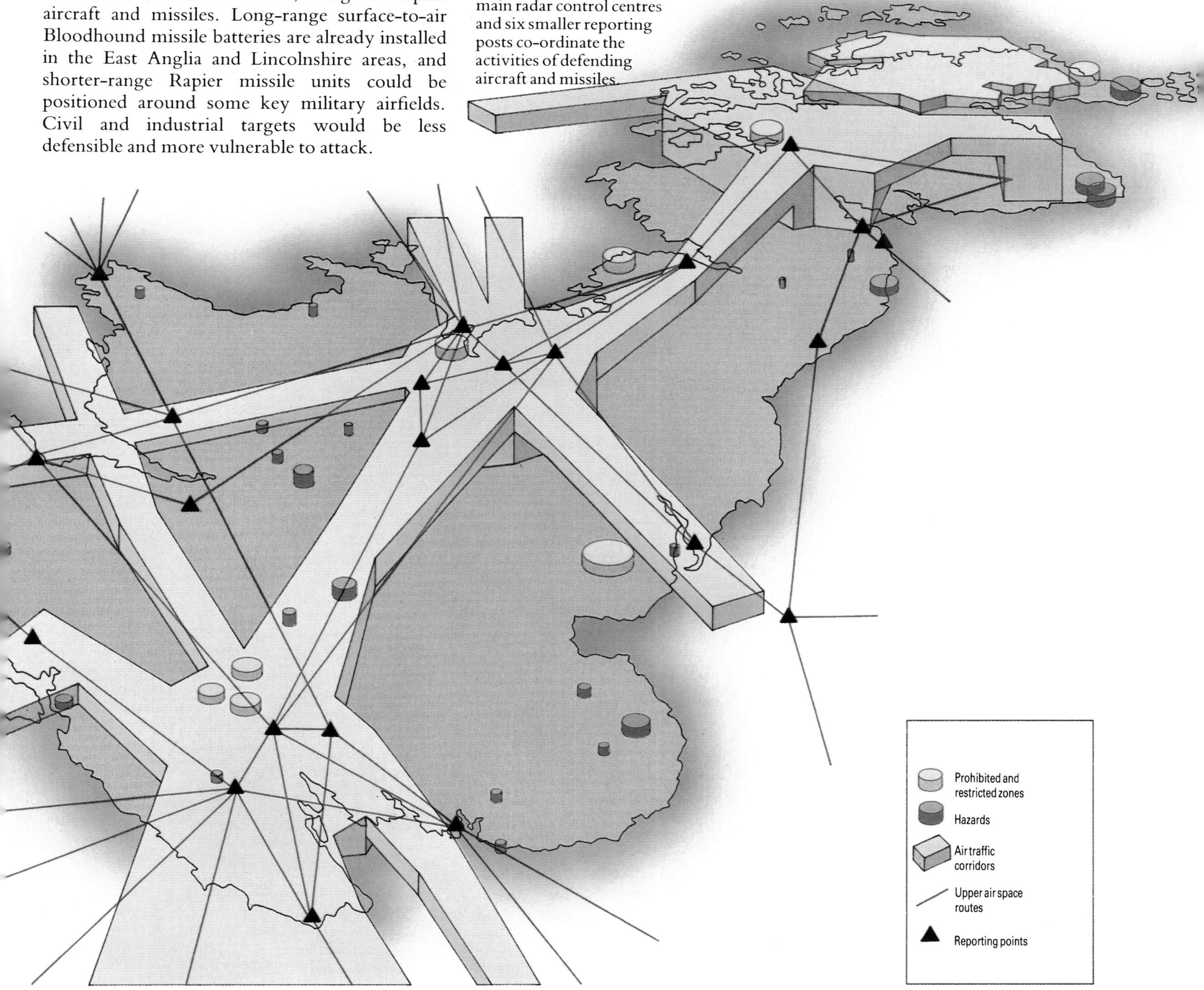

Prohibited and restricted zones

Hazards

Air traffic corridors

Upper air space routes

▲ Reporting points

POLICE, CRIME AND THE JUDICIARY

Britain has no national police force as such, though the Home Office co-ordinates training, research and development and mutual support between individual forces. The Home Office also runs a variety of central support services, including the maintenance of police communications, a forensic science service, and the operation of the Police National Computer (PNC) system, which is linked to all police forces in the country.

Except in London and Northern Ireland, police forces are financed and supervised by police authorities, composed partly of nominated councillors, and partly of magistrates. Most police forces cover the same area as a single county council (or, in Scotland, a regional council). There are also ten indirectly appointed joint police authorities, each serving two or more counties. Elected local government representatives may approve or disapprove police budgets, but are not permitted to consider 'operational' aspects of police work.

In London, where there is no local police authority, the Home Secretary is answerable to Parliament for the work of the Metropolitan Police. As well as policing London, the Metropolitan Police provides all or most of the members of some nationally organised police functions, such as the Fraud Squad, the National Drugs Intelligence Unit, the National Identification Bureau (formerly the Criminal Records Office), the Flying Squad, the Royalty and Diplomatic Protection Squads, and the Special Branch. There are also nine Regional Crime Squads in England and Wales and nine Regional Criminal Intelligence offices.

Crime and the judiciary

Crimes are divided into 'recordable' offences and lesser breaches of the law. Only recordable offences result in a personal record being created on the Police National Computer and at the Scotland Yard National Identification Bureau. Although minor traffic offences such as illegal parking may be tried in a magistrate's court together with much more serious breaches of the law, they are not usually regarded as recordable offences.

Judges and magistrates are normally appointed by the Lord Chancellor, who is a member of the government and Cabinet. However, constitutionally, party politics should not affect these appointments. The executive head of the judiciary is the Lord Chief Justice, a senior full-time judge.

Since 1945, Britain has taken a number of steps allowing international legal bodies to intervene in British legal decisions. As a member of the European Economic Community, Britain is subject to EEC law, which primarily affects industrial, employment and social matters. Britain has also ratified the European Convention on Human Rights, and is consequently subject to the judgements of the Court of Human Rights, in Strasbourg, France.

The courts

Most criminal offences are dealt with by magistrates' courts. But cases can be referred, on appeal or review, or for sentencing, to a crown court. Crown court judges may be barristers who sit as part-time recorders, or they may be senior High Court judges. High Court and Circuit judges periodically visit the major regional courts to deal with civil or criminal cases. Civil cases will often start in 'county' courts. From both crown and county courts, appeals may be taken to the High Court, or the Court of Appeal. After the Court of Appeal, a case may go the House of Lords for further review. Cases involving human rights or EEC law may go to the European Court of Human Rights or European Court of Justice.

Victims' survey

Many more crimes are known to be committed than are reported to the police, as these results of a 1981 Home Office survey show. The levels of reported crime vary widely as a proportion of the type of crime committed. For instance, because police 'clear-up' rates of burglaries and similar crimes tend to be very low, they are often reported only if the victim can make an insurance claim. Rape is also under-reported because of the fears and anxieties of some of the victims. Vandalism, the survey showed, accounted for more than a third of crimes experienced by those interviewed, yet only 8% of such crimes were reported.

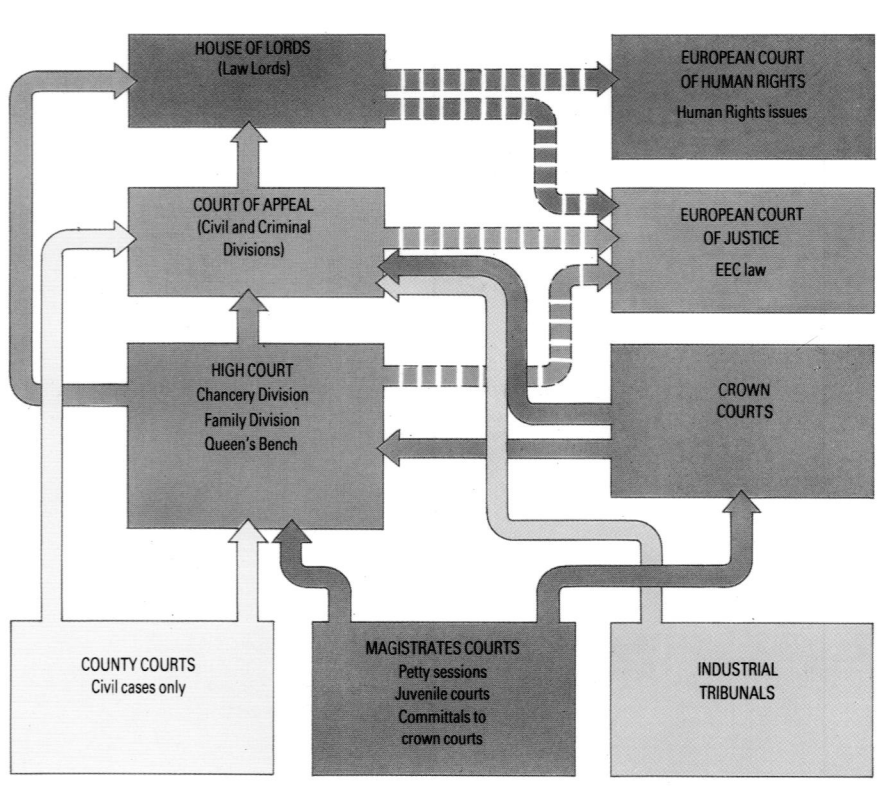

Police force boundaries

Following the 1964 Police Act, British police forces were extensively merged. There are now 43 police areas in England and Wales, and 8 in Scotland. (A single police force, the Royal Ulster Constabulary (RUC) covers Northern Ireland.) The highest courts in Britain, the Court of Appeal and the High Court are all located in London. In Scotland, there is a separate system of Sheriff and District Courts. The final Court of Criminal Appeal is the High Court of Justiciary, which meets in Edinburgh.

Police National Computer

Police officers can use the Police National Computer (PNC) to call up more than 47 million national records on people, vehicles and property. Computer records are consulted more than 70 million times a year. Terminals to PNC are located at all police force headquarters.

Types of crime

In 1983, more than 3 million criminal offences were notified to the police. They are shown below broken down by percentage. The average number of crimes recorded by the police per million population rose from 12,000 in the early 1950s to more than five times this level by the mid-1980s. There are major variations in crime levels between police force areas, especially between the metropolitan and non-metropolitan areas. In urban areas, for example, robbery and burglary are much more common than in rural districts. But this is not the case for serious offences of violence, or for sexual offences.

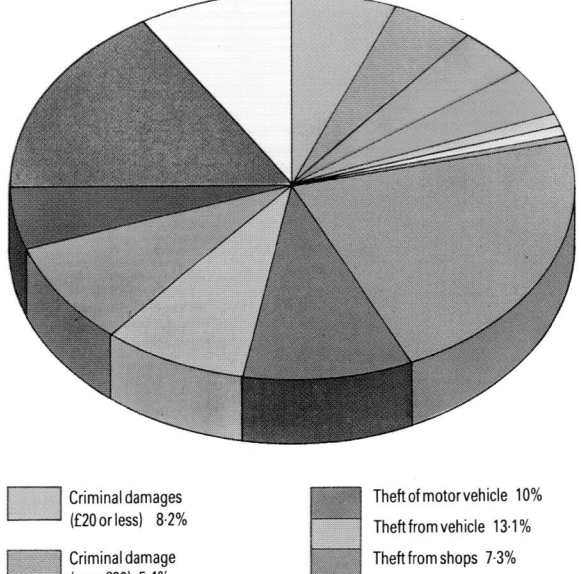

- Criminal damages (£20 or less) 8·2%
- Criminal damage (over £20) 5·4%
- Fraud/forgery 3·8%
- Violence against person 3·4%
- Robbery 0·7%
- Sexual offences 0·6%
- Theft of motor vehicle 10%
- Theft from vehicle 13·1%
- Theft from shops 7·3%
- Theft of bicycles 3·8%
- Burglary in a dwelling 13·3%
- Burglary in a building other than dwelling 11·7%
- Other theft/handling stolen goods 18·4%
- Other 0·3%

Circuits

District Courts

Northern
Grampian
Tayside
Central Scotland
Fife
Strathclyde
Lothian & Borders
Dumfries & Galloway
Northumbria
Cumbria
Durham
Cleveland
North Yorks
West Yorks
Humberside
Lancs
Merseyside
South Yorks
Greater Manchester
Cheshire
Derby
Lincs
North Wales
Notts
Staffs
Norfolk
Leics
West Midlands
Northants
Cambs
Dyfed-Powys
West Mercia
Warks
Suffolk
Beds
Herts
Essex
Glos
Thames Valley
Gwent
City of London
South Wales
Met
Avon & Somerset
Wilts
Surrey
Kent
Hants
Sussex
Devon & Cornwall
Dorset

The 'Met'

The Metropolitan Police is responsible for policing Greater London and parts of Essex, Surrey and Hertfordshire. In 1985, it was reorganised into 8 separate area commands.

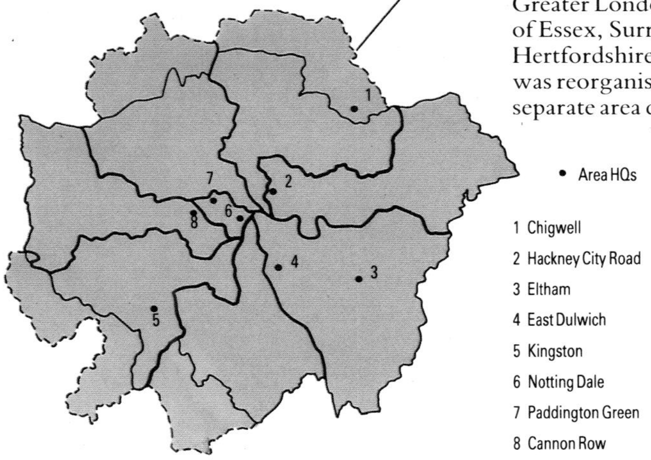

- Area HQs

1 Chigwell
2 Hackney City Road
3 Eltham
4 East Dulwich
5 Kingston
6 Notting Dale
7 Paddington Green
8 Cannon Row

POWER OUTSIDE THE GOVERNMENT

Apart from the formal power of the state, there are many other influences at work in Britain, as in other modern societies. These include business, the press, professional and industrial groups and other pressure groups. Some pressure groups are 'sectional': they represent people or organisations who share similar social or economic interests. The two most prominent and powerful of this type are the employers' organisation, the Confederation of British Industry (CBI) and the Trades Union Congress (TUC). Others include the Law Society, the British Medical Association (BMA) and the National Farmers' Union (NFU).

A second type of pressure group is the 'cause' organisation, whose members have common beliefs or aims but whose backgrounds and other interests may vary widely. Some of these groups, such as locally based campaigns on planning issues, are often transitory, but others, like the international aid charity Oxfam, the housing charity Shelter and the National Council for Civil Liberties (NCCL), have campaigned for decades.

Cause organisations achieve influence by publicity and by activities that might include lobbying councillors and MPs, holding demonstrations or exerting pressure on government departments by other means. Such campaigns may be particularly effective in the period before an election.

Confederation of British Industry

Many industrial firms belong to employers' organisations, often representing a single industry or section of an industry. Employers' organisations may negotiate collectively with trade unions on wages and conditions, as well as representing members' views to the government. Collectively, these employers' federations and other companies in the public and private sectors form the Confederation of British Industry, which is consulted by government departments.

The CBI's formal influence on government policy was consolidated in the 1960s when, with the TUC, its members were appointed to a new National Economic Development Council (NEDC). This tripartite government-union-industry body has many subsidiary development committees, all of which are charged with planning jointly for economic growth in a particular sector.

The Stock Exchange in the City of London has become a powerful institution and a major influence on national economic affairs.

The Church

About one in five Britons is a member of an established religion or faith, including Hinduism, Islam and other faiths. One in six people is a member of a Christian faith, though membership varies widely by region: in England 13% of the population, in Wales 23% and in Scotland 37%.

The Church of England is the main established church, having a formal place in the British state system. The monarch must be a member of the church, and appoints all its high officials – deans, bishops and archbishops – on the advice of the Prime Minister. Two Archbishops (York and Canterbury) and 24 bishops are members of the House of Lords. The governing body of the Church of England, the General Synod, includes the bishops, clergy and lay members of the Church, representing its 13,500 parishes. In Scotland, the presbyterian Church of Scotland is the established church. Its 1,765 churches are governed locally by Kirk Sessions, and nationally by a Scottish General Assembly.

Members of the Synod, seen here in session, are drawn from the clergy and laity. They consider both spiritual and administrative matters.

Trades Union Congress

The original Trades Union Congress of 1868 was little more than a debating shop. Today, about 10 million working people are members of the 93 trade unions affiliated to the TUC. Altogether, half of British workers belong to a trade union, a high proportion compared to other advanced industrial countries. The United States is 20% unionised, Japan 22% and West Germany 26%. A trade union's major function is collectively to represent workers in negotiating agreements on rates of pay and working conditions. In addition, many unions conduct research into health and safety at the workplace, organise industrial and professional education and training for their members and lobby government and other bodies.

During the 1980s, union membership declined as a consequence of increasing unemployment, and the trend by managers towards decentralised bargaining with workers and their representatives. However, the two largest unions still each represent more than a million members. These are the Transport and General Workers Union (TGWU), with 1·5 million members, and the Amalgamated Union of Engineering Workers (AUEW), with 1·2 million members. In Scotland, trade unions are represented by the Scottish TUC.

Members of the National Union of Mineworkers (NUM) demonstrate during the bitter, year-long miners' strike.

Non-aligned groups

The role of voluntary groups, unrelated to other established bodies or authorities, is widely recognised in Britain. The government both accepts voluntary groups and expects them to carry out functions ranging from running Citizens' Advice Bureaux (which are funded by the Department of Trade and Industry) to providing charitable services to assist the disabled, the elderly, or other disadvantaged groups. Many organisations of this kind are supported by local authority grants.

'Cause' organisations mount educational and publicity campaigns related to both charitable and political objectives. The non-aligned pressure groups that have received most publicity during the 1980s are those associated with campaigns on behalf of the environment, or against nuclear weapons. In Britain, the most prominent campaigns have been led by the Campaign for Nuclear Disarmament (CND), a movement calling for Britain to scrap its nuclear weapons, and the Greenpeace and Friends of the Earth (FoE) environmental groups. Recently, organisations raising funds to help feed the hungry in the Third World, such as Live Aid and Sport Aid, have attracted much public support.

Formed in the 1950s, CND was reborn as a mass peace movement in the 1980s with the appearance of a new generation of nuclear weapons.

SPORT

Many of the world's most popular sports originated in Britain. Golf, for example, began in Scotland in the 15th century, while the modern form of Association Football took shape in England in the 19th century.

Today, enthusiasm for sport remains strong, but assessing the degree of participation can present problems as many sports take place on an informal basis. However, there is a growing awareness of the benefits of sport in terms of health and as a social activity. As a result, successive governments have followed policies of supporting sport. A Parliamentary Under-Secretary in the Department of the Environment has the task of co-ordinating government policy on sport in England while the Secretaries of State for Wales and Scotland fulfil a similar role in their respective regions.

Government assistance to sport is the responsibility of three independent bodies – the Sports Council, the Sports Council for Wales and the Scottish Sports Council. The activities of the Welsh and Scottish Councils are restricted to their own countries, while the Sports Council deals both with England and with sporting matters that affect Britain as a whole.

Gambling

Betting and commercial gaming organisations together estimate that the British spend in excess of £6000 million annually on gambling. Horse and greyhound racing attract considerably more of this money than casinos, lotteries and licensed bingo and, apart from some cricket matches, are the only two sporting events where betting is allowed at the venue. However, most racing bets are placed at off-course and off-track betting offices, of which there are about 11,000.

'Doing the pools' is one of the most popular forms of gambling, though with average stakes of less than £1·20 a person, it is likely that few participants think of it as gambling at all. Between them, the two largest pools companies, Littlewoods and Vernons, accept about 10 million coupons a week in the football season, which suggests that about 15 million people are taking part. At the height of the season, pay-outs to prize winners amount to about £3 million a week.

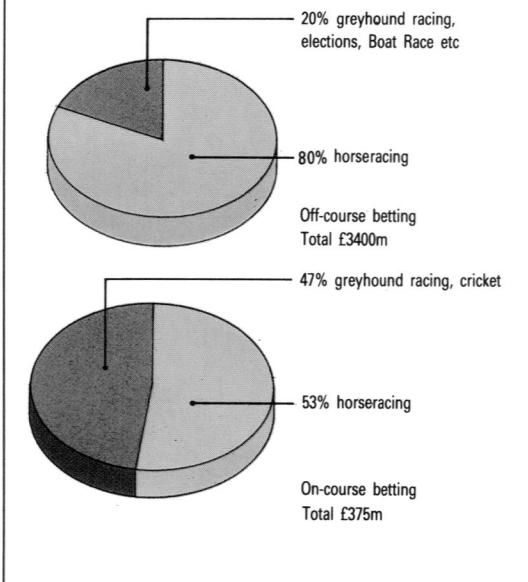

20% greyhound racing, elections, Boat Race etc

80% horseracing

Off-course betting
Total £3400m

47% greyhound racing, cricket

53% horseracing

On-course betting
Total £375m

Most popular sports on television

Sports coverage on television amounts to about 2500 hours a year. The relative sizes of audiences provide an indication of each sport's popularity. A snooker tournament, for example, may in its entirety attract up to 23 million viewers and a darts tournament may be watched by more than 12 million. Despite (or because of) falling attendances at matches, Association Football remains popular on television, with the BBC's Match of the Day having an average audience of about 8·5 million.

TOP TEN SPORTS –				
of people that watch sport on television,				
percentage interested (based on household survey 1984)				
Men	%		Women	%
1 Snooker	76		1 Tennis	56
2 Football	69		Skating	56
3 Athletics	52		3 Snooker	52
Boxing	52		4 Athletics	47
5 Motor car racing	49		5 Show jumping	46
Tennis	49		6 Swimming	36
7 Cricket	47		7 Snow sports	35
Darts	47		8 Darts	34
9 Golf	42		9 Football	33
10 Rugby Union	40		10 Golf	23

Participation

About 4 out of every 10 adults claim they take physical exercise at least once a month in summer. This figure is highest among young people – 6 out of 10 in the 16–24 age group. More men than women claim to take part in sport regularly.

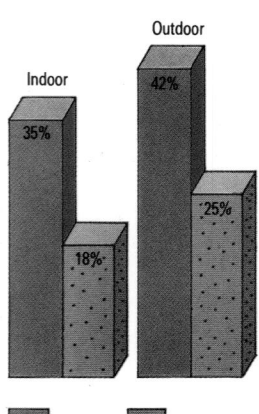

Indoor
35%
18%

Outdoor
42%
25%

Men Women

Of all the outdoor sports, fishing is by far the most popular. There are about 4 million sea and freshwater anglers in Britain. Of the latter, many fish for salmon and trout to eat, but in England and Wales some are competitive fish anglers, seeking coarse fish such as pike, carp and tench.

Run every summer, the London Marathon first took place in 1981, with 8000 entrants. Ten times the number applied in 1986, for 22,000 places. Anyone over 18 may enter. Marathons are also held in Southampton and Manchester.

Funding and sponsorship

The Sports Councils' aims include encouraging wider participation, providing better facilities and raising standards of performance. Between them the three councils allocated about £36 million of government funds in 1984–85. This included grants to the governing bodies of various sports, and loans and grants to voluntary bodies and local authorities. In addition, they finance the National Sports Centres (see map).

Sports facilities are mainly run by local authorities, whose total expenditure on recreation and sport in 1984–85 was about £800 million. This level of funding may change in future as a result of government reorganisation of local authorities, which came into effect in 1986. Local authorities provide facilities such as swimming baths, sports centres, playing fields, athletics stadia, tennis courts and parks. Schools and colleges also provide sports facilities, mainly to their own students.

Finance for sport is also found in the private sector. Sponsorship is playing an increasing role, with some £120 million in 1985 going mainly to sporting organisations and specific events.

Horseracing

Horseracing takes two main forms – flat racing and National Hunt (steeplechasing and hurdling). The most important races of the flat season (March to November) are the classics: the Derby and the Oaks at Epsom, the 2000 and the 1000 Guineas at Newmarket, and the St Leger at Doncaster. The highlight of the National Hunt season (end July to beginning of June) is the steeplechase Festival meeting at Cheltenham in March.

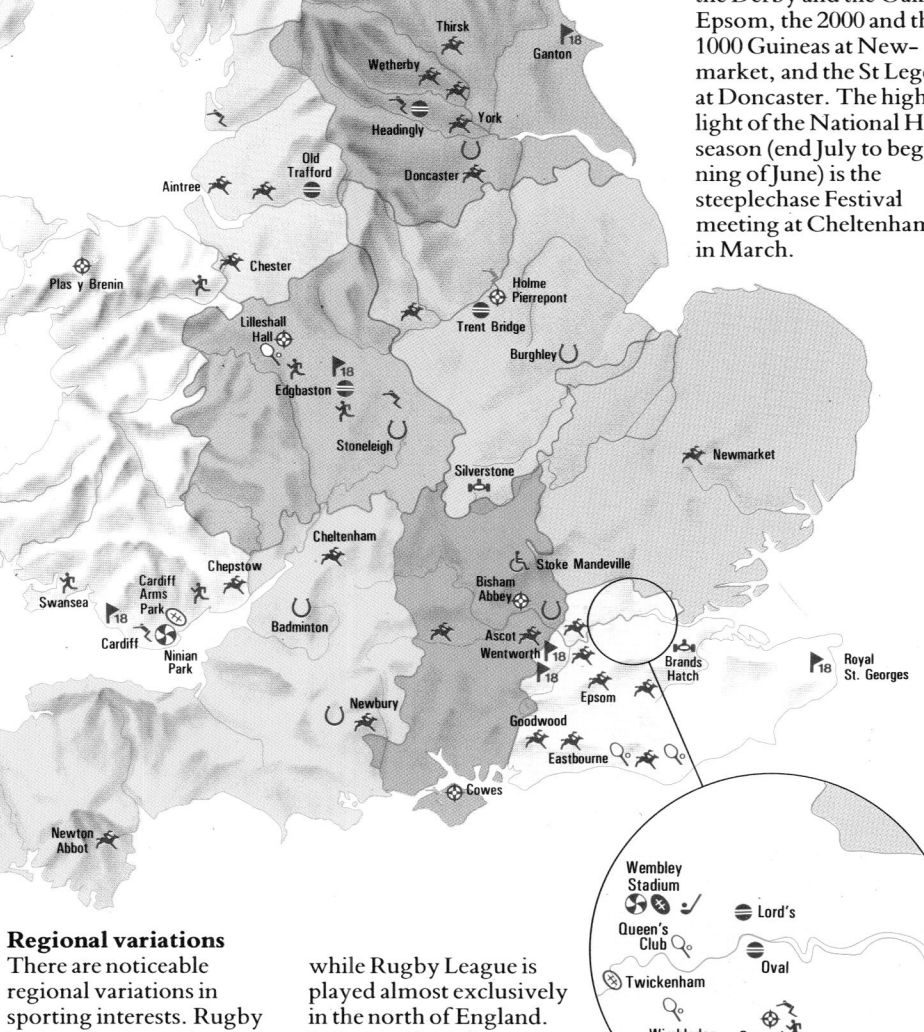

Sports Council Regions & Major Venues

- Northern Region
- North Western Region
- Yorkshire & Humberside
- East Midlands
- West Midlands
- Eastern Region
- Greater London and South East
- Southern Region
- South-West Region
- Scotland
- Wales

- National Sports Centres
- International Association Football Grounds
- Test Cricket Grounds
- Rugby League - ground used for finals
- Rugby Union - International Grounds
- Tennis Venues
- Motor Racing
- Sports for the Disabled
- Highland Games
- Swimming Pools used for International events
- Major Athletics Stadium
- Golf Courses
- Horse Racing
- Horse Riding
- Hockey
- Water Sports

Regional variations

There are noticeable regional variations in sporting interests. Rugby Union, for example, though played throughout Britain, is almost the national game of Wales, while Rugby League is played almost exclusively in the north of England. In Scotland, well over twice the proportion of adults play golf as in England.

TOURISM

In Britain, tourism is a major industry and an important part of the economy. Incorporating travel agents, tour operators, the hotel and catering trades, it employs more than one and a half million people. In financial terms, it has a vast turnover, with foreign currency earnings reaching over £4000 million in 1984. Income from tourism has for several years made up more than a tenth of all foreign currency earnings from invisible exports, which also include insurance and other financial services, and sea and air travel.

There is considerable government support for the industry. This is administered by the British Tourist Authority (BTA) and three tourist boards, the English, Welsh and Scottish. These, like the

BTA, are statutory bodies. The BTA is responsible for overseas promotion of British tourism, while the boards work within Britain. (The Scottish Tourist Board also does some promotion abroad, but it is the only national board to do so.)

As well as promoting tourism, tourist boards are responsible for developing and improving tourist accommodation and amenities, and administering grants and loans to help with this. The boards' work includes publishing accommodation guides for tourists and listing establishments that have taken part in a voluntary registration scheme. Information for tourists is given through information centres located in major towns and tourist areas, and via the Prestel information service.

Top 20 sites
The term 'tourist attraction' embraces everything from amusement parks to museums and galleries. There are 3000 such attractions open to the public in England alone – below are Britain's top 20 (1984).

1   Blackpool Pleasure Beach
     6,700,000
2   Tower of London
     4,087,000
3   British Museum (Lon)
     3,236,700
4   Science Museum (Lon)
     3,019,900
5   National Gallery (Lon)
     2,936,900
6   Natural History Museum (Lon)
     2,318,000
7   Madame Tussaud's (Lon)
     2,118,400
8   Alton Towers pleasure park
     1,956,000
9   Victoria & Albert Museum (Lon)
     1,692,800
10   Tate Gallery (Lon)
     1,265,600
11   London Zoo
     1,224,690
12   Bradgate Park pleasure park
     1,200,000
     Wicksteed Park pleasure park
     1,200,000
14   Burrell Collection (Glasgow)
     1,109,000
15   Kew Botanic Gardens
     1,084,290
16   Thorpe Park pleasure park
     1,020,000
17   Royal Academy of Arts (Lon)
     1,004,000
18   Camelot (Lancs)
     1,000,000
19   Roman Baths (Bath)
     931,170
20   National Railway Museum (York)
     889,500

In the past 10 years wildlife attractions such as Windsor Safari Park (above) have become increasingly popular with British tourists.

Numbers of visitors
The largest number of visitors to Britain from a single country is the 2·8 million from the United States. Recent years have seen a continual rise in visitors from North America as a whole, encouraged by favourable exchange rates.

Tourist economy
Although tourism brings in a large amount of foreign exchange, this is usually more than offset by British tourists' spending overseas. In the 1980s, almost every year has seen a deficit in what is known as the 'travel account' – usually around £300 million. Overseas tourists' spending in Britain is concentrated in England. Scottish receipts represent about 6% of the total, Welsh about 2%.

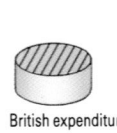

British expenditure overseas

Tourism income

Foreign

Home

£ thousand millions (£ billions)

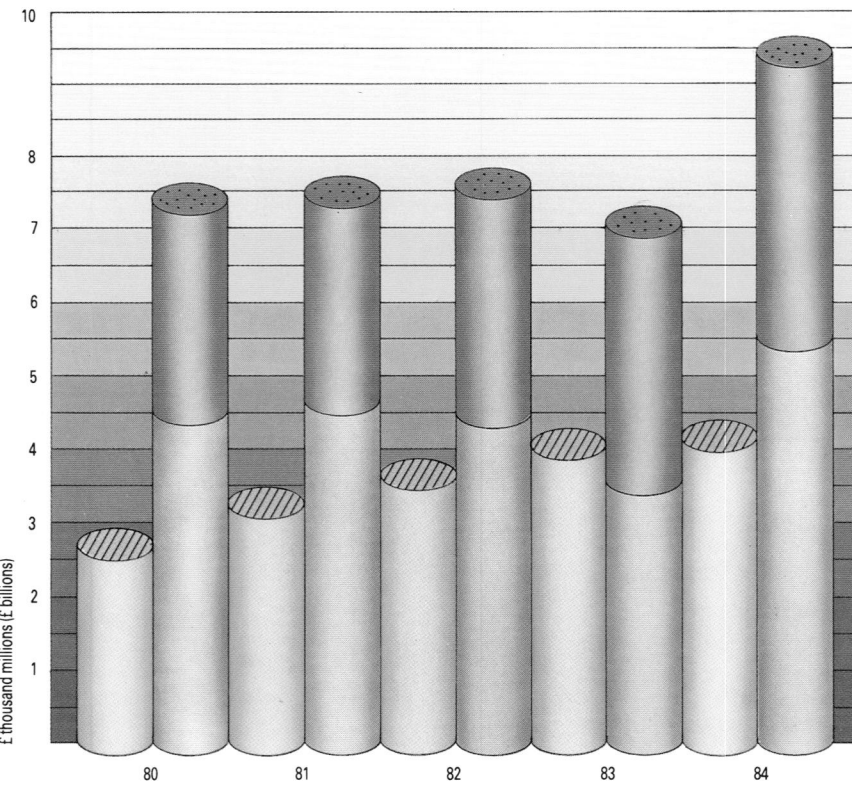

80   81   82   83   84

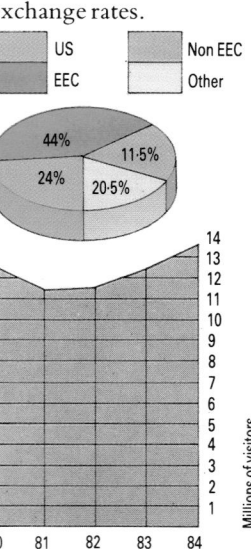

US   Non EEC
EEC   Other

44%   11·5%
24%   20·5%

Millions of visitors

14
13
12
11
10
9
8
7
6
5
4
3
2
1

80   81   82   83   84

The tourists

Currently, Britain attracts in a year about 14 million tourists from overseas, mainly from western Europe. For example, in 1984 the EEC group of countries provided 7·5 million tourists. Important as overseas tourism is, however, it is only part of the industry's concern. In the same year, tourist trips within Great Britain by British residents numbered some 140 million.

Most visitors to Britain choose to travel in summer, with August as the peak month. London, with some 40 million visits a year to its various tourist attractions, is more than twice as popular as any region in Britain. All historic towns seem to be especially popular with people from overseas. In both Winchester and Chester, for example, this group of tourists usually make up about a third of the total.

Tourist boards

The Welsh and Scottish Tourist Boards operate as two single bodies, but the English Tourist Board (ETB) sponsors and aids 12 regional boards (their boundaries are shown on the map). These work in partnership with the ETB, local trade interests and local government in promoting tourism in their areas.

Independent organisations such as the Automobile Association (AA) and Royal Automobile Club (RAC) supplement the work of the boards, providing tourists with sightseeing and accommodation information.

Tourism map

Britain's rich heritage comprises not only historic buildings, museums and art galleries but also nature reserves, National Parks and areas of natural beauty. Tourist sites of all kinds are managed by government-financed bodies such as English Heritage or by independent organisations, of which the National Trust, a charity with a million members, is the largest.

UK tourist trips

Tourism within Britain by British residents is far from restricted to holiday-making. In summer, the population makes about 600 million leisure day trips, only 15% of which are made while on holiday away from home. Most British holidaymakers stay with friends or relatives rather than rent holiday accommodation.

Map legend

- National Parks
- National Park Direction Areas (Scotland)
- Areas of Outstanding Natural Beauty / National Scenic Areas (Scotland)
- Heritage Coast and Coastal Conservation Zones (Scotland)
- Long Distance Footpaths
- Navigable rivers
- Canals
- Tourist Board Area boundaries
- Urban areas
- Regional proportion of total tourist nights spent in Britain 10mm=10%.
  - British visitors
  - Overseas visitors

Map labels

Durness, Ullapool, Golspie, Dornoch, Loch Torridon, Glen Affric, Banff, Fraserburgh, Speyside Way, Cairngorm, Stonehaven, Glen Nevis and Glencoe, SCOTLAND, Carnoustie, West Highland Way, St. Andrews, Trossachs, Helensburgh, Dunoon, Forth and Clyde Canal, Union Canal, North Berwick, Proposed Southern Upland Way, Brodick, Ayr, Berwick-on-Tweed, Northumberland, NORTHUMBRIA, Blyth, Tyne, Pennine Way, CUMBRIA, Tees, Redcar, Cleveland Way, Lake District, North York Moors, Whitby, Scarborough, Millennium Way, Lake Windermere, Ure, Yorkshire Dales, YORKSHIRE AND HUMBERSIDE, Filey, Douglas, Nidd, Bridlington, Morecambe, Wharfe, Liverpool Canal, Aire, Ouse, Wolds Way, Blackpool, Southport, Ribble, Leeds and, NORTH-, Cleethorpes, Mersey, WEST, Peak District, Llandudno, Colwyn Bay, Weaver Navi'g, Derwent, Witham Navigation, Skegness, Dee, Trent Navigation, EAST MIDLANDS, Sheringham, Cromer, Snowdonia, Shropshire Union Canal, Trent & Mersey Canal, Welland, Gt. Yarmouth, L. Bala, Offa's, Severn, Nene, The Broads, Barmouth, WALES, Dyke, HEART OF ENGLAND, Great Ouse, Lowestoft, Aberystwyth, Path, Stratford on Avon, Avon, EAST ANGLIA, Wye, Oxford Canal, Grand Union Canal, Felixstowe, Pembrokeshire Coast, Brecon Beacons, Uck, THAMES AND CHILTERNS, Clacton, Pembrokeshire Coast Path, Monmouth & Brecon Canal, Ridgeway, Thames, LONDON, Southend, Tenby, Barry, Avon, Kennet & Avon Canal, Kennet, Windsor, North Downs Way, Margate, Ramsgate, Ilfracombe, Minehead, Weston-super-Mare, Wey, Medway, Dover, Folkestone, Exmoor, Parrett, South Downs Way, SOUTH-EAST, WEST COUNTRY, Exe, SOUTHERN, Hastings, South-West Peninsula Path, Dartmoor, Poole, Bournemouth, Worthing, Brighton, Eastbourne, Lyme Regis, Weymouth, Swanage, Southsea, Shanklin, Ventnor, Teignmouth, Torbay, Newquay, South-West Peninsula Path

Visits by British residents

□ =1 million trips

- Cumbria
- Northumbria
- North West
- Yorkshire & Humbs
- Heart of England
- East Midlands
- Thames/Chiltern
- East Anglia
- London
- West Country
- Southern
- South East
- Scotland
- Wales

ARCHITECTURE

Britain's architectural heritage is among the richest in the world. It dates back at least to Roman times, though little remains of that period other than archeological sites. Of the buildings of the 4th to the 15th centuries, the most dramatic, and best-surviving, are the country's castles and cathedrals. Many of the castles were built soon after the Norman conquest of 1066 and most of the cathedrals were built during the latter part of the Middle Ages, when the Church (then Catholic) was most wealthy and powerful. However, over the centuries both have been modified and extended.

Later examples of architectural splendour are the stately homes of the aristocracy. Various styles are evident, from the detailed brick and timber work of the Elizabethan era to the graceful simplicity of Georgian times. Some of the styles reflect strong influences from France, Italy and Spain. The 19th century saw the rapid and extensive development of civic and industrial architecture – town halls, railway stations, factories – as the newly rich industrialists of the era put their mark on the cities they helped build and develop.

Today in Britain, buildings of special architectural or historical interest are protected by law. In England they are the responsibility of the Department of the Environment, through English Heritage. Similar bodies operate in both Scotland and Wales, through the Secretaries of State for Scotland and Wales respectively.

Churches and cathedrals
To build these, stone was frequently carried great distances – and occasionally imported from mainland Europe – to ensure that the very best materials were always used. Skilled stonemasons and glaziers were employed, and these are still to be found in many cathedral towns as restoration and repair work of ancient buildings is constantly needed.

Stately homes
Britain has several hundred stately homes. The original owners were usually rich enough to indulge in great splendour, and often eccentricity too. Some have magnificent landscaped gardens like Blenheim. Many stately homes have recently been opened to the public to help the present owners cover the high running costs.

Industrial towns
The 19th century saw an enormous amount of house-building in the industrial centres of Britain to accommodate the large numbers of factory and mine workers. Long rows of the typical terraced houses, built of stone or brick, can still be seen in many parts of Britain.

Georgian houses
The simple well-proportioned style of Georgian town houses (around 1720) was designed to appeal to the wealthy of the day. The best remaining examples are in Bath, Avon

Changing styles of architecture
In Britain, many styles of building have developed over the centuries in response to such influences as the availability of materials, the purpose of the building and, of course, fashion. The drawings below show a range of examples from around the country. Housing, in particular, displays 'vernacular architecture' – the native or regionally indigenous style of building.

Castles
These served as homes for nobles and soldiers, but the main criterion in their design was defensibility. Over the centuries, construction improved until they were virtually impregnable. The Norman motte and bailey style gradually gave way to a curtain wall and inner keep or tower design. Political changes eventually made castles unnecessary and after about 1500 very few were built simply as fortresses.

Traditional homes
These have often been made of locally available materials, of which stone has been the most commonly used. In the Highlands of Scotland, subsistence farmers, or crofters, used rough stone to make their simple homes. In the north of England, limestone, flint and cob have been used. In parts of southern England, timber and thatch houses are still to be seen. Thatch is one of the oldest roofing materials used. It is made from straw or reeds, tied in bundles.

Industrial buildings
From about 1815, industry gradually replaced craftsmanship as the basis for building. Even early examples of industrial architecture, such as the first road and rail bridges and dockland sites, were constructed from mass-produced building parts rather than being built by large gangs of labourers using traditional methods.

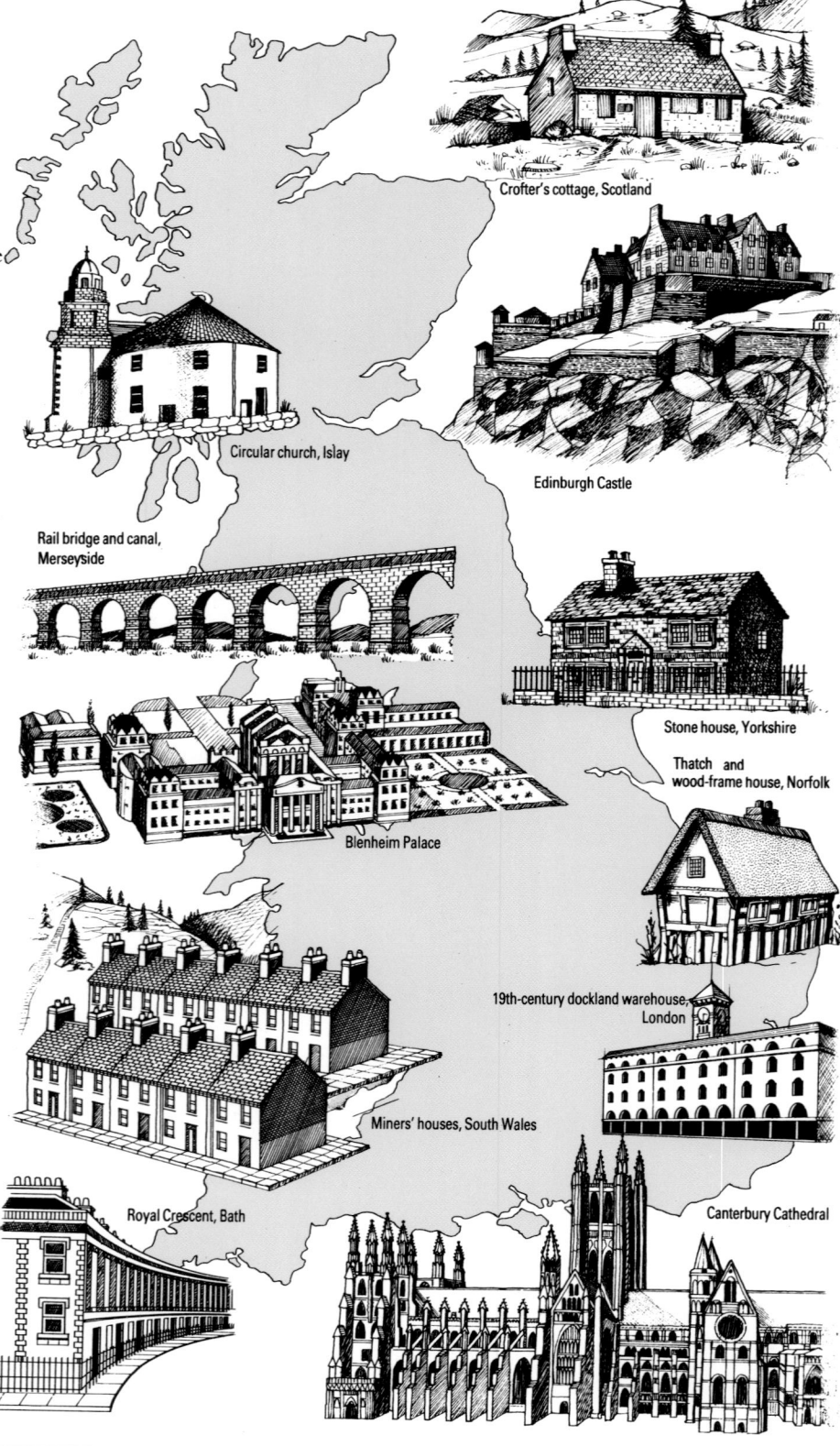

Crofter's cottage, Scotland

Circular church, Islay

Edinburgh Castle

Rail bridge and canal, Merseyside

Stone house, Yorkshire

Thatch and wood-frame house, Norfolk

Blenheim Palace

19th-century dockland warehouse, London

Miners' houses, South Wales

Royal Crescent, Bath

Canterbury Cathedral

Modern architecture

In Britain, the 20th century has seen great developments in building and architecture, especially in house building and town planning. Following World War I, whole new suburban housing estates and new towns were built, particularly in the then economically thriving Midlands and the south of England. They were to cope with the increasing population and to satisfy people's greater expectations of life in peacetime.

More new towns were established soon after World War II, and in the 1950s and 1960s slum clearance and the development of derelict and bombed areas took place on a large scale. The new approach to the housing problem was to build tower blocks of flats. However, high-rise housing has not worn well, and in recent years several tower blocks have been demolished as a result of being too costly to repair and for sociological reasons. Today's municipal housing is low-rise.

The 1980s have seen a further move in style towards 'post modernism', which combines both historical and modern references. Some modern British architects have adopted a 'high tech' approach, often creating a decoration that stems solely from expression of structure and services. The public, however, has often shown itself to be unimpressed by the architecture of the Modern Movement, and has more readily accepted the sympathetic planning of more traditionally designed buildings.

Organisation and standards

An independent body, the Royal Institute of British Architects (RIBA), and the Royal Incorporation of Architects in Scotland, with which it is allied, exercise controls over standards in architecture education. The Department of the Environment and the Royal Fine Art Commission exercise aesthetic control by means of planning laws. Finally, the British Standards Institute sets out performance and safety criteria.

Housing

In the mid-1970s the building of tower blocks, involving extensive use of prefabricated concrete and glass, gave way to low-rise housing exploiting more traditional materials such as brick and tile. This housing estate near Evesham, designed by British architects Darbourne and Darke, was built in the early 1980s. Many modern estates like this incorporate shops, libraries and schools built with the same materials and to the same style to create harmony.

Post modernism

The post modernist movement began in the early 1980s. British architects of this school include Jeremy Dickson, who has designed housing schemes based on the classical villa, and Terry Farrell, who designed the TV-am building in London (above). This is a renovated warehouse set alongside the Grand Union Canal. Colour and 'art deco' features are widely used.

High-tech buildings

The Renault Centre, Swindon, designed by architect Norman Foster, displays an undulating roof suspended from tubular steel poles by tension rods. Built as a warehouse, exhibition hall and offices, it has been described as 'humane high-tech'.

THE ARTS

The arts form one of Britain's most important tourist attractions. London is regarded as a major world centre for theatre, classical and popular music, opera, dance and fine art, and in recent years, as a result of government policy, the arts have become more available to the regions.

General arts policy is the responsibility of the Minister for the Arts, and government expenditure on national museums and art galleries is administered by the Office of Arts and Libraries in England and the Secretaries of State for Wales and Scotland in their respective countries. In 1984–85 this amounted to some £260 million. Additional funding comes from local authorities – in 1984–85 over £400 million was spent on public libraries, local museums and art galleries – and from sponsorship and patronage by industrial and commercial concerns – currently about £14·5 million a year. However, with the Arts Council and local authorities undergoing substantial change, support for the arts from private sources is likely to become an increasingly significant factor in the next two or three years. Consumer expenditure on the arts and entertainment amounts to about 5% of total annual household income.

Government funding

The largest portion of this – currently about 40% or some £100 million – goes to the Arts Council. This is an independent body, established in 1946, which gives financial help and advice to a large number of arts organisations, ranging from major opera and theatre companies to small dance and music groups. It also supports, together with local authorities, 15 regional arts associations in England and Wales, and subsidises the separate Scottish and Welsh Arts Councils.

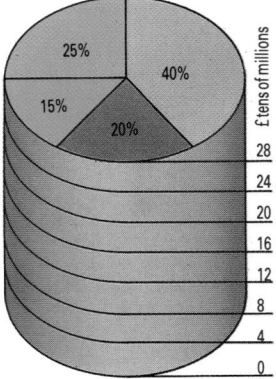

Arts Council
British Library
Others
National galleries and museums

£ tens of millions
28
24
20
16
12
8
4
0

Calendar of events

Many of the events shown here are held annually, often attracting both participants and audiences from all over the world. In addition, each year there are several hundred local events all over the country.

Festivals and exhibitions

There are some 240 professional arts festivals in Britain each year. The largest is the month-long Edinburgh International Festival, which annually stages about 200 performances of world-class theatre, opera and dance, and numerous 'fringe' events, in which amateur performers of all kinds take part. Important regional and cultural events include London's Notting Hill West Indian Carnival, and the Welsh Eisteddfods, of which the Royal National (below) is the largest.

Consumer spending on the arts

Despite government subsidies and continued support from overseas visitors, theatres and concert halls in Britain struggle to survive as people spend increasingly more on home entertainment and less on live performances of the arts.

1984-85

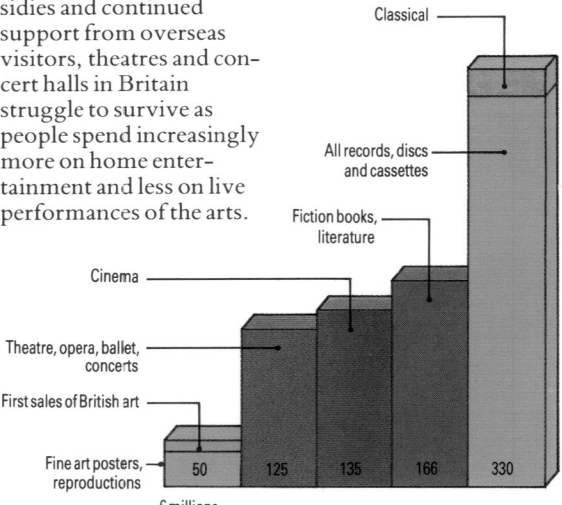

Classical

All records, discs and cassettes

Fiction books, literature

Cinema

Theatre, opera, ballet, concerts

First sales of British art

Fine art posters, reproductions

| 50 | 125 | 135 | 166 | 330 |

£ millions

Theatres

Of a total of 310 major theatres (those seating more than 200 people), 60 house resident theatre companies that receive state support. Arts Council funding of regional theatre is now being given priority over London's.

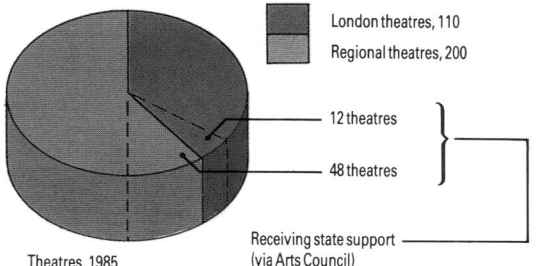

London theatres, 110
Regional theatres, 200

12 theatres
48 theatres

Receiving state support (via Arts Council)

Theatres, 1985

Covent Garden (above) once London's wholesale fruit and vegetable market, is now a major tourist attraction. It has become a focal point for street entertainers of all kinds.

Fine art

Interest and financial support for fine art is found throughout the country. The Burrell Collection in Glasgow is the newest major museum, featuring tapestries, paintings and *objets d'art*. The Third Eye Centre (right), also in Glasgow, is one of the many new small galleries that exhibit the work of young artists.

Cinema and television

There are some 1300 cinema screens in Britain. Attendances have declined drastically over the past 30 years, probably as a result of increased television viewing – the BBC and ITV together broadcast more than 60 hours of arts programmes on television each week – but also because of the way in which public funding for the film industry was until recently related to cinema attendances. Patterns of cinema-going in the last few years have been affected by the growth of the video market, which enables people to watch feature films in their homes.

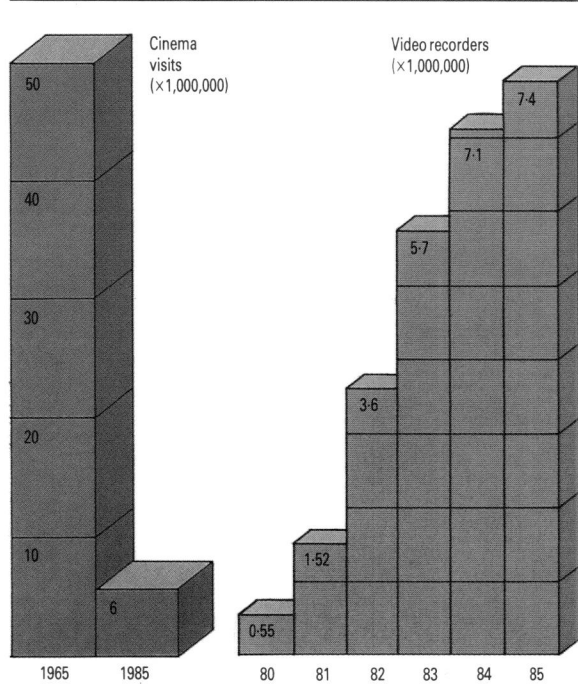

Cinema visits (×1,000,000)

50
40
30
20
10
6

1965   1985

Video recorders (×1,000,000)

7·4
7·1
5·7
3·6
1·52
0·55

80   81   82   83   84   85

Arts centres and performing groups

There are more than 200 arts centres and over 100 major museums and art galleries around Britain. Annually these attract more than 20 million visitors. The majority are in and around London, although the past five years have seen the establishment of important museums outside the capital – the National Railway Museum and Jorvik Viking Museum (York), the Ironbridge Gorge Museum, the Mary Rose Museum (Portsmouth) and the Open Air Museum (Durham).

In cinema and theatre, London's West End is the hub, although its Barbican Centre and South Bank arts complex are major sites, the Royal Shakespeare Company is based at Stratford upon Avon, and the National Museum of Photography, Film and Television is now well established in Bradford.

Britain has several international-class opera companies, including the English National, Welsh National, Royal Opera (at Covent Garden), Opera North (based in Leeds), and the Scottish Opera; symphony orchestras such as the London Symphony, Hallé (in Manchester) and the City of Birmingham; and dance companies, of which Sadler's Wells, the Royal Ballet, London Festival Ballet, Ballet Rambert, and London Contemporary Dance Theatre are best known.

Music and dance

In Britain, symphony orchestras, chamber orchestras and choral groups together number several hundred. A highlight of annual classical-music events is the season of Henry Wood Promenade Concerts, the Proms, in London's Albert Hall (below). Throughout the country, jazz, popular and folk music, ballet and other forms of dance are also popular, and there is a growing number of music events by ethnic groups, in particular Indian and West Indian.

ACKNOWLEDGEMENTS AND BIBLIOGRAPHY

The major thematic maps in the reference section were compiled by Peter Furtado, Lionel Bender, Mike March and Patrick Nugent from material provided by the authors. The maps were made and drawn by Clyde Surveys Ltd. of Maidenhead.

The editors and publishers would like to acknowledge the following as some major sources for these maps:

p11 Geology: Tectonic Map of Great Britain, the Institute of Geological Sciences 1966; and Oxford University Press.

p15 Climate: *The Climate of the British Isles* T J Chandler and S Gregory, Longman 1976.

p19 18th-century Britain: *An Historical Geography of England and Wales* ed R A Dodgshon and R A Butler, Academic Press 1978. *Man Made the Land* Alan R H Baker and J B Harley, David & Charles 1973.

p21 Industrial Revolution: *The Early Industrial Revolution* E Pawson, Batsford 1979.

p23 Workshop of the World: *The Movement of Population* C T Smith, Geographical Journal vol 117, 1951.

p30 Mineral Resources: *The Mineral Resources of Britain* John Blunden, Hutchinson 1975. *A Geography of Energy in the UK* John Fernie, Longman 1981.

p37 Nature Conservation: Countryside Commission, various official maps 1985.

p39, 41 Communications: BBC, IBA, Post Office and British Telecom Official Handbooks 1984–85.

p43 Agriculture: *Types of Farming in Britain* K Buchanan and D J Sinclair, Association of Agriculture 1966.

p47 Industry: *The Containment of Urban England* Peter Hall, George Allen & Unwin, 1974. *Britain 1985*, HMSO. *Regional Trends 1985* HMSO.

p57,59 Transport: British Rail and Ministry of Transport Official Maps 1961, 1985.

p69 Defence: *Defence Land Reviews*, HMSO 1973. Civil Aviation Authority published charts 1985; *Army, Navy and Air Force Lists* HMSO 1985.

p79 Tourism: English, Wales and Scottish Tourist Boards and the Nature Conservancy Council published data 1984–85.

Countless books have been written about the history, geography and countryside of Britain. The following titles (as well as those mentioned above) might be of interest about the geography of Britain:

The Personality of Britain Sir Cyril Fox and L F Chitty, National Museum of Wales 1932.

The UK Space ed J W House, Weidenfeld and Nicolson 1977.

The British Isles: A Systematic Geography J W Watson and J B Sissons, Nelson 1964.

Countryside Conservation Bryn Green, George Allen & Unwin 1985.

National Parks: Conservation or Cosmetics Ann and Malcolm McEwen. George Allen & Unwin 1982.

Britain's Structure and Scenery L D Stamp, Collins 1984.

Urban and Regional Planning Peter Hall, Penguin 1974.

Airport Strategy and Planning K R Sealy, Oxford University Press 1976.

Land Use and Living Space R H Best, Methuen 1981.

A Living History of the British Isles ed W G V Balchin, Country Life 1981.

A Natural History of the British Isles ed Pat Morris, Country Life 1979.

The Making of the English Landscape W G Hoskins, Penguin 1970.

Wales F V Emery, Longman 1969.

The Making of the Scottish Landscape R N Millman, Batsford 1975.

Editors Lionel Bender, Mike March, assisted by Madeleine Bender
Designer Patrick Nugent
Picture Researcher Juliet Brightmore
Typesetting Peter Furtado

ILLUSTRATORS
Alan Suttie: pages 10, 11, 12, 13, 20, 21, 26, 27, 28, 29, 50, 51, 52, 53, 56, 57, 64, 65, 70, 71, 81, 82
Bill Donohoe: pages 8, 9, 16, 17, 32, 33, 34, 35, 36, 37, 38, 39, 42, 43, 44, 45, 46, 47, 48, 49
Hayward Art Group: pages 18, 19, 22, 23, 24, 25, 30, 31, 54, 55, 58, 59, 62, 63, 66, 67, 72, 73, 76, 77, 78, 79, 83, 84
Chris Forsey: pages 14, 15
Make-up: Mike Pilley, Radius

PICTURE CREDITS
10 top and inset Institute of Geological Sciences, London; 12 British Geological Survey; 13 The Photo Source; 16 Dr John Mason; 18 top Mansell Collection; 18 bottom University of Reading, Institute of Agricultural History and Museum of English Rural Life; 21 Mansell Collection; 22 centre William Powell Frith *Many Happy Returns of the Day*, 1856. Harrogate Museums and Art Gallery; 22 bottom left Trades Union Congress Library; 22 bottom right BBC Hulton Picture Library; 24 centre *Punch*, April 20th, 1921; 24 bottom right Austin Rover; 26 Topham Picture Library; 32 British Nuclear Fuels, PLC; 34–35 top John McCormick; 35 bottom Thames Water; 36 The Photo Source; 38 British Telecom Photo Library; 40 Prestel, British Telecommunications PLC; 45 Haigh and Ringrose Ltd (part of Costain Group PLC); 49 Photograph by British Petroleum; 56 Aerofilms Ltd; 58 Flight International/Quadrant Picture Library; 60 Aerofilms Ltd; 63, 68 Illustrated London News Picture Library; 69 Jerry Mason; 70 Flight International/Quadrant Picture Library; 71 *Jane's Defence Weekly*/Hughes; 73 Central Office of Information. Crown copyright; 74 top The Stock Exchange; 74 bottom Robert Miles; 75 top Raissa Page/Format Photographers Picture Agency; 75 bottom Camera Press; 76 top–77 Frank Spooner Pictures; 76 bottom, 78 Britain on View Photographic Library; 81 top and centre Arcaid Photographic Library. Photo Richard Bryant; 81 bottom Foster Associates; 82 Wales Tourist Board Photographic Library; 83 top left Britain on View Photographic Library; 83 centre Scottish Tourist Board Photographic Library; 83 bottom right The Photo Source.

ORDNANCE SURVEY 1:250 000 Maps

Legend

ROADS ROUTES STRASSEN

The representation on this map of a road is no evidence of the existence of a right of way

Motorway with service area, service area
(limited access) and junction with junction
number
Autoroute avec aire de service, aire de service
(accès restreint) et échangeur avec son numéro
Autobahn mit Servicestation, Servicestation (mit
begrenztem Zugang) und Anschlussstelle mit
Nummer

Motorway junction with limited interchange
Echangeur à possibilités d'intercirculation restreintes
Anschlussstelle mit begrenztem Richtungswechsel

Motorway under construction
Autoroute en construction
Autobahn im Bau

A I (T) Dual carriageway

Trunk road with service area
Route à grande circulation avec aire de service
Fernverkehrsstrasse mit Servicestation

A I5 Double chaussée

Main road with roundabout or
multiple level junction
Route principale avec rond-point, sens
giratoire ou échangeur
Hauptstrasse mit Kreisverkehr
oder Anschlussstelle

B 4069 Zweibahnige Strasse

Secondary road
Route secondaire
Nebenstrasse

Road under construction
Route en construction
Strasse im Bau

Gradient 1 in 7 and steeper
Pente: 14% et plus
Steigungen: 14% und mehr

Toll

Toll   Road tunnel
Péage   Tunnel routier
Strassenbenutzungsgebühr   Strassentunnel

A 855   B 797

Narrow road with passing places
Route étroite avec voies de dépassment
Enge Strasse mit Ausweichstelle bzw. Uberholstelle

Other tarred road   Other minor road
Autre route goudronnée   Autre route
Sonstige asphaltierte Strasse Sonstige Nebenstrasse

18   23

Distances in miles between markers
Distances en miles les marques
Entfernungen in Meilen zwischen den Zeichen

Selected places of major traffic importance are known as Primary Route Destinations
and are shown on this map thus DERBY.   Distances and directions to such destinations are
repeated on traffic signs (see inside back cover).

TOURIST INFORMATION RENSEIGNEMENTS TOURISTIQUES TOURISTIKINFORMATION

Abbey, Cathedral, Priory
Abbaye, Cathédrale Prieuré
Abtei, Kathedrale, Priorei

Aquarium
Aquarium
Aquarium

Camp site
Terrain de camping
Campingplatz

Caravan site
Terrain pour caravanes
Wohnwagenplatz

Castle
Château
Schloss

Cave
Caverne
Höhle

Country park
Parc naturel
Landschaftspark

Craft centre
Centre artisanal
Zentrum für Kunsthandwerk

Garden
Jardin
Garten

Golf course or links
Terrain de golf
Golfplatz

Historic house
Manoir, Palais
Historisches Gebäude

Information centre
Bureau de renseignements
Informationsbüro

Motor racing
Courses automobiles
Autorennen

Museum
Musée
Museum

Nature or forest trail
Sentier signalisé pour piétons
Natur-oder Waldlehrpfad

Nature reserve
Réserve naturelle
Naturschutzgebiet

Other tourist feature
Autre site intéressant
Sonstige Sehenswurdigkeit

Picnic site
Emplacement de pique-nique
Picknickplatz

Preserved railway
Chemin de fer préservé
touristique
Museumseisenbahn

Racecourse
Hippodrome
Pferderennbahn

Skiing
Piste de ski
Skilaufen

Viewpoint
Belvédère
Aussichtspunkt

Wildlife park
Parc animalier
Wildpark

Zoo
Zoo
Tiergarten

GENERAL FEATURES

Buildings

Wood

Lighthouse
(in use)

Lighthouse
(disused)

Windmill

Radio or TV mast

Youth hostel

Civil aerodrome { with Customs facilities / without Customs facilities }

Heliport

Public telephone

Motoring organisation telephone

WATER FEATURES

Canal

Lake

Marsh

Bridge   Ferry

Short ferry routes
for vehicles

Transport for vehicles

(boat)   (hovercraft)

Ferry routes for vehicles
(subject to change)

Cliff

Slopes

Flat rock

Light-vessel

Low water mark

Foreshore

Dunes   High water mark

RAILWAYS

Standard gauge track

Narrow gauge track

Tunnel

Road crossing under or over

Level crossing

Station

ANTIQUITIES

ROMAN ROAD   Roman antiquity

Castle ·   Other antiquities

Native fortress

Site of battle (with date)

Roman road (course of)

Ancient Monuments and Historic Buildings
in the care of the Secretaries of State
for the Environment, for Scotland
and for Wales and that are open to the public.

BOUNDARIES

National

County, Region
or Islands Area

RELIEF

HEIGHTS IN FEET

Feet	Metres
3000	914
2000	610
1400	427
1000	305
600	183
200	61
0	0

·274
Heights in
feet above
mean sea level

Contours at
200ft intervals

To convert
feet to metres
multiply by 0·3048

1:250 000 Scale

4 centimetres to 10 kilometres (one grid square)

1 kilometre =0·6214 mile   1 mile = 1·61 kilometres

10   5   0   Kilometres 5   10   15

5   0   Miles   5   10

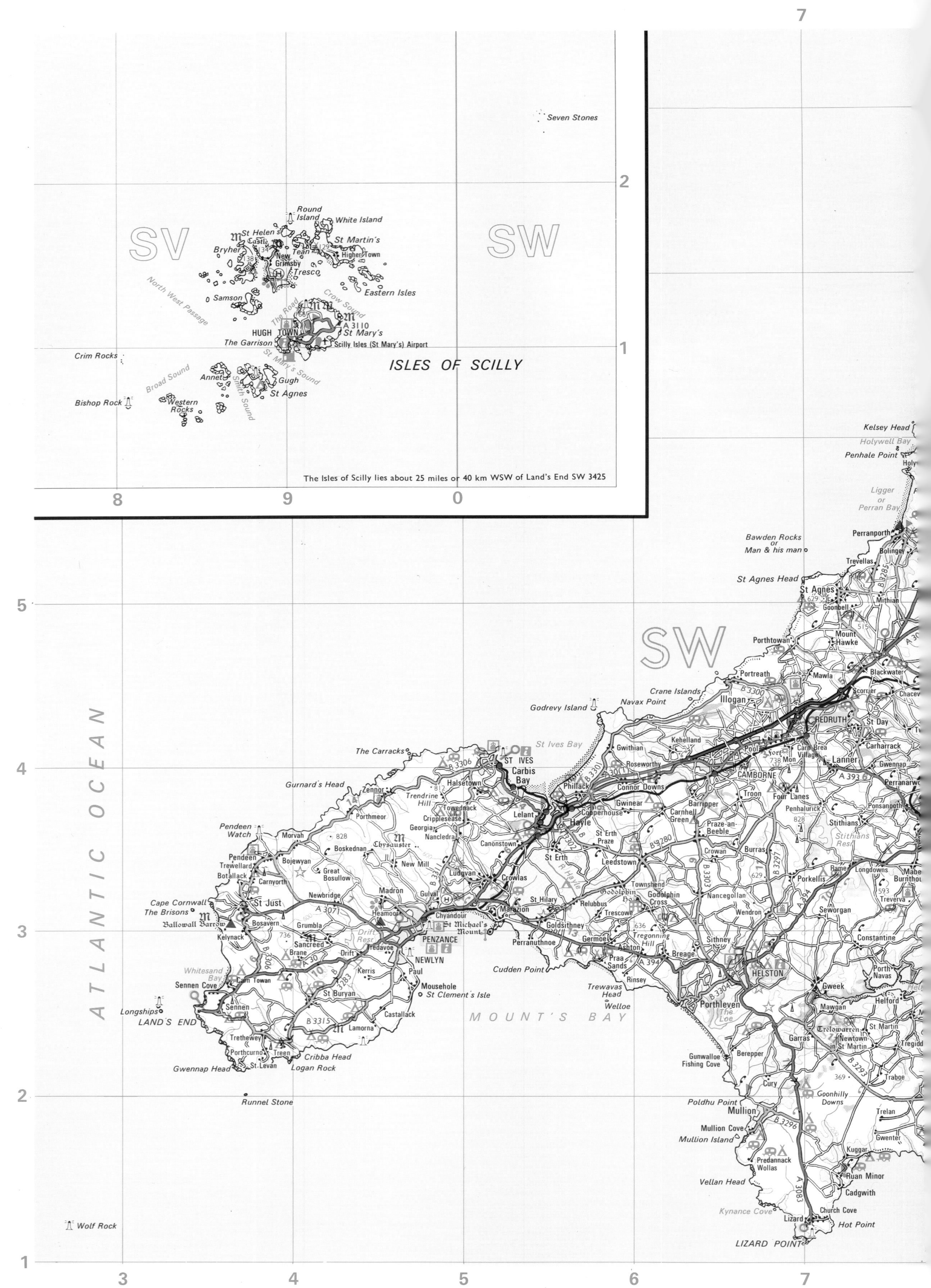

Seven Stones

SV   SW

Round Island
White Island
St Helen's
Castle
Bryher   Teän   St Martin's
New   Higher Town
Grimsby
Tresco
Samson   Eastern Isles
Crow Sound
The Road
North West Passage
HUGH TOWN   A 3110
St Mary's
The Garrison   Scilly Isles (St Mary's) Airport
Crim Rocks

ISLES OF SCILLY

Broad Sound   St Mary's Sound
Annet   Gugh
Bishop Rock   St Agnes
Western   South Sound
Rocks

The Isles of Scilly lies about 25 miles or 40 km WSW of Land's End SW 3425

8   9   0

Kelsey Head
Holywell Bay
Penhale Point
Holy
Ligger
or
Perran Bay
Bawden Rocks
or
Man & his man   Perranporth
Bolingey
Trevellas
St Agnes Head   B 3285
St Agnes
629
Goonbell   Mithian
515
Porthtowan   Mount
Hawke
SW
Portreath   Mawla   Blackwater
Crane Islands   Scorrier   Chacewe
Navax Point   B 3300   Illogan
Godrevy Island   REDRUTH   St Day
Carn Brea   Village   Lanner
St Ives Bay   Gwithian   Pool   738 Mon   Carharrack
The Carracks   ST IVES   Kehelland   CAMBORNE   Gwennap
Carbis   Roseworthy   A 393 6   Perranarw
Gurnard's Head   Bay   Troon   Four Lanes
Zennor   Halsetown   Phillack   Connor Downs   Barripper   Penhalurick
Trendrine   Gwinear   Carnhell   Praze-an-   Ponsanooth
Hill   Towednack   Copperhouse   Green   Beeble   Stithians
Porthmeor   Cripplesease   B 3302   Praze   Crowan   Burras   B 3297
Georgia   Hayle   St Erth   Leedstown   Townshend   Stithians
Pendeen   828   Nancledra   Praze   Resr
Watch   Boskednan   New Mill   Canonstown   Rame   Longdowns
Morvah   Ludgvan   St Erth   629   Porkellis   Mabe
Pendeen   Bojewyan   Chysauster   Crowlas   Relubbus   Godolphin   Nancegollan   Burnthou
Trewellard   Great Bosullow   Madron   Gulval   St Hilary   Cross   Wendron   593   Treverva
Botallack   Carnyorth   Newbridge   Marazion   Godolphin   Sithney   Seworgan
Cape Cornwall   Heamoor   St Michael's   Goldsithney   636   Constantine
The Brisons   St Just   A 307   Chyandour   Mount   Germoe   Tregonning   Porth
Ballowall Barrow   Bosavern   Grumbla   PENZANCE   Perranuthnoe   Ashton   Hill   HELSTON   Navas
Kelynack   736   Sancreed   NEWLYN   Praa   Breage
Drift   Paul   Sands   Rinsey   Gweek   Helford
Whitesand   Brane   30   Kerris   Cudden Point   Trewavas   Porthleven   Mawgan
Bay   Drift   Head   The   Garras   Trelowarren
Carn Towan   10   Welloe   Loe   Newtown   St Martin
Sennen Cove   St Buryan   Mousehole   in St Martin
Sennen   Castallack   St Clement's Isle   Gunwalloe   Berepper
Longships   B 3315   Lamorna   MOUNT'S BAY   Fishing Cove   Cury   Goonhilly   Tregidd
LAND'S END   Trethewey   Treen   Cribba Head   369   Downs   Trelan   Trabe
Porthcurno   St Levan   Logan Rock   Poldhu Point   Grabe
Gwennap Head   Mullion   B 3296
Runnel Stone   Mullion Cove   Gwenter
Mullion Island   Kuggar
Predannack   Ruan Minor
Wollas   Cadgwith
Wolf Rock   Vellan Head   A 3083
Kynance Cove   Church Cove
Lizard   Hot Point
LIZARD POINT

ATLANTIC OCEAN

3   4   5   6   7

ENGLISH CHANNEL

SX

87

PLYMOUTH to
Roscoff..............7-9 hrs
Santander.............24 hrs

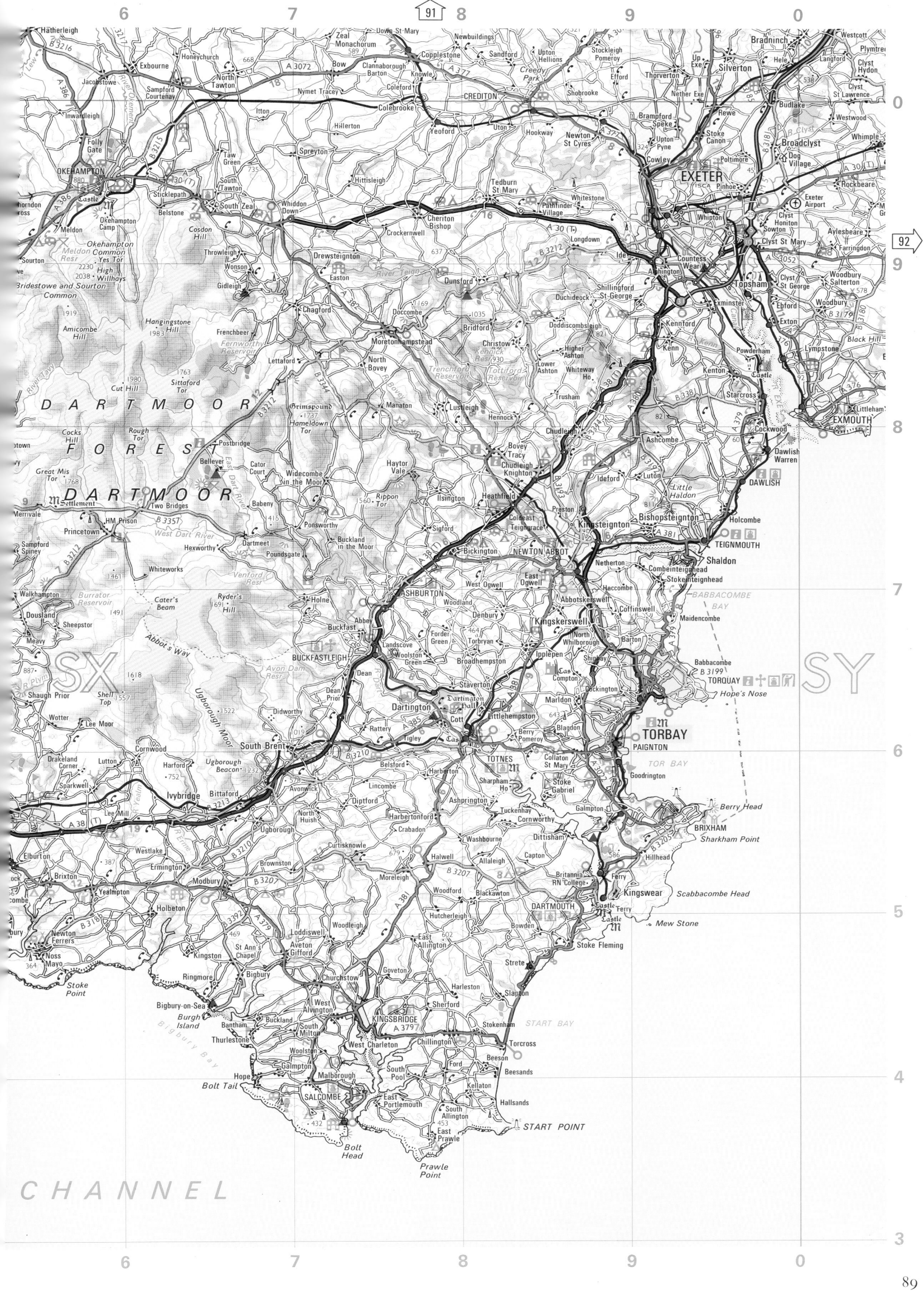

BRISTOL CHANNEL

ILFRAC

North West Point
LUNDY
466
South West Point Rat Island

Bull Point
Rockham Bay
Morte Point 451
Mortehoe
Lee
Sl

Woolacombe
654 688

Morte Bay

North
Buckland
Pickwell

Baggy Point

Croyde
Bay 518

Croyde Knowle

BARNSTAPLE Georgeham

Saunton

OR Braunton

Braunton Chivenor
Burrows Wrafton

Bideford BIDEFORD BAY
Bar Freming

Appledore Yella

Westward Ho! NORTHAM Tapeley
Westleigh
HARTLAND POINT Titchberry Windbury Abbotsham BIDEFORD Hor
Point East-the
Clovelly Water Woodtown
Stoke 564 Alvard
Hartland Hartland Clovelly Dykes Buck's Mills Fairy Cross Landcross
Quay Dyke 547 Littleham
Millford Philham Buck's Cross Parkham Weare
Elmscott 710 Parkham Buckland Giffard
South Woolfardisworthy Ash Brewer Monkleigh
Hole 709 Frithelstock
Knaps Welcombe Melbury
Longpeak 771 B 3227
Meddon Ashmansworthy East Putford Stibb Cross Little
708 West Putford Torring
Gooseham Eastcott Langtree
Morwenstow 512 Youlstone Dinworthy Bulkworthy Abbots A 388 616 Peters
Higher Sharpnose 734 Bradworthy Bickington Newton Marland Winsw
Point Shop 656 St Petrock
Woodford Upper Tamar Sutcombe Milton Damerel 560
Lower Sharpnose Lake Soldon Shebbear
Point Lower Tamar Alfardisworthy Cross Buckland
Coombe Lake 635 Holsworthy Thornbury Filleigh
Kilkhampton Beacon Bradford Sheepwas
BUDE Stibb B 39 B 3254 Holsworthy Cookbury Black 574
571 Chilsworthy Torrington Highampton
Poughill Grimscott 13
BAY Flexbury STRATTON Launcells Pancrasweek HOLSWORTHY Holemoor Graddon
Bude Haven BUDE 10 A 3072 632 Moor
216 Marhamchurch Bridgerule Pyworthy 531 Hollacombe Halwill
Widemouth Bay Launceston Junction
Coppathorne 440 632 Halwill Beaworthy
Dizzard Point Whitstone River Deer Clawton 917
Poundstock North Tamerton River Claw Quoditch
Tregole Week 18 Tetcott 388 Ashwater Eworthy B 3218
Cambeak 544 St Mary Lana Germansweek
Crackington Trewint B 3254 Luffincott Chapmans Bratton Bo
Wainhouse Jacobstow 578 Well Clovelly Cre
852 Corner 543 Clubworthy West Northcott Virginstow
South Curry Boyton East
Fire Beacon Point Wheatley 598 Bennacott Panson River Wolf
Marshgate Brazacott St Giles Broadwoodwidger
Boscastle 841 Warbstow on the Heath River Thrushel
Castle Lesnewth Camworthy North Polapit A 30
Tintagel Head Trevalga Otterham 641 Water Petherwin 469 Tamar Werrington Thrushelton
Bossiney Tremaine River Ottery Yeolmbridge Cross Green Lewdown
Tintagel 1009 Trewassa Tresmeer 464 Stowford 860
Treknow Trewarmett Davidstow Treneglos Langore Portgate Lewtrenchard
Start Point Tremail Egloskerry LAUNCESTON Lifton Castle
Treligga St Clether Tregeare St Stephens Tinhay Lydford
Trewassa A 395 Red Down Castle Coryton
Delabole Camelford Laneast Marystow
Port Isaac Helstone Crowdy Trewen Tregadillett Lawhitton Kelly Chillaton
Port Bay Reservoir River Inny Polyphant South Bradstone North
Isaac St Teath Altarnun Lewannick Petherwin 930 Brentor
Portgaverne Treligga Lezant Milton Abbot
Pendoggett Michaelstow Rough Brown Codda 1082 Dunterton 384
ellion Trelill 522 Tor Willy 1209 30 (T) 13
St Broward Garrow 1377
Tor

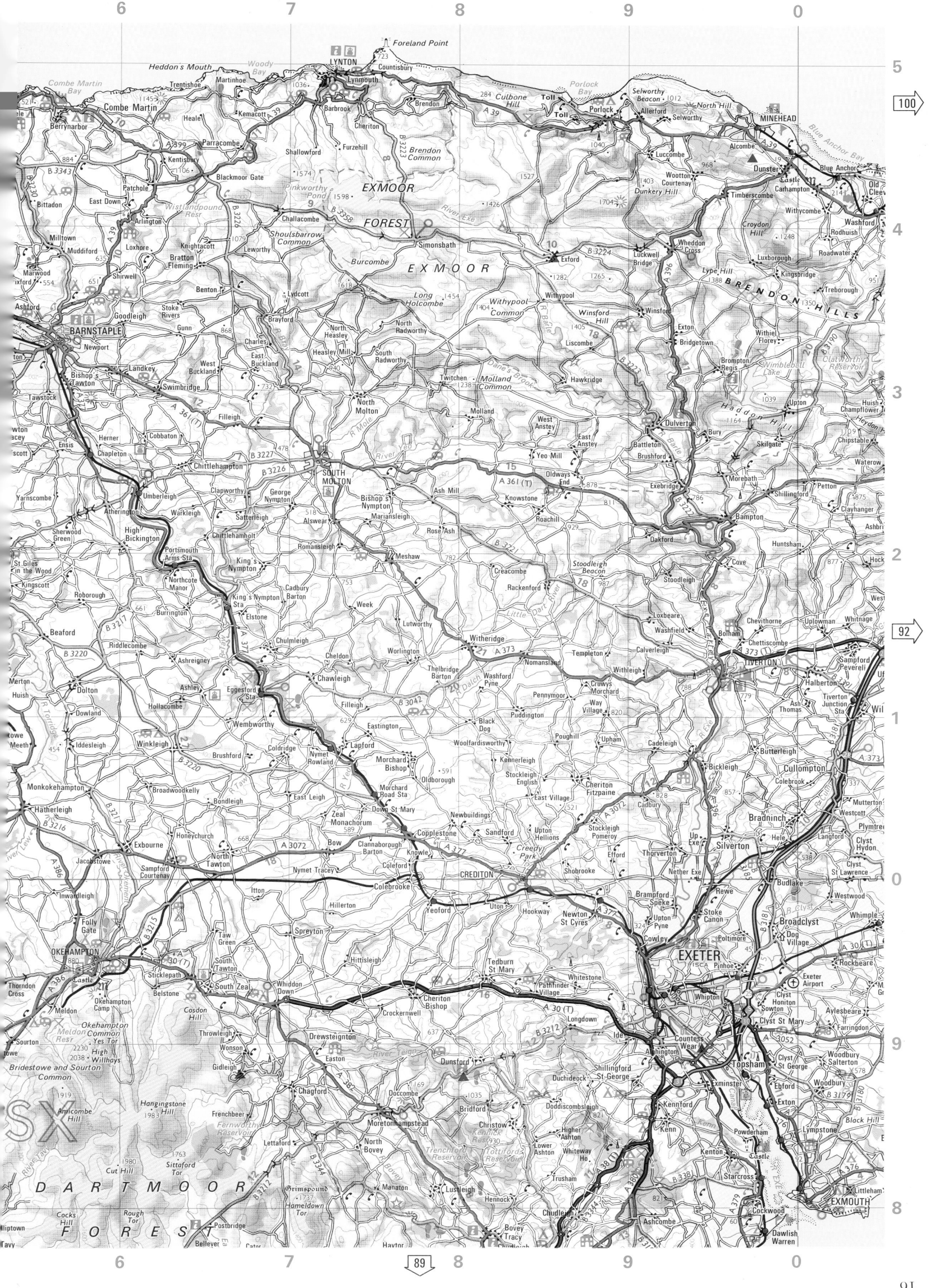

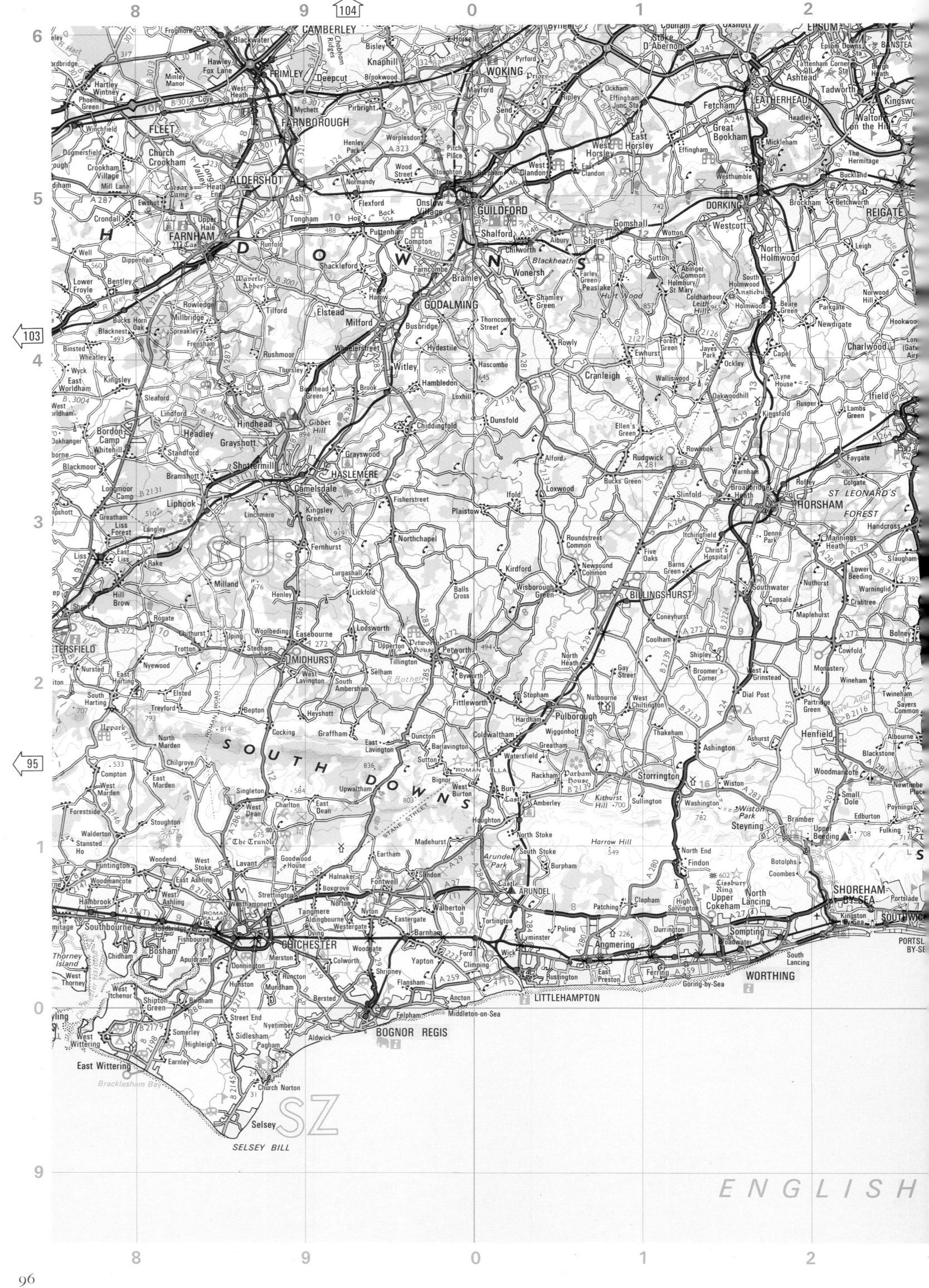

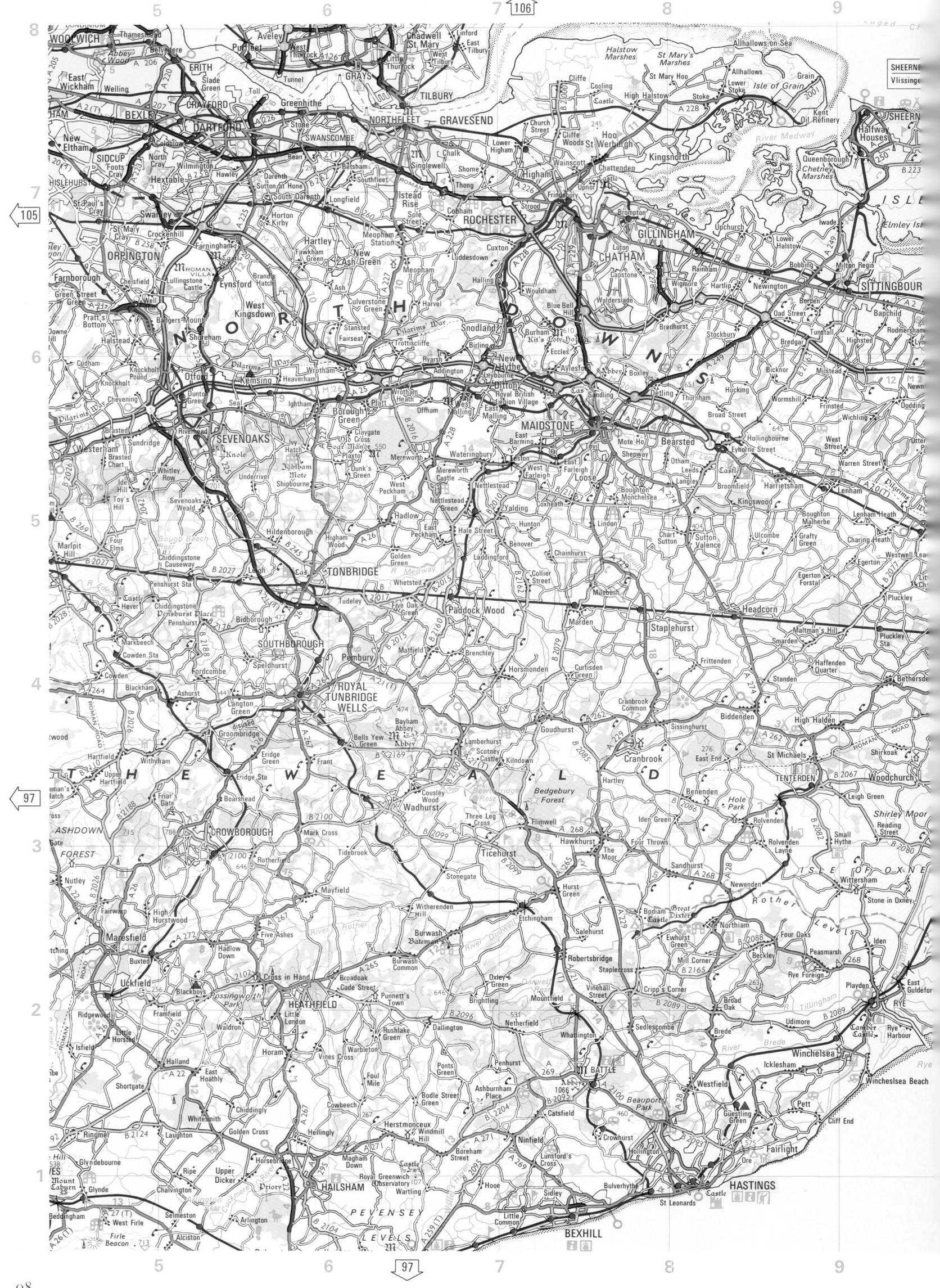

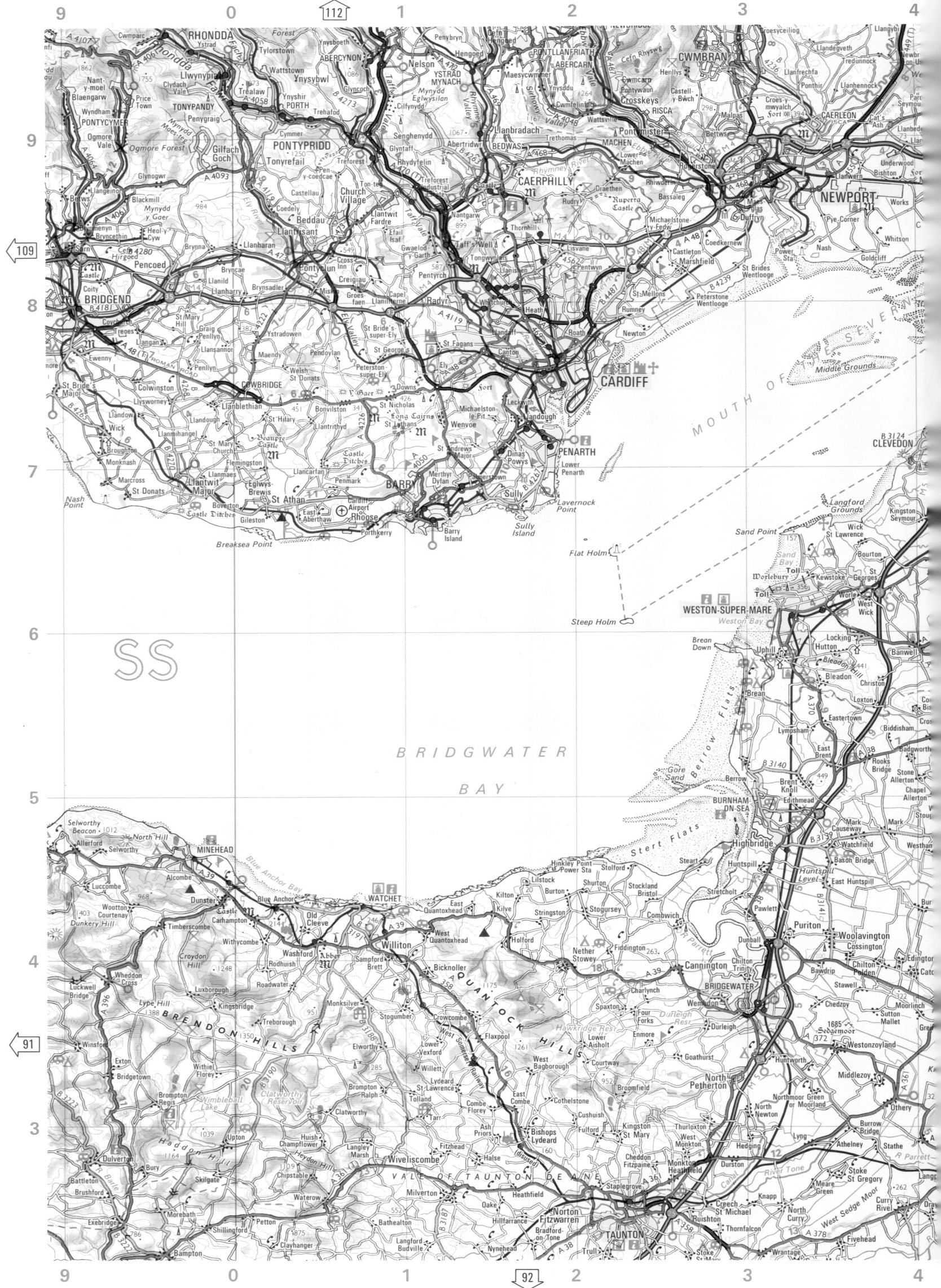

9   0   1   2   3   4

MOUTH OF THE SEVERN

SS

BRIDGWATER BAY

9   0   1   2   3   4

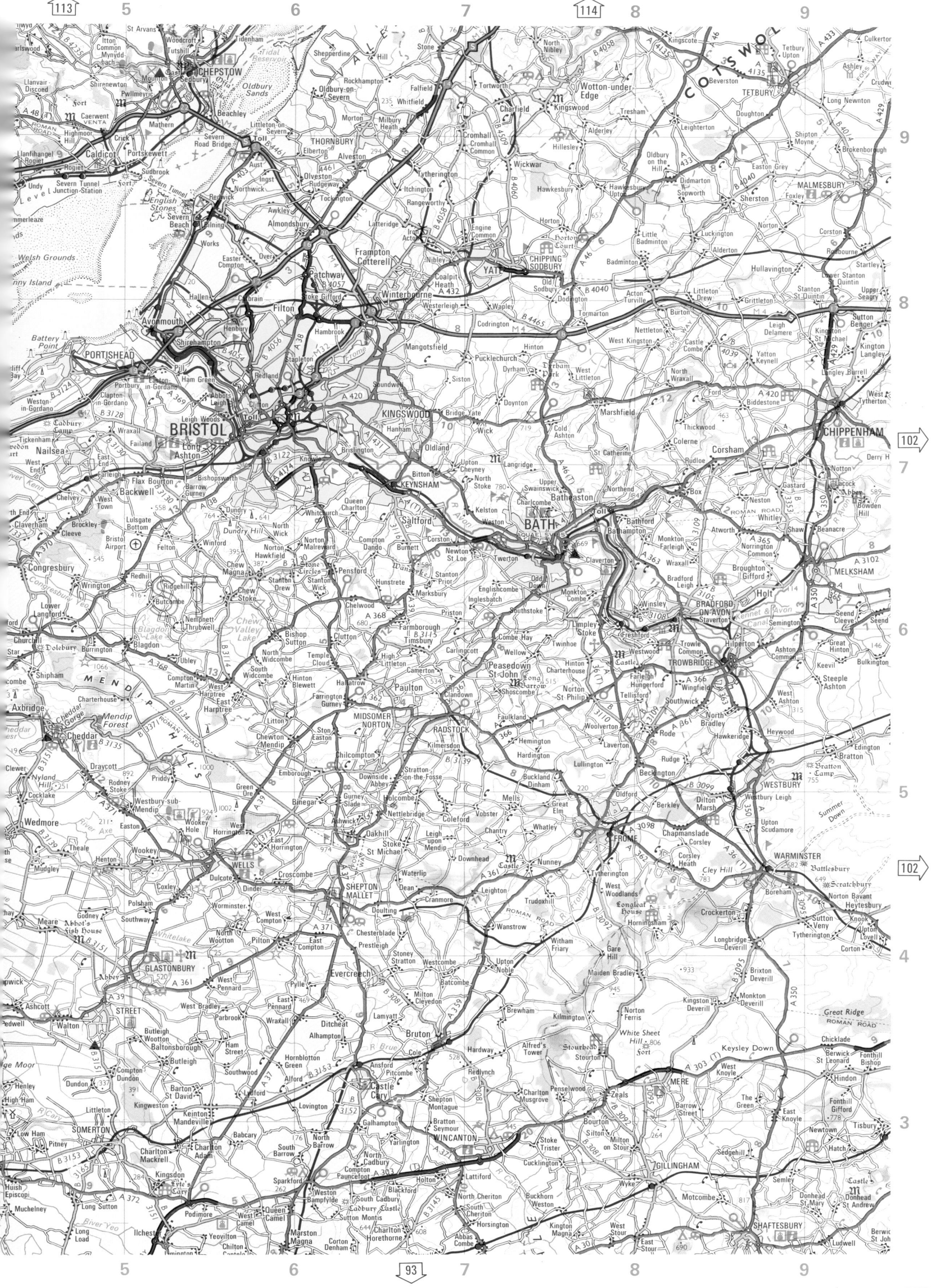

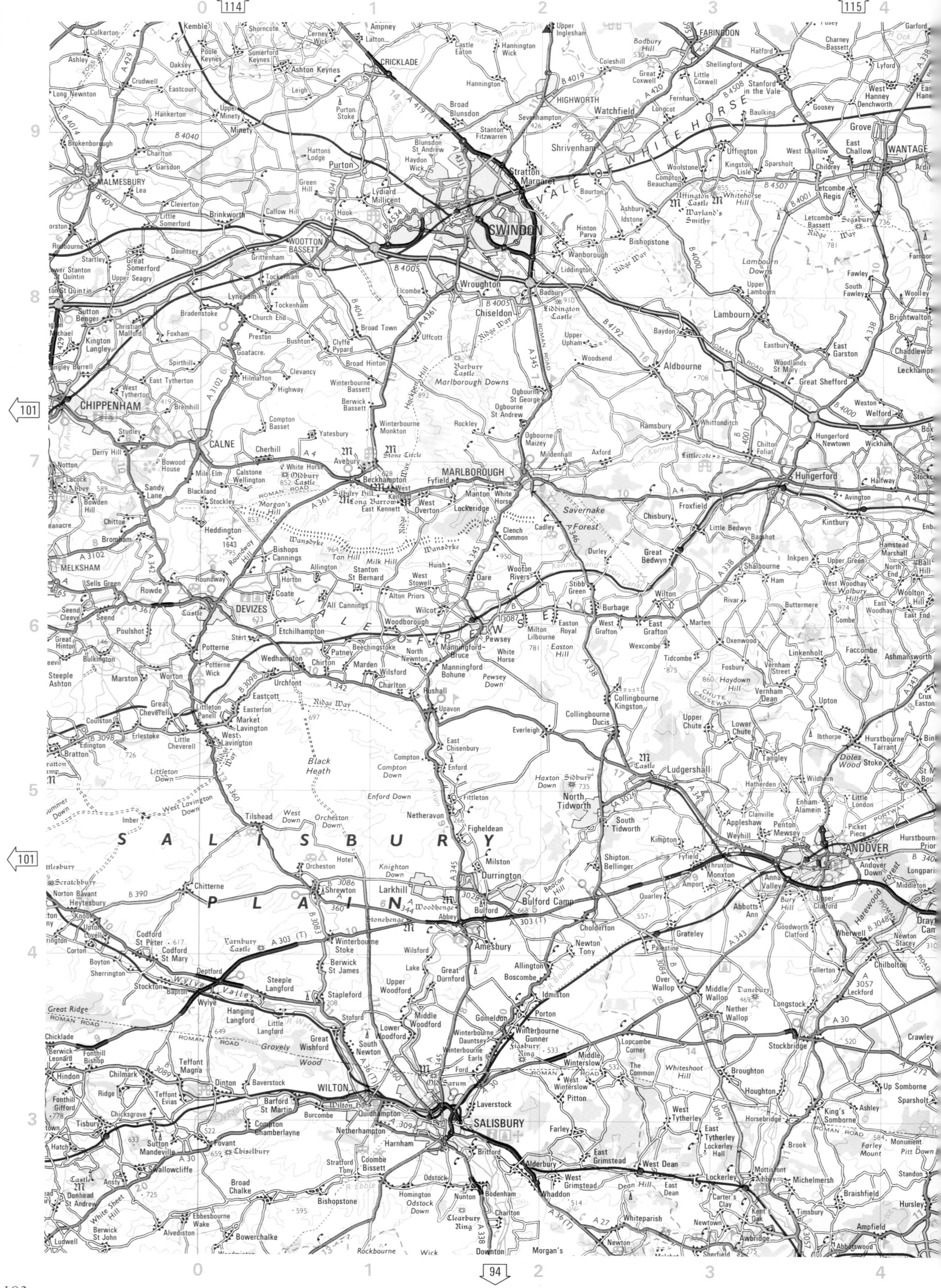

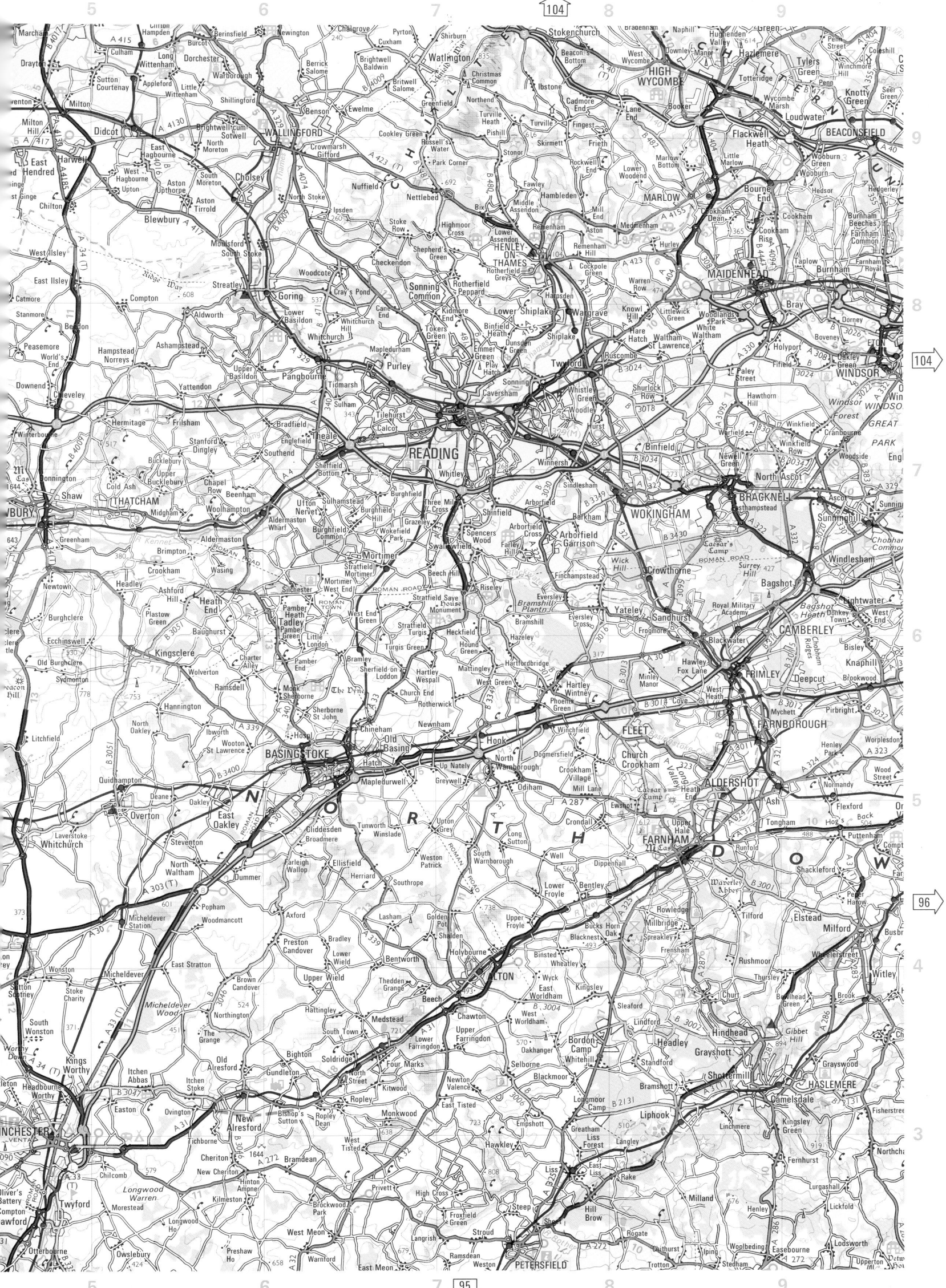

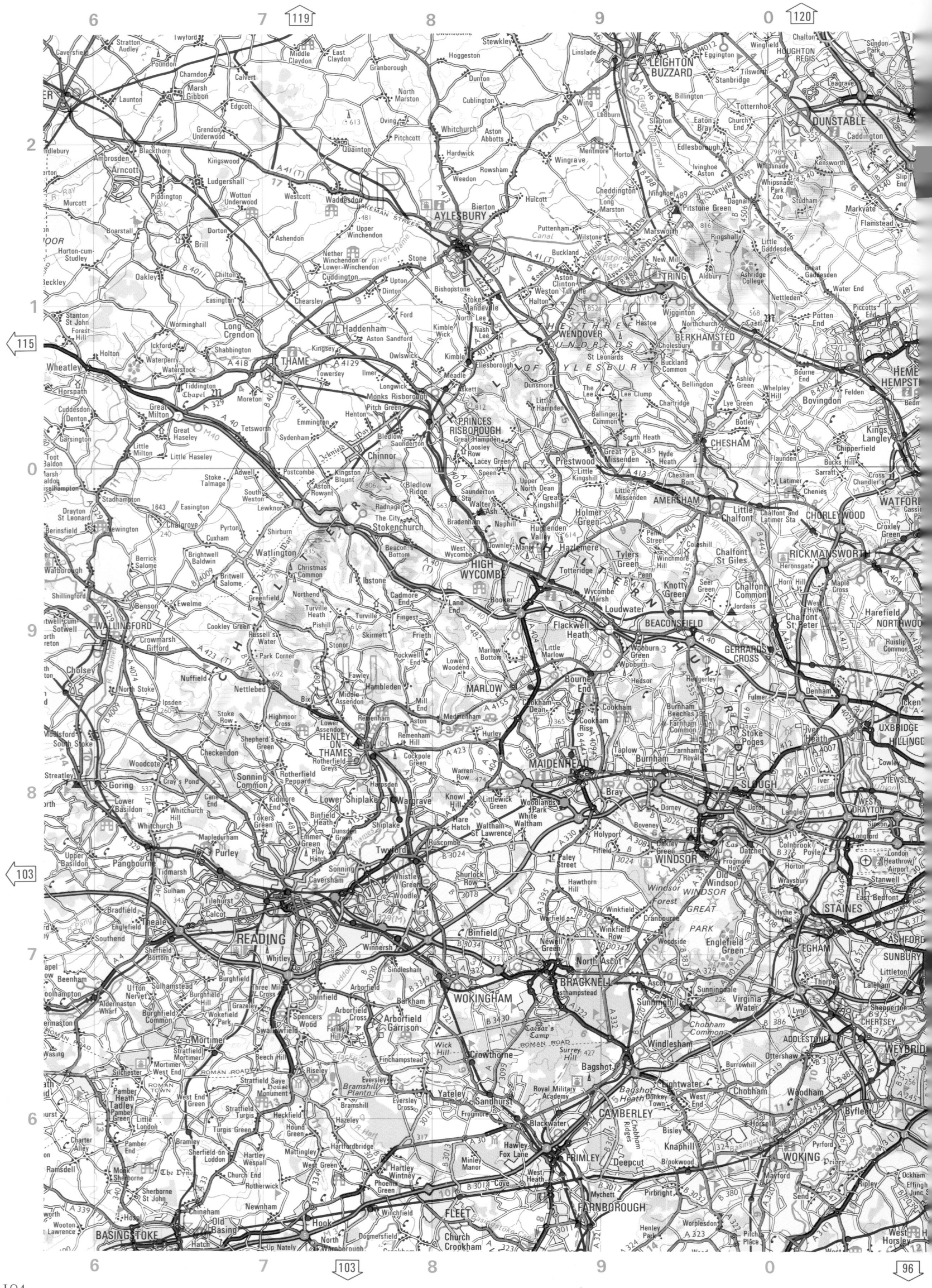

106
106

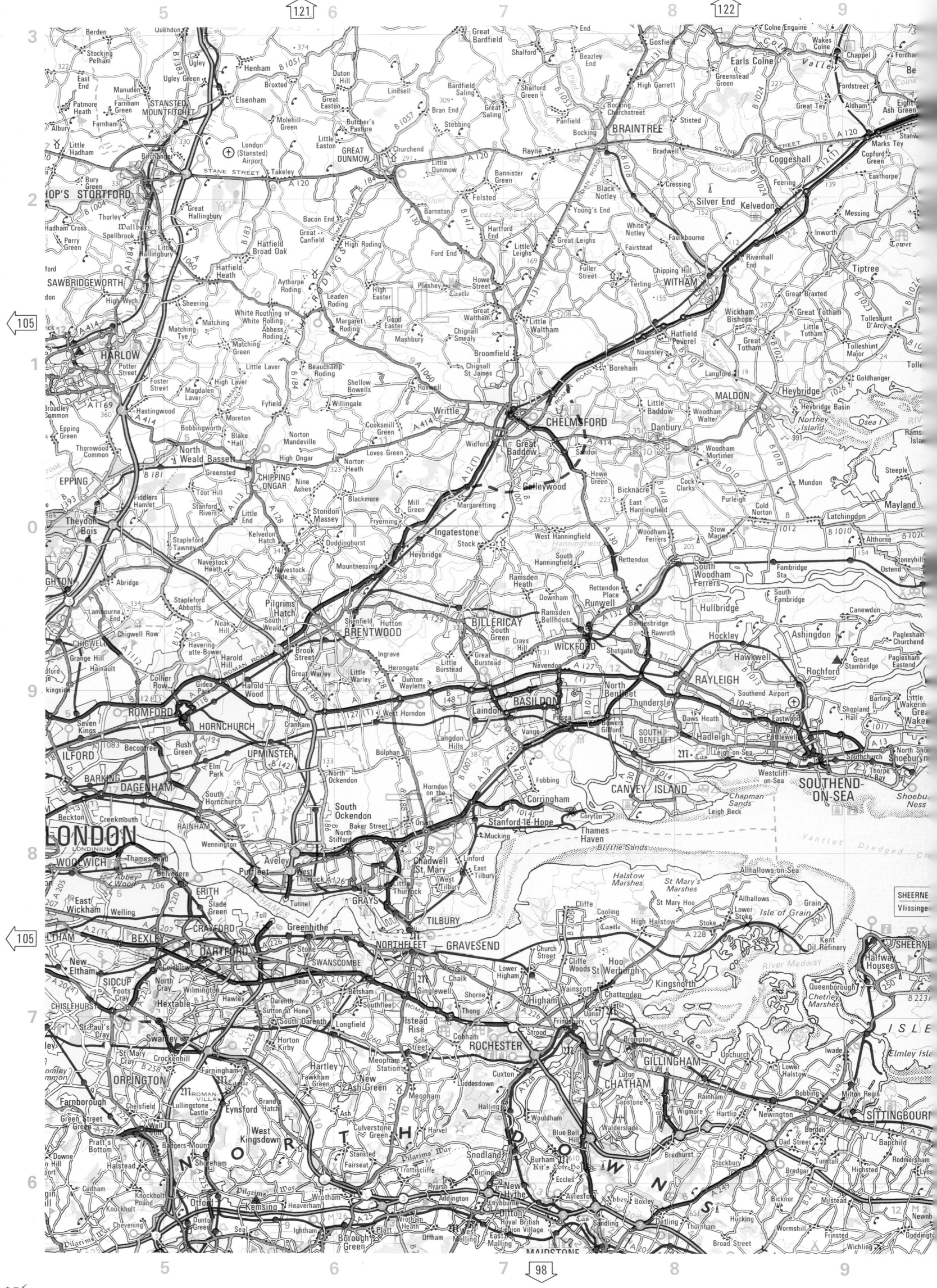

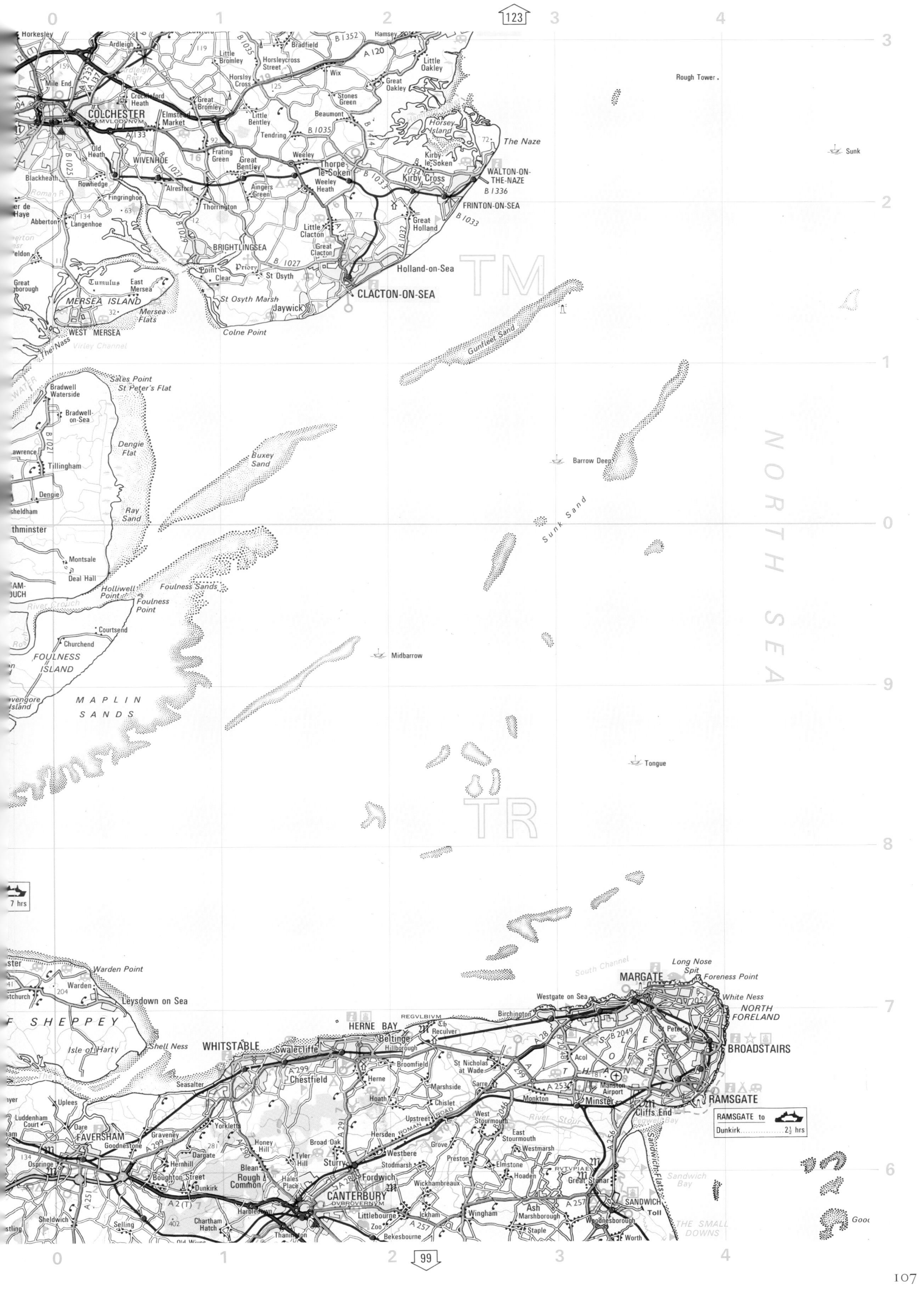

Horkesley
Ardleigh
Little Bromley
Bradfield
Hamsey
B 1352
A 120
Little Oakley
3

Mile End
COLCHESTER
CAMVLODVNVM
Crockleford Heath
Great Bromley
Horsley Cross
Wix
Great Oakley
Stones Green
125
Rough Tower .
119
Horsleycross Street

Old Heath
Elmstead Market
Frating Green
Great Bentley
Beaumont
Horsey Island
The Naze
Sunk

WIVENHOE
Alresford
Weeley
Thorpe le-Soken
Kirby le-Soken
72
WALTON-ON-THE-NAZE
B 1336
2

Rowhedge
Aingers Green
Weeley Heath
Kirby Cross
B 1034
FRINTON-ON-SEA
B 1033

Blackheath
Fingringhoe
Thorrington
B 1027
Little Clacton
Great Holland
B 1033

Langenhoe
63
12
BRIGHTLINGSEA
Great Clacton
B 1022
TM

Great
East Mersea
Tumulus
32
B 1027
Priory
St Osyth
Holland-on-Sea
1

MERSEA ISLAND
Mersea Flats
Point Clear
St Osyth Marsh
CLACTON-ON-SEA

WEST MERSEA
Jaywick

The Nass
Virley Channel
Colne Point
Gunfleet Sand

Sales Point
St Peter's Flat
0

Bradwell Waterside
Bradwell-on-Sea
Buxey Sand
Barrow Deep

Dengie Flat
Sunk Sand

Tillingham
Ray Sand

Dengie
Midbarrow
9

Montsale
Deal Hall
Foulness Sands

Holliwell Point
Foulness Point

Courtsend
Tongue
TR

Churchend
FOULNESS ISLAND

MAPLIN SANDS
8

7 hrs

Warden Point
Long Nose Spit
Foreness Point

Warden
MARGATE
White Ness
7

OF SHEPPEY
Leysdown on Sea
Westgate on Sea
NORTH FORELAND

Isle of Harty
Shell Ness
Birchington
St Peter's

WHITSTABLE
Swalecliffe
HERNE BAY
Beltinge
REGVLBIVM
Reculver
Acol
BROADSTAIRS

Seasalter
Chestfield
Herne
Hillborough
St Nicholas at Wade
Manston Airport
RAMSGATE

FAVERSHAM
Graveney
Hoath
Broomfield
Marshside
Sarre
Monkton
Minster
Cliffs End

Goodnestone
Dargate
Honey Hill
Broad Oak
Chislet
West Stourmouth
SANDWICH

Oare
Yorkletts
Tyler Hill
Sturry
Hersden
East Stourmouth
Westmarsh
RAMSGATE to Dunkirk .... 2½ hrs

Uplees
Blean
Hales Place
Westbere
Stodmarsh
Grove
Preston
Great Stonar

Osprige
Boughton Street
Rough Common
Fordwich
Wickhambreaux
Hoaden
Woodnesborough
Sandwich Bay

Sheldwich
Dunkirk
Harbledown
CANTERBURY
DVROVERNVM
Littlebourne
Ickham
Wingham
Ash
A 257
SANDWICH Toll

Selling
Chartham Hatch
Thanington
Bekesbourne
Staple
Marshborough
Worth
THE SMALL DOWNS

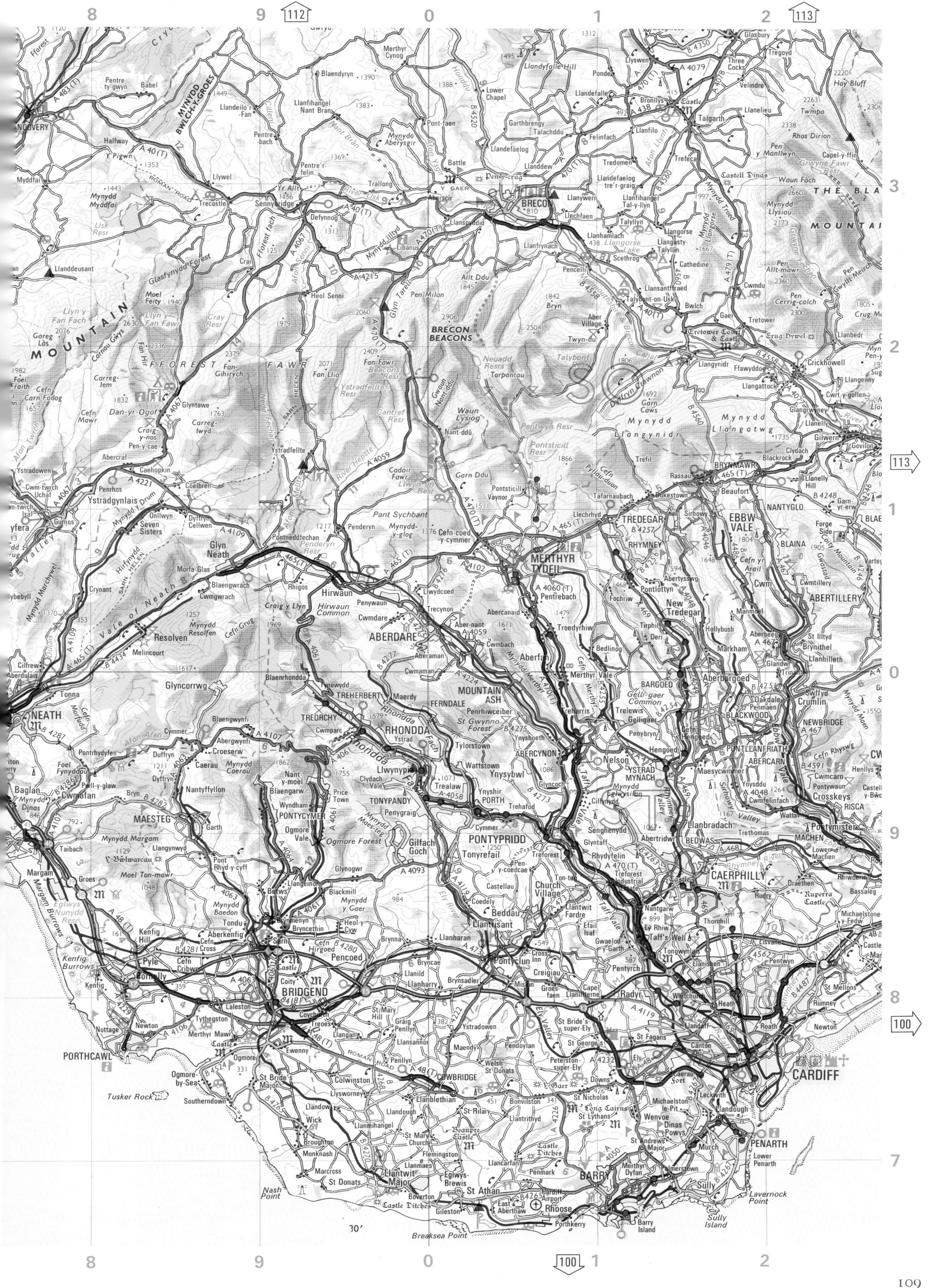

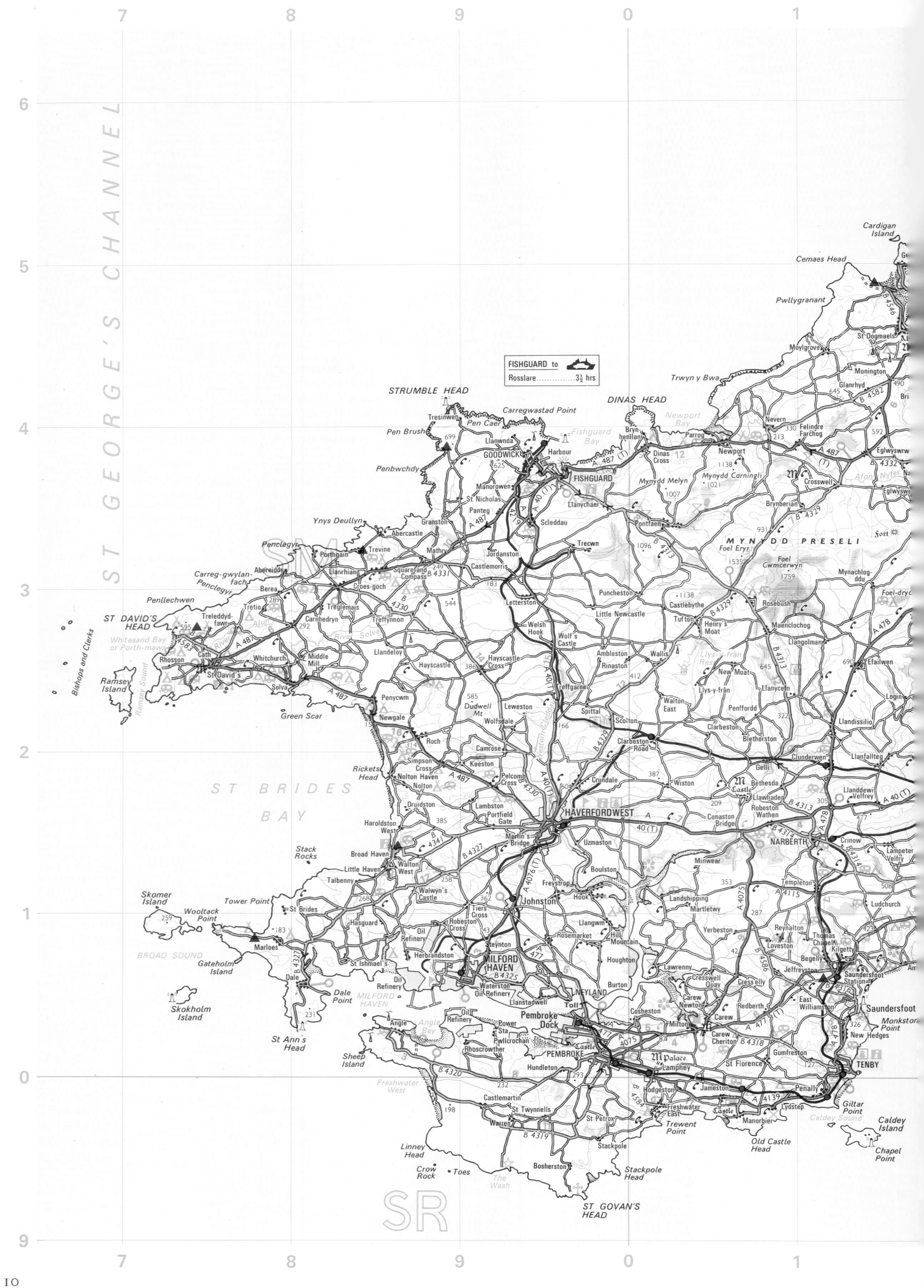

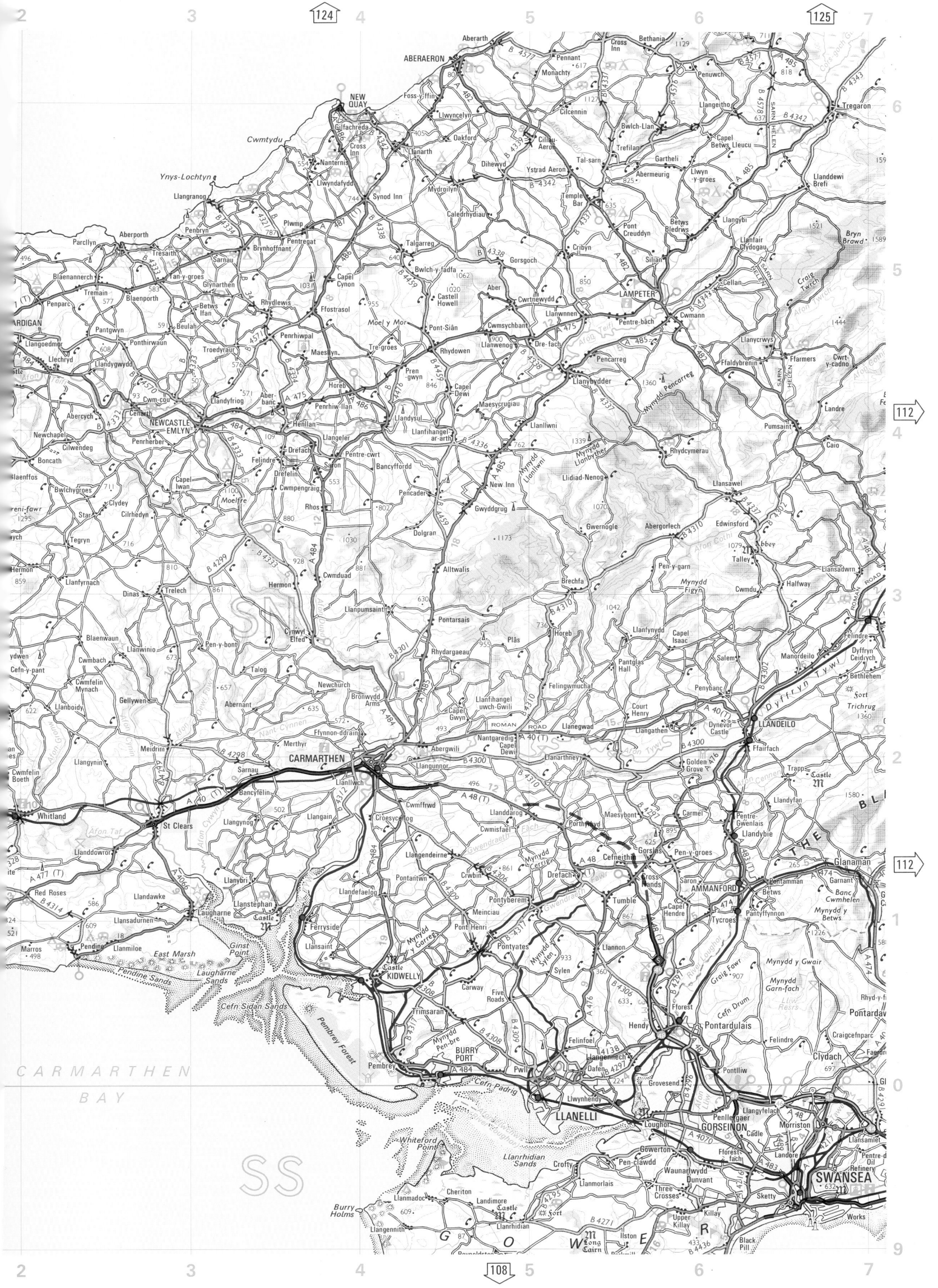

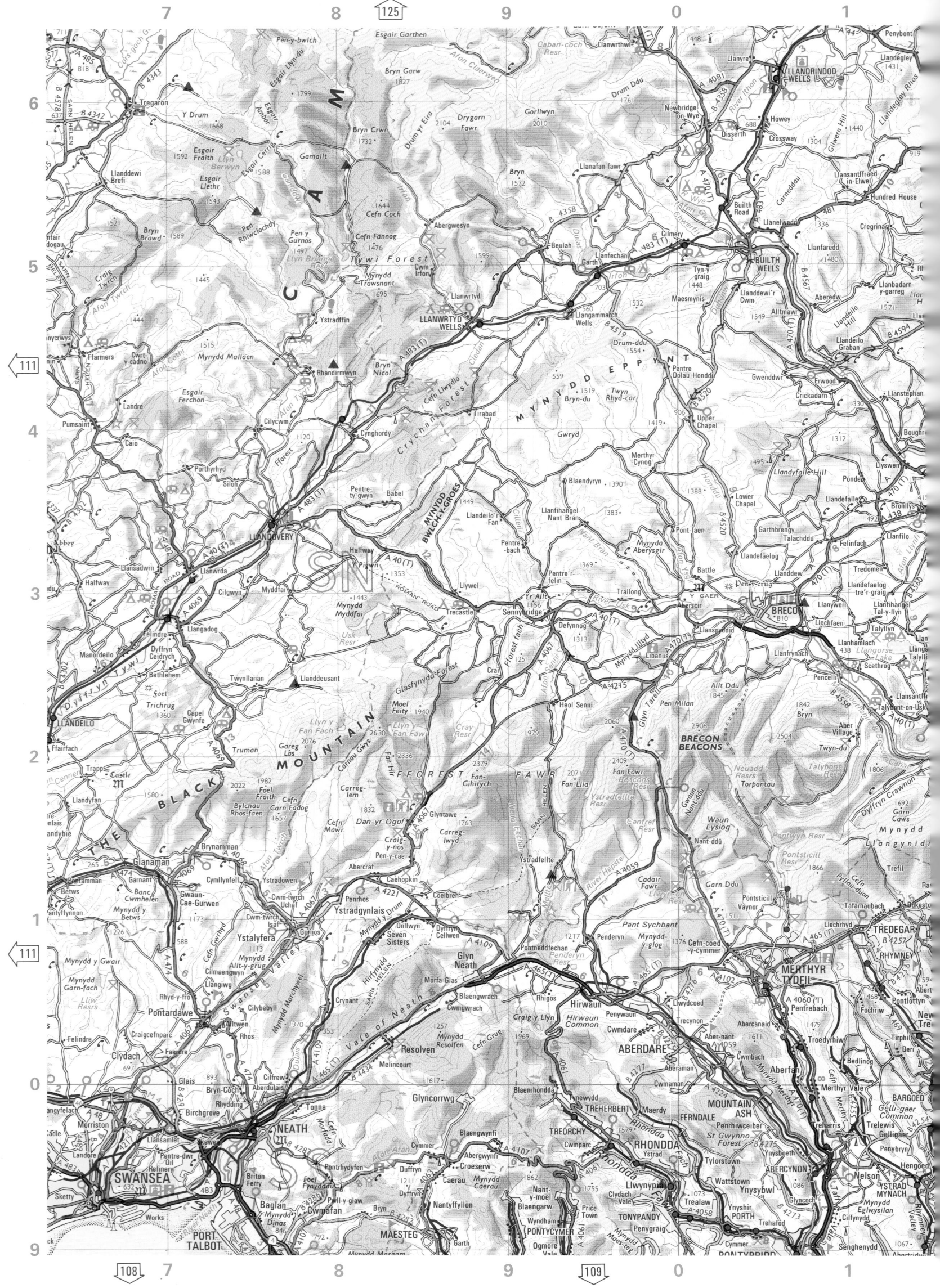

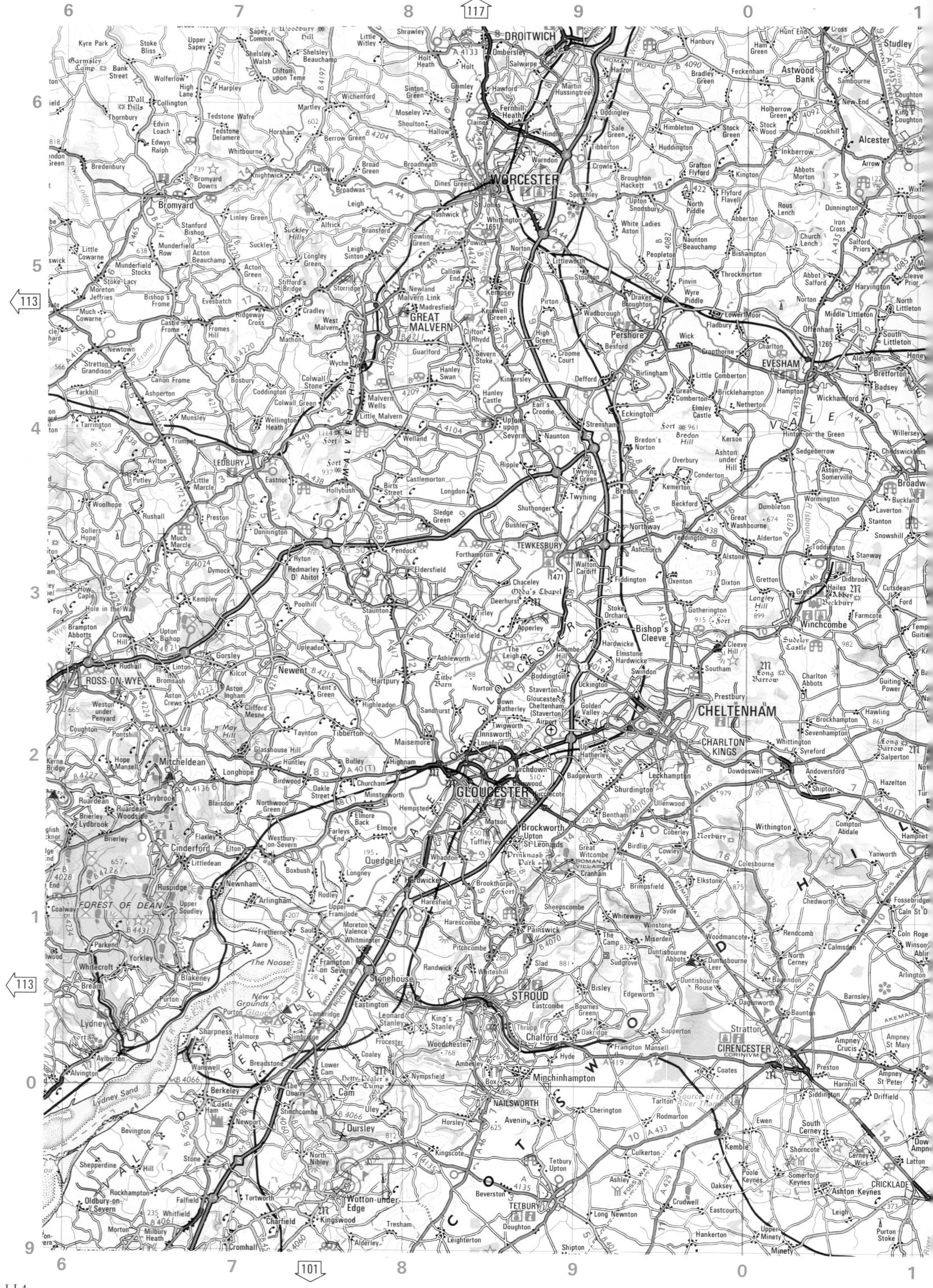

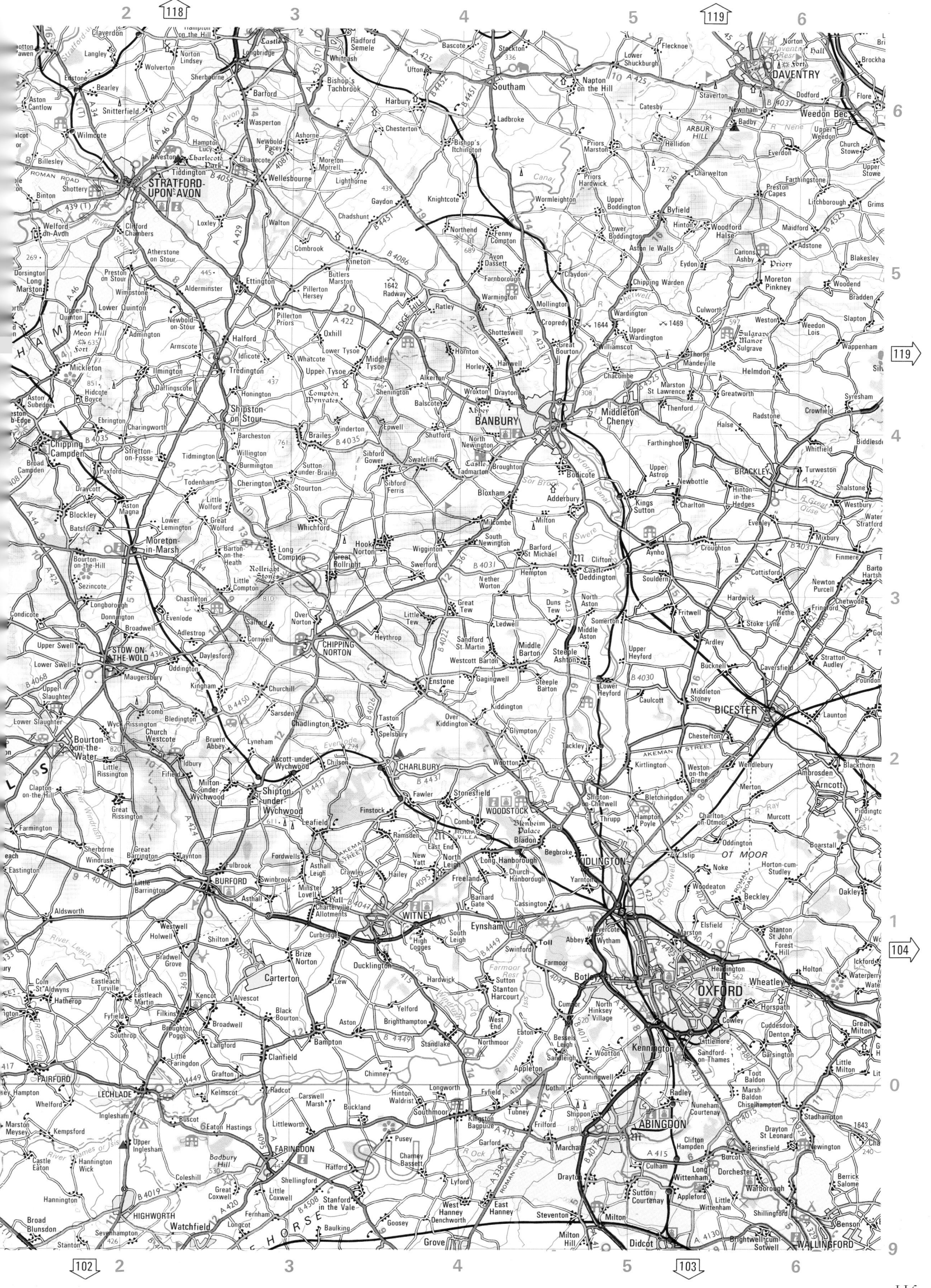

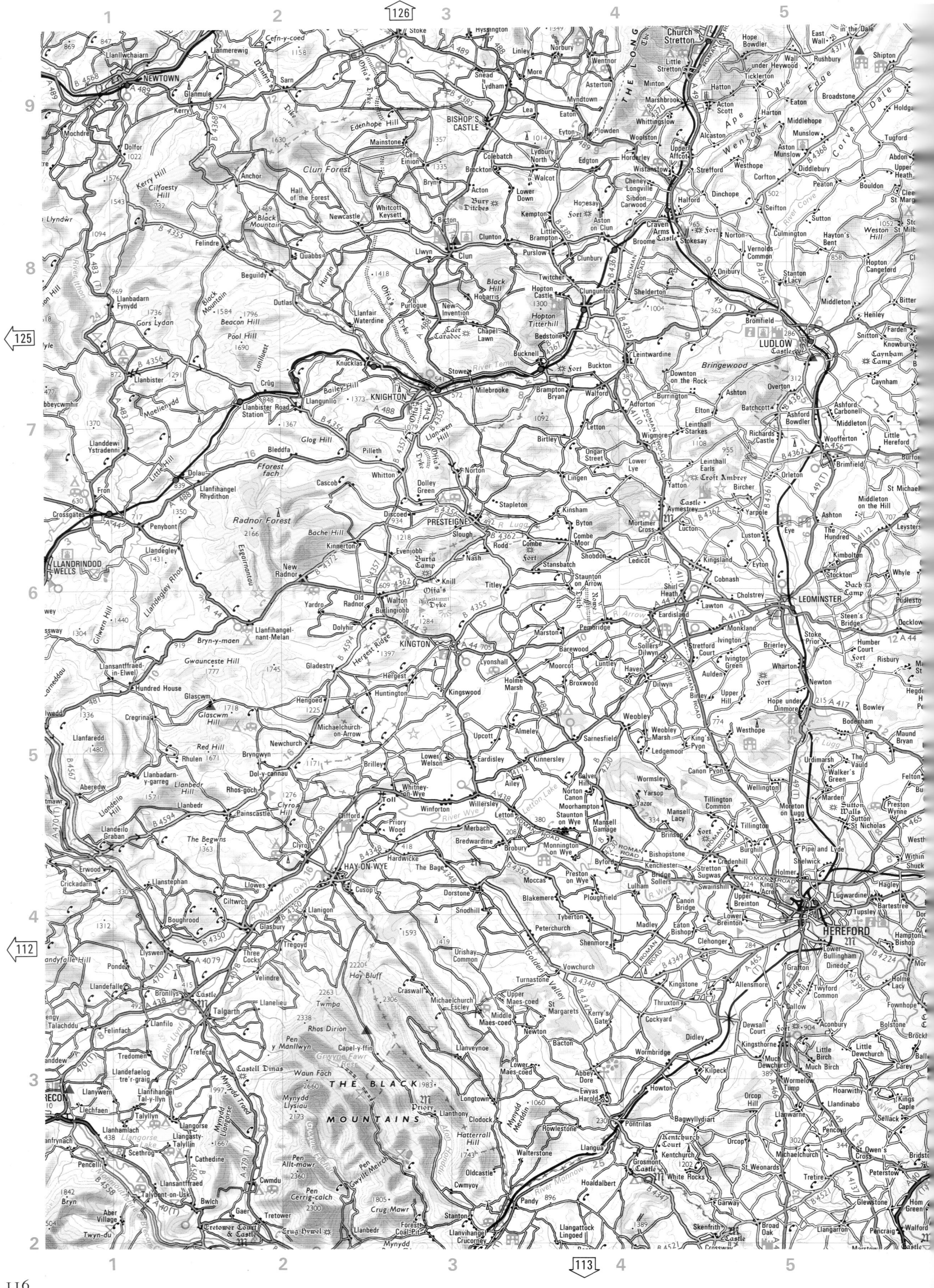

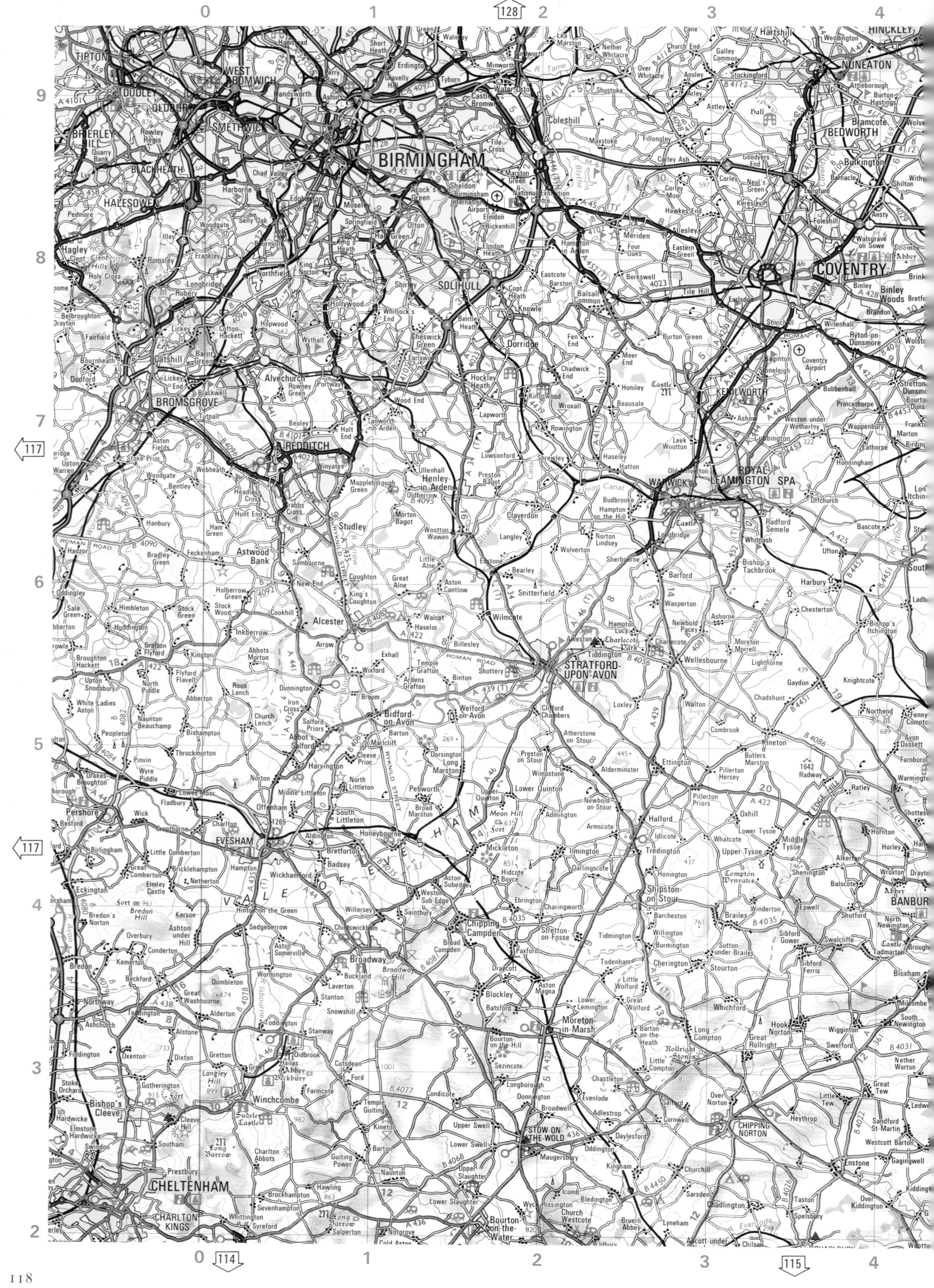

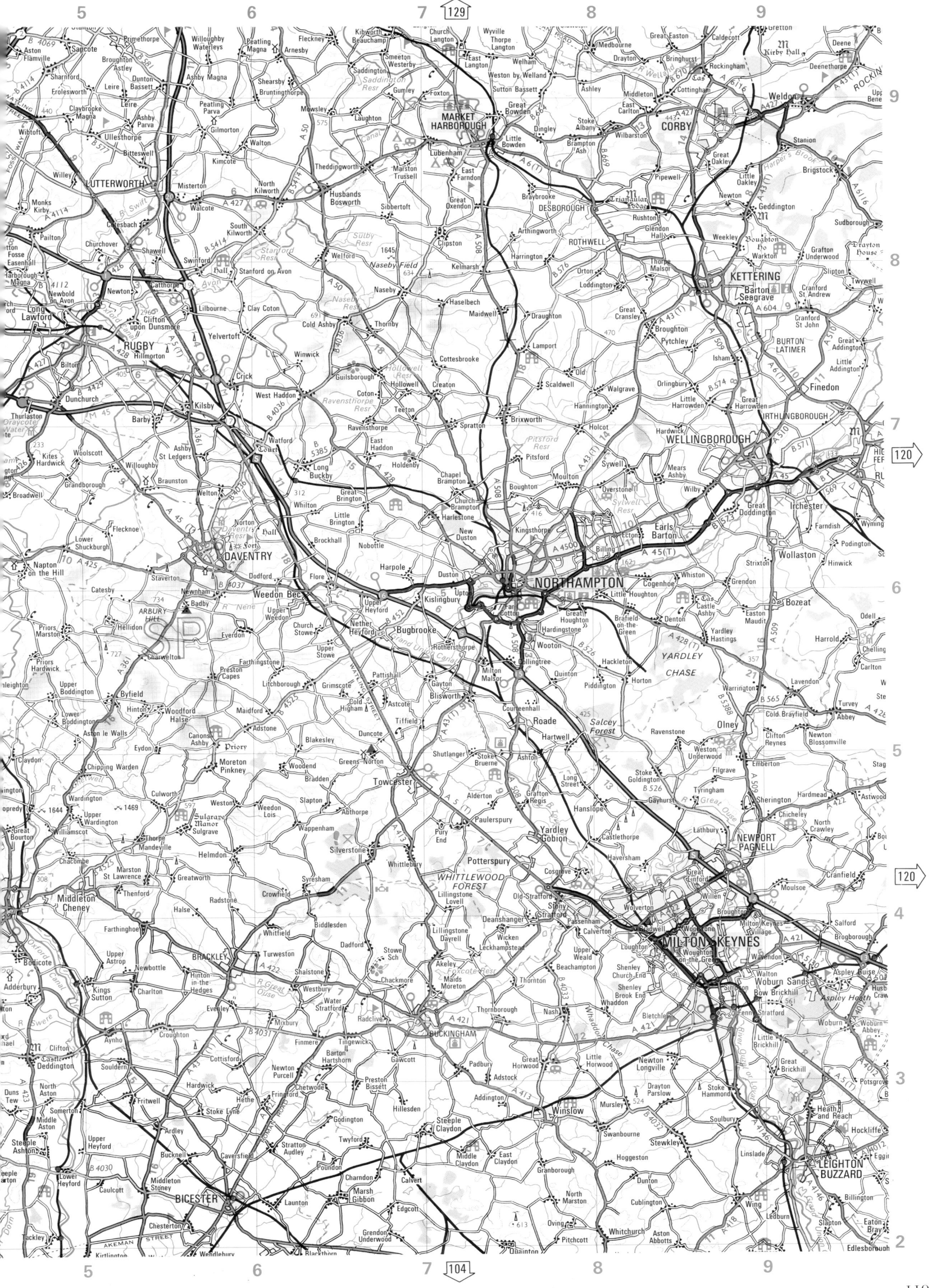

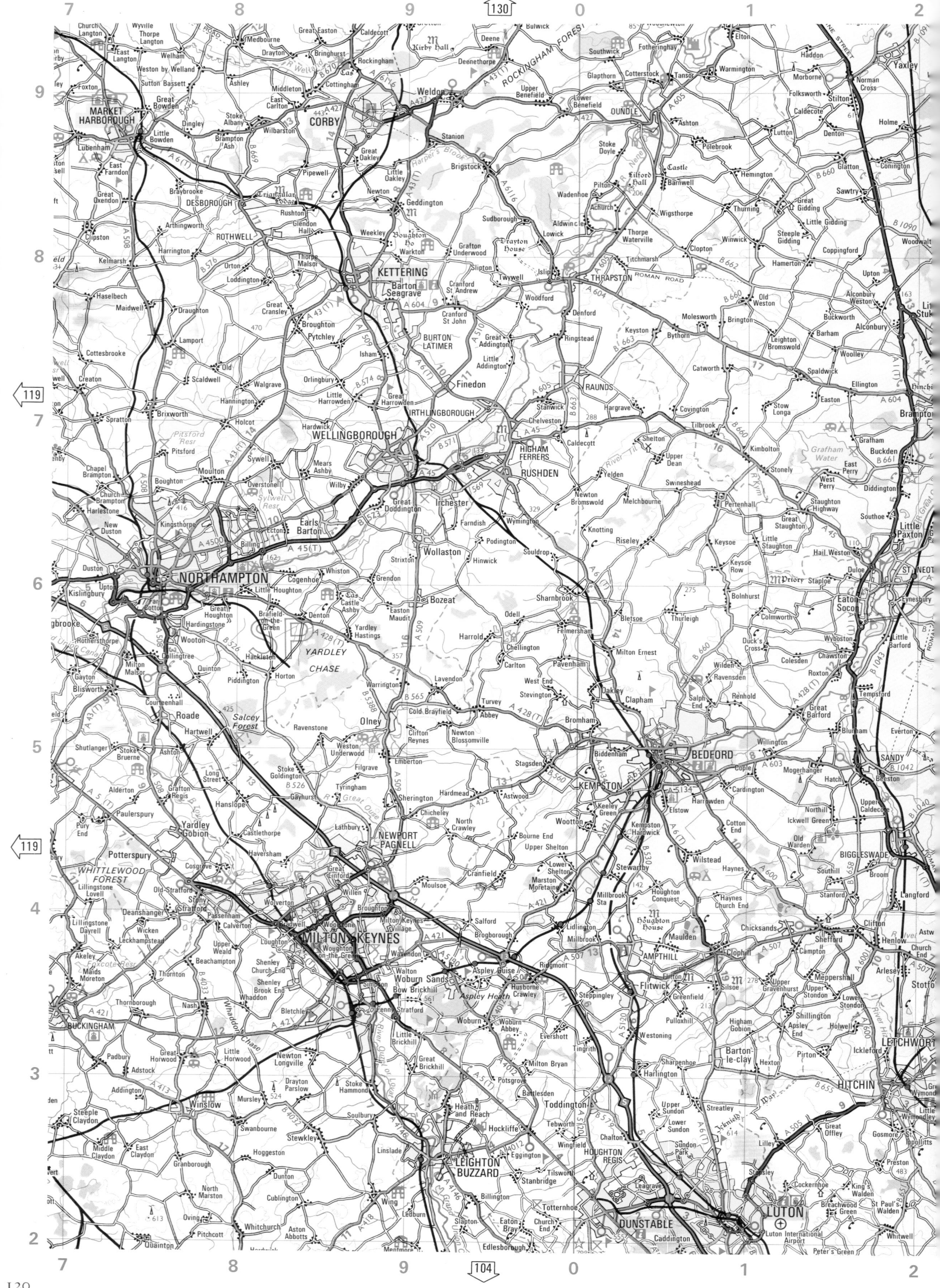

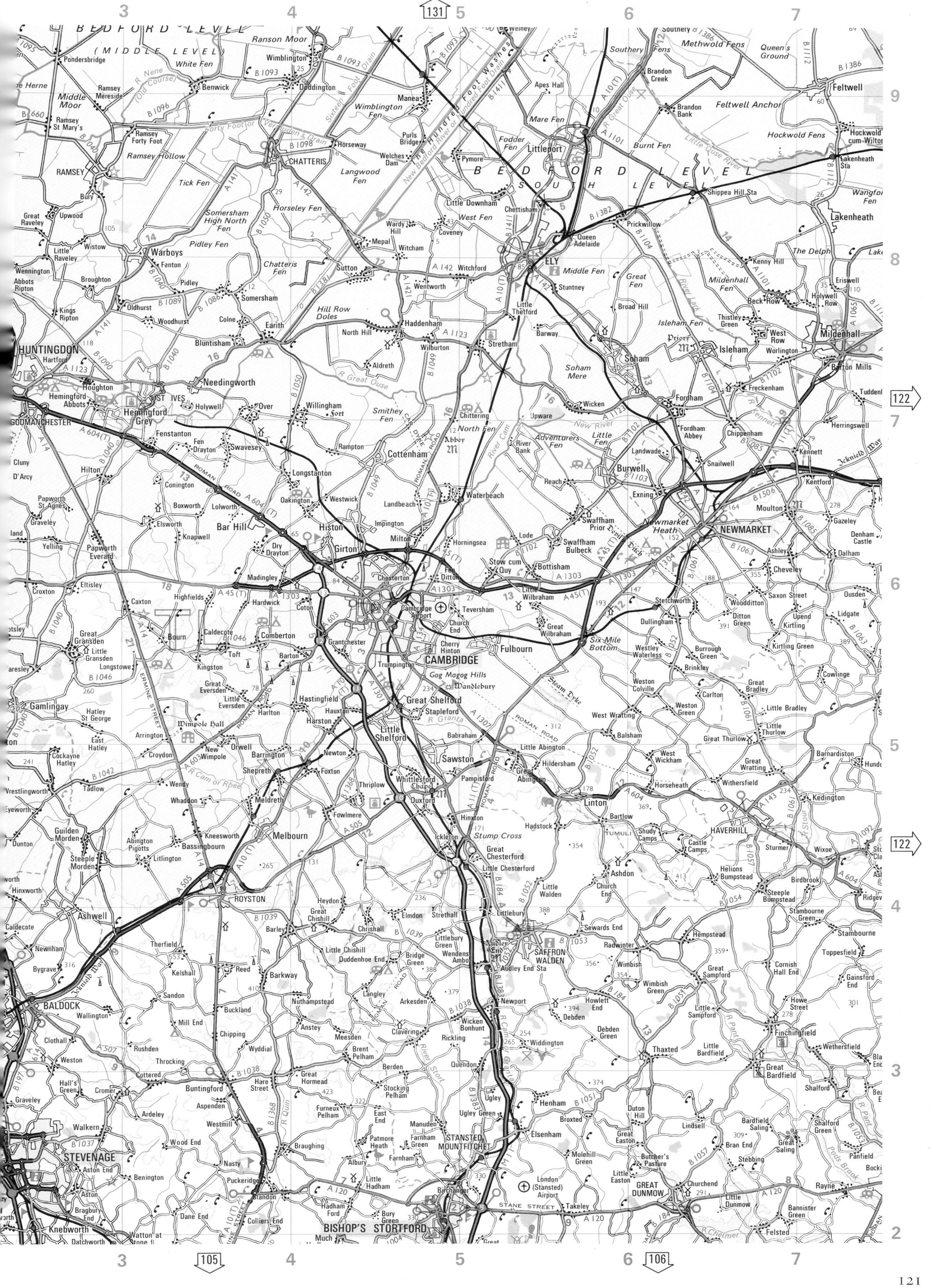

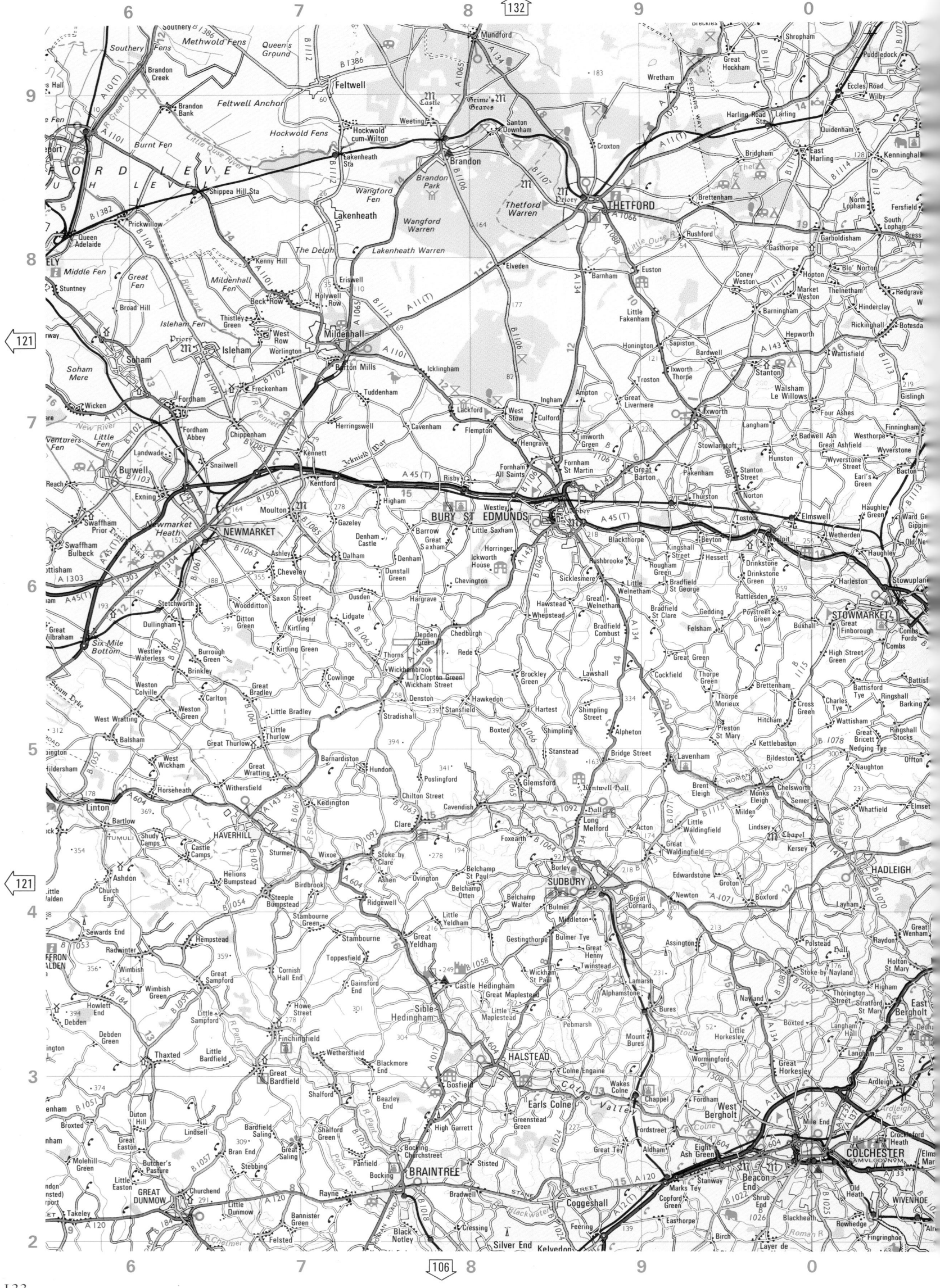

NORTH SEA

FELIXSTOWE to 🚢
Zeebrugge .... 5-8 hrs

HARWICH to 🚢
Hook of Holland 6¾-7½ hrs
Esbjerg .... 20 hrs
Kristiansand...... 22-24 hrs
Hamburg .... 21 hrs
Gothenburg............ 24 hrs

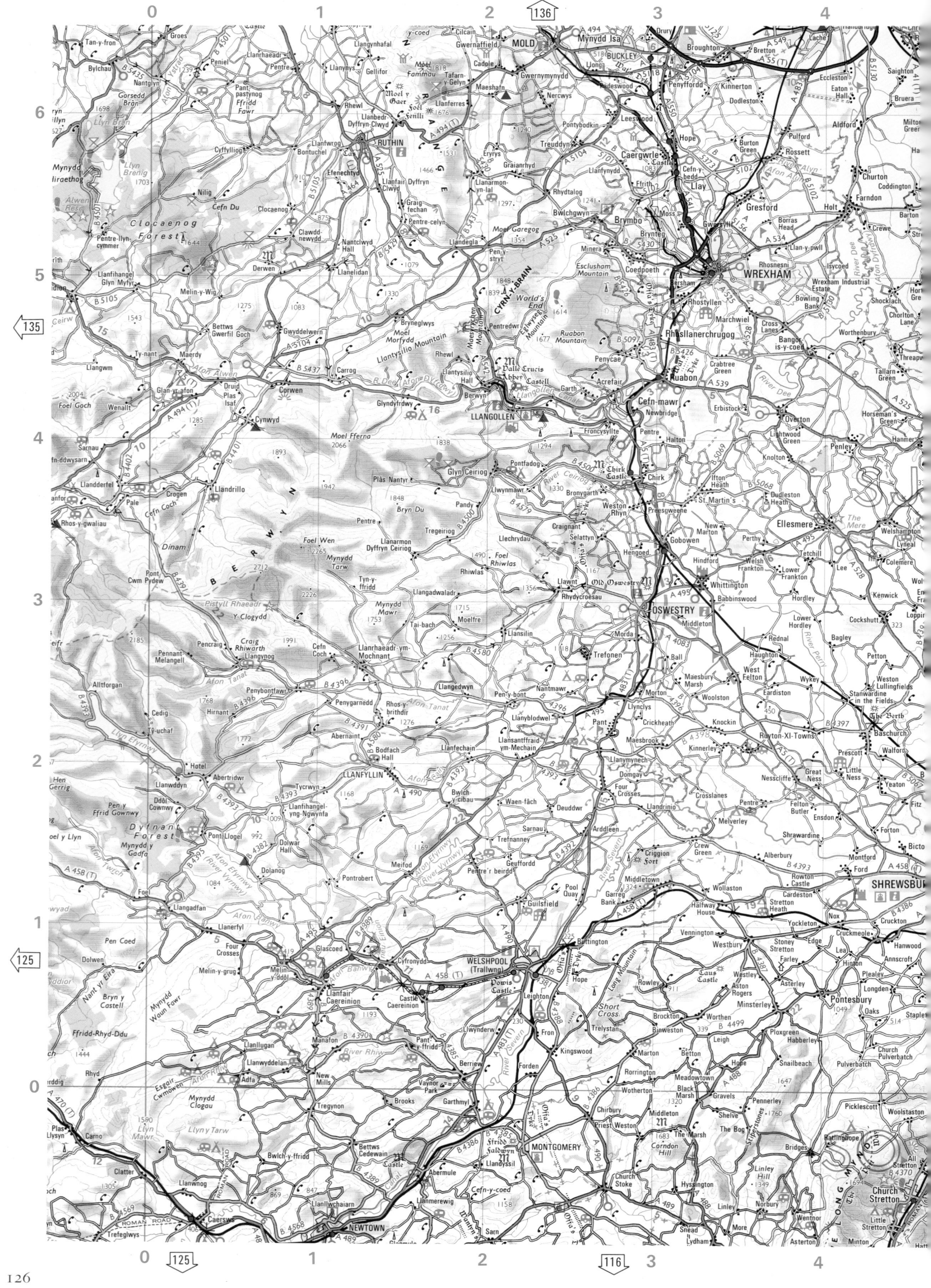

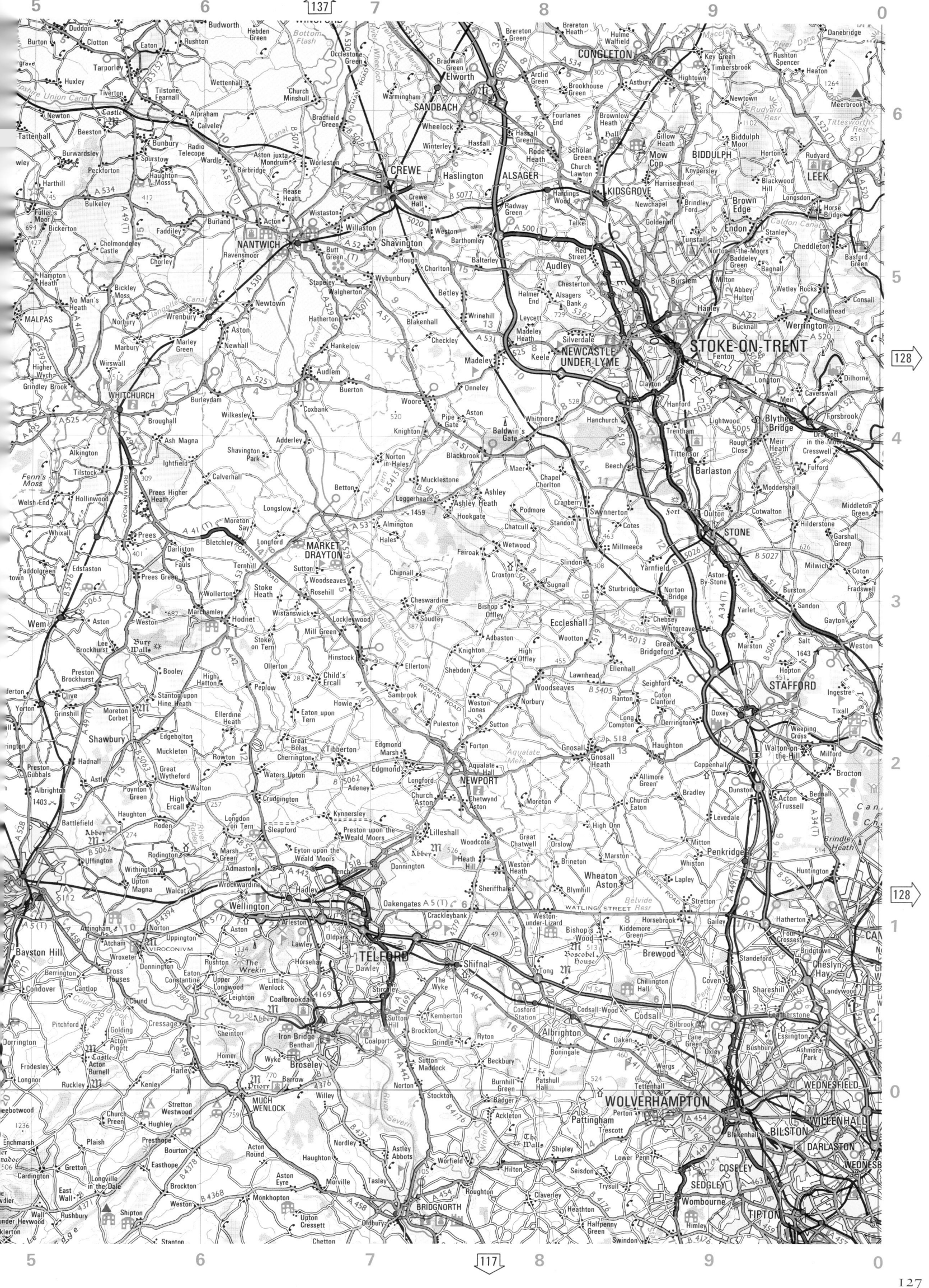

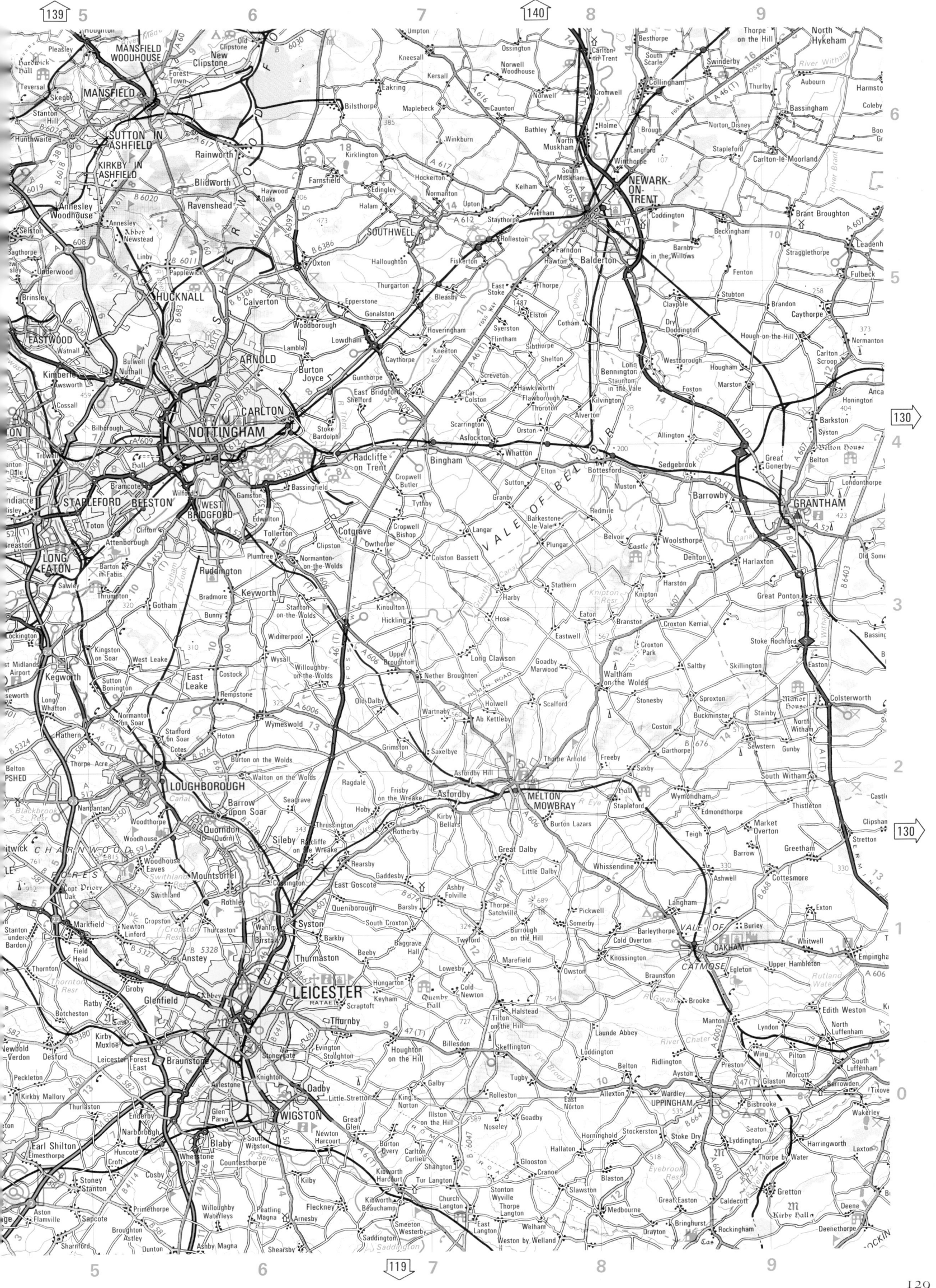

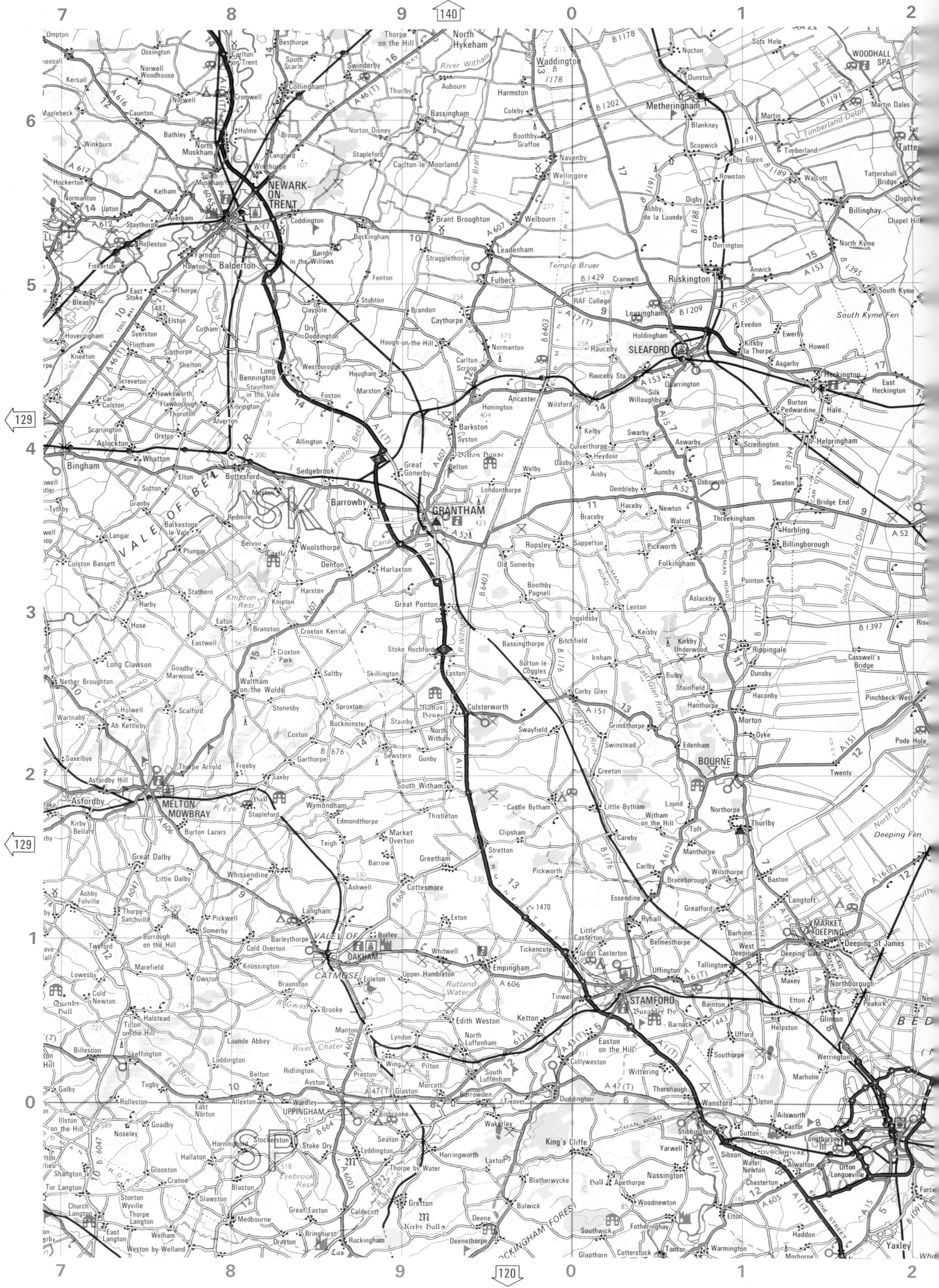

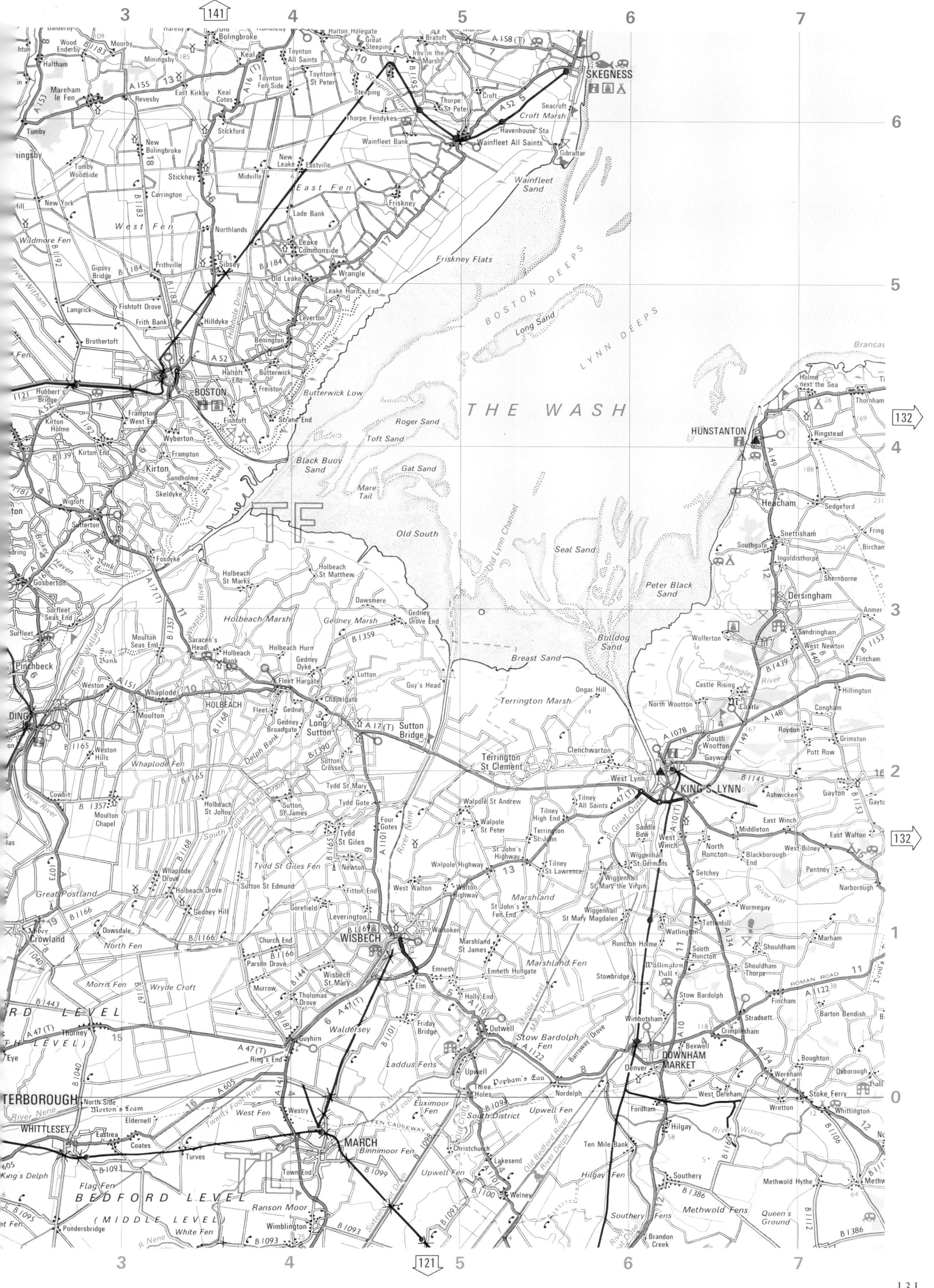

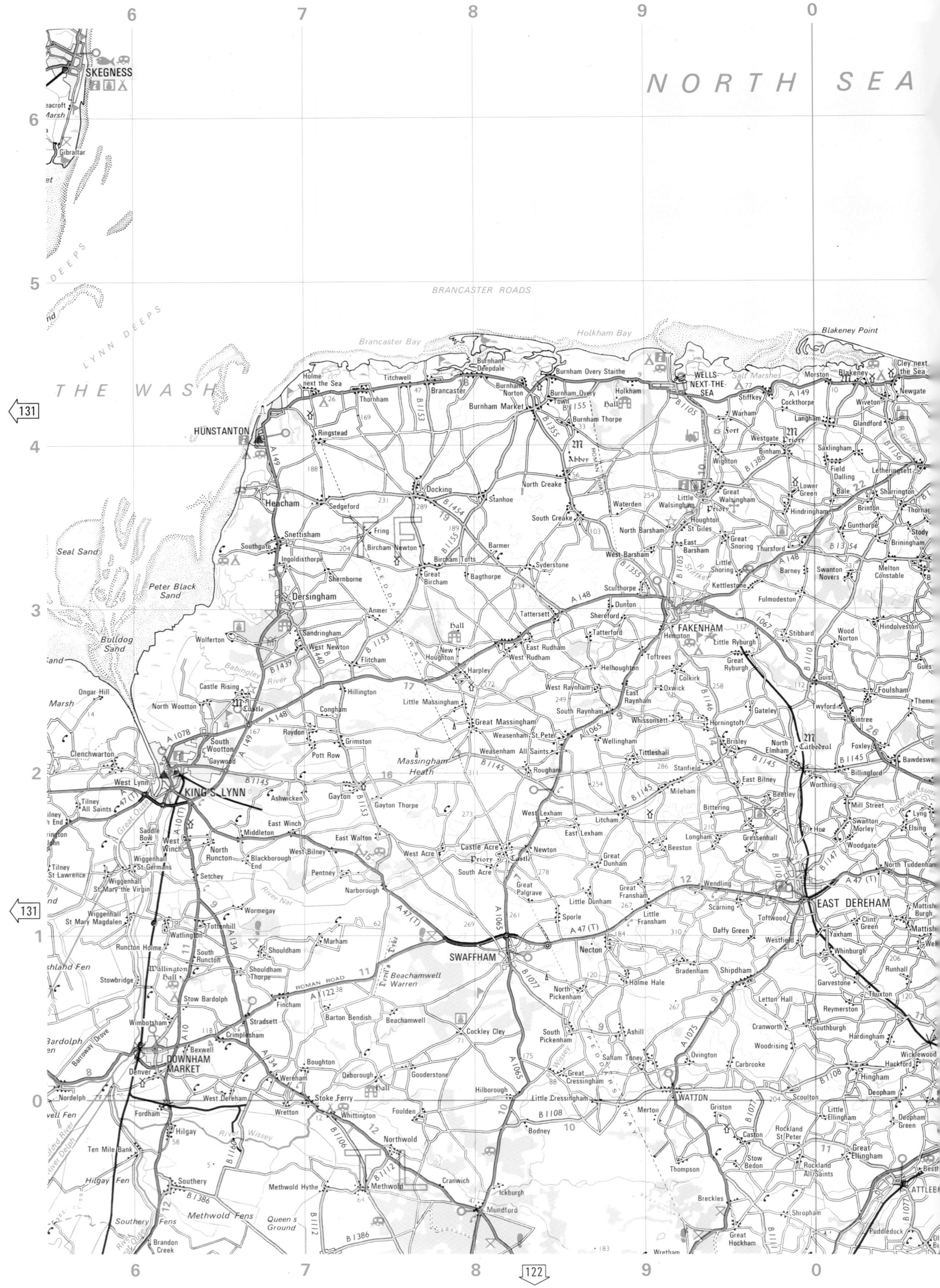

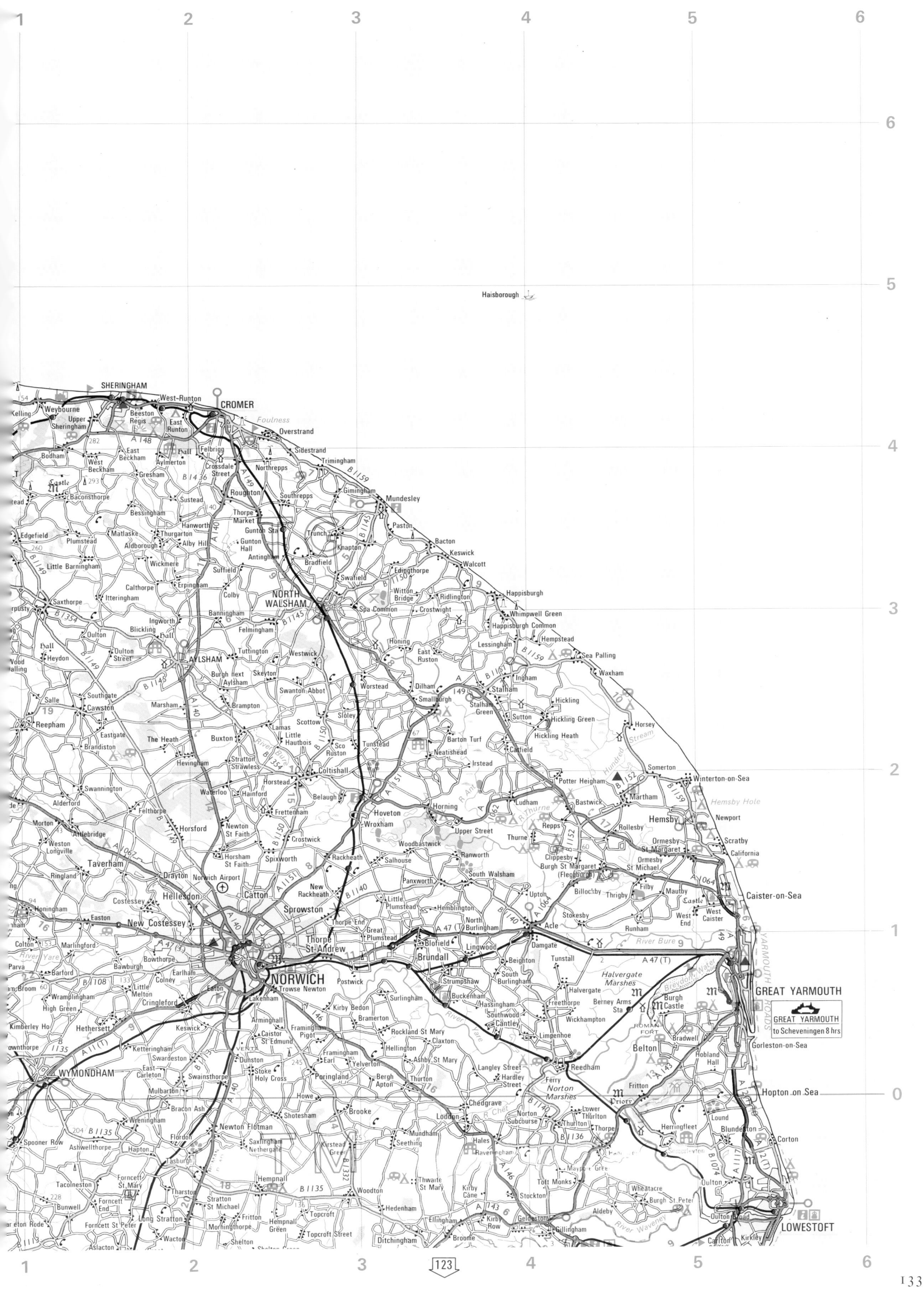

SHERINGHAM
West-Runton
CROMER
Foulness
Weybourne
Kelling
Upper
Sheringham
Beeston
Regis
East
Runton
Overstrand
A 148
Sidestrand
Bodham
East
Beckham
Felbrigg
Hall
Aylmerton
Northrepps
Trimingham
B 1159
West
Beckham
Gresham
Crossdale
Street
Castle
Baconsthorpe
Susted
Hanworth
Thorpe
Market
Roughton
Southrepps
Gimingham
Mundesley
Paston
Bessingham
A 140
Edgefield
Matlaske
Thurgarton
Hanworth
Guntton Sta.
Trunch
Knapton
Bacton
Keswick
Walcott
Plumstead
Aldborough
Alby Hill
Gunton
Hall
Antingham
Bradfield
Little Barningham
Wickmere
Suffield
Swafield
Saxthorpe
B 1354
Erpingham
Colby
NORTH
WALSHAM
Witton
Bridge
Edingthorpe
Happisburgh
Calthorpe
Itteringham
B 1145
Ridlington
Oulton
Ingworth
Blickling
Hall
Banningham
Spa Common
Crostwight
Happisburgh Common
Hall
Heydon
Oulton
Street
AYLSHAM
Felmingham
Honing
Lessingham
Hempstead
Tuttington
Westwick
East
Ruston
B 1159
Sea Palling
Salle
B 1145
Burgh next
Aylsham
Skeyton
Worstead
Dilham
Ingham
Waxham
Cawston
Marsham
Brampton
Smallburgh
Stalham
Hickling
Reepham
A 140
Scottow
Sloley
Stalham
Green
Sutton
Hickling Green
Eastgate
Buxton
Lamas
Little
Hautbois
Sco
Ruston
Tunstead
Barton Turf
Catfield
Hickling Heath
Horsey
Brandiston
The Heath
Hevingham
Stratton
Strawless
Coltishall
Neatishead
Irstead
Somerton
Swannington
Horstead
Belaugh
B 1152
Winterton-on-Sea
Alderford
Felthorpe
Waterloo
Hainford
Horning
Potter Heigham
Martham
B 1159
Hemsby Hole
Morton
Attlebridge
Horsford
Frettenham
Hoveton
Wroxham
Ludham
Bastwick
Hemsby
Newport
Weston
Longville
Newton
St. Faith
Crostwick
Upper Street
Thurne
Repps
Rollesby
Scratby
California
Ringland
Horsham
St. Faith
Spixworth
Woodbastwick
Ranworth
Clippesby
Ormesby
St. Margaret
Ormesby
St. Michael
Taverham
Drayton
Norwich Airport
Rackheath
Salhouse
South Walsham
Burgh St. Margaret
(Fleggburgh)
Filby
Caister-on-Sea
Hellesdon
Costessey
Catton
New
Rackheath
Panxworth
Upton
Billockby
Thrigby
Mautby
West
Caister
Honingham
Easton
Sprowston
Thorpe End
Great
Plumstead
Hemblington
North
Burlingham
Stokesby
West
End
Runham
New Costessey
Colton
Marlingford
A 47 (T)
Thorpe
St. Andrew
Blofield
Lingwood
Damgate
Acle
River Bure
A 149
GREAT YARMOUTH
Parva
Barford
Bowthorpe
Earlham
NORWICH
Postwick
Brundall
South
Burlingham
Beighton
Tunstall
A 47 (T)
Bawburgh
Colney
Trowse Newton
Strumpshaw
Buckenham
Halvergate
Marshes
Halvergate
Berney Arms
Sta.
Burgh
Castle
GREAT YARMOUTH
to Scheveningen 8 hrs
High Green
Cringleford
Lakenham
Kirby Bedon
Surlingham
Hassingham
Freethorpe
ROMAN
FORT
Gorleston-on-Sea
Kimberley Ho
Hethersett
Keswick
Arminghall
Caistor
St. Edmund
Bramerton
Rockland St. Mary
Southwood
Cantley
Wickhampton
Belton
Bradwell
Hobland
Hall
WYMONDHAM
A 11 (T)
Framingham
Pigot
Claxton
Limpenhoe
Swardeston
Framingham
Earl
Hellington
Langley Street
Reedham
Fritton
Hopton on Sea
East
Carleton
Dunston
Yelverton
Ashby St. Mary
Hardley
Street
Ferry
Spooner Row
Swainsthorpe
Mulbarton
Stoke
Holy Cross
Poringland
Bergh
Apton
Thurton
Norton
Marshes
Priory
Lound
Ashwellthorpe
Flordon
Howe
Chedgrave
Herringfleet
Blundeston
Bracon Ash
Shotesham
Brooke
Loddon
Norton
Subcourse
Lower
Thurlton
Thorpe
Corton
B 1135
Newton Flotman
Mundham
Hales
B 1136
Tacolneston
Hapton
Saxlingham
Nethergate
Kirstead
Green
Seething
Raveningham
Oulton
Broad
Bunwell
Tasburgh
Thwaite
St. Mary
Kirby
Cane
Stockton
Burgh St. Peter
Oulton Broad
Forncett
St. Mary
Hempnall
Woodton
Tott Monks
Wheatacre
LOWESTOFT
Aslacton
Forncett
End
Tharston
Stratton
St. Michael
Fritton
Hempnall
Green
Topcroft
Hedenham
B 1135
Aldeby
Forncett St. Peter
Long Stratton
Morningthorpe
Topcroft Street
Ellingham
Kirby
Row
Geldeston
Gillingham
Carlton
Kirkley
Wacton
Shelton
Ditchingham
Broome
Shelton Green
A 143

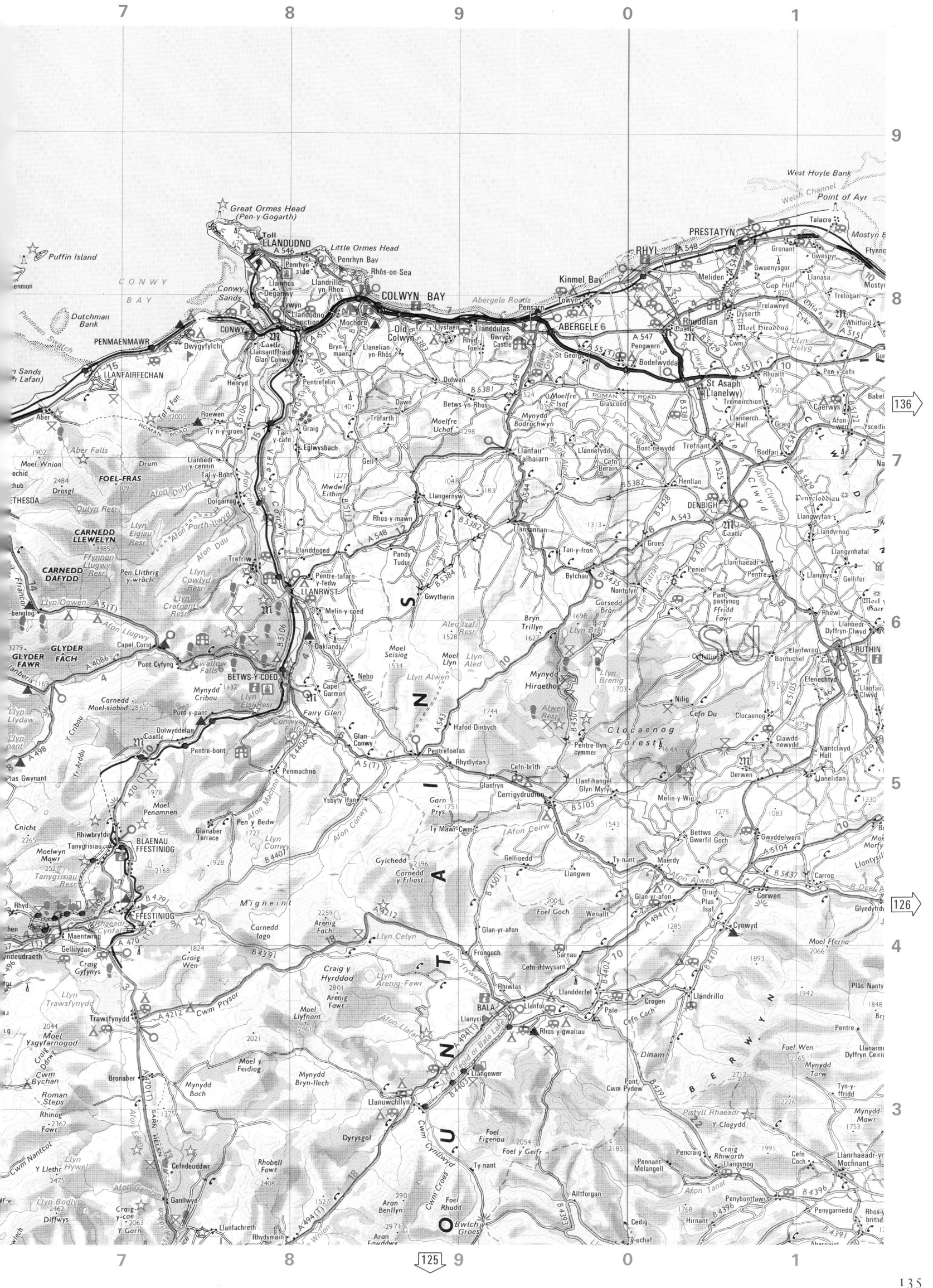

West Hoyle Bank
Welsh Channel
Point of Ayr

Puffin Island

Great Ormes Head
(Pen-y-Gogarth)
Toll
LLANDUDNO
A 546
Little Ormes Head
Penrhyn-side
Penrhyn Bay
Rhôs-on-Sea

PRESTATYN
RHYL A 548
Talacre
Mostyn B
Ffynnon
Gronant
Gwaenysgor
Gwespyr
Llanasa

CONWY
BAY
Conwy Sands
Llanrhos
Deganwy
Llandudno Junction
Llandrillo-yn-Rhos
COLWYN BAY
Abergele Roads
Kinmel Bay
Towyn
Pensarn
Meliden
Gop Hill 820
Trelawnyd
Dyserth
Moel Hiraddug
Llanasa
Trelogan
Whitford
Erke
A 5151

Penmaen Swatch

Dutchman Bank

PENMAENMAWR
Dwygyfylchi
CONWY
Castle
Llansantffraid
Glan Conwy
Bryn-y-maen
Mochdre
Old Colwyn
Llanelian-yn-Rhôs
Llysfaen
Llanddulas
Rhyd-y-foel
Gwrych Castle
ABERGELE 6
St George's
Pengwern
Bodelwyddan
A 55 (T)
RHUDDLAN
Castle
Dyserth
Moel Hiraddug
Clwyd
A 55 (T)
Pen-y-cefn
Gor

Aber Sands (y Lafan)
LLANFAIRFECHAN
Aber
Henryd
Pentrefelin
Dolwen
Betws-yn-Rhos
Moelfre Isaf
Glascoed
ROMAN ROAD
St Asaph (Llanelwy)
Tremeirchion
Llannerch Hall
Caerwys
Ysceifiog
Babel
A 5151

Moel Wnion
Roewen
Ty-n-y-groes
Tal y Fan 2000
ROMAN ROAD
Graig
Tal-y-cafn
Trofarth
Moelfre Uchaf 1298
Llanfair Talhaiarn
Llannefydd
Cefn Berain
Bont-newydd
Trefnant
Craig
Bodfari
A 541

Aber Falls 1902
Drum
Dawn
140
Llanddoged
Eglwysbach
Gell
Llangernyw
183
1048
A 544
Henllan
DENBIGH
Castle
Pen-y-cloddiau
Llangwyfan
Llandyrnog

FOEL-FRAS
Drosgl 2484
3091
Aton Dulyn
Dolgarrog
Mwdwl Eithin
1277
Rhos-y-mawn
B 5382
Llansannan
1313
Groes
A 543
Peniel
A 525
Llanrhaeadr
Pentre
Llanynys
Gellifor
Llangynhafal

CARNEDD LLEWELYN 3485
Ffynnon Llugwy Resr
Llyn Eigiau Resr
Afon 'Porth Llwyd
Trefriw
Pen Llithrig-y-wrâch
Llyn Cowlyd Resr
Pentre-tafarn-y-fedw
LLANRWST
Melin-y-coed
Gwytherin
Aled Isaf Resr
1528
Bryn Trillyn 1627
Llyn Bran
Gorsedd Bran
Nantglyn
Pant, pastynog
Ffridd Fawr
Rhewl
Moel Gaer

CARNEDD DAFYDD
Francon
Llyn Ogwen A 5 (T)
Llyn Crafnant Resr
Oaklands
Moel Seisiog 1534
Moel Llyn
Llyn Aled
Mynydd Hiraethog
Llyn Brenig 1703
Nilig
Cefn Du
Clocaenog
Llanfwrog
RUTHIN
Castle
Clawdd-newydd
Dyffryn-Clwyd

GLYDER FAWR
GLYDER FÂCH
Llanberis 1169
A 4086
Capel Curig
Pont Cyfyng
Swallow Falls
BETWS-Y-COED
Mynydd Cribau 1132
Carnedd Moel-siabod 2861
Pont-y-pant
A 5 (T)
Capel Garmon
Nebo
Moel Seisiog
Llyn Alwen
Hafod-Dinbych
1744
Alwen Resr
1644
Pentre-llyn-cymmer
Clocaenog Forest
Clawdd-newydd
Nantclwyd Hall
Derwen
Llanelidan
B 5429

Cnicht 2265
Llyn Llydaw
Llyn Nant
Plas Gwynant A 498
Dolwyddelan
Castle
Pentre-bont
Penmachno
Glan-Conwy
Conwy Falls
Fairy Glen
Rhydlydan
Pentrefoelas
A 5 (T)
Cefn-brith
Glasfryn
Cerrigydrudion
Llanfihangel
Glyn Myfyr
Melin-y-Wig
1275
1083
1330

Moel Penamnen
1978
Rhiwbryfdir
Tanygrisiau
BLAENAU FFESTINIOG
Glanaber Terrace
Pen y Bedw 1727
Afon Machno
Llyn Conwy 1928
B 4407
Ysbyty Ifan
Ty Mawr
Garn Prys 1751
Afon Ceirw
Cwm
Gellioedd
Bettws Gwerfil Goch
Gwyddelwern
B 5105
A 5104
Moel Morfydd

Moelwyn Mawr 2527
Tanygrisiau Resr 2168
Cwm Prysor
Gylchedd 2196
Carnedd y Filiast
Llangwm
Ty-nant
Maerdy
Afon Alwen
Glan-yr-afon
Druid
Plas Isaf
Carrog
B 5437
A Dee

Rhyd
FFESTINIOG
A 470
Maentwrog
Migneint
Arenig Fach 2259
Llyn Celyn
Glan-yr-afon
Foel Goch
Wenallt
2004
1543
Ty-nant
Glan-yr-afon
Corwen
A 494 (T)
Cynwyd
Moel Fferna 2066
Plâs Nanty

Gellilydan
Rhaeadr Cynfal
A 470
Craig Gyfynys
Graig Wen 1824
B 4391
Craig y Hyrddod 2801
Arenig Fawr 2461
Afon Llafar
Rhiwlas
Llandderfel
Pale
Crogen
Llandrillo
1893
1942
1848

Moel Ysgyfarnogod 2044
Craig Ddrwg
Cwm Bychan
Trawsfynydd
A 4212
Moel Llyfnant 2021
Llyn Trawsfynydd
BALA
Llanfor
Llanycil
Llyn Tegid or Bala Lake
Rhos-y-gwaliau
Cefn Coch
Dinam
Pont Cwm Pydew
Foel Wen 2265
Pentre
Mynydd Tarw 2712

Roman Steps
Rhinog Fawr 2362
Moel y Feidiog
Bronaber
SARN HELEN
Mynydd Bach
Moel y Feidiog
Mynydd Bryn-llech
Llanuwchllyn
Llangower
B 4403
Llanuwchllyn
Cwm Cynllwyd
Ty-nant
Pistyll Rhaeadr
Y Clogydd
Mynydd Mawr 2226
Tyn-y-ffridd

Llyn Hywel 2475
Y Llethr
Craig-y-cae 2063
Y Garn
Cefndeuddwr
Rhobell Fawr 2408
Dyrysgol
1527
Foel Figenau
Foel y Geifr 2054
2185
Pennant Melangell
Llangynog
1991
Cefn Coch
Llanrhaeadr-ym-Mochnant
Craig Rhiwarth
1753

Llyn Bodlyn 2462
Diffwys
Ganllwyd
Llanfachreth
Afon Gamlan
Rhydymain
Aran Benllyn 2901
Bwlch y Groes
Aran Fawddwy 2971
Foel Rhudd
Cwm Croes
Alltforgan
Cedig
Ty-uchaf
Aber
Hirnant
B 4391
Penybontfawr
B 4396
Pengarnedd
Rhos-brith
B 4396
1768

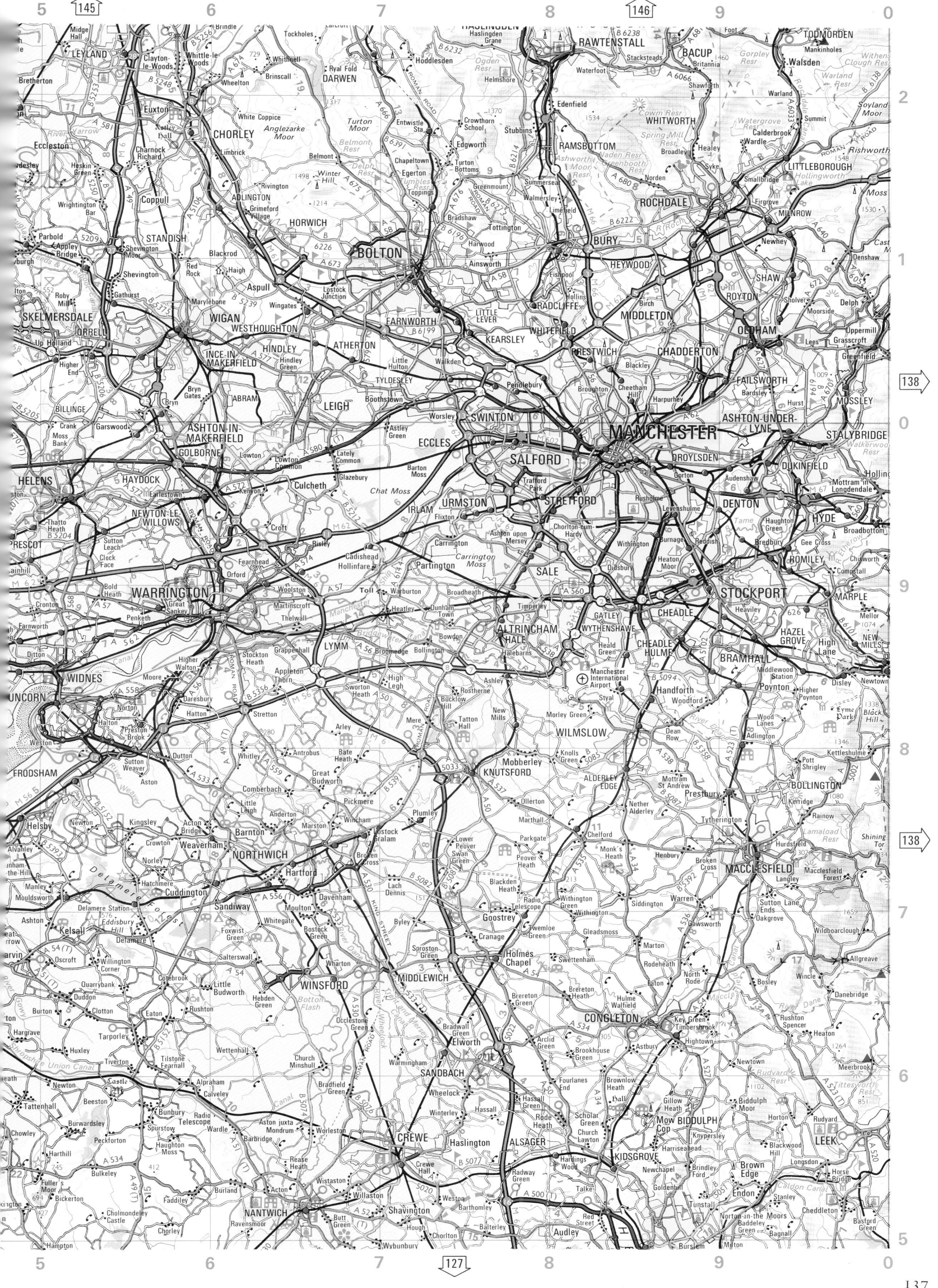

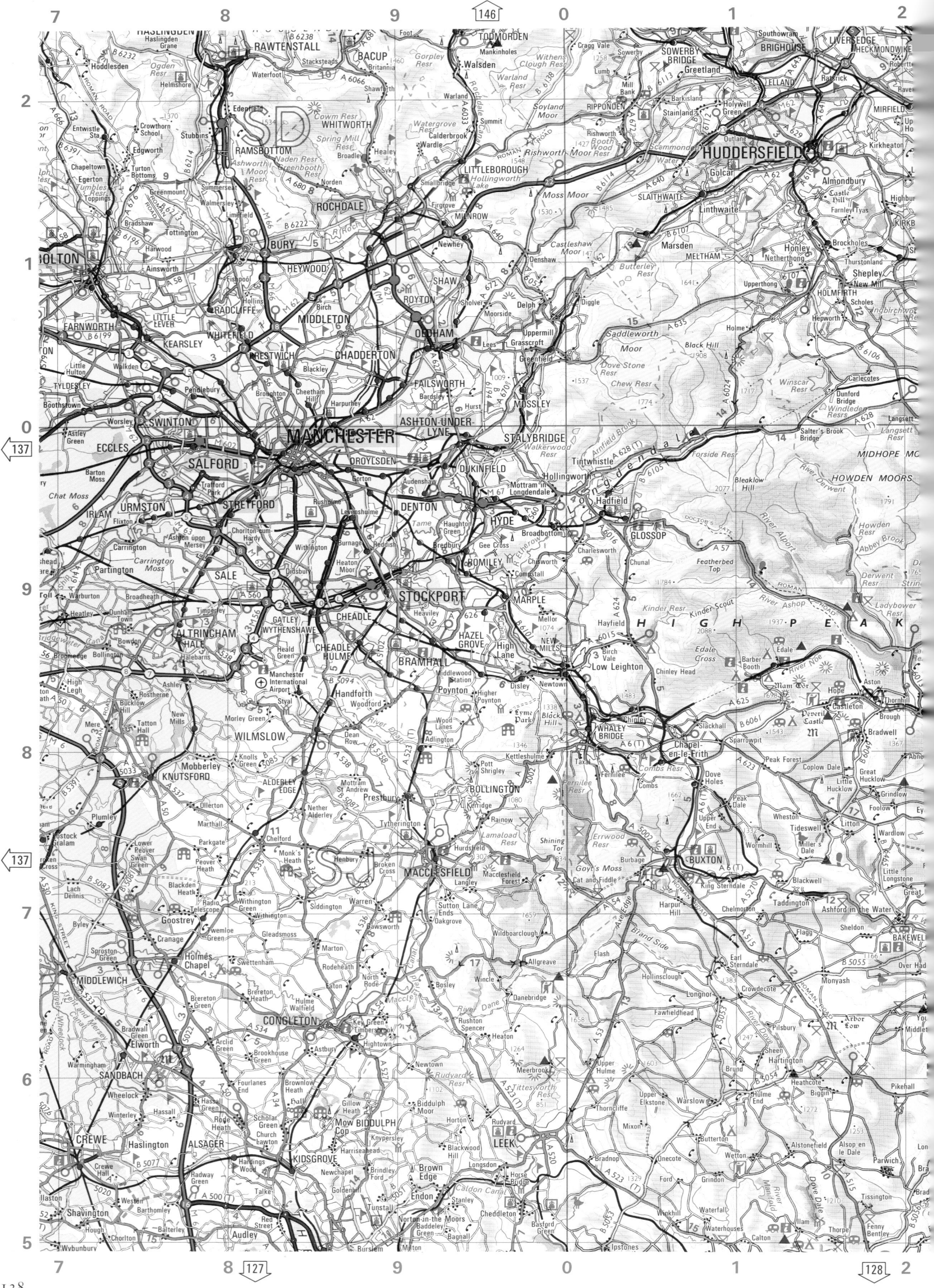

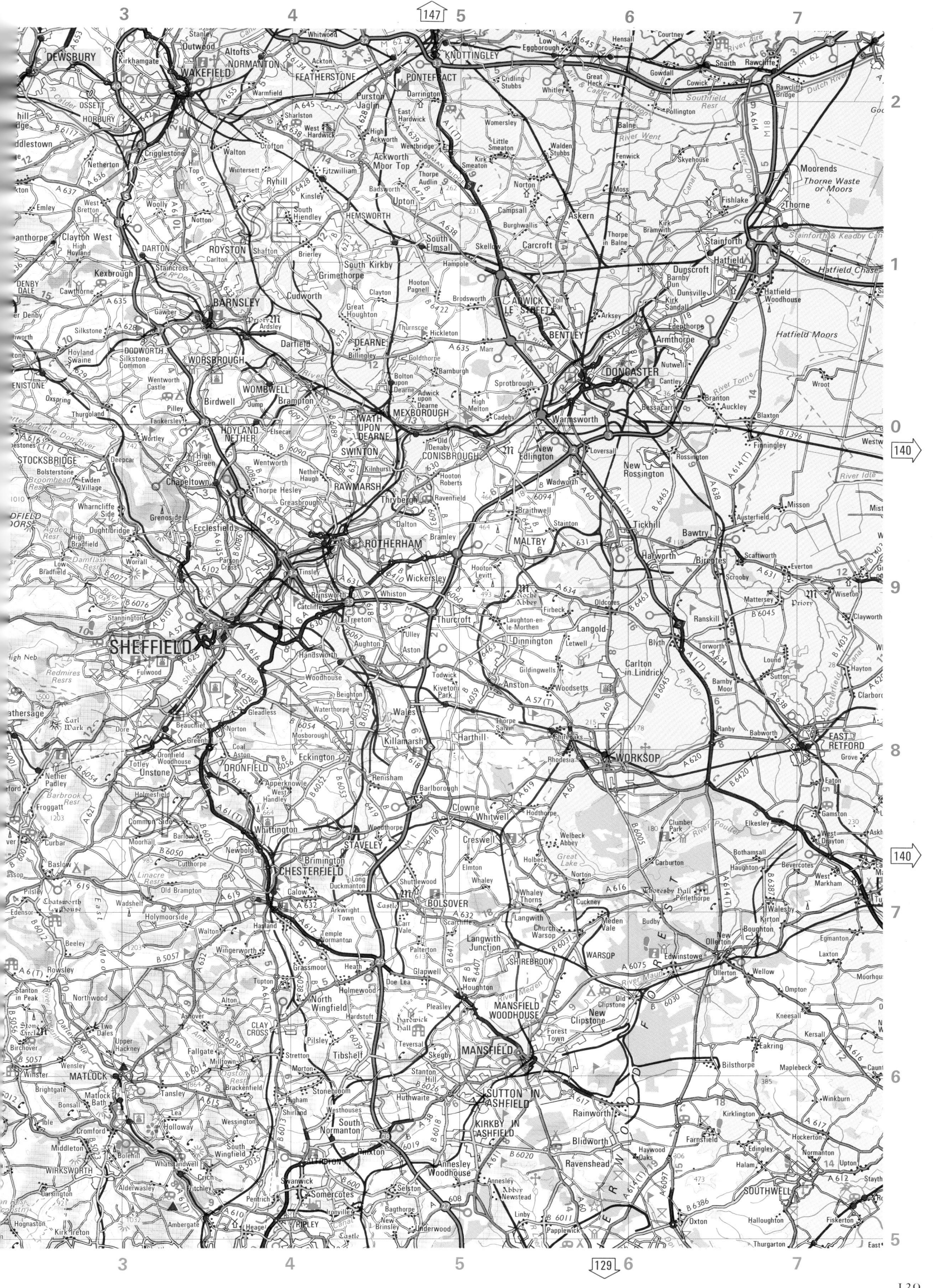

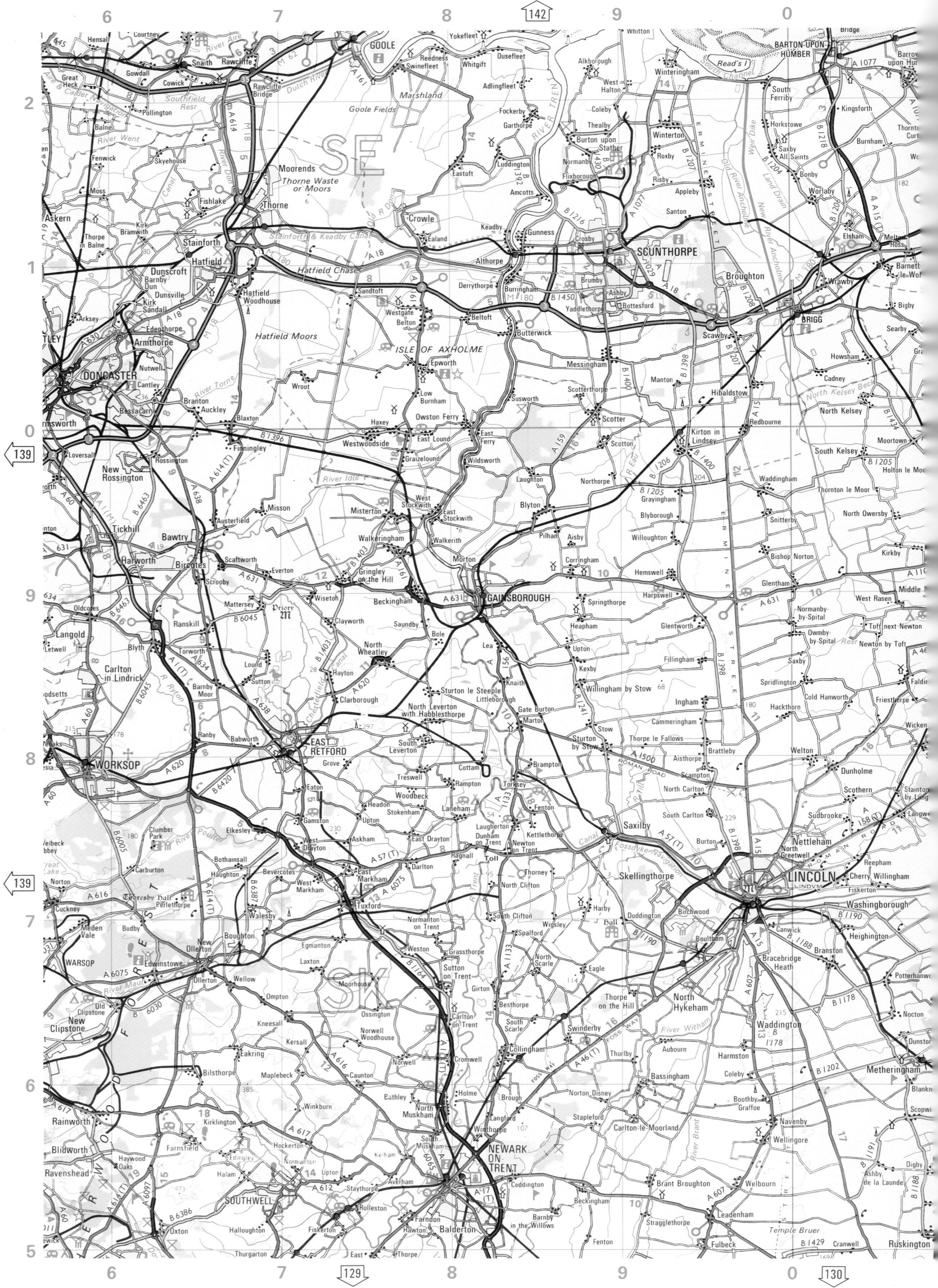

KINGSTON UPON HULL to
Rotterdam (Europoort)............14 hrs
Zeebrugge...........................15 hrs

NORTH SEA

SPURN HEAD

MOUTH OF THE HUMBER

RIVER HUMBER

GRIMSBY

CLEETHORPES

LOUTH

MABLETHORPE

Sutton on Sea

HORNCASTLE

ALFORD

SPILSBY

SKEGNESS

Ingoldmells

Chapel St Leonards

WOODHALL SPA

MARKET RASEN

THE WOLDS

East Fen

West Fen

Wildmore Fen

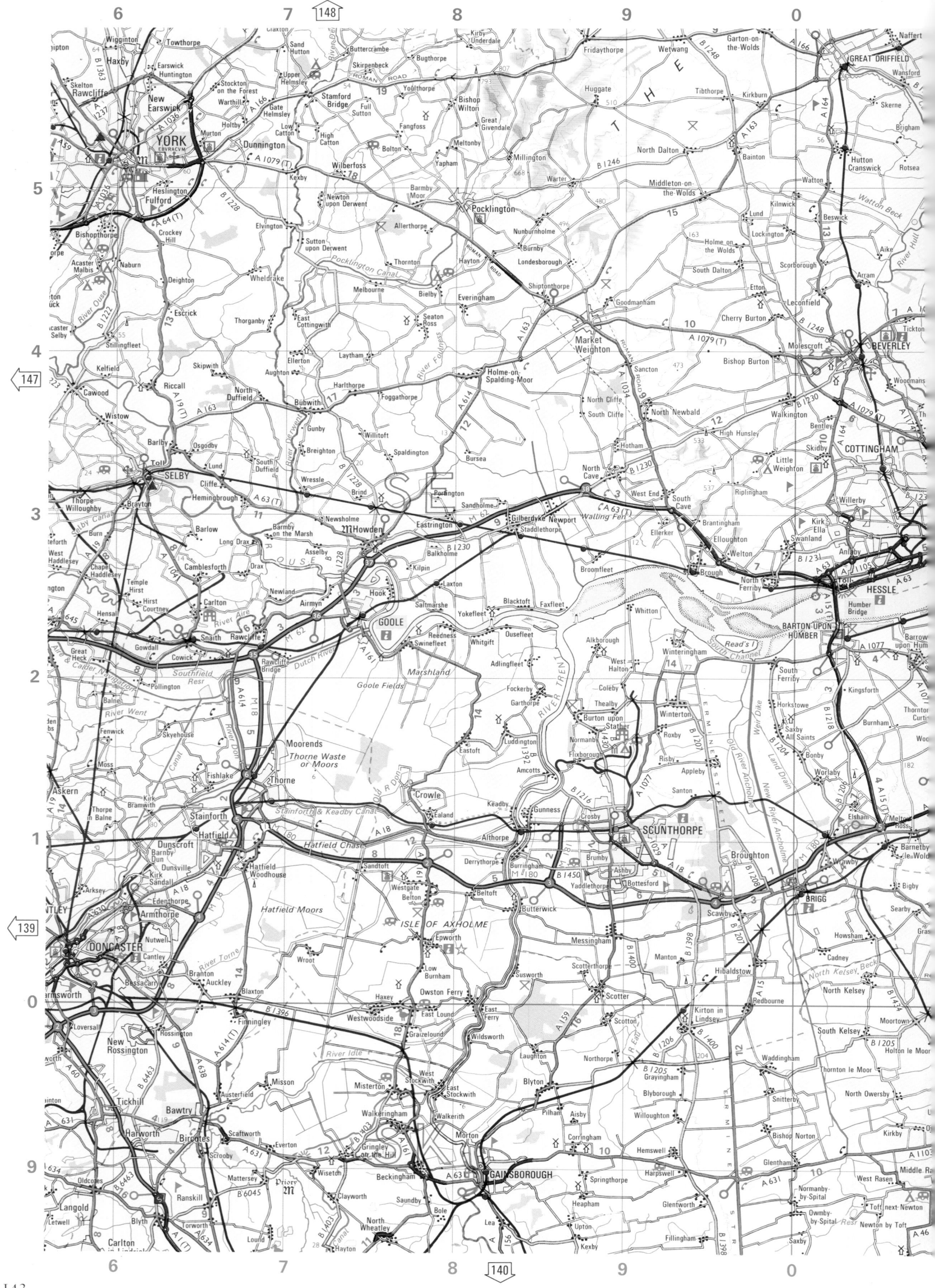

NORTH SEA

KINGSTON UPON HULL

HORNSEA

WITHERNSEA

SPURN HEAD

MOUTH OF THE HUMBER

RIVER HUMBER

GRIMSBY

CLEETHORPES

LOUTH

MARKET RASEN

MABLETHORPE

KINGSTON UPON HULL to	
Rotterdam (Europoort)	14 hrs
Zeebrugge	15 hrs

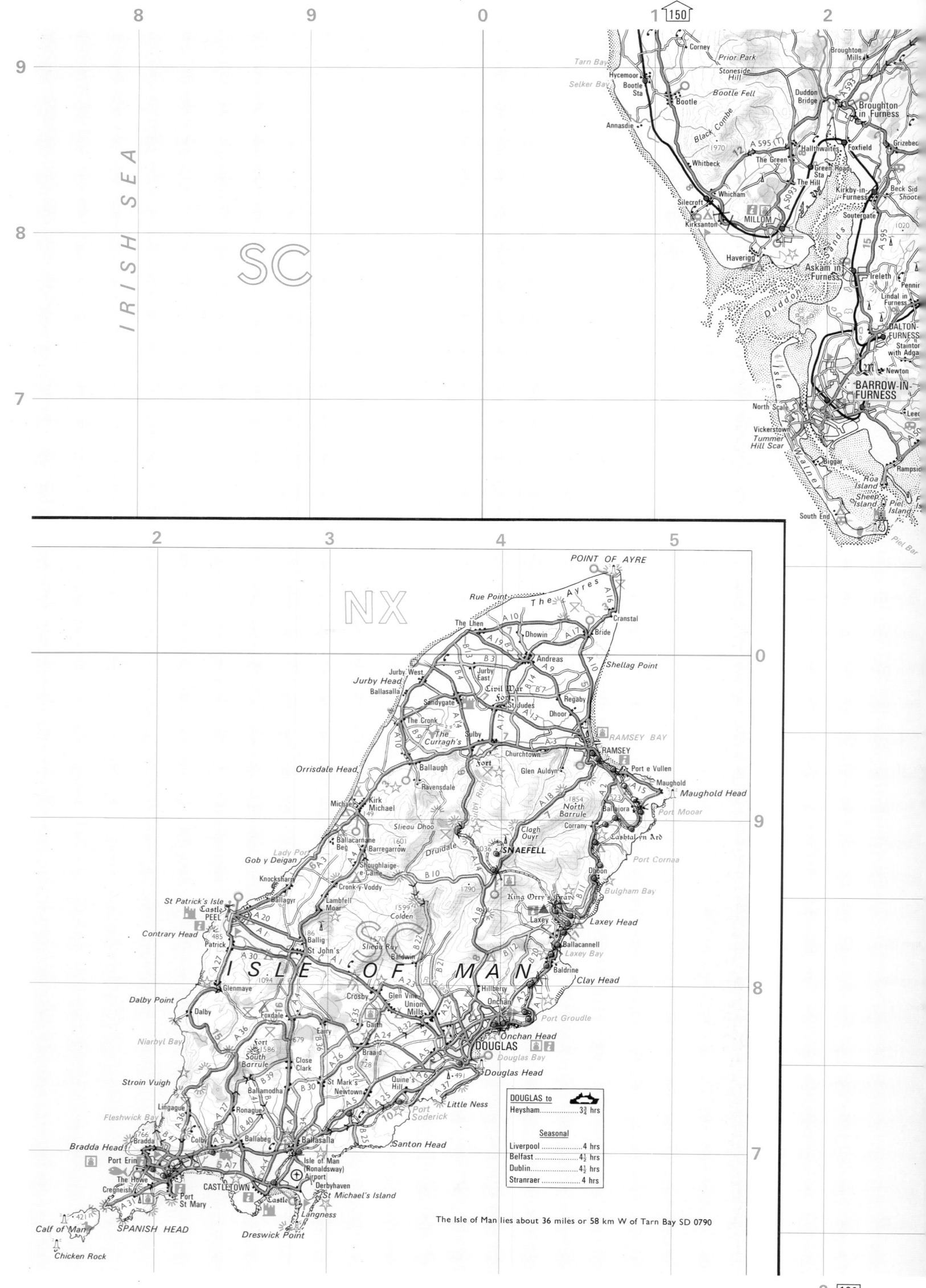

IRISH SEA

SC

150

Tarn Bay

Selker Bay

Corney
Prior Park
Broughton Mills
Hycemoor
Stoneside Hill
Bootle Sta
Bootle Fell
Duddon Bridge
Broughton in Furness
Bootle
Annasdie
Black Combe (1970)
Duddon Sands
Grizebeck
A 595 (T)
Whitbeck
Hallthwaites
Foxfield
The Green
Green Road Sta
Beck Side
Shoot
The Hill
Whicham
Kirkby-in-Furness
A 5093
Soutergate
Silecroft
MILLOM
Askam in Furness
Ireleth
Pennir
Kirksanton
Lindal in Furness
Haverigg
DALTON-FURNESS
Stainton with Adga
Newton
North Scale
BARROW-IN-FURNESS
Vickerstown
Tummer Hill Scar
Biggar
Rampsi
Roa Island
Sheep Island
Piel Island
South End
Piel Bar

NX

POINT OF AYRE

Rue Point
The Ayres
A 16
Cranstal
The Lhen
A 10
Dhowin
A 17
Bride
Jurby West
Jurby Head
Jurby East
Shellag Point
Jurby Head
Andreas
A 9
Ballasalla
Civil War Fort
Regaby
Sandygate
St Judes
Dhoor
The Cronk
Sulby
RAMSEY BAY
The Curragh's
Churchtown
RAMSEY
Orrisdale Head
Ballaugh
Fort
Glen Auldyn
Port e Vullen
Ravensdale
Maughold
Kirk Michael
Maughold Head
Michael
North Barrule 1854
Ballajora
Slieau Dhoo
Clagh Ouyr
Port Mooar
Ballacarnane Beg
Druidale
SNAEFELL 2036
Corrany
Barregarrow
Cashtal yn Ard
Lady Port
Gob y Deigan
Shoughlaige-e-Caine
B 10
Port Cornaa
Knocksharry
Cronk-y-Voddy
1790
Dhoon
Ballagyr
Lambfell Moar
Bulgham Bay
St Patrick's Isle
1599
King Orry's Grave
Castle
Colden
PEEL
Contrary Head
485
Ballig
Sloc Ray
Laxey
Patrick
St John's
Baldwin
Laxey Head
A 1
ISLE OF MAN
Ballacannell
Laxey Bay
Glenmaye
Crosby
Glen Vine
Baldrine
Dalby Point
Foxdale
Union Mills
Hillberry
Clay Head
Dalby
Garth
Onchan
Niarbyl Bay
Earry
1586
Port Groudle
Close Clark
Braaid
Onchan Head
DOUGLAS
Stroin Vuigh
Ballamodha
St Mark's
Quine's Hill
Douglas Bay
Lingague
Ronague
Newtown
Douglas Head
Fleshwick Bay
Colby
Ballabeg
Little Ness
Bradda Head
Ballasalla
Port Soderick
Port Erin
The Howe
Ballasalla
Santon Head
Cregneish
CASTLETOWN
Isle of Man (Ronaldsway) Airport
Port St Mary
Castle
Derbyhaven
Calf of Man
SPANISH HEAD
Langness
St Michael's Island
Chicken Rock
Dreswick Point

DOUGLAS to	
Heysham	3¾ hrs
Seasonal	
Liverpool	4 hrs
Belfast	4¾ hrs
Dublin	4½ hrs
Stranraer	4 hrs

The Isle of Man lies about 36 miles or 58 km W of Tarn Bay SD 0790

2 136

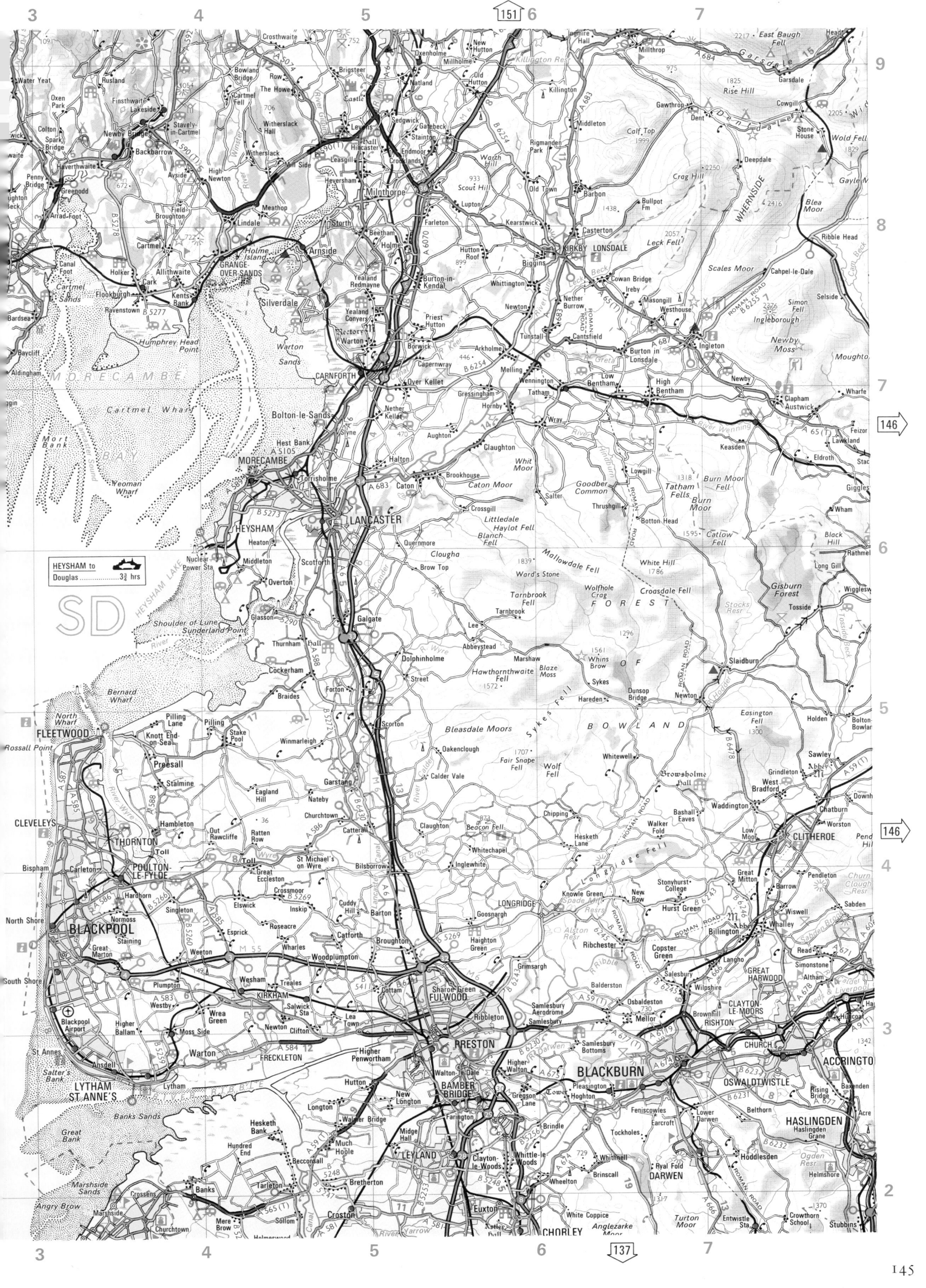

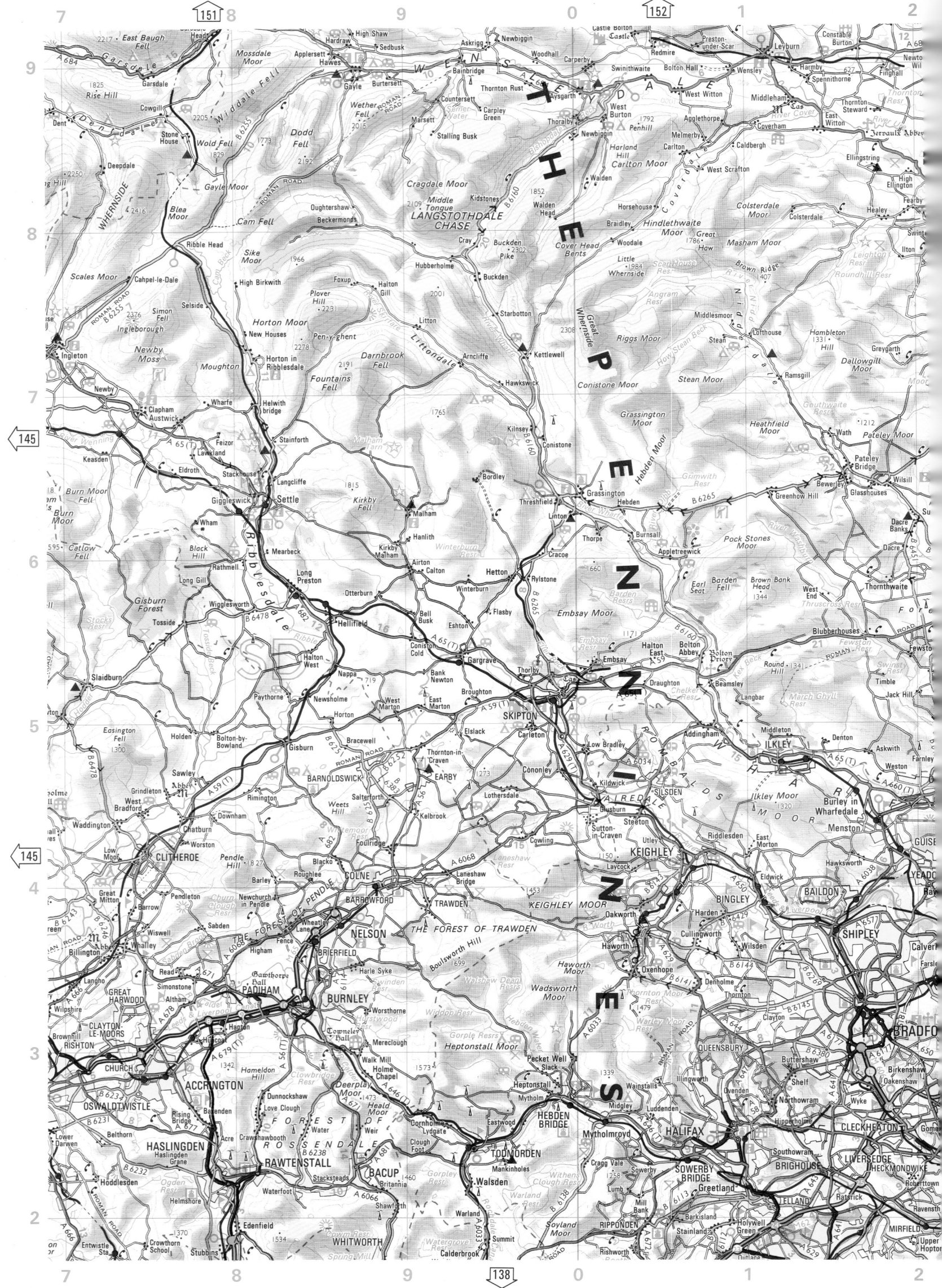

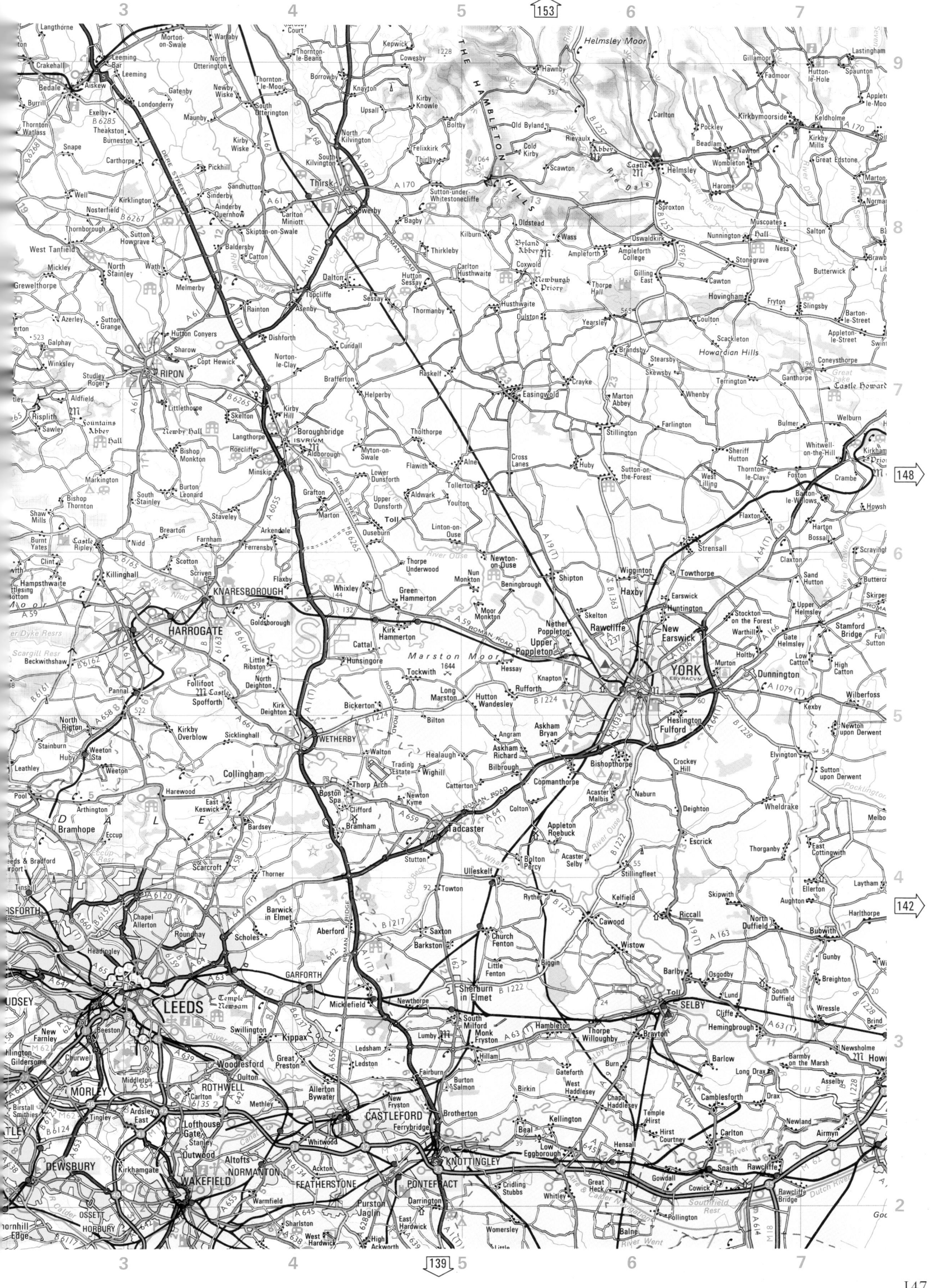

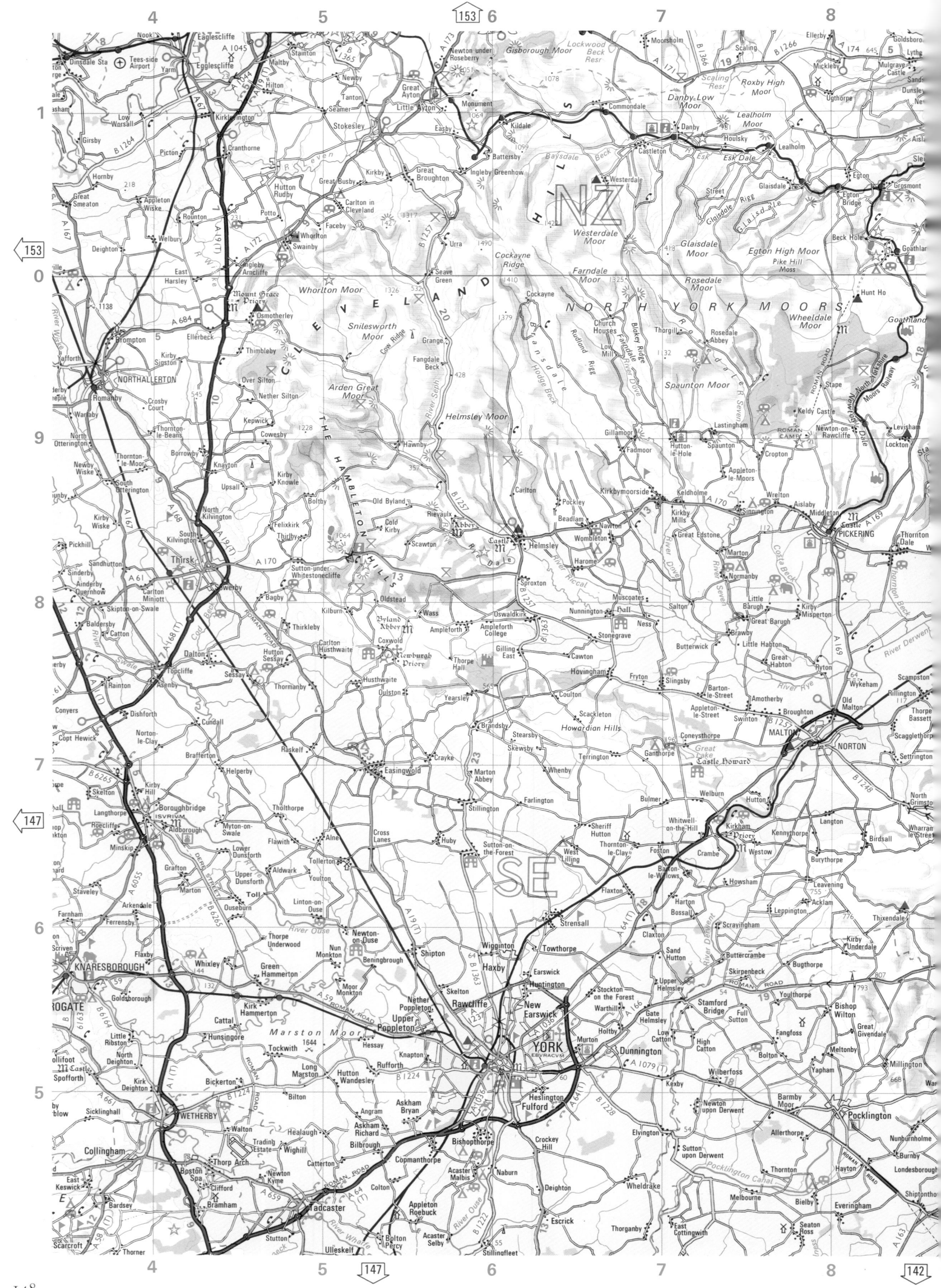

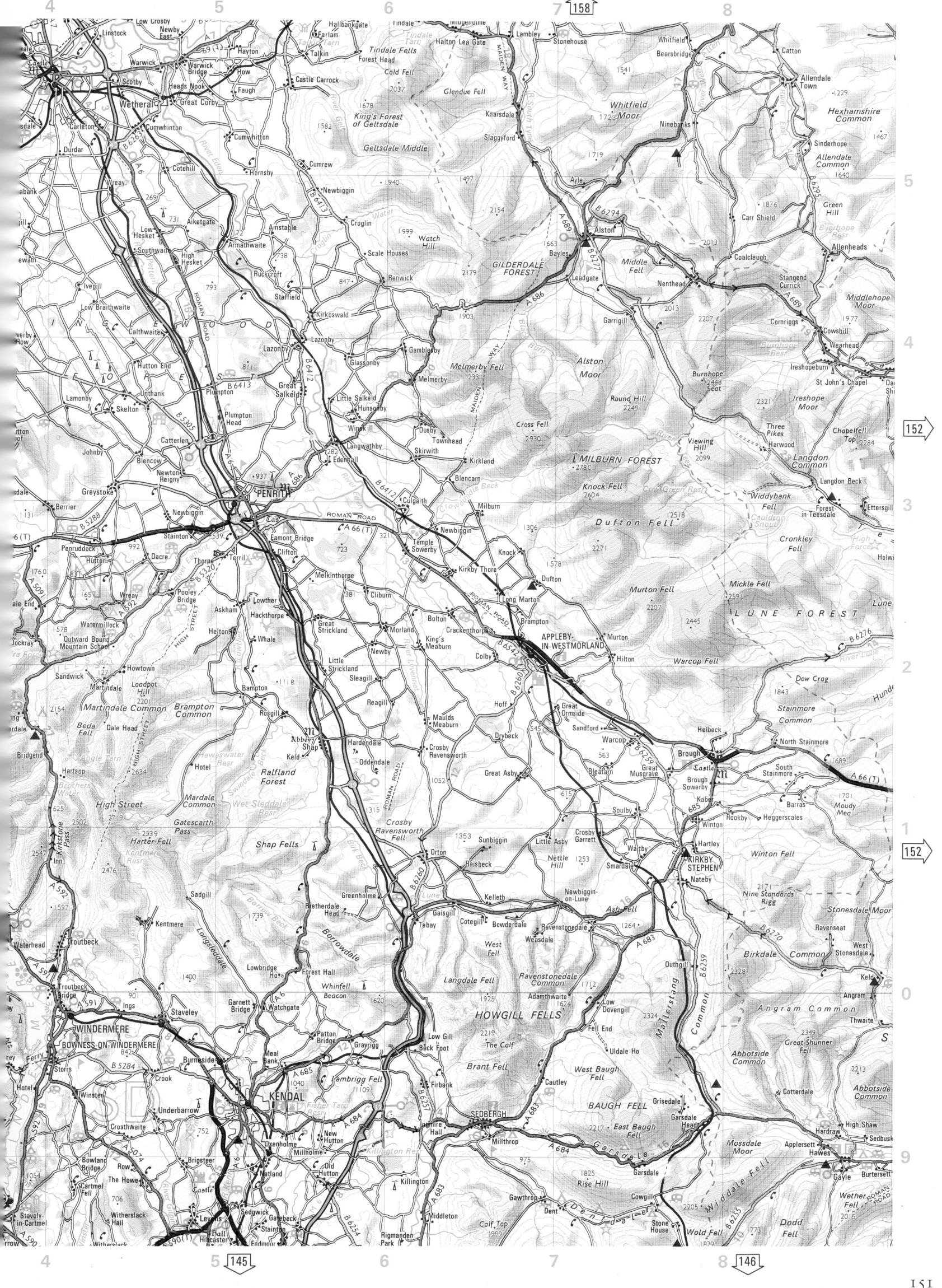

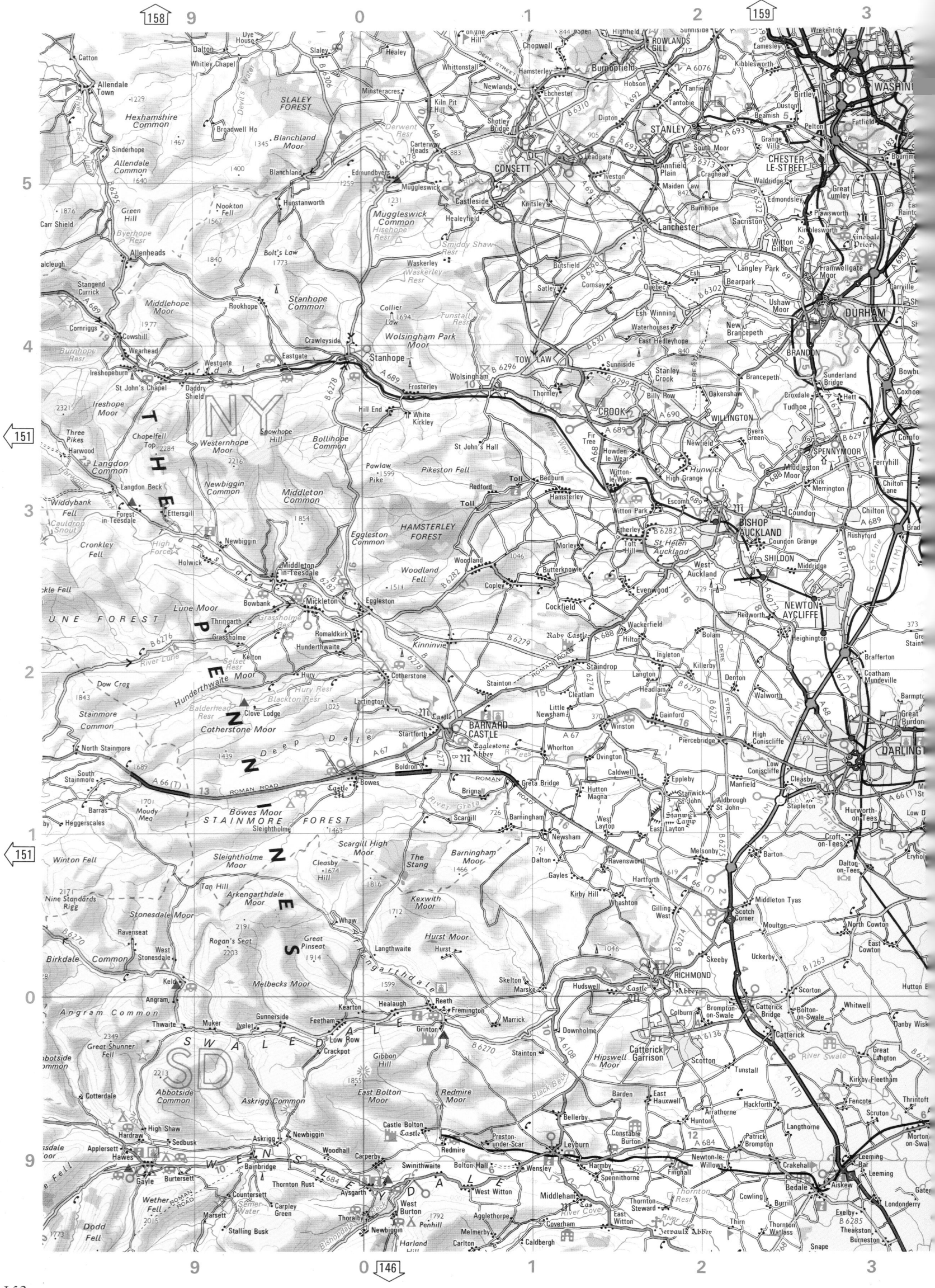

NORTH SEA

NZ

SE

NORTH YORK MOORS

CLEVELAND HILLS

THE HAMBLETON

SUNDERLAND
SEAHAM
PETERLEE
HARTLEPOOL
BILLINGHAM
STOCKTON-ON TEES
MIDDLESBROUGH
REDCAR
MARSKE-BY-THE-SEA
SALTBURN-BY-THE-SEA
BROTTON
LOFTUS
GUISBOROUGH
NORTHALLERTON

148 →

Ailsa Craig
Castle
1109

Matthew's Port
Dowhill
Dippie
Ladybank
Kilkerran
Dalquharran Castle
Daill
B 741
Killochan Castle
Maxwellston
Hadyard Hill
1060
Glenalla Field
1395
1408
Garleffin Fell
Old Dailly
Penkill
B 734
Black Hill
Woodland Bay
GIRVAN
Saugh Hill
971
Penwhapple Resr
Mull of Miljoan
1165
Dalquhairn
C A R R I C K
Byne Hill
Tormitchell
103
Barr
326
CHANGUE PLANTATION
Eldrick Hill
CARR FOREST
Kennedy's Pass
Grey Hill
975
Auchensoul
Pinmore
Polmaddie Hill
1854
Rig of the Shalloch
Currarie
Merkland
Cairn Hill
1572
966
Tarfessock
Lendalfoot
B 734
775
Mid Hill
1349
Knockinlochie
Greensides
1098
Bennane Head
612
A 77 (T)
A 765
Pinwherry
Bellamore
744
Pindonnan Craigs
Loch Moan
Kirriere
MERR
193
Colmonell
Pinwherry Hill
Standard
853
Knockdaw Hill
Knockdolian
Knockdolian Castle
Black Clauchrie
Garwall Hill
Palgowan
Benyel
BALLANTRAE BAY
B 7044
Knockdhu
756
Glen Tig
Barrhill
239
Laggan
GLENTROOL FOREST
Glencaird Hill
Glen Troo Lodge
Ballantrae
Cosses
752
Shiel Hill
Corwar Ho
534
Balkissock
B 7027
Glen
Downan Point
Glenapp Castle
1041
Strawarren Fell
Drumlamford Loch
Glentrool Village
Currarie Port
538
Beneraird
1439
Drumlamford Ho
Bargrennan
Carlock Hill
1046
Milljoan Hill
132
Chirmorrie
641
Loch Dornal
CAIRNRYAN to
Larne .... 2-2½ hrs
STRANRAER to
Larne .... 2½ hrs
Penderry Hill
High Murdonochee
606
Loch Maberry
Loch Ochiltree
938
Milleur Point
Glen App
844
Stab Hill
725
942
Craig Airie Fell
Polbae
Knowe
Corsewall Point
324
Mid Moile
Standing Stones
Urrall Fell
605
220
Barnhills
Finnart's Bay
Jamieson's Point
Penwhirn Resr
Quarter Fell
834
B 7027
North Cairn
Cairn Point
Lamb Hill
780
Arfield Fell
888
Eldrig Fell
Carseriggan
Challoch
South Cairn
Cairnryan
B 738
Knockcoid
Kirkcolm
A 77 (T)
Brdid Fell
Balmurrie
G A
NEWTON STEWART
Dounan Bay
314
Loch Connell
The Wig
New Luce
704
Benfield
Ervie
Portobello
LOCH RYAN
Cairnscarrow
Loch Heron
Drumphail
672
Loch Ronald
Barraer Fell
402
Slouchnawen Bay
NW
Knocknain
Leswalt
Innermessan
Bught Fell
Kirkcowan
High Moor of Killiemore
186
Lochnaw Castle
Lochinch Castle
Craig Fell
538
Gleniron Fell
Carscreugh
B 733
Carsegov
Glenstockadale
A 718
HE
Aird
White Loch
Black Loch
Dergoals
521
Dernaglar Loch
Knock Moss
428
B 733
Torhousemu Stone Circle
Broadsea Bay
B 738
STRANRAER
Castle Kennedy
Challoch Hill
484
Abbey
Castle of Park
A 747
THE
Bladn
Soulseat Loch
A 75 (T)
Dunragit
Glenluce
Whitefield Loch
MACH
Black Head
Craigenlee Fell
356
Lochans
596
Cairn Pat
Genoch Mains
A 757
Milton
Castle Loch
430
94
Portpatrick
Dunskey Castle
A 764
A 77
Bean Hill
A 716
A 715
Luce Sands
Craignarget Hill
23
Doon of May
Mochrum Loch
B 7005
B 7052
Port of Spittal Bay
Stoneykirk
Torrs Warren
Mochrum Fell
646
Whauphill
B 7042
H
Cairngarroch
Lake Cottage
Sandhead
Chapel Finian
432
Barrachan
Cairngarroch Bay
Meikle Float
Elrig
Mote of Druchtag
247
Money Head
A 714
Float Bay
Hole Stone Bay
Milton Point
A 747
Mochrum
Ardwell
Chapel Rossan Bay
Drumtroddan
Ardwell Point
A 716
L U C E   B A Y
Port William
Monreith Mains
B 702
Logan Mains
Balgowan Point
Monreith
Mull of Logan
Fort
Fell of Barhullion
Port Nessock or Port Logan Bay
Terally Point
Barsalloch Point
Monreith
Cairnywellan Head
Port Logan
Monreith Bay
Point of Cairndoon
11
Glasse
273
Clanyard Bay
B 7065
Kilstay Bay
480
Fell of Carle
Port Castle
Laggantalluch Head
Clanyard
Kirkmaiden
Drummore
Cailiness Point
537
Damnaglaur
Crammag Head
529
Maryport
Maryport Bay
Scares
Cairngaan
Port Kemin
MULL OF GALLOWAY

154

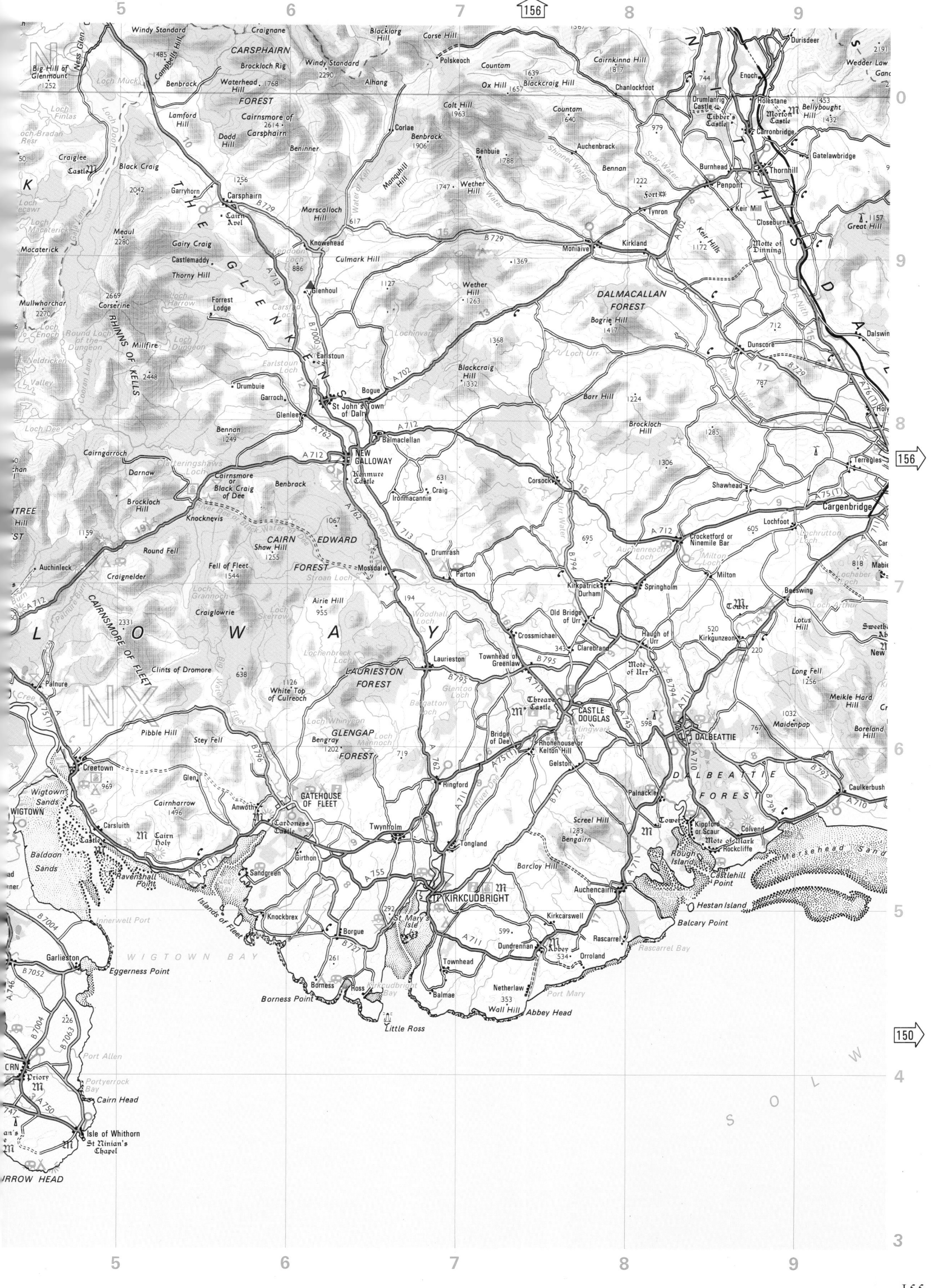

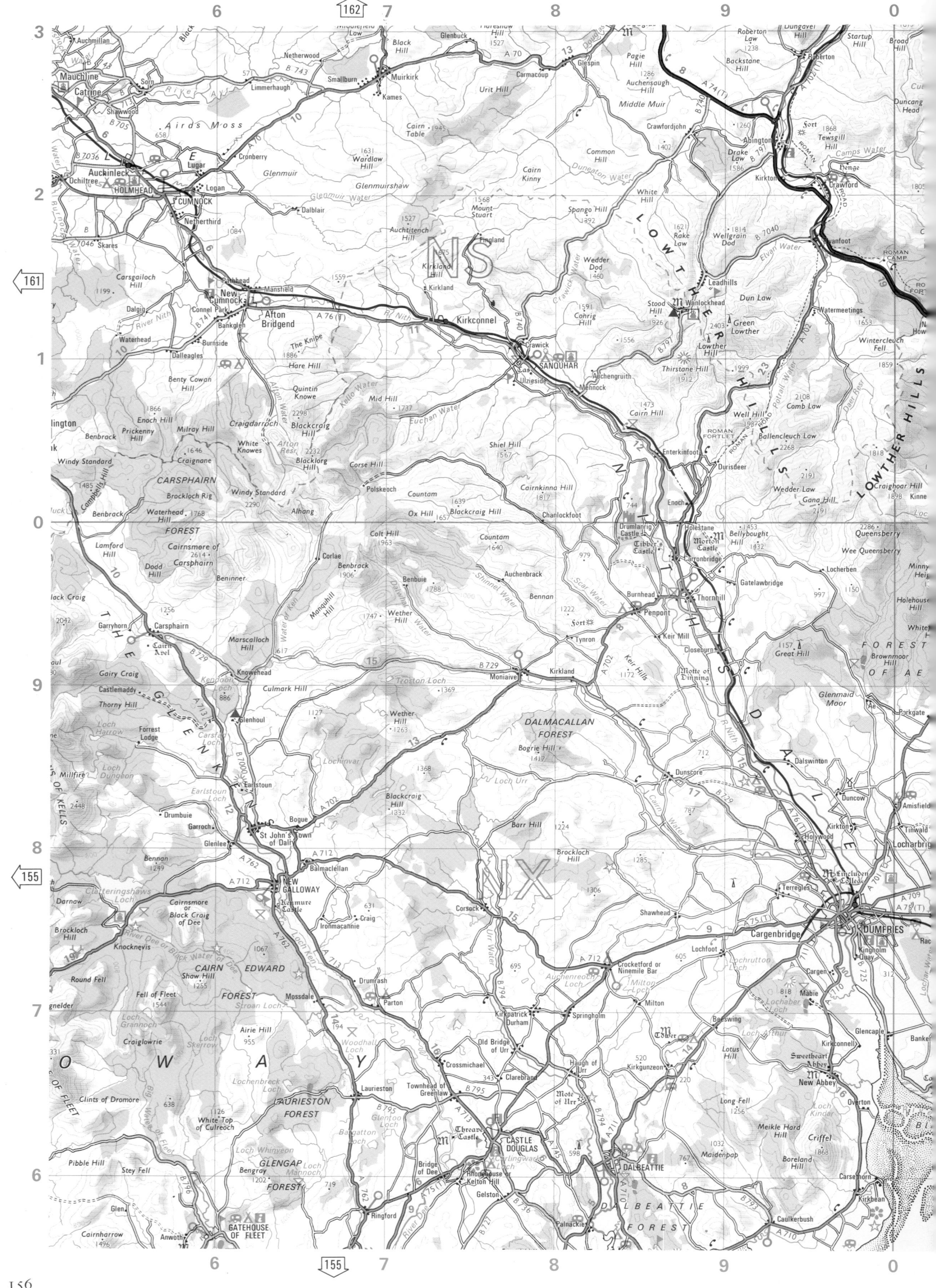

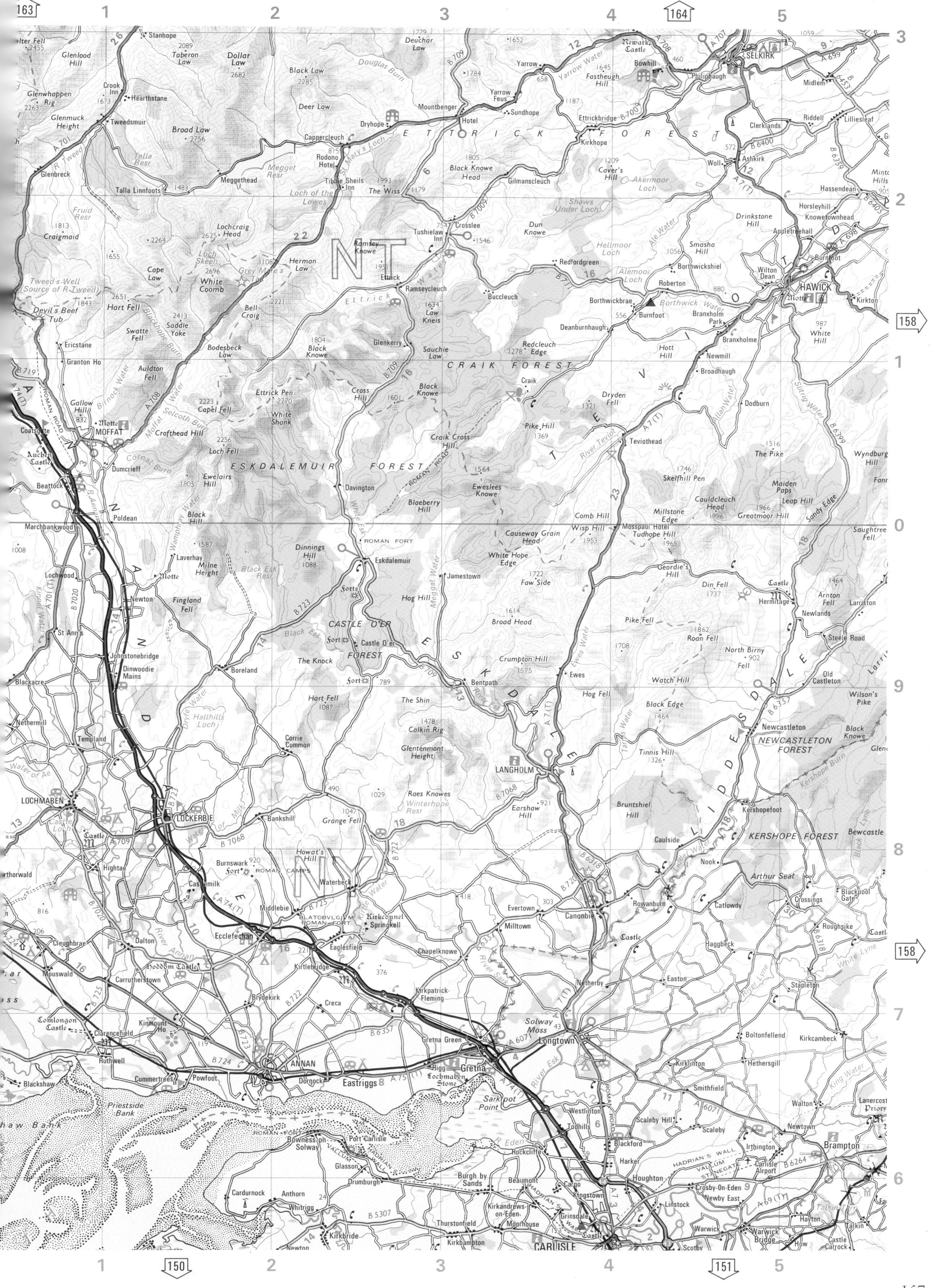

NORTH SEA

NEWCASTLE UPON TYNE to
Seasonal
Bergen.........................20-25 hrs
Esbjerg.......................18½-21 hrs
Stavanger....................17-18½ hrs
Gothenburg..................25-27½ hrs

KENNACRAIG to
Port Askaig.............. 2¾ hrs
Port Ellen .... 2¼ hrs
(seasonal)

SOUND OF BUTE

ISLAND OF BUTE

GIGHA ISLAND

ISLAND OF ARRAN

GOATFELL
2868

Brodick

CAMPBELTOWN

MULL OF KINTYRE

Sanda Island

Ailsa Craig

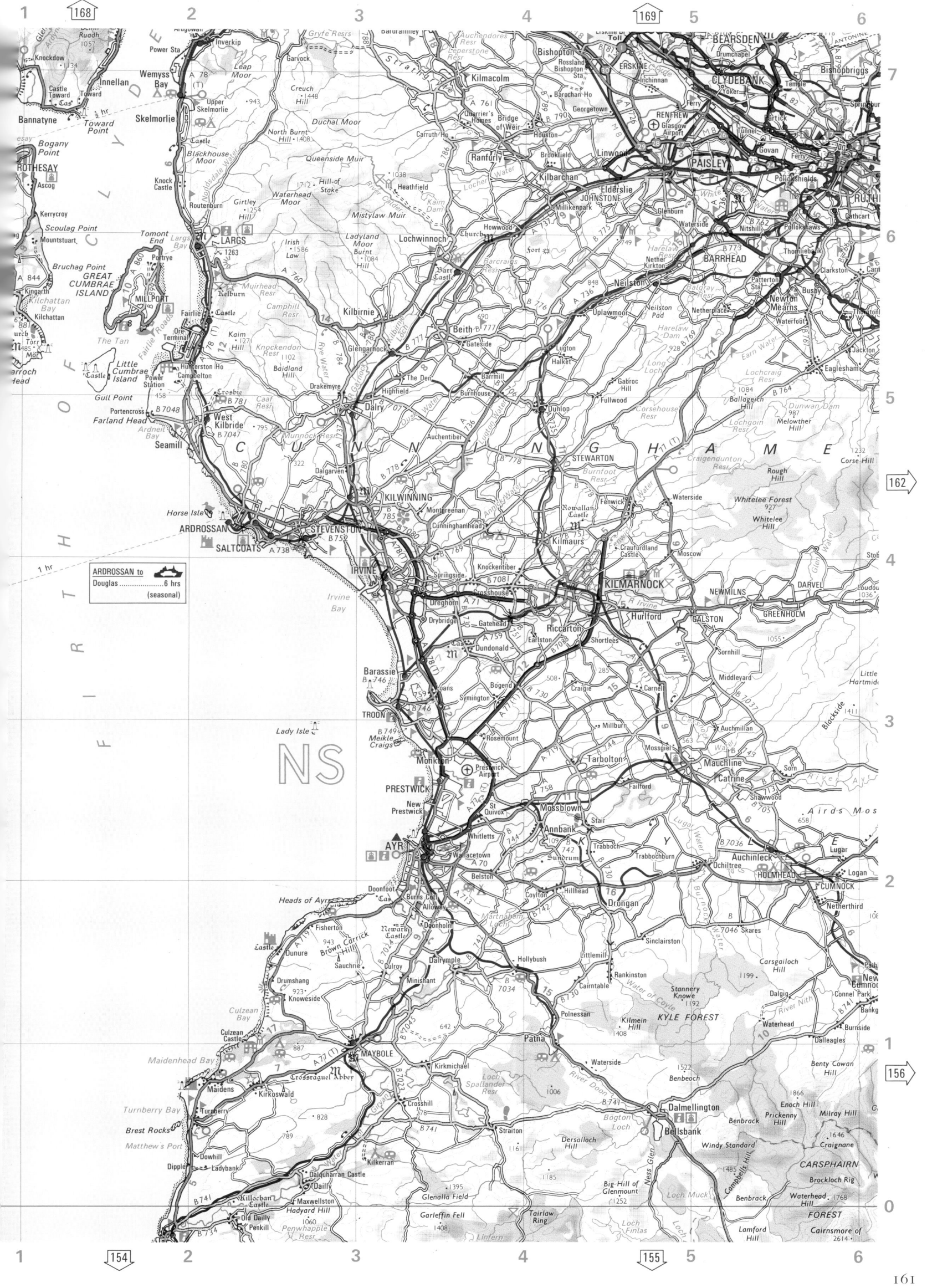

1   2   3   4   5   6

7

6

5

4

3

2

1

0

NS

ARDROSSAN to 🚢
Douglas ....6 hrs
(seasonal)

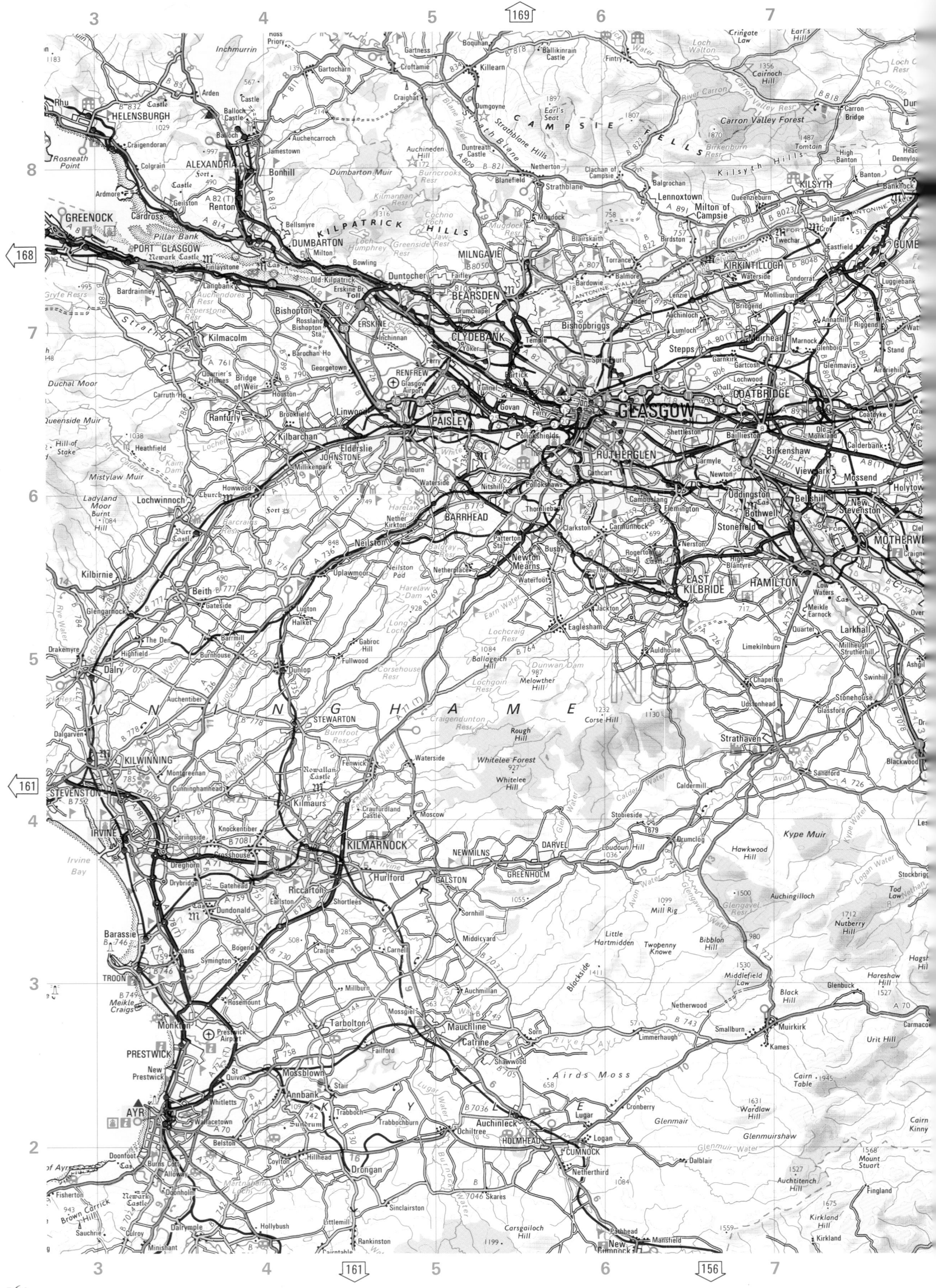

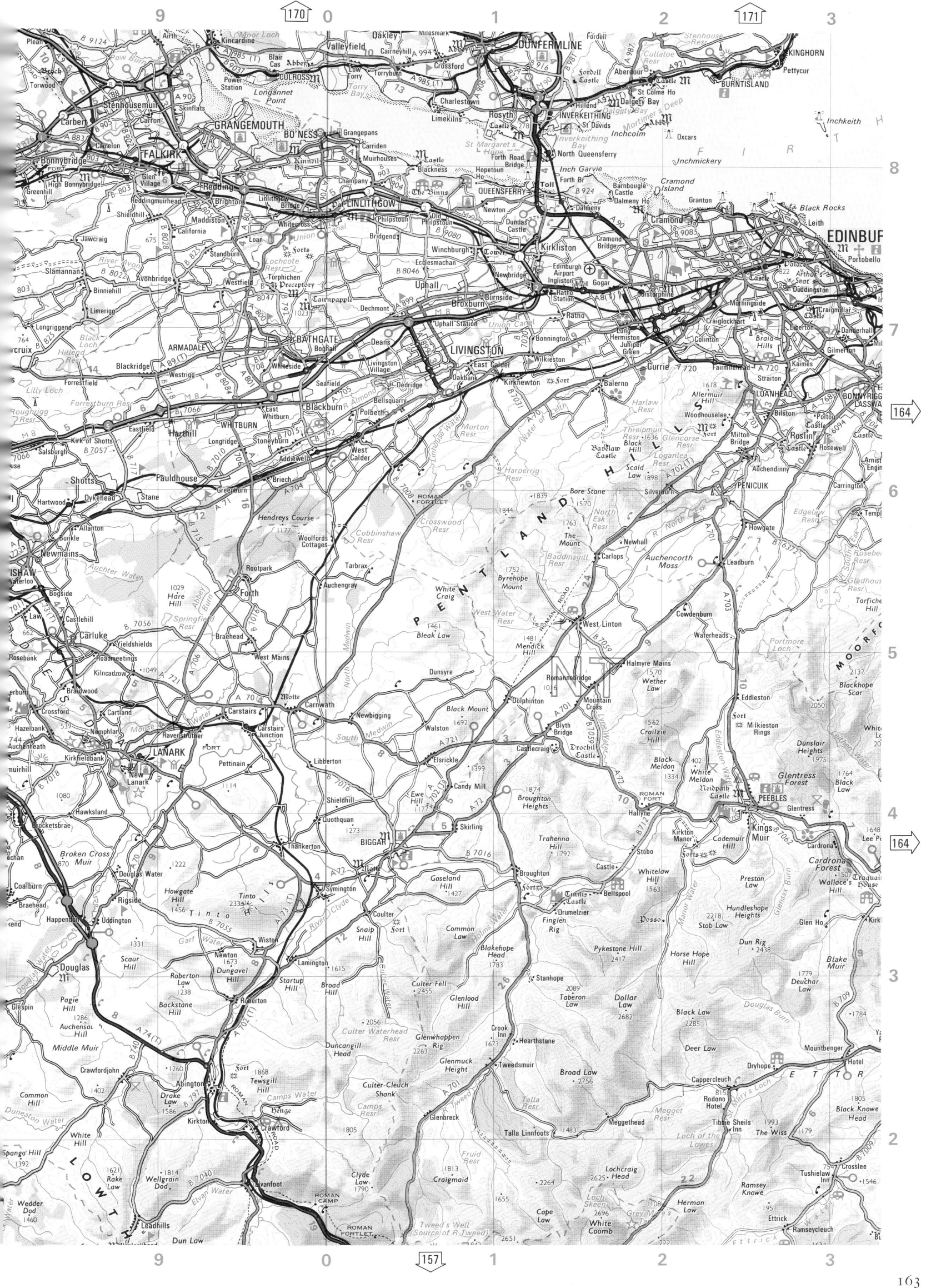

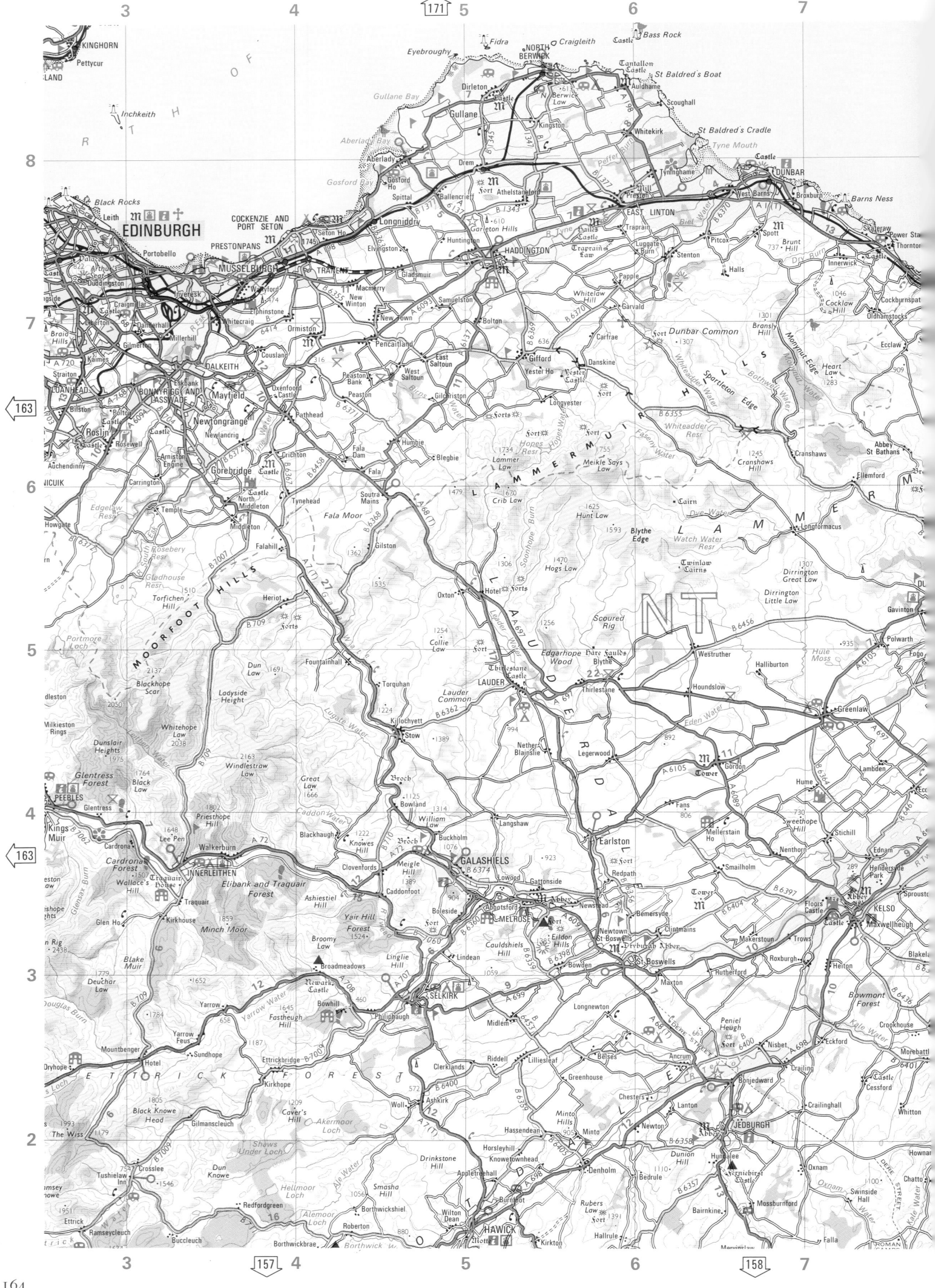

NM

Dubh
Artach

Port na
Cuilce
Rubh'a'
Geodha
Port Ceann
a' Ghàrraidh
Kiloran
Bay
Carnan
Balnahard
· 468
Eoin
Cailleach
Uragaig
Beinn
Breac
· 456
A 871
Kiloran
Kilchattan
An Rubha
Scalasaig
446
Port a' Bhàta
Port an Obain

COLONSAY

COLONSAY to
Oban.........2½ hrs

Rubha na h-
Uamha-sàile

Glende

Corpach
Bay

Beinn
Bhreac
· 1532

· 869

Eilean a'
Chladaich

Ardskenish
Garvard
Rubha Dubh
Meall an
Arbhair

· 1564

Allt an Tairbh
1487

Rainberg
Mòr

Shian Bay

Shian River

Dubh
Eilean
· 304
Priory
Eilean
Treadhrach

ORONSAY

Eilean
Ghaoideamal

Loch
Righ Mòr
575

J   U   R   A

Cruib
· 1036

Eilean
nan Ròn

Caolas Mòr

Ceann
Riobha

Rubh' an
t-Sàilein

Rubh'a'
Chrois-aoinidh
Loch Tarbert

Glenn

Post
Rocks

RUBH'
A'MHAIL

Rubh' Aird na
Sgitheich

Cnoc
an Ime
· 927

Rubha
Chàr

Rubha
Bholsa

Sgarbh
Breac
· 195

Allt na Gile

Glen
Batrick

Beinn
Bhreac

Loch
Lesgamaill
1029

A 846

Port Doir'a'
Chro-rain

Nave
Island

Eilean Beag

Ardnave
Point

Gortantaoid
Point

Sgairt
· 965
Sgàrbh
Dubh

Loch
Smigeadail

Bachlaig

Loch an
Aircill

Beinn
an Òir
· 2576

· 2477

An Dùnan

Carraig Bhàn

Tòn
Mhòr

Ardnave

Kilnave

Gortantaoid

· 1037
Giur-bheinn

Bunnahabhainn

Loch a'
Chnuic Bhric

PAPS OF JURA

Gleann Astàile

Corran R

JURA FOREST

Glas
· 839
Bheinn

Knockrome

Leargybreck

Loch
na Mile

Keils

Rubha
S
L

NR

An Clachan

Sanaigmore

Killinallan

Beinn
· 940
Bhreac

S
O
U
N
D

Caol Ila

Port Askaig

Inver
Cottage

Abhainn Gleann
Tubharnadeal

Craighouse

Small
Isles

Rubha
Lamanais
B 8018

Braigot

Ballinaby

Carnduncan

Gruinart

Craigens

Abhainn
Gleann Glas

River Drolsa

O
F

Loch
Finlaggan

Castle

Feolin
Ferry

Keills

Gleann Uillbh

Brat
· 123

Salgo
Bay

Loch
Gorm

B 8011

Foreland
Ho

Blackrock

Loch
Càm

A 846

Ballygrant

Loch
Ballygrant

Kilmeny

Glas
Eilean

Cabrach

Port na
Birlinne

Na Cùiltean

Coul Point

Kilchoman

Cnoc
Dubh

Conisby

Carraig
Dubh

Dun
Bhruichlinn

Esknish

Daill

Beinn
· 875
Dubh

Am Fraoch
Eilean

Jura Ho

Claig Castle
Brosdale
Island

Rubha na
Tràille

Machir
Bay

Bruichladdich

Islay
Ho.

Bridgend

I   S   L   A   Y

Dun
Nosebridge

Glas
· 1544
Bheinn

McArthur's
Head

2¾ hrs

Kilchiaran

Kilchiaran Bay

Rubha
Ghlamraidh

Tormisdale

Bowmore

Garfbreck

R
H
I
N
N
S

LOCH
INDAAL

A 847

Port
Charlotte

Mulindry

Kilennan R

Beinn
· 1544
Bhàn

Beinn
· 1612
Bheigier

Carraig Mhòr

Lossit Point

Lossit
Bay

Lossit

· 790

O
F

I
S
L
A
Y

Beinn
Tart a' Mhill

Nereabolls

Laggan
Point

R Laggan

A 8018

Duich
Lots

Duich R

A 846

Ardtalla

Gleann Leòra

Claggain
River
· 354

Claggain
Bay

Rubha na
Faing

Portnahaven

Ellister

Port Gleann
na Gaoidh

LAGGAN
BAY

Islay
(Port Ellen)
Aerodrome

Glenegedale

Allt nan Airighean

Beinn
· 1490
Uraraidh

Loch Beinn
Uraraidh

Cnoc Mòr
na Claigin

Aros Bay

Kintour
Kildalton
Cross

Ardmore
Point

Orsay

Port Wemyss

RHINNS
POINT

Knockangle
Point

Glenegedale R

Rubha Mòr

Kintra

Hotel

Kintra

Leorin

Beinn
· 1138
Sholum

Loch Leathann
an Sgorra

Ardmore

Eilean Craobhach
Eilean a' Chuirin

Eilean Bhrìde

2¾ hrs
(Summer only)

Craro I

Gre

Slugaide Glas

Maol
· 541
Buidhe

Cornabus

Port
Ellen

Kildalton
House

Ardbeg

Rubha na
Gainmhich

Dùn Mòr
Ghil

Glenastle

Cragabus

· 499

Laphroaig

Dunyvaig
Castle

Eilean
Imersay

Lower
Killeyan

T H E   O A

Carraig
Fhada

Texa

Loch
Kinnabus

· 401

Inerval

MULL OF OA

· 430

Beinn
· 661
Mhòr

Rubha na
Mèise Bàine

Rubha nan
Leacan

Port an Eas

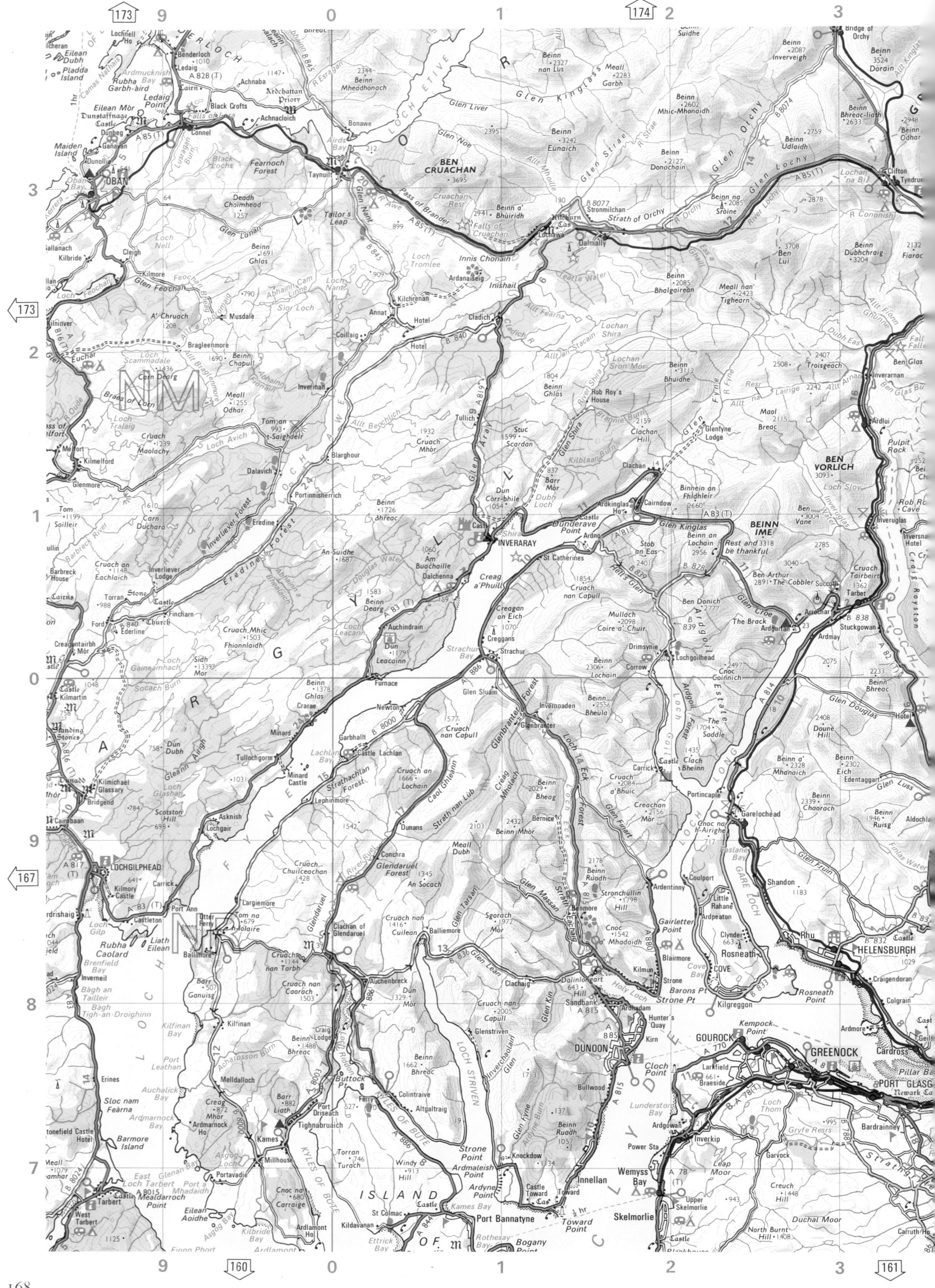

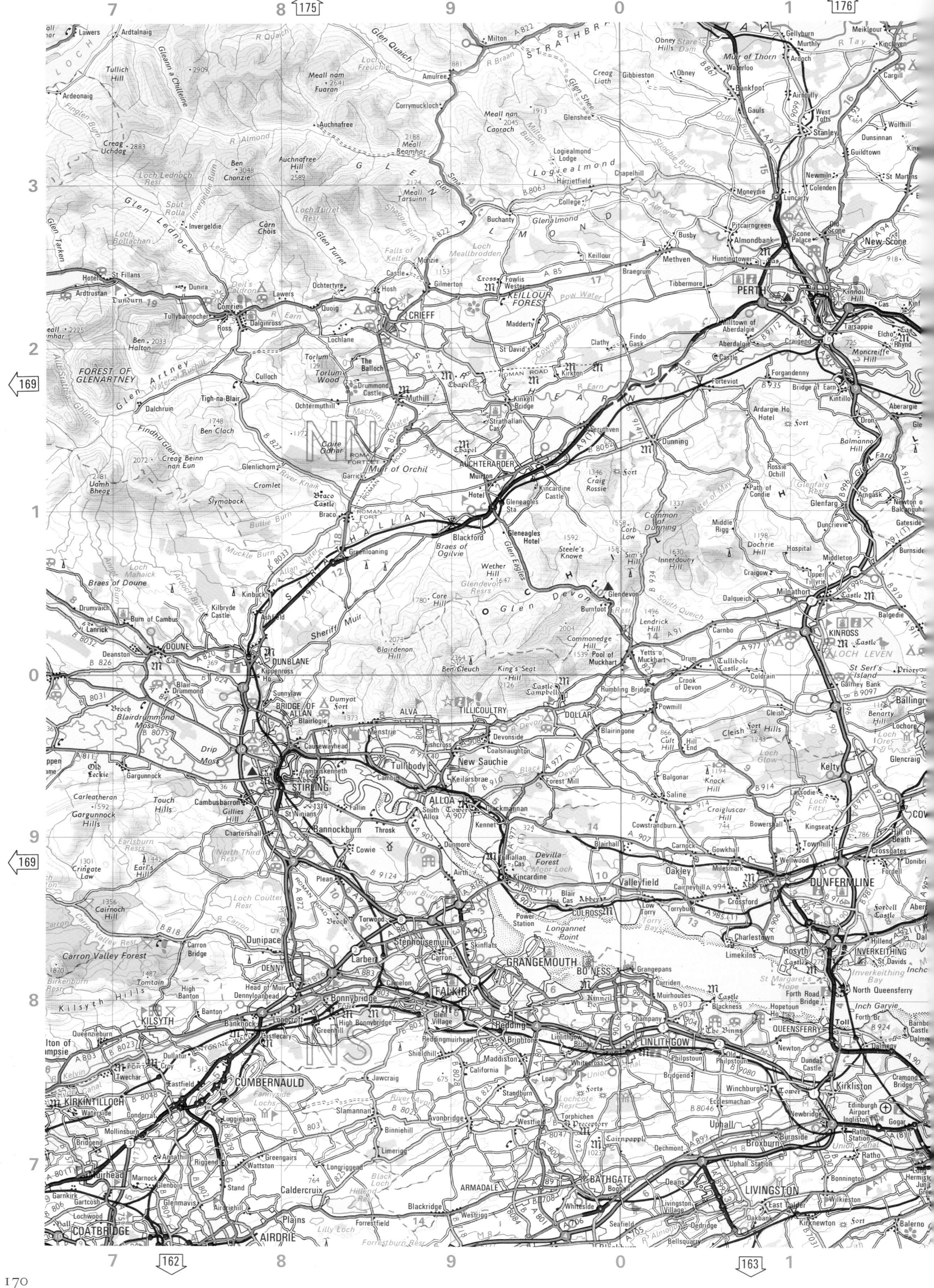

INNER HEBRIDES

COLL

Point
Ardnamurch

Cairns of Coll
Eag na Maoile
Eilean Mór
Rubha Mór
Rubh´ a
Bhinnein
Bousd
Sorisdale
1550
Cliad Bay
Gallanach
Arnabost
Grishipoll
Rubha Hogh
Ballyhaugh
Ben
340
Hogh
Loch
Cliad
239
Bagh Feisdlum
Quinish Point

Hogh Bay
Rubha a´
Ghraineig
Totronald
Arinagour
Rubha
an Aird
Port Mine
Feall Bay
Aileod
Acha
Castle
Breachacha
Castle
Friesland
Eilean
Ornsay
Loch Eatharna
M o r n i s h
Caliach Point
Calgary Point
Rubha Fàsachd
Port na
h-Eathar
Port nam
Partan
Calgary
544
Gunna
Crossapol
Bay
Soa
Port a´
Mhurain
Loch Breachacha
Rubha
nan Oirean
Urvaig
Vaul
Bay
Vaul
Salum
Rubha Dubh
Treshnish
Point
Ensay
Carn
1122
Rubha
Port Bhiosd
Balephetrish
Bay
Ruaig
Haunn
708
Cruachan
Odhar
839
Hough
Skerries
Clachan Mór
Rubha
Nead a´ Gheòidh
Rubh´
a´ Chaoil
Burg
Kiln
Hough
Bay
Balevullin
Rubha
Chràiginis
Gott Bay
Soa
Cairn na
Burgh Beg
Rubh´ an
t-Suibhein
L O C H   T U
389
Kilkenneth
Kenovay
Tiree
Airport
B 8068
Scarinish
Rubha na
Seann Charraige
Fladda
Moss
Heanish
TIREE
Lunga
337
Eilean
Dioghlum
Rubha na
Sròine
509
Fan
Port Mór
Middleton
Heylipol
Crossapol
Gometra
Maisgeir
Creaga
10
UL
Port Bharrapol
Barrapol
HYNISH
BAY
Rubha
Tràigh an Dùin
Treshnish Isles
Bac Mór or
Dutchman´s Cap
Bac Beag
Eilean
na Creiche
Little
Colonsay
201
Balephuil
Càrnan
462
Mór
Balemartine
Mannal
Staffa
Fingal´s Cave
Rinn
Thorbhais
Balephuil
Bay
Hynish
Erisgeir
Sger
Faoi
NL
Port Snoig

Rubha na
h-Uamha

Réidh
Eilean
Eilean
Annraidh
Rubha nan
Cearc
Garbh Phort
Abb
IONA
Baile
Mór
265
Aridhglas
Stac an Aoineidh
Creich
Sound of Iona
Fionnphort
Loch Poit
na h-
Eorabus
Ard
L assapol
Bunessan
ROSS   OF   M
Eilean na h-
Aon Chaorach
Greave
Fidden
Beinn a´
369
Ghlinne Mhóir
Soa
Island
Eilean
nam Muc
Erraid
246
Ardalanish
Uisken
Ardchiavaig
Eilean
a´ Chalmain
Beinn a´
Chaol-airigh
411
Ardalanish
Bay
Rubha nam
Maol Móra
Rubh´
Ardalanish

West Reef
Torran Rocks
Sgeir Dhoirbh
Dubh

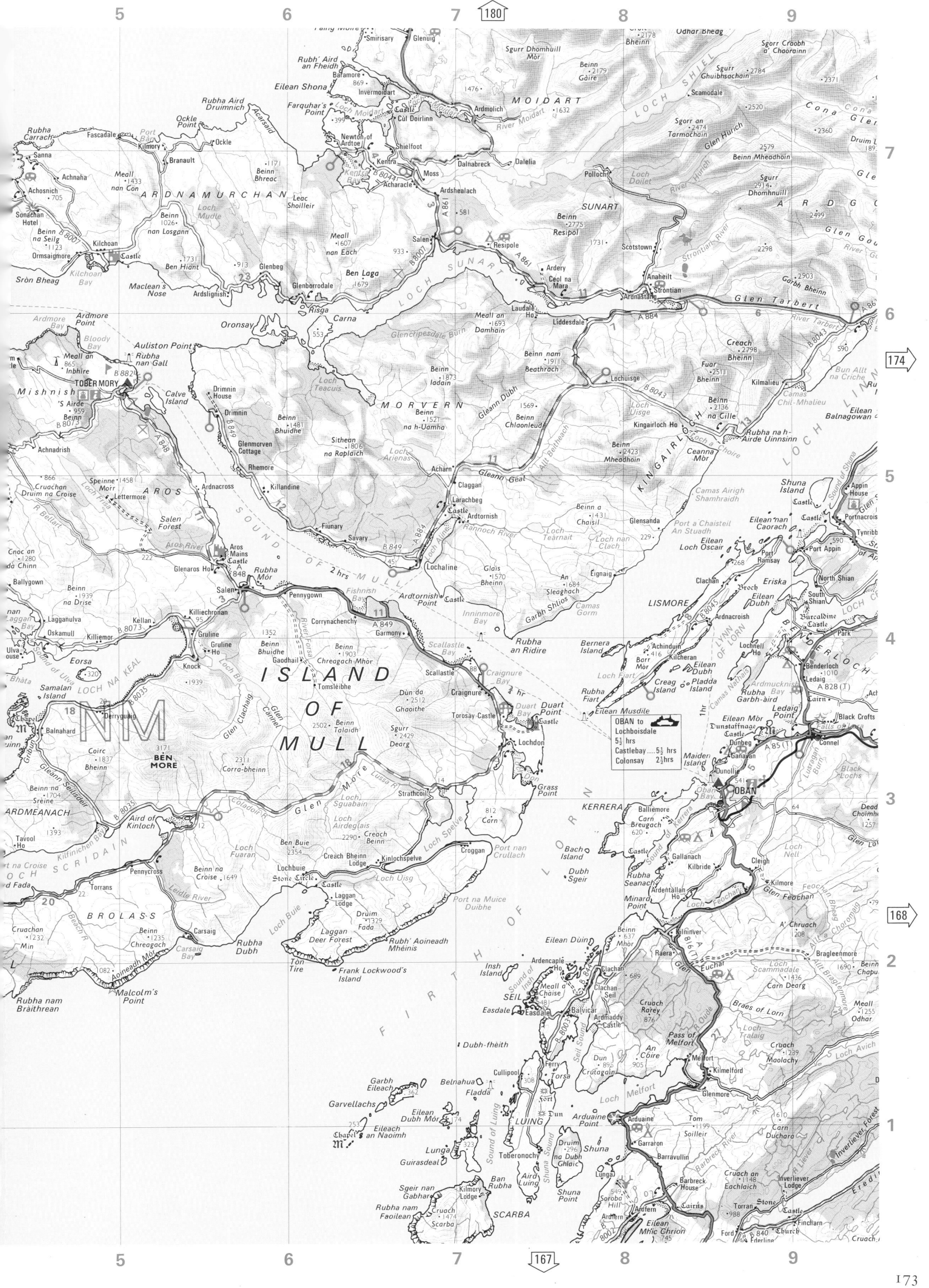

MOIDART

ARDNAMURCHAN

SUNART

LOCH SUNART

MORVERN

ISLAND
OF
MULL

BÉN
MORE

AROS

SOUND OF MULL

LOCH NA KEAL

BROLASS

ARDMEANACH

SCRIDAIN

KINGAIRLOCH

LISMORE

LYNN OF LORN

KERRERA

FIRTH OF LORN

OBAN

SEIL

LUING

SCARBA

OBAN to
Lochboisdale .... 5½ hrs
Castlebay ....5½ hrs
Colonsay ....2½ hrs

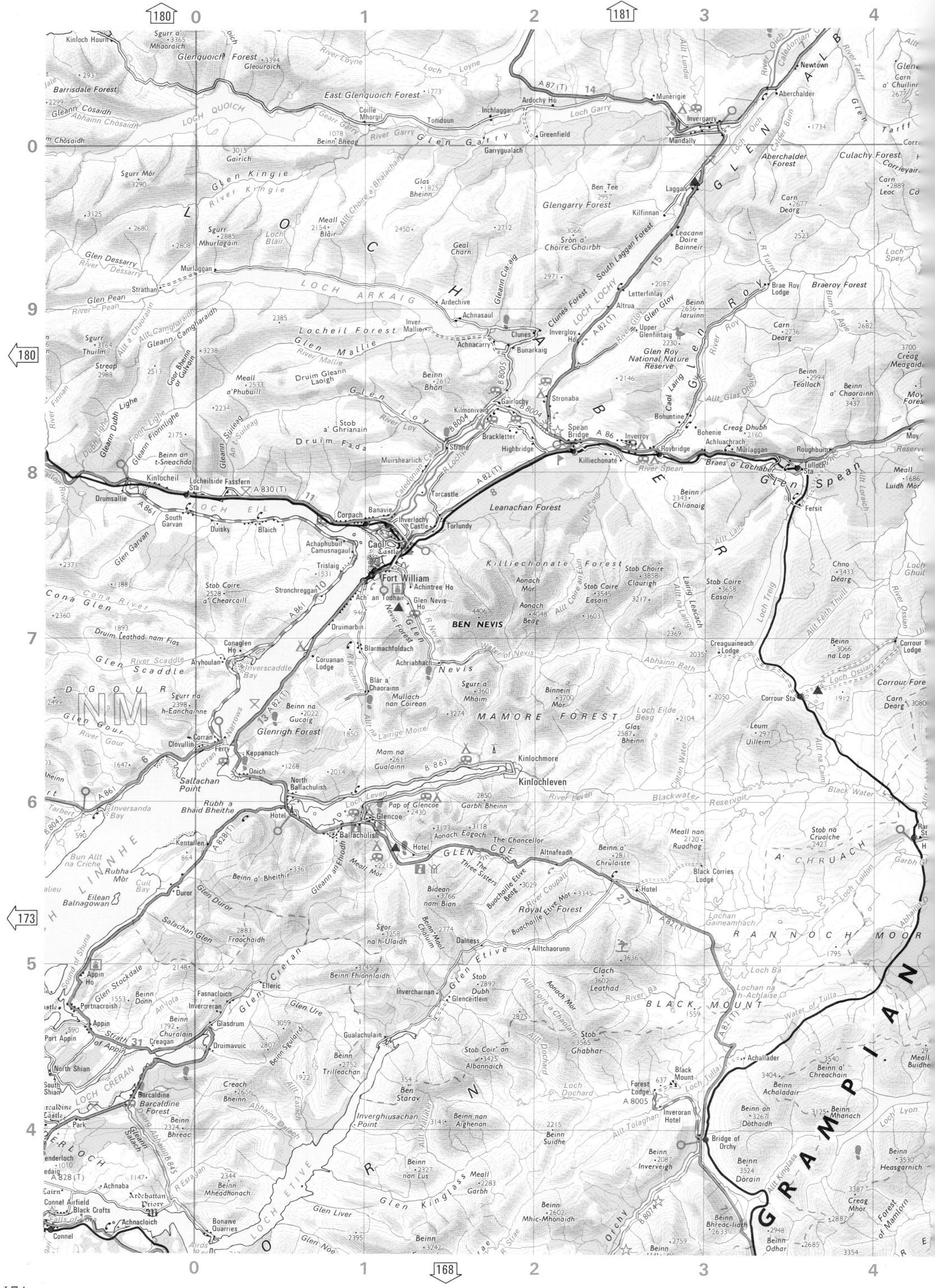

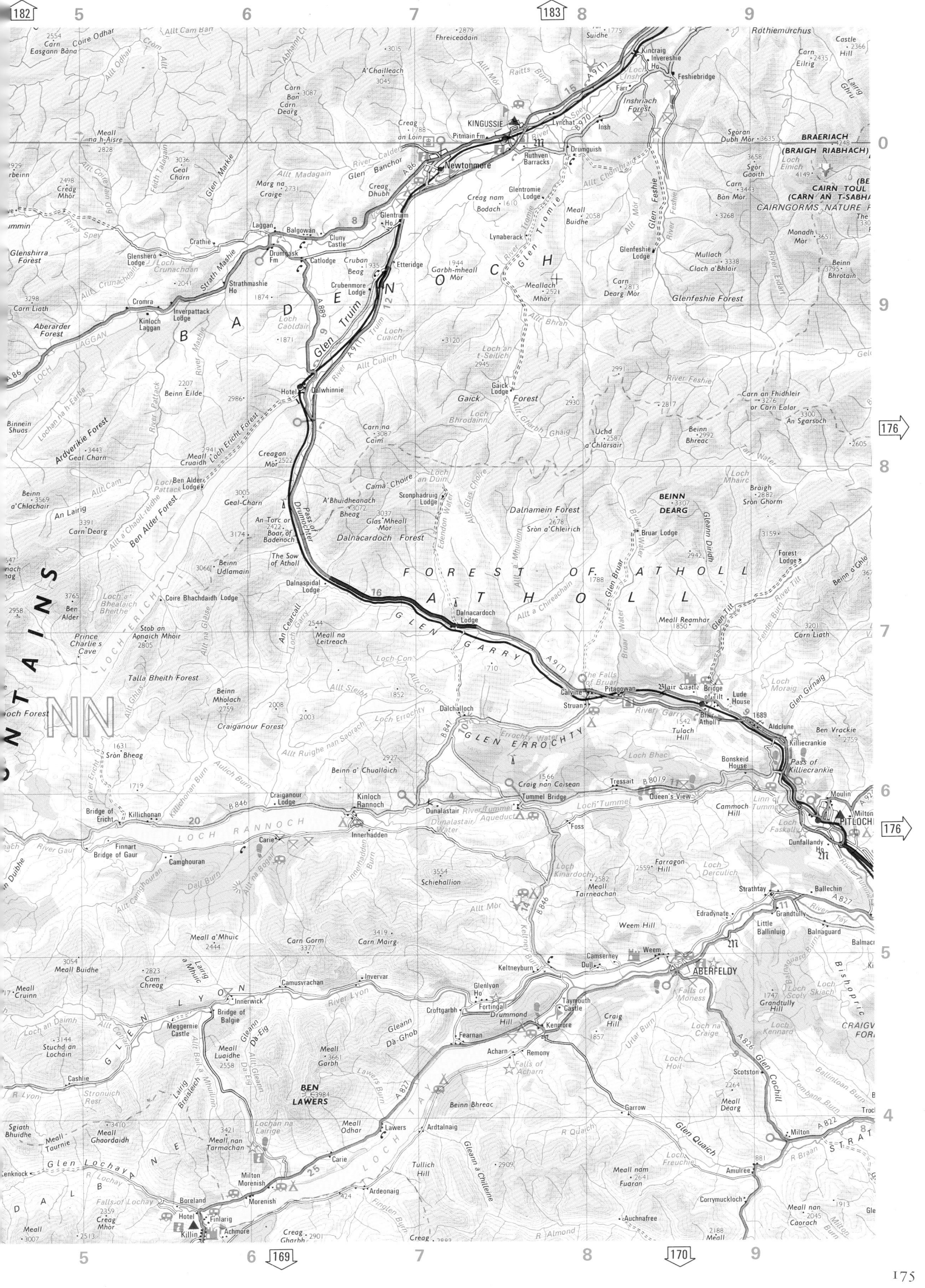

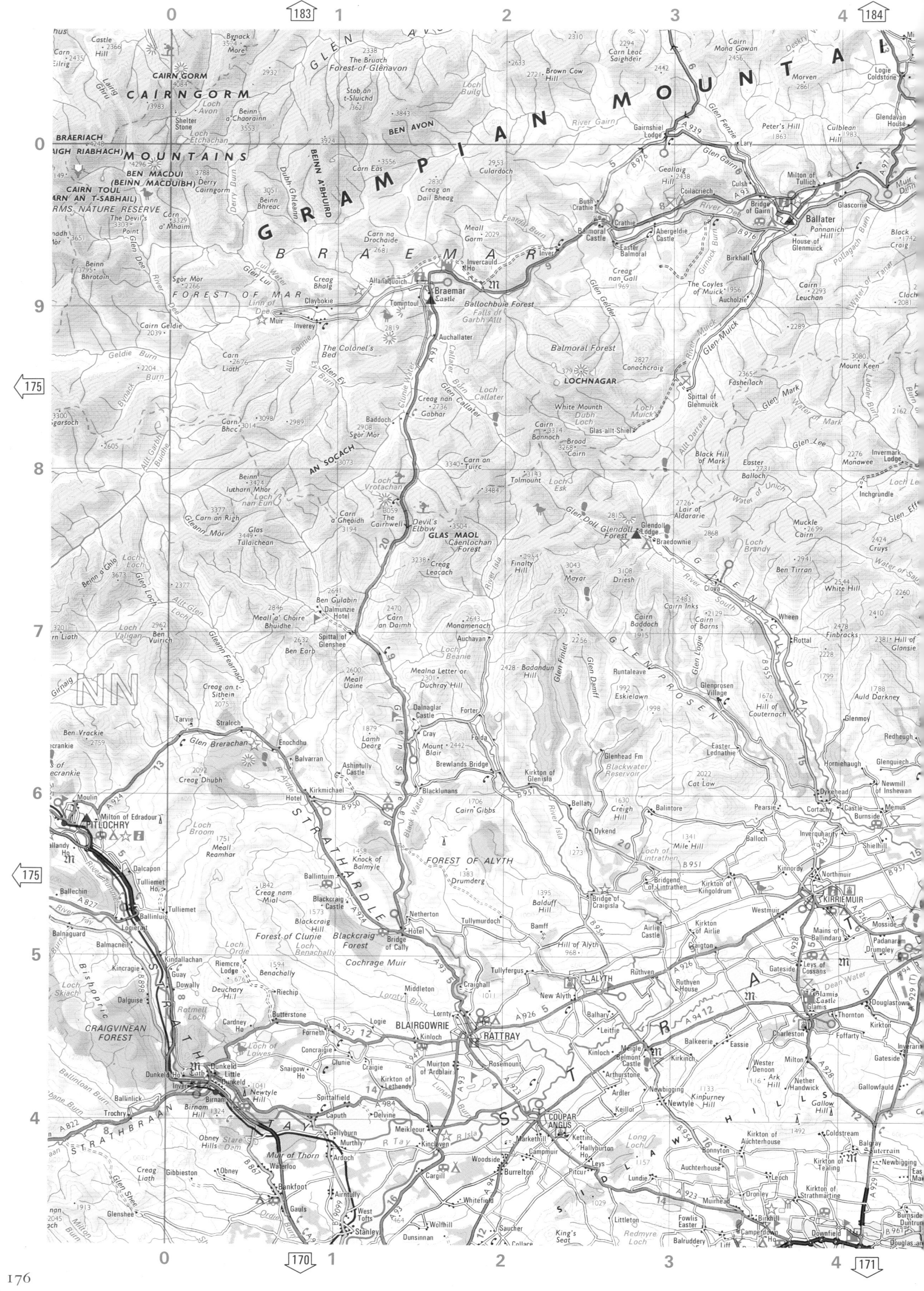

OUTER HEBRIDES

SOUTH UIST

ISLES OR WESTERN HEBRIDES

ATLANTIC OCEAN

SEA OF THE HEBRIDES

NF

NL

Wiay
Steisay
Ardivachar
Eochar
Loch Bee
Lochcarnan
A 6
865
Sandwick
Gasay
Glas-eileanan
Caltinish
Luirsay Dubh
West Gerinish
·285
·551
Loch Skipport
Stilligarry
B 890
Lochskipport
Ornish Island
4
Acairseid Falaich
Loch Druidibeg
·208
Mol a'Tuath
Howmore
Uisinish
HECLA
·576
Rubha Rossel
Verran Island
·1988
Snishival
Rubh' Aird-mhicheil
Stoneybridge
·1723
Rubha Bhilidh
Loch Coradale
12
Ormiclate Castle
Glen
BEINN
MHOR
Loch Ollay
·2033
Prince's Cave
·Buail a'Ghoill
Rubha Hellisdale
Rubha Ardvule
730
Calvay
Rubha Bolum
Loch Kildonan
Sheaval
Mingary
Loch Eynort
Gleann
Mór
·822
Loch Snigisclett
·1228
Askernish House
·412
Stulaval
Stuley
Layaval
Loch Stulaval
·1168
Daliburgh
A 865
Triuirebheinn
Rubha na Creige Móire
Crossdougal
Lochboisdale
Kilpheder
8
·902
LOCHBOISDALE to
Oban........................6 hrs
Boisdale
Loch Boisdale
Orosay
5
808?
Calvay
South Lochboisdale
Rubha Meall na Hoe
Smerclate
Garrynamonie
Easaval
Pollachar
Kilbride
·356
Rubha na h-Ordaig
Ludag
Ferry
Roneval
·661
Rubha na Hordaig
Sound of Eriskay
Sgeir a'Mhill
Lingay
Balla
Fiaray
Hornish
Ben
·610
Scrien
Hartamul
Sound of Fiaray
Scurrival Point
·291
Fuday
ERISKAY
Eilean Dallaig
Eoligarry
Rubha nan Eun
·403
·338
Stack Islands
Greian Head
Cleat
Ben
·680
Cliad
Orosay
Mhór
Oitir
Greanamul
Sgeir Liath
Cuier
·31
Gighay
Traigh
Mhór
·242
Hellisay
Borve Point
Bruernish
·352
FloddaY
Borve
North Bay
Fuiay
Doirlinn Head
Balnabodach
·309
Hotel
Tangasdale
Bruernish Point
Ben
·1090
Tangaval
Heaval
·1260
Earsary
BARRA
CASTLEBAY to
Oban........................6 hrs
Brevig
Caolis
Castlebay
Kiessimul
Castle
Rubha Mór
Biruaslum
Heishival
·624
Mór
Uinessan
VATERSAY
Vatersay
Vatersay Bay
Muldoanich
Vatersay
·279
·504
2 hrs
·327
Sound of Sandray
Flodday
Cairn
·678
Sandray
Galtar
Lingay
·269
Greanamul
Sound of Pabbay
Pabbay
·561
Rosinish
Heiskers
Sound of Mingulay
MINGULAY
·735
Mingulay
Bay
·896
Carnan
Sound of Berneray
·628
Berneray
Barra
Head

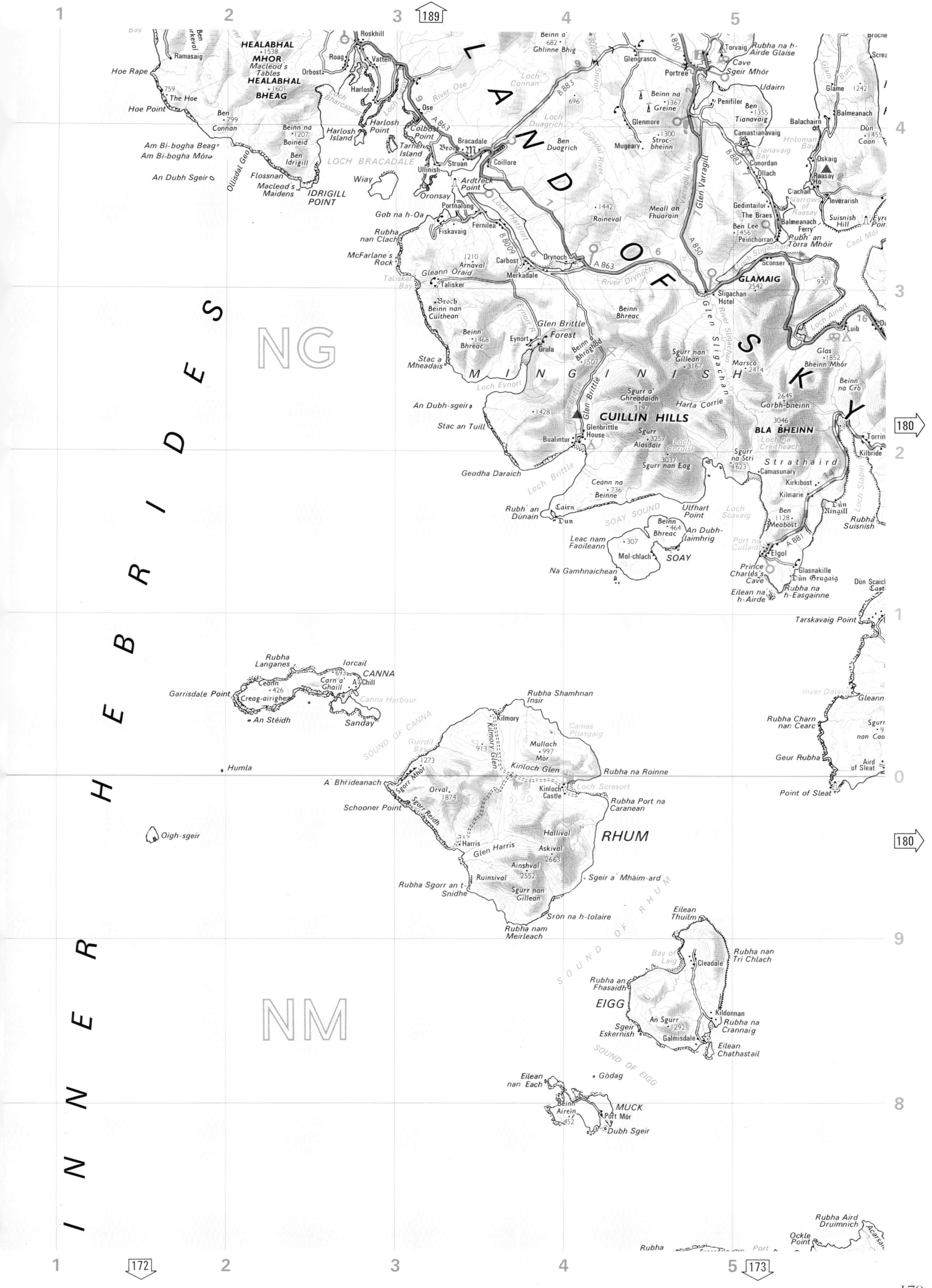

1 **2** **3** **4** **5**

Bay
Ben arkeval
Ramasaig

HEALABHAL
MHOR
·1538
Macleod's
Tables
HEALABHAL
BHEAG
·1601

Roskhill
Roag
Vatten

L A N D

Beinn a'
Ghlinne Bhig
682

Glengrasco

Torvaig
Rubha na h-
Airde Glaise
Cave
Sgeir Mhòr

A 850

Broch

Hoe Rape
Hoe Point
Hoe Point
759
The Hoe

River
River Sharcasaig
Ose

A 863

Harlosh
Orbost

Harlosh
Point
Colbost
Point
Tarner
Island
Broch

River Ose
Loch
Connan
696
B 88.5
9

Loch
Duagrich

Portree

Penifiler
Ben
Tianavaig
·1355

Udairn

Glame 1242

Balmeanach

Ben
Connan
·799

Beinn na
Boineid
·1207
Ben
Idrigill

Harlosh
Island

Ullinish
Struan
Bracadale
Coillore

Ben
Duagrich

·1442
Roineval

Ben Lee
·1456

Mugeary
Stroc-
bheinn
·1300

·1367
Greine

Glenmore

Camastianavaig
Conordan
Ollach

Tianavaig
Bay

Balachairn

B 883

Dùn
Caan
·1455

Inverarish

Oskaig

Raasay
Ho

Am Bi-bogha Beag
Am Bi-bogha Mór

An Dubh Sgeir

Flossnan
Macleod's
Maidens
IDRIGILL
POINT

Wiay

Oronsay

Gob na h-Oa
Rubha
nan Clach

Portnalong

Fiskavaig

Ardtreck
Point

Ferinlea

Loch Harport
B 8009

Meall an
Fhuarain

A 850
Gedintailor
The Braes
Balmeanach
Peinchorran
Pubh' an
Tòrra Mhóir

Glen Varragill
Varragill River

7

Narrows
of
Raasay

Holoman
Bay

Suisnish
Hill

Eyre
Poir..

Caol Mór

4

3

H E B R I D E S

NG

LOCH BRACADALE

McFarlane's
Rock

Gleann Oraid
Talisker
Taliske..
Bay

Broch
Beinn nan
Cuithean

Beinn
·1468
Bhreac

·1210
Arnaval
Merkadale

Carbost

Drynoch

Eynort
Grula

Glen Brittle
Forest

Beinn
Bhuidh
Beinn
Bhreac

Beinn
Bhrogaid
·1507

A 863

A 863

River Drynoch

Sgurr nan
Gillean
·3167

River Sligachan

Glen Sligachan

Sligachan
Hotel

Loch Sligachan
Sconser

GLAMAIG
·2542

Marsco
·2414

·930

Loch Ainort

Luib

16

Glas
Bheinn Mhòr

Beinn
na Cro

Du

Stac a
Mheadais

Loch Eynort

M I N I G I N I S H

An Dubh-sgeir

Stac an Tuill

·1428

Sgurr a'
Ghreadaidh
·3197

CUILLIN HILLS
·3046

Glen Brittle
Glenbrittle
House

Sgurr
Alasdair
·3257

Sgurr a'
·3037
Sgurr nan Eag

Harta Corrie

·2645
Garbh-bheinn

B L A B H E I N N

Sgurr
na Stri
·1623

Loch na
Creitheach

Loch Coruisk

S K Y

180

Torrin

Kilbride

2

Geodha Daraich

Loch Brittle

Bualintur

Ceann na
·736
Beinne

Rubh' an
Dùnain
Cairn
Dùn

SOAY SOUND

Leac nam
Faoileann
·307

Na Gamhnaichean

Beinn
Bhreac
·464

Mol-chlach

An Dubh-
Iaimhrig

SOAY

Ulfhart
Point

Loch Scavaig

S t r a t h a i r d

Camasunary

Kirkibost

Kilmarie

Ben
·1128
Meabòst

Elgol

Prince
Charles's
Cave

Glasnakille
Dùn Grugaig

Eilean na
h-Airde

Rubha na
h-Easgainne

Dùn Scaich
Cast..

Dùn
Ringill
Rubha
Suisnish

Tarskavaig Point

1

I N N E R

Rubha
Langanes
Iorcail
CANNA
A' Chill

Ceann
·426
Creag-airighe

Garrisdale Point

An Stéidh

Carn a'
Ghaill

Sanday

Canna Harbour

Guirdil
Bay

SOUND OF CANNA

913

Kilmory

Kilmory Glen

Mullach
·997
Mór

Rubha Shamhnan
Insir

Camas
Pliasgaig

Kinloch Glen

Kinloch
Castle

Loch Scresort

Rubha na Roinne

Rubha Port na
Caranean

Inver Dalavi..

Gleann

Rubha Charn
nan Cearc

Geur Rubha

Point of Sleat

Aird
of Sleat

Sgurr
9..
nan Cao..

0

Humla

Oigh-sgeir

A' Bhrideanach

Sgorr Mhòr
·1273

Orval
·874

Sgorr Reidh

Schooner Point

Harris

Glen Harris

Ruinsival
·2552

Rubha Sgorr an t-
Snidhe

Hallival
Askival
·2663

Ainshval
·2552

Sgurr nan
Gillean

RHUM

Sgeir a' Mhàim-ard

Sròn na h-Iolaire

Rubha nam
Meirleach

SOUND OF RHUM

Eilean
Thuilm

180

9

NM

Bay of
Laig

EIGG

Rubha an
Fhasaidh

Sgeir
Eskernish

An Sgurr
·1292

Galmisdale

Cleadale

Kildonnan

Rubha nan
Tri Chlach

Rubha na
Crannaig

Eilean
Chathastail

Eilean
nan Each

Beinn
Airein
·52

Gòdag

MUCK
Port Mór
y

Dubh Sgeir

SOUND OF EIGG

Rubha Aird
Druimnich

Ockle
Point

Rubha

Port

Alcarsa..

8

1 **2** **3** **4** **5**

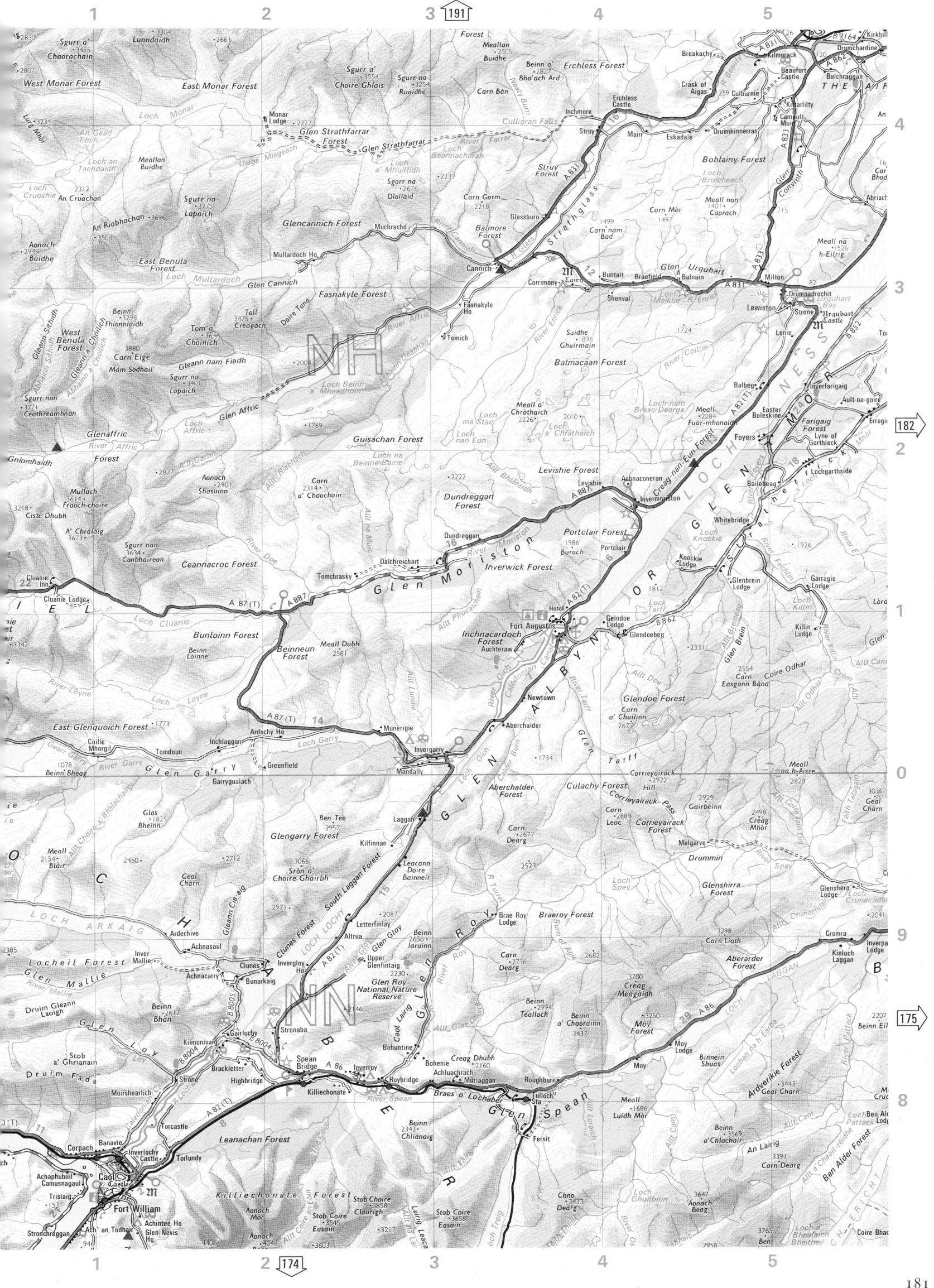

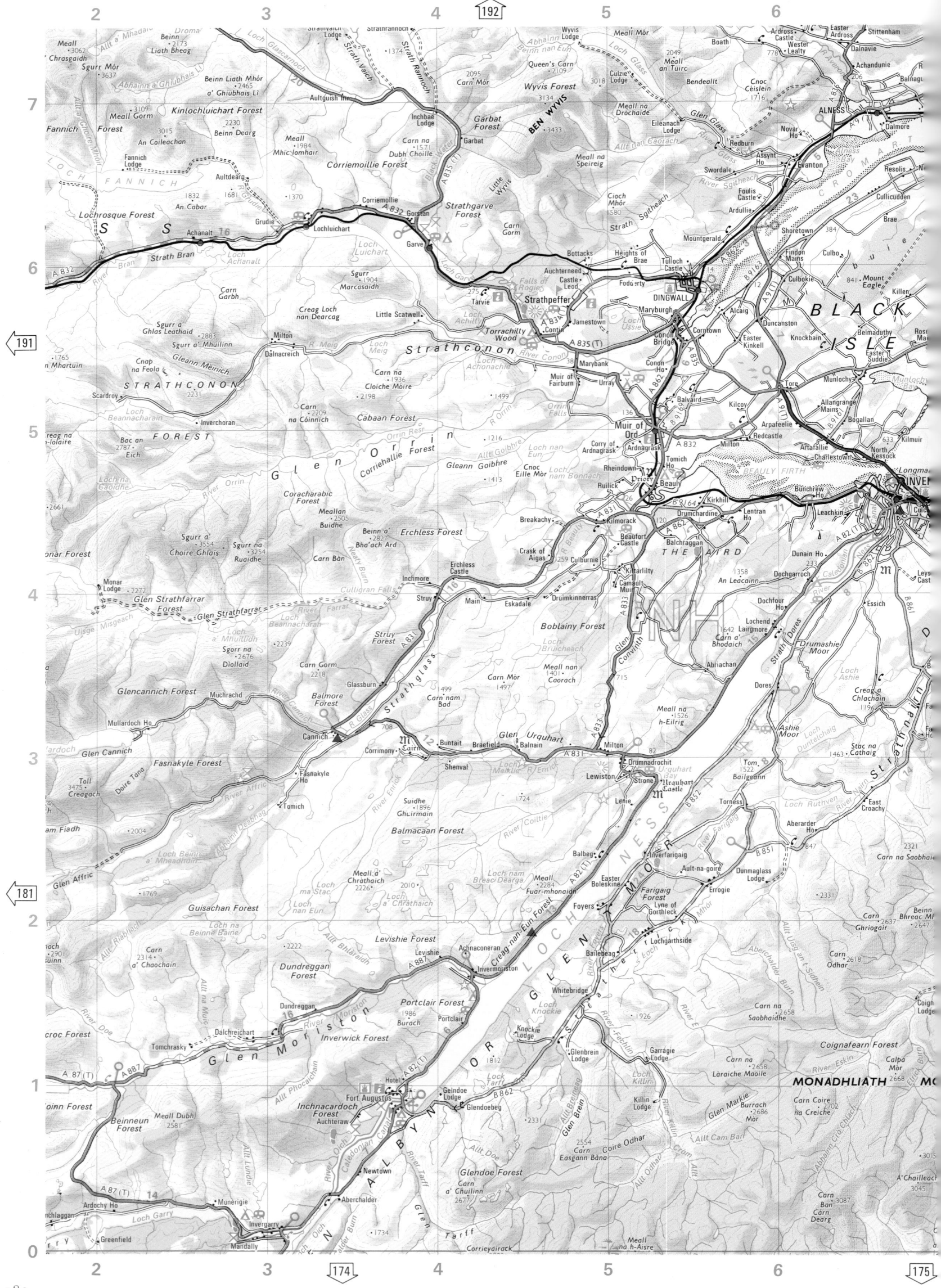

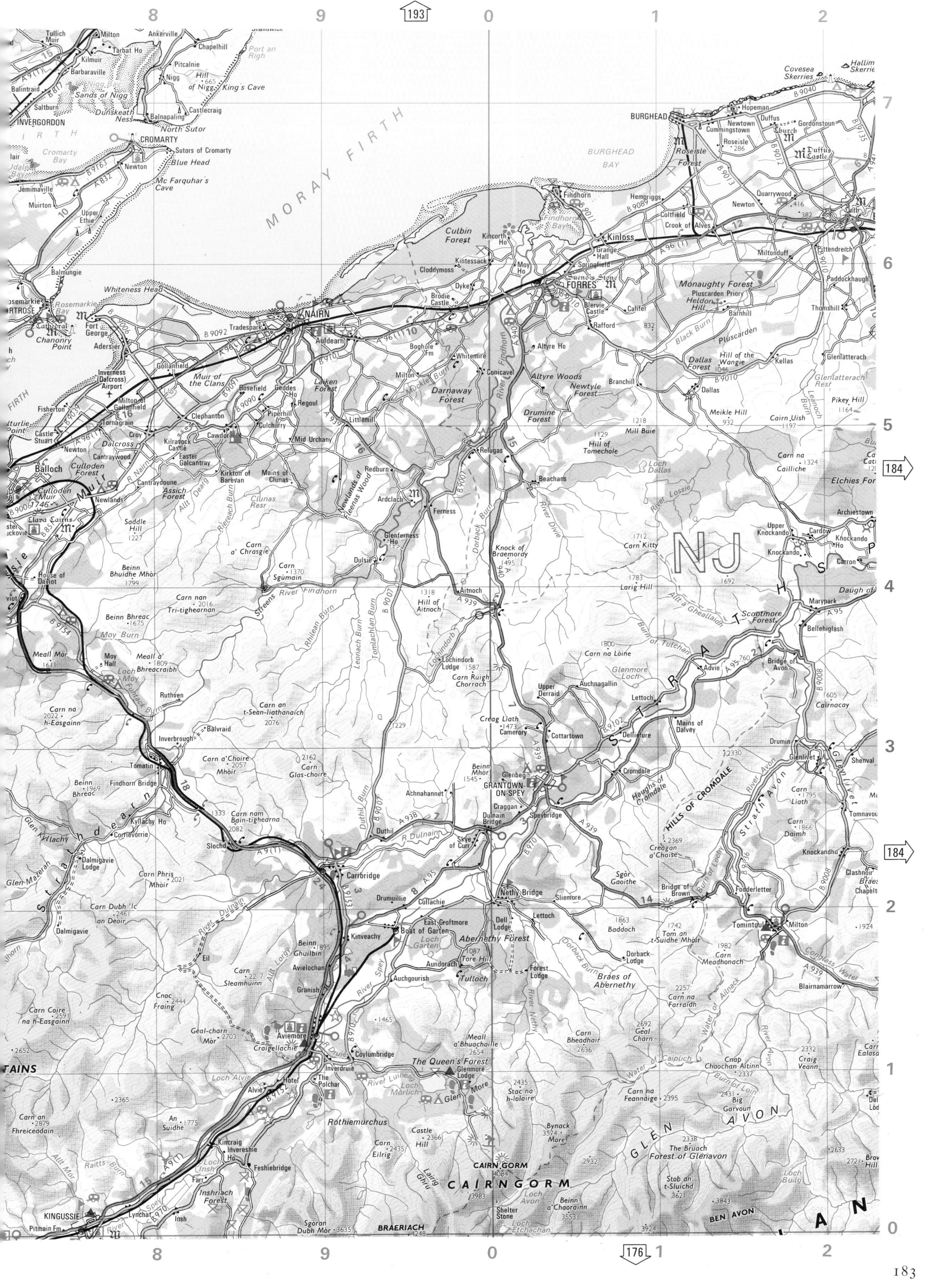

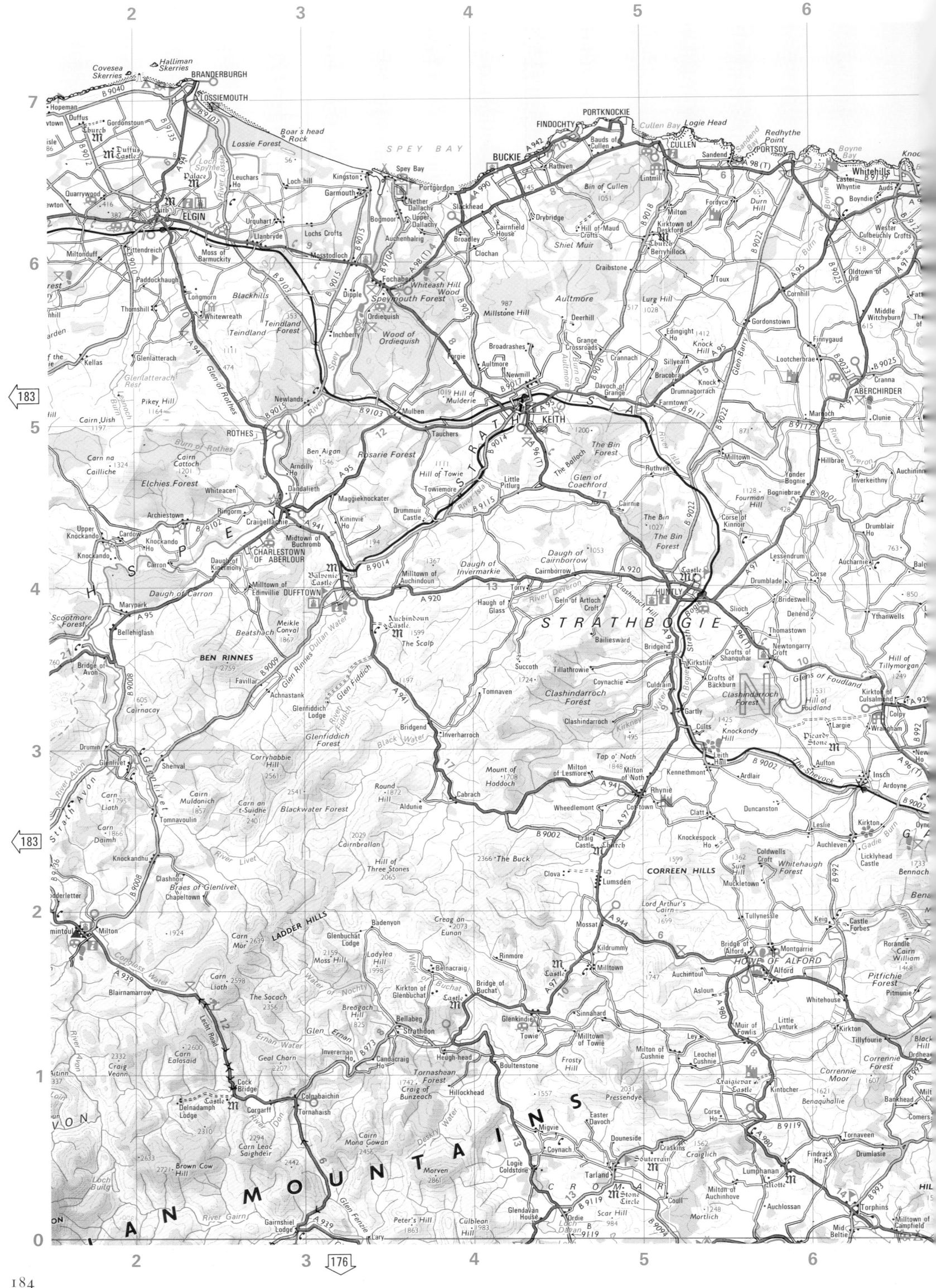

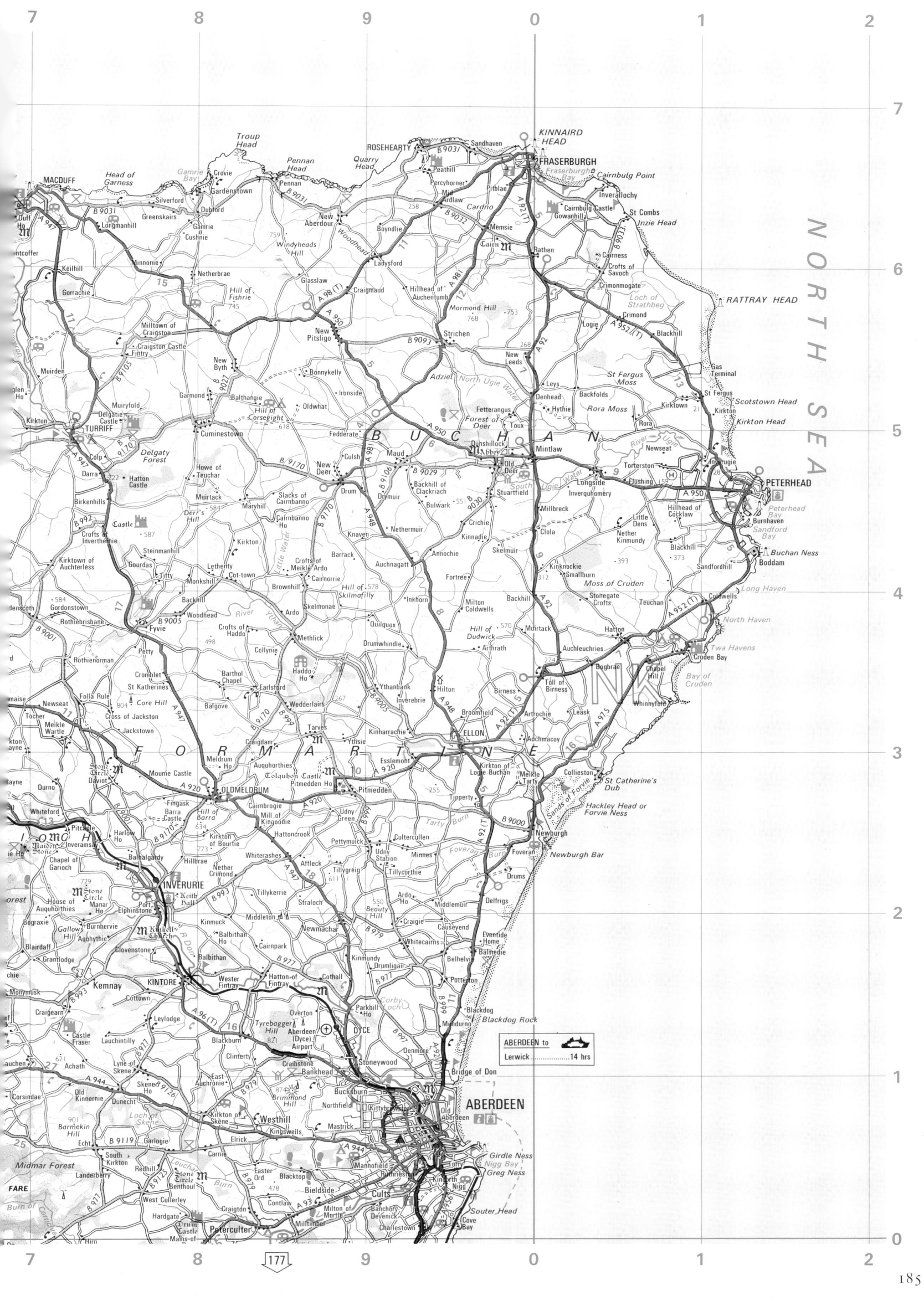

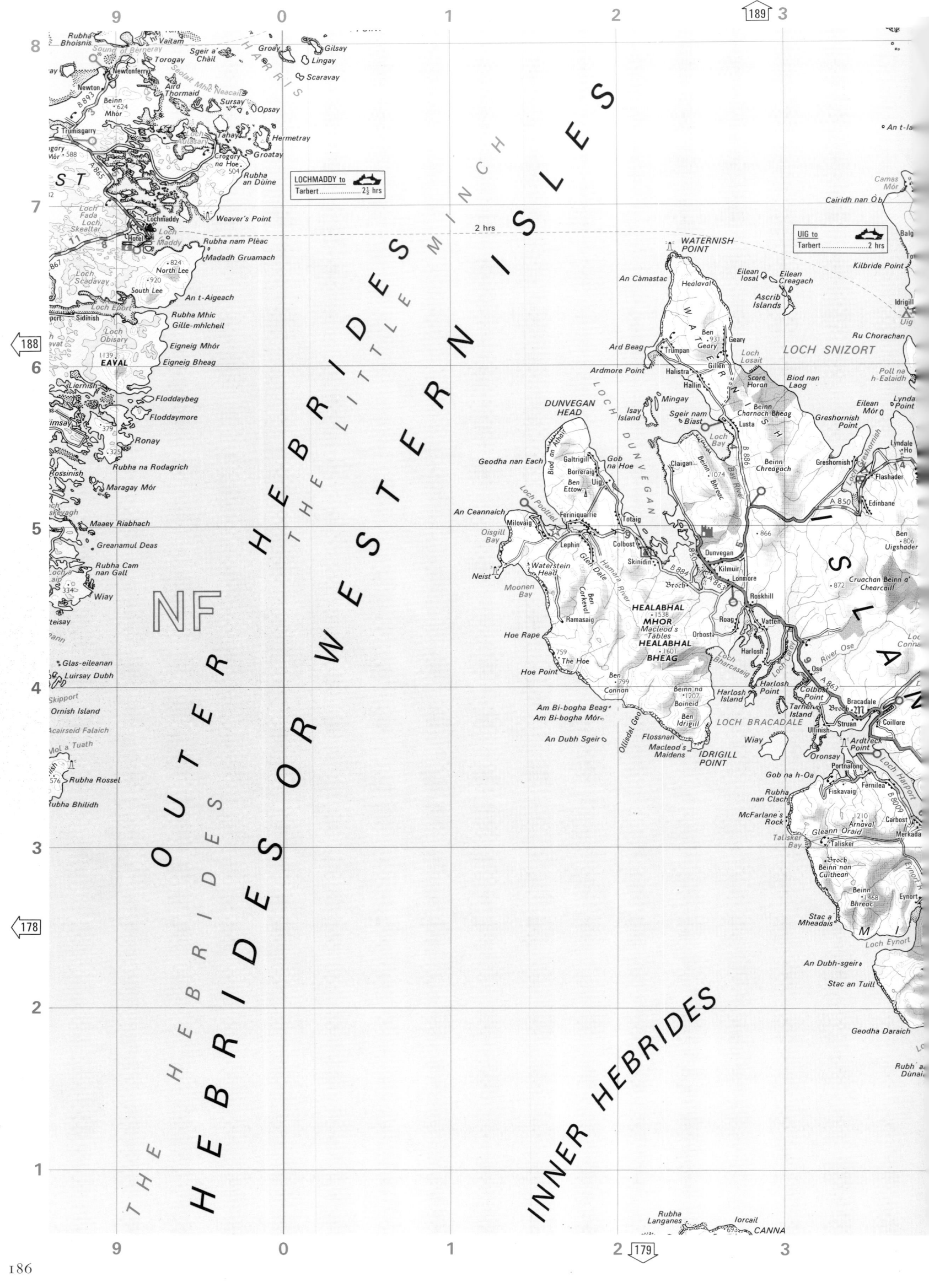

THE HEBRIDES OR WESTERN ISLES

INNER HEBRIDES

NF

THE LITTLE MINCH

OUTER HEBRIDES

LOCHMADDY to
Tarbert .... 2½ hrs

2 hrs

UIG to
Tarbert .... 2 hrs

EAVAL

WATERNISH
POINT

DUNVEGAN
HEAD

LOCH SNIZORT

LOCH BRACADALE

IDRIGILL
POINT

HEALABHAL
MHOR
Macleod's
Tables
HEALABHAL
BHEAG

188

178

179

THE WESTERN ISLES

PARK OR PAIRC

NB

NG

D E S O R   W E S T E R N   I S L E S

THE STORR

TROTTERNISH

S K Y E

I S L A N

ULLAPOOL to
Stornoway .... 3½ hrs

Eilean
Mullagrach
Isle Ristol
234
669
Polbain
Glas-leac Mór
268
Tanera
Beg
Summer
Isles
406
Tanera
Mór
Glas-leac Beag
Bottle
Island
Horse
Island
Eilean
Dubh
Priest Island
Càrr
Sgeir
Bodentarbal
Bay
Scoraig
Carnach
480
Cailleach Head
Leac D
LITTLE LO

Greenstone Point
Rubha Beag
Rubha Mór
Opinan
Stattic Point
Gob a' Chuaille
Mellon
Udrigle
478
Gruinard
Island
345
Badluarach
607
Achgarve
GRUINARD
BAY
Mungasdale
Gruinard
House
Inchina
Sròn a' Gheodha
Dhuibh
Eilean
Furadh Mór
Beinn • 513
Dearg Mhór
Laide
A 832
Durnamuck
Badcaul
Camas
Mór
271
340
Rubha
nan Sasan
Mellon
Charles
Sand
Coast
Little
Gruinard
985
Rubha Reigh
Cove
Ormiscaig
Bualnaluib
Tighnafiline
Drumchork
Beinn Dearg
Bad Chailleach
897
681
1283
Loch
an Draing
233
Aultbea
Carn nam
Buailtean
Sròn na Cléiter
972
An Cuaidh
Isle of
Ewe
Loch
Sguod
Loch
a' Bhaid
luachraich
Loch
Fada
1139
Melvaig
Inverasdale
LOCH EWE
593
Aird
Dhubh
Beinn a'
Chàisgein Beag
2230
Aultgrishan
Midtown
Rubha'
Ard na Bà
Meall
na Mèine
820
Fisherfield Forest
Beinn De
Mór
Seana
Chamas
962
Cnoc
Breac
Brae
Naast
Tournaig
Bad Bog
2802
Beinn a'
Chàisgein
Mór
Peterburn
Loch
Tallaidh
1140
1123
2595
Dubh
Loch
North
Erradale
Loch Bad
a' Chreamha
Lòndubh
Loch
Kernsary
Beinn
Airigh Charr
Port
Erradale
Poolewe
749
Rubha Bàn
Big Sand
R Sand
2817
Beinn Làir
Mh
Longa
Island
230
Caolas
Beag
B 8021
Lonemore
Strath
2595
Letterewe Forest
L
Gairloch
An Ard
Charlestown
1381
Meall
an Doirein
Letterewe
Beinn
Garbhaig
LOCH
GAIRLOCH
Eilean
Horrisdale
Eilean
Ruairidh
Mór
Eilean
Sùbhainn
Talladale
A 832
3215
SLIOCH
Port Henderson
9
264
Kerrysdale
Sròn na Carra
Badachro
Opinan
Shieldaig
River Kerry
Loch Bad
an Sgalaig
Loch
Maree
18
Rhu
Nòa
South
Erradale
B 8056
River Erradale
Loch
Clàir
Dubh
Loch
961
1312
Ananc
Redpoint
Flowerdale
Forest
Loch na h-
Oidhche
Beinn
an Eòin
Meall
Ghiubhais
2882
Kinlochewe
Sgeir Ghlas
Meall na
h-Uamha
2869
Shieldaig Forest
2805
2378
Ruadh-stac
Mór
3313
Beinn Eighe
National Nature
Reserve
A 896
Sgeir na Trian
Craig River
Beinn
Bhreac
2031
Loch a'
Bhealaich
W E S T E
3232
Beinn
Alligin
BEINN EIGHE
Loch
Clair
Coulin Lodge
Kilt Rock
Elishader
Valtos
Rubha nam
Brathairean
Culnaknock
Brackrey
Loch a' Bhraig
Rubha na
Fearn
Fearnmore
Lower
Diabaig
LIATHACH
11
Loch Diabalgas
Airde
3456
Torridon Forest
Glen Torridon
Sgurr
Dubh
2566
Coulin Forest
Port an
Fhearainn
410
Rubha
Chuaig
Fearnbeg
Arinacrinachd
Rechullin
Torridon Ho
A 896
Sgurr
Ruadh
3142
Leac
Tressirnish
ISLAND
OF
RONA
Eilean
Garbh
Cuaig
Kenmore
Ardheslaig
Loch a'
Chracaich
Alligin Shuas
Inveralligin
Torridon
UPPER
LOCH
TORRIDON
Annat
Abhainn
Thràil
3141
Loch
Coul
SOUND OF RAASAY
Eilean
Tigh
Garbh
Eilean
Kalnakill
Loch
Shieldaig
Balgy
Shieldaig
River Torridon
Ben-damph Forest
Beinn
Damh
2957
Beinn Liath Mhór
Coulin Lodge
Bearreraig
Bay
Loch a'
Sgurr
Abhainn Chuaig
Alltan t-Srathain
Alltan h-Eirigh
Lonbain
Loch
Gaineamhach
1619
Cròic-
bheinn
1692
Ben Shieldag
A 896
2410
Loch
an Eion
Sgorr
Ruadh
Holm
Island
833
Eilean
Fladday
Ard na
Claise Móire
Maol
Chean-dearg
3060
Achnashellach Sta
Prince
Charles's
Cave
Manish
Point
Torran
Loch
Arnish
2053
Glenshieldaig Forest
17
2332
Lair
Achna
F
Rubha na h-
Airde Glaise
Arnish
Brochel
Screapadal
Loch
nan Eun
Beinn a'
Chlachain
R Applecross
1682
Loch
Lundie
Loch
Coultrie
Sgurr a'
Gharaidh
2396
Balnacra
Coulags
Loch
Dùghaill
Achna
F
Udairn
Glame
1242
ISLAND
OF
RAASAY
Applecross Forest
2938
Beinn
Bhàn
Glas
Bheinn
2332
New
Kelso
Achintee
River Carron
Creag a' Chaora
Balachuirn
Balmeanach
Dùn
Caan
1455
Applecross Ho
Sgurr a'
Ghaorachain
Meall Gorm
2326
Sgurr a'
Ghaorachain
2539
Kirkton
A 896
Strathcarron
Carn
Geuradainn
1950
Creag a' Chaora
Ben
navaig
1355
tranavaig
Holoman
Bay
Applecross
Camusteel
Camusterrach
Ard-dhubh
Culduie
Loch
Bràigh an
Achaidh
Sanachan
Ardarroch
Lochcarron
1282
Attadale
Bearness
Loch
Lao
Oskaig
Rubha
Toscaig
Eilean na Bà
Toscaig
Achintraid
Loch Kishorn
Bendronai
Lodge

189
189
180

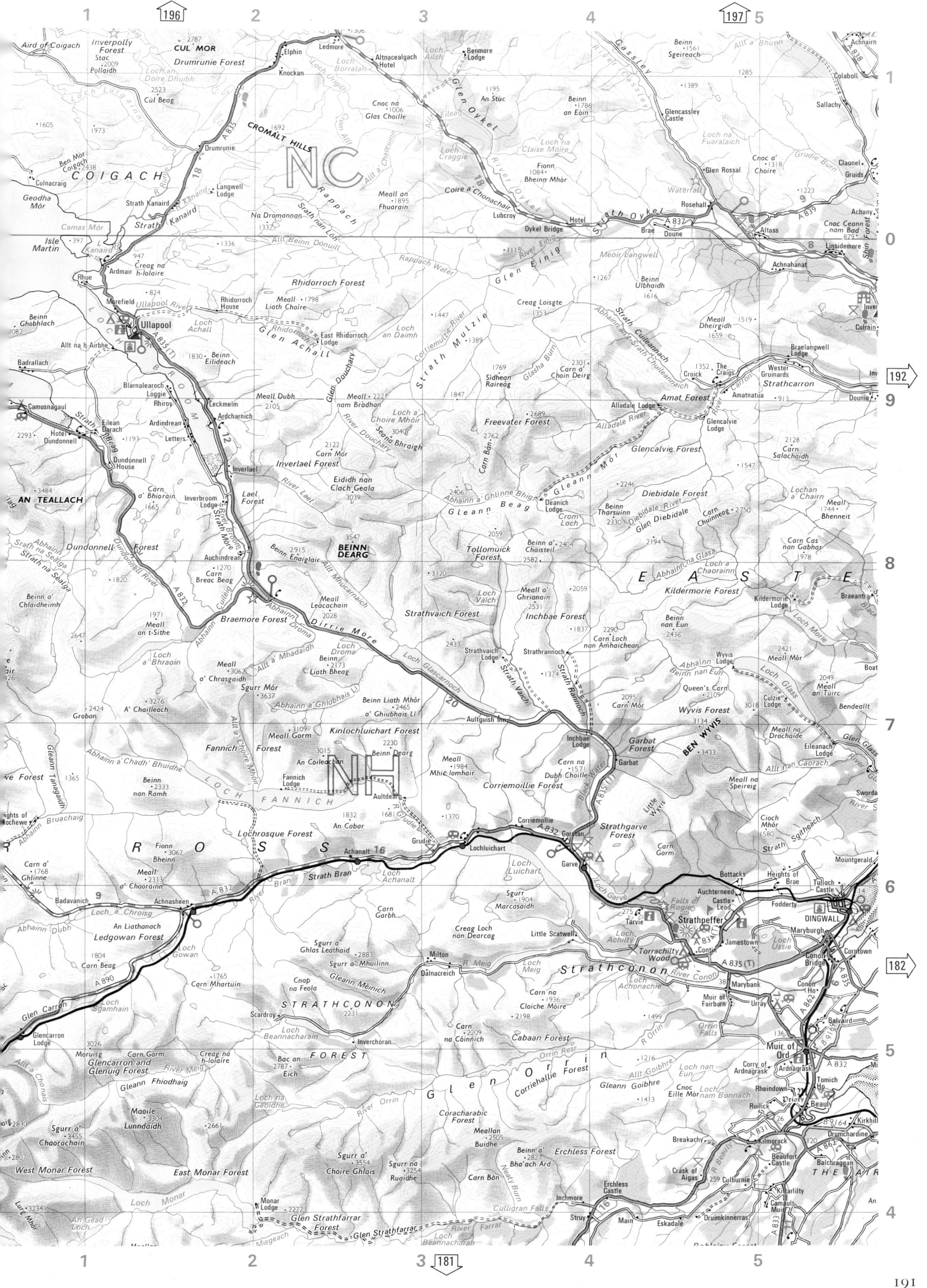

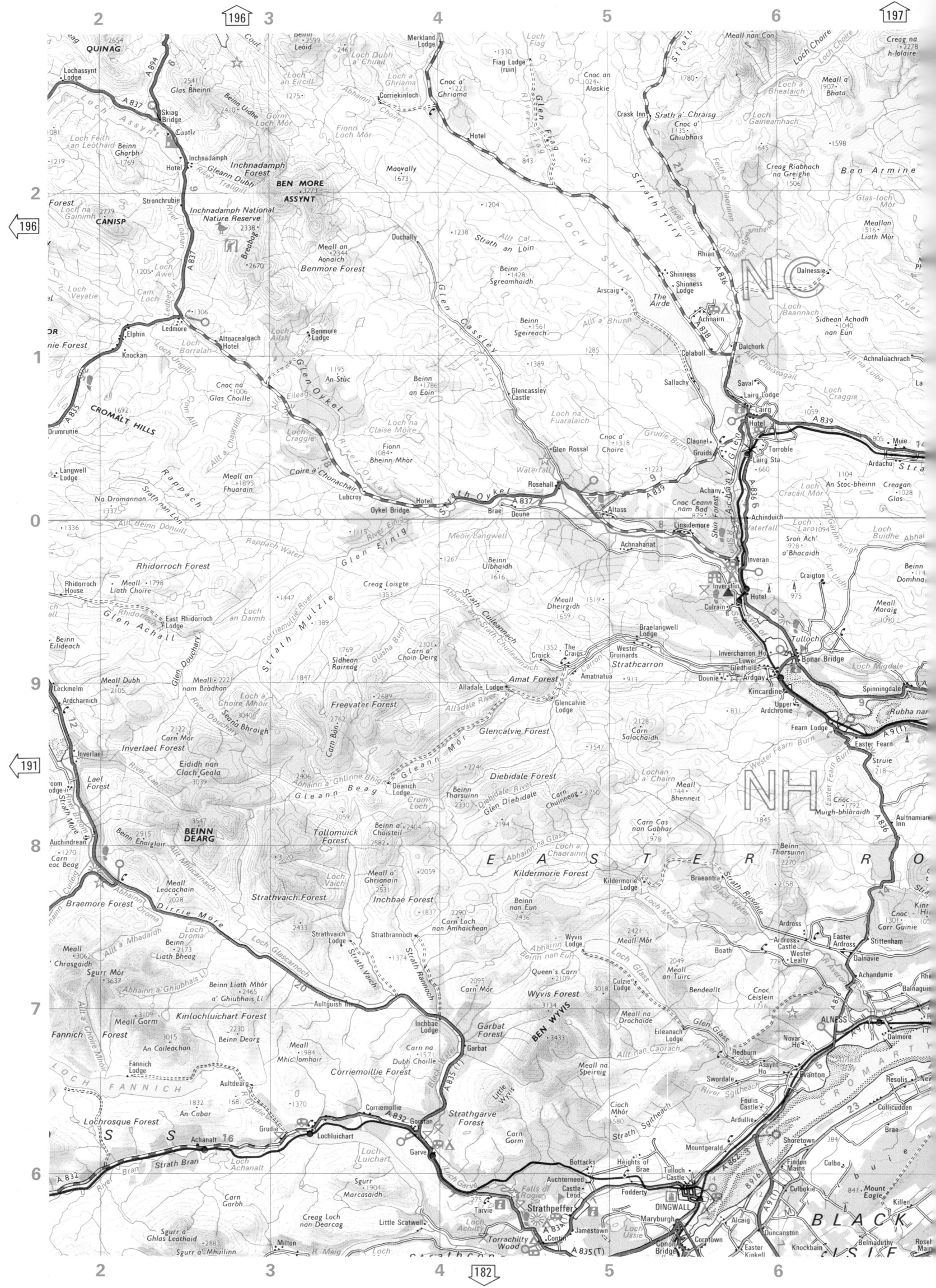

191

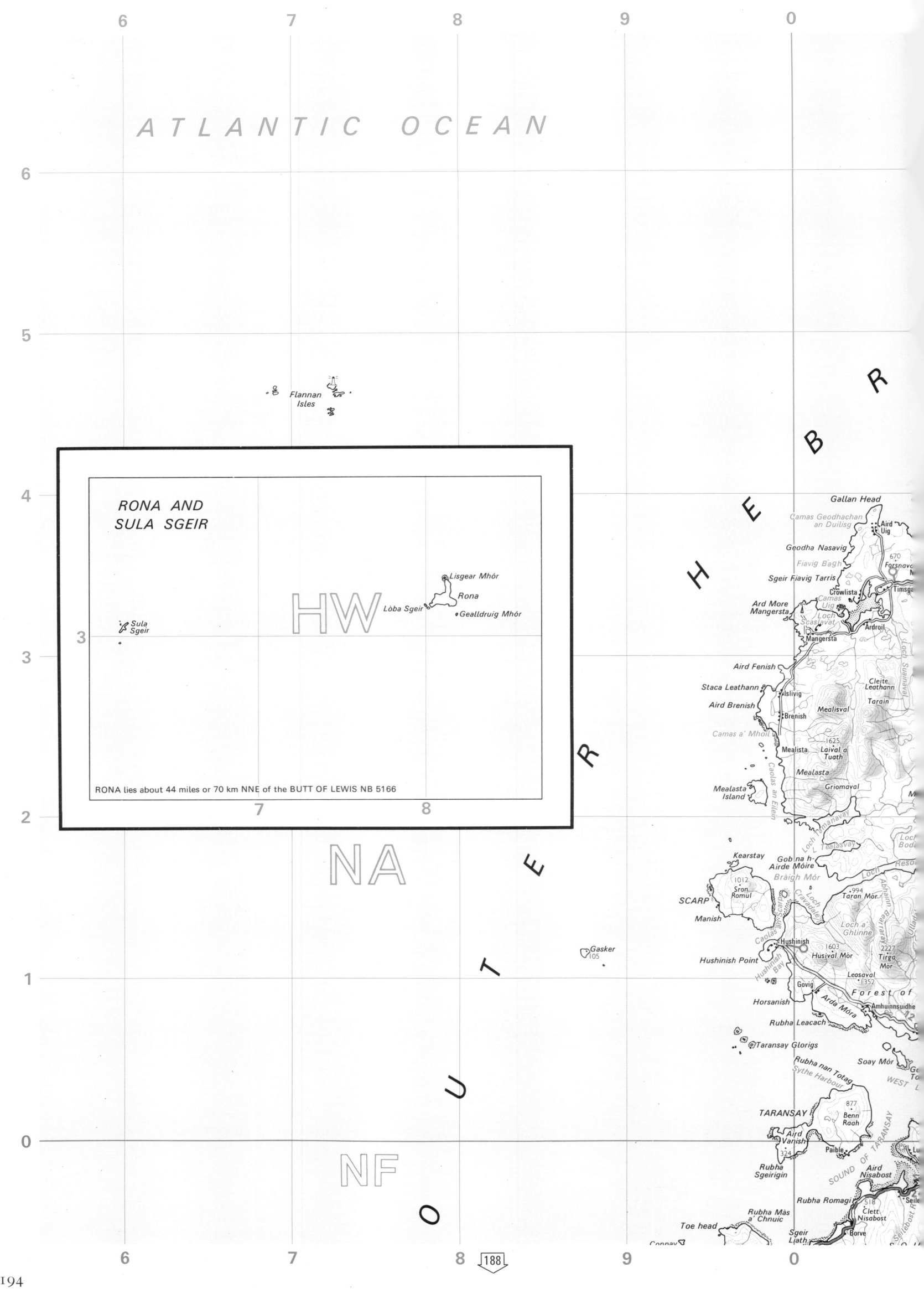

ATLANTIC OCEAN

H E B R

RONA AND
SULA SGEIR

HW

Flannan
Isles

Lisgear Mhór
Rona
Lòba Sgeir
Gealldruig Mhór

Sula
Sgeir

RONA lies about 44 miles or 70 km NNE of the BUTT OF LEWIS NB 5166

NA

NF

T E R

U

O

Gallan Head
Camas Geodhachan
an Duilisg
Aird
Uig
Geodha Nasavig
670
Forsnava
Fiavig Bagh
Sgeir Fiavig Tarris
Crowlista
Camas
Uig
Timsga
Ard More
Mangersta
Scaslavat
Ardroil
Mangersta

Aird Fenish

Staca Leathann
Islivig
Cleite
Leathann
Aird Brenish
Tarain
Brenish
Mealisval

Camas a' Mholl
1625
Mealista
Laival a
Tuath
Mealasta
Mealasta
Island
Griomaval

Loch
Bodo

Kearstay
Gob na h-
Airde Móire
Bràigh Mór
Loch
Reso

1012
Sron.
Romul
.994
Taran Mór
SCARP
Loch a'
Ghlinne
Manish

Gasker
105
Hushinish
1603
Hushinish Point
Husival Mór
2227
Tirga
Mór

1352
Govig
Leosaval
Horsanish
Arda Móra
Forest of
Amhuinnsuidhe
Rubha Leacach
Taransay Glorigs
Soay Mór
Rubha nan Totag
Sythe Harbour
WEST L

877
Benn
Raah
TARANSAY
Aird
Vanish
324
Paible
Rubha
Sgeirigin
Aird
Nisabost
SOUND OF TARANSAY
Rubha Romagi
518
Clett
Nisabost
Rubha Màs
a' Chnuic
Seile
Sgeir
Liath
Borve
Toe head
Connay

194
188

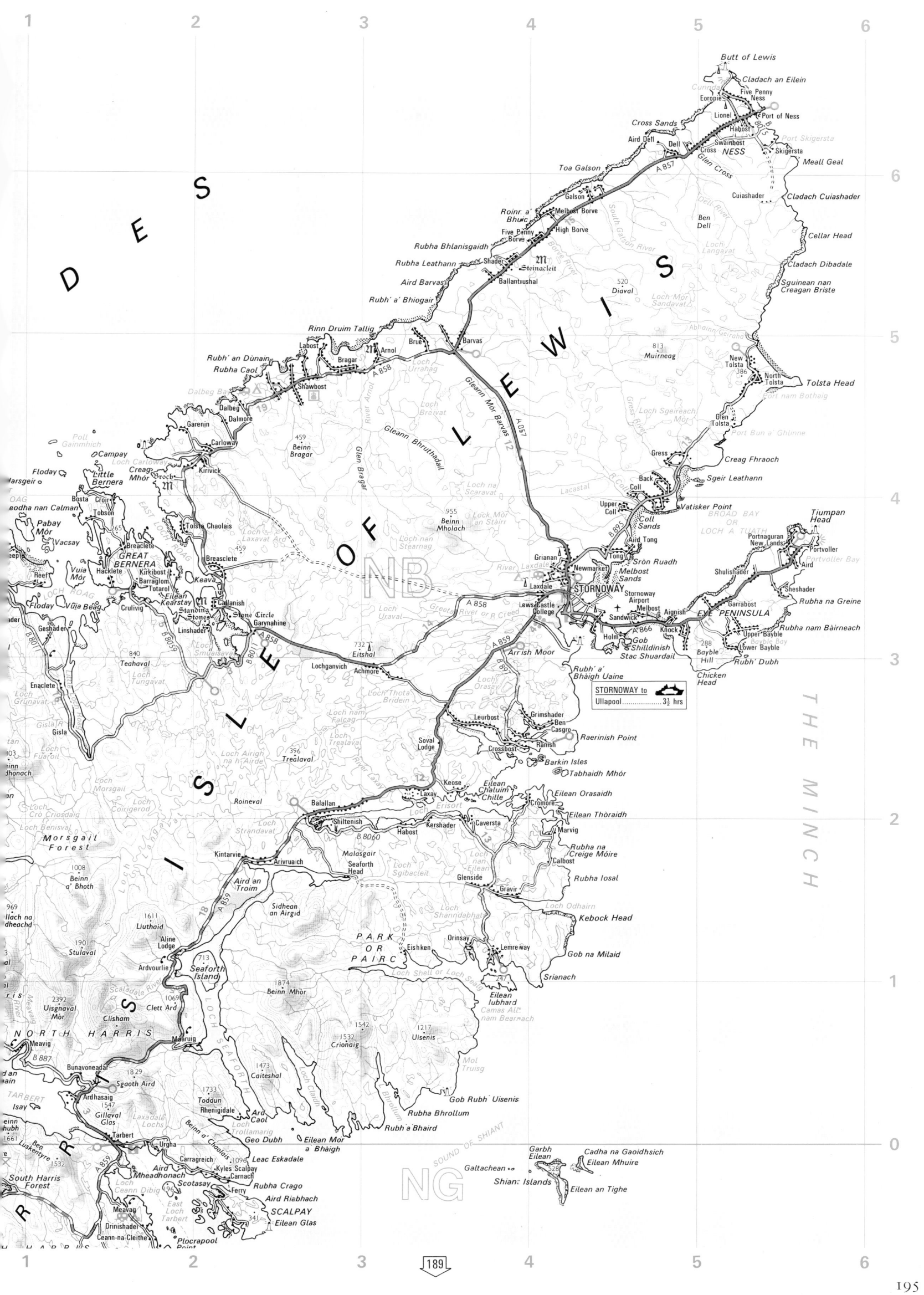

STACK SKERRY & SULE SKERRY

Sule Skerry

HX

Stack Skerry

Stack Skerry lies about 32 miles or 50 km N of WHITEN HEAD NC5068

6

NB

2

NB

THE MINCH

CAPE WRATH

Duslic

A' Chailleach
Am Bodach

Stack
Cló Kearvaig

An Garbh-eilean

Kearvaig

A' Ghoil

Faraid He

Geodha Ruadh
na Fola

976

Sgrìbhis-
bheinn

1216

Cnoc
a' Ghiubhais

984

Inshore

Loch
Inshore

726

Balnakeil

Bay of Keisgaig

Geodha Ruadh

498

Achiemore

Loch Airigh
na Beinne

911

Beinn an
Amair

Keoldale

Am Balg

505

Loch
Keisgaig

Fashven

1390

Beinn
Dearg

Sandwood
Loch

Creag
Riabhach

1592

1527

An Grianan

Strath Shinary

Abhainn an t-Strathain

598

Rubh' an
Fhir Lèithe

Loch na
Gainimh

Ghlas-
bheinn

1085

Farrmheall
709

Balchrick

828

1165

Droman
Oldshorebeg

202

Oldshoremore

An Socach

Gualin Ho

1034

A 838

19

Beinn
Spionnaidh

2535

Cranstackie

2630

Polla

Eilean an
Ròin Mór

Kinlochbervie

Badcall

B 801

Achriesgill

508

Loch na
Claise Càrnaich

1944

Loch Inchard

1605

Rubha na Leacaig

355

Achlyness

Hotel

Rhiconich

Strath Beag

Bàgh Loch
an Ròin

Loch Dughaill

Ceathramh Gàrbh

Ardmore Point

Ardmore

Ganu Mór

2980

1587

Rubha Ruadh

409

FOINAVEN

Fanagmore

Loch
Dionard

Loch 'a Garbh-
bhaid Mór

2553

Tarbet

Foindle

532

Loch an
Easain Uaine

1492

Handa Island

403

Loch
nam Brac

Laxford
Bridge

2580

Arkle

Scourie Bay

687

A 894

River Laxford

2548

Scourie

Gorm
Lochs

Lochstack
Lodge

Sàbhal
Beag

2393

Rubh' Aird
an t-Sionnaich

41

Loch
Stack

Abhainn an Lòin

Badcall

Ben Stack

2364

Strath Stack

Achfary

1093

Eilean a'
Bhreitheimh

Ben Auskaird

1265

18

Loch
Crocach

577

2627

Meallan Liath
Coire 'Mhic Dhughaill

2484

REAY FOREST

Lochmore
Lodge

1543

Meall Mór

Rubh' a'
Mhucard

Calbha
Beag

Ben
Strome

1374

Loch an
Leathaid Bhuain

Aultanrynie

Point of Stoer

Sgeir
nan Gall

Oldany
Island

EDDRACHILLIS BAY

Calbha
Mór

Allt nan Ramh

1777

Beinn
a' Bhùtha

Kinloch

A 838

1221

Cirean Geardail

530

Rubha nan Còsan

336

Eilean
Chrona

Kylestrome

Loch a' Chàirn Bhàin

Glendhu Forest

Loch More

1852

2010

Loch
Merkland

Cluas Deas

Clashnessie Bay

Drumbeg

353

Unapool

Loch Glendhu

Gleann Dubh

Beinn Aird
da Loch

Merkland
Lodge

Achnacarnin

B 869

Nedd

Newton

1722

Beinn

2599

246

Loch Dubh
a' Chuail

Balchladich

Clashmore

Clashnessie

337

Loch
Poll

Gleann Leireag

1722

Leoid

Cnoc

Rienachait

Loch a'
Leothaid

826

QUINAG

Glen Coul

2541

Loch an
Eircill

1275

Corriekinloch

Ghriam

Rubh' a' Mhill Dheirg

Stoer

Bay of Stoer

Clachtoll

2654

Lochassynt
Lodge

Glas Bheinn

A 894

Beinn
Udhe

2410

Gorm
Loch Mór

Fionn
Loch Mór

Rubha Leumair

681

Loch
Crocach

Skiag
Bridge

A 837

Achmelvich Bay

Rhicarn

Loch Beannach

Castle

Achmelvich

366

River Inver

1081

Loch Fèith
nan Leothaid

Beinn
Gharbh

Inchnadamph
Forest

Maovally

1673

Rubha Rodha

Baddidarach

Lochinver

Glencanisp
Lodge

1769

Hotel

Inchnadamph

Gleann Dubh

River Traligill

Soyea Island

Loch Inver

Loch Culag

1219

Stronchrubie

BEN MORE
ASSYNT

3273

Kirkaig Point

A' Chleit

Strathan

Abhainn na Clach Airigh

Glencanisp Forest

2779

Inchnadamph National
Nature Reserve

2338

Duchally

Loch Kirkaig

Inverkirkaig

Loch na
Gainimh

CANISP

Breabag

Rubha na Brèige

314

River Kirkaig

Fionn
Loch

SUILVEN

Meall an
Aonaich

2344

Rubha Coigeach

2399

Falls

641

Loch Veyatie

Loch
Awe

2670

Benmore Forest

Eilean Mór

262

ENARD BAY

Rubh' a'
Choin

Inverpolly
Lodge

Cam
Loch

Camas
Eilean Ghlais

Camas Coille

Inverpolly National
Nature Reserve

Ledbeg

1205

1306

1195

Rubha Mór

Brae of
Achnahaird

Loch Osgaig

Inverpolly
Forest

Stac
2009
Pollaidh

CUL MOR

2787

Drumrunie Forest

Elphin

Ledmore

Loch Urigill

Altnacealgach
Hotel

An Stùc

Reiff

Altandhu

234

Aird of Coigach

2523
Cul Beag

Knockan

Loch
Ailsh

Benmore
Lodge

Beinn

Eilean
Mullagrach

669

Polbain

Loch Bad
a' Ghaill

Loch
Doire Dhuibh

1605

Cnoc na
Glas Choille

1006

Glen Oykel

an Eoin

Isle Ristol

Glas-leac Mór

Badentarbat
Bay

Achiltibuie

1973

692

CROMALT HILLS

1786

Tanera
Beg

268

Polglass

A 835

Drumrunie

Loch
na

Summer
Isles

406

Tanera
Mór

ATLANTIC OCEAN

STRATHY POINT

Whiten Head or
An Ceann Geal

Geodh' a'
Bhrideoin

Eilean
Hoan

Rubha Thormaid

Port Allt a' Mhuilinn

Totegan

Eilean
Cluimhrig

Rispond

•603

Ben Hutig

Port Vasgo

Eilean nan Ròn

Ardmore
Point

Kirtomy
Point

•295

Strathy
Bay

Melvich
Bay

Red Point

Fresg

Dour

Heilam

Midfield

Neave or
Coomb Island

Farr
Point

Brawl

Baligill

Portskerra

Sandside Ho

•1338

Talmine

Skerray

Kirtomy

Altiphurst

Melvich

Bighouse

Rabbit
Islands

Armadale

Strathy

Hope

Lochside

•604

•632

Tongue
Bay

•361

Torrisdale

•369
Farr

Swordly

•643

Strathy
Forest

Bowside Lodge

Loch
Baligill

Golval

Drum
Hollistan
•608

Ben
Arnaboll

•756

Moine Ho

A 838

Skullomie
Coldbackie

Bettyhill
Achina

834

Beinn Ruadh

Loch
Akran

Loch
Meadie

Loch na
Seilge

Achuvoldrach

Borgie

Invernaver
Leckfurin

28

Loch
Buidhe Mòr

Beinn
nam Bò

•751

Achiemore

•746

Tongue Ho

A 836

•502

Strathy
Forest

Dalhalvaig

Cnoc Bad
Mhairtein

•747

Cno

Hotel

Tongue
Beinn
Bhreac

Skelpick

Loch Mòr na
Caorach

Loch
Meala

Trantlemore

Loch
Fhuarai

Ribigill

•577

•1018

Cnoc
1043
Craggie

Loch Craggie

•615

•620

Cnoc Badaireach
na Gaoithe

•692

Kinloch Lodge

•751

Beinn
Stumanadh

Rhifail

•963

Beinn
Rifa-gil

Loch
nan Clach

NC

Loch
na Seilg

•1962

Meallan
Liath

•1728

Skail

Loch
Strathy

Loch na
Saobhaidhe

•711

•918
Slethill Hill

Sle

BEN HOPE
3040

Loch
an Dherue

•2509

Ben
Loyal

•1828.
378

Loch Loyal
Lodge

Cnoc nan
Cuilean

Loch
Syre

Syre

Dalvina
Lodge

Allt Lon a' Chuill

•1110

•1133
Cnoc nan
Tri-chlach

Loch
Cròcach

Forsinain
Fm

Forsnain Burn

Alltnacaillich

•1364

Brock

•1167

Loch
Coulside

Loch
Haluim

Pole Hill

•965

Naver
Forest

•851

28

•1322

Loch Druim
a' Chliabhain

Ben Griam
Beg
•1902

Forsinard

•1210

Allnabad

Gobernuisgach
Lodge

•1143

Loch Meadie

Loch
Eileanach

B 873

856

Loch Naver

•887

Loch
Truderscaig

Hotel

640

Ben Griam
Mòr

•1331

Achentoul Forest

Lochside

Hotel

•1437

Loch a'
Ghorm-choire

•1821

•1302

Mudale

Altnaharra

270

Hotel

845

•933

Loch
Rimsdale

Loch
nan Clàr

Badanloch Forest

Loch
Badanloch

Badanloch
Lodge

•931

Loch
Achnamoine

Achentoul
1135

Knockfin
Heights

Fiag Lodge
(ruin)

•1330

Klibreck

Klibreck Burn

•1075

Allt an Achaidhean

Loch
Arichlinie

Kinbrace

Cnoc Coire
na Fearna
•1434

Meall an Fhuarain

•1549

BEN KLIBRECK
315·
•2367

Meall nan Con

Loch Choire
Lodge

Creag na
h-Iolaire
•2278

Cnoc an
Liath-bhaid Mhòir
•1423

River Helmsdale

Borrobol
Lodge

859

•912

Cnoc an
•1024
Alaskie

Loch a'
Bhealaich

Loch Choire Forest

Meall a'
Bhata
•1907

Ben Armine
•2311

Allt an Ealaidh

Gorm-loch
Beag

Borrobol Forest

Altanduin

Abhainn na Frithe

826

Kildonan Lodge

Beinn
•1365
Dubhain

Crask Inn

Srath a' Chràisg
Cnoc a'
Ghiubhais
1135

•1780

•1645

Creag
•2338
Mhòr

Gorm-loch
Mòr

•1598

Cnoc na
Bruen-choille
•1194

Creag
nam Fiadh
•1271

•1582

Ben Armine Forest

Strath of Kildonan or Strat

•843

•962

Creag Riabhach
na Greighe
•1506

Glas-loch
Mòr

•1253

Strath na Seilge

Ben Armine Lodge

Strath Skinsdale

Tuarie Burn

•1163

Craggie

Craggie Water

•1204

Meallan
Liath Mòr
•1516

Meall a'
Phiobaire
•1230

Coirefrois Burn

Black
Water

Cnoc
Meadhonach
•1134

•1581

Beinn
Dhorain
•2060

Loch
an Lòin

Rhian

Dalnessie

•783

•980

Brock

Meallan
Liath Beag
•1512

•1765

•1294

Shinness

Shinness
Lodge

Loch
Beannach

Sidhean Achadh
nan Eun
•1040

River Brora

Cnoc
961
Leamhnachd

Balnacoil

•1592

1765
Col-bheinn

Arscaig

The
Airde

Achnairn

Achnaluachrach

Grumby Rock
978

Strath Brora

Kilbraur
Hill

Loch
Brora

Gordonbush

Lothbeg

Colaboll

Dalchork

Glencassley
Castle

•1389

Sallachy

Saval

Lairg Lodge

West
Langwell

Dalreavoch

East
Langwell

Rhilochan

Farlary

Ben Horn
•1706

730
West Clyne

•1285

Lairg

Hotel

A 839

•1059

Loch
Craggie

•1063
Loch
Brora

Loch na
Fuaralaich

197

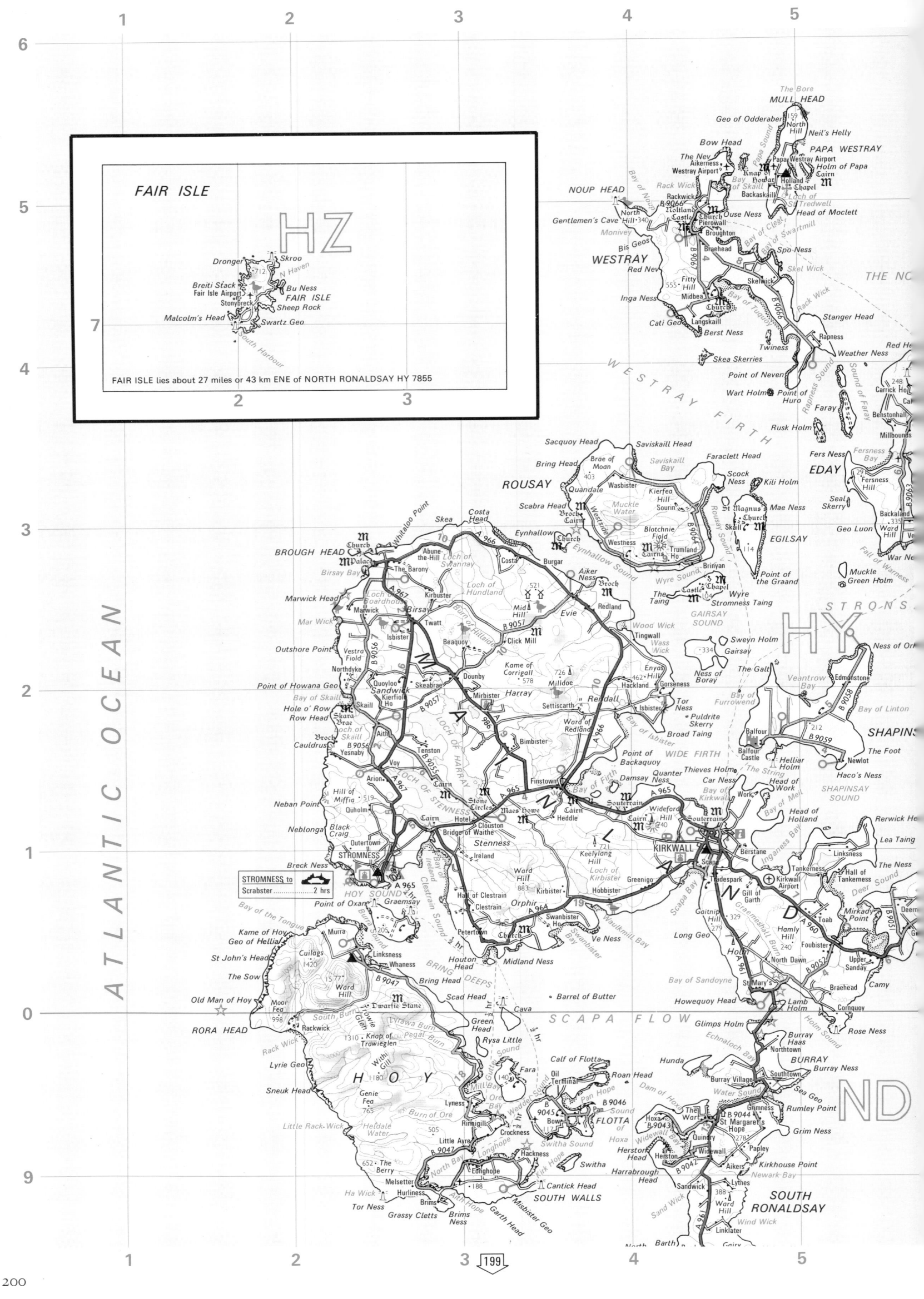

FAIR ISLE

HZ

Dronger
·712
Skroo
N Haven
Breiti Stack
Fair Isle Airport
Stonybreck
FAIR ISLE
Bu Ness
Sheep Rock
Malcolm's Head
Swartz Geo
South Harbour

FAIR ISLE lies about 27 miles or 43 km ENE of NORTH RONALDSAY HY 7855

ATLANTIC OCEAN

MULL HEAD
The Bore
Geo of Odderaber
59
North
Hill
Neil's Helly
Bow Head
The Nev
Aikerness
Westray Airport
Papa Westray Airport
PAPA WESTRAY
Holm of Papa
Cairn
Knap
of Skaill
Holland
Chapel
NOUP HEAD
North
Rackwick
Holland
Church
Ouse Ness
Pierowall
Head of Moclett
Gentlemen's Cave Hill ·340
B 9066
Braehead
Broughton
Spo Ness
Bay of Cleat
Head of Swartmill
Monivey
WESTRAY
Bis Geos
Red Nev
555
Fitty
Hill
Midbea
Skelwick
Rack Wick
B 9066
THE NO
Inga Ness
Church
Langskaill
Stanger Head
Cati Geo
Berst Ness
Twiness
Rapness
Red He
Skea Skerries
Weather Ness
Rapness Sound
248
Carrick Ho
Point of Neven
Wart Holm
Point of Huro
Faray
Benstonhall
WESTRAY FIRTH
Rusk Holm
Millbounds

Sacquoy Head
Saviskaill Head
Faraclett Head
Fers Ness
Fersness
Bay
B 9063
Bring Head
Brae of Moan
403
Saviskaill
Bay
EDAY
29
Fersness
Hill
Quandale
Wasbister
Scock
Ness
Kili Holm
Seal
Skerry
ROUSAY
Scabra Head
Kierfea
Hill
Sourin
St Magnus
Church
Mae Ness
Backaland
Broch
Cairn
Muckle
Water
Westside
Blotchnie
Field
B 9064
Geo Luon
Ward
Hill
Skea
Costa
Head
Eynhallow
Westness
Brinyan
EGILSAY
War Ne
BROUGH HEAD
Church
A 966
Church
Trumland
Ho
114
Point of
the Graand
Whitaloo Point
Abune-the-Hill
Costa
Burgar
Eynhallow Sound
Chapel
Muckle
Green Holm
Palace
The Barony
Loch of
Swannay
Aiker
Ness
Broch
The Taing
Wyre
STRONS
Birsay Bay
Kirbuster
Mid
Hill
Redland
Wyre Sound
Stromness Taing
Marwick Head
Marwick
Birsay
521
Evie
Wood Wick
GAIRSAY
SOUND
HY
Mar Wick
Isbister
Twatt
B 9057
Tingwall
Sweyn Holm
Gairsay
Ness of Or
Outshore Point
Beaquoy
Click Mill
Wass
Wick
·334
The Galt
Vestra
Fiold
Dounby
Kame of
Corrigall
Enyas
Hill
Ness of
Boray
Veantrow
Bay
Edmonstone
Point of Howana Geo
Northdyke
B 9056
578
Hackland
Gorseness
726
Bay of
Furrowend
Bay of Linton
Quoyloo
Skeabrae
462 Milldoe
Harray
Rendall
Tor
Ness
Puldrite
Skerry
B 9058
SHAPINS
Bay of Skaill
Sandwick
Kierfiold
Ho
B 9057
Mirbister
Settiscarth
Ward of
Redland
A 966
Broad Taing
Balfour
Bay of Isbister
B 9059
The Foot
Hole o' Row
Skaill
Bimbister
Point of
Backaquoy
WIDE FIRTH
Balfour
Castle
Helliar
Holm
Newlot
Row Head
Skara
Brae
Aith
Isbister
A 966
Damsay Ness
Thieves Holm
The String
Haco's Ness
Broch
Cauldrust
B 9056
Yesnaby
Tenston
Finstown
Quanter
Ness
Car Ness
Head of
Work
SHAPINSAY
SOUND
Voy
Cairn
A 965
Bay of Firth
Souterrain
Work
Head of
Holland
Arion
Stone
Circles
Maes Howe
Wideford
Hill
A 965
Souterrain
Rerwick He
Hill of
Miffia
519
Hotel
Cairn
Heddle
Cairn
KIRKWALL
Lea Taing
Neban Point
Quholm
Clouston
Bridge of Waithe
·240
Scapa
Berstane
Linkness
The Ness
Neblonga
Cairn
Ireland
Stenness
Keelylang
Hill
Loch of
Kirbister
Greenigo
Tradespark
Kirkwall
Airport
Hall of
Tankerness
Inganess Bay
Black
Craig
Outertown
STROMNESS
Ward
Hill
883
Hobbister
Gill of
Garth
Gaitnip
Hill
279
Mirkady
Point
Deer
Sound
Breck Ness
Hall of Clestrain
Kirbister
19
Hamly
Hill
240
Toab
B 9050
Deern
STROMNESS to
Scrabster............2 hrs
HOY SOUND
Point of Oxan
Graemsay
Clestrain
Orphir
A 964
Swanbister
Ho
Long Geo
Foubister
Upper
Sanday
Bay of the Tongue
Murra
205
Church
Petertown
Ve Ness
North Dawn
Holm
A 961
Kame of Hoy
Geo of Hellia
Linksness
Whaness
Houton
Head
Midland Ness
Swanbister
Bay
Bay of Sandoyne
St Mary's
Braehead
Camy
St John's Head
Cuilags
1420
Bring Head
Waulkmill Bay
Howequoy Head
Lamb
Holm
Corquoy
The Sow
15 77
Ward
Hill
Scad Head
Barrel of Butter
Glimps Holm
Burray
Haas
Rose Ness
Old Man of Hoy
B 9047
998
Moor
Fea
Dwarfie Stane
Cava
Green
Head
SCAPA FLOW
Northtown
Burray Ness
RORA HEAD
Rackwick
Trowie
Glen
Knap of
Trowieglen
1310
Rysa Little
Rysa
Sound
Echnaloch Bay
BURRAY
Lyrie Geo
Lyrawa Burn
Pegal Burn
Calf of Flotta
Roan Head
Hunda
Burray Village
Southtown
Sea Geo
Sneuk Head
HOY
1180
Genie
Fea
765
Withi Gill Burn
18
Fara
140
Oil
Terminal
Pan Hope
Water Sound
Rumley Point
Newark Bay
ND
Little Rack-Wick
Lyness
Ore
Bay
Wedder
Sound
B 9046
FLOTTA
Hoxa
The Wart
B 9044
Ghmness
Heldale
Water
505
Rinnigill
B 9045
Pan
Sound
of
Hoxa
St Margaret's
Hope
Grim Ness
Little Ayre
B 9047
Crockness
Herston
Head
Quindry
278
Papley
Ha Wick
652 The
Berry
Longhope
Hackness
Swithа Sound
Herston
B 9043
Widewall
B 9042
Aikers
Kirkhouse Point
Melsetter
Hurliness
Edinhope
Swithа
Harrabrough
Head
Sandwick
Lythes
Brims
Garth Head
Cantick Head
SOUTH WALLS
Sand Wick
388
Ward
Hill
Linklater
SOUTH
RONALDSAY
Tor Ness
Grassy Cletts
Brims
Ness
Misbister Geo
A 961
Wind Wick
North
Barth
Gairy

199
200

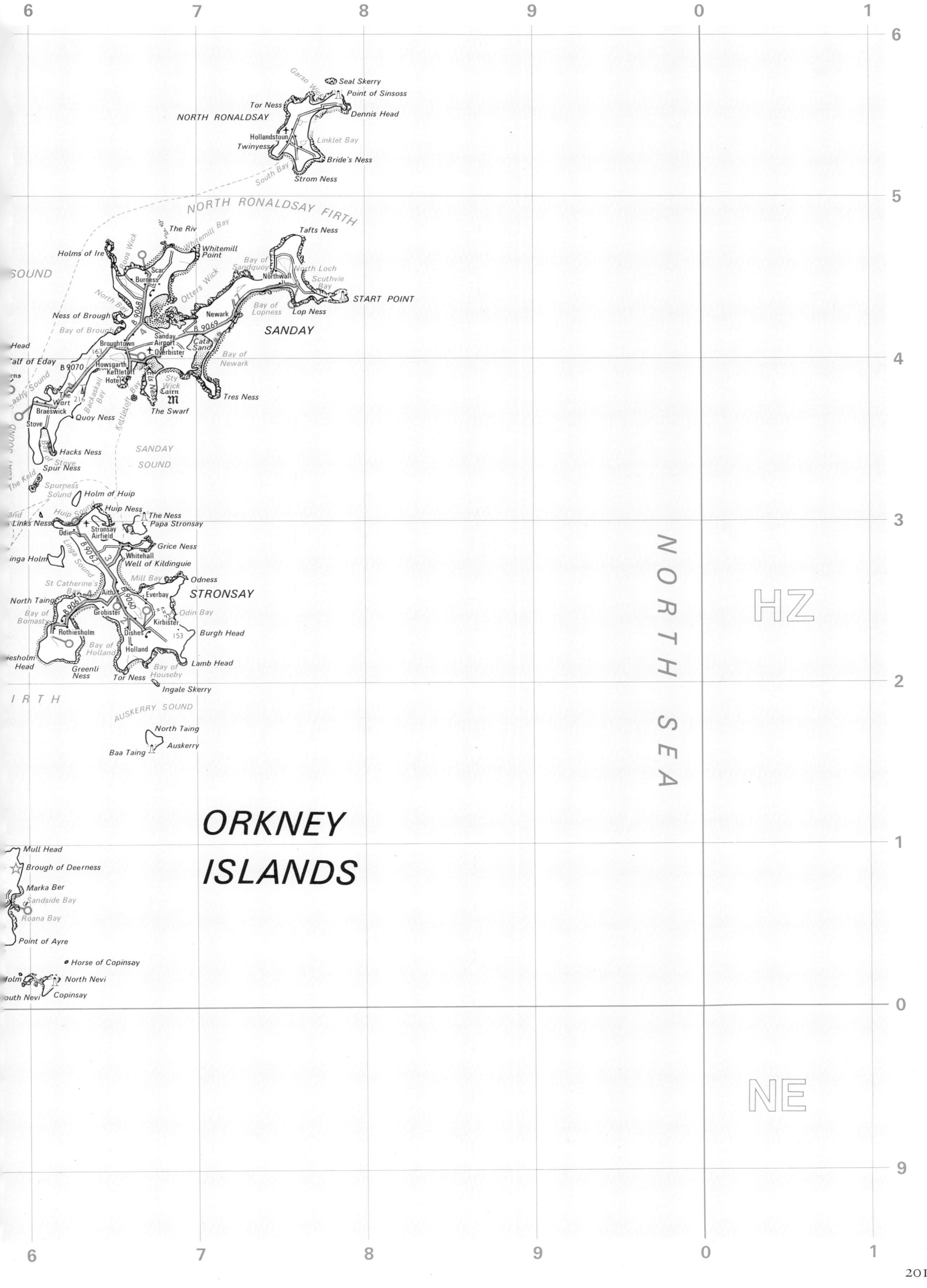

Garso Wick

Seal Skerry
Point of Sinsoss
Tor Ness
Dennis Head
NORTH RONALDSAY

Hollandstoun
Twinyess   Linklet Bay
Bride's Ness
Strom Ness
South Bay

NORTH RONALDSAY FIRTH

The Riv   Tafts Ness
Whitemill Bay
Holms of Ire   Whitemill
Point
SOUND   Scar   Bay of
Burness   Sandquoy   Warth Loch
Northwall   Scuthvie
Otters Wick   Bay
North Be   START POINT
Ness of Brough   Newark   Bay of   Lop Ness
B 9068   Lopness
Bay of Brough   B 9069   SANDAY
Head   Broughtown   Sanday   Cata
alf of Eday   Airport   Sand
B 9070   Howsgarth   Overbister   Bay of
ns   Kettletoft   Newark
Hotel   Sty
ashy Sound   Wick
The   216   Cairn
Wart   Tres Ness
Braeswick
Stove   Quoy Ness   The Swarf
SOUND
Hacks Ness   SANDAY
Stove   SOUND
The Keld   Spur Ness

Spurness
Sound   Holm of Huip
Huip Ness
and   Huip Sound   The Ness
Links Ness   Papa Stronsay
Odie   Stronsay
Airfield
inga Holm   B 9061   Grice Ness
Whitehall
Linga Sound   Well of Kildinguie
St Catherine's   Mill Bay   Odness
inga Holm   Aith   Everbay   STRONSAY
North Taing   B 9061   Odin Bay
Bay of   Grobister   Kirbister
Bomasty   Dishes   Burgh Head
Rothiesholm   153
Bay of
esholm   Holland   Holland
Head   Greenli   Lamb Head
Ness   Tor Ness   Bay of
Houseby
Ingale Skerry

IRTH
AUSKERRY SOUND

North Taing
Auskerry
Baa Taing

ORKNEY
ISLANDS

NORTH SEA

HZ

Mull Head
Brough of Deerness

Marka Ber
Sandside Bay
Roana Bay

Point of Ayre

Horse of Copinsay
olm   North Nevi
outh Nevi   Copinsay

NE

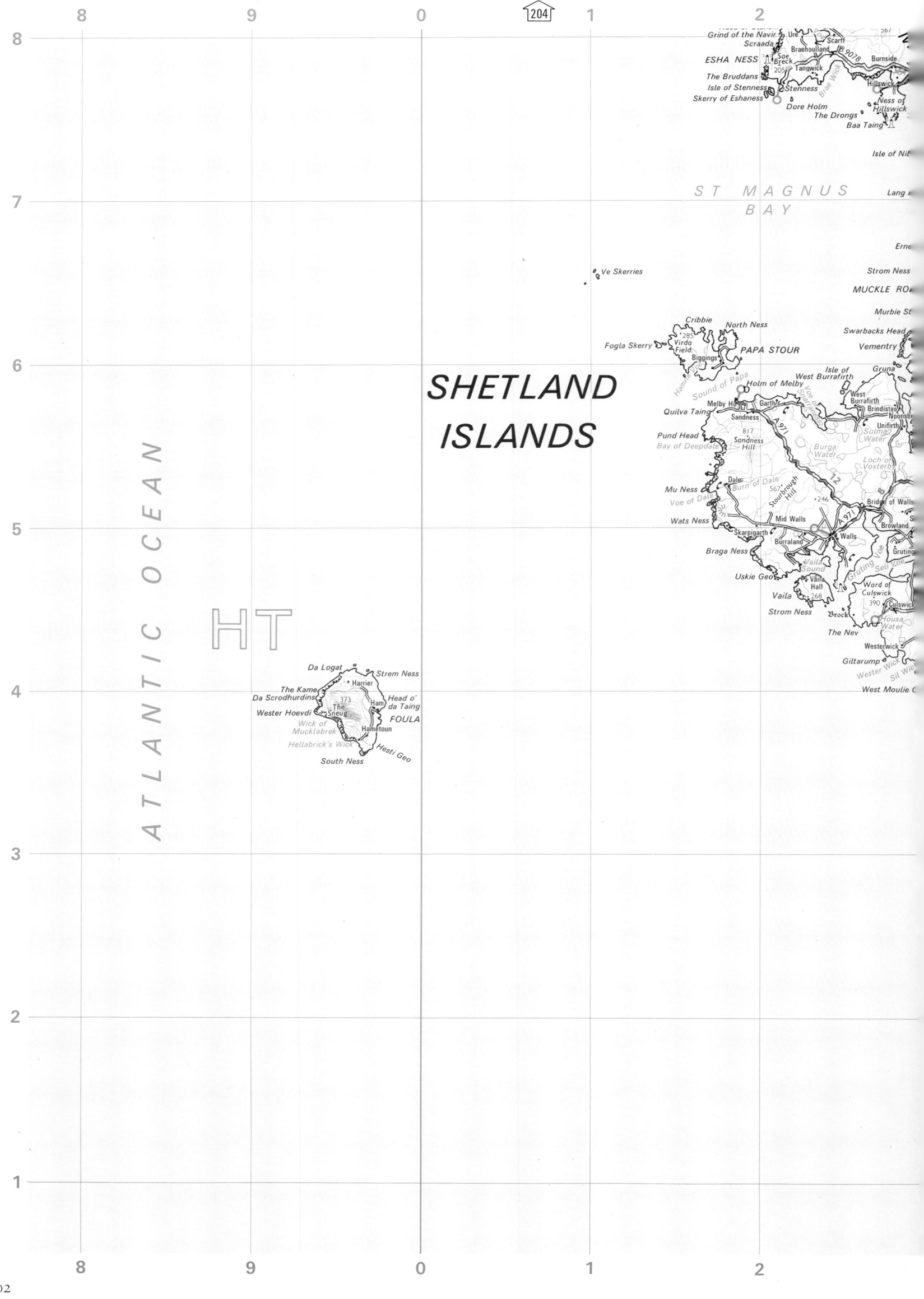

SHETLAND
ISLANDS

ST MAGNUS BAY

ATLANTIC OCEAN

ESHA NESS

Grind of the Navir   Ure
Scraada   Scarff
                     Braehoulland
Sae   Braehoulland   Burnside
Breck   Tangwick
The Bruddans
Isle of Stenness   Stenness
Skerry of Eshaness   Hillswick
Dore Holm   Ness of Hillswick
          The Drongs
                     Baa Taing

                                         Isle of Nib

                                         Lang

                                         Erne

                                         Strom Ness

                                         MUCKLE RO

                                         Murbie St

Ve Skerries

Cribbie   North Ness   Swarbacks Head
Fogla Skerry   Virda Field   PAPA STOUR   Vementry
                     Biggings   Gruna
                     Sound of Papa   Isle of West Burrafirth
                     Holm of Melby   West Burrafirth
Melby Ho   Garth   Brindister   Noonsb
Quilva Taing   Sandness   Unifirth   Sulma
Pund Head   Sandness Hill   Burga Water Loch o' Voxterb
Bay of Deepdale
Dale   Burn of Dale   Stourbrough Hill
Mu Ness   Voe of Dale   Bridge of Walls
Wats Ness   Mid Walls   Walls   Browland
Skarpigarth   Burraland   Gruting
Braga Ness   Waila Sound
Uskie Geo   Vaila Hall   Ward of Culswick
                     Vaila   Culswick
Strom Ness   Brock   Housa Water
The Nev   Westerwick
                                        Giltarump   Wester Wick   Sil Wic
                                                      West Moulie

HT

Da Logat   Strem Ness
The Kame   Harrier
Da Scrodhurdins   Head o' da Taing
Wester Hoevdi   The Sneug Ham
Wick of Mucklabrek   Hametoun FOULA
Hellabrick's Wick
South Ness   Hesti Geo

HO

ATLANTIC OCEAN

HT

Isle of Fet
Garmus Taing
Uyea 231
Burrier Wick
The Breck
Fugla Ness
South Wick
Nort
Roe
Hevdadale Head
Egga Field
564
Burn of Sandvoe
Lang Clodie Wick
644
Beorgs of
Skelberry
Gruna Stack
Turls Head
North Roe
The Faither
Roer
Watir
Muckle Ossa
351 Ketligill
Heillia Head
Stonga
Banks
Housetter
Ockran Head
Burries
Ness
740
Man
o' Scord
Collafirth
475
Ronas
Hill
South Head
Gluss
Water
Heylor
The
Clifts
Voe
Ollab
Whalwick Taing
Hamar
Faan
Hill
Head of Stanshi
Ure
Hamnavoe
567
Grind of the Navir
Scarff
Urafirth
B 9019
Scraada
Braehoulland
B 9078
Eela
Water
ESHA NESS
Sae
Breck
Burnside
10
A 970
Gluss
Bard
The Bruddans
205
Tangwick
Ness of
Olnesfirth
Isle of Stenness
Stenness
Hillswick
Burraland
Skerry of Eshaness
Dore Holm
Ness of
Hillswick
Blae Wick
389
Sullom
The Drongs
Ura Firth
Baa Taing
Isle of Nibon
Nibon
Cairn
ST MAGNUS
396
Mangaster
BAY
Lang Head
Egilsay
Islesburgh
Mavis
Grind
Turvalds Head
315
Erne Stack
Busta
Strom Ness
Roesound
MUCKLE ROE
555
South
Ward
Linga
Murbie Stacks
Little-ayre
Cribbie
North Ness
Swarbacks Minn
Swarbacks Head
Fogla Skerry
285
Virda
Field
Biggings
PAPA STOUR
Vementry
Cairn
498
Papa
Little
272
Isle of
West Burrafirth
Gruna

SHETLAND
ISLANDS

Holm of Melby
West
Burrafirth
Noonsbrough
Clousta
Loch
of
Vaara
Melby H
Garth
Quilva Taing
Sandness
Unifirth
Suma
Water
Brindister
Aith
817
A 971
Aittsting
Pund Head
Sandness
Hill
Burga
Water
313
Bay of Deepdal
Dale
Loch of
Voxterb
Twatt
Bixter
Mu Ness
567
Stourbrough
Hill
The Firth
Voe of Dale
Burn of Dale
246
Bridge of Walls
Effirth
Wats Ness
Mid Walls
Stanydale
Semblister
Tresta
Skarpigarth
Walls
Browland
B 9071
Ru
Braga Ness
Burraland
Gruting
A 971
Garderhouse
San
Uskie Geo
Vaila
Hall
Vaila
Sound
Gruting Voe
Sel
Ward of
Gossa

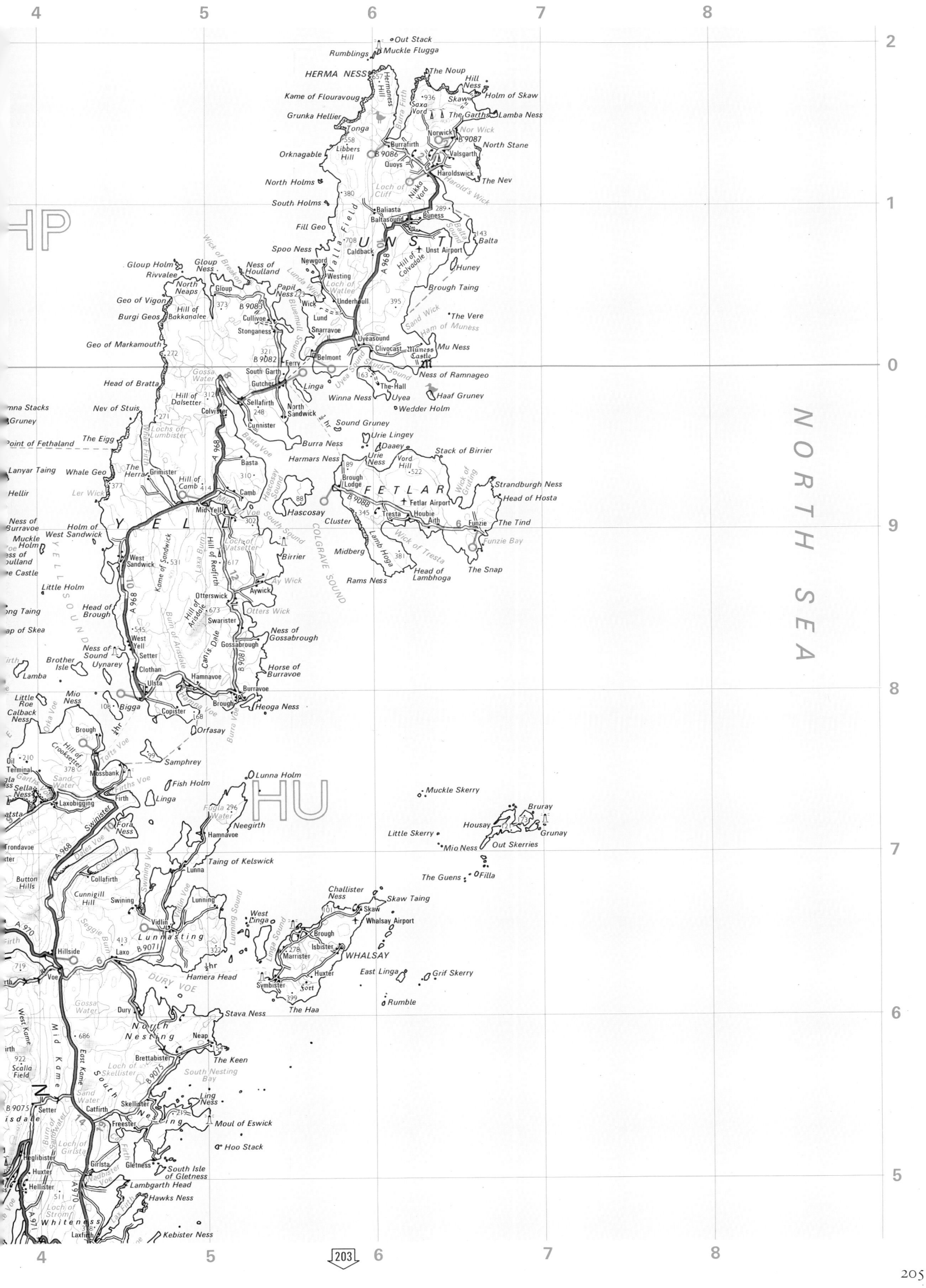

NORTH SEA

Out Stack
Rumblings
Muckle Flugga
HERMA NESS
Hermaness Hill 657
The Noup
Hill Ness
Kame of Flouravoug
936
Holm of Skaw
Saxa Vord
Skaw
Grunka Hellier
The Garths
Lamba Ness
Tonga
558
Norwick
Nor Wick
Orknagable
Burrafirth
B 9086
Burrafirth
Quoys
Valsgarth
B 9087
North Stane
Libbers Hill
Haroldswick
The Nev
North Holms
380
UNST
Loch of Cliff
Nikka Vord
South Holms
Fill Geo
Baliasta
Baltasound
Buness
289
Balta
143
Spoo Ness
708
Caldback
Gloup Holm
Gloup Ness
Ness of Houlland
Newgord
Unst Airport
Rivvalee
Gloup
Westing
Hill of Colvadale
Huney
North Neaps
Papil Ness
Loch of Watlee
Geo of Vigon
373
B 9083
Wick
Underhoull
Brough Taing
Burgi Geos
Hill of Bakkanalee
Cullivoe
Lund
395
Sand Wick
Stonganess
Snarravoe
Ham of Muness
Geo of Markamouth
272
321
Uyeasound
The Vere
B 9082
Clivocast
Muness Castle
Mu Ness
Head of Bratta
Gossa Water
Ferry
Belmont
Ness of Ramnageo
Hill of Dalsetter
South Garth
Skuda Sound
Nev of Stuis
312
Gutcher
63
Linga
The-Hall
Haaf Gruney
Point of Fethaland
271
Colvister
Sellafirth
248
Uyea
Wedder Holm
Lanyar Taing
The Eigg
Cunnister
North Sandwick
Winna Ness
Whale Geo
The Herra
Grimister
Hill of Camb
Basta
Sound Gruney
Hellier
Ler Wick
377
Camb
310
Burra Ness
89
Urie Lingey
Daaey
Stack of Birrier
Ness of Burravoe
Holm of West Sandwick
Mid Yell
414
Hascosay Sound
Harmars Ness
Urie Ness
Vord Hill
522
Wick of Gruting
Muckle Holm
YELL
302
Hascosay
88
Brough Lodge
FETLAR
Strandburgh Ness
Head of Hosta
Ness of Houlland
West Sandwick
Kame of Sandwick
531
Hill of Redfirth
617
12
Loch of Vatsetter
Birrier
B 9088
Cluster
345
Tresta
Fetlar Airport
Houbie
Aith
Funzie
The Tind
Little Holm
West Yell
Laxa Burn
Ay Wick
Midberg
Lamb Hoga
Funzie Bay
Brother Isle
Head of Brough
545
Otterswick
Aywick
Otters Wick
Rams Ness
381
Head of Lambhoga
The Snap
Lamba
Ness of Sound
A 968
Hill of Arisdale
673
Swarister
Ness of Gossabrough
Horse of Burravoe
Little Roe
Uynarey
Setter
Burn of Arisdale
Can's Dale
Gossabrough
Calback Ness
Clothan
B 9081
Mio Ness
108
Bigga
Copister
Ulsta
Hamnavoe
Burravoe
Heoga Ness
Brough
568
Orfasay
Samphrey
Brough
Hill of Crooksetter
Oil Terminal
210
378
Mossbank
Lunna Holm
Muckle Skerry
Bruray
Housay
Grunay
Out Skerries
Little Skerry
Mio Ness
HU
Sand Water
Fish Holm
Firths Voe
Linga
Fugla Water
296
Neegirth
Hamnavoe
Taing of Kelswick
The Guens
Filla
Laxobigging
Firth
Lunna
Swinister
Fora Ness
Trondavoe
A 968
Dales Voe
Collafirth
Lunning
Challister Ness
Skaw Taing
Button Hills
Cunnigill Hill
Swining
Lunning
Skaw
Whalsay Airport
A 970
Vidlin
West Linga
Brough
Collafirth
413
Lunnasting
Isbister
WHALSAY
Hillside
Laxo
B 9071
Marrister
278
East Linga
Grif Skerry
719
Voe
Gossa Water
Dury
Hamera Head
322
Huxter
Symbister
Sort
Rumble
North Nesting
Neap
399
The Haa
Stava Ness
West Kame
686
Brettabister
The Keen
922 Scalla Field
Mid Kame
East Kame
South Kame
Loch of Skellister
Loch of Girlsta
Sand Water
B 9075
South Nesting Bay
Setter
Catfirth
Skellister
Ling Ness
B 9075
Isdale
Freester
219
Moul of Eswick
Hoo Stack
Hegliabister
Huxter
Girlsta
Gletness
Hellister
Lambgarth Head
South Isle of Gletness
511
Hawks Ness
Whiteness
Laxfirth
Kebister Ness
A 971

INDEX TO 1:250 000 SCALE MAPS

Content

The index lists all the definitive names shown in the map section of the Atlas. For each entry the Atlas page number is listed and the National Grid map reference is given to the nearest kilometre of the feature to which the name applies.

For long linear features, such as the River Thames, more than one reference is given. For these multiple entries and where a name applies to more than one feature the County, Region or Island Area name is also given.

Abbreviations used in the index to identify the nature of certain named features and abbreviations for Counties used in the Index are listed here.

Method of Listing Names

Names are listed alphabetically in the index as they appear on the map. For example, 'Ashdown Forest' appears under 'A', while 'Forest of Bere' is under 'F'. Similarly, 'Beaulieu River' appers under 'B' but 'River Thames' is under 'R'. When the definite article precedes a name, the name appears first. Thus, 'The Wash' becomes 'Wash, The' and is listed under 'W'. An exception to this rule is made in the case of Gaelic and Welsh place names. These are listed under the initial letter of the Gaelic or Welsh definite article. For example, 'An Ceannaich' is listed under 'A' and 'Y Llethr' is listed under 'Y'.

How to use this Index   Example:

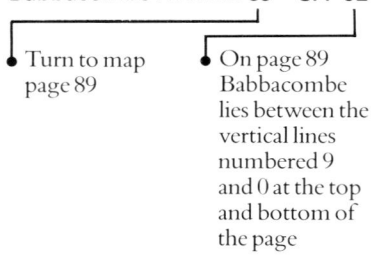

Babbacombe . . . . **89**   SX 92 65

- Turn to map page 89
- On page 89 Babbacombe lies between the vertical lines numbered 9 and 0 at the top and bottom of the page
- Babbacombe lies between the horizontal lines numbered 6 and 7 at left or right of the page

This reference system is a simplification of the National Grid system which allows one to pinpoint a place very accurately on the map and to find the same place on any other map of any scale using the same system. A full explanation is given with the National Grid map of Great Britain on the last endpaper.

List of County Names showing Abbreviations used in this Index

England

Avon	Avon
Bedfordshire	Beds
Berkshire	Berks
Buckinghamshire	Bucks
Cambridgeshire	Cambs
Cheshire	Ches
Cleveland	Cleve
Cornwall	Corn
Cumbria	Cumbr
Derbyshire	Derby
Devon	Devon
Dorset	Dorset
Durham	Durham
East Sussex	E. Susx
Essex	Essex
Gloucestershire	Glos
Greater London	G. Lon
Greater Manchester	G. Man
Hampshire	Hants
Hereford & Worcester	H & W
Hertfordshire	Herts
Humberside	Humbs
Isle of Wight	I. of W
Kent	Kent
Lancashire	Lancs
Leicestershire	Leic
Lincolnshire	Lincs
Merseyside	Mers
Norfolk	Norf

North Yorkshire	N. Yks
Northamptonshire	Northnts
Northumberland	Northum
Nottinghamshire	Notts
Oxfordshire	Oxon
Shropshire	Shrops
Somerset	Somer
South Yorkshire	S. Yks
Staffordshire	Staffs
Suffolk	Suff
Surrey	Surrey
Tyne and Wear	T. & W
Warwickshire	Warw
West Midlands	W. Mids
West Sussex	W. Susx
West Yorkshire	W. Yks
Wiltshire	Wilts

Other Areas

Isle of Man	I. of M
Isles of Scilly	I. Scilly

Wales

Clwyd	Clwyd
Dyfed	Dyfed
Gwent	Gwent
Gwynedd	Gwyn
Mid Glamorgan	M. Glam
Powys	Powys
South Glamorgan	S. Glam
West Glamorgan	W. Glam

Region & Island Area Names
Scotland
Regions

Borders	Border
Central	Central
Dumfries & Galloway	D & G
Fife	Fife
Grampian	Grampn
Highland	Highl
Lothian	Lothn
Strathclyde	Strath
Tayside	Tays

Island Areas

Orkney	Orkney
Shetland	Shetld
Western Isles	W. Isles

Feature codes

H	= Hill, mountain
F	= Forest, wood
W	= Water
T	= City, town, village
R	= Roman antiquity
A	= Non-Roman antiquity
P	= Town on Primary Route
Q	= Landmark on Primary Route

Adstock
Anstiebury

Adstock T 119 SP 7330
Adstone T 119 SP 5951
Adventurers Fen 121 TL 5568
Advie T 183 NJ 1234
Adwell T 104 SU 6999
Adwick le Street T 139 SE 5308
Adwick upon Dearne T 139 SE 4701
Adziel 185 NJ 9553
Ae T 156 NX 9889
Affleck T 185 NJ 8623
Affleck Castle A 177 NO 4938
Affpuddle T 93 SY 8093
Afon Aeron W 111 SN 5158
Afon Afan W 109 SS 8295
Afon Aled W 135 SH 9570
Afon Alun or River Alyn W 126 SJ 3756
Afon Alwen W 135 SJ 0343
Afon Banwy W 125 SJ 0510
Afon Banwy neu Einion W 126 SJ 1308
Afon Bidno W 125 SN 8783
Afon Biga W 125 SN 8689
Afon Cain W 126 SJ 1618
Afon Cefni W 134 SH 4572
Afon Ceirw W 135 SH 9447
Afon Cennen W 111 SN 6418
Afon Cerist W 125 SH 8416
Afon Claerwen W 125 SN 8862
Afon Cledwen W 135 SH 8964
Afon Clwyd or River Clwyd W 135 SJ 0376
Afon Clywedog, Clwyd W 135 SJ 0962
Afon Clywedog, Powys W 125 SN 9386
Afon Conwy W 135 SH 7768
Afon Cothi W 111 SN 6134
Afon Cynin W 111 SN 2718
Afon Cywyn W 111 SN 3115
Afon Ddu W 135 SH 7564
Afon Dewi Fawr W 111 SN 3023
Afon Duad W 111 SN 3729
Afon Dugoed, Gwyn W 125 SH 9012
Afon Dugoed, Powys W 125 SH 9012
Afon Dulas, Gwyn W 125 SH 7608
Afon Dulas, Powys W 125 SN 7898
Afon Dulyn W 135 SH 7267
Afon Dwyfach W 134 SH 4746
Afon Dwyfor W 134 SH 4941
Afon Dyfi W 125 SH 8816
Afon Dyfi or River Dovey W 125 SN 6696
Afon Dyfrdwy or River Dee, Ches W 126 SJ 4056
Afon Dyfrdwy or River Dee, Clwyd W 136 SJ 2380
Afon Dyfrdwy or River Dee, Clwyd W 126 SJ 3743
Afon Dyfrdwy or River Dee, Mers W 136 SJ 2380
Afon Dysynni W 125 SH 6407
Afon Eden W 135 SH 7129
Afon Efyrnwy or River Vyrnwy W 126 SJ 1714
Afon Gamlan W 125 SH 7124
Afon Glaslyn W 134 SH 5943
Afon Gronw W 111 SN 2221
Afon Gwydderig W 109 SN 8531
Afon Gwy or River Wye, Glos W 127 SO 5398
Afon Gwy or River Wye, Gwent W 127 SO 5398
Afon Gwy or River Wye, Powys W 112 SO 0153
Afon Honddu W 113 SO 2926
Afon Leri W 125 SN 6689
Afon Llafar W 135 SH 8734
Afon Lliw W 108 SS 5999
Afon Llugwy W 135 SH 7059
Afon Llwchwr or River Loughor W 108 SS 4897
Afon Llynfi W 109 SO 1432
Afon Lwyd W 113 SN 8690
Afon Machno W 135 SH 7849
Afon Marteg W 125 SO 0075
Afon Mawddach W 125 SH 7322
Afon Mellte W 109 SN 9211
Afon Mynwy or River Monnow, Gwent W 113 SO 4717
Afon Mynwy or River Monnow, H. & W W 113 SO 4717
Afon Nyfer W 110 SN 1237
Afon Porth-llwyd W 135 SH 7466
Afon Rheidol W 125 SN 6778
Afon Rhiw W 125 SJ 0401
Afon Senni W 109 SN 9225
Afon Taf W 111 SN 2515
Afon Tanat, Clwyd W 126 SJ 1524
Afon Tanat, Powys W 125 SJ 0425
Afon Teifi W 111 SN 5446
Afon Trannon W 125 SN 9491
Afon Troddi or River Trothy W 113 SO 4512
Afon Tryweryn W 135 SH 9138
Afon Twrch, Dyfed W 111 SN 6648
Afon Twrch, Dyfed W 109 SN 7715
Afon Twrch, Powys W 125 SH 9714
Afon Twrch, Powys W 109 SN 7715
Afon Twymyn W 125 SH 8801
Afon Tywi W 111 SN 5720
Afon-wen T 136 SJ 1371
Afon Wnion W 125 SH 8021
Afon Ysgir W 109 SO 0031
Afon Ystrad W 135 SJ 0163
Afon Ystwyth W 125 SN 6275
Afton Bridgend T 156 NS 6212
Afton Reservoir W 156 NS 6304
Afton Water W 156 NS 6308
Agden Resr W 139 SK 2692
Agglethorpe T 146 SE 0886
A' Ghairbhe W 190 NH 0259
A' Ghlas-bheinn H 180 NH 0023
A' Ghoil 196 NC 3571
Aignish T 195 NB 4832
Aike T 142 TA 0545
Aiker Ness, Orkney 200 HY 3826
Aikerness, Orkney T 200 HY 4552
Aikers T 200 ND 4590
Aiketgate T 151 NY 4846
Aikton T 150 NY 2753
Ailey T 113 SO 3448
Ailsa Craig 154 NX 0199
Ailworth T 130 TL 1198
Ainderby Quernhow T 147 SE 3481
Ainderby Steeple T 152 SE 3392
Aingers Green T 107 TM 1120
Ainsdale T 136 SD 3112
Ainshval H 179 NM 3794
Ainstable T 151 NY 5346
Ainsworth T 137 SD 7610
Aintree T 136 SJ 3798
Aira Force W 151 NY 3920
Aird, D. & G T 154 NX 0960
Aird, Strath T 167 NM 7600
Aird, W. Isles T 195 NB 5635
Aird a' Mhòrain 188 NF 8379
Aird an Rùnair 188 NF 6970
Aird an Troim 195 NB 2316
Aird Barvas 195 NB 3553
Aird Brenish 194 NA 9727
Aird Dell T 195 NB 4761
Aird-dhubh, Highld 180 NG 7040
Aird Dhubh, Highld 190 NG 9382
Airde, The 197 NC 5313
Aird Fada 173 NM 4424
Aird Fenish 194 NA 9929
Aird Luing 167 NM 7406
Aird Mhànais T 189 NG 1188
Aird Mheadhonach T 189 NG 1898
Aird Nisabost 188 NG 0497
Aird of Coigach 196 NC 0811
Aird of Kinloch 173 NM 5228
Aird of Sleat T 180 NG 5900
Aird Riabhach T 189 NG 2396
Airdrie T 162 NS 7665
Airdriehill T 162 NS 7867
Airds Bay W 168 NN 0032
Airds Moss 162 NS 6024
Airds, The, Highld T 187 NG 4052
Aird, The, Highld 187 NG 4376
Aird, The, Highld 182 NH 5642
Aird Thormaid 188 NF 9376
Aird Tong T 195 NB 4636
Aird Uig T 194 NB 0438
Aird Vanish 188 NF 9999
Aire & Calder Navigation, Humbs W 139 SE 5920
Aire & Calder Navigation, N. Yks W 139 SE 5920
Airedale 146 SE 0345
Airie Hill H 156 NX 6268
Airlie Castle 176 NO 2952
Airmyn T 142 SE 7225
Airntully T 170 NO 0935
Airor T 180 NG 7105
Airth T 170 NS 8987
Airton T 146 SD 9059
Aisby, Lincs T 140 SK 8792
Aisby, Lincs T 130 TF 0138
Aiskew T 147 SE 2788
Aislaby, N. Yks T 148 NZ 8608
Aislaby, N. Yks T 148 SE 7785
Aisthorpe T 140 SK 9480
Aith, Orkney 200 HY 2417
Aith, Orkney T 201 HY 6525
Aith, Shetld T 203 HU 3455
Aith, Shetld 205 HU 6390
Aith Hope W 199 ND 2988
Aith Ness 203 HU 5144
Aithsetter T 203 HU 4430
Aithsting 203 HU 3455
Aith Voe, Shetld W 203 HU 3458
Aith Voe, Shetld W 203 HU 4328
Aith Wick W 203 HU 4429
Aitnoch 183 NH 9839
Akeld T 165 NT 9529
Akeley T 119 SP 7037
Akeman Street, Bucks R 104 SP 7715
Akeman Street, Glos R 114 SP 0904
Akeman Street, Oxon R 115 SP 3314
Akenham T 123 TM 1448
Akermoor Loch W 164 NT 4021
Alavna Roman Fort R 150 NY 0337
Albaston T 88 SX 4270
Alberbury T 126 SJ 3614
Albourne T 96 TQ 2616
Albrighton, Shrops T 127 SJ 4918
Albrighton, Shrops T 127 SJ 8104
Alburgh T 123 TM 2687
Albury, Herts T 105 TL 4324
Albury, Surrey T 96 TQ 0447
Alby Hill T 133 TG 1934
Alcaig T 182 NH 5657
Alcaston T 116 SO 4587
Alcester T 118 SP 0857
Alciston T 97 TQ 5005
Alcombe T 91 SS 9745
Alconbury T 120 TL 1876
Alconbury Weston T 120 TL 1776
Aldbar Castle 177 NO 5757
Aldborough, Norf T 133 TG 1834
Aldborough, N. Yks T 147 SE 4066
Aldbourne T 102 SU 2675
Aldbrough T 143 TA 2438
Aldbrough St John T 152 NZ 2011
Aldbury T 104 SP 9612
Aldclune T 175 NN 8963
Aldeburgh T 123 TM 4656
Aldeburgh Bay W 123 TM 4755
Aldeby T 133 TM 4593
Aldenham T 105 TQ 1398
Alderbury T 94 SU 1827
Alderford T 133 TG 1218
Alderholt T 94 SU 1212
Alderley T 101 ST 7690
Alderley Edge T 137 SJ 8478
Aldermaston T 103 SU 5965
Aldermaston Wharf 103 SU 6067
Alderminster T 118 SP 2348
Aldershot T 103 SU 8650
Alderton, Glos T 114 SP 0033
Alderton, Northnts T 119 SP 7446
Alderton, Shrops T 127 SJ 4924
Alderton, Suff T 123 TM 3441
Alderton, Wilts T 101 ST 8483
Alderwasley T 128 SK 3153
Aldfield T 147 SE 2669
Aldford T 136 SJ 4259
Aldham T 122 TL 9125
Aldingbourne T 96 SU 9205
Aldingham T 145 SD 2871
Aldington, H. & W T 118 SP 0644
Aldington, Kent T 99 TR 0636
Aldington Frith T 99 TR 0436
Aldochlay T 168 NS 3591
Aldreth T 121 TL 4473
Aldridge T 128 SK 0500
Aldringham T 123 TM 4461
Aldsworth T 115 SP 1510
Aldunie T 184 NJ 3626
Aldwark, Derby T 139 SK 2257
Aldwark, N. Yks T 147 SE 4663
Aldwick T 96 SZ 9198
Aldwincle T 120 TL 0081
Aldworth T 103 SU 5579
Aled Isaf Reservoir W 135 SH 9159
Alemoor Loch W 157 NT 3914
Ale Water, Border W 157 NT 4318
Ale Water, Border W 165 NT 9064
Alexandria T 169 NS 3880
Alfardisworthy T 90 SS 2911
Alfington T 92 SY 1197
Alfold T 96 TQ 0334
Alford, Grampn T 184 NJ 5716
Alford, Lincs T 141 TF 4575
Alford, Somer T 93 ST 6032
Alfred's Tower 93 ST 7435
Alfreton T 128 SK 4155
Alfrick T 117 SO 7553
Alfriston T 97 TQ 5103
Alhampton T 93 ST 6234
Alhang, D. & G H 156 NS 6401
Alhang, Strath H 156 NS 6401
Aline Lodge 195 NB 1911
Alkborough T 142 SE 8821
Alkerton T 118 SP 3742
Alkham T 99 TR 2542
Alkington T 127 SJ 5339
Alkmonton T 128 SK 1838
Alladale Lodge 192 NH 4389
Alladale River W 191 NH 4088
Allaleigh T 89 SX 8153
Allanaquoich T 176 NO 1291
Allangrange Mains 182 NH 6251
Allanton, Border T 165 NT 8654
Allanton, Strath T 163 NS 8557
Allan Water, Border W 157 NT 4707
Allan Water, Central W 169 NN 8006
Allan Water, Tays W 169 NN 8006
Allardice T 177 NO 8174
All Cannings T 102 SU 1660
Allendale Common 151 NY 8345
Allendale Town T 151 NY 8355
Allenheads T 151 NY 8545
Allensmore T 113 SO 4636
Aller T 92 ST 4029
Allerby T 150 NY 0839
Aller Dean 165 NT 9947
Allerford T 91 SS 9046
Allermuir Hill H 163 NT 2266
Allerston T 149 SE 8782
Allerthorpe T 142 SE 7847
Allerton T 136 SJ 4085
Allerton Bywater T 147 SE 4227
Allesley T 118 SP 2981
Allestree T 128 SK 3439
Allexton T 130 SK 8100
Allgreave T 138 SJ 9767
Allhallow-on-Sea T 106 TQ 8478
Allhallows T 98 TQ 8377
Alligin Shuas T 190 NG 8357
Allimore Green T 127 SJ 8519
Allington, Lincs T 130 SK 8540
Allington, Wilts T 102 SU 0663
Allington, Wilts T 102 SU 2039
Allithwaite T 145 SD 3876
Allnabad 197 NC 4642
Alloa T 170 NS 8892
Allonby T 150 NY 0843
Allonby Bay W 150 NY 0742
Alloway T 161 NS 3318
All Saints South Elmham T 123 TM 3482
All Stretton T 126 SO 4695
Allt H 113 SO 2917
Allt a' Bhunn W 197 NC 5012
Allt Ach' a' Bhàthàich W 193 NC 8114
Allt a' Chaoil-rèidhe W 175 NN 5276
Allt a' Chaorainn W 174 NN 9688
Allt a' Chaoruinn W 191 NC 2704
Allt a' Chireachain W 175 NN 7772
Allt a' Choire Mhòir W 191 NH 1968
Allt a' Chonais W 191 NH 0747
Allt a' Choromaig W 168 NM 9221
Allt a' Chraois W 197 NC 4439
Allt à Gheallaidh, Grampn W 183 NJ 1238
Allt à Ghealaidh, Highld W 183 NJ 1238
Allt a' Ghiubhais W 190 NG 7968
Allt Airigh-dhamh W 198 NC 8237
Allt a' Mhadaidh W 191 NH 2374
Allt a' Mhuilinn, Highld W 193 NC 8313
Allt a' Mhuilinn, Tays W 175 NN 7675
Alltan Dearg W 197 NC 6460
Allt an Dùin W 198 NC 8124
Allt an Ealaidh W 198 NC 7227
Allt an Stacain W 168 NN 1320
Allt an Tairbh W 166 NR 5588
Allt an Tiaghaich W 196 NC 1523
Allt an t-Srathain W 190 NG 7156
Allt Arnan, Central W 168 NN 3018
Allt Arnan, Strath W 168 NN 3018
Allt Bail a' Mhuilinn W 175 NN 5743
Allt Beinn Dònuill W 191 NH 2299
Allt Beitheach W 173 NM 7552
Allt Beochlich W 168 NN 0315
Allt Bhlàraidh W 182 NH 3518
Allt Bhran W 175 NN 7889
Allt Braglenmore W 168 NM 9218
Allt Breineag W 182 NH 4708
Allt Cam, Highld W 175 NN 4477
Allt Cam, Highld W 175 NN 5178
Allt Cam Ban W 182 NH 5606
Allt Camgharaidh W 174 NM 9888
Allt Camghouran W 175 NN 5354
Allt Car W 197 NC 4417
Allt Chaiseagail W 197 NC 5909
Alltchaorunn 174 NN 1951
Allt Choire a' Bhalachain W 174 NN 1198
Allt Chomhraig W 175 NN 8197
Allt Cinn-locha W 167 NR 7879
Allt Coire a' Chaolain W 174 NN 2147
Allt Coire an Eòin W 174 NN 2273
Allt Coire Iain Oig W 175 NN 5197
Allt Coire na Saidhe Duibh W 197 NC 4835
Allt Con W 175 NN 6967
Allt Conait W 175 NN 5245
Allt Connie W 176 NO 0786
Allt Crunachdain W 175 NN 5291
Allt Cuaich W 175 NN 6786
Allt Darrarie W 176 NO 3283
Allt Ddu H 109 SO 0224
Allt Dearg W 183 NH 8246
Allt Dochard W 174 NN 2044
Allt Doe W 182 NH 4107
Allt Easach W 174 NN 0642
Allt Eigheach W 174 NN 4361
Allt Eileag W 191 NC 3007
Allt Fearna W 168 NN 1222
Allt Fèith Thuill W 174 NN 3771
Allt Fionn Ghlinne W 168 NN 3222
Alltforgan T 125 SH 9624
Allt Forsiescye W 199 ND 0258
Allt Garbh W 181 NH 1719
Allt Garbh-airigh W 192 NH 6398
Allt Garbh Buidhe W 176 NN 9981
Allt Gharbh Ghaig W 175 NN 7782
Allt Ghlas W 175 NN 5366
Allt Glas Choire W 175 NN 7376
Allt Glas Dhoire W 174 NN 3285
Allt Gleann Da-Eig W 175 NN 6042
Allt Gleann nam Meann W 169 NN 5212
Allt Gleann Udalain W 180 NG 8528
Allt Glen Loch W 176 NO 0171
Allt Goibhre W 182 NH 4348
Allt Hallater W 174 NN 1340
Allt Kinglass W 174 NN 3437
Allt Làire W 174 NN 3276
Allt Lon a' Chuil W 198 NC 7242
Allt Loraich W 174 NN 3978
Allt Lorgy W 183 NH 8716
Allt Lundie W 182 NH 2905
Allt Madagain W 175 NN 6398
Alltmawr T 112 SO 0746
Allt Mhoille W 168 NN 1231
Allt Mhucarnaich W 191 NH 2579
Allt Mòr, Highld W 180 NG 7221
Allt Mòr, Highld W 183 NH 7404
Allt Mòr, Highld W 175 NN 8295
Allt Mòr, Tays W 175 NN 7353
Allt na Bogair W 175 NN 6055
Alltnacaillich 197 NC 4545
Allt na Caim W 174 NN 3762
Allt na Doire Garbhe W 181 NH 0429
Allt na Gile W 166 NR 4877
Allt na Glaise W 175 NN 5769
Allt na h-Airbhe T 191 NH 1193
Allt na h-Eirigh W 190 NG 7053
Allt na Lairige, Highld W 174 NN 2872
Allt na Lairige, Strath W 168 NN 2517
Allt na Lairige Moire W 174 NN 1163
Allt na Lùibe W 192 NC 6608
Allt na Muic W 182 NH 2515
Allt nan Achaidhean W 198 NC 7928
Allt nan Airighean W 166 NR 3650
Allt nan Caorach W 182 NH 5267
Allt nan Ramh W 196 NC 2237
Allt-nan-Sugh T 180 NG 9029
Allt Odhar W 182 NH 5205
Allt Phocaichain W 182 NH 3211
Allt Riabhach W 182 NH 2118
Allt Riobain W 169 NN 4529
Allt Ruighe nan Saorach W 175 NN 6463
Allt Sleibh W 175 NN 6566
Allt Smeòrail W 193 NC 8512
Allt Srath à' Ghlinne W 169 NN 6717
Allt Tolaghan W 174 NN 2640
Allt Uisg an t-Sidhein W 182 NH 6117
Alltwalis T 111 SN 4431
Alltwen T 108 SN 7203
Almeley T 113 SO 3351
Almer T 93 SY 9199
Almington T 127 SJ 7034
Almondbank T 170 NO 0626
Almondbury T 138 SE 1615
Almondsbury T 101 ST 6084
Alne T 147 SE 4965
Alness T 182 NH 6569
Alness Bay W 182 NH 6467
Alnham T 159 NT 9910
Alnmouth T 159 NU 2410
Alnmouth Bay W 159 NU 2510
Alnwick P 159 NU 1813
Alphamstone T 122 TL 8735
Alpheton T 122 TL 8850
Alphington T 89 SX 9189
Alport T 139 SK 2264
Alpraham T 137 SJ 5859
Alresford T 107 TM 0621
Alrewas T 128 SK 1715
Alsager T 127 SJ 7955
Alsagers Bank T 127 SJ 8048
Alsop en le Dale T 128 SK 1655
Alston T 151 NY 7146
Alstone T 114 SO 9832
Alstonefield T 128 SK 1355
Alston Moor 151 NY 7240
Alston Reservoir W 145 SD 6136
Alswear T 91 SS 7222
Altandhu T 196 NB 9812
Altanduin 198 NC 8126
Altarnun T 87 SX 2281
Altass T 192 NC 5000
Alterwall T 199 ND 2865
Altgaltraig 168 NS 0473
Altham T 146 SD 7732
Althorne T 106 TQ 9199
Althorpe T 142 SE 8309
Altnabreac Station 198 ND 0045
Altnacealgach Hotel 196 NC 2610
Altnafeadh 174 NN 2256
Altnaharra T 197 NC 5635
Altofts T 147 SE 3723
Alton, Derby T 139 SK 3664
Alton, Hants T 103 SU 7239
Alton, Staffs T 128 SK 0742
Alton Pancras T 93 ST 6902
Alton Priors T 102 SU 1162
Alton Water Reservoir W 123 TM 1436
Altrincham T 137 SJ 7688
Altrua T 174 NN 2490
Alturlie Point 183 NH 7149
Altyre House 183 NJ 0254
Altyre Woods F 183 NJ 0253
Alum Bay W 94 SZ 3085
Alva T 170 NS 8897
Alvanley T 137 SJ 4974
Alvaston T 128 SK 3833
Alvechurch T 118 SP 0272
Alvecote T 128 SK 2404
Alvediston T 94 ST 9723
Alveley T 117 SO 7684
Alverdiscott T 90 SS 5125
Alverstoke T 95 SZ 6099
Alverstone T 95 SZ 5785
Alverton T 129 SK 7942
Alvescot T 115 SP 2704
Alveston, Avon T 101 ST 6388
Alveston, Warw T 118 SP 2356
Alvie T 183 NH 8609
Alvingham T 141 TF 3691
Alvington T 113 SO 6000
Alwalton T 130 TL 1395
Alwen Reservoir W 135 SH 9453
Alweston T 93 ST 6614
Alwinton T 158 NT 9206
Alyth T 176 NO 2448
Amat Forest 192 NH 4690
Amatnatua T 192 NH 4790
Am Balg 196 NC 1866
Ambergate T 128 SK 3551
Amber Hill T 131 TF 2346
Amberley, Glos T 114 SO 8501
Amberley, W. Susx T 96 TQ 0213
Am Bi-bogha Beag 186 NG 1938
Am Bi-bogha Mòr 186 NG 1838
Amble-by-the-Sea T 159 NU 2604
Amblecote T 117 SO 8985
Ambleside T 151 NY 3704
Ambleston T 110 SN 0025
Ambrosden T 115 SP 6019
Am Buachaille H 168 NN 0507
Amcotts T 142 SE 8514
Amersham P 104 SU 9798
Amesbury T 102 SU 1641
Am Fraoch Eilean 166 NR 4762
A' Mhoine 197 NC 5261
Amhuinnsuidhe T 188 NB 0408
Amicombe Hill H 89 SX 5687
Amington T 128 SK 2304
Amisfield T 156 NY 0082
Amlwch T 134 SH 4493
Amlwch Port T 134 SH 4593
Ammanford T 111 SN 6312
Amotherby T 148 SE 7473
Ampfield T 94 SU 4023
Ampleforth T 147 SE 5878
Ampleforth College 147 SE 5978
Ampney Crucis T 114 SP 0702
Ampney St Mary T 114 SP 0802
Ampney St Peter T 114 SP 0801
Amport T 102 SU 3044
Ampthill T 120 TL 0337
Ampton T 122 TL 8671
Amroth T 110 SN 1607
Amulree T 175 NN 9036
An Acairseid W 173 NM 4363
Anaheilt T 173 NM 8162
Anancaun T 190 NH 0262
An Ard T 190 NG 8075
An Cabar H 182 NH 2564
An Càmastac 186 NG 2365
An Caol T 190 NG 6152
Ancaster T 130 SK 9843
An Ceannaich 186 NG 1350
An Ceann Geal or Whiten Head 197 NC 5068
An Cearcall 175 NN 6270
Anchachork T 187 NG 4845
Anchor T 116 SO 1785
An Clachan 166 NR 2171
An Coileach H 189 NG 0892
An Coileachan H 182 NH 2468
An Coire 173 NM 8114
Ancroft T 165 NU 0045
An Cruachan, Highld H 181 NH 0935
An Cruachan, Strath H 167 NM 6900
Ancrum T 164 NT 6224
Ancton T 96 SU 9800
An Cuaidh H 190 NG 7689
Anderby T 141 TF 5275
Anderby Creek T 141 TF 5576
Anderson T 93 SY 8897
Anderton T 137 SJ 6475
Andover P 102 SU 3645
Andover Down T 102 SU 3946
Andoversford T 114 SP 0219
Andreas T 144 SC 4199
An Dubh-aird 180 NG 7833
An Dubh-laimhrig 187 NG 4715
An Dubh Sgeir, Highld 186 NG 1936
An Dubh-sgeir, Highld 186 NG 3422
An Dubh-sgeir, Strath 160 NR 6655
An Dùn 192 ND 1425
An Dùnan 166 NR 5773
An Fhaochag 180 NG 6903
An Garbh-eilean 196 NC 3373
An Gead Loch W 181 NH 1038
Angersleigh T 92 ST 1919
Angle T 110 SM 8603
Angle Bay W 110 SM 8803
Anglesey 134 SH 4179
Angle Tarn W 151 NY 4114
Anglezarke Moor 137 SD 6417
Angmering T 96 TQ 0704
Angram, N. Yks T 152 SD 8899
Angram, N. Yks T 147 SE 5248
Angram Common 152 SD 8499
Angram Resr W 146 SE 0476
An Grianan H 196 NC 2662
Angry Brow 136 SD 3019
Anie 169 NN 5810
An Iola W 174 NM 9847
Ankerville T 193 NH 8174
Anlaby T 142 TA 0328
An Lairig 175 NN 4977
An Leacainn H 182 NH 5741
An Lèan-chàrn H 197 NC 4252
An Liathanach H 191 NH 1357
Anmer T 132 TF 7429
Annan T 157 NY 1966
Annandale 157 NY 1294
Annaside T 144 SD 0986
Annat, Highld T 190 NG 8954
Annat, Strath T 168 NN 0322
Annat Bay W 190 NH 0396
Annathill T 169 NS 7270
Anna Valley T 102 SU 3444
Annbank T 161 NS 4022
Annesley T 129 SK 5053
Annesley Woodhouse T 129 SK 4953
Annet 86 SV 8608
Annet Burn W 169 NN 6906
Annfield Plain T 152 NZ 1651
Annick Water W 161 NS 3843
Annochie T 185 NJ 9342
Annscroft T 127 SJ 4508
An Riabhachan H 181 NH 1234
An Rubha 166 NR 3595
Ansdell T 145 SD 3428
Ansford T 93 ST 6433
An Sgarsoch, Grampn H 175 NN 9383
An Sgarsoch, Tays H 175 NN 9383
An Sgurr H 179 NM 4684
An Sleaghach H 173 NM 7643
Ansley T 128 SP 3091
Anslow T 128 SK 2125
Anslow Gate T 128 SK 1925
An Socach, Grampn H 176 NO 0980
An Socach, Highld H 196 NC 2658
An Socach, Strath H 168 NS 0587
An Stac H 180 NM 8688
An Stèidh 179 NG 2103
Anstey, Herts T 121 TL 4032
Anstey, Leic T 129 SK 5408
Anstiebury A 96 TQ 1544

Aylesham Bay of Laig

Aylesham T 99 TR 2352
Aylestone T 129 SK 5700
Aylmerton T 133 TG 1839
Aylsham T 133 TG 1926
Aylton T 117 SO 6637
Aymestrey T 116 SO 4265
Aynho T 115 SP 5133
Ayot St Lawrence T 105 TL 1916
Ayot St Peter T 105 TL 2115
Ayr P 161 NS 3320
Ayres, The 144 NX 4303
Aysgarth T 146 SE 0188
Ayside T 145 SD 3983
Ayston T 130 SK 8601
Aythorpe Roding T 106 TL 5915
Ayton, Border T 165 NT 9261
Ayton, N. Yks T 149 SE 9985
Aywick, Shetld T 205 HU 5386
Ay Wick, Shetld W 205 HU 5386
Azerley T 147 SE 2574

B

Baa Taing, Orkney 201 HY 6715
Baa Taing, Shetld 204 HU 2774
Babbacombe T 89 SX 9265
Babbacombe Bay W 89 SX 9568
Babbet Ness 171 NO 5914
Babbinswood T 126 SJ 3330
Babcary T 93 ST 5628
Babel T 109 SN 8335
Babell T 136 SJ 1573
Babeny 89 SX 6775
Babingley River W 132 TF 6725
Babraham T 121 TL 5150
Babworth T 140 SK 6880
Bac an Eich H 182 NH 2248
Bac Beag 172 NM 2337
Bach Camp A 113 SO 5460
Bache Hill H 116 SO 2163
Bach Island 173 NM 7726
Bachlaig 166 NR 4175
Back T 195 NB 4840
Backaland T 200 HY 5630
Backaskail Bay W 201 HY 6438
Backaskaill 200 HY 4850
Backbarrow T 145 SD 3584
Backburn T 177 NO 8592
Backfolds T 185 NK 0252
Backford T 136 SJ 3971
Backhill, Grampn T 185 NJ 7939
Backhill, Grampn T 185 NK 0039
Backhill of Clackriach T 185 NJ 9246
Backhill of Trustach T 177 NO 6397
Backies T 193 NC 8302
Backlass T 199 ND 2053
Backmuir of New Gilston T 171 NO 4308
Back of Keppoch T 180 NM 6588
Backstane Hill H 163 NS 9128
Backwell T 101 ST 4868
Backworth T 159 NZ 3072
Bac Mór or Dutchman's Cap 172 NM 2438
Bacon End T 106 TL 6018
Baconsthorpe T 133 TG 1237
Bacton, H. & W T 113 SO 3732
Bacton, Norf T 133 TG 3433
Bacton, Suff T 122 TM 0567
Bacup T 146 SD 8623
Bad a' Chreamha H 180 NG 8536
Badachro T 190 NG 7873
Badandun Hill H 176 NO 2067
Badanloch Forest 198 NC 8035
Badanloch Lodge 198 NC 7933
Badavanich 191 NH 1058
Bad Bog 190 NG 9281
Badbury T 102 SU 1980
Badbury Hill H 115 SU 2694
Badbury Rings A 94 ST 9503
Badby T 119 SP 5659
Badcall, Highld T 196 NC 1542
Badcall, Highld T 196 NC 2455
Badcall Bay W 196 NC 1641
Badcaul T 190 NH 0191
Baddeley Green T 127 SJ 9051
Baddesley Ensor T 128 SP 2798
Baddidarach T 196 NC 0823
Baddinsgill Reservoir W 163 NT 1255
Baddoch, Grampn 176 NO 1382
Baddoch, Highld H 183 NJ 0819
Badenoch 175 NN 7091
Badenscoth T 185 NJ 7038
Badentarbat Bay W 190 NC 0108
Badenyon 184 NJ 3419
Badger T 127 SO 7699
Badgers Mount T 105 TQ 4961
Badgeworth T 114 SO 9019
Badgworth T 100 ST 3952
Badicaul T 180 NG 7529
Badingham T 123 TM 3068
Badlesmere T 99 TR 0054
Badlipster 199 ND 2449
Badluarach T 190 NG 9994
Badminton T 101 ST 8082
Badninish T 193 NH 7694
Badrallach T 191 NH 0691
Badsey T 118 SP 0743
Badsworth T 139 SE 4614
Badwell Ash T 122 TL 9969
Bagby T 147 SE 4680
Bagendon T 114 SP 0106
Bage, The T 113 SO 2943
Baggrave Hall 129 SK 6908
Baggy Point 90 SS 4140
Bàgh an Tailleir W 168 NR 8580
Bàgh Feisdlum W 172 NM 2558
Bàgh Loch an Ròin W 196 NC 1954
Bàgh na Doide W 167 NR 7076
Bàgh nam Faoilean W 188 NF 8345
Bàgh nan Gunnaichean W 187 NG 4574
Bàgh Tigh-an-Droighinn W 168 NR 8579
Bagillt T 136 SJ 2275
Bagillt Bank 136 SJ 2276
Baginton T 118 SP 3475
Baglan T 109 SS 7592
Bagley T 126 SJ 4027
Bagnall T 127 SJ 9251
Bagshot, Surrey T 104 SU 9163
Bagshot, Wilts T 102 SU 3165
Bagshot Heath F 104 SU 9161
Bagthorpe, Norf T 132 TF 7932
Bagthorpe, Notts T 129 SK 4751
Bagworth T 129 SK 4408
Bagwyllydiart T 113 SO 4426
Baidland Hill H 161 NS 2552
Baildon T 146 SE 1539
Baile T 188 NF 9381
Bailebeag T 182 NH 5018
Baile Boidheach T 167 NR 7473
Baile Mór T 172 NM 2824
Bailey Hill H 116 SO 2472
Bailieward 184 NJ 4737
Baillieston T 162 NS 6763
Bail Uachdraich T 188 NF 8160
Bainbridge T 152 SD 9390
Bainton, Cambs T 130 TF 0906
Bainton, Humbs T 149 SE 9652
Bairnkine T 158 NT 6515
Bait or St Mary's Island 159 NZ 3575
Bakers End T 105 TL 3917
Baker Street T 106 TQ 6381
Bakethin Reservoir W 158 NY 6391
Bakewell T 138 SK 2168
Bala P 135 SH 9236
Balachuirn T 180 NG 5540
Balaglas T 188 NF 8457
Bala Lake or Llyn Tegid W 135 SH 9133
Balallan T 195 NB 2920
Balbeg T 182 NH 4224
Balbeggie T 170 NO 1629
Balbegno Castle 177 NO 6473
Balbithan T 185 NJ 7917
Balbithan House 185 NJ 8118
Balblair T 183 NH 7066
Balcary Point 155 NX 8249
Balcherry T 193 NH 8182
Balchladich T 196 NC 0330
Balchraggan T 182 NH 5343
Balchrick T 196 NC 1960
Balcombe T 97 TQ 3130
Balcomie 171 NO 6209
Balcurvie T 171 NO 3401
Balderhead Reservoir W 152 NY 9218
Baldersby T 147 SE 3578
Balderstone T 145 SD 6332
Balderton T 130 SK 8251
Baldhu T 86 SW 7743
Baldinnie T 171 NO 4211
Baldock T 121 TL 2433
Baldoon Sands 155 NX 4653
Baldrine T 144 SC 4281
Balduff Hill H 176 NO 2253
Baldwin T 144 SC 3581
Baldwinholme T 150 NY 3352
Baldwin's Gate T 127 SJ 7940
Bale T 132 TG 0136
Balemartine T 172 NL 9841
Balephetrish Bay W 172 NM 0047
Balephuil T 172 NL 9640
Balephuil Bay W 172 NL 9440
Balerno T 163 NT 1666
Baleshare 188 NF 7861
Balevullin T 172 NL 9546
Balfield T 177 NO 5468
Balfour T 200 HY 4716
Balfour Castle 200 HY 4716
Balfron T 169 NS 5488
Balgaveny T 184 NJ 6640
Balgavies 177 NO 5351
Balgedie T 170 NO 1604
Balgonar T 170 NT 0293
Balgove T 185 NJ 8133
Balgowan T 175 NN 6394
Balgowan Point 154 NX 1242
Balgown T 186 NG 3868
Balgray T 176 NO 4038
Balgray Reservoir W 161 NS 5157
Balgrochan T 169 NS 6278
Balgy T 190 NG 8454
Balhalgardy T 185 NJ 7623
Balhary 176 NO 2646
Baliasta T 205 HP 6009
Baligill T 198 NC 8566
Balintore, Highld T 193 NH 8675
Balintore, Tays 176 NO 2859
Balintraid T 183 NH 7370
Balivanich T 188 NF 7755
Balkeerie 176 NO 3244
Balkholme T 142 SE 7928
Balkissock T 154 NX 1381
Ball T 126 SJ 3026
Balla T 178 NF 7811
Ballabeg T 144 SC 2470
Ballacannell T 144 SC 4382
Ballacarnane Beg T 144 SC 3088
Ballachulish T 174 NN 0858
Ballageich Hill H 161 NS 5350
Ballagyr T 144 SC 2684
Ballajora T 144 SC 4790
Ballamodha T 144 SC 2773
Ballantrae T 154 NX 0882
Ballantrae Bay W 154 NX 0783
Ballantrushal T 195 NB 3753
Ballard Point 94 SZ 0481
Ballasalla, I. of M T 144 SC 2769
Ballasalla, I. of M T 144 SC 3497
Ballater T 176 NO 3695
Ballaugh T 144 SC 3493
Ballechin 175 NN 9353
Balleigh T 193 NH 7084
Ballencleuch Law H 156 NS 9304
Ballencreiff T 171 NT 4878
Ball Hill T 102 SU 4263
Balliekine T 160 NR 8739
Balliemore, Strath T 173 NM 8328
Balliemore, Strath 168 NS 0584
Ballig T 144 SC 2882
Ballikinrain Castle 169 NS 5687
Ballimore, Central 169 NN 5317
Ballimore, Strath 168 NR 9283
Ballinaby T 166 NR 2267
Ballindean 171 NO 2529
Ballinger Common T 104 SP 9103
Ballingham T 113 SO 5731
Ballingry T 170 NT 1797
Ballinlick 176 NN 9840
Ballinloan Burn W 176 NN 9542
Ballinluig T 176 NN 9752
Ballintuim T 176 NO 1054
Balloch, Highld T 183 NH 7347
Balloch, Strath T 169 NS 3982
Balloch, Tays 176 NO 3557
Ballochan T 177 NO 5290
Ballochbuie Forest F 176 NO 1990
Balloch Castle 169 NS 3983
Ballochroy 160 NR 7252
Balloch, The H 184 NJ 4748
Ballo Reservoir W 171 NO 2204
Ballowall Barrow A 86 SW 3531
Balls Cross T 96 SU 9826
Ballygown T 173 NM 4343
Ballygrant T 166 NR 3966
Ballyhaugh 172 NM 1758
Ballymichael T 160 NR 9231
Balmacaan Forest 182 NH 4025
Balmacara T 180 NG 8127
Balmacara Square T 180 NG 8028
Balmaclellan T 156 NX 6579
Balmacneil 176 NN 9750
Balmae T 155 NX 6845
Balmaha T 169 NS 4290
Balmalcolm 171 NO 3108
Balmanno Hill H 170 NO 1414
Balmartin T 188 NF 7273
Balmeanach, Highld 187 NG 5234
Balmeanach, Highld 180 NG 5540
Balmedie T 185 NJ 9617
Balmerino T 171 NO 3524
Balmer Lawn T 94 SU 3003
Balmoral Castle 176 NO 2595
Balmoral Forest 176 NO 2487
Balmore T 169 NS 6073
Balmore Forest 182 NH 3333
Balmullo T 171 NO 4220
Balmungie 183 NH 7459
Balmurrie 154 NX 2066
Balnabodach T 178 NF 7101
Balnacoil T 193 NC 8011
Balnacra T 190 NG 9846
Balnafoich 183 NH 6835
Balnagown Castle 193 NH 7675
Balnaguard T 175 NN 9451
Balnaguard Burn W 175 NN 9249
Balnaguisich T 192 NH 6771
Balnahard, Strath T 173 NM 4534
Balnahard, Strath 166 NR 4199
Balnain T 182 NH 4430
Balnakeil T 196 NC 3968
Balnakeil Bay W 196 NC 3869
Balnaknock T 187 NG 4162
Balnamoon 177 NO 5563
Balnapaling T 183 NH 7969
Balne T 139 SE 5919
Balquhidder T 169 NN 5320
Balranald T 188 NF 7169
Balruddery Farm 171 NO 3132
Balsall Common T 118 SP 2377
Balscote T 118 SP 3941
Balsham T 121 TL 5850
Balta 205 HP 6608
Baltasound, Shetld T 205 HP 6208
Balta Sound, Shetld W 205 HP 6508
Balterley T 127 SJ 7450
Balthangie T 185 NJ 8351
Baltonsborough T 93 ST 5434
Balvaird T 182 NH 5351
Balvarran 176 NO 0762
Balvenie Castle A 184 NJ 3240
Balvicar T 173 NM 7616
Balvraid T 183 NH 8331
Bamber Bridge T 145 SD 5626
Bamburgh T 165 NU 1834
Bamff 176 NO 2251
Bamford T 138 SK 2083
Bampton, Cumbr T 151 NY 5118
Bampton, Devon T 91 SS 9522
Bampton, Oxon T 115 SP 3103
Bampton Common 151 NY 4716
Banavie T 174 NN 1177
Banbury P 119 SP 4540
Banc Cwmhelen H 108 SN 6811
Banchory T 177 NO 7095
Banchory-Devenick T 177 NJ 9002
Banc Nant-rhys H 125 SN 8279
Bancyfelin T 111 SN 3218
Bancyffordd T 111 SN 4037
Bandirran House 171 NO 1930
Banff T 185 NJ 6864
Bangor P 134 SH 5771
Bangor-is-y-coed T 126 SJ 3945
Banham T 122 TM 0687
Bank T 94 SU 2807
Bankend, D. & G T 156 NY 0268
Bankend, Strath T 163 NS 8033
Bankfoot T 170 NO 0635
Bankglen T 156 NS 5912
Bankhead, Grampn T 184 NJ 6608
Bankhead, Grampn T 185 NJ 8910
Bank Newton T 146 SD 9153
Banknock T 169 NS 7879
Banks, Cumbr T 158 NY 5664
Banks, Lancs T 136 SD 3920
Bankshill T 157 NY 1982
Banks Sands 145 SD 3624
Bank Street T 117 SO 6362
Banningham T 133 TG 2129
Banniskirk House 199 ND 1657
Bannister Green T 106 TL 6920
Bannockburn T 169 NS 8190
Ban Rubha 167 NM 7106
Banstead T 105 TQ 2559
Bantham T 89 SX 6643
Banton T 169 NS 7579
Banwell T 100 ST 3959
Baosbheinn H 190 NG 8665
Bapchild T 98 TQ 9262
Bapton T 102 ST 9938
Baramore T 173 NM 6474
Barassie T 161 NS 3232
Barbaraville T 193 NH 7472
Barber Booth T 138 SK 1184
Barbon T 145 SD 6282
Barbreck House 167 NM 8306
Barbreck River W 173 NM 8407
Barbridge T 137 SJ 6165
Barbrook T 91 SS 7147
Barbrook Resr W 139 SK 2877
Barbury Castle A 102 SU 1576
Barby T 119 SP 5470
Barcaldine T 174 NM 9641
Barcaldine Castle A 173 NM 9040
Barcaldine Forest F 174 NM 9640
Barcheston T 118 SP 2639
Barcloy Hill H 155 NX 7552
Barcombe T 97 TQ 4114
Barcombe Cross T 97 TQ 4215
Barcraigs Reservoir W 161 NS 3957
Barden T 152 SE 1493
Barden Fell 146 SE 0858
Barden Reservoirs W 146 SE 0257
Bardfield Saling T 122 TL 6828
Bard Head 203 HU 5135
Bardister 204 HU 3577
Bardney T 141 TF 1169
Bardon Mill 158 NY 7764
Bardowie T 169 NS 5873
Bardrainney T 168 NS 3473
Bardsea T 145 SD 3074
Bardsey T 147 SE 3643
Bardsey Island or Ynys Enlli 124 SH 1222
Bardsey Sound W 124 SH 1324
Bardsley T 137 SD 9201
Bardwell T 122 TL 9473
Barewood T 113 SO 3856
Barford, Norf T 133 TG 1107
Barford, Warw T 118 SP 2761
Barford St Martin T 94 SU 0531
Barford St Michael T 115 SP 4332
Barfrestone T 99 TR 2650
Bargatton Loch W 156 NX 6961
Bargoed T 109 ST 1599
Bargrennan T 154 NX 3576
Barham, Cambs T 120 TL 1375
Barham, Kent T 99 TR 2050
Barham, Suff T 123 TM 1451
Bar Hill T 121 TL 3863
Barholm T 130 TF 0810
Barkby T 129 SK 6309
Barkestone-le-Vale T 129 SK 7835
Barkham T 104 SU 7867
Barking, G. Lon T 105 TQ 4785
Barking, Suff T 122 TM 0753
Barkingside T 105 TQ 4489
Barkin Isles 195 NB 4023
Barkisland T 138 SE 0519
Barkston, Lincs T 130 SK 9241
Barkston, N. Yks T 147 SE 4936
Barkway T 121 TL 3835
Barkwith T 141 TF 1681
Barlaston T 127 SJ 8938
Barlavington T 96 SU 9716
Barlborough T 139 SK 4777
Barlby T 147 SE 6334
Barlestone T 128 SK 4205
Barley, Herts T 121 TL 3938
Barley, Lancs T 146 SD 8240
Barleythorpe T 130 SK 8409
Barling T 106 TQ 9289
Barlow, Derby T 139 SK 3474
Barlow, N. Yks T 147 SE 6428
Barlow, T. & W T 159 NZ 1560
Barmby Moor T 148 SE 7848
Barmby on the Marsh T 142 SE 6928
Barmekin Hill H 185 NJ 7207
Barmer T 132 TF 8133
Barmoor Castle 165 NT 9939
Barmore Island 168 NR 8771
Barmouth T 124 SH 6116
Barmouth Bay W 124 SH 5913
Barmpton T 152 NZ 3118
Barmston T 149 TA 1659
Barnack T 130 TF 0704
Barnacle T 118 SP 3884
Barnard Castle T 152 NZ 0516
Barnard Gate T 115 SP 4010
Barnardiston T 122 TL 7148
Barnbougle Castle 170 NT 1678
Barnburgh T 139 SE 4803
Barnby T 123 TM 4789
Barnby Dun T 139 SE 6109
Barnby in the Willows T 130 SK 8652
Barnby Moor T 139 SK 6684
Barnes T 105 TQ 2276
Barnet T 105 TQ 2496
Barnetby le Wold T 142 TA 0509
Barney T 132 TF 9932
Barnham, Suff T 122 TL 8779
Barnham, W. Susx T 96 SU 9604
Barnham Broom T 133 TG 0807
Barnhead T 177 NO 6657
Barnhill T 183 NJ 1457
Barnhills 154 NW 9871
Barningham, Durham T 152 NZ 0810
Barningham, Suff T 122 TL 9676
Barningham Moor 152 NZ 0608
Barnoldby le Beck T 143 TA 2303
Barnoldswick T 146 SD 8746
Barns Green T 96 TQ 1226
Barnsley, Glos T 114 SP 0705
Barnsley, S. Yks P 139 SE 3406
Barns Ness 164 NT 7277
Barnstaple P 91 SS 5533
Barnstaple or Bideford Bay W 90 SS 3432
Barnston, Essex T 106 TL 6419
Barnston, Mers T 136 SJ 2883
Barnt Green T 118 SP 0073
Barnton T 137 SJ 6375
Barnwell T 120 TL 0484
Barnwood T 114 SO 8618
Barochan House 161 NS 4168
Barons Point 168 NS 2281
Barony, The T 200 HY 2627
Barr T 154 NX 2794
Barra 178 NF 6801
Barra Castle 185 NJ 7925
Barrachan T 154 NX 3649
Barrack T 185 NJ 8942
Barraer Fell H 154 NX 3761
Barraglom T 195 NB 1634
Barra Head 178 NL 5579
Barrahormid T 167 NR 7183
Barrapol T 172 NL 9543
Barras, Cumbr T 151 NY 8411
Barras, Grampn T 177 NO 8480
Barrasford T 158 NY 9173
Barravullin T 173 NM 8207
Barr Castle A 161 NS 3458
Barregarrow T 144 SC 3288
Barrel of Butter 200 HY 3500
Barr Ganuisg H 168 NR 9280
Barr Glen 160 NR 6937
Barrhead T 161 NS 5058
Barr Hill, D. & G H 156 NX 7881
Barrhill, Strath T 154 NX 2382
Barrington, Cambs T 121 TL 3949
Barrington, Somer T 92 ST 3918
Barripper T 86 SW 6238
Barrisdale Bay W 180 NG 8605
Barr Liath H 168 NR 9773
Barrmill T 161 NS 3651
Barr Mór, Strath H 173 NM 8138
Barr Mór, Strath H 168 NN 1312
Barrock T 199 ND 2571
Barrock House 199 ND 2862
Barrow, Lancs T 145 SD 7338
Barrow, Leic T 130 SK 8915
Barrow, Shrops T 127 SJ 6500
Barrow, Suff T 122 TL 7663
Barroway Drove T 131 TF 5703
Barrowby T 130 SK 8836
Barrow Deep (lightship) 107 TM 3003
Barrowden T 130 SK 9400
Barrowford T 146 SD 8539
Barrow Gurney T 101 ST 5367
Barrow-in-Furness P 144 SD 1969
Barrow Street T 93 ST 8330
Barrow upon Humber T 142 TA 0721
Barrow upon Soar T 129 SK 5717
Barrow upon Trent T 128 SK 3528
Barr Water W 160 NR 6937
Barry, S. Glam T 109 ST 1167
Barry, Tays T 171 NO 5334
Barry Island T 109 ST 1166
Barry Links 171 NO 5432
Barry Links Station 171 NO 5433
Barsalloch Point 154 NX 3441
Barsby T 129 SK 6911
Barsham T 123 TM 3989
Barston T 118 SP 2078
Bartestree T 113 SO 5641
Bartford St Martin T 94 SU 0531
Bar, The, Dyfed 124 SN 5781
Bar, The, Gwyn 134 SH 4160
Bar, The, Gwyn 124 SH 6014
Barth Head 199 ND 4285
Barthol Chapel T 185 NJ 8134
Barthomley T 127 SJ 7652
Bartley T 94 SU 3112
Bartlow T 121 TL 5845
Barton, Cambs T 121 TL 4055
Barton, Ches T 126 SJ 4454
Barton, Devon T 89 SX 9067
Barton, Glos T 114 SP 1025
Barton, Lancs T 145 SD 5137
Barton, N. Yks T 152 NZ 2308
Barton, Warw T 118 SP 1051
Barton Bendish T 132 TF 7105
Barton Hartshorn T 119 SP 6430
Barton in Fabis T 129 SK 5232
Barton in the Beans T 128 SK 3906
Barton-le-Clay T 120 TL 0831
Barton-le-Street T 148 SE 7274
Barton-le-Willows T 148 SE 7163
Barton Mills T 122 TL 7173
Barton Moss T 137 SJ 7397
Barton on Sea T 94 SZ 2393
Barton-on-the-Heath T 115 SP 2532
Barton Seagrave T 120 SP 8977
Barton Stacey T 102 SU 4341
Barton St David T 93 ST 5431
Barton Turf T 133 TG 3522
Barton-under-Needwood T 128 SK 1818
Barton-upon-Humber T 142 TA 0322
Barvas T 195 NB 3649
Barway T 121 TL 5475
Barwell T 129 SP 4496
Barwick T 93 ST 5613
Barwick in Elmet T 147 SE 4037
Baschurch T 126 SJ 4222
Bascote T 118 SP 4063
Basford Green T 128 SJ 9951
Bashall Eaves T 145 SD 7043
Bashley T 94 SZ 2497
Basildon P 106 TQ 7088
Basingstoke P 103 SU 6352
Basingstoke Canal W 103 SU 8453
Baslow T 139 SK 2572
Bason Bridge T 100 ST 3445
Bassaleg T 100 ST 2787
Bassenthwaite T 150 NY 2332
Bassenthwaite Lake W 150 NY 2129
Bassett T 94 SU 4216
Bassingbourn T 121 TL 3344
Bassingfield T 129 SK 6137
Bassingham T 140 SK 9159
Bassingthorpe T 130 SK 9628
Bass Rock 171 NT 6087
Basta T 205 HU 5294
Basta Voe W 205 HU 5296
Baston T 130 TF 1114
Bastwick T 133 TG 4217
Batchcott T 116 SO 4971
Batcombe, Dorset T 93 ST 6104
Batcombe, Somer T 101 ST 6939
Bate Heath T 137 SJ 6879
Bateman's A 97 TQ 6723
Bath P 101 ST 7464
Bathampton T 101 ST 7766
Bathealton T 92 ST 0724
Batheaston T 101 ST 7867
Bathford T 101 ST 7966
Bathgate T 163 NS 9768
Bathley T 140 SK 7759
Bathpool T 88 SX 2874
Batley T 147 SE 2424
Batsford T 115 SP 1834
Battersby T 153 NZ 5907
Battersea T 105 TQ 2876
Battery Point 101 ST 4677
Battisford T 122 TM 0554
Battisford Tye T 122 TM 0254
Battle, E. Susx T 97 TQ 7416
Battle, Powys T 109 SO 0131
Battlefield T 127 SJ 5116
Battlesbridge T 106 TQ 7794
Battlesbury A 101 ST 8945
Battlesden T 120 SP 9628
Battleton T 91 SS 9127
Battramsley T 94 SZ 3098
Bauds of Cullen T 184 NJ 4867
Baugh Fell 151 SD 7393
Baughurst T 103 SU 5861
Baulking T 102 SU 3191
Baumber T 141 TF 2274
Baunton T 114 SP 0204
Bavelaw Castle A 163 NT 1662
Baverstock T 94 SU 0232
Bawburgh T 133 TG 1508
Bawden Rocks or Man & his man 86 SW 7053
Bawdeswell T 132 TG 0420
Bawdrip T 100 ST 3439
Bawdsey T 123 TM 3440
Bawtry P 139 SK 6593
Baxenden T 146 SD 7726
Baxterley T 128 SP 2897
Bayble Bay W 195 NB 5330
Bayble Hill H 195 NB 5030
Baycliff T 145 SD 2872
Baydon T 102 SU 2878
Bayford T 105 TL 3008
Bayham Abbey T 97 TQ 6436
Bayhead T 188 NF 7468
Bayles T 151 NY 7045
Baylham T 123 TM 1051
Bay of Backaland W 200 HY 5730
Bay of Bomasty W 201 HY 6123
Bay of Brough W 201 HY 6541
Bay of Cleat W 200 HY 4646
Bay of Cruden W 185 NK 0935
Bay of Deepdale W 202 HU 1754
Bay of Firth W 200 HY 3814
Bay of Fladdabister W 203 HU 4432
Bay of Furrowend W 200 HY 4719
Bay of Holland W 201 HY 6423
Bay of Houseby W 201 HY 6821
Bay of Ireland W 200 HY 2809
Bay of Isbister W 200 HY 3918
Bay of Keisgaig W 196 NC 2469
Bay of Kirkwall W 200 HY 4413
Bay of Laig W 179 NM 4688

Bermondsey Bloxworth

Bermondsey T 105 TQ 3579
Bernard Wharf 145 SD 3451
Bernera T 180 NG 8020
Bernera Island 173 NM 7939
Berneray, W. Isles 188 NF 9181
Berneray, W. Isles 178 NL 5580
Berney Arms Station 133 TG 4605
Bernice 168 NS 1391
Bernisdale T 187 NG 4050
Berrick Salome T 104 SU 6293
Berriedale T 193 ND 1222
Berriedale Water W 199 ND 0730
Berrier T 151 NY 4029
Berriew T 126 SJ 1800
Berrington, Northum T 165 NU 0043
Berrington, Shrops T 127 SJ 5307
Berrow T 100 ST 2952
Berrow Flats 100 ST 2854
Berrow Green T 117 SO 7458
Berry Head 89 SX 9456
Berry Hill T 113 SO 5712
Berryhillock T 184 NJ 5060
Berryl's Point 87 SW 8467
Berrynarbor T 91 SS 5646
Berry Pomeroy T 89 SX 8261
Berry, The H 200 ND 2490
Berry Top H 177 NO 8696
Bersham T 126 SJ 3049
Berstane 200 HY 4610
Bersted T 96 SU 9200
Berst Ness 200 HY 4441
Berth, The A 126 SJ 4323
Bervie Bay W 177 NO 8372
Bervie Water W 177 NO 8074
Berwick T 97 TQ 5105
Berwick Bassett T 102 SU 1073
Berwick Hill T 159 NZ 1775
Berwick St James T 102 SU 0739
Berwick St John T 94 ST 9422
Berwick St Leonard T 93 ST 9233
Berwick-upon-Tweed P 165 NT 9953
Berwyn, Clwyd H 135 SJ 0431
Berwyn, Clwyd T 126 SJ 1943
Berwyn, Gwyn H 135 SJ 0431
Berwyn, Powys H 135 SJ 0431
Bescar Lane Station 136 SD 3914
Besford T 117 SO 9145
Bessacarr T 139 SE 6101
Bessels Leigh T 115 SP 4501
Bessingham T 133 TG 1636
Besthorpe, Norf T 132 TM 0695
Besthorpe, Notts T 140 SK 8264
Beswick T 149 TA 0148
Betchworth T 96 TQ 2150
Bethania, Dyfed T 124 SN 5763
Bethania, Gwyn T 135 SH 6250
Bethel T 134 SH 5265
Bethersden T 98 TQ 9240
Bethesda, Dyfed T 110 SN 0918
Bethesda, Gwyn T 135 SH 6266
Bethlehem T 108 SN 6825
Bethnal Green T 105 TQ 3482
Betley T 127 SJ 7548
Betsham T 98 TQ 6071
Betteshanger T 99 TR 3152
Bettiscombe T 92 SY 3999
Bettisfield T 126 SJ 4635
Betton, Shrops T 126 SJ 3102
Betton, Shrops T 127 SJ 6937
Bettws, Gwent T 113 SO 2919
Bettws, Gwent T 100 ST 2990
Bettws Cedewain T 126 SO 1296
Bettws Gwerfil Goch T 135 SJ 0346
Bettws Newydd T 113 SO 3606
Bettyhill T 197 NC 7062
Betws, Dyfed T 111 SN 6311
Betws, M. Glam T 109 SS 9087
Betws Bledrws T 111 SN 5951
Betws Garmon T 134 SH 5357
Betws Ifan T 111 SN 3047
Betws-y-Coed P 135 SH 7956
Betws-yn-Rhos T 135 SH 9073
Beulah, Dyfed T 111 SN 2946
Beulah, Powys T 112 SN 9251
Beul an Toim W 188 NF 7857
Bevendean T 97 TQ 3406
Bevercotes T 140 SK 6972
Beverley T 142 TA 0339
Beverston T 114 ST 8693
Bevington T 114 ST 6697
Bewaldeth T 150 NY 2134
Bewcastle T 158 NY 5674
Bewcastle Fells H 158 NY 5681
Bewdley T 117 SO 7875
Bewerley T 146 SE 1564
Bewholme T 149 TA 1650
Bewl Bridge Reservoir W 97 TQ 6832
Bexhill T 97 TQ 7407
Bexley T 105 TQ 4775
Bexwell T 132 TF 6303
Beyton T 122 TL 9362
Biargar 203 HU 3635
Bibblon Hill H 162 NS 6632
Bibury T 114 SP 1106
Bicester T 115 SP 5822
Bickenhall T 92 ST 2818
Bickenhill T 118 SP 1882
Bicker T 131 TF 2237
Bicker Haven 131 TF 2533
Bickerstaffe T 136 SD 4404
Bickerton, Ches T 127 SJ 5052
Bickerton, N. Yks T 147 SE 4550
Bickington, Devon T 91 SS 5332
Bickington, Devon T 89 SX 7972
Bickleigh, Devon T 91 SS 9407
Bickleigh, Devon T 89 SX 5262
Bickleton T 90 SS 5031
Bickley T 105 TQ 4268
Bickley Moss T 127 SJ 5449
Bicknacre T 106 TL 7802
Bicknoller T 100 ST 1139
Bicknor T 98 TQ 8658
Bickton T 94 SU 1412
Bicton, Shrops T 126 SJ 4415
Bicton, Shrops T 116 SO 2982
Bidborough T 97 TQ 5643
Biddenden T 98 TQ 8438
Biddenham T 120 TL 0250
Biddestone T 101 ST 8673
Biddisham T 100 ST 3853
Biddlesden T 119 SP 6340
Biddlestone T 158 NT 9608
Biddulph T 137 SJ 8857
Biddulph Moor T 137 SJ 9058
Bidean nam Bian H 174 NN 1454
Bideford P 90 SS 4526
Bideford Bar 90 SS 4333
Bideford or Barnstaple Bay W 90 SS 3432
Bidford-on-Avon T 118 SP 1052
Bielby T 142 SE 7843
Bieldside T 177 NJ 8802
Biel Water W 171 NT 6375
Bierley T 95 SZ 5178
Bierton T 104 SP 8315
Bigbury T 89 SX 6646
Bigbury Bay W 89 SX 6342
Bigbury-on-Sea T 89 SX 6544
Bigby T 142 TA 0507
Bigga 205 HU 4479
Biggar, Cumbr T 144 SD 1966
Biggar, Strath T 163 NT 0437
Big Garvoun H 183 NJ 1408
Bigges's Pillar H 159 NU 1207
Biggin, Derby T 128 SK 1559
Biggin, Derby T 128 SK 2648
Biggin, N. Yks T 147 SE 5434
Biggings T 202 HU 1760
Biggin Hill T 105 TQ 4158
Biggin Hill Airport 105 TQ 4160
Biggins T 145 SD 6078
Biggleswade T 120 TL 1944
Big Hill of Glenmount H 155 NS 4500
Bighouse 198 NC 8964
Bighton T 95 SU 6134
Bignor T 96 SU 9814
Big Sand T 190 NG 7579
Bigton T 203 HU 3721
Big Water of Fleet W 156 NX 5662
Bilberry T 87 SX 0160
Bilborough T 129 SK 5141
Bilbrook T 127 SJ 8803
Bilbrough T 147 SE 5346
Bilbster T 199 ND 2853
Bildeston T 122 TL 9949
Billericay T 106 TQ 6794
Billesdon T 129 SK 7102
Billesley T 118 SP 1456
Billia Field H 205 HU 3786
Billing T 119 SP 8062
Billingborough T 130 TF 1134
Billinge T 137 SD 5300
Billingford, Norf T 132 TG 0120
Billingford, Suff T 123 TM 1678
Billingham T 153 NZ 4623
Billinghay T 130 TF 1555
Billingley T 139 SE 4304
Billingshurst T 96 TQ 0825
Billingsley T 117 SO 7085
Billington, Beds T 104 SP 9422
Billington, Lancs T 145 SD 7235
Billockby T 133 TG 4213
Bill of Portland 93 SY 6768
Billsmoor Park 158 NY 9496
Billy Row T 152 NZ 1637
Bilsborrow T 145 SD 5140
Bilsby T 141 TF 4776
Bilsington T 99 TR 0434
Bilsthorpe T 139 SK 6460
Bilston, Lothn T 163 NT 2664
Bilston, W. Mids T 128 SO 9597
Bilstone T 128 SK 3605
Bilting T 99 TR 0549
Bilton, Humbs T 143 TA 1633
Bilton, Northum T 159 NU 2210
Bilton, N. Yks T 147 SE 4750
Bilton, Warw T 119 SP 4873
Bimbister T 200 HY 3216
Binbrook T 141 TF 2193
Bincombe T 93 SY 6884
Binegar T 101 ST 6149
Binfield T 104 SU 8471
Binfield Heath T 104 SU 7478
Bin Forest, The F 184 NJ 5143
Bingfield T 159 NY 9772
Bingham T 129 SK 7039
Bingham's Melcombe A 93 ST 7702
Bingley T 146 SE 1139
Binham T 132 TF 9839
Binley, Hants T 102 SU 4253
Binley, W. Mids T 118 SP 3777
Binley Woods T 118 SP 3977
Binnein an Fhidhleir H 168 NN 2110
Binnein Mòr H 174 NN 2166
Binnein Shuas H 175 NN 4682
Binniehill T 170 NS 8572
Binnimoor Fen 131 TL 4497
Binns, The A 170 NT 0578
Bin of Cullen H 184 NJ 4864
Binsey H 150 NY 2235
Binstead T 95 SZ 5791
Binsted T 103 SU 7740
Bin, The H 184 NJ 5043
Binton T 118 SP 1454
Bintree T 132 TG 0123
Binweston T 126 SJ 3004
Bioda Buidhe H 187 NG 4366
Biod an Athair H 186 NG 1554
Biod nan Laog 186 NG 2958
Birch, Essex T 106 TL 9419
Birch, G. Man T 137 SD 8507
Bircham Newton T 132 TF 7633
Bircham Tofts T 132 TF 7732
Birchanger T 105 TL 5122
Bircher T 116 SO 4765
Birch Green T 106 TL 9419
Birchgrove T 108 SS 7098
Birchington T 99 TR 2969
Birchover T 139 SK 2462
Birch Vale T 138 SK 0286
Birchwood T 140 SK 9369
Bircotes T 139 SK 6391
Birdbrook T 122 TL 7041
Birdham T 95 SU 8200
Birdingbury T 118 SP 4368
Birdlip T 114 SO 9214
Birdsall T 148 SE 8165
Birdsgreen T 117 SO 7685
Birdston T 169 NS 6575
Birdwell T 139 SE 3401
Birdwood T 114 SO 7418
Birgham T 165 NT 7839
Birk Beck W 151 NY 5907
Birkdale T 136 SD 3215
Birkdale Common 151 NY 8302
Birkenburn Reservoir W 169 NS 6780
Birkenhead P 136 SJ 3288
Birkenhills T 185 NJ 7445
Birkenshaw, Strath T 162 NS 6961
Birkenshaw, W. Yks T 146 SE 2028
Birker Force W 150 SD 1899
Birkhall T 176 NO 3493
Birkhill T 171 NO 3534
Birkin T 147 SE 5327
Birley T 113 SO 4553
Birling, Kent T 98 TQ 6860
Birling, Northum T 159 NU 2406
Birlingham T 117 SO 9343
Birmingham P 118 SP 0787
Birmingham International Airport 118 SP 1784
Birnam T 176 NO 0341
Birnam Hill H 176 NO 0340
Birness T 185 NJ 9933
Birnock Water W 157 NT 1008
Birns Water W 164 NT 4865
Birsay 200 HY 2825
Birsay Bay W 200 HY 2427
Birse T 177 NO 5597
Birsemore T 177 NO 5297
Birstall T 129 SK 5909
Birstall Smithies T 147 SE 2225
Birstwith T 147 SE 2359
Birtley, H. & W T 116 SO 3669
Birtley, Northum T 158 NY 8778
Birtley, T. & W T 152 NZ 2756
Birts Street T 117 SO 7836
Biruaslum 178 NL 6096
Bisbrooke T 130 SP 8899
Bis Geos 200 HY 4147
Bishampton T 118 SO 9951
Bishop Auckland P 152 NZ 2029
Bishopbriggs T 169 NS 6170
Bishop Burton T 142 SE 9839
Bishopdale Beck W 146 SD 9885
Bishop Hill H 170 NO 1804
Bishop Middleham T 152 NZ 3331
Bishop Monkton T 147 SE 3266
Bishop Norton T 140 SK 9892
Bishopric 176 NN 9647
Bishop Rock 86 SV 8006
Bishops and Clerks 110 SM 6625
Bishopsbourne T 99 TR 1852
Bishops Cannings T 102 SU 0364
Bishop's Castle T 116 SO 3288
Bishop's Caundle T 93 ST 6913
Bishop's Cleeve T 114 SO 9527
Bishop's Frome T 117 SO 6648
Bishop's Itchington T 118 SP 3957
Bishops Lydeard T 92 ST 1629
Bishop's Nympton T 91 SS 7523
Bishop's Offley T 127 SJ 7829
Bishop's Stortford P 105 TL 4821
Bishop's Sutton T 95 SU 6131
Bishop's Tachbrook T 118 SP 3161
Bishop's Tawton T 91 SS 5630
Bishopsteignton T 89 SX 9073
Bishopstoke T 95 SU 4719
Bishopston T 108 SS 5889
Bishopstone, Bucks T 104 SP 8010
Bishopstone, E. Susx T 97 TQ 4701
Bishopstone, H. & W T 113 SO 4143
Bishopstone, Wilts T 94 SU 0725
Bishopstone, Wilts T 102 SU 2483
Bishop Sutton T 101 ST 5859
Bishop's Waltham T 95 SU 5517
Bishopswood, Somer T 92 ST 2512
Bishop's Wood, Staffs T 127 SJ 8309
Bishopsworth T 101 ST 5768
Bishop Thornton T 147 SE 2663
Bishopthorpe T 147 SE 5947
Bishopton, Durham T 153 NZ 3621
Bishopton, Strath T 169 NS 4371
Bishopton Station 169 NS 4370
Bishop Wilton T 148 SE 7955
Bishton T 100 ST 3987
Bisley, Glos T 114 SO 9006
Bisley, Surrey T 104 SU 9559
Bispham T 145 SD 3040
Bissoe T 86 SW 7741
Bisterne Close T 94 SU 2302
Bitchfield T 130 SK 9828
Bittadon T 91 SS 5441
Bittaford T 89 SX 6657
Bittering T 132 TF 9317
Bitterley T 116 SO 5677
Bitterne T 95 SU 4413
Bitteswell T 119 SP 5385
Bitteswell Aerodrome 119 SP 5184
Bitton T 101 ST 6869
Bix T 104 SU 7285
Bixter T 203 HU 3352
Bla Bheinn H 187 NG 5221
Blaby T 129 SP 5697
Blacka Burn W 158 NY 7878
Blackacre T 157 NY 0490
Blackadder T 165 NT 8552
Blackadder Water W 165 NT 8252
Blackawton T 89 SX 8051
Black Bay W 160 NR 7726
Black Beck W 152 SE 1093
Blackborough T 92 ST 0909
Blackborough End T 132 TF 6613
Black Bourton T 115 SP 2804
Blackboys T 97 TQ 5120
Blackbrook T 127 SJ 7639
Blackbrook Reservoir W 129 SK 4517
Black Buoy Sand 131 TF 4139
Black Burn, Cumbr W 151 NY 6940
Black Burn, Grampn W 183 NJ 1256
Blackburn, Grampn T 185 NJ 8212
Blackburn, Lancs P 145 SD 6828
Blackburn, Lothn T 163 NS 9865
Blackburn Common 158 NY 8092
Blackburn Rig 165 NT 7966
Blackbury Castle A 92 SY 1892
Black Callerton T 159 NZ 1769
Black Clauchrie T 154 NX 2984
Black Combe 144 SD 1486
Black Corries Lodge 174 NN 2956
Black Craig, D. & G H 155 NX 5095
Black Craig, Grampn H 176 NO 4394
Black Craig, Orkney 200 HY 2111
Blackcraig Castle 176 NO 1053
Blackcraig Forest F 176 NO 1151
Blackcraig Hill, D. & G H 156 NS 7401
Blackcraig Hill, D. & G H 156 NX 7082
Blackcraig Hill, Strath H 156 NS 6406
Blackcraig Hill, Tays H 176 NO 0952
Black Craig of Dee or Cairnsmore H 156 NX 5875
Black Crofts T 168 NM 9234
Blackden Heath T 137 SJ 7871
Black Devon, Central W 170 NS 9693
Black Devon, Fife W 170 NS 9693
Black Dog, Devon T 91 SS 8009
Blackdog, Grampn T 185 NJ 9514
Blackdog Rock 185 NJ 9613
Black Down, Devon H 92 ST 0906
Black Down, Devon 88 SX 5081
Black Down, Dorset H 93 SY 6187
Black Down Hills H 92 ST 1616
Black Edge, Border H 157 NY 4288
Black Edge, D. & G H 157 NY 4288
Black Esk W 157 NY 2293
Black Esk Reservoir W 157 NY 2096
Black Fell H 158 NY 7173
Blackfield T 95 SU 4401
Blackford, Cumbr T 157 NY 3962
Blackford, Somer T 100 ST 4147
Blackford, Somer T 93 ST 6526
Blackford, Tays T 170 NN 8909
Blackfordby T 128 SK 3318
Blackgang T 95 SZ 4876
Blackgang Chine 95 SZ 4876
Blackhall T 177 NO 6795
Blackhall Colliery 153 NZ 4539
Blackhall Forest F 177 NO 6695
Blackhall Rocks T 153 NZ 4638
Blackham T 97 TQ 5039
Blackhaugh T 164 NT 4238
Black Head, Corn 86 SW 7716
Black Head, Corn 87 SX 0348
Black Head, D. & G 154 NW 9856
Blackheath, Essex T 107 TM 0021
Blackheath, Surrey 96 TQ 0446
Black Heath, Wilts 102 SU 0751
Blackheath, W. Mids T 118 SO 9786
Black Hill, Ches H 138 SJ 9982
Black Hill, Derby H 138 SE 0704
Black Hill, Devon H 92 SY 0285
Black Hill, D. & G H 157 NT 1500
Black Hill, Grampn H 184 NJ 6712
Blackhill, Grampn T 185 NK 0755
Blackhill, Grampn T 185 NK 0843
Black Hill, Lothn H 163 NT 1863
Black Hill, N. Yks H 146 SD 7760
Black Hill, Shrops H 116 SO 3279
Black Hill, Strath H 162 NS 7029
Black Hill, Strath H 154 NX 3896
Black Hill, W. Yks H 138 SE 0704
Black Hill of Mark, Grampn H 176 NO 3281
Black Hill of Mark, Tays H 176 NO 3281
Blackhills 184 NJ 2758
Blackhope Burn W 157 NT 1311
Blackhope Scar H 164 NT 3148
Blackhouse Moor 161 NS 2064
Black Islands 180 NG 7529
Black Isle 182 NH 6556
Black Knowe, Border H 157 NT 2210
Black Knowe, Border H 157 NT 2807
Black Knowe, Border H 158 NY 5487
Black Knowe, D. & G H 157 NT 2807
Black Knowe, Northum H 158 NY 5891
Black Knowe, Northum H 158 NY 6481
Black Knowe Head H 164 NT 3122
Blackland T 102 SU 0168
Black Law, Border H 163 NT 2127
Black Law, Border H 164 NT 3042
Blackley T 137 SD 8602
Black Loch, Central W 170 NS 8670
Black Loch, D. & G W 154 NX 1161
Black Loch, Strath W 170 NS 8670
Black Lochs W 168 NM 9231
Blacklorg Hill H 156 NS 6504
Blacklunans T 176 NO 1460
Black Lyne W 158 NY 5481
Blackman's Law H 158 NY 7498
Black Marsh T 126 SO 3299
Black Meldon H 163 NT 2042
Blackmill T 109 SS 9386
Blackmoor T 95 SU 7733
Blackmoor Gate 91 SS 6443
Blackmoor Vale 93 ST 7315
Blackmore T 106 TL 6001
Blackmore End T 122 TL 7330
Black Mount, Highld 174 NN 2947
Black Mount, Strath T 174 NN 2842
Black Mount, Strath 174 NN 2947
Black Mount, Strath H 163 NT 0846
Black Mountain, Powys H 116 SO 1677
Black Mountain, Shrops H 116 SO 1983
Black Mountains, The, Gwent H 113 SO 2427
Black Mountains, The, H. & W H 113 SO 2427
Black Mountains, The, Powys H 113 SO 2427
Black Mountain, The, Dyfed H 109 SN 7618
Black Mountain, The, Powys H 109 SN 7618
Blackness T 170 NT 0579
Blacknest T 103 SU 7941
Black Notley T 106 TL 7620
Blacko T 146 SD 8641
Black Pill T 108 SS 6190
Black Point 160 NR 7104
Blackpool P 145 SD 3035
Blackpool Airport 145 SD 3231
Blackpool Gate T 158 NY 5377
Blackridge T 163 NS 8967
Blackrock, Gwent T 109 SO 2112
Blackrock, Strath T 166 NR 3063
Black Rocks, Lothn 171 NT 2777
Black Rocks, N. Yks T 149 TA 0486
Blackrod T 137 SD 6110
Black Sail Pass 150 NY 1811
Blackshaw T 157 NY 0465
Blackshaw Bank 157 NY 0462
Blackside H 162 NS 5930
Blackstone T 96 TQ 2316
Blackthorn T 104 SP 6219
Blackthorpe T 122 TL 9063
Blacktoft T 142 SE 8424
Blackton Reservoir W 152 NY 9418
Blacktop T 185 NJ 8604
Black Torrington T 90 SS 4605
Blackwater, Corn T 86 SW 7346
Black Water, Grampn W 184 NJ 3530
Blackwater, Hants T 104 SU 8460
Black Water, Highld W 193 NC 7815
Black Water, Highld W 182 NH 4066
Black Water, Highld W 192 NH 5776
Black Water, Highld W 174 NN 3861
Blackwater, I. of W T 95 SZ 5086
Black Water, Tays W 176 NO 1459
Blackwaterfoot T 160 NR 8928
Blackwater Forest 184 NJ 3126
Black Water of Dee or River Dee W 156 NX 5973
Blackwater Reservoir, Highld W 174 NN 3060
Blackwater Reservoir, Tays W 176 NO 2560
Blackwater River W 104 SU 7364
Blackwell, Derby T 138 SK 1272
Blackwell, H. & W T 118 SO 9972
Blackwood, Gwent T 109 ST 1797
Blackwood, Strath T 162 NS 7943
Blackwood Hill T 127 SJ 9255
Blacon T 136 SJ 3868
Bladerstone T 145 SD 6232
Bladnoch T 155 NX 4254
Bladon T 115 SP 4414
Blaeberry Hill H 157 NT 2801
Blaenannerch T 111 SN 2549
Blaenau Ffestiniog T 135 SH 7045
Blaenavon T 113 SO 2509
Blaendyryn T 112 SN 9337
Blaenffos T 111 SN 1937
Blaengarw T 109 SS 9092
Blaengwrach T 109 SN 8705
Blaengwynfi T 109 SS 8996
Blaenpennal T 125 SN 6364
Blaenplwyf T 124 SN 5775
Blaenporth T 111 SN 2648
Blaenrhondda T 109 SS 9299
Blaenwaun T 111 SN 2327
Blagdon, Avon T 101 ST 5058
Blagdon, Devon T 89 SX 8560
Blagdon Hill T 92 ST 2118
Blagdon Lake W 101 ST 5159
Blaich T 174 NN 0377
Blaina T 109 SO 2008
Blair Atholl T 175 NN 8765
Blair Castle, Fife 170 NS 9685
Blair Castle, Tays A 175 NN 8666
Blairdaff T 185 NJ 6917
Blairdenon Hill, Central H 170 NN 8601
Blairdenon Hill, Tays H 170 NN 8601
Blair Drummond 169 NS 7398
Blairdrummond Moss 169 NS 7197
Blairgowrie T 176 NO 1745
Blairhall T 170 NT 0089
Blairingone T 170 NS 9896
Blairlogie T 169 NS 8296
Blairmore T 168 NS 1982
Blairnamarrow 184 NJ 2115
Blairskaith T 169 NS 5975
Blaisdon T 114 SO 7017
Blakebrook T 117 SO 8176
Blakedown T 117 SO 8878
Blake Hall 105 TL 5305
Blakehope Fell H 158 NY 8494
Blakehope Head H 163 NT 1030
Blakelaw T 164 NT 7730
Blakeman's Law H 158 NY 8795
Blakemere T 113 SO 3641
Blake Muir 164 NT 3030
Blakeney, Glos T 114 SO 6707
Blakeney, Norf T 132 TG 0243
Blakeney Point 132 TG 0046
Blakenhall, Ches T 127 SJ 7247
Blakenhall, W. Mids T 127 SO 9197
Blakeshall T 117 SO 8381
Blakesley T 119 SP 6250
Blakey Ridge H 148 SE 6897
Blanch Fell 145 SD 5760
Blanchland T 152 NY 9650
Blanchland Moor 152 NY 9553
Blandford Camp T 93 ST 9108
Blandford Forum P 93 ST 8806
Blandford St Mary T 93 ST 8805
Bland Hill T 146 SE 2053
Blanefield T 169 NS 5579
Blane Water W 169 NS 5183
Blankney T 140 TF 0760
Blàr a' Chaorainn 174 NN 1066
Blàr Dearg 199 ND 0454
Blarghour 168 NM 9913
Blarmachfoldach T 174 NN 0969
Blarnalearoch T 191 NH 1490
Blary Hill H 160 NR 7136
Blashford T 94 SU 1506
Blaston T 129 SP 8095
Blatherwycke T 130 SP 9795
Blatobulgium R 157 NY 2175
Blawith T 145 SD 2888
Blaxhall T 123 TM 3657
Blaxton T 139 SE 6700
Blaydon T 159 NZ 1762
Blaze Moss H 145 SD 6153
Bleadon T 100 ST 3456
Bleadon Hill H 100 ST 3557
Bleak Law H 163 NT 0651
Bleaklow Hill H 138 SK 1096
Blea Moor 146 SD 7782
Blean T 99 TR 1261
Bleasby T 129 SK 7149
Bleasdale Moors 145 SD 5648
Blea Tarn, Cumbr W 150 NY 2914
Bleatarn, Cumbr T 151 NY 7313
Bleaval H 188 NG 0391
Blebocraigs T 171 NO 4315
Bleddfa T 116 SO 2068
Bledington T 115 SP 2422
Bledlow T 104 SP 7702
Bledlow Ridge T 104 SU 7997
Blegbie T 164 NT 4761
Blencarn T 151 NY 6331
Blencathra or Saddleback H 150 NY 3127
Blencogo T 150 NY 1948
Blencow T 151 NY 4532
Blendworth T 95 SU 7013
Blenheim Palace A 115 SP 4416
Blennerhasset T 150 NY 1741
Blervie Castle 183 NJ 0757
Bletchingdon T 115 SP 5017
Bletchingley T 97 TQ 3250
Bletchley, Bucks T 120 SP 8634
Bletchley, Shrops T 127 SJ 6233
Bletherston T 110 SN 0721
Bletsoe T 120 TL 0258
Blewbury T 103 SU 5385
Blickling T 133 TG 1728
Blidworth T 129 SK 5956
Blindburn 158 NT 8210
Blindcrake T 150 NY 1434
Blindley Heath T 97 TQ 3646
Blisland T 87 SX 1073
Blissford T 94 SU 1713
Bliss Gate T 117 SO 7472
Blisworth T 119 SP 7253
Blithfield Reservoir W 128 SK 0524
Blockley T 115 SP 1635
Blofield T 133 TG 3309
Blo' Norton T 122 TM 0179
Bloody Bay W 173 NM 4858
Bloodybush Edge H 158 NT 9014
Blore T 128 SK 1349
Blorenge H 113 SO 2712
Blotchnie Field H 200 HY 4128
Blovid 203 HU 4119
Bloxham T 115 SP 4235
Bloxwich T 128 SK 0002
Bloxworth T 93 SY 8894

Blubberhouses Bretherdale Head

Blubberhouses T 146 SE 1755
Blue Anchor T 100 ST 0243
Blue Anchor Bay W 100 ST 0145
Blue Bell Hill T 98 TQ 7462
Blue Head 183 NH 8166
Bluemull Sound W 205 HP 5502
Blundellsands T 136 SJ 3099
Blundeston T 133 TM 5197
Blunham T 120 TL 1551
Blunsdon St Andrew T 102 SU 1389
Bluntisham T 121 TL 3674
Blyborough T 140 SK 9394
Blyford T 123 TM 4276
Blymhill T 127 SJ 8112
Blyth, Northum T 159 NZ 3181
Blyth, Notts T 139 SK 6286
Blyth Bridge T 163 NT 1345
Blythburgh T 123 TM 4575
Blythe T 164 NT 5849
Blythe Bridge T 128 SJ 9541
Blythe Edge H 164 NT 6056
Blythe Sands 106 TQ 7580
Blyton T 140 SK 8594
Boarhills T 171 NO 5614
Boarhunt T 95 SU 6008
Boar of Badenoch or An Torc, Highld H 175 NN 6276
Boar of Badenoch or An Torc, Tays H 175 NN 6276
Boarshead T 97 TQ 5332
Boar's Head Rock 184 NJ 2968
Boars of Duncansby W 199 ND 3775
Boarstall T 104 SP 6214
Boasley Cross T 88 SX 5093
Boath T 192 NH 5774
Boat of Garten T 183 NH 9419
Bobbing T 98 TQ 8864
Bobbington T 117 SO 8090
Boblainy Forest F 182 NH 4938
Bocaddon T 87 SX 1758
Boch-ailean 193 ND 1020
Bochastle 169 NN 6107
Bockhampton T 93 SY 7291
Bocking T 106 TL 7523
Bocking Churchstreet T 122 TL 7625
Boconnoc 87 SX 1460
Boddam, Grampn T 185 NK 1342
Boddam, Shetld T 203 HU 3915
Boddington T 114 SO 8925
Boddin Point 177 NO 7153
Bodedern T 134 SH 3380
Bodelwyddan T 135 SJ 0075
Bodenham, H. & W T 113 SO 5351
Bodenham, Wilts T 94 SU 1626
Bodesbeck Law H 157 NT 1610
Bodewryd T 134 SH 4090
Bodfach Hall 126 SJ 1320
Bodfari T 135 SJ 0970
Bodffordd T 134 SH 4276
Bodham T 133 TG 1240
Bodiam T 98 TQ 7825
Bodicote T 119 SP 4638
Bodieve T 87 SW 9973
Bodior 134 SH 2876
Bodle Street Green T 97 TQ 6514
Bodmin P 87 SX 0767
Bodmin Moor 87 SX 1876
Bodmin Parkway Station 87 SX 1164
Bodney T 132 TL 8398
Bodorgan 134 SH 3867
Bodorgan Station 134 SH 3870
Boduan T 134 SH 3237
Bogallan T 182 NH 6350
Bogany Point 161 NS 1065
Bogbrae T 185 NK 0335
Bogend T 161 NS 3932
Bogh a' Chùirn 167 NR 6893
Boghall T 163 NS 9968
Boghole Farm 183 NH 9755
Bogmoor T 184 NJ 3563
Bogniebrae T 184 NJ 5945
Bognor Regis P 96 SZ 9399
Bograxie T 185 NJ 7119
Bogrie Hill H 156 NX 7885
Bogside 163 NS 8354
Bog, The T 126 SO 3598
Bogton T 184 NJ 6751
Bogton Loch W 161 NS 4605
Bogue 156 NX 6481
Bohenie T 174 NN 2982
Bohortha T 87 SW 8632
Bohuntine T 174 NN 2983
Boisdale T 178 NF 7417
Bojewyan T 86 SW 3934
Bolam T 152 NZ 1922
Bolam Lake W 159 NZ 0881
Bold Heath T 137 SJ 5389
Boldon T 159 NZ 3561
Boldon Colliery 159 NZ 3462
Boldre T 94 SZ 3198
Boldron T 152 NZ 0314
Bole T 140 SK 8286
Bolehill T 128 SK 2955
Boleside T 164 NT 4933
Bolham T 91 SS 9514
Bolham Water T 92 ST 1612
Bolingey T 86 SW 7653
Bollihope Common 152 NY 9834
Bollington, Ches T 137 SJ 7286
Bollington, Ches T 137 SJ 9377
Bolney T 96 TQ 2623
Bolnhurst T 120 TL 0859
Bolshan 177 NO 6252
Bolsover T 139 SK 4770
Bolsterstone T 139 SK 2796
Bolstone T 113 SO 5532
Boltby T 147 SE 4986
Bolt Head 89 SX 7236
Bolton, Cumbr T 151 NY 6323
Bolton, G. Man P 137 SD 7108
Bolton, Humbs T 148 SE 7752
Bolton, Lothn T 171 NT 5070
Bolton, Northum T 159 NU 1013
Bolton Abbey T 146 SE 0754
Bolton-by-Bowland T 146 SD 7849
Boltonfellend T 157 NY 4768
Boltongate T 150 NY 2340
Bolton Hall 152 SE 0789
Bolton-le-Sands T 145 SD 4868
Bolton-on-Swale T 152 SE 2599
Bolton Percy T 147 SE 5341
Bolton Priory A 146 SE 0754
Bolton upon Dearne T 139 SE 4502
Bolt's Law H 152 NY 9545
Bolt Tail 89 SX 6639
Bolventor T 87 SX 1876
Bomere Heath T 127 SJ 4719
Bonar Bridge T 192 NH 6191
Bonawe T 168 NN 0033
Bonby T 142 TA 0015
Boncath T 111 SN 2038
Bonchester Bridge T 158 NT 5812
Bondleigh T 91 SS 6504
Bonehill T 128 SK 1902
Bo'Ness T 170 NS 9981
Bonhill T 169 NS 3979
Boningale T 127 SJ 8102
Bonjedward T 164 NT 6523
Bonkle T 163 NS 8356
Bonnington, Kent T 99 TR 0535
Bonnington, Northnts T 170 NT 1269
Bonnington Smiddy 177 NO 5739
Bonnybank 171 NO 3503
Bonnybridge T 169 NS 8280
Bonnykelly T 185 NJ 8653
Bonnyrigg and Lasswade T 164 NT 3065
Bonnyton, Tays 176 NO 3338
Bonnyton, Tays T 177 NO 6655
Bonsall T 139 SK 2858
Bonskeid House 175 NN 8961
Bont T 113 SO 3819
Bontddu T 125 SH 6718
Bont Dolgadfan T 125 SH 8800
Bont-goch or Elerch T 125 SN 6886
Bont-newydd, Clwyd T 135 SJ 0170
Bontnewydd, Gwyn T 134 SH 4860
Bont Newydd, Gwyn T 125 SH 7720
Bontuchel T 135 SJ 0857
Bonvilston T 109 ST 0674
Booker T 104 SU 8491
Booley T 127 SJ 5725
Boosbeck T 153 NZ 6617
Boot T 150 NY 1701
Boothby Graffoe T 140 SK 9859
Boothby Pagnell T 130 SK 9730
Boothstown T 137 SD 7200
Booth Wood Reservoir T 144 SD 1088
Bootle, Cumbr T 144 SD 1088
Bootle, Mers P 136 SJ 3394
Bootle Fell 144 SD 1488
Bootle Station 150 SD 0989
Boquhan 169 NS 5387
Boraston T 117 SO 6170
Borcheston T 129 SK 4804
Borden T 98 TQ 8862
Bordley T 146 SD 9364
Bordon Camp T 95 SU 7936
Boreham, Essex T 106 TL 7509
Boreham, Wilts T 101 ST 8844
Boreham Street T 97 TQ 6611
Borehamwood T 105 TQ 1996
Boreland, Central 169 NN 5534
Boreland, D. & G T 157 NY 1791
Boreland Hill H 156 NX 9460
Boreray, W. Isles 188 NF 8581
Bore Stane 163 NT 1459
Bore, The W 200 HY 4956
Borgie T 197 NC 6759
Borgie Forest F 197 NC 6654
Borgue, D. & G T 155 NX 6348
Borgue, Highld T 199 ND 1325
Borle Brook W 117 SO 7088
Borley T 122 TL 8442
Bornesketaig T 186 NG 3771
Borness T 155 NX 6145
Borness Point 155 NX 6144
Boroughbridge T 147 SE 3966
Borough Green T 97 TQ 6057
Borras Head T 126 SJ 3653
Borreraig T 186 NG 1853
Borrobol Forest 198 NC 7925
Borrobol Lodge 198 NC 8626
Borrodale Burn W 180 NM 7086
Borrow Beck W 151 NY 5205
Borrowby T 153 SE 4289
Borrowdale, Cumbr 150 NY 2516
Borrowdale, Cumbr 151 NY 5603
Borrowdale Fells 150 NY 2613
Borrowfield 177 NO 8393
Borrowwash T 128 SK 4134
Borth T 124 SN 6190
Borthwickbrae T 157 NT 4113
Borthwickshiels T 157 NT 4315
Borthwick Water W 157 NT 4513
Borth-y-Gest T 134 SH 5637
Borve, Highld T 187 NG 4448
Borve, W. Isles T 178 NF 6501
Borve, W. Isles T 188 NF 9181
Borve, W. Isles T 188 NG 0394
Borve Point 178 NF 6401
Borve River W 195 NB 4254
Borwick T 145 SD 5273
Bosavern T 86 SW 3630
Bosbury T 117 SO 6943
Boscastle T 88 SX 0990
Boscobel House A 127 SJ 8308
Boscombe, Dorset T 94 SZ 1191
Boscombe, Wilts T 102 SU 2038
Bosham T 95 SU 8004
Bosherton T 110 SR 9694
Boskednan T 86 SW 4434
Bosley T 137 SJ 9165
Bossall T 148 SE 7160
Bossiney T 88 SX 0688
Bossingham T 99 TR 1549
Bosta T 195 NB 1440
Bostock Green T 137 SJ 6769
Boston P 131 TF 3244
Boston Deeps W 131 TF 5450
Boston Spa T 147 SE 4245
Boswinger T 87 SW 9941
Botallack T 86 SW 3632
Botany Bay T 105 TQ 2999
Botesdale T 122 TM 0575
Bothal T 159 NZ 2386
Bothamsall T 139 SK 6773
Bothel T 150 NY 1839
Bothenhampton T 93 SY 4691
Bothwell T 162 NS 7058
Bothwell Water W 164 NT 6865
Botley, Bucks T 104 SP 9802
Botley, Hants T 95 SU 5113
Botley, Oxon T 115 SP 4805
Botolphs T 96 TQ 1909
Bottacks T 182 NH 4960
Bottesford, Humbs T 142 SE 8907
Bottesford, Leic T 129 SK 8039
Bottisham T 121 TL 5460
Bottle Island 190 NB 9502
Bottomcraig T 171 NO 3624
Bottom Flash W 137 SJ 6665
Botton Head 145 SD 6661
Botusfleming T 88 SX 4061
Botwnnog T 134 SH 2631
Bough Beech Reservoir W 97 TQ 4948
Boughrood T 112 SO 1239
Boughspring T 113 ST 5597
Boughton, Norf T 132 TF 6902
Boughton, Northnts T 119 SP 7565
Boughton, Notts T 139 SK 6768
Boughton Aluph T 99 TR 0348
Boughton House A 120 SP 9081
Boughton Lees T 99 TR 0247
Boughton Malherbe T 98 TQ 8849
Boughton Monchelsea T 97 TQ 7651
Boughton Street T 99 TR 0659
Boulby T 153 NZ 7619
Bouldon T 116 SO 5485
Boulmer T 159 NU 2614
Boulmer Haven W 159 NU 2613
Boulston T 110 SM 9712
Boulsworth Hill H 146 SD 9336
Boultenstone 184 NJ 4111
Boultham T 140 SK 9669
Bourn T 121 TL 3256
Bourne T 130 TF 0920
Bourne End, Beds T 120 SP 9644
Bourne End, Bucks T 104 SU 8987
Bourne End, Herts T 104 TL 0206
Bournemouth (Hurn) Airport 94 SZ 1198
Bournemouth P 94 SZ 0991
Bournes Green T 114 SO 9104
Bourneville T 118 SP 0481
Bournheath T 118 SO 9574
Bournmoor T 152 NZ 3151
Bourton, Avon T 100 ST 3864
Bourton, Dorset T 93 ST 7730
Bourton, Oxon T 102 SU 2387
Bourton, Shrops T 127 SO 5996
Bourton on Dunsmore T 118 SP 4370
Bourton-on-the-Hill T 115 SP 1732
Bourton-on-the-Water T 115 SP 1620
Bousd 172 NM 2563
Boveney T 104 SU 9377
Boverton T 109 SS 9868
Bovey Tracey T 89 SX 8178
Bovingdon T 104 TL 0103
Bovington Camp T 93 SY 8388
Bow, Devon T 91 SS 7201
Bow, G. Lon T 105 TQ 3783
Bow, Orkney T 200 ND 3693
Bowbank T 152 NY 9423
Bow Brickhill T 120 SP 9034
Bowburn T 152 NZ 3038
Bowcombe T 95 SZ 4686
Bowd T 92 SY 1090
Bowden, Border T 164 NT 5530
Bowden, Devon T 89 SX 8449
Bowden Hill T 102 ST 9367
Bowderdale T 151 NY 6704
Bowdon T 137 SJ 7586
Bower 158 NY 7583
Bowerchalke T 94 SU 0223
Bowermadden T 199 ND 2464
Bowers Gifford T 106 TQ 7588
Bowershall T 170 NT 0991
Bowertower T 199 ND 2362
Bowes T 152 NY 9913
Bowes Moor 152 NY 9211
Bow Head 200 HY 4553
Bowhill T 164 NT 4227
Bowland T 164 NT 4540
Bowland Bridge T 151 SD 4189
Bowley T 113 SO 5452
Bowlhead Green T 96 SU 9138
Bowling T 169 NS 4473
Bowling Bank T 126 SJ 3948
Bowling Green T 117 SO 8251
Bowmanstead T 150 SD 3096
Bowmont Forest F 164 NT 7328
Bowmont Water W 165 NT 8124
Bowmore T 166 NR 3159
Bowness-on-Solway T 157 NY 2262
Bowness-on-Windermere T 151 SD 4096
Bow of Fife 171 NO 3212
Bowood House 102 ST 9770
Bowsden T 165 NT 9941
Bowside Lodge 198 NC 8361
Bow Street T 125 SN 6284
Bowthorpe T 133 TG 1709
Box, Glos T 114 SO 8600
Box, Wilts T 101 ST 8268
Boxbush T 114 SO 7413
Boxford, Berks T 102 SU 4271
Boxford, Suff T 122 TL 9640
Boxgrove T 95 SU 9007
Boxley T 98 TQ 7758
Boxted, Essex T 122 TL 9933
Boxted, Suff T 122 TL 8251
Boxworth T 121 TL 3464
Boylestone T 128 SK 1835
Boyndie T 184 NJ 6464
Boyndie Bay W 184 NJ 6765
Boyndlie T 185 NJ 9062
Boyne Bay W 184 NJ 6266
Boynton T 149 TA 1368
Boysack 177 NO 6249
Boyton, Corn T 88 SX 3191
Boyton, Suff T 123 TM 3747
Boyton, Wilts T 102 ST 9539
Bozeat T 120 SP 9059
Braaid T 144 SC 3276
Braal Castle 199 ND 1360
Brabling Green T 123 TM 2964
Brabourne T 99 TR 1041
Brabourne Lees T 99 TR 0840
Brabster T 199 ND 3269
Bracadale T 186 NG 3538
Braceborough T 130 TF 0813
Bracebridge Heath T 140 SK 9867
Braceby T 130 TF 0135
Bracewell T 146 SD 8648
Brackenfield T 139 SK 3759
Bracklesham Bay W 95 SZ 8195
Brackletter T 174 NN 1882
Brackley, Northnts T 119 SP 5837
Brackley, Strath T 160 NR 7942
Bracknell T 104 SU 8668
Brack, The H 168 NN 2403
Braco T 169 NN 8309
Bracobrae T 184 NJ 5053
Braco Castle 169 NN 8211
Bracon Ash T 133 TM 1899
Bracora T 180 NM 7192
Bracorina T 180 NM 7292
Bradbourne T 128 SK 2052
Bradbury T 152 NZ 3128
Bradda T 144 SC 1970
Bradda Head 144 SC 1869
Bradden T 119 SP 6448
Braddock T 87 SX 1662
Bradenham, Bucks T 104 SU 8297
Bradenham, Norf T 132 TF 9208
Bradenstoke T 102 SU 0079
Bradfield, Berks T 103 SU 6072
Bradfield, Essex T 123 TM 1430
Bradfield, Norf T 133 TG 2733
Bradfield Combust T 122 TL 8957
Bradfield Green T 137 SJ 6859
Bradfield Moors 139 SK 2392
Bradfield St Clare T 122 TL 9057
Bradfield St George T 122 TL 9160
Bradford, Devon T 90 SS 4207
Bradford, Northum T 165 NU 1532
Bradford, W. Yks P 146 SE 1633
Bradford Abbas T 93 ST 5814
Bradford Leigh T 101 ST 8362
Bradford-on-Avon T 101 ST 8260
Bradford-on-Tone T 92 ST 1722
Bradford Peverell T 93 SY 6592
Brading T 95 SZ 6086
Bradley, Derby T 128 SK 2246
Bradley, Hants T 103 SU 6341
Bradley, Humbs T 143 TA 2406
Bradley, Staffs T 127 SJ 8818
Bradley Green T 118 SO 9961
Bradley in the Moors T 128 SK 0641
Bradmore T 129 SK 5831
Bradninch T 91 SS 9903
Bradnop T 128 SK 0155
Bradpole T 93 SY 4794
Bradshaw T 137 SD 7312
Bradstone T 88 SX 3880
Bradwall Green T 137 SJ 7563
Bradwell, Bucks T 120 SP 8339
Bradwell, Derby T 138 SK 1781
Bradwell, Essex T 106 TL 8023
Bradwell, Norf T 133 TG 5003
Bradwell Grove T 115 SP 2408
Bradwell-on-Sea T 107 TM 0006
Bradwell Waterside T 107 TL 9907
Bradworthy T 90 SS 3214
Brae, Highld 192 NC 4301
Brae, Highld T 190 NG 8185
Brae, Highld T 183 NH 6663
Brae, Shetld T 204 HU 3568
Braeantra T 192 NH 5678
Braedownie 176 NO 2875
Braefield T 182 NH 4130
Braegrum 170 NO 0025
Braehead, D. & G T 155 NX 4252
Braehead, Orkney T 200 HY 4447
Braehead, Orkney 200 HY 5101
Braehead, Strath T 163 NS 8134
Braehead, Strath T 163 NS 9550
Braehead, Tays T 177 NO 6852
Braehoulland T 204 HU 2479
Braelangwell Lodge 192 NH 5192
Braemar P 176 NO 1591
Braemore T 199 ND 0830
Braemore Forest 191 NH 2276
Brae of Achnahaird T 196 NC 0013
Brae of Glenbervie 177 NO 7684
Brae of Moan H 200 HY 3733
Braeriach or Braigh Riabhach, Grampn H 175 NN 9499
Braeriach or Braigh Riabhach, Highld H 175 NN 9499
Braeroy Forest 174 NN 3791
Brae Roy Lodge T 174 NN 3391
Braeside T 168 NS 2375
Braes of Abernethy 183 NJ 0715
Braes of Balquhidder 169 NN 4921
Braes of Doune 169 NN 6905
Braes of Glenlivet 184 NJ 2421
Braes of Lorn 168 NM 8716
Braes of Ogilvie 170 NN 8907
Braes of the Carse 171 NO 2429
Braes o' Lochaber 174 NN 3180
Braes, The T 187 NG 5234
Braeswick T 201 HY 6137
Brae Wick W 204 HU 2478
Brafferton, Durham T 152 NZ 2921
Brafferton, N. Yks T 147 SE 4370
Brafield-on-the-Green T 120 SP 8258
Braga Ness 202 HU 1948
Bragar T 195 NB 2947
Bragbury End T 105 TL 2621
Bragleenmore 168 NM 9020
Braich Anelog 124 SH 1427
Braich y Pwll 124 SH 1325
Braides T 145 SD 4451
Braid Fell H 154 NX 1166
Braid Hills H 171 NT 2569
Braidley T 146 SE 0380
Braidon Bay W 177 NO 8677
Braidwood T 163 NS 8447
Bràigh Mòr W 194 NB 0016
Bràigh-nam-bàgh 189 NG 0889
Braigh Riabhach or Braeriach, Grampn H 175 NN 9499
Braigh Riabhach or Braeriach, Highld H 175 NN 9499
Bràigh Sròn Ghorm H 175 NN 9078
Braigo 166 NR 2369
Brailes T 118 SP 3139
Brailsford T 128 SK 2541
Braintree T 106 TL 7523
Braiseworth T 123 TM 1371
Braishfield T 94 SU 3723
Braithwaite T 150 NY 2324
Braithwell T 139 SK 5394
Bramber T 96 TQ 1910
Bramcote T 129 SK 5037
Bramdean T 95 SU 6128
Bramerton T 133 TG 2904
Bramfield, Herts T 105 TL 2915
Bramfield, Suff T 123 TM 4074
Bramford T 122 TM 1246
Bramhall T 137 SJ 8985
Bramham T 147 SE 4243
Bramhope T 147 SE 2543
Bramley, Hants T 104 SU 6559
Bramley, Surrey T 96 TQ 0044
Bramley, S. Yks T 139 SK 4992
Brampford Speke T 89 SX 9298
Brampton, Cambs T 120 TL 2070
Brampton, Cumbr T 158 NY 5361
Brampton, Cumbr T 151 NY 6723
Brampton, Lincs T 140 SK 8479
Brampton, Norf T 133 TG 2224
Brampton, Suff T 123 TM 4381
Brampton, S. Yks T 139 SE 4101
Brampton Abbots T 113 SO 6026
Brampton Ash T 119 SP 7987
Brampton Bryan T 116 SO 3772
Brampton Station 123 TM 4183
Bramshall T 128 SK 0633
Bramshaw T 94 SU 2615
Bramshill 104 SU 7461
Bramshill Plantation F 104 SU 7562
Bramshott T 95 SU 8432
Branault 173 NM 5269
Brancaster T 132 TF 7743
Brancaster Bay W 132 TF 7646
Brancaster Roads W 132 TF 8049
Brancepeth T 152 NZ 2238
Branchill T 183 NJ 0952
Branderburgh T 184 NJ 2371
Brandesburton T 143 TA 1147
Brandeston T 123 TM 2460
Brandiston T 133 TG 1321
Brandon, Durham T 152 NZ 2339
Brandon, Lincs T 130 SK 9048
Brandon, Northum T 159 NU 0417
Brandon, Suff T 122 TL 7886
Brandon, Warw T 118 SP 4076
Brandon Bank T 122 TL 6288
Brandon Creek T 122 TL 6091
Brandon Park 122 TL 7784
Brandon Parva T 132 TG 0707
Brandsby T 147 SE 5872
Brands Hatch 105 TQ 5764
Brand Side 138 SK 0468
Brane T 86 SW 4028
Bran End T 122 TL 6525
Branksome T 94 SZ 0692
Branksome Park T 94 SZ 0590
Brannie Burn W 168 NN 1616
Branscombe T 92 SY 1988
Bransdale 153 SE 6296
Bransford T 117 SO 7952
Bransgore T 94 SZ 1898
Bransly Hill H 171 NT 6770
Branston, Leic T 130 SK 8129
Branston, Lincs T 140 TF 0267
Branston, Staffs T 128 SK 2221
Branstone T 95 SZ 6583
Brant Broughton T 130 SK 9154
Brant Fell 151 SD 6795
Brantham T 120 TL 1034
Branthwaite T 150 NY 2937
Brantingham T 142 SE 9429
Branton, Northum T 159 NU 0416
Branton, S. Yks T 139 SE 6401
Branxholme T 157 NT 4611
Branxholm Park T 157 NT 4612
Branxton T 165 NT 8937
Brassington T 128 SK 2354
Brasted T 97 TQ 4755
Brasted Chart T 97 TQ 4653
Brat Bheinn H 166 NR 4966
Brathens T 177 NO 6798
Bratoft T 141 TF 4764
Brattleby T 140 SK 9480
Bratton T 101 ST 9152
Bratton Camp A 101 ST 9051
Bratton Clovelly T 88 SX 4691
Bratton Fleming T 91 SS 6437
Bratton Seymour T 93 ST 6729
Braughing T 121 TL 3925
Braunston, Leic T 130 SK 8306
Braunston, Northnts T 119 SP 5466
Braunstone T 129 SK 5502
Braunton T 90 SS 4836
Braunton Burrows 90 SS 4535
Brawby T 148 SE 7378
Brawl T 198 NC 8166
Brawlbin T 199 ND 0757
Bray T 104 SU 9079
Braybrooke T 119 SP 7684
Brayford T 91 SS 6834
Bray Shop T 88 SX 3374
Braystones T 150 NY 0005
Brayton T 147 SE 6030
Brazacott T 88 SX 2690
Breabag H 196 NC 2917
Breachacha Castle 172 NM 1553
Breachwood Green T 105 TL 1522
Breaclete T 195 NB 1536
Breadalbane 169 NN 4735
Breadstone T 114 SO 7100
Breagach Hill H 184 NJ 3313
Breage T 86 SW 6128
Breakachy T 182 NH 4644
Breakerie Water W 160 NR 6510
Breakish T 180 NG 6823
Breaksea Point 109 ST 0265
Bream T 113 SO 6005
Breamore T 94 SU 1519
Breamore House A 94 SU 1519
Brean T 100 ST 2955
Brean Down H 100 ST 2858
Brearton T 147 SE 3261
Breasclete T 195 NB 2135
Breaston T 129 SK 4633
Breast Sand 131 TF 5427
Brechfa T 111 SN 5230
Brechin T 177 NO 5960
Breckles T 132 TL 9494
Breck Ness 200 HY 2209
Breckrey T 187 NG 5162
Breck, The 204 HU 3292
Brecon P 109 SO 0428
Brecon Beacons H 109 SO 0121
Bredbury T 137 SJ 9291
Brede T 98 TQ 8218
Bredenbury T 113 SO 6156
Bredfield T 123 TM 2653
Bredgar T 98 TQ 8860
Bredhurst T 98 TQ 7962
Bredon T 117 SO 9236
Bredon Hill H 118 SO 9639
Bredon's Norton T 117 SO 9339
Bredwardine T 113 SO 3344
Breedon on the Hill T 128 SK 4022
Breich T 163 NS 9660
Breighton T 142 SE 7034
Breiti Stack 201 HZ 2072
Brei Wick W 203 HU 4740
Bremenium R 158 NY 8398
Bremhill T 102 ST 9873
Brenchley T 97 TQ 6741
Brendon T 91 SS 7648
Brendon Common 91 SS 7645
Brendon Hills H 92 ST 0135
Brenfield Bay W 168 NR 8582
Brenish T 194 NA 9926
Brenish Point 188 NF 9089
Brent Eleigh T 122 TL 9447
Brentford T 105 TQ 1778
Brent Knoll T 100 ST 3350
Brent Pelham T 121 TL 4331
Brentwood T 106 TQ 5993
Brenzett T 99 TR 0027
Brereton T 128 SK 0516
Brereton Green T 137 SJ 7764
Brereton Heath T 137 SJ 8164
Bressay 203 HU 5040
Bressay Sound W 203 HU 4841
Bressingham T 123 TM 0881
Brest Rocks 161 NS 1905
Bretby T 128 SK 2923
Bretford T 118 SP 4277
Bretforton T 118 SP 0944
Bretherdale Head T 151 NY 5705

Bretherton Burneside

Bretherton T 137 SD 4720
Brettabister T 203 HU 4857
Brettenham, Norf T 122 TL 9383
Brettenham, Suff T 122 TL 9653
Bretton T 136 SJ 3563
Brevig T 178 NL 6998
Brewham T 93 ST 7236
Brewlands Bridge T 176 NO 1961
Brewood T 127 SJ 8808
Breydon Water W 133 TG 4907
Briantspuddle T 93 SY 8193
Brickendon T 105 TL 3208
Bricket Wood T 105 TL 1202
Bricklehampton T 118 SO 9842
Bride T 144 NX 4401
Bridekirk T 150 NY 1133
Bridell T 110 SN 1742
Bride's Ness 201 HY 7752
Bridestowe T 88 SX 5189
Bridestowe and Sourton Common 89 SX 5588
Brideswell T 184 NJ 5839
Bridford T 89 SX 8186
Bridge T 99 TR 1854
Bridge End T 130 TF 1436
Bridgefoot T 150 NY 0529
Bridge Green T 121 TL 4637
Bridgemary T 95 SU 5803
Bridgend, Cumbr T 151 NY 3914
Bridgend, Fife T 171 NO 3911
Bridgend, Grampn T 184 NJ 3731
Bridgend, Grampn T 184 NJ 5135
Bridgend, Lothn T 170 NT 0475
Bridgend, M. Glam T 109 SS 9080
Bridgend, Strath T 166 NR 3362
Bridgend, Strath T 168 NR 8592
Bridgend, Strath T 169 NS 6870
Bridgend, Tays T 177 NO 5368
Bridgend of Lintrathen T 176 NO 2854
Bridge of Alford T 184 NJ 5617
Bridge of Allan T 169 NS 7997
Bridge of Avon T 184 NJ 1835
Bridge of Balgie 175 NN 5746
Bridge of Brown T 183 NJ 1220
Bridge of Buchat 184 NJ 4015
Bridge of Cally T 176 NO 1451
Bridge of Canny T 177 NO 6597
Bridge of Craigisla 176 NO 2553
Bridge of Dee T 156 NX 7360
Bridge of Don T 185 NJ 9410
Bridge of Dun T 177 NO 6658
Bridge of Dye T 177 NO 6586
Bridge of Earn T 170 NO 1318
Bridge of Ericht 175 NN 5258
Bridge of Feugh T 177 NO 7095
Bridge of Forss T 199 ND 0368
Bridge of Gairn T 176 NO 3597
Bridge of Gaur 175 NN 5056
Bridge of Muchalls T 177 NO 8991
Bridge of Orchy T 174 NN 2939
Bridge of Tilt 175 NN 8765
Bridge of Waithe 200 HY 2811
Bridge of Walls T 202 HU 2651
Bridge of Weir T 161 NS 3865
Bridgerule T 90 SS 2702
Bridges T 126 SO 3996
Bridge Sollers T 113 SO 4142
Bridge Street T 122 TL 8749
Bridgetown T 91 SS 9233
Bridge Trafford T 136 SJ 4571
Bridgewater Canal, Ches W 137 SJ 7287
Bridgewater Canal, G. Man W 137 SJ 7287
Bridge Yate T 101 ST 6873
Bridgham T 122 TL 9686
Bridgnorth T 127 SO 7193
Bridgtown T 128 SJ 9808
Bridgwater P 92 ST 3037
Bridgwater Bay W 100 ST 1852
Bridlington P 149 TA 1866
Bridlington Bay W 149 TA 2065
Bridport T 93 SY 4692
Bridstow T 113 SO 5824
Brierfield T 146 SD 8436
Brierley, Glos T 113 SO 6215
Brierley, H. & W T 113 SO 4956
Brierley, S. Yks T 139 SE 4110
Brierley Hill T 117 SO 9287
Briga Head 199 ND 1875
Brigg T 142 TA 0007
Brigham, Cumbr T 150 NY 0830
Brigham, Humbs T 149 TA 0753
Brighouse T 146 SE 1423
Brighstone T 94 SZ 4282
Brighstone Bay W 94 SZ 4380
Brightgate T 139 SK 2659
Brighthampton T 115 SP 3803
Brightling T 97 TQ 6821
Brightlingsea T 107 TM 0816
Brighton, Corn T 87 SW 9054
Brighton, E. Susx P 97 TQ 3104
Brightons T 170 NS 9377
Brightstone Forest F 94 SZ 4384
Brightwalton T 102 SU 4279
Brightwell T 123 TM 2543
Brightwell Baldwin T 104 SU 6595
Brightwell-cum-Sotwell T 103 SU 5890
Brignall T 152 NZ 0612
Brig o' Turk T 169 NN 5306
Brigsley T 143 TA 2501
Brigsteer T 151 SD 4889
Brigstock T 120 SP 9485
Brill T 104 SP 6513
Brilley T 113 SO 2649
Brimfield T 116 SO 5268
Brimington T 139 SK 4073
Brimmond Hill H 185 NJ 8509
Brimpsfield T 114 SO 9312
Brimpton T 103 SU 5564
Brims T 199 ND 2888
Brims Ness, Highld 199 ND 0471
Brims Ness, Orkney 199 ND 2988
Brinacory T 180 NM 7591
Brind T 142 SE 7431
Brindister, Shetld T 202 HU 2857
Brindister, Shetld T 203 HU 4336
Brindle T 145 SD 5924
Brindley Ford T 127 SJ 8854
Brindley Heath 128 SJ 9914
Brineton T 127 SJ 8013
Bring Deeps W 200 HY 2902
Bringewood, H. & W F 116 SO 4673
Bringewood, Shrops F 116 SO 4673
Bring Head, Orkney 200 HY 2702
Bring Head, Orkney 200 HY 3733
Bringhurst T 120 SP 8492
Brington T 120 TL 0875
Briningham T 132 TG 0334
Brinkburn Priory A 159 NZ 1198
Brinkhill T 141 TF 3773
Brinkley T 122 TL 6254
Brinklow T 118 SP 4379
Brinkworth T 102 SU 0184
Brinscall T 145 SD 6221
Brinsley T 129 SK 4649
Brinsop T 113 SO 4444
Brinsworth T 139 SK 4290
Brinton T 132 TG 0335
Brinyan T 200 HY 4327
Brisley T 132 TF 9521
Brislington T 101 ST 6270
Brisons, The 86 SW 3431
Bristol P 101 ST 5973
Bristol Airport 101 ST 5065
Bristol Channel W 108 SS 5167
Briston T 132 TG 0632
Britannia T 146 SD 8821
Britford T 94 SU 1628
Briton Ferry T 109 SS 7494
Britwell Salome T 104 SU 6793
Brixham T 89 SX 9255
Brixton, Devon T 89 SX 5552
Brixton, G. Lon T 105 TQ 3175
Brixton Deverill T 101 ST 8638
Brixworth T 119 SP 7470
Brize Norton T 115 SP 3007
Broad Bay or Loch a Tuath W 195 NB 5036
Broad Bench 93 SY 8978
Broad Blunsden T 102 SU 1590
Broadbottom T 138 SJ 9894
Broadbridge T 95 SU 8105
Broadbridge Heath T 96 TQ 1431
Broadbury 88 SX 4697
Broad Cairn, Grampn H 176 NO 2481
Broad Cairn, Tays H 176 NO 2481
Broad Campden T 118 SP 1637
Broad Chalke T 94 SU 0325
Broadclyst T 89 SX 9897
Broad Down H 92 SY 1793
Broadford T 180 NG 6423
Broadford Bay W 180 NG 6523
Broad Green T 117 SO 7756
Broadhaugh 157 NT 4509
Broad Haven T 110 SM 8613
Broad Head H 157 NY 3494
Broadheath, G. Man T 137 SJ 7689
Broad Heath, H. & W T 117 SO 6665
Broadheath, H. & W T 117 SO 8056
Broadhembury T 92 ST 1004
Broadhempston T 89 SX 8066
Broad Hill, Cambs T 122 TL 5976
Broad Hill, Strath H 163 NT 0029
Broad Hinton T 102 SU 1076
Broadlands House 94 SU 3520
Broad Law H 163 NT 1423
Broad Laying T 102 SU 4362
Broadley, Grampn T 184 NJ 3961
Broadley, Lancs T 137 SD 8816
Broadley Common T 105 TL 4206
Broad Marston T 118 SP 1446
Broadmayne T 93 SY 7286
Broadmeadows T 164 NT 4130
Broadmere T 103 SU 6247
Broad Oak, Dorset T 93 ST 7812
Broadoak, Dorset T 93 SY 4396
Broad Oak, E. Susx T 97 TQ 6022
Broad Oak, E. Susx T 98 TQ 8220
Broad Oak, H. & W T 113 SO 4821
Broad Oak, Kent T 99 TR 1661
Broadrashes T 184 NJ 4354
Broadsea Bay W 154 NW 9759
Broad Sound W 110 SM 7307
Broad Sound W 86 SV 8309
Broadstairs T 99 TR 3967
Broadstone, Dorset T 94 SZ 0095
Broadstone, Shrops T 116 SO 5489
Broad Street T 98 TQ 8356
Broad Taing 200 HY 4217
Broad Town T 102 SU 0978
Broadwas T 117 SO 7655
Broadwater T 96 TQ 1404
Broadway, H. & W T 118 SP 1037
Broadway, Somer T 92 ST 3215
Broadway Hill H 118 SP 1136
Broadwell, Glos T 113 SO 5911
Broadwell, Glos T 115 SP 2027
Broadwell, Oxon T 115 SP 2504
Broadwell, Warw T 119 SP 4565
Broadwell House 152 NY 9153
Broadwey T 93 SY 6683
Broadwindsor T 93 ST 4302
Broadwoodkelly T 91 SS 6105
Broadwoodwidger T 88 SX 4189
Brobury T 113 SO 3444
Brochel T 190 NG 5846
Brockbridge T 95 SU 6118
Brockdish T 123 TM 2079
Brockenhurst T 94 SU 2902
Brocketsbrae T 163 NS 8239
Brockford Street T 123 TM 1166
Brockhall T 119 SP 6362
Brockham T 96 TQ 1949
Brockhampton, Glos T 114 SP 0322
Brockhampton, H. & W T 113 SO 5932
Brockholes T 138 SE 1511
Brocklesby T 143 TA 1311
Brockley T 101 ST 4666
Brockley Green T 122 TL 8254
Brockloch Hill, D. & G H 155 NX 5173
Brockloch Hill, D. & G H 156 NX 8179
Brockloch Rig H 156 NS 5801
Brockton, Shrops T 126 SJ 3104
Brockton, Shrops T 127 SJ 7203
Brockton, Shrops T 116 SO 3285
Brockton, Shrops T 127 SO 5793
Brockweir T 113 SO 5401
Brockwood Park T 95 SU 6226
Brockworth T 114 SO 8916
Brocolitia R 158 NY 8571
Brocton T 128 SJ 9619
Brodick T 160 NS 0135
Brodick Bay W 160 NS 0237
Brodie Castle 183 NH 9857
Brodsworth T 139 SE 5007
Brogborough T 120 SP 9638
Brokenborough T 101 ST 9189
Broken Cross, Ches T 137 SJ 6873
Broken Cross, Ches T 137 SJ 8973
Broken Cross Muir 163 NS 8537
Brolass 173 NM 5023
Bromborough T 136 SJ 3582
Bromcote T 118 SP 4088
Brome T 123 TM 1376
Brome Street T 123 TM 1576
Bromeswell T 123 TM 3050
Bromfield, Cumbr T 150 NY 1747
Bromfield, Shrops T 116 SO 4877
Bromham, Beds T 120 TL 0051
Bromham, Wilts T 102 ST 9665
Bromley T 105 TQ 4069
Bromley Common 105 TQ 4266
Bromley Green T 99 TR 0036
Brompton, Kent T 98 TQ 7768
Brompton, N. Yks T 153 SE 3796
Brompton, N. Yks T 149 SE 9482
Brompton-on-Swale T 152 SE 2199
Brompton Ralph T 92 ST 0832
Brompton Regis T 91 SS 9531
Bromsash T 114 SO 6424
Bromsgrove P 118 SO 9670
Bromyard T 117 SO 6554
Bromyard Downs T 117 SO 6655
Bronaber T 135 SH 7131
Bronington T 127 SJ 4839
Bronllys T 109 SO 1435
Bronnant T 125 SN 6467
Bronwydd Arms T 111 SN 4123
Bronygarth T 126 SJ 2637
Brook, Hants T 94 SU 2714
Brook, Hants T 94 SU 3428
Brook, I. of W T 94 SZ 3883
Brook, Kent T 99 TR 0644
Brook, Surrey T 96 SU 9337
Brooke, Leic T 130 SK 8505
Brooke, Norf T 133 TM 2899
Brookfield T 161 NS 4164
Brookhouse T 145 SD 5464
Brookhouse Green T 137 SJ 8161
Brookland T 99 TQ 9825
Brookmans Park T 105 TL 2404
Brooks T 126 SO 1499
Brook Street T 105 TQ 5792
Brookthorpe T 114 SO 8312
Brookwood T 96 SU 9557
Broom, Beds T 120 TL 1743
Broom, Warw T 118 SP 0953
Broome, H. & W T 117 SO 9078
Broome, Norf T 123 TM 3491
Broome, Shrops T 116 SO 4081
Broomedge T 137 SJ 7086
Broome Park T 159 NU 1112
Broomer's Corner T 96 TQ 1221
Broomfield, Essex T 106 TL 7010
Broomfield, Grampn T 185 NJ 9532
Broomfield, Kent T 98 TQ 8352
Broomfield, Kent T 99 TR 1966
Broomfield, Somer T 92 ST 2231
Broomfleet T 142 SE 8827
Broomhead Reservoir W 139 SK 2696
Broom Hill, Dorset T 94 SU 0302
Broomhill, Northum T 159 NU 2401
Broomlee Lough W 158 NY 7969
Broomy Law H 164 NT 4131
Broomy Lodge 94 SU 2111
Brora T 193 NC 9004
Brosdale Island 166 NR 4962
Broseley T 127 SJ 6702
Brother Isle 205 HU 4281
Brothers Water W 151 NY 4012
Brothertoft T 131 TF 2746
Brotherton T 147 SE 4826
Brotton T 153 NZ 6819
Broubster T 199 ND 0360
Brough, Cumbr P 151 NY 7914
Brough, Derby T 138 SK 1882
Brough, Highld T 199 ND 2273
Brough, Humbs T 142 SE 9426
Brough, Notts T 140 SK 8358
Brough, Shetld T 205 HU 4377
Brough, Shetld T 203 HU 5141
Brough, Shetld T 205 HU 5179
Brough, Shetld T 203 HU 5564
Broughall T 127 SJ 5641
Brough Head, Highld 199 ND 3763
Brough Head, Orkney 200 HY 2328
Brough Lodge 205 HU 5892
Brough Ness 199 ND 4482
Brough of Deeness 201 HY 5908
Brough Sowerby T 151 NY 7912
Brough Taing 205 HP 6304
Brough, The T 204 HU 2982
Broughton, Border T 163 NT 1135
Broughton, Bucks T 120 SP 8940
Broughton, Cambs T 121 TL 2878
Broughton, Clwyd T 136 SJ 3463
Broughton, Cumbr T 150 NY 0731
Broughton, G. Man T 137 SD 8201
Broughton, Hants T 94 SU 3033
Broughton, Humbs T 142 SE 9608
Broughton, Lancs T 145 SD 5235
Broughton, M. Glam T 109 SS 9271
Broughton, Northnts T 120 SP 8375
Broughton, N. Yks T 146 SD 9451
Broughton, N. Yks T 148 SE 7673
Broughton, Orkney T 200 HY 4448
Broughton, Oxon T 118 SP 4238
Broughton Astley T 119 SP 5292
Broughton Beck T 145 SD 2882
Broughton Gifford T 101 ST 8763
Broughton Hackett T 117 SO 9254
Broughton Heights H 163 NT 1241
Broughton in Furness T 144 SD 2187
Broughton Mills T 150 SD 2290
Broughton Moor T 150 NY 0533
Broughton Poggs T 115 SP 2304
Broughtown T 201 HY 6641
Broughty Ferry T 171 NO 4630
Browland T 202 HU 2650
Brown Bank Head H 146 SE 1058
Brown Candover T 103 SU 5739
Brown Carrick Hill H 161 NS 2916
Brown Caterthun 177 NO 5566
Brown Clee Hill H 117 SO 5985
Brown Cow Hill H 184 NJ 2304
Brown Edge T 127 SJ 9053
Brown Head 160 NR 9025
Brownhill, Grampn T 185 NJ 8640
Brownhill, Lancs T 145 SD 6830
Brownhills T 128 SK 0505
Brownieside T 165 NU 1623
Brownlow Heath T 137 SJ 8360
Brownmoor Hill H 156 NX 9991
Brown Ridge H 146 SE 1077
Brownsea Island 94 SZ 0288
Brownston T 89 SX 6952
Brown Willy H 87 SX 1579
Browsholme Hall A 145 SD 6845
Brow Top T 145 SD 5258
Broxbourne T 105 TL 3607
Broxburn, Lothn T 170 NT 0772
Broxburn, Lothn T 164 NT 6977
Broxted T 121 TL 5727
Broxwood T 113 SO 3654
Bruach, The H 183 NJ 1105
Bruan T 199 ND 3139
Bruar Lodge 175 NN 8376
Bruar Water W 175 NN 8273
Bruchag Point 161 NS 1157
Bruddans, The 204 HU 2077
Brue T 195 NB 3449
Bruera T 136 SJ 4360
Bruern Abbey T 115 SP 2620
Bruernish T 178 NF 7202
Bruernish Point 178 NF 7300
Bruichladdich T 166 NR 2661
Bruisyard T 123 TM 3266
Brumby T 142 SE 8909
Brund T 138 SK 1061
Brundall T 133 TG 3208
Brundish T 123 TM 2669
Brundish Street T 123 TM 2671
Brunerican Bay W 160 NR 6907
Brunt Hill H 164 NT 6874
Brunton, Fife T 171 NO 3220
Brunton, Northum T 165 NU 2024
Bruntshiel Hill H 157 NY 4182
Bruray 205 HU 6972
Brushford, Devon T 91 SS 6707
Brushford, Somer T 91 SS 9225
Bruton T 93 ST 6834
Bruxie Hill H 177 NO 8280
Bryanston T 93 ST 8706
Brydekirk T 157 NY 1870
Bryher 86 SV 8714
Brymbo T 126 SJ 2953
Bryn, G. Man T 137 SD 5600
Bryn, Powys H 112 SN 9055
Bryn, Powys H 109 SO 0722
Bryn, Shrops T 116 SO 2985
Bryn, W. Glam T 109 SS 8192
Bryn Amlwg H 125 SN 9297
Brynamman T 108 SN 7114
Brynberian T 110 SN 1035
Bryn Brawd H 112 SN 6952
Bryncae T 109 SS 9982
Bryncethin T 109 SS 9184
Bryncir T 134 SH 4844
Bryn-côch T 109 SS 7499
Bryncroes T 134 SH 2231
Bryncrug T 124 SH 6103
Bryn Crwn H 112 SN 8258
Bryn Du, Clwyd H 126 SJ 1436
Bryn-du, Powys H 112 SN 9442
Bryneglwys T 126 SJ 1447
Brynford T 136 SJ 1774
Bryn Garw, Dyfed H 125 SN 8077
Bryn Garw, Powys H 125 SN 8361
Bryn Gates T 137 SD 5901
Brynglas Station 125 SH 6303
Bryngwran T 134 SH 3577
Bryngwyn, Gwent T 113 SO 3909
Bryngwyn, Powys T 113 SO 1849
Bryn-henllan T 110 SN 0039
Brynhoffnant T 111 SN 3351
Brynithel T 109 SO 2101
Bryn Llyndŵr H 125 SO 0683
Brynmawr T 109 SO 1912
Brynmenyn T 109 SS 9084
Brynna T 109 SS 9883
Bryn Nicol H 112 SN 8344
Brynrefail T 134 SH 4886
Brynsadler T 109 ST 0380
Brynsiencyn T 134 SH 4867
Brynteg, Clwyd T 126 SJ 3052
Brynteg, Gwyn T 134 SH 4982
Bryn, The T 113 SO 3309
Bryn Titli H 125 SN 9375
Bryn Trillyn H 135 SH 9459
Bryn y Castell H 125 SH 9705
Bryn y Fan H 125 SN 9388
Bryn-y-maen, Clwyd T 135 SH 8376
Bryn-y-maen, Powys H 113 SO 1657
Buachaille Etive Beag H 174 NN 1854
Buachaille Etive Mór H 174 NN 2153
Buail' a' Ghoill 178 NF 8130
Bualintur T 187 NG 4020
Bualnaluib T 190 NG 8690
Bubbenhall T 118 SP 3672
Bubwith T 142 SE 7136
Buccleuch T 157 NT 3214
Buchan 185 NJ 9749
Buchanan Smithy 169 NS 4689
Buchan Burn W 155 NX 4282
Buchan Hill H 155 NX 4281
Buchan Ness 185 NK 1342
Buchanty 170 NN 9328
Buchlyvie T 169 NS 5793
Buckabank T 151 NY 3749
Buckden, Cambs T 120 TL 1967
Buckden, N. Yks T 146 SD 9477
Buckden Pike H 146 SD 9678
Buckenham T 133 TG 3505
Buckerell T 92 ST 1200
Buckfast T 89 SX 7467
Buckfastleigh T 89 SX 7366
Buckhaven T 171 NT 3598
Buckholm T 164 NT 4838
Buckhorn Weston T 93 ST 7524
Buckhurst Hill T 105 TQ 4193
Buckie T 184 NJ 4265
Buckies T 199 ND 1163
Buckingham T 119 SP 6933
Buckland, Bucks T 104 SP 8812
Buckland, Devon T 89 SX 6743
Buckland, Glos T 118 SP 0836
Buckland, Herts T 121 TL 3533
Buckland, Kent T 99 TR 3042
Buckland, Oxon T 115 SU 3498
Buckland, Surrey T 96 TQ 2250
Buckland Abbey A 88 SX 4866
Buckland Brewer T 90 SS 4120
Buckland Common T 104 SP 9206
Buckland Dinham T 101 ST 7551
Buckland Filleigh T 90 SS 4609
Buckland in the Moor T 89 SX 7273
Buckland Monochorum T 88 SX 4868
Buckland Newton T 93 ST 6905
Buckland St Mary T 92 ST 2713
Bucklebury T 103 SU 5570
Bucklerheads 177 NO 4636
Bucklers Hard T 94 SU 4000
Bucklesham T 123 TM 2441
Buckley T 136 SJ 2864
Bucklow Hill T 137 SJ 7383
Buckminster T 130 SK 8722
Bucknall, Lincs T 141 TF 1769
Bucknall, Staffs T 127 SJ 9047
Bucknell, Oxon T 115 SP 5625
Bucknell, Shrops T 116 SO 3574
Bucksburn T 185 NJ 8909
Buck's Cross T 90 SS 3422
Bucks Green T 96 TQ 0732
Bucks Hill T 104 TL 0500
Bucks Horn Oak T 103 SU 8041
Buck's Mills T 90 SS 3523
Buck, The H 184 NJ 4123
Buckton, H. & W T 116 SO 3873
Buckton, Northum T 165 NU 0838
Buckworth T 120 TL 1576
Budbrooke T 118 SP 2665
Budby T 139 SK 6270
Buddo Ness 171 NO 5515
Buddon Ness 171 NO 5430
Bude P 90 SS 2106
Bude Bay W 90 SS 1706
Bude Haven W 90 SS 1906
Budlake T 89 SS 9800
Budle T 165 NU 1535
Budle Bay W 165 NU 1535
Budleigh Salterton T 92 SY 0682
Budock Water T 87 SW 7832
Buerton T 127 SJ 6843
Bugbrooke T 119 SP 6757
Bugeilyn W 125 SN 8292
Bught Fell H 154 NX 2062
Bugle T 87 SX 0159
Bugthorpe T 148 SE 7758
Buidhe Bheinn H 180 NG 9508
Builg Burn W 177 NO 6786
Builth Road T 112 SO 0253
Builth Wells P 112 SO 0451
Bulbarrow Hill H 93 ST 7705
Bulby T 130 TF 0526
Buldoo T 198 NC 9967
Bulford T 102 SU 1743
Bulford Camp T 102 SU 1843
Bulg H 177 NO 5476
Bulgham Bay W 144 SC 4585
Bulkeley T 127 SJ 5354
Bulkington, Warw T 118 SP 3986
Bulkington, Wilts T 102 ST 9458
Bulkworthy T 90 SS 3914
Bull (lightship) 143 TA 3809
Bull Bay W 134 SH 4394
Bulldog Sand 132 TF 6027
Bulley T 114 SO 7619
Bullie Burn W 169 NN 7909
Bull Point 90 SS 4646
Bullpot Farm 145 SD 6681
Bullwood T 168 NS 1674
Bulmer, Essex T 122 TL 8440
Bulmer, N. Yks T 148 SE 6967
Bulmer Tye T 122 TL 8438
Bulphan T 106 TQ 6385
Bulverhythe T 98 TQ 7708
Bulwark T 185 NJ 9345
Bulwell T 129 SK 5345
Bulwick T 130 SP 9694
Bumble's Green T 105 TL 4005
Bunacaimb T 180 NM 6588
Bun Allt na Criche W 173 NM 9256
Bun an Leoib W 172 NM 4023
Bunarkaig T 174 NN 1887
Bunavoneadar T 189 NB 1303
Bunbury T 137 SJ 5658
Bunchrew House 182 NH 6245
Bundalloch T 180 NG 8927
Buness, Shetld 205 HP 6209
Bu Ness, Shetld 201 HZ 2272
Bunessan T 172 NM 3821
Bungay T 123 TM 3389
Bunloinn Forest 181 NH 1707
Bunnahabhainn T 166 NR 4273
Bunny T 129 SK 5829
Buntait T 182 NH 4030
Buntingford T 121 TL 3629
Bunwell T 133 TM 1193
Burach H 182 NH 3814
Burbage, Derby T 138 SK 0472
Burbage, Leic T 119 SP 4492
Burbage, Wilts T 102 SU 2361
Burcombe, Somer 91 SS 7538
Burcombe, Wilts T 94 SU 0730
Burcot T 115 SU 5696
Burdale T 149 SE 8762
Bures T 122 TL 9034
Burfa Camp A 116 SO 2861
Burford, Oxon T 115 SP 2512
Burford, Shrops T 116 SO 5868
Burg T 172 NM 3845
Burgar 200 HY 3427
Burga Water W 202 HU 2354
Burgess Hill T 97 TQ 3119
Burgh, Strath 173 NM 4226
Burgh, Suff T 123 TM 2351
Burgh by Sands T 157 NY 3259
Burgh Castle T 133 TG 4804
Burghclere T 103 SU 4761
Burghead T 183 NJ 1169
Burghead Bay W 183 NJ 0867
Burghfield T 104 SU 6668
Burghfield Common T 104 SU 6566
Burghfield Hill T 104 SU 6667
Burgh Head 201 HY 6923
Burgh Heath T 96 TQ 2457
Burghill T 113 SO 4844
Burgh Island 89 SX 6443
Burgh le Marsh T 141 TF 5064
Burghley House A 130 TF 0406
Burgh next Aylsham T 133 TG 2125
Burgh on Bain T 141 TF 2286
Burgh St Margaret or Fleggburgh T 133 TG 4414
Burgh St Peter T 133 TM 4693
Burghwallis T 139 SE 5311
Burgi Geos 205 HP 4703
Burham T 98 TQ 7262
Burifa' Hill H 199 ND 2075
Buriton T 95 SU 7320
Burland T 127 SJ 6153
Burlawn T 87 SW 9970
Burlescombe T 92 ST 0716
Burleston T 93 SY 7794
Burley, Hants T 94 SU 2103
Burley, Leic T 130 SK 8810
Burleydam T 127 SJ 6042
Burley Gate T 113 SO 5947
Burley in Wharfedale T 146 SE 1646
Burley Lodge 94 SU 2405
Burley Street T 94 SU 2404
Burlingjobb T 113 SO 2558
Burlton T 126 SJ 4526
Burmarsh T 99 TR 1031
Burmington T 118 SP 2638
Burn T 147 SE 5928
Burnage T 137 SJ 8692
Burnaston T 128 SK 2832
Burnby T 142 SE 8346
Burncrooks Reservoir, Central W 169 NS 4879
Burncrooks Reservoir, Strath W 169 NS 4879
Burneside T 151 SD 5095

Burness

Capstone

Burness T 201 HY 6644
Burneston T 147 SE 3085
Burnett T 101 ST 6665
Burn Farm 177 NO 6072
Burnfoot, Border T 157 NT 4113
Burnfoot, Border T 158 NT 5116
Burnfoot, Tays 170 NN 9804
Burnfoot Reservoir W 161 NS 4544
Burnham, Berks T 104 SU 9381
Burnham, Humbs T 142 TA 0517
Burnham Beeches F 104 SU 9585
Burnham Deepdale T 132 TF 8043
Burnham Green T 105 TL 2616
Burnham Market T 132 TF 8342
Burnham Norton T 132 TF 8243
Burnham-on-Crouch T 106 TQ 9496
Burnham-on-Sea T 100 ST 3049
Burnham Overy Staithe T 132 TF 8444
Burnham Overy Town T 132 TF 8443
Burnham Thorpe T 132 TF 8541
Burnhaven T 185 NK 1244
Burnhead T 156 NX 8695
Burnhervie T 185 NJ 7319
Burnhill Green T 127 SJ 7900
Burnhope T 152 NZ 1848
Burnhope Reservoir W 151 NY 8438
Burnhope Seat H 151 NY 7837
Burnhouse T 161 NS 3850
Burn Howe Rigg 149 SE 9198
Burniston T 149 TA 0193
Burnley P 146 SD 8432
Burn Moor, Lancs 145 SD 6964
Burn Moor, N. Yks 145 SD 6964
Burn Moor Fell 145 SD 7064
Burnmoor Tarn W 150 NY 1804
Burnmouth T 165 NT 9560
Burnock Water W 161 NS 5017
Burn of Acharole W 199 ND 2251
Burn of Agie W 174 NN 3790
Burn of Arisdale W 205 HU 4883
Burn of Aultmore W 184 NJ 4553
Burn of Boyne W 184 NJ 6064
Burn of Branny W 176 NO 4483
Burn of Calletar W 177 NO 4969
Burn of Cambus T 169 NN 7003
Burn of Cattie W 177 NO 5795
Burn of Corrichie W 177 NJ 7101
Burn of Dale W 202 HU 2053
Burn of Hillside W 200 HY 3124
Burn of Houstry W 199 ND 1534
Burn of Laxdale W 203 HU 4131
Burn of Lochy W 183 NJ 1323
Burn of Loin W 183 NJ 1409
Burn of Lyth W 199 ND 2961
Burn of Ore W 200 ND 2893
Burn of Rothes W 184 NJ 2448
Burn of Sandvoe W 204 HU 3590
Burn of Sandwater W 203 HU 4153
Burn of Sheeoch W 177 NO 7490
Burn of Tennet W 177 NO 5183
Burn of Tulchan W 183 NJ 1036
Burn of Turret W 177 NO 5480
Burnopfield T 152 NZ 1656
Burnsall T 146 SE 0361
Burns Cottage 161 NS 3318
Burnside, Fife T 170 NO 1608
Burnside, Lothn T 170 NT 0972
Burnside, Shetld T 204 HU 2778
Burnside, Strath T 156 NS 5811
Burnside, Tays 176 NO 4259
Burnside, Tays 177 NO 5050
Burnside of Duntrune T 171 NO 4434
Burnswark 157 NY 1979
Burnt Fen 122 TL 6087
Burn, The 177 NO 5971
Burnt Hill H 161 NS 3058
Burntisland T 171 NT 2385
Burntwood T 128 SK 0509
Burnt Yates T 147 SE 2561
Burpham, Surrey T 96 TQ 0152
Burpham, W. Susx T 96 TQ 0408
Burrach Mór H 182 NH 5808
Burradon, Northum 159 NT 9806
Burradon, T. & W T 159 NZ 2772
Burrafirth, Shetld T 205 HP 6113
Burra Firth, Shetld W 205 HP 6115
Burraland, Shetld 202 HU 2249
Burraland, Shetld 204 HU 3475
Burra Ness 205 HU 5595
Burras T 86 SW 6734
Burra Sound W 200 HY 2404
Burrator Reservoir W 89 SX 5568
Burravoe, Shetld T 203 HU 3567
Burra Voe, Shetld W 204 HU 3688
Burravoe, Shetld T 205 HU 5279
Burra Voe, Shetld W 205 HU 5279
Burray 200 ND 4796
Burray Haas 200 ND 4998
Burray Ness 200 ND 5096
Burray Village T 200 ND 4695
Burrelton T 176 NO 2037
Burridge T 95 SU 5110
Burrier Wick W 204 HU 3192
Burries Ness 204 HU 2783
Burrill T 147 SE 2387
Burringham T 142 SE 8309
Burrington, Avon T 101 ST 4859
Burrington, Devon T 91 SS 6316
Burrington, H. & W T 116 SO 4472
Burrough Green T 122 TL 6355
Burrough on the Hill T 129 SK 7510
Burrow Bridge T 92 ST 3530
Burrow Head 155 NX 4534
Burrowhill T 104 SU 9763
Burry Holms 108 SS 4092
Burry Port T 108 SN 4401
Burscough T 136 SD 4310
Burscough Bridge T 136 SD 4411
Bursea T 142 SE 8033
Burshill T 149 TA 0948
Bursledon T 95 SU 4809
Burslem T 127 SJ 8749
Burstall T 123 TM 0944
Burstock T 93 ST 4202
Burston, Norf T 123 TM 1383
Burston, Staffs T 127 SJ 9430
Burstow T 97 TQ 3041
Burstwick T 143 TA 2227
Burtersett T 152 SD 8989
Burtle T 100 ST 4043
Burton, Ches T 136 SJ 3174
Burton, Ches T 137 SJ 5164
Burton, Dorset T 94 SZ 1694
Burton, Dyfed T 110 SM 9805
Burton, Lincs T 140 SK 9674
Burton, Northum T 165 NU 1633
Burton, Somer T 100 ST 1944
Burton, Wilts T 101 ST 8179
Burton Agnes T 149 TA 1063
Burton Bradstock T 93 SY 4889
Burton Constable T 143 TA 1836
Burton Fleming T 149 TA 0872
Burton Green, Clwyd T 136 SJ 3458
Burton Green, Warw T 118 SP 2675
Burton Hastings T 118 SP 4189
Burton-in-Kendal T 145 SD 5376
Burton in Lonsdale T 145 SD 6572
Burton Joyce T 129 SK 6443
Burton Latimer T 120 SP 9074
Burton Lazars T 129 SK 7616
Burton-le-Coggles T 130 SK 9725
Burton Leonard T 147 SE 3263
Burton on the Wolds T 129 SK 5820
Burton Overy T 129 SP 6798
Burton Pedwardine T 130 TF 1142
Burton Pidsea T 143 TA 2531
Burton Salmon T 147 SE 4927
Burton upon Stather T 142 SE 8717
Burton upon Trent P 128 SK 2423
Burton Wood T 137 SJ 5692
Burwardsley T 127 SJ 5156
Burwarton T 117 SO 6285
Burwash T 97 TQ 6724
Burwash Common T 97 TQ 6423
Burwell, Cambs T 121 TL 5866
Burwell, Lincs T 141 TF 3579
Burwick, Orkney 199 ND 4384
Bur Wick, Shetld W 203 HU 3940
Burwick, Shetld 203 HU 3940
Bury, Cambs T 121 TL 2883
Bury, G. Man T 137 SD 8010
Bury, Somer T 91 SS 9427
Bury, W. Susx T 96 TQ 0113
Bury Ditches A 116 SO 3283
Bury Green T 105 TL 4521
Bury Hill H 102 SU 3443
Bury St Edmunds P 122 TL 8564
Burythorpe T 148 SE 7964
Bury Walls A 127 SJ 5727
Busbridge T 96 SU 9842
Busby, Strath T 162 NS 5756
Busby, Tays 170 NO 0326
Buscot T 115 SU 2397
Bushbury T 127 SJ 9203
Bush Crathie T 176 NO 2596
Bushey T 105 TQ 1495
Bushey Heath T 105 TQ 1594
Bush Green T 123 TM 2187
Bushley T 114 SO 8734
Bushton T 102 SU 0677
Bushy Park 105 TQ 1569
Buss Craig 165 NT 9465
Busta T 203 HU 3466
Busta Voe W 203 HU 3566
Butcher's Pasture T 106 TL 6024
Butcombe T 101 ST 5161
Butleigh T 93 ST 5233
Butleigh Wootton T 93 ST 5035
Butlers Marston T 118 SP 3250
Butley T 123 TM 3650
Butser Hill H 95 SU 7120
Butsfield T 152 NZ 1045
Butterburn 158 NY 6774
Buttercrambe T 148 SE 7358
Butterknowle T 152 NZ 1025
Butterleigh T 91 SS 9708
Butterley W 138 SE 0410
Buttermel Fell 150 NY 1915
Buttermere, Cumbr T 150 NY 1716
Buttermere, Cumbr W 150 NY 1815
Buttermere, Wilts T 102 SU 3461
Buttershaw T 146 SE 1329
Butterstone T 176 NO 0645
Butterton T 128 SK 0756
Butterwick, Humbs T 142 SE 8305
Butterwick, Lincs T 131 TF 3845
Butterwick, N. Yks T 148 SE 7377
Butterwick, N. Yks T 149 SE 9971
Butterwick Low 131 TF 4243
Butt Green T 127 SJ 6651
Buttington T 126 SJ 2508
Buttock Point 168 NS 0175
Butt of Lewis 195 NB 5166
Button Hills H 205 HU 3968
Buttonoak T 117 SO 7578
Buxey Sand 107 TM 1102
Buxhall T 122 TM 0057
Buxted T 97 TQ 4923
Buxton, Derby P 138 SK 0673
Buxton, Norf T 133 TG 2322
Bwlch T 109 SO 1522
Bwlchgwyn T 126 SJ 2653
Bwlch-Llan T 111 SN 5758
Bwlch Mawr H 134 SH 4247
Bwlchtocyn T 124 SH 3126
Bwlch-y-cibau T 126 SJ 1717
Bwlch-y-fadfa T 111 SN 4349
Bwlch-y-ffridd T 125 SO 0695
Bwlchygroes, Dyfed T 111 SN 2436
Bwlch y Groes, Gwyn 125 SH 9123
Bwlch-y-sarnau T 125 SO 0374
Byerhope Reservoir W 151 NY 8546
Byers Green T 152 NZ 2234
Byfield T 119 SP 5253
Byfleet T 104 TQ 0661
Byford T 113 SO 3943
Bygrave T 121 TL 2636
Byker T 159 NZ 2764
Byland Abbey A 147 SE 5478
Bylchau T 135 SH 9763
Bylchau Rhos-faen H 109 SN 7517
Byley T 137 SJ 7269
Bynack Burn W 176 NN 9784
Bynack More H 183 NJ 0406
Byne Hill H 154 NX 1794
Byrehope Mount H 163 NT 1054
Bythorn T 120 TL 0575
Byton T 116 SO 3764
Byworth T 96 SU 9821

C

Caaf Reservoir W 161 NS 2550
Cabaan Forest 182 NH 3650
Caban-coch Reservoir W 125 SN 9163
Cabourne T 143 TA 1401
Cabrach, Grampn T 184 NJ 3827
Cabrach, Strath 166 NR 4964
Cadair Fawr H 109 SN 9812
Cadair Idris H 125 SH 7013
Cadbury T 91 SS 9104
Cadbury Barton T 91 SS 6917
Cadbury Camp A 101 ST 4572
Cadbury Castle A 93 ST 6225
Cadder T 169 NS 6172
Caddington T 104 TL 0619
Caddonfoot T 164 NT 4434
Caddon Water W 164 NT 4140
Cadeby, Leic T 128 SK 4202
Cadeby, S. Yks T 139 SE 5100
Cadeleigh T 91 SS 9107
Cademuir Hill H 163 NT 2337
Cade Street T 97 TQ 6020
Cadgwith T 86 SW 7214
Cadham 171 NO 2702
Cadha na Gaoidhsich 189 NG 4399
Cadishead T 137 SJ 7092
Cadle T 108 SS 6297
Cadley T 102 SU 2066
Cadmore End T 104 SU 7892
Cadnam T 94 SU 2913
Cadney T 142 TA 0103
Cadole T 136 SJ 2062
Cae Afon H 125 SH 8114
Caeathro T 134 SH 5061
Caehopkin T 109 SN 8212
Caenlochan Forest 176 NO 1875
Caerau, M. Glam T 109 SS 8594
Caerau, S. Glam T 109 ST 1375
Caer Caradoc, Shrops A 116 SO 3175
Caer Caradoc, Shrops A 127 SO 4795
Caerdeon T 125 SH 6518
Caergeiliog T 134 SH 3078
Caergwrle T 136 SJ 3057
Caerlaverock Castle A 156 NY 0265
Caerleon T 100 ST 3391
Caer Llan T 113 SO 4908
Caernarfon P 134 SH 4862
Caernarfon Bay W 134 SH 3056
Caerphilly T 109 ST 1587
Caersws T 125 SO 0392
Caerwent T 101 ST 4790
Caerwys T 136 SJ 1373
Caesar's Camp A 103 SU 8350
Caethle T 124 SN 6099
Cagar Feosaig H 193 NC 8404
Cailiness Point 154 NX 1535
Cailleach Head 190 NG 9898
Cailleach Uragaig 166 NR 3898
Caio T 112 SN 6739
Cairidh nan Òb 186 NG 3570
Cairnacay H 184 NJ 2032
Cairn Avel A 155 NX 5592
Cairnbaan T 167 NR 8390
Cairn Baddoch H 176 NO 2770
Cairn Bannoch, Grampn H 176 NO 2282
Cairn Bannoch, Tays H 176 NO 2282
Cairnbanno House 185 NJ 8444
Cairnborrow T 184 NJ 4640
Cairnbrallan H 184 NJ 3324
Cairnbrogie T 185 NJ 8527
Cairnbulg Castle 185 NK 0164
Cairn Cattoch H 184 NJ 2347
Cairncross, Border T 165 NT 8963
Cairncross, Tays T 177 NO 4979
Cairndow T 168 NN 1810
Cairn Edward Forest F 156 NX 6072
Cairness 185 NK 0360
Cairneyhill T 170 NT 0486
Cairnfield House 184 NJ 4162
Cairngaan T 154 NX 1232
Cairn Galtar H 178 NL 6491
Cairngarroch, D. & G T 154 NX 0549
Cairngarroch, D. & G H 155 NX 4977
Cairngarroch Bay W 154 NX 0449
Cairn Geldie H 176 NN 9988
Cairn Gibbs H 176 NO 1859
Cairn Gorm, Grampn H 183 NJ 0004
Cairn Gorm, Highld H 183 NJ 0004
Cairngorm Mountains, Grampn H 176 NJ 0000
Cairngorm Mountains, Highld H 176 NJ 0000
Cairngorms Nature Reserve, Grampn 175 NN 9498
Cairngorms Nature Reserve, Highld 175 NN 9498
Cairnharrow H 155 NX 5356
Cairn Head 155 NX 4838
Cairn Hill, D. & G H 156 NS 8507
Cairnhill, Grampn T 184 NJ 6632
Cairn Hill, Strath H 154 NX 3090
Cairn Holy A 155 NX 5154
Cairnie T 184 NJ 4844
Cairn Inks H 176 NO 3072
Cairnkinna Hill H 156 NS 7901
Cairn Kinny H 162 NS 7821
Cairn Leuchan H 176 NO 3891
Cairn Mona Gowan H 184 NJ 3305
Cairn-mon-earn H 177 NO 7892
Cairn Muldonich H 184 NJ 2326
Cairn na Burgh Beg 172 NM 3044
Cairnoch Hill H 169 NS 6985
Cairn of Barns H 176 NO 3271
Cairn o' Mount 177 NO 6480
Cairnorrie T 185 NJ 8641
Cairnpapple A 170 NS 9871
Cairnpark 185 NJ 8318
Cairn Pat H 154 NX 0456
Cairn Point 154 NX 0668
Cairnryan T 154 NX 0668
Cairnscarrow H 154 NX 1364
Cairnsmore of Carsphairn H 156 NX 5998
Cairnsmore of Fleet 155 NX 5065
Cairnsmore or Black Craig of Dee H 156 NX 5875
Cairns of Coll 172 NM 2866
Cairn Table H 162 NS 7224
Cairn Toul or Carn an t-Sabhail H 176 NN 9697
Cairn Uish H 184 NJ 1750
Cairn Water W 156 NX 8682
Cairnwell, The, Grampn H 176 NO 1377
Cairnwell, The, Tays H 176 NO 1377
Cairn William H 184 NJ 6516
Cairnywellan Head 154 NX 0940
Caisteal Abhail H 160 NR 9644
Caister-on-Sea T 133 TG 5112
Caistor T 143 TA 1101
Caistor St Edmund T 133 TG 2303
Caistron T 159 NT 9901
Caiteshal H 189 NB 2404
Calair Burn W 169 NN 5319
Calback Ness 205 HU 3977
Calbha Beag 196 NC 1537
Calbha Mór 196 NC 1637
Calbost T 195 NB 4117
Calbourne T 94 SZ 4286
Calcot T 104 SU 6671
Caldback 205 HP 6006
Caldbeck T 150 NY 3239
Caldbergh T 146 SE 0985
Caldecote, Cambs T 120 TL 1488
Caldecote, Cambs T 121 TL 3457
Caldecote, Herts T 121 TL 2338
Caldecott, Leic T 130 SP 8693
Caldecott, Northnts T 120 SP 9868
Calderbank T 162 NS 7662
Calder Bridge T 150 NY 0305
Calderbrook T 137 SD 9418
Calder Burn W 174 NH 3401
Caldercruix T 163 NS 8167
Calder Mains T 199 ND 0959
Caldermill T 162 NS 6641
Calder Vale T 145 SD 5345
Calder Water W 162 NS 6242
Caldey Island 110 SS 1496
Caldey Sound W 110 SS 1298
Caldhame 177 NO 4748
Caldicot T 101 ST 4888
Caldicot Level 101 ST 4285
Caldon Canal W 127 SJ 9453
Caldwell, Derby T 128 SK 2517
Caldwell, N. Yks T 152 NZ 1613
Caldy T 136 SJ 2285
Caledonian Canal W 182 NH 3406
Caledrhydiau T 111 SN 4753
Calf of Eday 201 HY 5839
Calf of Flotta 200 ND 3896
Calf of Man 144 SC 1565
Calfsound, Orkney T 200 HY 5738
Calf Sound, Orkney W 200 HY 5739
Calf, The H 151 SD 6697
Calf Top H 145 SD 6685
Calgary T 172 NM 3751
Calgary Bay W 172 NM 3650
Calgary Point 172 NM 1052
Caliach Point 172 NM 3454
Califer T 183 NJ 0857
California, Central T 170 NS 9076
California, Norf T 133 TG 5114
Calke T 128 SK 3722
Calkin Rig H 157 NY 2987
Callaly T 159 NU 0509
Callander T 169 NN 6207
Callanish T 195 NB 2133
Callater Burn W 176 NO 1685
Callestick T 86 SW 7750
Calligarry T 180 NG 6203
Callington T 88 SX 3669
Callop River W 180 NM 9279
Callow T 113 SO 4934
Callow End T 117 SO 8349
Callow Hill, H. & W T 117 SO 7473
Callow Hill, Wilts T 102 SU 0384
Callows Grave T 117 SO 5967
Calmore T 94 SU 3414
Calmsden T 114 SP 0408
Calne T 102 SU 0070
Caln St Dennis T 114 SP 0811
Calow T 139 SK 4171
Calpa Mór H 183 NH 6610
Calshot T 95 SU 4701
Calshot Castle A 95 SU 4802
Calshot Spit (lightship) 95 SU 5001
Calstock T 88 SX 4368
Calstone Wellington T 102 SU 0268
Calthorpe T 133 TG 1831
Calthwaite T 151 NY 4640
Caltinish T 188 NF 8341
Calton, N. Yks T 146 SD 9159
Calton, Staffs T 128 SK 1050
Calvay, W. Isles 178 NF 7728
Calvay, W. Isles 178 NF 8218
Calve Island 173 NM 5254
Calveley T 137 SJ 5958
Calver T 139 SK 2474
Calverhall T 127 SJ 6037
Calver Hill T 113 SO 3748
Calverleigh T 91 SS 9214
Calverley T 146 SE 2036
Calvert T 104 SP 6824
Calverton, Bucks T 119 SP 7939
Calverton, Notts T 129 SK 6149
Calvine T 175 NN 8065
Cam T 114 ST 7599
Cama' Choire 175 NN 6878
Camas Airigh Shamhraidh W 173 NM 8449
Camas Allt nam Bearnach W 189 NB 3608
Camas a' Mhoil W 194 NA 9825
Camas Barabhaig W 180 NG 6909
Camas Chil-Mhalieu W 173 NM 9055
Camas Coille W 196 NC 0016
Camas Eilean Ghlais W 196 NB 9615
Camas Geodhachan an Duilisg W 194 NB 0438
Camas Ghaoideil W 180 NM 6683
Camas Gorm W 173 NM 7742
Camas-luinie T 180 NG 9428
Camas Mór, Highld W 191 NC 1000
Camas Mór, Highld W 186 NG 3770
Camas Mór, Highld W 190 NG 7591
Camas na Ceardaich W 160 NR 9162
Camas Nathais W 173 NM 8737
Camas Pliasgaig W 179 NG 4002
Camastianavaig T 187 NG 5039
Camas Uig W 194 NB 0233
Camasunary T 187 NG 5118
Camault Muir T 182 NH 5040
Camb T 205 HU 5192
Cambeak 88 SX 1296
Cam Beck W 146 SD 7978
Camber T 99 TQ 9618
Camber Castle A 98 TQ 9218
Camberley T 104 SU 8860
Camberwell T 105 TQ 3376
Camblesforth T 147 SE 6426
Cambo T 159 NZ 0285
Camboglanna R 158 NY 6166
Cambois T 159 NZ 3083
Cambo Ness 171 NO 6011
Camborne T 86 SW 6440
Cambrian Mountains, Clwyd H 125 SH 8809
Cambrian Mountains, Dyfed H 125 SH 8809
Cambrian Mountains, Gwyn H 125 SH 8809
Cambrian Mountains, Powys H 125 SH 8809
Cambridge, Cambs P 121 TL 4558
Cambridge, Glos T 114 SO 7503
Cambridge Airport 121 TL 4858
Cambus T 170 NS 8593
Cambusavie Farm 193 NH 7796
Cambusbarron T 169 NS 7792
Cambuscurrie Bay W 193 NH 7285
Cambuskenneth T 169 NS 8094
Cambuslang T 162 NS 6459
Cambusmore Lodge 193 NH 7697
Cam Chreag H 175 NN 5349
Camddwr W 112 SN 7755
Camden Town T 105 TQ 2984
Camelford T 88 SX 1083
Camelon T 170 NS 8680
Camelsdale T 95 SU 8932
Cameron Burn W 171 NO 5112
Cameron Reservoir W 171 NO 4711
Camerory T 183 NJ 0231
Camerton, Avon T 101 ST 6857
Camerton, Cumbr T 150 NY 0331
Cam Fell 146 SD 8180
Camghouran 175 NN 5456
Cam Loch, Highld W 196 NC 2113
Càm Loch, Strath W 167 NR 8287
Camlo Hill H 125 SO 0469
Cammachmore T 177 NO 9094
Cammachmore Bay W 177 NO 9295
Cammeringham T 140 SK 9482
Cammoch Hill H 175 NN 8959
Campay 195 NB 1442
Campbells Hill H 161 NS 5202
Campbelton T 161 NS 1950
Campbeltown P 160 NR 7120
Campbeltown Loch W 160 NR 7420
Camperdown House 171 NO 3532
Camphill Reservoir W 161 NS 2655
Campmuir 176 NO 2137
Campsall T 139 SE 5413
Campsey Ash T 123 TM 3255
Campsie Fells, Central H 169 NS 6083
Campsie Fells, Strath H 169 NS 6083
Camps Reservoir W 163 NT 0022
Camps Water W 163 NS 9722
Camp, The T 114 SO 9109
Campton T 120 TL 1338
Camrose T 110 SM 9220
Camserney 175 NN 8149
Camster T 199 ND 2641
Camster Burn W 199 ND 2446
Camulodunum R 122 TM 0025
Camus Geodhachan an Duilisg W 194 NB 0438
Camus-Luinie H 180 NG 9428
Camusnagaul, Highld T 191 NH 0689
Camusnagaul, Highld T 174 NN 0975
Camusrory T 180 NM 8595
Camusteel T 190 NG 7042
Camusterrach T 190 NG 7141
Camusvrachan 175 NN 6147
Camy 200 HY 5401
Canada T 94 SU 2918
Canal Foot T 145 SD 3177
Candacraig House 184 NJ 3411
Candlesby T 141 TF 4567
Candy Mill T 163 NT 0741
Cane End T 104 SU 6779
Canewdon T 106 TQ 8994
Canford Cliffs 94 SZ 0689
Canford Heath 94 SZ 0295
Canis Dale 205 HU 5082
Canisp H 196 NC 2018
Cann T 93 ST 8721
Canna 179 NG 2505
Canna Harbour W 179 NG 2704
Cann Common T 93 ST 8820
Cannich T 182 NH 3331
Cannington T 100 ST 2539
Cannock P 128 SJ 9810
Cannock Chase 128 SK 0016
Cannock Wood T 128 SK 0412
Cannon Street Station 105 TQ 3280
Canonbie T 157 NY 3976
Canon Bridge T 113 SO 4341
Canon Frome T 117 SO 6543
Canon Pyon T 113 SO 4649
Canons Ashby T 119 SP 5650
Canonstown T 86 SW 5335
Canterbury P 99 TR 1557
Cantick Head 200 ND 3489
Cantley, Norf T 133 TG 3803
Cantley, S. Yks T 139 SE 6202
Cantlop T 127 SJ 5205
Canton T 109 ST 1676
Cantraydoune T 183 NH 7946
Cantraywood T 183 NH 7847
Cantref Reservoir W 109 SN 9916
Cantsfield T 145 SD 6273
Canvey Island T 106 TQ 7983
Canwell Hall 128 SK 1400
Canwick T 140 SK 9869
Canworthy Water T 88 SX 2291
Caol T 174 NN 1176
Caola Bàn W 172 NM 1151
Caolas T 172 NM 0848
Caolas a' Mhòrain W 188 NF 8480
Caolas an Eilein W 194 NA 9821
Caolas an Scarp W 194 NA 9912
Caolas Beag W 190 NG 7578
Caolas Mór, Highld W 180 NG 7035
Caolas Mór, Strath W 166 NR 3687
Caolas Scalpay W 180 NG 6027
Caol Ghleann 168 NS 0693
Caol Ila T 166 NR 4269
Caolis T 178 NL 6297
Caol Lairig 174 NN 2785
Caol Mór W 180 NG 5833
Caol Raineach W 197 NC 6464
Caol Rona W 190 NG 6153
Cape Cornwall 86 SW 3431
Capel T 96 TQ 1440
Cape Law H 157 NT 1315
Capel Bangor T 125 SN 6580
Capel Betws Lleucu T 111 SN 6058
Capel Carmel T 124 SH 1628
Capel Coch T 134 SH 4682
Capel Curig T 135 SH 7258
Capel Cynon T 111 SN 3849
Capel Dewi T 111 SN 4542
Capel Fell, Border H 157 NT 1606
Capel Fell, D. & G H 157 NT 1606
Capel Garmon T 135 SH 8155
Capel Gwyn, Dyfed T 111 SN 4622
Capel Gwyn, Gwyn T 134 SH 3475
Capel Gwynfe T 108 SN 7222
Capel Hendre T 111 SN 5911
Capel Isaac T 111 SN 5827
Capel Iwan T 111 SN 2936
Capel-le-Ferne T 99 TR 2538
Capel Llanillterne T 109 ST 0980
Capel Parc T 134 SH 4487
Capel St Mary T 123 TM 0938
Capel-y-ffin T 113 SO 2531
Capenhurst T 136 SJ 3673
Capernwray T 145 SD 5371
Cape Wrath 196 NC 2574
Capheaton T 159 NZ 0380
Capler Camp A 113 SO 5933
Caplestone Fell H 158 NY 5988
Cappercleuch T 163 NT 2423
Capstone T 98 TQ 7665

Capton
Chapel Haddlesey

Capton *T* 89 SX 8353
Caputh *T* 176 NO 0840
Caradon Hill *H* 88 SX 2770
Cara Island 160 NR 6444
Carbis Bay *T* 86 SW 5238
Carbost, Highld *T* 186 NG 3731
Carbost, Highld *T* 187 NG 4248
Carbrooke *T* 132 TF 9402
Carburton *T* 139 SK 6173
Carcary 177 NO 6455
Carclew 87 SW 7838
Car Colston *T* 129 SK 7242
Carcroft *T* 139 SE 5410
Cardenden *T* 171 NT 2194
Cardeston *T* 126 SJ 3912
Cardiff *P* 109 ST 1876
Cardiff Airport 109 ST 0667
Cardigan *P* 111 SN 1846
Cardigan Bay *W* 124 SN 3793
Cardigan Island 110 SN 1651
Cardington, Beds *T* 120 TL 0847
Cardington, Shrops *T* 127 SO 5095
Cardinham *T* 87 SX 1268
Cardney House 176 NO 0545
Cardno 185 NJ 9663
Cardoness Castle *A* 155 NX 5855
Cardow *T* 184 NJ 1943
Cardrona *T* 164 NT 3039
Cardrona Forest *F* 164 NT 3036
Cardross, Strath *T* 168 NS 3477
Cardross, Strath 169 NS 6097
Cardurnock *T* 157 NY 1758
Car Dyke, Cambs *R* 130 TF 1508
Car Dyke, Cambs *R* 121 TL 4769
Car Dyke, Lincs *R* 130 TF 1437
Careby *T* 130 TF 0216
Careston 177 NO 5258
Carew *T* 110 SN 0403
Carew Cheriton *T* 110 SN 0402
Carew Newton *T* 110 SN 0404
Carey *T* 113 SO 5631
Carfrae *T* 171 NT 5769
Cargen *T* 156 NX 9672
Cargenbridge *T* 156 NX 9474
Cargill 176 NO 1536
Cargo *T* 157 NY 3659
Cargreen *T* 88 SX 4362
Carham *T* 165 NT 7938
Carhampton *T* 91 ST 0042
Carharrack *T* 86 SW 7341
Carie, Tays 175 NN 6157
Carie, Tays 175 NN 6437
Carinbulg Point 185 NK 0366
Carines 87 SW 7959
Carisbrooke *T* 95 SZ 4888
Carishader *T* 195 NB 0933
Cark *T* 145 SD 3676
Carland Cross 87 SW 8453
Carlby *T* 130 TF 0414
Carleatheran *H* 169 NS 6891
Carlecotes *T* 138 SE 1703
Carleton, Cumbr *T* 151 NY 4252
Carleton, Lancs *T* 145 SD 3440
Carleton, N. Yks *T* 146 SD 9749
Carleton Forehoe *T* 133 TG 0905
Carleton Rode *T* 123 TM 1192
Carlingcott *T* 101 ST 6958
Carlingwark Loch *W* 156 NX 7661
Carlin Tooth *H* 158 NT 6302
Carlisle *P* 151 NY 4055
Carlisle Airport 157 NY 4860
Carlock Hill *H* 154 NX 0877
Carlops *T* 163 NT 1655
Carloway *T* 195 NB 2042
Carlton, Beds *T* 120 SP 9555
Carlton, Cambs *T* 122 TL 6453
Carlton, Cleve *T* 153 NZ 3921
Carlton, Leic *T* 128 SK 3904
Carlton, Notts *T* 129 SK 6141
Carlton, N. Yks *T* 146 SE 0684
Carlton, N. Yks *T* 147 SE 6186
Carlton, N. Yks *T* 147 SE 6424
Carlton, Suff *T* 123 TM 3864
Carlton, S. Yks *T* 139 SE 3609
Carlton, W. Yks *T* 147 SE 3327
Carlton Colville *T* 123 TM 5190
Carlton Curlieu *T* 129 SP 6997
Carlton Husthwaite *T* 147 SE 4976
Carlton in Cleveland *T* 153 NZ 5004
Carlton in Lindrick *T* 139 SK 5884
Carlton-le-Moorland *T* 140 SK 9057
Carlton Miniott *T* 147 SE 4081
Carlton Moor 146 SE 0384
Carlton-on-Trent *T* 140 SK 7963
Carlton Scroop *T* 130 SK 9444
Carluke *T* 163 NS 8450
Carl Wark *A* 139 SK 2681
Carmacoup *T* 162 NS 7927
Carmarthen *P* 111 SN 4120
Carmarthen Bay *W* 108 SN 2500
Carmel, Clwyd *T* 136 SJ 1776
Carmel, Dyfed *T* 111 SN 5816
Carmel, Gwyn *T* 134 SH 3882
Carmel, Gwyn *T* 134 SH 4955
Carmel Head 134 SH 2993
Carminish *T* 188 NG 0284
Carminish Islands 188 NG 0185
Carmont 177 NO 8084
Carmunnock *T* 162 NS 5957
Carmyle *T* 162 NS 6561
Carmyllie *T* 177 NO 5542
Carna 173 NM 6259
Carn a' Bhiorain *H* 191 NH 1483
Carn a' Bhodaich *H* 182 NH 5737
Carnaby *T* 149 TA 1465
Carnach, Highld *T* 190 NH 0196
Carnach, Highld *T* 180 NH 0228
Carnach, W. Isles *T* 189 NG 2297
Carn a' Chaochain *H* 182 NH 2318
Carn a' Choin Deirg *H* 191 NH 3992
Carn a' Choire Mhóir *H* 183 NH 8429
Carn a' Chrasgie *H* 183 NH 8643
Carn a' Chuilinn *H* 182 NH 4103
Carn a' Ghaill *H* 179 NG 2606
Carn a' Gheòidh, Grampn *H* 176 NO 1076
Carn a' Gheòidh, Tays *H* 176 NO 1076
Carn a' Ghlinne *H* 191 NH 0660
Carn a' Mhaim *H* 176 NN 9995
Carnan *H* 178 NL 5582
Carn an Daimh *H* 176 NO 1371
Carnan Eoin *H* 166 NR 4098
Carn an Fhidhleir or Carn Ealar, Grampn *H* 175 NN 9084
Carn an Fhidhleir or Carn Ealar, Highld *H* 175 NN 9084
Carn an Fhidhleir or Carn Ealar, Tays *H* 175 NN 9084
Carn an Fhreiceadain *H* 183 NH 7207
Carnan Mór *H* 172 NL 9640
Carn an Righ *H* 176 NO 0277
Carn an t-Sabhail or Cairn Toul *H* 176 NN 9697
Carn an t-Sean-liathanaich *H* 183 NH 8632
Carn an t-Suidhe *H* 184 NJ 2726
Carn an Tuirc *H* 176 NO 1780
Carnau Gŵys *H* 109 SN 8120
Carn Bàn, Highld *H* 183 NH 3341
Carn Bàn, Highld *H* 191 NH 3387
Carn Bàn, Highld *H* 182 NH 6303
Carn Bàn, Strath *H* 173 NM 7228
Carn Bàn Mór *H* 175 NN 8997
Carn Beag *H* 191 NH 1055
Carnbee *T* 171 NO 5306
Carn Bhac, Grampn *H* 176 NO 0482
Carn Bhac, Tays *H* 176 NO 0482
Carn Bheadhair *H* 183 NJ 0511
Carnbo *T* 170 NO 0503
Carn Breac *H* 191 NH 0453
Carn Breac Beag *H* 191 NH 1779
Carn Brea Village *T* 86 SW 6841
Carn Breugach *H* 173 NM 8127
Carn Cas nan Gabhar *H* 192 NH 5280
Càrn Chois *H* 169 NN 7927
Càrn Chuinneag *H* 192 NH 4883
Carn Coire na Creiche *H* 182 NH 6208
Carn Coire na h-Easgainn *H* 183 NH 7313
Carn Daimh *H* 184 NJ 1825
Carn Dearg, Highld *H* 175 NH 6302
Carn Dearg, Highld *H* 174 NN 4166
Carn Dearg, Highld *H* 175 NN 5076
Carn Dearg, Strath *H* 168 NM 8919
Carn Dearg, Tays *H* 174 NN 4166
Carn Dearg Mór *H* 175 NN 8291
Carn Dubh 'Ic an Deòir *H* 183 NH 7719
Carn Duchara *H* 168 NM 8910
Carnduncan 166 NR 2467
Carne 87 SW 9138
Carn Ealar or Carn an Fhidhleir, Grampn *H* 175 NN 9084
Carn Ealar or Carn an Fhidhleir, Highld *H* 175 NN 9084
Carn Ealar or Carn an Fhidhleir, Tays *H* 175 NN 9084
Carn Ealasaid *H* 184 NJ 2211
Càrn Èas *H* 176 NO 1198
Carn Easgann Bàna *H* 182 NH 4806
Carneddau *H* 112 SO 0654
Carnedd Dafydd *H* 135 SH 6663
Carnedd Iago *H* 135 SH 7840
Carnedd Llewelyn *H* 135 SH 6864
Carnedd Moel-siabod *H* 135 SH 7054
Carnedd y Filiast *H* 135 SH 8744
Carn Eige *H* 181 NH 1226
Carn Eilrig *H* 183 NH 9305
Carnell *T* 161 NS 4632
Car Ness 200 HY 4614
Carn Fadrun *A* 134 SH 2835
Carnferg *H* 177 NO 5293
Carnforth *T* 145 SD 4970
Carn Gafallt *H* 125 SN 9464
Carn Garbh *H* 182 NH 2858
Carn Geuradainn *H* 180 NG 9839
Carn Ghriogair *H* 182 NH 6520
Carn Glas-choire *H* 183 NH 8929
Carn-gorm, Highld *T* 180 NG 9520
Carn Gorm, Highld *H* 191 NH 1350
Carn Gorm, Highld *H* 182 NH 3235
Carn Gorm, Highld *H* 182 NH 4362
Carn Gorm, Tays *H* 175 NN 6350
Carnhedryn *T* 110 SM 8027
Carnhell Green *T* 86 SW 6137
Carnie *T* 185 NJ 8005
Carnish *T* 188 NF 8160
Carn Kitty *H* 183 NJ 0942
Carn Leac *H* 174 NN 4097
Carn Leac Saighdeir *H* 184 NJ 2706
Carn Liath, Grampn *H* 184 NJ 1826
Carn Liath, Grampn *H* 184 NJ 2515
Carn Liath, Grampn *H* 176 NO 0386
Carn Liath, Highld *H* 175 NN 4790
Carn Liath, Tays *H* 175 NN 9369
Carn Loch nan Amhaichean *H* 192 NH 4175
Carn Mairg *H* 175 NN 6851
Carn Meadhonach *H* 183 NJ 1417
Carn Mhartuin *H* 191 NH 1754
Carn Mór, Grampn *H* 184 NJ 2618
Carn Mór, Highld *H* 191 NH 2487
Carn Mór, Highld *H* 192 NH 4271
Carn Mór, Highld *H* 182 NH 4334
Carn Mór, Highld *H* 180 NM 9090
Carn Mór, Strath *H* 172 NM 3948
Carn na Caillich *H* 183 NJ 1847
Carn na Caim, Highld *H* 175 NN 6782
Carn na Caim, Tays *H* 175 NN 6782
Carn na Cloiche Móire *H* 182 NH 3753
Carn na Còinnich *H* 182 NH 3251
Carn na Drochaide *H* 176 NO 1293
Carn na Dubh Choille *H* 182 NH 3867
Carn na Farraich *H* 183 NJ 1114
Carn na Feannaige *H* 183 NJ 1008
Carn na h-Easgainn *H* 183 NH 7432
Carn na Làraiche Maoile *H* 182 NH 5811
Carn na Lòine *H* 183 NJ 0736
Carn nam Bad *H* 183 NH 4033
Carn nam Bain-tighearna *H* 183 NH 8425
Carn nam Buailtean *H* 190 NH 0086
Carn nan Iomairean *H* 180 NG 9135
Carn nan Sgeir 190 NC 0101
Carn nan Tri-tighearnan *H* 183 NH 8239
Carn na Saobhaidh *H* 183 NH 6724
Carn na Saobhaidhe *H* 182 NH 6014
Carn na Sean-lùibe *H* 180 NH 0235
Carno *T* 125 SN 9696
Carnock *T* 170 NT 0488
Carn Odhar *H* 182 NH 6317
Carnon Downs *T* 87 SW 7940
Carnousie *T* 184 NJ 6650
Carnoustie *T* 171 NO 5634
Carn Phris Mhóir *H* 183 NH 8021
Carn Ruigh Chorrach *H* 183 NH 9934
Carn Salachaidh *H* 192 NH 5187
Carn Sgùlain *H* 183 NH 6909
Carn Sgùmain *H* 183 NH 8740
Carn Sleamhuinn *H* 183 NH 8516
Carn Towan *T* 86 SW 3626
Carnwath *T* 163 NS 9846
Carnyorth *T* 86 SW 3733
Carperby *T* 152 SE 0089
Carpley Green *T* 146 SD 9487
Carracks, The 86 SW 4640
Carradale *T* 160 NR 8138
Carradale Bay *W* 160 NR 8037
Carradale Point 160 NR 8136
Carradale Water *W* 160 NR 7843
Carragreich *T* 189 NG 1998
Carraig Bhàn *W* 166 NR 2572
Carraig Dubh 166 NR 3062
Carraig Fhada 166 NR 3444
Carraig Mhór 166 NR 4656
Carrbridge *T* 183 NH 9022
Carr Brigs 171 NO 6411
Carreg Ddu 134 SH 2742
Carreg-gwylan-fach 110 SM 7730
Carreglefn *T* 134 SH 3889
Carreg-lem *H* 109 SN 8017
Carreg-lwyd *H* 109 SN 8615
Carreg Ti-pw 124 SN 5370
Carregwastad Point 110 SM 9240
Carreg yr Imbill 134 SH 3834
Carr End 165 NU 2232
Carrick, Fife 171 NO 4422
Carrick, Strath 168 NR 9087
Carrick, Strath *T* 168 NS 1994
Carrick, Strath 154 NX 3294
Carrick Forest *F* 154 NX 4093
Carrick House 200 HY 5638
Carrick Roads *W* 87 SW 8335
Carriden *T* 170 NT 1081
Carrine 160 NR 6609
Carrington, G. Man *T* 137 SJ 7492
Carrington, Lincs *T* 131 TF 3155
Carrington, Lothn *T* 164 NT 3160
Carrington Moss 137 SJ 7491
Carrog *T* 126 SJ 1143
Carron, Central *T* 170 NS 8882
Carron, Grampn *T* 184 NJ 2241
Carron Bridge, Central 169 NS 7483
Carronbridge, D. & G *T* 156 NX 8798
Carron Valley Forest, Central *F* 169 NS 6982
Carron Valley Forest, Strath *F* 169 NS 6982
Carron Valley Reservoir, Central *W* 169 NS 6983
Carron Valley Reservoir, Strath *W* 169 NS 6983
Carrot Hill *H* 176 NO 4540
Carr Shield *T* 151 NY 8047
Carrs, The 149 SE 9779
Carrutherstown *T* 157 NY 1071
Carruth House 161 NS 3566
Carr Vale *T* 139 SK 4669
Carrville *T* 152 NZ 3043
Carrycoats Hall 158 NY 9279
Carsaig *T* 173 NM 5421
Carsaig Bay *W* 173 NM 5421
Carscreugh 154 NX 2259
Carsegowan *T* 155 NX 4258
Carse Gray 177 NO 4653
Carse House 160 NR 7461
Carse of Gowrie 171 NO 2624
Carseriggan 154 NX 3167
Carsethorn *T* 156 NX 9959
Carsfad Loch *W* 156 NX 6086
Carsgailoch Hill *H* 161 NS 5514
Carshalton *T* 105 TQ 2764
Carsington *T* 128 SK 2553
Carsington Reservoir *W* 128 SK 2552
Carskiey *T* 160 NR 6508
Carsluith *T* 155 NX 4854
Carsphairn *T* 156 NX 5693
Carsphairn Forest *F* 156 NS 5701
Carstairs *T* 163 NS 9346
Carstairs Junction *T* 163 NS 9545
Carswell Marsh *T* 115 SU 3299
Carter Bar, Border 158 NT 6906
Carter Bar, Northum 158 NT 6906
Carter's Clay *T* 94 SU 3024
Carterton *T* 115 SP 2807
Carterway Heads *T* 152 NZ 0451
Carthagena Bank 171 NO 2722
Carthew *T* 87 SX 0055
Carthorpe *T* 147 SE 3083
Cartington *T* 159 NU 0304
Cartland *T* 163 NS 8646
Cartmel *T* 145 SD 3878
Cartmel Fell *T* 145 SD 4188
Cartmel Sands 145 SD 3376
Cartmel Wharf 145 SD 3668
Carway *T* 111 SN 4606
Cas *T* 160 NR 7064
Cascob *T* 116 SO 2466
Cashel Dhu 197 NC 4549
Cashlie 175 NN 4941
Cashmoor *T* 94 ST 9713
Cashtal yn Ard *A* 144 SC 4689
Cassington *T* 115 SP 4510
Cassiobury Park *T* 104 TQ 0997
Casswell's Bridge *T* 130 TF 1627
Castallack *T* 86 SW 4525
Castellau *T* 109 ST 0586
Castell Dinas *A* 109 SO 1730
Castell Howell *T* 111 SN 4448
Castell Odo *A* 124 SH 1828
Castell y Bere *A* 125 SH 6708
Castell-y-bŵch *T* 100 ST 2792
Casterton *T* 145 SD 6279
Castle 200 HY 2113
Castle Acre *T* 132 TF 8115
Castle an Dinas *A* 87 SW 9462
Castle Ashby *T* 120 SP 8659
Castlebay *T* 178 NL 6698
Castle Bolton *T* 152 SE 0391
Castle Bromwich *T* 118 SP 1590
Castle Bytham *T* 130 SK 9818
Castlebythe *T* 110 SN 0229
Castle Caereinion *T* 126 SJ 1605
Castle Campbell *A* 170 NS 9699
Castle Camps *T* 122 TL 6343
Castle Carrock *T* 151 NY 5455
Castle Cary, Somer *T* 93 ST 6332
Castlecary, Strath *T* 169 NS 7878
Castle Combe *T* 101 ST 8477
Castlecraig, Border *T* 163 NT 1344
Castlecraig, Highld *T* 183 NH 8269
Castle Ditches, Hants *A* 94 SU 1219
Castle Ditches, S. Glam *A* 109 SS 9667
Castle Ditches, S. Glam *A* 109 ST 0670
Castle Donington *T* 129 SK 4427
Castle Douglas *T* 156 NX 7662
Castle Eaton *T* 115 SU 1495
Castle Eden *T* 153 NZ 4237
Castle Forbes 184 NJ 6219
Castleford *T* 147 SE 4225
Castle Fraser 185 NJ 7212
Castle Frome *T* 117 SO 6645
Castle Gresley *T* 128 SK 2818
Castle Haven *W* 177 NO 8884
Castle Heaton *T* 165 NT 9041
Castle Hedingham *T* 122 TL 7835
Castlehill, Highld 199 ND 1968
Castle Hill, Highld *H* 183 NH 9505
Castlehill, Strath *T* 163 NS 8451
Castle Hill, Suff *T* 123 TM 1547
Castle Hill, W. Yks *A* 138 SE 1514
Castlehill Point 155 NX 8552
Castle Howard 148 SE 7170
Castle Huntly 171 NO 3029
Castle Kennedy *T* 154 NX 1059
Castle Lachlan 168 NS 0195
Castle Leod 182 NH 4859
Castell y Bere *A* 125 SH 6608
Castle Loch, D. & G *W* 154 NX 2853
Castle Loch, D. & G *W* 157 NY 0881
Castlemaddy 155 NX 5589
Castlemartin *T* 110 SR 9198
Castlemilk *T* 157 NY 1577
Castlemorris *T* 110 SM 9031
Castlemorton *T* 117 SO 7937
Castle O'er *T* 157 NY 2492
Castle O'er Forest *F* 157 NY 2493
Castle of Mey 199 ND 2973
Castle of Old Wick *A* 199 ND 3748
Castle of Park *A* 154 NX 1857
Castle Point 165 NU 1441
Castle Ring *A* 128 SK 0412
Castle Rising *T* 132 TF 6624
Castleshaw Moor 138 SD 9911
Castle Side *T* 152 NZ 0748
Castle Stuart 183 NH 7449
Castle Sween *A* 167 NR 7178
Castle, The 205 HU 3787
Castlethorpe *T* 119 SP 7944
Castleton, Derby *T* 138 SK 1583
Castleton, Gwent *T* 100 ST 2583
Castleton, N. Yks *T* 148 NZ 6807
Castleton, Strath *T* 168 NR 8884
Castle Toward 161 NS 1168
Castletown, Highld *T* 199 ND 1968
Castletown, I. of M *T* 144 SC 2667
Castletown, T. & W *T* 159 NZ 3558
Caston *T* 132 TL 9597
Castor *T* 130 TL 1298
Catacol *T* 160 NR 9149
Catacol Bay *W* 160 NR 9049
Cat and Fiddle 138 SK 0071
Cata Sand 201 HY 7040
Catbrain *T* 101 ST 5780
Catcleugh Reservoir *W* 158 NT 7303
Catcliffe *T* 139 SK 4288
Catcott *T* 100 ST 3939
Cateran Hill *H* 165 NU 1023
Caterham *T* 97 TQ 3455
Cater's Beam 89 SX 6369
Catesby *T* 119 SP 5259
Catfield *T* 133 TG 3821
Catfirth, Shetld *T* 203 HU 4354
Cat Firth, Shetld *W* 203 HU 4552
Catford *T* 105 TQ 3872
Catforth *T* 145 SD 4735
Cath *T* 110 SM 7525
Cathcart *T* 162 NS 5860
Cathedine *T* 109 SO 1425
Catherington *T* 95 SU 7014
Catherton *T* 117 SO 6578
Cati Geo 200 HY 4342
Cat Law *H* 176 NO 3161
Catlodge *T* 175 NN 6392
Catlowdy *T* 157 NY 4576
Catlow Fell 145 SD 7160
Catmore *T* 103 SU 4580
Caton *T* 145 SD 5364
Caton Moor 145 SD 5763
Cator Court 89 SX 6877
Catrine *T* 161 NS 5225
Cat's Ash *T* 100 ST 3790
Catsfield *T* 97 TQ 7213
Catshill *T* 118 SO 9674
Cattal *T* 147 SE 4454
Cattawade *T* 123 TM 1033
Catterall *T* 145 SD 4942
Catterick *T* 152 SE 2497
Catterick Bridge *T* 152 SE 2299
Catterick Garrison *T* 152 SE 1897
Catterlen *T* 151 NY 4833
Catterline *T* 177 NO 8678
Catterton *T* 147 SE 5146
Catthorpe *T* 119 SP 5578
Cattistock *T* 93 SY 5999
Catton, Norf *T* 133 TG 2312
Catton, Northum *T* 151 NY 8257
Catton, N. Yks *T* 147 SE 3778
Catton Hall 128 SK 2015
Catwick *T* 143 TA 1345
Catworth *T* 120 TL 0873
Caulcott *T* 115 SP 5024
Cauldcleuch Head *H* 157 NT 4500
Cauldcots 177 NO 6547
Cauldhame *T* 169 NS 6494
Cauldon *T* 128 SK 0749
Cauldron Snout *W* 151 NY 8228
Cauldrus 200 HY 2116
Cauldshiels Hill *H* 164 NT 5131
Caulkerbush *T* 150 NX 9257
Caulside *T* 157 NY 4480
Caunsall *T* 117 SO 8581
Caunton *T* 140 SK 7460
Causamul 188 NF 6670
Caus Castle *A* 126 SJ 3307
Causeway Grain Head, Border *H* 157 NY 3598
Causeway Grain Head, D. & G *H* 157 NY 3598
Causewayhead *T* 169 NS 8095
Causeyend *T* 185 NJ 9419
Causey Park 159 NZ 1795
Causey Park Bridge *T* 159 NZ 1994
Causey Pike *H* 150 NY 2120
Cautley *T* 151 SD 6995
Cava 200 ND 3299
Cavendish *T* 122 TL 8046
Cavenham *T* 122 TL 7669
Caversfield *T* 115 SP 5825
Caversham *T* 104 SU 7175
Caver's Hill *H* 164 NT 3921
Caversta *T* 195 NB 3619
Caverswall *T* 128 SJ 9543
Caw *H* 150 SD 2394
Cawdor *T* 183 NH 8450
Caw Fell *H* 150 NY 1310
Cawood *T* 147 SE 5737
Cawsand *T* 88 SX 4350
Cawston *T* 133 TG 1323
Cawthorne *T* 139 SE 2808
Cawton *T* 147 SE 6476
Caxton *T* 121 TL 3058
Caynham *T* 116 SO 5573
Caynham Camp *A* 116 SO 5473
Caythorpe, Lincs *T* 130 SK 9348
Caythorpe, Notts *T* 129 SK 6845
Cayton *T* 149 TA 0583
Cayton Bay *W* 149 TA 0684
Ceannacroc Forest 181 NH 1713
Ceanna Mór 173 NM 8551
Ceann Creag-airighe *H* 179 NG 2205
Ceann Ear 188 NF 6462
Ceann Leathad nam Bò 199 ND 1324
Ceann na Beinne *H* 187 NG 4217
Ceann-na-Cleithe *T* 189 NG 1794
Ceann Riobha 166 NR 3585
Ceathramh Garbh 196 NC 2251
Cedig 125 SH 9922
Cefn Berain *T* 135 SH 9969
Cefn-brîth *T* 135 SH 9350
Cefn Bryn *H* 108 SS 5089
Cefn Carnedd *A* 125 SO 0190
Cefn Carn Fadog *H* 109 SN 7616
Cefn Cenarth *H* 125 SN 9676
Cefn Coch, Clwyd *H* 135 SJ 0035
Cefn Coch, Gwyn *H* 135 SJ 0035
Cefn Coch, Powys *T* 125 SJ 1026
Cefn Coch, Powys *H* 112 SN 8253
Cefn-coed-y-cymmer *T* 109 SO 0308
Cefn Cribwr *T* 109 SS 8582
Cefn-crin *H* 125 SO 0272
Cefn Cross *T* 109 SS 8682
Cefn Crug *H* 109 SN 8802
Cefn-ddwysarn 135 SH 9638
Cefndeuddwr 125 SH 7326
Cefn Drum *H* 111 SN 6104
Cefn Du *H* 135 SJ 0454
Cefn Einion *T* 116 SO 2886
Cefneithin *T* 111 SN 5513
Cefn Fannog *H* 112 SN 8251
Cefn Gwrhyd *H* 108 SN 7308
Cefn Hengoed *T* 109 ST 1496
Cefn Hirgoed *H* 109 SS 9383
Cefni Reservoir *W* 134 SH 4477
Cefn Llwydlo *H* 112 SN 8542
Cefn-mawr, Clwyd *T* 126 SJ 2842
Cefn Mawr, Powys *H* 109 SN 7915
Cefn Merthyr *H* 109 SO 0800
Cefn Morfudd *H* 109 SS 7997
Cefn Padrig 108 SN 4800
Cefn Pyllau-duon *H* 109 SO 1012
Cefn Rhyswg *H* 113 ST 2394
Cefn Sidan Sands 111 SN 3405
Cefn-y-bedd *T* 126 SJ 3156
Cefn-y-coed *H* 126 SO 1993
Cefn-y-pant *T* 111 SN 1925
Cefn yr Arail *H* 109 SO 0519
Cefnyresgair *H* 125 SN 7589
Ceidio 134 SH 4185
Ceint *T* 134 SH 4975
Cellan *T* 111 SN 6149
Cellarhead, Staffs *T* 128 SJ 9547
Cellar Head, W. Isles 195 NB 5656
Cemaes *T* 134 SH 3793
Cemaes Bay *W* 134 SH 3694
Cemaes Head 110 SN 1350
Cemlyn Bay *W* 134 SH 3393
Cemmaes *T* 125 SH 8406
Cemmaes Road *T* 125 SH 8204
Cenarth *T* 111 SN 2741
Cennin *T* 134 SH 4645
Ceol na Mara 173 NM 7561
Ceres *T* 171 NO 4011
Cerne Abbas *T* 93 ST 6601
Cerney Wick *T* 114 SU 0796
Cerrigceinwen *T* 134 SH 4273
Cerrigydrudion *T* 135 SH 9548
Cessford *T* 164 NT 7323
Cessnock Water *W* 161 NS 5028
Chaceley *T* 114 SO 8530
Chacewater *T* 86 SW 7544
Chackmore *T* 119 SP 6835
Chacombe *T* 119 SP 4943
Chadderton *T* 137 SD 9005
Chaddesden *T* 128 SK 3737
Chaddesley Corbett *T* 117 SO 8973
Chaddleworth *T* 102 SU 4177
Chadlington *T* 115 SP 3322
Chadshunt *T* 118 SP 3453
Chad Valley *T* 118 SP 0485
Chadwell St Mary *T* 106 TQ 6478
Chadwick End *T* 118 SP 2073
Chaffcombe *T* 92 ST 3510
Chagford *T* 89 SX 7087
Chailey *T* 97 TQ 3919
Chainhurst *T* 97 TQ 7347
Chaipaval *H* 188 NF 9792
Chalbury Common *T* 94 SU 0206
Chaldon *T* 97 TQ 3255
Chaldon Down *H* 93 SY 7882
Chaldon Herring or East Chaldon *T* 93 SY 7983
Chale *T* 95 SZ 4877
Chale Bay *W* 95 SZ 4677
Chale Green *T* 95 SZ 4879
Chalfont and Latimer Station 104 SU 9997
Chalfont Common *T* 104 TQ 0091
Chalfont St Giles *T* 104 SU 9893
Chalfont St Peter *T* 104 TQ 0090
Chalford *T* 114 SO 8902
Chalgrove *T* 104 SU 6396
Chalk *T* 98 TQ 6772
Challacombe *T* 91 SS 6940
Challister Ness 203 HU 5767
Challoch *T* 154 NX 3867
Challoch Hill *H* 154 NX 1657
Challock *T* 99 TR 0150
Chalton, Beds *T* 120 TL 0326
Chalton, Hants *T* 95 SU 7316
Chalvington *T* 97 TQ 5209
Champany *T* 170 NT 0278
Chancellor, The *H* 174 NN 1658
Chandler's Cross *T* 104 TQ 0698
Chandler's Ford *T* 94 SU 4320
Changue Forest *F* 154 NX 3093
Chanlockfoot 156 NS 7900
Channerwick *T* 203 HU 4023
Chanonry Point 183 NH 7555
Chantry, Somer *T* 101 ST 7146
Chantry, Suff *T* 123 TM 1443
Chapel *T* 171 NT 2593
Chapel Allerton, Somer *T* 100 ST 4050
Chapel Allerton, W. Yks *T* 147 SE 3037
Chapel Amble *T* 87 SW 9975
Chapel Brampton *T* 119 SP 7266
Chapel Chorlton *T* 127 SJ 8138
Chapel-en-le-Frith *T* 138 SK 0580
Chapelfell Top *H* 152 NY 8734
Chapel Finian *A* 154 NX 2748
Chapelgate *T* 131 TF 4124
Chapel Haddlesey *T* 147 SE 5826

Chapelhall Clotton

Chapelhall T 162 NS 7862
Chapel Hill, Grampn T 185 NK 0635
Chapel Hill, Gwent T 113 SO 5300
Chapelhill, Highld 193 NH 8273
Chapel Hill, Lincs T 130 TF 2054
Chapelhill, Tays T 170 NO 0130
Chapelhill, Tays 171 NO 2021
Chapelknowe T 157 NY 3173
Chapel Lawn T 116 SO 3176
Chapel-le-Dale T 145 SD 7377
Chapel Ness 171 NT 4899
Chapel of Garioch T 185 NJ 7124
Chapel Point, Corn 87 SX 0243
Chapel Point, Dyfed 110 SS 1495
Chapel Rossan Bay W 154 NX 1145
Chapel Row T 103 SU 5769
Chapel Site T 150 NY 3205
Chapel St Leonards T 141 TF 5572
Chapelton, Devon T 91 SS 5726
Chapelton, Strath T 162 NS 6848
Chapelton, Tays T 177 NO 6247
Chapeltown, Grampn T 184 NJ 2421
Chapeltown, Lancs T 137 SD 7315
Chapeltown, S. Yks T 139 SK 3696
Chapman Sands 106 TQ 8383
Chapmanslade T 101 ST 8247
Chapmans Well T 88 SX 3593
Chappel T 122 TL 8928
Chard T 92 ST 3208
Chardstock T 92 ST 3104
Charfield T 101 ST 7292
Charing T 98 TQ 9549
Charing Cross Station 105 TQ 3080
Charing Heath T 98 TQ 9249
Charingworth T 118 SP 2039
Charlbury T 115 SP 3519
Charlcombe T 101 ST 7467
Charlecote T 118 SP 2656
Charlecote Park A 118 SP 2656
Charles T 91 SS 6832
Charleston T 176 NO 3845
Charlestown, Corn T 87 SX 0351
Charlestown, Dorset T 93 SY 6579
Charlestown, Fife T 170 NT 0683
Charlestown, Grampn T 177 NJ 9300
Charlestown, Highld T 190 NG 8174
Charlestown, Highld T 182 NH 6448
Charlestown of Aberlour T 184 NJ 2642
Charles Tye T 122 TM 0252
Charlesworth T 138 SK 0092
Charleton House 171 NO 4503
Charlton, G. Lon T 105 TQ 4278
Charlton, H. & W T 118 SP 0145
Charlton, Northnts T 115 SP 5235
Charlton, Wilts T 93 ST 9022
Charlton, Wilts T 102 ST 9689
Charlton, Wilts T 102 SU 1156
Charlton, Wilts T 94 SU 1723
Charlton, W. Susx T 95 SU 8812
Charlton Abbots T 114 SP 0324
Charlton Adam T 93 ST 5328
Charlton Down H 93 ST 8700
Charlton Horethorne T 93 ST 6623
Charlton Kings T 114 SO 9620
Charlton Mackrell T 93 ST 5228
Charlton Marshall T 93 ST 9003
Charlton Musgrove T 93 ST 7231
Charlton-on-Otmoor T 115 SP 5912
Charlwood T 96 TQ 2441
Charlynch T 92 ST 2337
Charminster T 93 SY 6892
Charmouth T 92 SY 3693
Charndon T 104 SP 6724
Charney Bassett T 115 SU 3895
Charnock Richard T 137 SD 5515
Charnwood Forest F 129 SK 4814
Charsfield T 123 TM 2556
Charter Alley T 103 SU 5957
Charterhouse T 101 ST 4955
Chartershall T 169 NS 8090
Charterville Allotments T 115 SP 3110
Chartham T 99 TR 1055
Chartham Hatch T 99 TR 1056
Chartridge T 104 SP 9303
Chart Sutton T 98 TQ 7950
Charwelton T 119 SP 5356
Chase Terrace T 128 SK 0409
Chasetown T 128 SK 0508
Chasewater W 128 SK 0307
Chastleton T 115 SP 2429
Chatburn T 146 SD 7644
Chatcull T 127 SJ 7934
Chatham T 98 TQ 7567
Chathill T 165 NU 1827
Chat Moss 137 SJ 7096
Chatsworth House A 139 SK 2870
Chattenden T 98 TQ 7572
Chatteris T 121 TL 3985
Chatteris Fen 121 TL 3980
Chattisham T 123 TM 0942
Chatto T 158 NT 7717
Chatton T 165 NU 0528
Chawleigh T 91 SS 7112
Chawston T 120 TL 1556
Chawton T 95 SU 7037
Cheadle, G. Man T 137 SJ 8688
Cheadle, Staffs T 128 SK 0143
Cheadle Hulme T 137 SJ 8786
Cheam T 105 TQ 2463
Chearsley T 104 SP 7110
Chebsey T 127 SJ 8628
Checkendon T 104 SU 6683
Checkley, Ches T 127 SJ 7346
Checkley, Staffs T 128 SK 0237
Chedburgh T 122 TL 7957
Cheddar T 101 ST 4553
Cheddar Gorge 101 ST 4754
Cheddar Reservoir W 101 ST 4453
Cheddington T 104 SP 9116
Cheddleton T 128 SJ 9752
Cheddon Fitzpaine T 92 ST 2427
Chedgrave T 133 TM 3699
Chedington T 93 ST 4805
Chediston T 123 TM 3577
Chedworth T 114 SP 0512
Chedzoy T 92 ST 3337
Cheeseman's Green T 99 TR 0238
Cheetham Hill T 137 SD 8400
Cheldon T 91 SS 7313
Chelford T 137 SJ 8174
Chelker Reservoir W 146 SE 0551
Chellaston T 128 SK 3730
Chellington T 120 SP 9555
Chelmarsh T 117 SO 7288
Chelmarsh Reservoir W 117 SO 7387
Chelmondiston T 123 TM 2037
Chelmorton T 138 SK 1170
Chelmsford P 106 TL 7007
Chelsea T 105 TQ 2778
Chelsfield T 105 TQ 4864
Chelsworth T 122 TL 9848
Cheltenham P 114 SO 9522
Chelveston T 120 SP 9969
Chelvey T 101 ST 4668
Chelwood T 101 ST 6361
Chelwood Gate T 97 TQ 4129
Cheney Longville T 116 SO 4285
Chenies T 104 TQ 0198
Chepstow P 113 ST 5393
Chepstow Park Wood F 113 ST 4997
Cherhill T 102 SU 0370
Cherington, Glos T 114 ST 9098
Cherington, Warw T 118 SP 2936
Cheriton, Devon 91 SS 7346
Cheriton, Devon T 92 ST 1001
Cheriton, Hants T 95 SU 5828
Cheriton, W. Glam T 108 SS 4593
Cheriton Bishop T 89 SX 7793
Cheriton Fitzpaine T 91 SS 8606
Cherrington T 127 SJ 6620
Cherry Burton T 142 SE 9942
Cherry Cobb Sands 143 TA 2221
Cherry Hinton T 121 TL 4856
Cherry Willingham T 140 TF 0372
Chertsey T 104 TQ 0466
Cheselbourne T 93 SY 7699
Chesham T 104 SP 9501
Chesham Bois T 104 SU 9699
Cheshunt T 105 TL 3602
Chesil Beach 93 SY 6180
Cheslyn Hay T 128 SJ 9807
Chessington T 105 TQ 1863
Chester P 136 SJ 4066
Chesterblade T 101 ST 6641
Chesterfield, Derby P 139 SK 3871
Chesterfield, Staffs T 128 SK 1005
Chesterfield Canal W 140 SK 7284
Chester-le-Street T 152 NZ 2751
Chesters, Border T 164 NT 6022
Chesters, Border T 158 NT 6210
Chesterton, Cambs T 130 TL 1295
Chesterton, Cambs T 121 TL 4660
Chesterton, Oxon T 115 SP 5521
Chesterton, Staffs T 127 SJ 8349
Chesterton, Warw T 118 SP 3558
Chestfield T 99 TR 1366
Cheswardine T 127 SJ 7229
Cheswick T 165 NU 0346
Cheswick Black Rocks 165 NU 0347
Cheswick Green T 118 SP 1376
Chetney Marshes 98 TQ 8871
Chetnole T 93 ST 6007
Chettiscombe T 91 SS 9614
Chettisham T 121 TL 5482
Chettle T 94 ST 9513
Chetton T 117 SO 6690
Chetwode T 119 SP 6429
Chetwynd Aston T 127 SJ 7517
Cheveley T 122 TL 6860
Chevening T 97 TQ 4857
Chevington T 122 TL 7859
Cheviot Hills, The, Border H 158 NT 8212
Cheviot Hills, The, Northum H 158 NT 8212
Cheviot, The H 158 NT 9020
Chevithorne T 91 SS 9715
Chew Magna T 101 ST 5763
Chew Resr W 138 SE 0301
Chew Stoke T 101 ST 5561
Chewton Mendip T 101 ST 5953
Chew Valley Lake W 101 ST 5659
Cheynies 203 HU 3438
Chicheley T 120 SP 9045
Chichester P 95 SU 8604
Chichester Harbour W 95 SU 7600
Chicken Head 195 NB 5029
Chicken Rock 144 SC 1463
Chickerell T 93 SY 6480
Chicklade T 93 ST 9134
Chicksands T 120 TL 1139
Chicksgrove T 94 ST 9729
Chidden T 95 SU 6517
Chiddingfold T 96 SU 9635
Chiddingly T 97 TQ 5414
Chiddingstone T 97 TQ 4945
Chiddingstone Causeway 97 TQ 5246
Chideock T 93 SY 4292
Chidham T 95 SU 7903
Chieveley T 103 SU 4773
Chignall Smealy T 106 TL 6611
Chignall St James T 106 TL 6709
Chigwell T 105 TQ 4493
Chigwell Row T 105 TQ 4693
Chilbolton T 102 SU 3939
Chilcombe T 93 SY 5291
Chilcompton T 101 ST 6451
Chilcote T 128 SK 2811
Childer Thornton T 136 SJ 3677
Child Okeford T 93 ST 8312
Childrey T 102 SU 3687
Child's Ercall T 127 SJ 6625
Childswickham T 118 SP 0738
Childwall T 136 SJ 4189
Chilfrome T 93 SY 5898
Chilgrove T 95 SU 8314
Chilham T 99 TR 0653
Chillaton T 88 SX 4381
Chillenden T 99 TR 2753
Chillerton T 95 SZ 4884
Chillesford T 123 TM 3852
Chillingham T 165 NU 0626
Chillington, Devon T 89 SX 7942
Chillington, Somer T 92 ST 3811
Chillington Hall 127 SJ 8607
Chilmark T 94 ST 9732
Chilson T 115 SP 3119
Chilsworthy, Corn T 88 SX 4172
Chilsworthy, Devon T 90 SS 3206
Chiltern Hills, Bucks H 104 SU 7799
Chiltern Hills, Oxon H 104 SU 7799
Chiltern Hundreds 104 SU 9588
Chilthorne Domer T 93 ST 5218
Chilton, Bucks T 104 SP 6811
Chilton, Durham T 152 NZ 2829
Chilton, Oxon T 103 SU 4885
Chilton Cantelo T 93 ST 5721
Chilton Chine 94 SZ 4082
Chilton Foliat T 102 SU 3270
Chilton Lane T 152 NZ 3031
Chilton Polden T 100 ST 3739
Chilton Street T 122 TL 7546
Chilton Trinity T 100 ST 2939
Chilworth, Hants T 94 SU 4118
Chilworth, Surrey T 96 TQ 0247
Chimney T 115 SP 3500
Chineham T 103 SU 6554
Chingford T 105 TQ 3893
Chinley T 138 SK 0482
Chinley Head T 138 SK 0584
Chinnor T 104 SP 7500
Chipchase Castle 158 NY 8875
Chipnall T 127 SJ 7231
Chippenham, Cambs T 122 TL 6669
Chippenham, Wilts P 101 ST 9173
Chipperfield T 104 TL 0402
Chipping, Herts T 121 TL 3531
Chipping, Lancs T 145 SD 6243
Chipping Campden T 118 SP 1539
Chipping Hill T 106 TL 8115
Chipping Norton T 115 SP 3127
Chipping Ongar T 105 TL 5503
Chipping Sodbury T 101 ST 7382
Chipping Warden T 119 SP 4948
Chipstable T 92 ST 0427
Chipstead T 96 TQ 2757
Chirbury T 126 SO 2698
Chirdon Burn W 158 NY 7683
Chirk T 126 SJ 2938
Chirk Castle A 126 SJ 2638
Chirmorie 154 NX 2076
Chirnside T 165 NT 8756
Chirnsidebridge T 165 NT 8556
Chirton T 102 SU 0757
Chisbury T 102 SU 2766
Chiselborough T 93 ST 4614
Chiselbury A 94 SU 0128
Chiseldon T 102 SU 1879
Chiselhampton T 115 SU 5998
Chislehurst T 105 TQ 4470
Chislet T 99 TR 2264
Chiswell Green T 105 TL 1304
Chiswick T 105 TQ 2077
Chisworth T 138 SJ 9891
Chitcomb T 95 SU 5020
Chithurst T 95 SU 8423
Chittering T 121 TL 4970
Chitterne T 102 ST 9944
Chittlehamholt T 91 SS 6420
Chittlehampton T 91 SS 6325
Chittoe T 102 ST 9566
Chivenor T 90 SS 5034
Chno Dearg H 174 NN 3774
Chobham T 104 SU 9762
Chobham Common 104 SU 9665
Chobham Ridges H 104 SU 9159
Cholderton T 102 SU 2342
Cholesbury T 104 SP 9306
Chollerton T 158 NY 9372
Cholmondeley Castle 127 SJ 5351
Cholsey T 103 SU 5886
Cholstrey T 113 SO 4659
Choppington T 159 NZ 2583
Chopwell T 159 NZ 1258
Chorley, Ches T 127 SJ 5751
Chorley, Lancs T 137 SD 5817
Chorley, Shrops T 117 SO 6983
Chorley, Staffs T 128 SK 0711
Chorleywood, Bucks T 104 TQ 0295
Chorleywood, Herts T 104 TQ 0295
Chorlton T 127 SJ 7250
Chorlton-cum-Hardy T 137 SJ 8193
Chorlton Lane T 126 SJ 4547
Chowley T 127 SJ 4756
Chrishall T 121 TL 4439
Christchurch, Cambs T 131 TL 4996
Christchurch, Dorset T 94 SZ 1592
Christchurch, Glos T 113 SO 5713
Christchurch Bay W 94 SZ 2292
Christian Malford T 102 ST 9678
Christleton T 136 SJ 4465
Christmas Common T 104 SU 7193
Christon T 100 ST 3757
Christon Bank T 165 NU 2122
Christow T 89 SX 8384
Christ's Hospital 96 TQ 1428
Chudleigh T 89 SX 8679
Chudleigh Knighton T 89 SX 8477
Chulmleigh T 91 SS 6814
Chunal T 138 SK 0391
Church, Lancs T 145 SD 7428
Church, N. Yks T 153 SE 6697
Churcham T 114 SO 7618
Church Aston T 127 SJ 7417
Church Bay W 134 SH 2989
Church Brampton T 119 SP 7165
Church Broughton T 128 SK 2033
Church Cove T 86 SW 7112
Church Crookham T 103 SU 8152
Churchdown T 114 SO 8820
Church Eaton T 127 SJ 8417
Church End, Beds T 104 SP 9921
Church End, Beds T 120 TL 1937
Church End, Cambs T 131 TF 3909
Church End, Cambs T 121 TL 4857
Church End, Essex T 121 TL 5841
Churchend, Essex T 106 TL 6322
Churchend, Essex T 107 TR 0092
Church End, Hants T 103 SU 6756
Church End, Warw T 118 SP 2992
Church End, Wilts T 102 SU 0278
Church Fenton T 147 SE 5136
Church Gresley T 128 SK 2918
Church Hanborough T 115 SP 4212
Churchill, Avon T 101 ST 4459
Churchill, Devon T 92 ST 2901
Churchill, H. & W T 117 SO 8879
Churchill, Oxon T 115 SP 2824
Churchinford T 92 ST 2112
Church Knowle T 94 SY 9381
Church Langton T 129 SP 7293
Church Lawford T 119 SP 4476
Church Lawton T 127 SJ 8255
Church Leigh T 128 SK 0235
Church Lench T 118 SP 0251
Church Minshull T 137 SJ 6660
Church Norton T 95 SZ 8795
Churchover T 119 SP 5180
Church Preen T 127 SO 5498
Church Pulverbatch T 126 SJ 4302
Churchstanton T 92 ST 1914
Church Stoke T 126 SO 2794
Churchstow T 89 SX 7145
Church Stowe T 119 SP 6357
Church Street T 98 TQ 7174
Church Stretton T 126 SO 4593
Churchtown, I. of M T 144 SC 4294
Churchtown, Lancs T 145 SD 4843
Churchtown, Mers T 136 SD 3518
Church Village T 109 ST 0886
Church Warsop T 139 SK 5668
Churchwell T 147 SE 2729
Church Westcote T 115 SP 2120
Churn Clough Reservoir W 146 SD 7838
Churnsike Lodge 158 NY 6677
Churt T 103 SU 8538
Churton T 126 SJ 4156
Churwell T 147 SE 2729
Chute Causeway R 102 SU 2955
Chwerfri W 112 SO 0052
Chwilog T 134 SH 4338
Chyandour T 86 SW 4731
Chysauster A 86 SW 4535
Ciaran Water W 174 NN 2862
Cilan Uchaf T 124 SH 2923
Cilcain T 136 SJ 1765
Cilcennin T 111 SN 5260
Cilfaesty Hill H 116 SO 1384
Cilfor T 135 SH 6237
Cilfrew T 109 SN 7700
Cilfynydd T 109 ST 0892
Cilgerran T 111 SN 1943
Cilgwyn T 109 SN 7429
Ciliau-Aeron T 111 SN 5058
Cilleni W 109 SN 9034
Cilmaengwyn T 109 SN 7406
Cilmery T 112 SO 0051
Cilrhedyn T 111 SN 2835
Ciltwrch T 113 SO 1640
Cilurnum R 158 NY 9170
Cilwendeg T 111 SN 2238
Cilybebyll T 109 SN 7404
Cilycwm T 112 SN 7540
Cinderford T 114 SO 6514
Cioch Mhór H 182 NH 5063
Cirean Geardail 196 NC 0134
Cirencester P 114 SP 0201
Cir Mhór H 160 NR 9743
Cissbury Ring A 96 TQ 1308
Ciste Dhubh H 181 NH 0616
City Dulas T 134 SH 4787
City of London P 105 TQ 3281
City, The T 104 SU 7896
Clachaig T 168 NS 1181
Clachaig Water W 160 NR 7041
Clachan, Highld T 187 NG 5436
Clachan, Strath T 173 NM 7819
Clachan, Strath T 173 NM 8643
Clachan, Strath 168 NN 1812
Clachan, Strath T 160 NR 7656
Clachan-a-Luib T 188 NF 8163
Clachan Burn W 198 NC 7360
Clachan Hill H 168 NN 1815
Clachan Mór 172 NL 9747
Clachan of Campsie T 169 NS 6079
Clachan of Glendaruel T 168 NR 9984
Clachan-Seil T 173 NM 7818
Clachan Yell H 176 NO 4491
Clach Bheinn H 168 NS 2195
Clachbreck T 167 NR 7776
Clach Leathad H 174 NN 2349
Clachtoll T 196 NC 0427
Clackmannan T 170 NS 9191
Clacton-on-Sea P 107 TM 1714
Cladach an Eilein 195 NB 5365
Cladach Cuiashader 195 NB 5558
Cladach Dibadale 195 NB 5554
Claddach Kirkibost T 188 NF 7865
Cladich 168 NN 0921
Cladich River W 168 NN 1020
Claerwen Reservoir W 125 SN 8565
Claggain Bay W 166 NR 4653
Claggain River W 166 NR 4354
Claggan T 173 NM 6949
Clagh Ouyr H 144 SC 4188
Claife Heights 151 SD 3797
Claigan T 186 NG 2353
Claig Castle 166 NR 4762
Claines T 117 SO 8558
Clandown T 101 ST 6855
Clanfield, Hants T 95 SU 6916
Clanfield, Oxon T 115 SP 2802
Clannaborough Barton 91 SS 7402
Clanville T 102 SU 3149
Clanyard T 154 NX 1037
Clanyard Bay W 154 NX 0938
Claonaig T 160 NR 8756
Claonel T 192 NC 5604
Claonig Bay W 160 NR 8755
Clapgate T 94 SU 0102
Clapham, Beds T 120 TL 0253
Clapham, G. Lon T 105 TQ 2875
Clapham, N. Yks T 145 SD 7469
Clapham, W. Susx T 96 TQ 0906
Clappers T 165 NT 9455
Clappersgate T 150 NY 3603
Clapton T 92 ST 4106
Clapton-in-Gordano T 101 ST 4774
Clapton-on-the-Hill T 115 SP 1618
Clapworthy T 91 SS 6724
Clarbeston T 110 SN 0421
Clarbeston Road T 110 SN 0121
Clarborough T 140 SK 7383
Clardon T 199 ND 1568
Clardon Head 199 ND 1570
Clare T 122 TL 7745
Clarebrand T 156 NX 7666
Clarencefield T 157 NY 0968
Clarkston T 162 NS 5756
Clashindarroch 184 NJ 4831
Clashindarroch Forest F 184 NJ 4633
Clashmach Hill H 184 NJ 4938
Clashmore, Highld T 196 NC 0331
Clashmore, Highld T 193 NH 7489
Clashmore Wood F 193 NH 7491
Clashnessie T 196 NC 0530
Clashnessie Bay W 196 NC 0631
Clashnoir T 184 NJ 2222
Clathy 170 NN 9920
Clatt T 184 NJ 5426
Clatter T 125 SN 9994
Clatterin' Brig 177 NO 6678
Clatteringshaws Loch W 155 NX 5476
Clatto Hill H 171 NO 3506
Clatto Reservoir W 171 NO 3607
Clatworthy T 92 ST 0530
Clatworthy Reservoir W 92 ST 0431
Clauchlands Point 160 NS 0532
Claughton, Lancs T 145 SD 5342
Claughton, Lancs T 145 SD 5666
Clava Cairns A 183 NH 7544
Claverdon T 118 SP 1964
Claverham T 101 ST 4466
Clavering T 121 TL 4731
Claverley T 127 SO 7593
Claverton T 101 ST 7864
Clawdd-du-bach H 125 SN 8770
Clawdd-newydd T 135 SJ 0852
Clawton T 88 SX 3599
Claxby, Lincs T 141 TF 1194
Claxby, Lincs T 141 TF 4571
Claxton, Norf T 133 TG 3303
Claxton, N. Yks T 148 SE 6960
Claybokie T 176 NO 0890
Claybrooke Magna T 119 SP 4988
Clay Coton T 119 SP 5977
Clay Cross T 139 SK 3963
Claydon, Oxon T 119 SP 4550
Claydon, Suff T 123 TM 1350
Claygate T 105 TQ 1563
Claygate Cross T 97 TQ 6155
Clayhanger, Devon T 92 ST 0222
Clayhanger, W. Mids T 128 SK 0404
Clay Head 144 SC 4480
Clayhidon T 92 ST 1615
Clayock T 199 ND 1659
Clay of Allan 193 NH 8276
Claypole T 130 SK 8549
Clayton, Staffs T 127 SJ 8543
Clayton, S. Yks T 139 SE 4507
Clayton, W. Susx T 97 TQ 3014
Clayton, W. Yks T 146 SE 1231
Clayton-le-Moors T 145 SD 7431
Clayton-le-Woods T 145 SD 5622
Clayton West T 139 SE 2510
Clayworth T 140 SK 7388
Cleadale T 179 NM 4789
Cleadon T 159 NZ 3862
Clearbury Ring A 94 SU 1625
Clearwell T 113 SO 5708
Cleasby T 152 NZ 2513
Cleasby Hill H 152 NY 9707
Cleat, Orkney T 199 ND 4584
Cleat, W. Isles T 178 NF 6604
Cleatlam T 152 NZ 1118
Cleator T 150 NY 0113
Cleator Moor T 150 NY 0214
Cleckheaton T 146 SE 1825
Cledan W 112 SN 8845
Cleedownton T 116 SO 5880
Cleehill T 117 SO 5975
Clee St Margaret T 116 SO 5684
Cleethorpes T 143 TA 3008
Cleeton St Mary T 117 SO 6178
Cleeve T 101 ST 4565
Cleeve Hill T 114 SO 9826
Cleeve Prior T 118 SP 0849
Clehonger T 113 SO 4638
Cleigh T 168 NM 8725
Cleish T 170 NT 0998
Cleish Hills H 170 NT 0796
Cleite Leathann H 194 NB 0428
Cleland T 162 NS 7958
Clench Common T 102 SU 1765
Clenchwarton T 132 TF 5920
Clent T 117 SO 9379
Clent Hills H 117 SO 9479
Cleobury Mortimer T 117 SO 6776
Cleobury North T 117 SO 6287
Cleongart 160 NR 6734
Clephanton T 183 NH 8150
Clerklands T 164 NT 5024
Clestrain T 200 HY 3006
Clestrain Sound W 200 HY 2806
Clett 199 ND 1071
Clett Ard H 189 NB 1908
Clett Nisabost H 188 NG 0495
Clettraval H 190 NG 7572
Cleughbrae T 157 NY 0673
Clevancy T 102 SU 0575
Clevedon T 100 ST 4074
Clevedon Court A 101 ST 4271
Cleveland 153 NZ 6213
Cleveland Hills H 153 SE 5899
Cleveleys T 145 SD 3143
Cleverton T 102 ST 9785
Clewer T 101 ST 4351
Cley Hill H 101 ST 8344
Cley next the Sea T 132 TG 0443
Cliad Bay W 172 NM 1960
Cliasmol T 189 NB 0706
Cliburn T 151 NY 5824
Click Mill 200 HY 3222
Cliddesden T 103 SU 6349
Cliffe, Kent T 98 TQ 7376
Cliffe, N. Yks T 147 SE 6632
Cliffe Hill H 97 TQ 4310
Cliff End T 98 TQ 8813
Cliffe Woods T 98 TQ 7373
Clifford, H. & W T 113 SO 2445
Clifford, W. Yks T 147 SE 4244
Clifford Chambers T 118 SP 1952
Clifford's Mesne T 114 SO 7023
Cliffs End T 99 TR 3464
Clift Hills H 203 HU 3931
Clifton, Avon T 101 ST 5773
Clifton, Beds T 120 TL 1639
Clifton, Central T 168 NN 3230
Clifton, Cumbr T 151 NY 5326
Clifton, Derby T 128 SK 1644
Clifton, H. & W T 117 SO 8446
Clifton, Lancs T 145 SD 4630
Clifton, Northum T 159 NZ 2082
Clifton, Notts T 129 SK 5534
Clifton, Oxon T 115 SP 4831
Clifton Campville T 128 SK 2510
Clifton Hampden T 115 SU 5495
Clifton Reynes T 120 SP 9051
Clifton upon Dunsmore T 119 SP 5376
Clifton upon Teme T 117 SO 7161
Clift Sound W 203 HU 3933
Clifts, The 204 HU 3281
Climping T 96 SU 9902
Clint T 147 SE 2559
Clintburn 158 NY 7179
Clinterty 185 NJ 8311
Clint Green T 132 TG 0210
Clintmains T 164 NT 6132
Clints Dod H 164 NT 6268
Clints of Dromore H 155 NX 5464
Clippesby T 133 TG 4214
Clipsham T 130 SK 9716
Clipston, Northnts T 119 SP 7181
Clipston, Notts T 129 SK 6334
Clisham H 189 NB 1507
Clitheroe T 145 SD 7441
Clive T 127 SJ 5124
Clivocast T 205 HP 6000
Clocaenog T 135 SJ 0854
Clocaenog Forest F 135 SJ 0153
Clochan T 184 NJ 4061
Cloch Point 168 NS 2076
Clock Face T 137 SJ 5291
Cloddymoss T 183 NH 9860
Clodock T 113 SO 3227
Clola T 185 NK 0043
Clophill T 120 TL 0838
Clopton, Northnts T 120 TL 0680
Clopton, Suff T 123 TM 2252
Clopton Green T 122 TL 7654
Closeburn T 156 NX 8992
Close Clark T 144 SC 2775
Clothall T 121 TL 2731
Clothan 205 HU 4581
Clotton T 137 SJ 5263

Clougha Cottam

Clougha H 145 SD 5459
Clough Foot T 146 SD 9023
Cloughton T 149 TA 0094
Cloughton Newlands T 149 TA 0195
Cloughton Wyke W 149 TA 0295
Clousta T 203 HU 3157
Clouston T 200 HY 3011
Clova, Grampn 184 NJ 4522
Clova, Tays T 176 NO 3273
Clovelly T 90 SS 3124
Clovelly Dykes A 90 SS 3123
Clove Lodge T 152 NY 9317
Clovenfords T 164 NT 4436
Clovenstone T 185 NJ 7717
Clovullin T 174 NN 0063
Clowbridge Reservoir W 146 SD 8228
Clowne T 139 SK 4975
Clows Top T 117 SO 7171
Cluanie Forest 181 NH 0409
Cluanie Inn 181 NH 0711
Cluanie Lodge 181 NH 0910
Cluas Deas 196 NC 0032
Clubworthy T 88 SX 2792
Cluer T 189 NG 1490
Clumber Park 139 SK 6274
Clun T 116 SO 3081
Clunas Resr W 183 NH 8646
Clunbury T 116 SO 3780
Clunderwen T 110 SN 1219
Clunes T 174 NN 2088
Clunes Forest F 174 NN 2189
Clun Forest 116 SO 2286
Clungunford T 116 SO 3978
Clunie, Grampn T 184 NJ 6350
Clunie, Tays 176 NO 1144
Clunie Water W 176 NO 1485
Clunton T 116 SO 3381
Cluny T 171 NT 2495
Cluny Castle, Grampn 185 NJ 6812
Cluny Castle, Highld 175 NN 6494
Cluster 205 HU 5990
Clutton, Avon T 101 ST 6259
Clutton, Ches T 126 SJ 4654
Clwydian Range, Clwyd H 136 SJ 1464
Clwydian Range, Clwyd H 136 SJ 1564
Clwyt-y-bont T 134 SH 5763
Clydach, Gwent T 109 SO 2213
Clydach, W. Glam T 108 SN 6901
Clydach Vale T 109 SS 9793
Clydebank T 169 NS 5069
Clyde Law H 156 NT 0217
Clydesdale 163 NS 8347
Clydey T 111 SN 2535
Clyffe Pypard T 102 SU 0776
Clynder T 168 NS 2484
Clynelish T 193 NC 8905
Clynnog-fawr T 134 SH 4149
Clyro T 113 SO 2143
Clyro Hill H 113 SO 2046
Clyst Honiton T 89 SX 9893
Clyst Hydon T 92 ST 0301
Clyst St George T 89 SX 9888
Clyst St Lawrence T 92 ST 0200
Clyst St Mary T 89 SX 9790
Clyth T 199 ND 2837
Cnap Chaochan Aitinn H 183 NJ 1410
Cnap na Feola H 182 NH 2254
Cnicht H 135 SH 6446
Cnoc a' Bhaile-shios H 160 NR 8662
Cnoc a' Chapuill H 160 NR 9630
Cnoc a' Choire H 192 NC 5004
Cnoc a' Ghiubhais, Highld H 196 NC 2670
Cnoc a' Ghiubhais, Highld H 197 NC 5423
Cnoc a' Ghriama H 196 NC 4026
Cnoc a' Mhadaidh H 168 NS 1684
Cnoc an Alaskie H 197 NC 4926
Cnocan Conachreag H 199 ND 1136
Cnoc an dà Chinn H 173 NM 4445
Cnoc an Earrannaiche H 199 ND 2441
Cnoc an Eireannaich H 198 NC 9527
Cnoc an Fhuarain Bhàin H 198 NC 9553
Cnoc an Ime H 166 NR 5880
Cnoc an Liath-bhaid Mhóir H 198 NC 7629
Cnoc an t-Sabhail H 192 NH 6978
Cnoc Badaireach na Gaoithe H 198 NC 8452
Cnoc Bad Mhairtein H 198 NC 9354
Cnoc Breac H 190 NG 7884
Cnoc Buidhe H 160 NR 6930
Cnoc Ceann nam Bad H 192 NC 5500
Cnoc Cèislein H 182 NH 5870
Cnoc Coinnich H 168 NN 2300
Cnoc Coire na Feàrna H 198 NC 9329
Cnoc Corr Guinie H 192 NH 6775
Cnoc Craggie H 197 NC 6052
Cnoc Creagach H 160 NR 8455
Cnoc Donn H 160 NR 7453
Cnoc Dubh H 166 NR 2362
Cnoc Eille Mòr H 182 NH 4547
Cnoc Fraing H 183 NH 8014
Cnoc Leamhnachd H 193 NC 7511
Cnoc Loch Mhadadh H 198 NC 9932
Cnoc Meadhonach H 193 NC 8417
Cnoc Mòr H 160 NR 6809
Cnoc Mòr na Claigin H 166 NR 4553
Cnoc Moy H 160 NR 6115
Cnoc Muigh-bhlàraidh H 192 NH 6382
Cnoc na Breun-choille H 198 NC 7824
Cnoc na Carraige H 160 NR 9768
Cnoc na Glas Choille H 191 NC 2708
Cnoc na h' Airighe H 168 NS 2290
Cnoc na Maoile H 193 ND 0021
Cnoc na Mèine H 160 NR 9060
Cnoc nan Craobh H 160 NR 7345
Cnoc nan Cùilean H 197 NC 5946
Cnoc nan Gabhar H 160 NR 8039
Cnoc nan Tri-chlach H 198 NC 7943
Cnoc Odhar H 160 NR 6612
Cnoc Preas a' Mhadaidh H 198 NC 9848
Cnoc Reamhar, Strath H 167 NR 7691
Cnoc Reamhar, Strath H 160 NR 9224
Cnoc Stighseir H 167 NR 7176
Cnwch Coch T 125 SN 6775
Coad's Green T 88 SX 2976
Coal Aston T 139 SK 3679
Coalbrookdale T 127 SJ 6604
Coalburn T 163 NS 8134
Coalcleugh T 151 NY 8045
Coaley T 114 SO 7701
Coall Head 203 HU 4433
Coalpit Heath T 101 ST 6780
Coalport T 127 SJ 6902
Coalsnaughton T 170 NS 9295
Coaltown of Balgonie T 171 NT 3099
Coaltown of Wemyss T 171 NT 3295
Coalville T 128 SK 4213
Coalway T 113 SO 5910
Coast T 190 NG 9290
Coatbridge T 162 NS 7365
Coatdyke T 162 NS 7564
Coate T 102 SU 0461
Coates, Cambs T 131 TL 3097
Coates, Glos T 114 SO 9801
Coatham T 153 NZ 5925
Coatham Mundeville T 152 NZ 2820
Coatsgate T 157 NT 0605
Cobbaton T 91 SS 6126
Cobbin's Brook W 105 TL 4001
Cobbinshaw Reservoir W 163 NT 0158
Cobbler, The H 168 NN 2505
Coberley T 114 SO 9616
Cobham, Kent T 98 TQ 6768
Cobham, Surrey T 105 TQ 1060
Cobnash T 113 SO 4560
Cochno Reservoir W 169 NS 4976
Cochrage Muir 176 NO 1349
Cockayne T 153 SE 6198
Cockayne Hatley T 121 TL 2649
Cockayne Ridge 153 NZ 6100
Cock Beck W 147 SE 4739
Cock Bridge T 184 NJ 2509
Cockburnspath T 164 NT 7771
Cock Cairn, Grampn H 177 NO 4688
Cock Cairn, Tays H 177 NO 4688
Cock Clarks T 106 TL 8102
Cockenzie and Port Seton T 171 NT 4075
Cockerham T 145 SD 4652
Cockerington T 141 TF 3790
Cockermouth P 150 NY 1230
Cockernhoe T 105 TL 1223
Cockfield, Durham T 152 NZ 1224
Cockfield, Suff T 122 TL 9054
Cockfosters T 105 TQ 2796
Cock Hill H 177 NO 5387
Cocking T 95 SU 8717
Cockington T 89 SX 8963
Cocklake T 101 ST 4449
Cock Law H 158 NT 8517
Cocklaw Hill H 164 NT 7271
Cockley Beck T 150 NY 2401
Cockley Cley T 132 TF 7904
Cock of Arran 160 NR 9552
Cockpole Green T 104 SU 7981
Cocks Hill H 89 SX 5678
Cockshutt T 126 SJ 4329
Cockthorpe T 132 TF 9842
Cockwood T 89 SX 9780
Cockyard T 113 SO 4134
Cod Beck W 147 SE 4277
Codda 87 SX 1878
Coddenham T 123 TM 1354
Coddington, Ches T 126 SJ 4555
Coddington, H. & W T 117 SO 7242
Coddington, Notts T 130 SK 8354
Codford St Mary T 102 ST 9739
Codford St Peter T 102 ST 9640
Codicote T 105 TL 2118
Codnor T 128 SK 4149
Codrington T 101 ST 7278
Codsall T 127 SJ 8703
Codsall Wood T 127 SJ 8405
Coedely T 109 ST 0286
Coedkernew T 100 ST 2783
Coedpoeth T 126 SJ 2851
Coed-y-gaer H 125 SO 0084
Coed-y-paen T 113 ST 3398
Coed Ystumgwern T 124 SH 5824
Coelbren T 109 SN 8511
Coffinswell T 89 SX 8968
Cofton Hackett T 118 SP 0075
Cogenhoe T 120 SP 8260
Coggeshall T 106 TL 8523
Cogra Moss W 150 NY 0919
Coigach 191 NC 1104
Coignafearn Forest 182 NH 6412
Coignafearn Lodge 183 NH 6815
Coilacriech T 176 NO 3297
Coilantogle 169 NN 5906
Coileach H 189 NG 0892
Coillaig 168 NN 0220
Coille Mhorgil T 174 NH 1001
Coillore T 186 NG 3537
Coirc Bheinn H 173 NM 4832
Coire a' Chonachair 191 NC 3302
Coire Bhachdaidh Lodge 175 NN 5472
Coirefrois Burn W 197 NC 7015
Coire na Beinne H 199 ND 1540
Coire Odhar, Highld 182 NH 5006
Coire Odhar, Tays 169 NN 8213
Coire Thomag 167 NR 7974
Coity T 109 SS 9281
Coity Mountain H 113 SO 2307
Colaboll T 197 NC 5610
Coladoir River W 173 NM 5829
Colan T 87 SW 8661
Colaton Raleigh T 92 SY 0787
Col-bheinn H 193 NC 8811
Colbost T 186 NG 2149
Colbost Point 186 NG 3039
Colburn T 152 SE 1999
Colby, Cumbr T 151 NY 6620
Colby, I. of M T 144 SC 2370
Colby, Norf T 133 TG 2231
Colchester P 122 TM 0025
Cold Ash T 103 SU 5170
Cold Ashby T 119 SP 6576
Cold Ashton T 101 ST 7572
Cold Aston T 115 SP 1319
Coldbackie T 197 NC 6160
Coldblow T 105 TQ 5173
Cold Brayfield T 120 SP 9252
Coldean T 97 TQ 3308
Coldeast T 89 SX 8174
Colden H 144 SC 3484
Colden Common T 95 SU 4822
Coldfair Green T 123 TM 4361
Cold Fell H 151 NY 6055
Cold Hanworth T 140 TF 0383
Coldharbour T 96 TQ 1543
Cold Hesledon T 153 NZ 4047
Cold Higham T 119 SP 6653
Coldingham T 165 NT 9065
Coldingham Bay W 165 NT 9166
Coldingham Moor 165 NT 8667
Cold Kirby T 147 SE 5384
Cold Law H 165 NT 9523
Cold Newton T 129 SK 7106
Cold Norton T 106 TL 8400
Cold Overton T 130 SK 8110
Coldrain 170 NO 0800
Coldred T 99 TR 2746
Coldridge T 91 SS 6907
Coldsmouth Hill H 165 NT 8528
Coldstream, Border P 165 NT 8439
Coldstream, Tays 176 NO 3939
Coldwaltham T 96 TQ 0216
Coldwells T 185 NK 1039
Coldwells Croft T 184 NJ 5622
Cole T 93 ST 6733
Colebatch T 116 SO 3287
Colebrook T 91 ST 0006
Colebrooke T 89 SS 7700
Coleburn T 152 SE 2098
Coleby, Humbs T 142 SE 8919
Coleby, Lincs T 140 SK 9760
Coleford, Devon T 91 SS 7701
Coleford, Glos T 113 SO 5710
Coleford, Somer T 101 ST 6849
Colehill T 94 SU 0200
Coleman's Hatch T 97 TQ 4533
Colemere T 126 SJ 4332
Colenden T 170 NO 1029
Coleorton T 128 SK 4017
Colerne T 101 ST 8171
Colesbourne T 114 SO 9913
Colesden T 120 TL 1255
Coleshill, Bucks T 104 SU 9495
Coleshill, Oxon T 115 SU 2393
Coleshill, Warw T 118 SP 2089
Colgate T 97 TQ 2332
Colgrain T 168 NS 3280
Colgrave Sound W 205 HU 5790
Colinsburgh T 171 NO 4703
Colinton T 171 NT 2169
Colintraive T 168 NS 0374
Colkirk T 132 TF 9126
Coll, Strath 172 NM 2057
Coll, W. Isles T 195 NB 4640
Collace 171 NO 2032
Collafirth, Shetld T 204 HU 3483
Colla Firth, Shetld W 204 HU 3683
Collafirth, Shetld 205 HU 4268
Colla Firth, Shetld W 205 HU 4469
Collaton St Mary T 89 SX 8760
College Burn W 165 NT 8825
Collessie T 171 NO 2813
Collie Law H 164 NT 4850
Collier Law H 152 NZ 0141
Collier Row T 105 TQ 4991
Colliers End T 105 TL 3720
Collier Street T 97 TQ 7145
Collieston T 185 NK 0428
Colliford Lake Reservoir W 87 SX 1772
Collin T 156 NY 0275
Collingbourne Ducis T 102 SU 2453
Collingbourne Kingston T 102 SU 2355
Collingham, Notts T 140 SK 8361
Collingham, W. Yks T 147 SE 3845
Collington T 117 SO 6560
Collingtree T 119 SP 7555
Colliston T 177 NO 6046
Coll Sands 195 NB 4638
Collynie 185 NJ 8436
Collyweston T 130 SK 9902
Colmonell T 154 NX 1486
Colmworth T 120 TL 1058
Colnabaichin T 184 NJ 2908
Colnbrook T 104 TQ 0277
Colne, Cambs T 121 TL 3775
Colne, Lancs T 146 SD 8940
Colne Engaine T 122 TL 8530
Colne Point 107 TM 1012
Colne Valley 122 TL 8629
Colney T 133 TG 1707
Colney Heath T 105 TL 2005
Colney Street T 105 TL 1502
Coln Rogers T 114 SP 0809
Coln St Aldwyns T 115 SP 1405
Coln St Dennis T 114 SP 0810
Colonel's Bed, The 176 NO 0887
Colonsay 166 NR 3794
Colp 185 NJ 7448
Colpy T 184 NJ 6432
Colsay 203 HU 3618
Colsterdale T 146 SE 1281
Colsterdale Moor 146 SE 1181
Colsterworth T 130 SK 9324
Colston Bassett T 129 SK 6933
Colt Crag Reservoir W 158 NY 9378
Coltfield T 183 NJ 1163
Colt Hill H 156 NX 6999
Coltishall T 133 TG 2720
Colton, Cumbr T 145 SD 3186
Colton, Norf T 133 TG 1009
Colton, N. Yks T 147 SE 5444
Colton, Staffs T 128 SK 0520
Colvend T 155 NX 8654
Colvister T 205 HU 5197
Colwall Green T 117 SO 7541
Colwall Stone T 117 SO 7542
Colwell T 158 NY 9575
Colwell Bay W 94 SZ 3288
Colwich T 128 SK 0121
Colwinston T 109 SS 9475
Colworth T 96 SU 9102
Colwyn Bay T 135 SH 8479
Colyford T 92 SY 2492
Colyton T 92 SY 2494
Combe, Berks T 102 SU 3761
Combe, H. & W T 116 SO 3463
Combe, Oxon T 115 SP 4116
Combe Florey T 92 ST 1431
Combe Hay T 101 ST 7359
Combeinteignhead T 89 SX 9071
Combe Martin T 91 SS 5846
Combe Martin Bay W 91 SS 5748
Combe Moor T 116 SO 3663
Combe Raleigh T 92 ST 1502
Comberbach T 137 SJ 6477
Comberton T 121 TL 3856
Combe St Nicholas T 92 ST 3011
Comb Fell H 158 NT 9118
Comb Hill H 157 NT 3900
Comb Law H 156 NS 9407
Combpyne T 92 SY 2992
Combrook T 118 SP 3051
Combs, Derby T 138 SK 0478
Combs, Suff T 122 TM 0456
Combs Fords T 122 TM 0557
Combs Resr W 138 SK 0379
Combwich T 100 ST 2542
Comers T 184 NJ 6707
Comlongon Castle A 157 NY 0769
Commins Coch T 125 SH 8403
Commondale T 153 NZ 6610
Commonedge Hill H 170 NN 9801
Common Hill H 163 NS 8222
Common Law H 163 NT 0832
Common Moor T 87 SX 2469
Common of Dunning 170 NO 0109
Common Side T 139 SK 3375
Common, The T 94 SU 2432
Compstall T 138 SJ 9691
Compton, Berks T 103 SU 5379
Compton, Devon T 89 SX 8664
Compton, Hants T 95 SU 4625
Compton, Surrey T 96 SU 9547
Compton, Wilts T 102 SU 1352
Compton, W. Susx T 95 SU 7714
Compton Abbas T 93 ST 8718
Compton Abdale T 114 SP 0616
Compton Basset T 102 SU 0372
Compton Bay W 94 SZ 3684
Compton Beauchamp T 102 SU 2887
Compton Bishop T 100 ST 3955
Compton Chamberlayne T 94 SU 0229
Compton Dando T 101 ST 6464
Compton Down H 102 SU 1051
Compton Dundon T 93 ST 4932
Compton Martin T 101 ST 5457
Compton Pauncefoot T 93 ST 6425
Compton Valence T 93 SY 5993
Compton Wynyates A 118 SP 3342
Comrie T 169 NN 7722
Conachcraig H 176 NO 2887
Cona Glen 174 NM 9372
Conaglen House 174 NN 0269
Cona River W 174 NM 9472
Conaston Bridge 110 SN 0615
Conchra T 168 NS 0289
Concraigie 176 NO 1044
Conderton T 118 SO 9637
Condicote T 115 SP 1528
Condorrat T 169 NS 7373
Condover T 127 SJ 4906
Coneyhurst T 96 TQ 1023
Coneysthorpe T 148 SE 7171
Coney Weston T 122 TL 9577
Congerstone T 128 SK 3605
Congham T 132 TF 7123
Conglass Water W 184 NJ 2016
Congleton P 137 SJ 8663
Congresbury T 101 ST 4363
Congresbury Yeo W 101 ST 4662
Conicavel T 183 NH 9953
Conic Hill H 169 NS 4392
Conie Glen 160 NR 6911
Conieglen Water W 160 NR 6912
Coningsby T 141 TF 2257
Conington, Cambs T 120 TL 1786
Conington, Cambs T 121 TL 3266
Conisbrough T 139 SK 5098
Conisby T 166 NR 2661
Conisholme T 141 TF 4095
Coniston, Cumbr T 150 SD 3097
Coniston, Humbs T 143 TA 1535
Coniston Cold T 146 SD 9055
Conistone T 146 SD 9867
Conistone Moor 146 SE 0170
Coniston Water W 150 SD 3094
Connah's Quay T 136 SJ 2969
Connel T 168 NM 9134
Connel Park T 156 NS 6012
Connor Downs T 86 SW 5939
Conon Bridge T 182 NH 5455
Conon House 182 NH 5353
Cononley T 146 SD 9847
Conordan T 187 NG 5038
Conrig Hill H 156 NS 8112
Consall T 128 SJ 9848
Consett P 152 NZ 1051
Constable Burton T 152 SE 1690
Constantine T 86 SW 7329
Constantine Bay W 87 SW 8574
Contin T 182 NH 4556
Contlaw 177 NJ 8402
Contrary Head 144 SC 2282
Conwy P 135 SH 7778
Conwy Bay W 135 SH 7180
Conwy Falls W 135 SH 8053
Conwy Sands 135 SH 7680
Conyer T 99 TQ 9664
Cookbury T 90 SS 4006
Cookham T 104 SU 8985
Cookham Dean T 104 SU 8785
Cookham Rise T 104 SU 8885
Cookhill T 118 SP 0558
Cookley, H. & W T 117 SO 8480
Cookley, Suff T 123 TM 3575
Cookley Green T 104 SU 6990
Cookney T 177 NO 8793
Cooksbridge T 97 TQ 4013
Cooksmill Green T 106 TL 6406
Coolham T 96 TQ 1222
Cooling T 98 TQ 7576
Coombe, Corn T 90 SS 2011
Coombe, Corn T 87 SW 9551
Coombe Abbey A 118 SP 4079
Coombe Bissett T 94 SU 1126
Coombe Hill T 114 SO 8827
Coombe Keynes T 93 SY 8484
Coombes T 96 TQ 1908
Coomb Island or Neave 197 NC 6664
Cooran Lane W 155 NX 4782
Copdock T 123 TM 1141
Copeland Forest F 150 NY 1507
Copford Green T 106 TL 9222
Copinsay 201 HY 6101
Copister T 205 HU 4879
Cople T 120 TL 1048
Copley T 152 NZ 0825
Coplow Dale T 138 SK 1679
Copmanthorpe T 147 SE 5547
Coppathorne T 88 SS 2000
Coppay 188 NF 9393
Coppenhall T 127 SJ 9119
Copperhouse T 86 SW 5738
Coppingford T 120 TL 1680
Copplestone T 91 SS 7702
Coppull T 137 SD 5614
Copsale T 96 TQ 1725
Copster Green T 145 SD 6733
Copt Heath T 118 SP 1777
Copt Hewick T 147 SE 3471
Copthorne T 97 TQ 3139
Copt Oak T 129 SK 4812
Copythorne T 94 SU 3014
Coquetdale 159 NU 0800
Coquet Island 159 NU 2904
Coracharabic Forest 182 NH 3245
Corb Law H 170 NO 0009
Corbridge P 159 NY 9964
Corby P 120 SP 8888
Corby Glen T 130 SK 9924
Corby Loch W 185 NJ 9214
Corby Pike H 158 NT 8401
Core Hill, Grampn H 185 NJ 7633
Core Hill, Tays H 170 NN 8804
Coreley T 117 SO 6174
Corfe T 92 ST 2319
Corfe Castle T 94 SY 9681
Corfe Mullen T 94 SY 9896
Corfe River W 94 SY 9685
Corfton T 116 SO 4985
Corgarff T 184 NJ 2808
Corhampton T 95 SU 6120
Corinium R 114 SP 0201
Corlae T 156 NX 6597
Corlan-fraith H 125 SH 6300
Corley T 118 SP 3085
Corley Ash T 118 SP 2986
Corley Moor T 118 SP 2885
Cornabus 166 NR 3346
Cornal Burn W 157 NT 1304
Corndon Hill H 126 SO 3096
Cornelly T 109 SS 8281
Corney T 150 SD 1191
Cornforth T 152 NZ 3134
Corngafallt 125 SN 9464
Cornhill T 184 NJ 5858
Cornhill-on-Tweed T 165 NT 8539
Corn Holm 201 HY 5901
Cornholme T 146 SD 9026
Cornish Hall End T 122 TL 6836
Cornquoy 200 ND 5299
Cornriggs T 151 NY 8441
Cornsay T 152 NZ 1443
Corntown T 182 NH 5555
Cornwell T 115 SP 2727
Cornwood T 89 SX 6059
Cornworthy T 89 SX 8255
Corpach T 174 NN 0977
Corpach Bay W 166 NR 5691
Corpusty T 133 TG 1130
Corra-bheinn H 173 NM 5732
Corran, Highld T 180 NG 8509
Corran, Highld T 174 NN 0163
Corran Narrows W 174 NN 0163
Corran River W 166 NR 5373
Corrany T 144 SC 4589
Correen Hills H 184 NJ 5222
Corrennie Forest F 184 NJ 6410
Corrennie Moor 184 NJ 6110
Corrie T 160 NS 0243
Corrie Common T 157 NY 2085
Corriehallie Forest 182 NH 3748
Corriekinloch 196 NC 3625
Corriemoillie T 182 NH 3563
Corriemoillie Forest 182 NH 3467
Corriemulzie River W 191 NH 3193
Corrievorrie 183 NH 7724
Corrieyairack Forest 174 NN 4396
Corrieyairack Hill H 174 NN 4299
Corrieyairack Pass 174 NN 4198
Corrimony T 182 NH 3730
Corringham, Essex T 106 TQ 7083
Corringham, Lincs T 140 SK 8791
Corris T 125 SH 7507
Corris Uchaf T 125 SH 7408
Corrour Forest 174 NN 4167
Corrour Shooting Lodge 174 NN 4169
Corrour Station 174 NN 3566
Corrow 168 NN 1800
Corry T 180 NG 6424
Corryhabbie Hill H 184 NJ 2829
Corrymuckloch 170 NN 8934
Corrynachenchy 173 NM 6441
Corry of Ardnagrask T 182 NH 5048
Corscombe T 93 ST 5105
Corse T 184 NJ 6040
Corse Hill, D. & G H 156 NS 6803
Corse Hill, Strath H 162 NS 5946
Corse House 184 NJ 5407
Corsehouse Reservoir W 161 NS 4850
Corse of Kinnoir 184 NJ 5543
Corserine H 155 NX 4987
Corsewall Point 154 NW 9772
Cors Fochno 125 SN 6493
Cors-goch Glan Teifi W 125 SN 6964
Corsham T 101 ST 8770
Corsindae T 185 NJ 6808
Corsley T 101 ST 8246
Corsley Heath T 101 ST 8245
Corsock T 156 NX 7576
Corston, Avon T 101 ST 6965
Corston, Wilts T 101 ST 9284
Corstopitum R 159 NY 9864
Corstorphine T 171 NT 1972
Cortachy 176 NO 3959
Corton, Suff T 133 TM 5497
Corton, Wilts T 102 ST 9340
Corton Denham T 93 ST 6322
Coruanan Lodge 174 NN 0668
Corve Dale 116 SO 5488
Corwar House 154 NX 2780
Corwen T 135 SJ 0743
Coryton, Devon T 88 SX 4583
Coryton, Essex T 106 TQ 7482
Cosby T 129 SP 5494
Cosdon Hill H 89 SX 6391
Coseley T 127 SO 9494
Cosford Station 127 SJ 7905
Cosgrove T 119 SP 7942
Cosham T 95 SU 6505
Cosheston T 110 SN 0003
Cossall T 129 SK 4842
Cosses 154 NX 1182
Cossington, Leic T 129 SK 6013
Cossington, Somer T 100 ST 3540
Costa T 200 HY 3328
Costa Beck W 148 SE 7682
Costa Head 200 HY 3130
Costessey T 133 TG 1711
Costock T 129 SK 5726
Coston T 130 SK 8422
Cotebrook T 137 SJ 5765
Cotegill T 151 NY 6504
Cotehele House A 88 SX 4268
Cotehill T 151 NY 4650
Cotes, Leic T 129 SK 5520
Cotes, Staffs T 127 SJ 8434
Côtesbach T 119 SP 5382
Cotgrave T 129 SK 6435
Cothall T 185 NJ 8715
Cotham T 129 SK 7947
Cothelstone T 92 ST 1831
Cotherstone T 152 NZ 0119
Cotherstone Moor 152 NY 9316
Cothill T 115 SU 4699
Cotleigh T 92 ST 2002
Coton, Cambs T 121 TL 4058
Coton, Northnts T 119 SP 6771
Coton, Staffs T 128 SJ 9832
Coton Clanford T 127 SJ 8723
Coton in the Elms T 128 SK 2415
Cotswold Hills H 114 SO 9707
Cott T 89 SX 7861
Cottam, Lancs T 145 SD 5032
Cottam, Notts T 140 SK 8180

Cottartown Cruach Rarey

Cottartown T 183 NJ 0331
Cottenham T 121 TL 4567
Cotterdale T 151 SD 8394
Cottered T 121 TL 3129
Cotterstock T 120 TL 0490
Cottesbrooke T 119 SP 7173
Cottesmore T 130 SK 9013
Cottingham, Humbs T 142 TA 0532
Cottingham, Northnts T 120 SP 8490
Cottisford T 115 SP 5931
Cotton, Staffs T 128 SK 0646
Cotton, Suff T 122 TM 0767
Cotton End T 120 TL 0845
Cot-town, Grampn T 184 NJ 5026
Cottown, Grampn T 185 NJ 7715
Cot-town, Grampn T 185 NJ 8240
Cotwalton T 127 SJ 9234
Coughton, H. & W T 113 SO 5921
Coughton, Warw T 118 SP 0860
Coulags T 190 NG 9645
Coulin Forest 190 NH 0054
Coulin Lodge 190 NH 0056
Coull T 177 NJ 5102
Coul Point 166 NR 1864
Coulport T 168 NS 2087
Coulsdon T 105 TQ 3059
Coulston T 102 ST 9554
Coulter T 163 NT 0233
Coulton T 147 SE 6374
Cound T 127 SJ 5504
Cound Brook W 127 SJ 5305
Coundon T 152 NZ 2429
Coundon Grange T 152 NZ 2228
Countam, D. & G H 156 NS 7102
Countam, D. & G H 156 NX 7698
Countersett T 146 SD 9187
Countess Wear T 89 SX 9489
Countesthorpe T 129 SP 5895
Countisbury T 91 SS 7449
Coupar Angus T 176 NO 2240
Coupland T 165 NT 9331
Cour T 160 NR 8248
Cour Bay W 160 NR 8248
Courteachan T 180 NM 6897
Courteenhall T 119 SP 7653
Cour, The W 174 NN 2377
Court Henry T 111 SN 5522
Courtsend T 107 TR 0293
Courtway T 92 ST 2033
Cousland T 164 NT 3768
Cousley Wood T 97 TQ 6533
Cove, Devon T 91 SS 9519
Cove, Hants T 103 SU 8455
Cove, Highld T 190 NG 8090
Cove, Strath T 168 NS 2282
Cove Bay, Grampn T 177 NJ 9501
Cove Bay, Strath W 168 NS 2282
Covehithe T 123 TM 5281
Coven T 127 SJ 9107
Coveney T 121 TL 4882
Covenham Reservoir W 141 TF 3496
Covenham St Bartholomew T 141 TF 3394
Covenham St Mary T 141 TF 3394
Coventry P 118 SP 3379
Coventry Airport 118 SP 3574
Coventry Canal, Warw W 128 SP 3196
Coventry Canal, Warw W 118 SP 3786
Cove Point 160 NR 7107
Coverack T 87 SW 7818
Coverdale 146 SE 0683
Coverham T 146 SE 1086
Cover Head Bents 146 SE 0078
Covesea Skerries 184 NJ 1971
Covington T 120 TL 0570
Cowan Bridge T 145 SD 6376
Cowbeech T 97 TQ 6114
Cowbit T 131 TF 2617
Cowbridge T 109 SS 9974
Cowden T 97 TQ 4640
Cowdenbeath T 170 NT 1691
Cowdenburn 163 NT 2052
Cowden Station 97 TQ 4741
Cowes T 95 SZ 4995
Cowesby T 153 SE 4689
Cowes Roads W 95 SZ 5097
Cowfold T 96 TQ 2122
Cowgask Burn W 170 NN 9620
Cowgill T 146 SD 7587
Cow Green Reservoir, Cumbr W 151 NY 8030
Cow Green Reservoir, Durham W 151 NY 8030
Cowick T 147 SE 6521
Cowie T 169 NS 8489
Cowie Water W 177 NO 7888
Cowley, Devon T 89 SX 9095
Cowley, G. Lon T 104 TQ 0582
Cowley, Glos T 114 SO 9614
Cowley, Oxon T 115 SP 5504
Cowling, N. Yks T 146 SD 9643
Cowling, N. Yks T 147 SE 2387
Cowlinge T 122 TL 7254
Cown Reservoir W 137 SD 8818
Cowpen Bewley T 153 NZ 4824
Cowplain T 95 SU 6911
Cow Ridge H 153 SE 5496
Cowshill T 151 NY 8540
Cowstrandburn T 170 NT 0390
Coxbank T 127 SJ 6541
Coxbench T 128 SK 3743
Cox Common T 123 TM 4082
Coxheath T 97 TQ 7451
Coxhoe T 152 NZ 3136
Coxley T 101 ST 5243
Coxwold T 147 SE 5377
Coychurch T 109 SS 9379
Coyles of Muick, The H 176 NO 3391
Coylton 161 NS 4114
Coylumbridge T 183 NH 9110
Coynach T 184 NJ 4405
Coynachie 184 NJ 4934
Crabadon 89 SX 7555
Crabbs Cross T 118 SP 0464
Crab Rocks 149 TA 2074
Crabtree T 96 TQ 2225
Crabtree Green T 126 SJ 3345
Crackenthorpe T 151 NY 6622
Crackington T 88 SX 1595
Crackleybank T 127 SJ 7611
Crackpot T 152 SD 9796
Cracoe T 146 SD 9760
Cradley T 117 SO 7347
Crafthole T 88 SX 3654
Cragabus 166 NR 3245
Cragdale Moor 146 SD 9182
Craggan T 183 NJ 0226
Craggie 193 NC 8719
Craggie Water W 193 NC 8918
Cragg Vale T 146 SE 0123
Craghead T 152 NZ 2150
Crag Hill H 145 SD 6983
Crag Lough W 158 NY 7668
Crai T 109 SN 8924
Craibstone, Grampn 184 NJ 4959
Craibstone, Grampn T 185 NJ 8611
Craichie T 177 NO 5047
Craig, D. & G T 156 NX 6875
Craig, Highld T 190 NH 0349
Craigairie Fell H 154 NX 2373
Craiganour Forest 175 NN 6064
Craiganour Lodge 175 NN 6159
Craig Castle T 184 NJ 4724
Craigcefnparc T 108 SN 6703
Craigdallie 171 NO 2528
Craigdam T 185 NJ 8430
Craigdarroch 156 NS 6306
Craig Ddrwg H 135 SH 6533
Craigearn T 185 NJ 7214
Craigellachie, Grampn T 184 NJ 2945
Craigellachie, Highld H 183 NH 8811
Craigend 170 NO 1120
Craigendoran T 168 NS 3181
Craigendunton Reservoir W 161 NS 5246
Craigenlee Fell H 154 NX 0257
Craigens 166 NR 2967
Craig Fell H 154 NX 1761
Craig Goch Reservoir W 125 SN 8969
Craig Gyfynys H 135 SH 6838
Craighall 176 NO 1748
Craighat 169 NS 4984
Craig Hill H 175 NN 8145
Craighoar Hill H 156 NT 0002
Craighouse T 166 NR 5267
Craigie, Grampn T 185 NJ 9119
Craigie, Strath T 161 NS 4232
Craigie, Tays 176 NO 1143
Craigievar Castle A 184 NJ 5609
Craiglee H 155 NX 4796
Craigleith 171 NT 5587
Craiglich H 184 NJ 5305
Craiglockhart T 171 NT 2270
Craig Lodge 169 NS 0077
Craiglowrie H 155 NX 5467
Craigluscar Hill H 170 NT 0690
Craigmahandle H 177 NO 4990
Craigmaid H 157 NT 0717
Craigmaud T 185 NJ 8958
Craigmillar T 171 NT 2971
Craig nan Caisean H 175 NN 7760
Craignane H 156 NS 5804
Craignant T 126 SJ 2535
Craignarget Hill H 154 NX 2652
Craignelder H 155 NX 5070
Craigneuk, Strath T 162 NS 7656
Craigneuk, Strath T 162 NS 7865
Craignish Castle 167 NM 7701
Craignish Point 167 NR 7599
Craignure T 173 NM 7137
Craignure Bay W 173 NM 7237
Craigo T 177 NO 6864
Craig of Bunzeach H 184 NJ 3609
Craig of Dalfro H 177 NO 6789
Craigow 170 NO 0806
Craig Rhiwarth H 125 SJ 0527
Craig River W 190 NG 7963
Craig Rossie H 170 NN 9812
Craigrothie T 171 NO 3710
Craig Royston 168 NN 3405
Craigruie 169 NN 4920
Craigs, The 192 NH 4790
Craigston Castle 185 NJ 7655
Craigton, Grampn T 177 NJ 8301
Craigton, Highld 192 NH 6296
Craigton, Tays T 176 NO 3250
Craigton, Tays T 177 NO 5138
Craigtown T 198 NC 8956
Craig Twrch H 111 SN 6649
Craig Veann H 184 NJ 1911
Craigvinean Forest F 176 NN 9845
Craig-y-cae H 125 SH 7023
Craig y Hyrddod H 135 SH 8237
Craig y Llyn H 109 SN 9103
Craig-y-nos H 109 SN 8415
Craig yr Hyrddod H 135 SH 8237
Craik T 157 NT 3408
Craik Cross Hill, Border H 157 NT 3004
Craik Cross Hill, D. & G H 157 NT 3004
Craik Forest F 157 NT 3409
Craik Moor 158 NT 8118
Crail T 171 NO 6107
Crailing T 164 NT 6824
Crailinghall T 164 NT 6922
Crailzie Hill H 163 NT 1945
Crakehall T 152 SE 2490
Cramalt T 163 NT 1922
Crambe T 148 SE 7364
Cramlington T 159 NZ 2676
Crammag Head 154 NX 0834
Cramond T 170 NT 1876
Cramond Bridge T 170 NT 1775
Cramond Island 171 NT 1978
Cranage T 137 SJ 7568
Cranberry T 127 SJ 8236
Cranborne T 94 SU 0513
Cranbourne T 104 SU 9272
Cranbourne Chase 94 ST 9417
Cranbrook T 98 TQ 7736
Cranbrook Common T 98 TQ 7938
Crane Islands 86 SW 6344
Cranfield T 120 SP 9642
Cranford T 105 TQ 1077
Cranford St Andrew T 120 SP 9277
Cranford St John T 120 SP 9276
Cranham, G. Lon T 105 TQ 5787
Cranham, Glos T 114 SO 8913
Crank T 137 SJ 5099
Cranleigh T 96 TQ 0638
Cranmore, I. of W T 94 SZ 3990
Cranmore, Somer T 101 ST 6643
Cranna T 184 NJ 6353
Crannach T 184 NJ 4954
Cranoe T 129 SP 7695
Cransford T 123 TM 3164
Cranshaw Hill H 164 NT 6761
Cranshaws T 164 NT 6961
Cranstackie H 196 NC 3555
Cranstal T 144 NX 4602
Cranthorne T 153 NZ 4407
Crantock T 87 SW 7960
Cranwell T 130 TF 0349
Cranwich T 132 TL 7894
Cranworth T 132 TF 9804
Crapstone T 88 SX 5067
Crarae 168 NR 9997
Craro Island 160 NR 6247
Crask Inn 197 NC 5224
Craskins T 184 NJ 5106
Crask of Aigas T 182 NH 4642
Craster T 159 NU 2519
Craswall T 113 SO 2836
Cratfield T 123 TM 3175
Crathes T 177 NO 7596
Crathes Castle A 177 NO 7396
Crathie, Grampn T 176 NO 2695
Crathie, Highld T 175 NN 5894
Craufurdland Castle 161 NS 4540
Craven Arms T 116 SO 4382
Crawcrook T 159 NZ 1363
Crawford T 156 NS 9520
Crawfordjohn T 163 NS 8823
Crawick T 156 NS 7711
Crawick Water W 156 NS 8014
Crawleside T 152 NY 9940
Crawley, Hants T 94 SU 4234
Crawley, Oxon T 115 SP 3412
Crawley, W. Susx P 96 TQ 2736
Crawley Down T 97 TQ 3437
Crawshawbooth T 146 SD 8125
Crawton T 177 NO 8779
Crawton Bay W 177 NO 8779
Cray, N. Yks T 146 SD 8479
Cray, Tays 176 NO 1463
Crayford T 105 TQ 5175
Crayke T 147 SE 5670
Cray Reservoir W 109 SN 8821
Crays Hill T 106 TQ 7192
Cray's Pond T 104 SU 6380
Creachan Mòr H 168 NS 1891
Creach Beinn H 173 NM 6427
Creach Bheinn, Highld H 173 NM 8657
Creach Bheinn, Strath H 173 NM 4229
Creach Bheinn, Strath H 174 NM 0242
Creach Bheinn Lodge 173 NM 6425
Creacombe T 91 SS 8119
Creag a' Chaorainn H 190 NH 0043
Creag a Chlachain H 182 NH 6533
Creag a' Lain H 187 NG 4658
Creagan 174 NM 9744
Creagan a' Chaise H 183 NJ 1024
Creagan an Eich H 168 NN 1003
Creag an Dail Bheag H 176 NO 1596
Creag an Eunan H 184 NJ 3819
Creagan Glas H 192 NC 6701
Creag an Lòin H 175 NH 6901
Creagan Mòr H 175 NN 6180
Creagantairbh Mhòr 167 NM 8401
Creag an t-Sithein H 176 NO 0365
Creag a' Phuill 168 NN 1005
Creag Beinn nan Eun H 169 NN 7213
Creag Bhalg H 176 NO 0991
Creag Bhàn, Highld H 180 NM 7884
Creag Bhan, Strath H 160 NR 6451
Creag Dhubh, Highld H 175 NH 6797
Creag Dhubh, Tays H 176 NO 0161
Creag Fhraoch 195 NB 5142
Creag Gharbh H 169 NN 6332
Creag Island 173 NM 8337
Creag Leacach H 176 NO 1574
Creag Liath, Highld H 193 NH 7295
Creag Liath, Highld H 183 NJ 0031
Creag Liath, Tays H 176 NN 9837
Creag Loch nan Dearcag H 182 NH 3356
Creag Loisgte H 191 NH 3695
Creag Meagaidh H 174 NN 4187
Creag Mholach 168 NS 1093
Creag Mhòr, Central H 174 NN 3936
Creag Mhòr, Central H 169 NN 5134
Creag Mhòr, Highld H 197 NC 6924
Creag Mhòr, Highld H 175 NN 4897
Creag Mhòr, Strath H 167 NM 8202
Creag Mhòr, Strath H 168 NR 9273
Creag Mhòr, Tays H 174 NN 3936
Creag Mhòr, W. Isles H 195 NB 1841
Creag na h-Iolaire, Highld H 197 NC 6728
Creag na h-Iolaire, Highld H 191 NH 1398
Creag na h-Iolaire, Highld H 191 NH 1749
Creag nam Bodach H 175 NN 7596
Creag nam Fiadh H 193 NC 8423
Creag nam Mial H 176 NO 0554
Creag-nan-Eun Forest F 182 NH 4619
Creag nan Gabhar H 176 NO 1584
Creag nan Gall H 176 NO 2692
Creagorry T 188 NF 7948
Creag Riabhach H 196 NC 2763
Creag Riabhach na Greighe H 197 NC 6120
Creag Scalabsdale H 198 NC 9724
Creaguaineach Lodge 174 NN 3068
Creag Uchdag, Central H 169 NN 7032
Creag Uchdag, Tays H 169 NN 7032
Creaton T 119 SP 7072
Creca T 157 NY 2270
Credenhill T 113 SO 4543
Crediton T 89 SS 8300
Creech St Michael T 92 ST 2725
Creed T 87 SW 9347
Creedy Park 91 SS 8301
Creekmouth T 105 TQ 4581
Creeting St Mary T 122 TM 0758
Creeton T 130 TF 0120
Creetown T 155 NX 4758
Creggans T 168 NN 0802
Cregneish T 144 SC 1867
Cregrina T 112 SO 1252
Creich, Fife T 171 NO 3221
Creich, Strath 172 NM 3124
Creigh Hill H 176 NO 2759
Creigiau T 109 ST 0881
Cressage T 127 SJ 5904
Cresselly T 110 SN 0606
Cressing T 106 TL 7920
Cresswell, Northum T 159 NZ 2993
Cresswell, Staffs T 128 SJ 9739
Cresswell Quay T 110 SN 0506
Creswell T 139 SK 5274
Cretingham T 123 TM 2260
Cretshengan T 160 NR 7167
Creuch Hill H 161 NS 2668
Crewe, Ches T 137 SJ 4253
Crewe, Ches T 127 SJ 7055
Crewe Hall 127 SJ 7354
Crew Green T 126 SJ 3215
Crewkerne T 93 ST 4409
Crews Hill T 105 TQ 3199
Crianlarich P 169 NN 3825
Cribba Head 86 SW 4022
Cribbie 202 HU 1562
Cribin Fawr H 125 SH 7915
Crib Law H 164 NT 5259
Cribyn T 111 SN 5251
Criccieth T 134 SH 5038
Crich T 128 SK 3554
Crichie T 185 NJ 9745
Crichton T 164 NT 3862
Crick, Gwent T 101 ST 4890
Crick, Northnts T 119 SP 5872
Crickadarn T 112 SO 0942
Cricket St Thomas T 92 ST 3708
Crickheath T 126 SJ 2923
Crickhowell T 109 SO 2118
Cricklade T 114 SU 1093
Cridling Stubbs T 147 SE 5221
Crieff T 170 NN 8621
Criffel H 156 NX 9561
Crigdon Hill H 158 NT 8605
Criggion T 126 SJ 2915
Crigglestone T 139 SE 3116
Crimond T 185 NK 0556
Crimonmogate 185 NK 0458
Crimplesham T 132 TF 6503
Crim Rocks 86 SV 8009
Crinan T 167 NR 7894
Crinan Canal W 167 NR 8390
Cringate Law H 169 NS 6888
Cringleford T 133 TG 1905
Crinow T 110 SN 1214
Crionaig H 189 NB 2905
Cripplesease T 86 SW 5036
Cripp's Corner T 98 TQ 7720
Croasdale Fell H 145 SD 6857
Crockenhill T 105 TQ 5067
Crockernwell T 89 SX 7592
Crockerton T 101 ST 8642
Crocketford or Ninemile Bar T 156 NX 8372
Crockey Hill T 147 SE 6246
Crockham Hill T 97 TQ 4450
Crockleford Heath T 122 TM 0426
Crockness 200 ND 3192
Croeserw T 109 SS 8695
Croes-goch T 110 SM 8230
Croesor T 135 SH 6344
Croesyceiliog T 113 ST 3096
Croesyceiliog T 111 SN 4016
Croes-y-mwyalch T 100 ST 3092
Croft, Ches T 137 SJ 6393
Croft, Leic T 129 SP 5195
Croft, Lincs T 141 TF 5061
Croft Ambrey A 116 SO 4466
Croftamie T 169 NS 4785
Croftgarbh 175 NN 7246
Crofthead Hill H 157 NT 1305
Croft Marsh 141 TF 5360
Crofton T 139 SE 3817
Croft-on-Tees T 152 NZ 2809
Crofts of Backburn T 184 NJ 5434
Crofts of Benachielt T 199 ND 1838
Crofts of Haddo T 185 NJ 8337
Crofts of Inverthernie T 185 NJ 7344
Crofts of Meikle Ardo T 185 NJ 8541
Crofts of Savoch T 185 NK 0459
Crofts of Shanquhar T 184 NJ 5435
Crofty T 108 SS 5295
Crogary Mòr H 188 NF 8673
Crogary na Hoe H 188 NF 9772
Crogen 135 SJ 0036
Croggan T 173 NM 7027
Croglin T 151 NY 5747
Croglin Water W 151 NY 5646
Cròic-bheinn H 190 NG 7652
Croick 192 NH 4591
Croir T 195 NB 1539
Croit Bheinn H 180 NM 8177
Crom Allt, Highld W 191 NC 2406
Cròm Allt, Highld W 182 NH 5405
Cromalt Hills H 191 NC 2205
Cromar 184 NJ 4703
Cromarty T 183 NH 7867
Cromarty Bay W 183 NH 7466
Cromarty Firth W 183 NH 6767
Cromblet 185 NJ 7835
Cromdale T 183 NJ 0728
Cromer, Herts T 121 TL 2928
Cromer, Norf P 133 TG 2142
Cromer Point 149 TA 0392
Cromford T 128 SK 2956
Cromhall T 101 ST 6990
Cromhall Common T 101 ST 6989
Cromlet H 169 NN 7812
Crom Loch W 191 NH 3982
Cromore T 195 NB 4021
Cromra T 175 NN 5390
Cromwell T 140 SK 7961
Cronberry T 162 NS 6022
Crondall T 103 SU 7948
Cronkley Fell 151 NY 8427
Cronk Sumark A 144 SC 3994
Cronk, The T 144 SC 3395
Cronk-y-Voddy T 144 SC 3086
Cronton T 137 SJ 4988
Croofoot Reservoir, Cleve W 153 NZ 4331
Croofoot Reservoir, Durham W 153 NZ 4331
Crook, Cumbr T 151 SD 4695
Crook, Durham T 152 NZ 1635
Crookedshaws Hill H 165 NT 8024
Crookham, Berks T 103 SU 5464
Crookham, Northum T 165 NT 9138
Crookham Village T 103 SU 7952
Crookhouse T 164 NT 7626
Crook Inn 163 NT 1126
Crooklands T 145 SD 5383
Crook of Alves T 183 NJ 1362
Crook of Devon T 170 NO 0300
Croome Court 117 SO 8844
Cropredy T 119 SP 4646
Cropston T 129 SK 5511
Cropston Reservoir W 129 SK 5410
Cropthorne T 118 SO 9944
Cropton T 148 SE 7589
Cropwell Bishop T 129 SK 6835
Cropwell Butler T 129 SK 6837
Crosbie A 161 NS 2150
Crosby, Cumbr T 150 NY 0738
Crosby, Humbs T 142 SE 8711
Crosby, I. of M T 144 SC 3279
Crosby, Mers T 136 SJ 3198
Crosby Channel W 136 SJ 2799
Crosby Court 153 SE 3991
Crosby Garrett T 151 NY 7209
Crosby-on-Eden T 157 NY 4459
Crosby Ravensworth T 151 NY 6214
Crosby Ravensworth Fell 151 NY 6010
Croscombe T 101 ST 5944
Crosdale Fell H 145 SD 6857
Cross, Somer T 100 ST 4154
Cross, W. Isles T 195 NB 5061
Crossaig 160 NR 8351
Crossaig Glen 160 NR 8251
Crossapol T 172 NL 9943
Crossapol Bay W 172 NM 1352
Cross Ash T 113 SO 4019
Crossbost T 195 NB 3924
Crosscanonby T 150 NY 0739
Crossdale Street T 133 TG 2239
Crossdougal T 178 NF 7520
Cross Drain W 130 TF 1613
Crossens T 136 SD 3719
Cross Fell H 151 NY 6834
Crossford, Fife T 170 NT 0686
Crossford, Strath T 163 NS 8246
Crossgates, Fife T 170 NT 1488
Crossgates, Powys T 125 SO 0965
Crossgill T 145 SD 5562
Cross Green, Devon T 88 SX 3888
Cross Green, Suff T 122 TL 9852
Crosshands, Dyfed T 111 SN 1922
Cross Hands, Dyfed T 111 SN 5612
Cross Hill, Border H 157 NT 2507
Crosshill, Fife T 170 NT 1796
Crosshill, Strath T 161 NS 3206
Crosshouse T 161 NS 3938
Cross Houses T 127 SJ 5407
Crossings T 157 NY 5076
Cross in Hand T 97 TQ 5621
Cross Inn, Dyfed T 111 SN 3957
Cross Inn, Dyfed T 124 SN 5464
Cross Inn, M. Glam T 109 ST 0583
Crosskeys T 109 ST 2292
Crosskirk T 199 ND 0370
Cross Lanes, Clwyd T 126 SJ 3747
Cross Lanes, N. Yks T 147 SE 5264
Crosslanes, Shrops T 126 SJ 3218
Cross Law H 165 NT 8768
Crosslee T 157 NT 3018
Crossmichael T 156 NX 7366
Crossmoor T 145 SD 4438
Cross of Jackston T 185 NJ 7432
Crossraguel Abbey A 161 NS 2708
Crossroads T 177 NO 7594
Cross Sands 195 NB 4962
Cross Water of Luce W 154 NX 1867
Crossway T 113 SO 4519
Crossway Green T 117 SO 8468
Crossways T 93 SY 7688
Crosswell T 110 SN 1236
Crosswood Reservoir W 163 NT 0657
Crosthwaite T 151 SD 4391
Croston T 137 SD 4819
Crostwick T 133 TG 2515
Crostwight T 133 TG 3430
Croughton T 115 SP 5433
Crovie T 185 NJ 8065
Crowan T 86 SW 6434
Crowborough T 97 TQ 5130
Crowcombe T 92 ST 1336
Crowdecote T 138 SK 1065
Crowdundle Beck W 151 NY 6530
Crowdy Reservoir W 88 SX 1483
Crowfield, Northnts T 119 SP 6141
Crowfield, Suff T 123 TM 1557
Crow Hill T 114 SO 6427
Crowhurst, E. Susx T 97 TQ 7512
Crowhurst, Surrey T 97 TQ 3947
Crowland T 131 TF 2410
Crowlas T 86 SW 5133
Crowle, Humbs T 142 SE 7712
Crowle, H. & W T 117 SO 9256
Crowlin Islands 180 NG 6934
Crowlista T 194 NB 0433
Crowmarsh Gifford T 104 SU 6189
Crownhill T 88 SX 4857
Crownthorpe T 133 TG 0803
Crow Rock 110 SR 8894
Crow Sound W 86 SV 9312
Crowthorne T 104 SU 8364
Crowthorn School T 137 SD 7418
Crowton T 137 SJ 5774
Croxall T 128 SK 1913
Croxdale T 152 NZ 2636
Croxden T 128 SK 0639
Croxley Green T 104 TQ 0795
Croxton, Cambs T 121 TL 2459
Croxton, Humbs T 143 TA 0912
Croxton, Norf T 122 TL 8786
Croxton, Staffs T 127 SJ 7832
Croxton Kerrial T 130 SK 8329
Croxton Park T 130 SK 8227
Croy, Highld T 183 NH 7949
Croy, Strath T 169 NS 7275
Croyde T 90 SS 4439
Croyde Bay W 90 SS 4239
Croydon, Cambs T 121 TL 3149
Croydon, G. Lon P 105 TQ 3365
Croydon Hill H 91 SS 9740
Cruach a' Bhuic H 168 NS 1693
Cruachan H 168 NN 3507
Cruachan Beinn a' Chearcaill H 186 NG 3546
Cruachan Druim na Croise H 173 NM 4550
Cruach an Eachlaich H 168 NM 8606
Cruach an Locha H 160 NR 7865
Cruach an Lochain H 168 NS 0493
Cruachan Min H 173 NM 4421
Cruachan Odhar H 172 NM 3846
Cruachan Reservoir W 168 NN 0828
Cruach an Tailleir H 167 NR 7469
Cruach an Uillt Fheàrna H 167 NR 6290
Cruach a' Phubuill H 167 NR 8276
Cruach Brenfield H 167 NR 8283
Cruach Chuilceachan H 168 NR 9887
Cruach Ionnastail H 167 NR 6491
Cruach Lagain H 160 NR 7466
Cruach Lusach H 167 NR 7883
Cruach Maolachy H 168 NM 8914
Cruach Mhic Fhionnlaidh H 168 NM 9402
Cruach Mhic-Gougain H 160 NR 7550
Cruach Mhòr H 168 NN 0514
Cruach nam Fiadh, Strath H 167 NR 8085
Cruach nam Fiadh, Strath H 160 NR 8256
Cruach nan Caorach H 168 NR 9980
Cruach nan Capull, Strath H 168 NN 1405
Cruach nan Capull, Strath H 168 NS 0797
Cruach nan Capull, Strath H 168 NS 0979
Cruach nan Cuilean H 168 NS 0484
Cruach nan Gabhar H 160 NR 7542
Cruach nan Tarbh H 168 NR 9782
Cruach na Seilcheig H 167 NR 6898
Cruach Rarey H 173 NM 8116

Gleniron Fell Great Yeldham

Gleniron Fell *H*	154	NX 1962
Glenkens, The	156	NX 5786
Glenkerry *T*	157	NT 2811
Glen Kin	168	NS 1380
Glenkindie *T*	184	NJ 4313
Glen Kingie	174	NM 0397
Glen Kinglas	168	NN 2009
Glen Kinglass	168	NN 1335
Glen Kyllachy	183	NH 7424
Glenlatterach	184	NJ 5454
Glenlatterach Reservoir *W*	184	NJ 1953
Glen Lean	168	NS 0982
Glen Lednock	169	NN 7328
Glenlee, D. & G *T*	156	NX 6080
Glen Lee, Tays	176	NO 3881
Glenlichorn	169	NN 7912
Glen Liver	168	NN 0835
Glenlivet, Grampn *T*	184	NJ 1929
Glenlivet, Grampn	184	NJ 2027
Glen Loch	176	NN 9972
Glen Lochay	175	NN 5037
Glen Lochy	168	NN 2630
Glen Logie	176	NO 3168
Glen Lonan	168	NM 9427
Glenlood Hill *H*	163	NT 0828
Glen Loth	193	NC 9412
Glen Loy	174	NN 1183
Glenluce *T*	154	NX 1957
Glen Lui	176	NO 0592
Glen Luss	168	NS 3393
Glen Lussa	160	NR 7326
Glenlussa Water *W*	160	NR 7326
Glen Lyon	175	NN 5446
Glenlyon House	175	NN 7347
Glenmaid Moor	156	NX 9689
Glen Mallie	174	NN 0887
Glen Mark	176	NO 3684
Glen Markie, Highld	182	NH 5507
Glen Markie, Highld	175	NN 5897
Glen Massan	168	NS 1286
Glenmavis *T*	162	NS 7567
Glenmaye *T*	144	SC 2379
Glen Mazeran	183	NH 7221
Glenmore, Highld *T*	187	NG 4340
Glen More, Highld	180	NG 8818
Glen More, Highld	183	NH 9809
Glen More, Strath	173	NM 6230
Glenmore, Strath	173	NM 8412
Glenmore Loch *W*	183	NJ 0833
Glenmore Lodge	183	NH 9809
Glenmore River *W*	180	NG 8917
Glen Moriston	182	NH 2411
Glen Mòr or Glen Albyn	182	NH 4211
Glenmorven Cottage	173	NM 5651
Glenmoy *T*	176	NO 4064
Glenmuck Height *H*	163	NT 0724
Glen Muick	176	NO 3288
Glenmuir	162	NS 6322
Glenmuirshaw	156	NS 6919
Glenmuir Water *W*	156	NS 6719
Glen Nant	168	NN 0128
Glen Nevis	174	NN 1368
Glen Nevis House	174	NN 1272
Glen Noe	168	NN 0733
Glen of Artloch Croft	184	NJ 4839
Glen of Coachford	184	NJ 4646
Glen of Rothes	184	NJ 2552
Glen Ogle	169	NN 5726
Glen Orchy	168	NN 2433
Glen Orrin	182	NH 3649
Glen Oykel	191	NC 3108
Glen Parva *T*	129	SP 5798
Glen Pean	174	NM 9490
Glen Prosen	176	NO 2967
Glenprosen Village *T*	176	NO 3265
Glen Quaich	175	NN 8638
Glenquiech	176	NO 4261
Glen Quoich	180	NH 0107
Glenquoich Forest	180	NH 0106
Glenridding *T*	151	NY 3717
Glenrigh Forest	174	NN 0664
Glen Rinnes	184	NJ 2935
Glenrisdell *T*	160	NR 8658
Glen Rosa	160	NR 9838
Glen Rossal	192	NC 4604
Glenrothes *T*	171	NO 2700
Glen Roy	174	NN 3088
Glen Roy National Nature Reserve	174	NN 2888
Glensanda	173	NM 8246
Glen Sannox	160	NR 9944
Glensaugh	177	NO 6778
Glensax Burn *W*	163	NT 2635
Glen Scaddle	174	NM 9668
Glen Shee, Tays	170	NN 9734
Glenshee, Tays	170	NN 9834
Glen Shee, Tays	176	NO 1462
Glenshero Lodge	175	NN 5593
Glen Shiel	180	NH 0211
Glenshieldaig Forest	190	NG 8449
Glenshiel Forest	180	NG 9414
Glen Shira	168	NN 1314
Glenshirra Forest	175	NN 4793
Glenside *T*	195	NB 3615
Glen Sletdale	193	NC 9113
Glen Sligachan	187	NG 4927
Glen Sluain	168	NS 0999
Glens of Foudland	184	NJ 6034
Glen Spean	174	NN 3580
Glenstockadale	154	NX 0161
Glen Stockdale	174	NM 9549
Glen Strae	168	NN 1631
Glen Strathfarrar	182	NH 3039
Glen Strathfarrar Forest	182	NH 2338
Glenstriven	168	NS 0778
Glen Tanar	177	NO 4694
Glen Tanar House	177	NO 4795
Glen Tarbert	173	NM 8960
Glen Tarff	174	NH 3901
Glen Tarken	169	NN 6626
Glen Tarsan	168	NS 0785
Glentenmont Height *H*	157	NY 2885
Glentham *T*	140	TF 0090
Glen Tig	154	NX 1382
Glen Tilt	175	NN 8870
Glen Tolsta	195	NB 5244
Glentoo Loch *W*	156	NX 7062
Glen Torridon	190	NG 9356
Glentress *T*	163	NT 2839
Glentress Forest *F*	163	NT 2842
Glen Tromie	175	NN 7795
Glentromie Lodge	175	NN 7796
Glen Trool	154	NX 4180
Glentrool Forest *F*	154	NX 3681
Glen Trool Lodge *T*	154	NX 4080
Glentrool Village *T*	154	NX 3578
Glentrosdale Bay *W*	167	NM 6700
Glen Truim	175	NN 6789
Glentruim House	175	NN 6895
Glen Turret	169	NN 8225
Glentworth *T*	140	SK 8488
Glenuig *T*	180	NM 6777
Glenuig Bay *W*	180	NM 6777
Glen Ure	174	NN 0647
Glen Urquhart	182	NH 4430
Glen Varragill	187	NG 4737
Glen Village *T*	170	NS 8878
Glen Vine *T*	144	SC 3378
Glen Water *W*	162	NS 5740
Glenwhappen Rig *H*	163	NT 0625
Gleouraich *H*	180	NH 0305
Glespin *T*	163	NS 8028
Gletness *T*	203	HU 4651
Glevum *R*	114	SO 8318
Glewstone *T*	113	SO 5622
Glims Holm	200	ND 4799
Glinton *T*	130	TF 1505
Glog Hill *H*	116	SO 2269
Glooston *T*	129	SP 7595
Glossop *T*	138	SK 0394
Gloster Hill *T*	159	NU 2504
Gloucester *P*	114	SO 8318
Gloucester & Cheltenham (Staverton) Airport	114	SO 8821
Gloucester & Sharpness Canal *W*	114	SO 7406
Gloup *T*	205	HP 5004
Gloup Holm	205	HP 4806
Gloup Ness	205	HP 5006
Glusburn *T*	146	SE 0044
Gluss *T*	204	HU 3477
Gluss Isle	205	HU 3778
Gluss Voe *W*	204	HU 3678
Gluss Water *W*	204	HU 2581
Glutt Lodge	198	NC 9936
Glutt Water *W*	198	ND 0036
Glyder Fâch *H*	135	SH 6558
Glyder Fawr *H*	135	SH 6458
Glympton *T*	115	SP 4221
Glynarthen *T*	111	SN 3148
Glyn Ceiriog *T*	126	SJ 2038
Glyncoch *T*	109	ST 0792
Glyncorrwg *T*	109	SS 8799
Glynde *T*	97	TQ 4508
Glyndebourne *T*	97	TQ 4510
Glyndyfrdwy *T*	126	SJ 1542
Glyn Neath *T*	109	SN 8806
Glynogwr *T*	109	SS 9587
Glyntaff *T*	109	ST 0889
Glyn Tarell	109	SN 9722
Glyntawe	109	SN 8416
Glyntrefnant	125	SN 9192
Gnosall *T*	127	SJ 8321
Gnosall Heath *T*	127	SJ 8220
Goadby *T*	129	SP 7598
Goadby Marwood *T*	129	SK 7826
Goatacre *T*	102	SU 0177
Goat Fell *H*	160	NR 9941
Goathill *T*	93	ST 6717
Goathland *T*	148	NZ 8301
Goathland Moor	148	SE 8598
Goathurst *T*	92	ST 2534
Gob a' Chuaille	190	NG 8496
Gob Aird an Tolmachain	189	NB 0904
Gob Dubh	167	NR 6385
Gobernuisgach Lodge	197	NC 4341
Gob na h-Airde Móire	194	NB 0117
Gob na h-Oa	186	NG 3134
Gob na Hoe	186	NG 1954
Gob na Milaid	195	NB 4211
Gobowen *T*	126	SJ 3033
Gob Rubh' Uisenis	189	NB 3503
Gob Shilldinish	195	NB 4631
Gob y Deigan	144	SC 2887
Gòdag	179	NM 4181
Godalming *T*	96	SU 9743
Godington *T*	119	SP 6327
Godmanchester *T*	121	TL 2470
Godmanstone *T*	93	SY 6697
Godmersham *T*	99	TR 0650
Godney *T*	101	ST 4842
Godolphin Cross *T*	86	SW 6031
Godolphin House *A*	86	SW 6031
Godre'r-graig *T*	109	SN 7507
Godrevy Island	86	SW 5743
Godshill, Hants *T*	94	SU 1715
Godshill, I. of W *T*	95	SZ 5281
Godstone *T*	97	TQ 3451
Godstone Station	97	TQ 3648
Goff's Oak *T*	105	TL 3203
Gogar *T*	170	NT 1672
Goginan *T*	125	SN 6981
Gog Magog Hills *H*	121	TL 4953
Golan *T*	134	SH 5242
Golant *T*	87	SX 1254
Golberdon *T*	88	SX 3271
Golborne *T*	137	SJ 6198
Golcar *T*	138	SE 1016
Goldcliff *T*	100	ST 3683
Golden Cross *T*	97	TQ 5312
Golden Green *T*	97	TQ 6348
Golden Grove *T*	111	SN 5919
Goldenhill *T*	127	SJ 8553
Golden Pot *T*	103	SU 7143
Golden Valley, Glos *T*	114	SO 9022
Golden Valley, H. & W	113	SO 3636
Golders Green *T*	105	TQ 2488
Goldhanger *T*	106	TL 9009
Golding *T*	127	SJ 5403
Goldsborough, N. Yks *T*	153	NZ 8314
Goldsborough, N. Yks *T*	147	SE 3856
Goldsithney *T*	86	SW 5430
Goldthorpe *T*	139	SE 4604
Gollanfield *T*	183	NH 8153
Golspie *T*	193	NC 8300
Golspie Burn *W*	193	NC 8202
Golval	198	NC 8962
Gomeldon *T*	94	SU 1835
Gomersal *T*	146	SE 2026
Gometra	172	NM 3641
Gomshall *T*	96	TQ 0847
Gonalston *T*	129	SK 6747
Gon Firth, Shetld *W*	203	HU 3662
Gonfirth, Shetld *T*	203	HU 3761
Goodber Common	145	SD 6263
Good Easter *T*	106	TL 6012
Gooderstone *T*	132	TF 7602
Goodie Water *W*	169	NS 6499
Goodleigh *T*	91	SS 5934
Goodmanham *T*	142	SE 8843
Goodnestone, Kent *T*	99	TR 0461
Goodnestone, Kent *T*	99	TR 2554
Goodrich *T*	113	SO 5719
Goodrington *T*	89	SX 8858
Goodwick *T*	110	SM 9438
Goodwin Sands	99	TR 4555
Goodwood House	95	SU 8808
Goodworth Clatford *T*	102	SU 3642
Goodyers End *T*	118	SP 3486
Goole *T*	142	SE 7423
Goole Fields	142	SE 7519
Goonbell *T*	86	SW 7249
Goonhavern *T*	87	SW 7853
Goonhilly Downs	86	SW 7120
Gooseham *T*	90	SS 2216
Goosetrey *T*	137	SJ 7769
Goosey *T*	102	SU 3591
Goosnargh *T*	145	SD 5536
Goostrey *T*	137	SJ 7770
Gop Hill *H*	135	SJ 0880
Gordon *T*	164	NT 6443
Gordonbush *T*	193	NC 8409
Gordonstoun	184	NJ 1869
Gordonstown, Grampn *T*	184	NJ 5656
Gordonstown, Grampn *T*	185	NJ 7138
Gorebridge *T*	164	NT 3461
Gorefield *T*	131	TF 4111
Gore Sand	100	ST 2851
Goring *T*	103	SU 6081
Goring-by-Sea *T*	96	TQ 1103
Gorleston-on-Sea *T*	133	TG 5203
Gorllwyn *H*	112	SN 9259
Gorm Loch *W*	196	NC 2144
Gorm-loch Beag *W*	197	NC 7027
Gorm Loch Mór, Highld *W*	196	NC 3124
Gorm-loch Mór, Highld *W*	193	NC 7123
Gorple Reservoirs *W*	146	SD 9231
Gorpley Reservoir *W*	146	SD 9123
Gorrachie	185	NJ 7358
Gorran Haven *T*	87	SX 0141
Gors *T*	125	SN 6377
Gorsedd *T*	136	SJ 1576
Gorsedd Brân *H*	135	SH 9760
Gorseinon *T*	108	SS 5898
Gorseness *T*	200	HY 4119
Gorsgoch, Dyfed *T*	111	SN 4850
Gors Goch, Powys *H*	125	SN 9393
Gorslas *T*	111	SN 5713
Gorsley *T*	114	SO 6826
Gors Lydan *H*	116	SO 1276
Gorstan *T*	182	NH 3862
Gortantaoid	166	NR 3373
Gortantaoid Point	166	NR 3374
Gorton *T*	137	SJ 8896
Gosbeck *T*	123	TM 1655
Gosberton *T*	131	TF 2331
Goseland Hill *H*	163	NT 0735
Gosfield *T*	122	TL 7829
Gosford Bay *W*	171	NT 4478
Gosford House	171	NT 4578
Gosforth, Cumbr *T*	150	NY 0703
Gosforth, T. & W *T*	159	NZ 2368
Gosmore *T*	120	TL 1827
Gosport *T*	95	SZ 6199
Gossabrough *T*	205	HU 5283
Gossa Water, Shetld *W*	203	HU 3045
Gossa Water, Shetld *W*	203	HU 4360
Gossa Water, Shetld *W*	205	HU 4899
Goswick *T*	165	NU 0545
Gote o' Tram *W*	199	ND 3648
Gotham *T*	129	SK 5330
Gotherington *T*	114	SO 9629
Gott	203	HU 4345
Gott Bay *W*	172	NM 0546
Goudhurst *T*	97	TQ 7237
Goulceby *T*	141	TF 2579
Gourdas *T*	185	NJ 7741
Gourdon *T*	177	NO 8270
Gourock *T*	168	NS 2477
Gouthwaite Reservoir *W*	146	SE 1369
Govan *T*	161	NS 5464
Goveton *T*	89	SX 7546
Govig *T*	194	NB 0109
Govilon *T*	113	SO 2614
Gowanhill *T*	185	NK 0363
Gowdall *T*	147	SE 6222
Gower	108	SS 5290
Gowerton *T*	108	SS 5996
Gowkhall *T*	170	NT 0589
Goxhill, Humbs *T*	143	TA 1021
Goxhill, Humbs *T*	143	TA 1844
Goyle Hill *H*	177	NO 6882
Goyt's Moss	138	SK 0172
Graddon Moor	90	SS 4602
Graemeshall Burn *W*	200	HY 4704
Graemsay	200	HY 2505
Graffham *T*	96	SU 9217
Grafham *T*	120	TL 1669
Grafham Water *W*	120	TL 1468
Grafton, H. & W *T*	113	SO 4937
Grafton, H. & W *T*	116	SO 5861
Grafton, N. Yks *T*	147	SE 4163
Grafton, Oxon *T*	115	SP 2700
Grafton Flyford *T*	118	SO 9656
Grafton Regis *T*	119	SP 7546
Grafton Underwood *T*	120	SP 9280
Grafty Green *T*	98	TQ 8748
Graianrhyd *T*	126	SJ 2156
Graig, Clwyd *T*	135	SJ 0872
Graig, Gwyn *T*	135	SH 8071
Graig Fawr *H*	111	SN 6106
Graig-fechan *T*	126	SJ 1454
Graig Goch *H*	125	SH 7108
Graig Penllyn *T*	109	SS 9777
Graig Wen *H*	135	SH 7439
Grain *T*	98	TQ 8876
Grainsby *T*	143	TF 2799
Grainthorpe *T*	141	TF 3897
Graizelound *T*	142	SK 7798
Grampian Mountains, Grampn *H*	175	NN 7785
Grampian Mountains, Highld *H*	175	NN 7785
Grampian Mountains, Strath *H*	175	NN 7785
Grampian Mountains, Tays *H*	175	NN 7785
Grampound *T*	87	SW 9348
Grampound Road *T*	87	SW 9150
Gramsdale *T*	188	NF 8155
Granborough *T*	119	SP 7625
Granby *T*	129	SK 7536
Grandborough *T*	119	SP 4966
Grandtully *T*	175	NN 9153
Grandtully Hill *H*	175	NN 9147
Grand Union Canal, Bucks *W*	104	SP 9220
Grand Union Canal, Warw *W*	118	SP 2466
Grange, Cumbr *T*	150	NY 2517
Grange, Mers *T*	136	SJ 2286
Grange, N. Yks *T*	153	SE 5796
Grange, Tays	171	NO 2725
Grange Crossroads *T*	184	NJ 4754
Grange Fell *H*	157	NY 2481
Grange Hall	183	NJ 0660
Grange Heath	93	SY 9083
Grange Hill *T*	105	TQ 4492
Grange Moor *T*	139	SE 2216
Grangemouth *T*	170	NS 9381
Grange of Lindores	171	NO 2516
Grange-over-Sands *T*	145	SD 4077
Grangepans *T*	170	NT 0081
Grange, The	95	SU 5636
Grangetown *T*	153	NZ 5520
Grange Villa *T*	152	NZ 2352
Granish *T*	183	NH 8915
Gransmoor *T*	149	TA 1259
Granston *T*	110	SM 8934
Grantchester *T*	121	TL 4356
Grantham *P*	130	SK 9135
Grantham Canal *W*	129	SK 7431
Grantley *T*	147	SE 2369
Grantlodge *T*	185	NJ 7017
Granton *T*	171	NT 2376
Granton House	157	NT 0709
Grantown-on-Spey *T*	183	NJ 0327
Grantshouse *T*	165	NT 8165
Grappenhall *T*	137	SJ 6386
Grasby *T*	142	TA 0804
Grasmere, Cumbr *W*	150	NY 3306
Grasmere, Cumbr *T*	150	NY 3307
Grasmoor *H*	150	NY 1720
Grasscroft *T*	138	SD 9704
Grassendale *T*	136	SJ 3985
Grassholme *T*	152	NY 9221
Grassholme Reservoir *W*	152	NY 9422
Grassington *T*	146	SE 0064
Grassington Moor	146	SE 0368
Grassmoor *T*	139	SK 4066
Grass Point	173	NM 7430
Grassthorpe *T*	140	SK 7967
Grassy Cletts	199	ND 2887
Grateley *T*	102	SU 2641
Gratwich *T*	128	SK 0231
Graveley, Cambs *T*	121	TL 2464
Graveley, Herts *T*	121	TL 2327
Gravelly Hill *T*	118	SP 1090
Gravels *T*	126	SJ 3300
Graveney *T*	99	TR 0562
Gravesend *T*	98	TQ 6473
Gravir *T*	195	NB 3715
Grayingham *T*	140	SK 9396
Grayrigg *T*	151	SD 5797
Grays *T*	98	TQ 6177
Grayshott *T*	95	SU 8735
Grayswood *T*	96	SU 9134
Graythorp *T*	153	NZ 5127
Grazeley *T*	104	SU 6966
Grèabhal *H*	188	NG 0089
Greanamul, W. Isles	178	NF 7305
Greanamul, W. Isles	178	NL 6289
Greanamul Deas	188	NF 8848
Greasbrough *T*	139	SK 4295
Greasby *T*	136	SJ 2587
Great Abington *T*	121	TL 5348
Great Addington *T*	120	SP 9675
Great Alne *T*	118	SP 1259
Great Altcar *T*	136	SD 3206
Great Amwell *T*	105	TL 3612
Great Asby *T*	151	NY 6712
Great Ashfield *T*	122	TM 0068
Great Ayton *T*	153	NZ 5611
Great Baddow *T*	106	TL 7204
Great Bank	145	SD 3323
Great Bardfield *T*	122	TL 6730
Great Barford *T*	120	TL 1352
Great Barr *T*	128	SP 0495
Great Barrington *T*	115	SP 2113
Great Barrow *T*	137	SJ 4768
Great Barton *T*	122	TL 8667
Great Barugh *T*	148	SE 7479
Great Bavington *T*	159	NY 9880
Great Bedwyn *T*	102	SU 2764
Great Bentley *T*	107	TM 1121
Great Bernera	195	NB 1635
Great Bealings *T*	123	TM 2348
Great Bircham *T*	132	TF 7632
Great Blakenham *T*	123	TM 1250
Great Bolas *T*	127	SJ 6621
Great Bookham *T*	96	TQ 1354
Great Borne *H*	150	NY 1216
Great Bosullow *T*	86	SW 4133
Great Bourton *T*	119	SP 4545
Great Bowden *T*	119	SP 7588
Great Bradley *T*	122	TL 6653
Great Braxted *T*	106	TL 8614
Great Bricett *T*	122	TM 0350
Great Brickhill *T*	120	SP 9030
Great Bridgeford *T*	127	SJ 8827
Great Brington *T*	119	SP 6665
Great Bromley *T*	123	TM 0826
Great Broughton *T*	153	NZ 5406
Great Budworth *T*	137	SJ 6677
Great Burbo Bank	136	SJ 2698
Great Burdon *T*	152	NZ 3116
Great Burstead *T*	106	TQ 6892
Great Busby *T*	153	NZ 5205
Great Calva *H*	150	NY 2931
Great Canfield *T*	106	TL 5918
Great Carlton *T*	141	TF 4185
Great Casterton *T*	130	TF 0009
Great Chart *T*	99	TQ 9842
Great Chatwell *T*	127	SJ 7914
Great Chesterford *T*	121	TL 5042
Great Cheverell *T*	102	ST 9854
Great Chishill *T*	121	TL 4238
Great Clacton *T*	107	TM 1716
Great Clifton *T*	150	NY 0429
Great Coates *T*	143	TA 2310
Great Comberton *T*	118	SO 9542
Great Corby *T*	151	NY 4754
Great Cornard *T*	122	TL 8840
Great Coxwell *T*	115	SU 2793
Great Cransley *T*	120	SP 8376
Great Cressingham *T*	132	TF 8501
Great Crosby *T*	136	SJ 3299
Great Cubley *T*	128	SK 1638
Great Cumbrae Island	161	NS 1656
Great Dalby *T*	129	SK 7414
Great Dixter *A*	98	TQ 8125
Great Dodd *H*	150	NY 3420
Great Doddington *T*	120	SP 8864
Great Driffield *T*	149	TA 0257
Great Dunham *T*	132	TF 8714
Great Dunmow *T*	106	TL 6221
Great Durnford *T*	102	SU 1338
Great Easton, Essex *T*	122	TL 6025
Great Easton, Leic *T*	130	SP 8493
Great Eau *W*	141	TF 4484
Great Eccleston *T*	145	SD 4340
Great Edstone *T*	148	SE 7084
Great Ellingham *T*	132	TM 0197
Great Elm *T*	101	ST 7449
Great End *H*	150	NY 2208
Great Eversden *T*	121	TL 3653
Great Fen	122	TL 6078
Great Finborough *T*	122	TM 0157
Greatford *T*	130	TF 0811
Great Fransham *T*	132	TF 8913
Great Gable *H*	150	NY 2110
Great Gaddesden *T*	104	TL 0211
Great Gidding *T*	120	TL 1183
Great Givendale *T*	148	SE 8153
Great Glemham *T*	123	TM 3461
Great Glen *T*	129	SP 6597
Great Gonerby *T*	130	SK 8938
Great Gransden *T*	121	TL 2755
Great Green *T*	122	TL 9155
Great Habton *T*	148	SE 7576
Great Hallingbury *T*	105	TL 5119
Greatham, Cleve *T*	153	NZ 4927
Greatham, Hants *T*	95	SU 7731
Greatham, W. Susx	96	TQ 0415
Great Hampden *T*	104	SP 8401
Great Harrowden *T*	120	SP 8870
Great Harwood *T*	145	SD 7332
Great Haseley *T*	104	SP 6401
Great Hatfield *T*	143	TA 1842
Great Haw *H*	146	SE 0779
Great Haywood *T*	128	SK 0022
Great Heck *T*	147	SE 5921
Great Henny *T*	122	TL 8637
Great Hill *H*	156	NX 9492
Great Hinton *T*	101	ST 9059
Great Hockham *T*	122	TL 9592
Great Holland *T*	107	TM 2119
Great Horkesley *T*	122	TL 9729
Great Hormead *T*	121	TL 4030
Great Horwood *T*	119	SP 7731
Great Houghton, Northnts *T*	119	SP 7958
Great Houghton, S. Yks *T*	139	SE 4306
Great Hucklow *T*	138	SK 1777
Great Kelk *T*	149	TA 1058
Great Kingshill *T*	104	SU 8898
Great Lake, Notts *W*	139	SK 5773
Great Lake, N. Yks *W*	148	SE 7170
Great Langton *T*	152	SE 2996
Great Law *H*	164	NT 4041
Great Leighs *T*	106	TL 7317
Great Limber *T*	143	TA 1308
Great Linford *T*	120	SP 8541
Great Livermere *T*	122	TL 8871
Great Longstone *T*	138	SK 2071
Great Lumley *T*	152	NZ 2949
Great Lyth *T*	126	SJ 4507
Great Malvern *T*	117	SO 7846
Great Maplestead *T*	122	TL 8034
Great Marton *T*	145	SD 3335
Great Massingham *T*	132	TF 7922
Great Mew Stone	88	SX 5047
Great Milton *T*	104	SP 6302
Great Missenden *T*	104	SP 8901
Great Mis Tor *H*	89	SX 5676
Great Mitton *T*	145	SD 7139
Great Mongeham *T*	99	TR 3451
Greatmoor Hill *H*	157	NT 4800
Great Moulton *T*	123	TM 1690
Great Musgrave *T*	151	NY 7613
Great Ness *T*	126	SJ 3919
Great Oakley, Essex *T*	123	TM 1927
Great Oakley, Northnts *T*	120	SP 8785
Great Offley *T*	120	TL 1426
Great Ormes Head or Pen-y-Gogarth	135	SH 7584
Great Ormside *T*	151	NY 7017
Great Orton *T*	150	NY 3254
Great Oxendon *T*	119	SP 7383
Great Palgrave *T*	132	TF 8312
Great Parndon *T*	105	TL 4308
Great Paxton *T*	120	TL 2163
Great Pinseat *H*	152	NY 9602
Great Plumstead *T*	133	TG 3010
Great Ponton *T*	130	SK 9230
Great Postland *T*	131	TF 2612
Great Preston *T*	147	SE 4029
Great Raveley *T*	121	TL 2581
Great Ridge	94	ST 9336
Great Rissington *T*	115	SP 1917
Great Rollright *T*	115	SP 3231
Great Ryburgh *T*	132	TF 9527
Great Ryle *T*	159	NU 0212
Great Saling *T*	122	TL 7025
Great Salkeld *T*	151	NY 5536
Great Sampford *T*	122	TL 6435
Great Sankey *T*	137	SJ 5788
Great Saxham *T*	122	TL 7862
Great Shefford *T*	102	SU 3875
Great Shelford *T*	121	TL 4652
Great Shunner Fell *H*	151	SD 8497
Great Smeaton *T*	153	NZ 3404
Great Snoring *T*	132	TF 9434
Great Somerford *T*	102	ST 9682
Great Stainton *T*	152	NZ 3322
Great Stambridge *T*	106	TQ 9091
Great Staughton *T*	120	TL 1264
Great Steeping *T*	141	TF 4364
Great Stonar *T*	99	TR 3359
Greatstone-on-Sea *T*	99	TR 0822
Great Stour *W*	99	TR 0651
Great Strickland *T*	151	NY 5522
Great Stukeley *T*	121	TL 2274
Great Sturton *T*	141	TF 2176
Great Swinburne *T*	158	NY 9375
Great Tew *T*	115	SP 3929
Great Tey *T*	122	TL 8926
Great Thurlow *T*	122	TL 6750
Great Torrington *T*	90	SS 4919
Great Tosson *T*	159	NU 0200
Great Totham, Essex *T*	106	TL 8511
Great Totham, Essex *T*	106	TL 8713
Great Wakering *T*	106	TQ 9587
Great Waldingfield *T*	122	TL 9043
Great Walsingham *T*	132	TF 9437
Great Waltham *T*	106	TL 6913
Great Warley *T*	105	TQ 5890
Great Washbourne *T*	114	SO 9834
Great Welnetham *T*	122	TL 8859
Great Wenham *T*	122	TM 0738
Great Whernside	146	SE 0074
Great Whittington *T*	159	NZ 0070
Great Wigborough *T*	107	TL 9615
Great Wilbraham *T*	121	TL 5457
Great Wishford *T*	94	SU 0835
Great Witcombe *T*	114	SO 9114
Great Witley *T*	117	SO 7566
Great Wolford *T*	115	SP 2534
Greatworth *T*	119	SP 5542
Great Wratting *T*	122	TL 6848
Great Wymondley *T*	120	TL 2128
Great Wyrley *T*	128	SJ 9907
Great Wytheford *T*	127	SJ 5719
Great Yarmouth *P*	133	TG 5207
Great Yeldham *T*	122	TL 7638

Greave Harmby

Greave 172 NM 2420
Greeb Point 87 SW 8733
Greenbooth Reservoir *W* 137 SD 8515
Greenburn *T* 163 NS 9360
Greendykes *T* 165 NU 0628
Greenfield, Beds *T* 120 TL 0534
Greenfield, Clwyd *T* 136 SJ 1977
Greenfield, G. Man *T* 138 SD 9904
Greenfield, Highld *T* 174 NH 2000
Greenfield, Oxon *T* 104 SU 7191
Greenford *T* 105 TQ 1382
Greengairs *T* 169 NS 7870
Greenham *T* 103 SU 4865
Green Hammerton *T* 147 SE 4657
Greenhaugh *T* 158 NY 7987
Greenhead, Cumbr *T* 158 NY 6665
Green Head, Orkney 200 ND 3099
Greenhill, Central *T* 169 NS 8278
Greenhill, G. Lon *T* 105 TQ 1688
Green Hill, Northum *H* 152 NY 8647
Greenhill, S. Yks *T* 139 SK 3481
Green Hill, Wilts *T* 102 SU 0686
Greenhithe *T* 98 TQ 5974
Greenholm *T* 161 NS 5337
Greenholme *T* 151 NY 5905
Greenhouse *T* 164 NT 5523
Greenhow Hill *T* 146 SE 1164
Greenigo *T* 200 HY 4007
Greenland *T* 199 ND 2467
Green Law, Border *H* 158 NT 6706
Greenlaw, Border *T* 164 NT 7146
Greenlee Lough *W* 158 NY 7769
Greenli Ness 201 HY 6221
Greenloaning *T* 169 NN 8307
Green Lowther *H* 156 NS 9012
Greenmount *T* 137 SD 7714
Greenmow *T* 203 HU 4428
Greenock *P* 168 NS 2776
Greenodd *T* 145 SD 3182
Green Ore *T* 101 ST 5750
Green Road Station 144 SD 1883
Green Scar 110 SM 7922
Greenside *T* 159 NZ 1462
Greensidehill *T* 159 NT 9716
Greenside Reservoir *W* 169 NS 4775
Greensides *W* 154 NX 2788
Greenskairs *T* 185 NJ 7863
Greens Norton *T* 119 SP 6649
Greenstead Green *T* 122 TL 8227
Greensted *T* 105 TL 5303
Greenstone Point 190 NG 8698
Green Street *T* 105 TQ 1998
Green Street Green *T* 105 TQ 4563
Green, The, Cumbr *T* 144 SD 1784
Green, The, Wilts *T* 93 ST 8731
Greenwich *T* 105 TQ 4077
Greet *T* 114 SP 0230
Greeta River or River
Creed *W* 195 NB 3932
Greete *T* 116 SO 5770
Greetham, Leic *T* 130 SK 9214
Greetham, Lincs *T* 141 TF 3070
Greetland *T* 146 SE 0821
Greg Ness 185 NJ 9704
Gregson Lane *T* 145 SD 5926
Greian Head 178 NF 6404
Greinton *T* 92 ST 4136
Gremista 203 HU 4643
Grendon, Northnts *T* 120 SP 8760
Grendon, Warw *T* 128 SP 2799
Grendon Common *T* 128 SP 2798
Grendon Green *T* 113 SO 5957
Grendon Underwood *T* 104 SP 6820
Grenitote *T* 188 NF 8275
Grenoside *T* 139 SK 3393
Gresford *T* 126 SJ 3555
Gresham *T* 133 TG 1638
Greshornish *T* 186 NG 3353
Greshornish Point 186 NG 3456
Gress *T* 195 NB 4942
Gressenhall *T* 132 TF 9616
Gressingham *T* 145 SD 5669
Gress River *W* 195 NB 4644
Greta Bridge *T* 152 NZ 0813
Greta River *W* 150 NY 3225
Gretna *T* 157 NY 3167
Gretna Green *T* 157 NY 3168
Gretton, Glos *T* 114 SP 0130
Gretton, Northnts *T* 130 SP 8994
Gretton, Shrops *T* 127 SO 5195
Grewelthorpe *T* 147 SE 2376
Grey Cairns *A* 199 ND 2644
Greygarth *T* 146 SE 1872
Grey Head 201 HY 5840
Grey Hill *H* 154 NX 1692
Grey Mare's Tail *W* 157 NT 1814
Greysouthen *T* 150 NY 0729
Greystoke *T* 151 NY 4331
Greystone *T* 177 NO 5343
Greywell *T* 103 SU 7151
Grianan *T* 195 NB 4135
Gribbin Head 87 SX 0949
Gribun 173 NM 4433
Grice Ness 201 HY 6728
Griff *T* 118 SP 3588
Griffithstown *T* 113 ST 2999
Grif Skerry 203 HU 6362
Grike *T* 150 NY 0814
Grimeford Village *T* 137 SD 6112
Grime's Graves *A* 122 TL 8189
Grimethorpe *T* 139 SE 4109
Griminish *T* 188 NF 7751
Griminish Point 188 NF 7276
Grimister *T* 205 HU 4693
Grimley *T* 117 SO 8360
Grimness, Orkney *T* 200 ND 4793
Grim Ness, Orkney 200 ND 4992
Grimoldby *T* 141 TF 3988
Grimsargh *T* 145 SD 5834
Grimsay 188 NF 8656
Grimsby *P* 143 TA 2709
Grimscote *T* 119 SP 6553
Grimscott *T* 90 SS 2606
Grimshader *T* 195 NB 4025
Grimspound *A* 89 SX 7080
Grimsthorpe *T* 130 TF 0422
Grimston, Leic *T* 129 SK 6821
Grimston, Norf *T* 132 TF 7221
Grimstone *T* 93 SY 6394
Grimwith Reservoir *W* 146 SE 0664
Grindale *T* 149 TA 1371
Grindiscol *T* 203 HU 4939
Grindleford *T* 139 SK 2477
Grindleton *T* 146 SD 7545
Grindley Brook *T* 127 SJ 5243
Grindlow *T* 138 SK 1877
Grind of the Navir 204 HU 2180
Grindon, Northum *T* 165 NT 9144
Grindon, Staffs *T* 128 SK 0854
Grindstone Law *H* 158 NT 7607
Gringle *T* 127 SJ 7503
Gringley on the Hill *T* 140 SK 7390
Grinsdale *T* 157 NY 3658
Grinshill *T* 127 SJ 5223
Grinton *T* 152 SE 0498
Griomaval *H* 194 NB 0122
Grisedale, Cumbr 151 NY 3715
Grisedale, Cumbr *T* 151 SD 7793
Grisedale Pike *H* 150 NY 1922
Grisedale Tarn *W* 150 NY 3412
Grishipoll 172 NM 1959
Griskerry 203 HU 3622
Gristhorpe *T* 149 TA 0882
Griston *T* 132 TL 9499
Gritley 200 HY 5604
Grittenham *T* 102 SU 0382
Grittleton *T* 101 ST 8680
Grizebeck *T* 144 SD 2385
Grizedale *T* 150 SD 3394
Grizedale Forest *F* 150 SD 3394
Groatay 188 NF 9773
Groban *H* 191 NH 0970
Gròb Bàgh *W* 160 NR 6346
Grobister *T* 201 HY 6524
Groby *T* 129 SK 5207
Groes, Clwyd *T* 135 SJ 0064
Groes, W. Glam *T* 109 SS 7987
Groes-faen *T* 109 ST 0781
Groeslon *T* 134 SH 4755
Grogport *T* 160 NR 8044
Gromford *T* 123 TM 3858
Gronant *T* 135 SJ 0983
Groombridge *T* 97 TQ 5337
Grosebay *T* 189 NG 1593
Grosmont, Gwent *T* 113 SO 4024
Grosmont, N. Yks *T* 148 NZ 8205
Groton *T* 122 TL 9541
Grove, Dorset *T* 93 SY 6972
Grove, Kent *T* 99 TR 2362
Grove, Notts *T* 140 SK 7379
Grove, Oxon *T* 102 SU 4090
Grovely Wood *F* 94 SU 0534
Grove Park *T* 105 TQ 4172
Grovesend *T* 108 SN 5900
Grudie *T* 182 NH 3062
Grudie Burn *W* 192 NC 5305
Grudie River *W* 196 NC 3362
Gruids *T* 192 NC 5703
Gruinard Bay *W* 190 NG 9293
Gruinard House 190 NG 9692
Gruinard Island 190 NG 9494
Gruinard River *W* 190 NG 9788
Gruinart 166 NR 2866
Grula 186 NG 3826
Gruline *T* 173 NM 5440
Gruline House 173 NM 5539
Grumbla *T* 86 SW 4029
Grumby Rock *H* 197 NC 7010
Gruna 202 HU 2859
Grunasound *T* 203 HU 3733
Gruna Stack 204 HU 2886
Grunay 205 HU 6971
Grundisburgh *T* 123 TM 2250
Gruney 205 HU 3896
Grunka Hellier 205 HP 5815
Gruting *T* 202 HU 2749
Gruting Voe *W* 202 HU 2647
Grutness 203 HU 4009
Grut Wick *W* 203 HU 5138
Grwyne Fawr Reservoir *W*
113 SO 2331
Grwyne Fechan *W* 109 SO 2225
Gryfe Reservoirs *W* 168 NS 2871
Gualachulain 174 NN 1145
Gualann *H* 169 NS 4594
Gualin House 196 NC 3056
Guallann Mhòr *H* 160 NR 9062
Guardbridge *T* 171 NO 4518
Guarlford *T* 117 SO 8145
Guay 176 NO 0049
Guens, The 205 HU 6568
Guestling Green *T* 98 TQ 8513
Guestwick *T* 132 TG 0627
Gugh 86 SV 8908
Guide Post *T* 159 NZ 2585
Guilden Morden *T* 121 TL 2744
Guilden Sutton *T* 136 SJ 4468
Guildford *P* 96 SU 9949
Guildtown *T* 170 NO 1331
Guile Point *W* 165 NU 1340
Guillamon Island 180 NG 6327
Guilsborough *T* 119 SP 6773
Guilsfield *T* 126 SJ 2211
Guirasdeal 173 NM 6907
Guirdil Bay *W* 179 NG 3101
Guisachan Forest 182 NH 2821
Guisborough *T* 153 NZ 6015
Guiseley *T* 146 SE 1942
Guist *T* 132 TF 9925
Guiting Power *T* 114 SP 0924
Gulber Wick *W* 203 HU 4438
Gulf of Corryvreckan *W* 167 NM 6902
Gulland Rock 87 SW 8778
Gullane *T* 171 NT 4882
Gullane Bay *W* 171 NT 4783
Gull Point 161 NS 1450
Gulval *T* 86 SW 4831
Gumfreston *T* 110 SN 1001
Gumley *T* 119 SP 6890
Gunby, Humbs *T* 142 SE 7135
Gunby, Lincs *T* 130 SK 9121
Gundleton *T* 95 SU 6133
Gunfleet Sand 107 TM 2611
Gunn *T* 91 SS 6333
Gunna 172 NM 1051
Gunnerside *T* 152 SD 9598
Gunnerton *T* 158 NY 9075
Gunness *T* 142 SE 8411
Gunnislake *T* 88 SX 4371
Gunnista *T* 203 HU 5043
Gunthorpe, Norf *T* 132 TG 0134
Gunthorpe, Notts *T* 129 SK 6844
Gunton Hall 133 TG 2234
Gunton Station 133 TG 2535
Gunver Head 87 SW 8977
Gunwalloe Fishing Cove *T*
86 SW 6522
Gurnard *T* 95 SZ 4796
Gurnard Bay *W* 95 SZ 4795
Gurnard's Head 86 SW 4338
Gurn Ddu *H* 134 SH 4046
Gurney Slade *T* 101 ST 6249
Gurnos *T* 109 SN 7709
Gussage All Saints *T* 94 SU 0010
Gussage St Michael *T* 94 ST 9811
Guston *T* 99 TR 3242
Gutcher *T* 205 HU 5499
Guthrie *T* 177 NO 5650
Gutter Sound *W* 200 ND 3196
Guyhirn *T* 131 TF 3903
Guy's Head *T* 131 TF 4825
Guy's Marsh *T* 93 ST 8420
Guyzance *T* 159 NU 2103
Gwaelod-y-Garth *T* 109 ST 1183
Gwaenysgor *T* 135 SJ 0781
Gwalchmai *T* 134 SH 3976
Gwastad *H* 113 SO 2305
Gwastedyn Hill *H* 125 SN 9866
Gwaun-Cae-Gurwen *T* 108 SN 7011
Gwaunceste Hill *H* 113 SO 1655
Gwaun Nant-ddu *H* 109 SO 0017
Gwbert *T* 110 SN 1650
Gweek *T* 86 SW 7026
Gwehelog *T* 113 SO 3804
Gwenddwr *T* 112 SO 0643
Gwendraeth *W* 111 SN 3806
Gwendraeth Fâch *W* 111 SN 4915
Gwendraeth Fawr *W* 111 SN 5212
Gwennap *T* 86 SW 7340
Gwennap Head 86 SW 3621
Gwenter *T* 86 SW 7417
Gwernaffield *T* 136 SJ 2064
Gwernesney *T* 113 SO 4101
Gwernogle *T* 111 SN 5334
Gwernymynydd *T* 136 SJ 2162
Gwersyllt *T* 126 SJ 3153
Gwespyr *T* 136 SJ 1183
Gwinear *T* 86 SW 5937
Gwithian *T* 86 SW 5841
Gwrych Castle 135 SH 9277
Gwryd *H* 112 SN 9339
Gwyddelwern *T* 135 SJ 0746
Gwyddgrug *T* 111 SN 4635
Gwytherin *T* 135 SH 8761
Gylchedd *H* 135 SH 8544
Gypsey Race *W* 149 TA 0970

H

Haaf Gruney 205 HU 6398
Haa, The 203 HU 5560
Habberley, H. & W *T* 117 SO 8077
Habberley, Shrops *T* 126 SJ 3903
Habitancum *R* 158 NY 8986
Habost, W. Isles *T* 195 NB 3219
Habost, W. Isles *T* 195 NB 5162
Habrough *T* 143 TA 1413
Haccombe *T* 89 SX 8970
Haceby *T* 130 TF 0336
Hacheston *T* 123 TM 3059
Hackford *T* 132 TG 0502
Hackforth *T* 152 SE 2493
Hackland 200 HY 3920
Hacklete *T* 195 NB 1534
Hackleton *T* 119 SP 8055
Hackley Head or Forvie Ness
185 NK 0226
Hackness, N. Yks *T* 149 SE 9690
Hackness, Orkney *T* 200 ND 3390
Hackney *T* 105 TQ 3585
Hackpen Hill, Devon *H* 92 ST 1112
Hackpen Hill, Wilts *H* 102 SU 1375
Hacks Ness 201 HY 6134
Hackthorn *T* 140 SK 9982
Hackthorpe *T* 151 NY 5422
Haconby *T* 130 TF 1025
Haco's Ness 200 HY 5214
Hadden *T* 165 NT 7836
Haddenham, Bucks *T* 104 SP 7408
Haddenham, Cambs *T* 121 TL 4675
Haddington *T* 171 NT 5173
Haddiscoe *T* 133 TM 4496
Haddock Sands *W* 203 HU 3343
Haddo House 185 NJ 8634
Haddon *T* 120 TL 1392
Haddon Hall *A* 139 SK 2366
Haddon Hill *H* 91 SS 9828
Hademore *T* 128 SK 1708
Hadfield *T* 138 SK 0296
Hadham Cross *T* 105 TL 4218
Hadham Ford *T* 105 TL 4322
Hadleigh, Essex *T* 106 TQ 8187
Hadleigh, Suff *T* 122 TM 0242
Hadley *T* 127 SJ 6712
Hadley End *T* 128 SK 1320
Hadlow *T* 97 TQ 6350
Hadlow Down *T* 97 TQ 5324
Hadnall *T* 127 SJ 5220
Hadrian's Wall, Cumbr *R*
157 NY 4661
Hadrian's Wall, Northum *R*
158 NY 9669
Hadstock *T* 121 TL 5544
Hadston Carrs 159 NU 2800
Hadyard Hill *H* 154 NX 2699
Hadzor *T* 117 SO 9162
Haffenden Quarter *T* 98 TQ 8840
Hafod-Dinbych *T* 135 SH 8953
Haggbeck *T* 157 NY 4773
Haggerston *T* 165 NU 0443
Hagley, H. & W *T* 113 SO 5641
Hagley, H. & W *T* 117 SO 9180
Hagshaw Hill *H* 162 NS 7830
Hagworthingham *T* 141 TF 3469
Haigh *T* 137 SD 6009
Haighton Green *T* 145 SD 5634
Haile *T* 150 NY 0308
Hailes *T* 114 SP 0530
Hailes Castle *A* 171 NT 5775
Hailey, Herts *T* 105 TL 3611
Hailey, Oxon *T* 115 SP 3512
Hailsham *T* 97 TQ 5909
Hail Weston *T* 120 TL 1662
Hainault *T* 105 TQ 4691
Hainford *T* 133 TG 2218
Hainton *T* 141 TF 1884
Haisborough (lightship) 133 TG 4049
Haisthorpe *T* 149 TA 1264
Halam *T* 129 SK 6754
Halberry Head 199 ND 3037
Halberton *T* 91 ST 0012
Halcro *T* 199 ND 2360
Halcro Head 199 ND 4785
Hale, Ches *T* 136 SJ 4682
Hale, G. Man *T* 137 SJ 7786
Hale, Hants *T* 94 SU 1919
Hale, Lincs *T* 130 TF 1442
Hale Bank *T* 137 SJ 4883
Halebarns *T* 137 SJ 7985
Hales, Norf *T* 133 TM 3897
Hales, Staffs *T* 127 SJ 7134
Halesowen *T* 118 SO 9683
Hales Place *T* 99 TR 1459
Hale Street *T* 97 TQ 6749
Halesworth *T* 123 TM 3877
Halewood *T* 136 SJ 4485
Halford, Shrops *T* 116 SO 4383
Halford, Warw *T* 118 SP 2645
Halfpenny Green *T* 117 SO 8292
Halfway, Berks *T* 102 SU 4068
Halfway, Dyfed *T* 111 SN 6430
Halfway, Powys *T* 109 SN 8332
Halfway House *T* 126 SJ 3411
Halfway Houses *T* 98 TQ 9372
Halidon Hill *H* 165 NT 9654
Halifax *P* 146 SE 0925
Halistra *T* 186 NG 2459
Halket *T* 161 NS 4252
Halkirk *T* 199 ND 1359
Halkyn *T* 136 SJ 2171
Halkyn Mountain *H* 136 SJ 1972
Halladale River *W* 198 NC 8953
Halland *T* 97 TQ 5016
Hallaton *T* 129 SP 7896
Hallatrow *T* 101 ST 6357
Hallbankgate *T* 158 NY 5859
Hall Dunnerdale *T* 150 SD 2195
Hallen *T* 101 ST 5580
Hall Green *T* 118 SP 1181
Hallhills Loch *W* 157 NY 1688
Halliburton *T* 164 NT 6748
Halliman Skerries 184 NJ 2172
Hallin *T* 186 NG 2558
Halling *T* 98 TQ 7064
Hallington *T* 159 NY 9875
Hallington Reservoirs *W* 159 NY 9776
Hallival *H* 179 NM 3996
Hall of Clestrain 200 HY 2907
Hall of Tankerness 200 HY 5208
Hall of the Forest *T* 116 SO 2183
Halloughton *T* 129 SK 6851
Hallow *T* 117 SO 8258
Hall Road Station 136 SD 3000
Hallrule *T* 158 NT 5914
Halls *T* 171 NT 6572
Hallsands *T* 89 SX 8138
Hall, The 205 HU 6098
Hallthwaites *T* 144 SD 1785
Hallworthy *T* 88 SX 1887
Hallyburton House 176 NO 2438
Hallyne *T* 163 NT 1940
Halmer End *T* 127 SJ 8049
Halmore *T* 114 SO 6902
Halmyre Mains *T* 163 NT 1749
Halnaker *T* 96 SU 9108
Halsall *T* 136 SD 3710
Halse, Northnts *T* 119 SP 5640
Halse, Somer *T* 92 ST 1427
Halsetown *T* 86 SW 5038
Halsham *T* 143 TA 2727
Halsinger *T* 90 SS 5138
Halstead, Essex *T* 122 TL 8130
Halstead, Kent *T* 105 TQ 4861
Halstead, Leic *T* 129 SK 7405
Halstock *T* 93 ST 5308
Halstow Marshes 106 TQ 7778
Haltham *T* 141 TF 2463
Haltoft End *T* 131 TF 3645
Halton, Bucks *T* 104 SP 8710
Halton, Ches *T* 137 SJ 5482
Halton, Clwyd *T* 126 SJ 3039
Halton, Lancs *T* 145 SD 5064
Halton East *T* 146 SE 0454
Halton Gill *T* 146 SD 8776
Halton Holegate *T* 141 TF 4165
Halton Lea Gate *T* 158 NY 6558
Halton West *T* 146 SD 8454
Haltwhistle *T* 158 NY 7064
Halvergate *T* 133 TG 4106
Halvergate Marshes 133 TG 4707
Halwell *T* 89 SX 7753
Halwill *T* 88 SX 4299
Halwill Junction *T* 88 SS 4400
Ham, G. Lon *T* 105 TQ 1772
Ham, Glos *T* 114 ST 6898
Ham, Highld *T* 199 ND 2373
Ham, Kent 99 TR 3254
Ham, Shetld *T* 202 HT 9738
Ham, Wilts *T* 102 SU 3362
Hamar 205 HU 5136
Hamara River *W* 186 NG 1947
Hamble *T* 95 SU 4607
Hambleden *T* 104 SU 7886
Hambledon, Hants *T* 95 SU 6414
Hambledon, Surrey *T* 96 SU 9638
Hambleton, Lancs *T* 145 SD 3742
Hambleton, N. Yks *T* 147 SE 5530
Hambleton Hill *H* 146 SE 1473
Hambleton Hills, The *H* 153 SE 5089
Hambridge *T* 92 ST 3921
Hambrook, Avon *T* 101 ST 6479
Hambrook, W. Susx *T* 95 SU 7806
Hameldon Hill *H* 146 SD 8128
Hameldown Tor *H* 89 SX 7080
Hamera Head 203 HU 4862
Hameringham *T* 141 TF 3068
Hamerton *T* 120 TL 1379
Hametoun *T* 202 HT 9637
Hamford Water *W* 123 TM 2225
Ham Green, Avon *T* 101 ST 5375
Ham Green, H. & W *T* 118 SP 0163
Ham Hill *A* 93 ST 4816
Hamilton *T* 162 NS 7255
Hamly Hill *H* 200 HY 4904
Hammersmith *T* 105 TQ 2279
Hammerwich *T* 128 SK 0607
Hammond Beck *W* 130 TF 2038
Hammond Street *T* 105 TL 3304
Hammoon *T* 93 ST 8114
Hamna Voe, Shetld *W* 202 HU 1659
Hamna Voe, Shetld *W* 202 HU 2380
Hamnavoe, Shetld 204 HU 2380
Hamnavoe, Shetld *T* 203 HU 3735
Hamna Voe, Shetld *W* 205 HU 4879
Hamnavoe, Shetld 205 HU 4971
Hamnavoe, Shetld *T* 205 HU 4980
Ham of Muness *W* 205 HP 6301
Hampden Park *T* 97 TQ 6002
Hampnett *T* 114 SP 1015
Hampole *T* 139 SE 5010
Hampreston *T* 94 SZ 0598
Hampstead *T* 105 TQ 2485
Hampstead Norreys *T* 103 SU 5276
Hampsthwaite *T* 147 SE 2658
Hampton, G. Lon *T* 105 TQ 1369
Hampton, H. & W *T* 118 SP 0243
Hampton, Shrops *T* 117 SO 7486
Hampton Bishop *T* 113 SO 5538
Hampton Court *A* 105 TQ 1568
Hampton Heath *T* 127 SJ 4949
Hampton in Arden *T* 118 SP 2081
Hampton Lovell *T* 117 SO 8865
Hampton Lucy *T* 118 SP 2557
Hampton on the Hill *T* 118 SP 2564
Hampton Poyle *T* 115 SP 5015
Hamsey *T* 97 TQ 4012
Hamstall Ridware *T* 128 SK 1019
Hamstead, I. of W *T* 94 SZ 3991
Hamstead, W. Mids *T* 128 SP 0493
Hamstead Marshall *T* 102 SU 4165
Hamsterley, Durham *T* 152 NZ 1131
Hamsterley, Durham *T* 152 NZ 1156
Hamsterley Forest *F* 152 NZ 0428
Hamstreet, Kent *T* 99 TR 0033
Ham Street, Somer *T* 93 ST 5534
Hamworthy *T* 94 SY 9991
Hanbury, H. & W *T* 118 SO 9663
Hanbury, Staffs *T* 128 SK 1727
Hanchurch *T* 127 SJ 8441
Handa Island 196 NC 1348
Handbridge *T* 136 SJ 4165
Handcross *T* 96 TQ 2629
Handfast Point or The
Foreland 94 SZ 0582
Handforth *T* 137 SJ 8583
Handley *T* 136 SJ 4657
Handsacre *T* 128 SK 0916
Handsworth, S. Yks *T* 139 SK 4186
Handsworth, W. Mids *T* 118 SP 0390
Hanford *T* 127 SJ 8742
Hanging Langford *T* 94 SU 0337
Hanham *T* 101 ST 6472
Haningstone Hill *H* 89 SX 6186
Hankelow *T* 127 SJ 6745
Hankerton *T* 102 ST 9790
Hankham *T* 97 TQ 6105
Hanley *T* 127 SJ 8847
Hanley Castle *T* 117 SO 8442
Hanley Child *T* 117 SO 6465
Hanley Swan *T* 117 SO 8142
Hanley William *T* 117 SO 6766
Hanlith *T* 146 SD 9061
Hanmer *T* 126 SJ 4539
Hanningfield Reservoir *W*
106 TQ 7398
Hannington, Hants *T* 103 SU 5455
Hannington, Northnts *T* 120 SP 8171
Hannington, Wilts *T* 115 SU 1793
Hannington Wick *T* 115 SU 1795
Hanslope *T* 119 SP 8046
Hanthorpe *T* 130 TF 0823
Hanwell *T* 118 SP 4343
Hanwood *T* 126 SJ 4409
Hanworth, G. Lon *T* 105 TQ 1271
Hanworth, Norf *T* 133 TG 1935
Happendon *T* 163 NS 8533
Happisburgh *T* 133 TG 3831
Happisburgh Common *T* 133 TG 3729
Hapsford *T* 137 SJ 4774
Hapton, Lancs *T* 146 SD 7931
Hapton, Norf *T* 133 TM 1796
Harberton *T* 89 SX 7758
Harbertonford *T* 89 SX 7856
Harbledown *T* 99 TR 1357
Harborne *T* 118 SP 0284
Harborough Magna *T* 119 SP 4779
Harbottle *T* 158 NT 9304
Harbury *T* 118 SP 3759
Harby, Leic *T* 129 SK 7431
Harby, Notts *T* 140 SK 8870
Harcombe *T* 92 SY 1590
Harden *T* 146 SE 0838
Hardendale *T* 151 NY 5814
Hardgate *T* 177 NJ 7901
Hardham *T* 96 TQ 0417
Hardhorn *T* 145 SD 3538
Hardingham *T* 132 TG 0403
Hardingstone *T* 119 SP 7657
Hardings Wood *T* 127 SJ 8254
Hardington *T* 101 ST 7452
Hardington Mandeville *T* 93 ST 5111
Hardington Marsh *T* 93 ST 5009
Hardknott Pass 150 NY 2301
Hardley *T* 94 SU 4204
Hardley Street *T* 133 TG 3801
Hardmead *T* 120 SP 9347
Hardraw *T* 152 SD 8691
Hardstoft *T* 139 SK 4463
Hardway, Hants *T* 95 SU 6001
Hardway, Somer *T* 93 ST 7234
Hardwick, Bucks *T* 104 SP 8019
Hardwick, Cambs *T* 121 TL 3758
Hardwick, Norf *T* 123 TM 2289
Hardwick, Northnts *T* 120 SP 8569
Hardwick, Oxon *T* 115 SP 3706
Hardwick, Oxon *T* 115 SP 5729
Hardwicke, Glos *T* 114 SO 8012
Hardwicke, Glos *T* 114 SO 9127
Hardwicke, H. & W *T* 113 SO 2743
Hardwick Hall *A* 139 SK 4663
Hareby *T* 141 TF 3365
Hareden *T* 145 SD 6450
Hare Faulds *A* 164 NT 5849
Harefield *T* 104 TQ 0590
Hare Hatch *T* 104 SU 8077
Hare Hill, Strath *H* 156 NS 6509
Hare Hill, Strath *H* 163 NS 9053
Harehope *T* 159 NU 0920
Harelaw Dam *W* 161 NS 4753
Harelaw Reservoir *W* 161 NS 4859
Hare Ness 177 NO 9599
Harescombe *T* 114 SO 8410
Haresfield *T* 114 SO 8110
Hareshaw Hill *H* 162 NS 7629
Hare Street *T* 121 TL 3929
Harewood *T* 147 SE 3245
Harewood Forest *F* 102 SU 4044
Harford *T* 89 SX 6359
Hargrave, Ches *T* 137 SJ 4862
Hargrave, Northnts *T* 120 TL 0370
Hargrave, Suff *T* 122 TL 7759
Harker *T* 157 NY 3960
Harkstead *T* 123 TM 1834
Harland Hill *H* 146 SE 0284
Harlaston *T* 128 SK 2110
Harlaw House 185 NJ 7424
Harlaxton *T* 130 SK 8832
Harlech *T* 134 SH 5831
Harlesden *T* 105 TQ 2183
Harleston, Devon *T* 89 SX 7945
Harleston, Norf *T* 123 TM 2483
Harleston, Suff *T* 122 TM 0160
Harlestone *T* 119 SP 7064
Harle Syke *T* 146 SD 8635
Harley *T* 127 SJ 5901
Harling Road Station 122 TL 9788
Harlington *T* 120 TL 0330
Harlosh *T* 186 NG 2841
Harlosh Island 186 NG 2739
Harlosh Point 186 NG 2840
Harlow *P* 105 TL 4510
Harlow Hill *T* 159 NZ 0768
Harlow Reservoir *W* 163 NT 1864
Harlthorpe *T* 142 SE 7437
Harlton *T* 121 TL 3852
Harman's Cross *T* 94 SY 9880
Harmars Ness 205 HU 5894
Harmby *T* 152 SE 1289

Harmer Green High Grange

Harmer Green T 105 TL 2516
Harmer Hill T 127 SJ 4922
Harmston T 140 SK 9762
Harnham T 94 SU 1328
Harnhill T 114 SP 0700
Harold Hill T 105 TQ 5391
Haroldston West T 110 SM 8615
Haroldswick, Shetld T 205 HP 6312
Harold's Wick, Shetld W 205 HP 6411
Harold Wood T 105 TQ 5590
Harome T 147 SE 6482
Harpenden T 105 TL 1314
Harperleas Reservoir W 171 NO 2105
Harperrig Reservoir W 163 NT 0961
Harper's Brook W 120 SP 9286
Harpford T 92 SY 0990
Harpham T 149 TA 0961
Harpley, H. & W T 117 SO 6861
Harpley, Norf T 132 TF 7826
Harpole T 119 SP 6960
Harpsdale T 199 ND 1356
Harpsden T 104 SU 7680
Harpswell T 140 SK 9389
Harpurhey T 137 SD 8601
Harpur Hill T 138 SK 0671
Harrabrough Head 200 ND 4190
Harrapool T 180 NG 6523
Harray 200 HY 3319
Harrier 202 HT 9540
Harrietfield T 170 NN 9829
Harrietsham T 98 TQ 8652
Harrington, Cumbr T 150 NX 9925
Harrington, Lincs T 141 TF 3671
Harrington, Northnts T 119 SP 7780
Harringworth T 130 SP 9197
Harris, Highld 179 NM 3395
Harris, W. Isles 189 NG 1198
Harriseahead T 127 SJ 8656
Harrogate P 147 SE 3055
Harrold T 120 SP 9557
Harrow T 105 TQ 1588
Harrowbarrow T 88 SX 4070
Harrowden T 120 TL 0747
Harrow Hill H 96 TQ 0809
Harrow on the Hill T 105 TQ 1586
Harsgeir 195 NB 1140
Harston, Cambs T 121 TL 4250
Harston, Leic T 130 SK 8431
Hart T 153 NZ 4634
Harta Corrie 187 NG 4723
Hartamul 178 NF 8311
Hartburn T 159 NZ 0986
Harter Fell, Cumbr 151 NY 4609
Harter Fell, Cumbr 150 SD 2199
Hartest T 122 TL 8352
Hart Fell, D. & G H 157 NT 1113
Hart Fell, D. & G H 157 NY 2389
Hartfield T 97 TQ 4735
Hartford, Cambs T 121 TL 2572
Hartford, Ches T 137 SJ 6472
Hartfordbridge T 103 SU 7757
Hartford End T 106 TL 6817
Hartforth T 152 NZ 1706
Harthill, Ches T 127 SJ 5055
Harthill, Strath T 163 NS 9064
Harthill, S. Yks T 139 SK 4980
Harthope Burn W 165 NT 9623
Hartington T 138 SK 1260
Hartland T 90 SS 2624
Hartland Point 90 SS 2227
Hartland Quay T 90 SS 2224
Hartlebury T 117 SO 8470
Hartlepool P 153 NZ 5132
Hartlepool Bay W 153 NZ 5231
Hartley, Cumbr T 151 NY 7808
Hartley, Kent T 98 TQ 6166
Hartley, Kent T 97 TQ 7634
Hartley, Northum T 159 NZ 3375
Hartley Wespall T 104 SU 6958
Hartley Wintney T 103 SU 7656
Hartlip T 98 TQ 8364
Harton, N. Yks T 148 SE 7061
Harton, Shrops T 116 SO 4888
Harton, T. & W T 159 NZ 3764
Hartpury T 114 SO 8025
Hartshill T 128 SP 3294
Hartshorne T 128 SK 3221
Hartshorn Pike H 158 NT 6201
Hartsop T 151 NY 4013
Hartwell T 119 SP 7850
Hartwood T 163 NS 8459
Harvel T 98 TQ 6563
Harvington T 118 SP 0549
Harwell T 103 SU 4989
Harwich P 123 TM 2632
Harwich Harbour W 123 TM 2633
Harwood, Durham T 151 NY 8233
Harwood, G. Man T 137 SD 7411
Harwood Beck W 151 NY 8321
Harwood Dale T 149 SE 9695
Harwood Forest F 159 NY 9894
Harworth T 139 SK 6191
Hascombe T 96 SU 9940
Hascosay 205 HU 5592
Hascosay Sound W 205 HU 5492
Haselbech T 119 SP 7177
Haselbury Plucknett T 93 ST 4710
Haseley T 118 SP 2367
Haselor T 118 SP 1257
Hasfield T 114 SO 8227
Hasguard T 110 SM 8509
Haskayne T 136 SD 3508
Haskeir Eagach 188 NF 5980
Haskeir Island 188 NF 6182
Hasketon T 123 TM 2550
Hasland T 139 SK 3969
Haslemere T 95 SU 9032
Haslingden T 146 SD 7823
Haslingden Grane T 146 SD 7522
Haslingfield T 121 TL 4052
Haslington T 127 SJ 7356
Hassall T 137 SJ 7657
Hassall Green T 137 SJ 7858
Hassell Street T 99 TR 0946
Hassendean T 158 NT 5420
Hassingham T 133 TG 3705
Hassocks T 97 TQ 3015
Hassop T 139 SK 2272
Hastigrow T 199 ND 2661
Hastingleigh T 99 TR 0944
Hastings P 98 TQ 8109
Hastingwood T 105 TL 4807
Hastoe T 104 SP 9109
Haswell T 153 NZ 3743
Hatch, Beds T 120 TL 1547
Hatch, Hants T 103 SU 6752
Hatch, Wilts T 93 ST 9228
Hatch Beauchamp T 92 ST 3020
Hatch End T 105 TQ 1391
Hatching Green T 105 TL 1312
Hatchmere T 137 SJ 5571
Hatcliffe T 143 TA 2100
Hatfield, Herts P 105 TL 2208
Hatfield, H. & W T 113 SO 5959
Hatfield, S. Yks T 139 SE 6509
Hatfield Broad Oak T 105 TL 5416
Hatfield Chase 142 SE 7110
Hatfield Heath T 105 TL 5215
Hatfield House A 105 TL 2308
Hatfield Moors 142 SE 7006
Hatfield Peverel T 106 TL 7911
Hatfield Woodhouse T 142 SE 6808
Hatford T 115 SU 3394
Hatherden T 102 SU 3450
Hatherleigh T 91 SS 5404
Hathern T 129 SK 5022
Hatherop T 115 SP 1505
Hathersage T 139 SK 2381
Hatherton, Ches T 127 SJ 6847
Hatherton, Staffs T 128 SJ 9510
Hatley St George T 121 TL 2851
Hatt T 88 SX 3961
Hatterrall Hill H 113 SO 3025
Hattingley T 95 SU 6437
Hatton, Ches T 137 SJ 5982
Hatton, Derby T 128 SK 2130
Hatton, G. Lon T 104 TQ 0975
Hatton, Grampn T 185 NK 0537
Hatton, Lincs T 141 TF 1776
Hatton, Shrops T 116 SO 4690
Hatton, Warw T 118 SP 2467
Hatton Castle 185 NJ 7546
Hattoncrook T 185 NJ 8424
Hatton Heath T 136 SJ 4561
Hatton of Fintray T 185 NJ 8416
Hattons Lodge 102 SU 0688
Haugham T 141 TF 3381
Haugh Head T 165 NU 0026
Haughley T 122 TM 0262
Haughley Green T 122 TM 0364
Haugh of Glass T 184 NJ 4239
Haugh of Urr T 156 NX 8066
Haughs of Cromdale 183 NJ 0927
Haughton, Notts T 139 SK 6772
Haughton, Shrops T 126 SJ 3727
Haughton, Shrops T 127 SJ 5516
Haughton, Shrops T 127 SO 6896
Haughton, Staffs T 127 SJ 8620
Haughton Common 158 NY 8072
Haughton Green T 137 SJ 9393
Haughton Moss T 127 SJ 5756
Haunn 172 NM 3447
Haunton T 128 SK 2310
Hauxley T 159 NU 2703
Hauxley Haven W 159 NU 2802
Hauxton T 121 TL 4352
Havant T 95 SU 7106
Haven T 113 SO 4054
Havengore Island 107 TQ 9789
Havenstreet T 95 SZ 5690
Haven, The W 131 TF 3541
Haverfordwest P 110 SM 9515
Haverhill T 122 TL 6745
Haverigg T 144 SD 1578
Havering-atte-Bower T 105 TQ 5193
Haversham T 120 SP 8242
Haverthwaite T 145 SD 3483
Hawarden T 136 SJ 3165
Hawarden Airport 136 SJ 3565
Hawes T 152 SD 8789
Haweswater Reservoir W 151 NY 4814
Hawford T 117 SO 8460
Hawick, Border T 157 NT 5014
Ha Wick, Orkney W 200 ND 2489
Hawkchurch T 92 ST 3400
Hawkedon T 122 TL 7952
Hawkeridge T 101 ST 8653
Hawkerland T 92 SY 0588
Hawkesbury T 101 ST 7687
Hawkesbury Upton T 101 ST 7887
Hawkes End T 118 SP 2982
Hawkhill T 159 NU 2212
Hawkhope 158 NY 7189
Hawkhurst T 97 TQ 7630
Hawkinge T 99 TR 2140
Hawkley T 95 SU 7429
Hawkridge T 91 SS 8630
Hawkridge Reservoir W 92 ST 2036
Hawkshead T 150 SD 3598
Hawksland T 163 NS 8439
Hawks Ness 203 HU 4648
Hawkswick T 146 SD 9570
Hawksworth, Notts T 129 SK 7543
Hawksworth, W. Yks T 146 SE 1641
Hawkwell T 106 TQ 8491
Hawkwood Hill H 162 NS 6837
Hawley, Hants T 104 SU 8558
Hawley, Kent T 105 TQ 5571
Hawling T 114 SP 0623
Hawnby T 153 SE 5489
Haworth T 146 SE 0337
Haworth Moor 146 SE 0035
Hawsker T 149 NZ 9207
Hawstead T 122 TL 8659
Hawthorn T 153 NZ 4145
Hawthorn Hill T 104 SU 8774
Hawthornthwaite Fell H 145 SD 5751
Hawton T 129 SK 7851
Haxby T 147 SE 6057
Haxey T 142 SK 7699
Haxton Down H 102 SU 2050
Hay Bluff H 113 SO 2436
Haycock H 150 NY 1410
Haydock T 137 SJ 5696
Haydon T 93 ST 6715
Haydon Bridge T 158 NY 8464
Haydon Dean 165 NT 9844
Haydon Wick T 102 SU 1387
Haydown Hill H 102 SU 3156
Haye T 88 SX 3469
Hayes, G. Lon T 104 TQ 0980
Hayes, G. Lon T 105 TQ 4066
Hayfield T 138 SK 0387
Hayhillock 177 NO 5242
Hayle T 86 SW 5637
Hayling Bay W 95 SZ 7198
Hayling Island 95 SU 7201
Haylot Fell 145 SD 5961
Haynes T 120 TL 0942
Haynes Church End T 120 TL 0841
Hay-on-Wye T 113 SO 2342
Hayscastle T 110 SM 8925
Hayscastle Cross T 110 SM 9125
Hay Stacks 150 NY 1913
Hayton, Cumbr T 150 NY 1041
Hayton, Cumbr T 151 NY 5057
Hayton, Humbs T 142 SE 8245
Hayton, Notts T 140 SK 7284
Hayton's Bent T 116 SO 5280
Haytor Vale T 89 SX 7777
Haywards Heath T 97 TQ 3324
Haywood Oaks T 129 SK 6055
Hazelbank T 163 NS 8344
Hazelbury Bryan T 93 ST 7408
Hazeley T 104 SU 7459
Hazel Grove T 137 SJ 9286
Hazelrigg T 165 NU 0533
Hazelslade T 128 SK 0212
Hazelton Walls 171 NO 3322
Hazelwood T 128 SK 3246
Hazlemere T 104 SU 8995
Hazlerigg T 159 NZ 2372
Hazleton T 114 SP 0818
Heacham T 132 TF 6737
Headbourne Worhty T 95 SU 4932
Headcorn T 98 TQ 8344
Headingley T 147 SE 2836
Headington T 115 SP 5407
Headlam T 152 NZ 1818
Headless Cross T 118 SP 0365
Headley, Hants T 103 SU 5162
Headley, Hants T 95 SU 8236
Headley, Surrey T 96 TQ 2054
Head o' da Taing 202 HT 9739
Head of Bratta 205 HU 4799
Head of Brough 205 HU 4484
Head of Garness 185 NJ 7465
Head of Holland 200 HY 4912
Head of Hosta 205 HU 6791
Head of Lambhoga 205 HU 6287
Head of Moclett 200 HY 4949
Head of Muir T 169 NS 8181
Head of Stanshi 204 HU 2180
Head of Work 200 HY 4814
Headon T 140 SK 7477
Heads Nook T 151 NY 4955
Heads of Ayre 161 NS 2818
Heage T 128 SK 3750
Healabhal Bheag H 186 NG 2242
Healabhal Mhòr H 186 NG 2244
Healaugh, N. Yks T 152 SE 0199
Healaugh, N. Yks T 147 SE 5047
Healaval H 186 NG 2464
Heald Green T 137 SJ 8585
Heald Moor 146 SD 8826
Heale 91 SS 6446
Healey, Lancs T 137 SD 8815
Healey, Northum T 159 NZ 0158
Healey, N. Yks T 146 SE 1880
Healeyfield T 152 NZ 0648
Healing T 143 TA 2110
Heamoor T 86 SW 4631
Heanish T 172 NM 0343
Heanor T 128 SK 4346
Heanton Punchardon T 90 SS 5035
Heapham T 140 SK 8788
Hearnish 188 NF 6263
Hearthstane T 163 NT 1126
Heart Law H 164 NT 7166
Heasley Mill T 91 SS 7332
Heast T 180 NG 6417
Heath, Derby T 139 SK 4466
Heath, S. Glam T 109 ST 1779
Heath and Reach T 120 SP 9228
Heathcote T 138 SK 1460
Heath End, Hants T 103 SU 5962
Heath End, Hants T 103 SU 8449
Heather T 128 SK 3810
Heathfield, Devon T 89 SX 8376
Heathfield, E. Susx T 97 TQ 5821
Heathfield, Somer T 92 ST 1626
Heathfield, Strath T 161 NS 3262
Heathfield Moor 146 SE 1167
Heath Hayes T 128 SK 0110
Heath Hill T 127 SJ 7614
Heath House T 100 ST 4146
Heath, The T 133 TG 1821
Heathton T 117 SO 8192
Heatley T 137 SJ 7088
Heaton, Lancs T 145 SD 4460
Heaton, Staffs T 138 SJ 9562
Heaton, T. & W T 159 NZ 2766
Heaton Moor T 137 SJ 8791
Heaval H 178 NL 6799
Heaverham T 105 TQ 5758
Heaviley T 137 SJ 9088
Hebburn T 159 NZ 3164
Hebden T 146 SE 0263
Hebden Bridge T 146 SD 9927
Hebden Green T 137 SJ 6365
Hebden Moor 146 SE 0466
Hebden Water W 146 SD 9631
Hebrides or Western Isles, Highld 178 NG 0239
Hebrides or Western Isles, Strath 178 NG 0239
Hebrides or Western Isles, W. Isles 178 NG 0239
Hebron T 159 NZ 1989
Heckfield T 104 SU 7260
Heckington T 130 TF 1444
Heckmondwike T 146 SE 2123
Hecla H 178 NF 8234
Heddington T 102 ST 9966
Heddle T 200 HY 3512
Heddon-on-the-Wall T 159 NZ 1366
Heddon's Mouth 91 SS 6549
Hedenham T 133 TM 3193
Hedge End T 95 SU 4912
Hedgehope Hill H 158 NT 9419
Hedgerley T 104 SU 9787
Hedging T 92 ST 3029
Hedley on the Hill T 159 NZ 0759
Hednesford T 128 SK 0012
Hedon T 143 TA 1828
Hedsor T 104 SU 9086
Hegdon Hill T 113 SO 5854
Heggerscales T 151 NY 8210
Heglibister T 203 HU 3851
Heighington, Durham T 152 NZ 2422
Heighington, Lincs T 140 TF 0369
Heights of Brae T 182 NH 5161
Heights of Kinlochewe T 191 NH 0764
Heilam 197 NC 4560
Heillia 204 HU 2684
Heishival Mòr H 178 NL 6296
Heisker or Monach Islands 188 NF 6262
Heiskers 178 NL 5886
Heiton T 164 NT 7130
Helbeck T 151 NY 7915
Heldale Water W 200 ND 2592
Heldon Hill 183 NJ 1358
Hele, Devon T 91 SS 5347
Hele, Devon T 91 SS 9902
Helensburgh T 168 NS 2982
Helford T 86 SW 7526
Helford River W 86 SW 7626
Helhoughton T 132 TF 8626
Helions Bumpstead T 122 TL 6541
Hellabrick's Wick W 202 HT 9636
Helland T 87 SX 0770
Hellesdon T 133 TG 2012
Helliar Holm 200 HY 4815
Hellidon T 119 SP 5158
Hellifield T 146 SD 8556
Helli Ness 203 HU 4628
Hellingly T 97 TQ 5912
Hellington T 133 TG 3103
Hellir 205 HU 3892
Hellisay 178 NF 7504
Hellister T 203 HU 3949
Hellmoor Loch W 157 NT 3816
Hell's Glen 168 NN 1706
Hell's Mouth or Porth Neigwl W 124 SH 2626
Helman Head 199 ND 3646
Helmdon T 119 SP 5843
Helmingham T 123 TM 1957
Helmsdale T 193 ND 0215
Helmshore T 146 SD 7821
Helmsley T 147 SE 6183
Helmsley Moor 153 SE 5991
Helperby T 147 SE 4369
Helperthorpe T 149 SE 9570
Helpringham T 130 TF 1340
Helpston T 130 TF 1205
Helsby T 137 SJ 4875
Helston P 86 SW 6527
Helstone T 87 SX 0881
Helton T 151 NY 5122
Helvellyn H 150 NY 3415
Helwick (lightship) 108 SS 3280
Helwith Bridge T 146 SD 8169
Hemblington T 133 TG 3411
Hembury A 92 ST 1103
Hemel Hempstead T 104 TL 0507
Hemingbrough T 147 SE 6730
Hemingby T 141 TF 2374
Hemingford Abbots T 121 TL 2970
Hemingford Grey T 121 TL 2970
Hemingstone T 123 TM 1553
Hemington, Northnts T 120 TL 0985
Hemington, Somer T 101 ST 7253
Hemley T 123 TM 2842
Hempholme T 149 TA 0850
Hempnall T 133 TM 2494
Hempnall Green T 133 TM 2493
Hempriggs T 183 NJ 1064
Hempriggs House 199 ND 3547
Hempstead, Essex T 122 TL 6338
Hempstead, Norf T 133 TG 1037
Hempstead, Norf T 133 TG 4028
Hempsted T 114 SO 8117
Hempton, Norf T 132 TF 9129
Hempton, Oxon T 115 SP 4431
Hemsby T 133 TG 4917
Hemsby Hole W 133 TG 5117
Hemswell T 140 SK 9390
Hemsworth T 139 SE 4213
Hemyock T 92 ST 1313
Henbury, Avon T 101 ST 5678
Henbury, Ches T 137 SJ 8873
Hendersyde Park 164 NT 7435
Hendon, G. Lon T 105 TQ 2389
Hendon, T. & W T 153 NZ 4055
Hendre T 136 SJ 1967
Hendreys Course H 163 NS 9758
Hendy T 111 SN 5803
Heneglwys T 134 SH 4276
Henfield T 96 TQ 2115
Hen Gerrig H 125 SH 9518
Hengistbury Head 94 SZ 1790
Hengoed, M. Glam T 109 ST 1595
Hengoed, Powys T 113 SO 2253
Hengoed, Shrops T 126 SJ 2933
Hengrave T 122 TL 8268
Henham T 121 TL 5428
Henley, Shrops T 116 SO 5476
Henley, Somer T 93 ST 4332
Henley, Suff T 123 TM 1551
Henley, W. Susx T 95 SU 8925
Henley-in-Arden T 118 SP 1566
Henley-on-Thames T 104 SU 7682
Henley Park T 96 SU 9352
Henllan, Clwyd T 135 SJ 0268
Henllan, Dyfed T 111 SN 3540
Henllan Amgoed T 111 SN 1820
Henllys T 113 ST 2694
Henlow T 120 TL 1738
Hennock T 89 SX 8380
Henryd T 135 SH 7774
Henry's Moat T 110 SN 0427
Hensall T 147 SE 5923
Hensbarrow Downs H 87 SW 9957
Henshaw T 158 NY 7664
Henstead T 123 TM 4986
Henstridge T 93 ST 7219
Henstridge Marsh T 93 ST 7420
Henton, Oxon T 104 SP 7602
Henton, Somer T 100 ST 4050
Henwood T 88 SX 2673
Heogan T 203 HU 4743
Heoga Ness 205 HU 5379
Heol Senni T 109 SN 9223
Heol-y-Cyw T 109 SS 9484
Hepburn T 165 NU 0624
Hepple T 159 NT 9800
Hepscott T 159 NZ 2284
Heptonstall T 146 SD 9828
Heptonstall Moor 146 SD 9430
Hepworth, Suff T 122 TL 9874
Hepworth, W. Yks T 138 SE 1606
Herbrandston T 110 SM 8707
Hereford P 113 SO 5140
Hergest T 113 SO 2755
Hergest Ridge, H. & W H 113 SO 2556
Hergest Ridge, Powys H 113 SO 2556
Heriot T 164 NT 3952
Herma Ness 205 HP 6018
Hermaness Hill H 205 HP 6017
Herman Law, Border H 157 NT 2115
Herman Law, D. & G H 157 NT 2115
Hermetray 188 NF 9874
Hermitage, Berks T 103 SU 5173
Hermitage, Border T 157 NY 5095
Hermitage, Dorset T 93 ST 6407
Hermitage, W. Susx T 95 SU 7505
Hermitage, The T 96 TQ 2253
Hermon, Dyfed T 111 SN 2131
Hermon, Dyfed T 111 SN 3630
Hermon, Gwyn T 134 SH 3969
Herne T 99 TR 1865
Herne Bay T 99 TR 1768
Herner T 91 SS 5826
Herne, The 121 TL 2490
Hernhill T 99 TR 0660
Herodsfoot T 87 SX 2160
Herongate T 106 TQ 6391
Heronsgate T 104 TQ 0294
Herra, The 205 HU 4693
Herriard T 103 SU 6645
Herringfleet T 133 TM 4797
Herringswell T 122 TL 7169
Herrington T 153 NZ 3653
Herscha Hill H 177 NO 7380
Hersden T 99 TR 2062
Hersham T 105 TQ 1164
Herstmonceux T 97 TQ 6312
Herston T 200 ND 4191
Herston Head 200 ND 4191
Hertford P 105 TL 3212
Hertford Heath T 105 TL 3511
Hertingfordbury T 105 TL 3012
Hesketh Bank T 145 SD 4423
Hesketh Lane T 145 SD 6141
Hesket Newmarket T 150 NY 3438
Heskin Green T 137 SD 5315
Hesleden T 153 NZ 4438
Hesleyside 158 NY 8183
Heslington T 147 SE 6250
Hessay T 147 SE 5253
Hessenford T 88 SX 3057
Hessett T 122 TL 9361
Hessle T 142 TA 0326
Hestan Island 155 NX 8350
Hest Bank T 145 SD 4766
Hesti Geo 202 HT 9736
Heston T 105 TQ 1277
Heswall T 136 SJ 2782
Hethe T 115 SP 5929
Hethersett T 133 TG 1505
Hethersgill T 157 NY 4767
Hethpool T 165 NT 8928
Hett T 152 NZ 2836
Hetton T 146 SD 9658
Hetton-le-Hole T 153 NZ 3547
Hetty Pegler's Tump A 114 SO 7900
Heugh T 159 NZ 0873
Heugh-head T 184 NJ 3811
Hevdadale Head 204 HU 3089
Heveningham T 123 TM 3372
Hever T 97 TQ 4744
Heversham T 145 SD 4983
Hevingham T 133 TG 1921
Hewelsfield T 113 SO 5602
Hewish, Avon T 100 ST 4064
Hewish, Somer T 93 ST 4208
Hexham P 158 NY 9364
Hexhamshire Common 152 NY 8853
Hextable T 105 TQ 5170
Hexton T 120 TL 1030
Hexworthy T 89 SX 6572
Heybridge, Essex T 106 TL 8508
Heybridge, Essex T 106 TQ 6498
Heybridge Basin T 106 TL 8707
Heybrook Bay T 88 SX 4949
Heydon, Cambs T 121 TL 4340
Heydon, Norf T 133 TG 1127
Heydon Hill H 92 ST 0327
Heydour T 130 TF 0039
Heylipol T 172 NL 9743
Heylor T 204 HU 2881
Heysham T 145 SD 4161
Heysham Lake W 145 SD 3758
Heyshott T 95 SU 8918
Heytesbury T 101 ST 9242
Heythrop T 115 SP 3527
Heywood, G. Man T 137 SD 8510
Heywood, Wilts T 101 ST 8753
Hibaldstow T 142 SE 9702
Hickleton T 139 SE 4805
Hickling, Norf T 133 TG 4124
Hickling, Notts T 129 SK 6928
Hickling Green T 133 TG 4023
Hickling Heath T 133 TG 4022
Hidcote Boyce T 118 SP 1742
High Ackworth T 139 SE 4417
Higham, Derby T 139 SK 3959
Higham, Kent T 98 TQ 7171
Higham, Lancs T 146 SD 8036
Higham, Suff T 122 TL 7465
Higham, Suff T 122 TM 0335
Higham Dykes T 159 NZ 1375
Higham Ferrers T 120 SP 9668
Higham Gobion T 120 TL 1032
Higham on the Hill T 128 SP 3895
Highampton T 90 SS 4804
Higham Wood T 97 TQ 6048
High Banton 169 NS 7480
High Beach T 105 TQ 4097
High Bentham T 145 SD 6669
High Bickington T 91 SS 6020
High Birkwith T 146 SD 8077
High Blantyre T 162 NS 6856
High Bonnybridge T 169 NS 8379
High Borve T 195 NB 4156
High Bradfield T 139 SK 2692
Highbridge, Highld T 174 NN 1981
Highbridge, Somer T 100 ST 3147
Highbrook T 97 TQ 3430
Highburton T 138 SE 1913
Highbury T 101 ST 6949
High Buston T 159 NU 2308
High Callerton T 159 NZ 1670
High Catton T 148 SE 7153
Highclere T 102 SU 4360
Highclere Castle 103 SU 4458
Highcliffe T 94 SZ 2093
High Cogges T 115 SP 3709
High Coniscliffe T 152 NZ 2215
High Cross, Hants T 95 SU 7126
High Cross, Herts T 105 TL 3618
High Cross Bank T 128 SK 2817
High Easter T 106 TL 6214
High Ellington T 146 SE 1983
Higher Ashton T 89 SX 8584
Higher Ballam T 145 SD 3630
High Ercall T 127 SJ 5917
Higher End T 137 SD 5303
Higher Penwortham T 145 SD 5128
Higher Poynton T 137 SJ 9483
Higher Sharpnose Point 90 SS 1914
Higher Tale T 92 ST 0601
Higher Town T 86 SV 9315
Higher Walreddon T 88 SX 4871
Higher Walton, Ches T 137 SJ 5985
Higher Walton, Lancs T 145 SD 5727
Higher Wych T 127 SJ 4943
Highfield, Northum 158 NY 7391
Highfield, Strath T 161 NS 3050
Highfield, T. & W T 159 NZ 1458
Highfields T 121 TL 3558
High Force W 152 NY 8727
High Garrett T 122 TL 7726
High Grange T 152 NZ 1731

Huby Kelly Bray

Huby, N. Yks T 147 SE 2747
Huby, N. Yks T 147 SE 5665
Hucclecote T 114 SO 8717
Hucking T 98 TQ 8458
Hucknall T 129 SK 5349
Huddersfield P 138 SE 1416
Huddington T 117 SO 9457
Hudswell T 152 NZ 1400
Huggate T 149 SE 8855
Hughenden Valley T 104 SU 8696
Hughley T 127 SO 5698
Hugh Town T 86 SV 9010
Huip Ness 201 HY 6430
Huip Sound W 201 HY 6330
Huish, Devon T 91 SS 5311
Huish, Wilts T 102 SU 1463
Huish Champflower T 92 ST 0429
Huish Episcopi T 93 ST 4326
Hulcott T 104 SP 8516
Hule Moss W 164 NT 7149
Hulland T 128 SK 2446
Hulland Ward T 128 SK 2547
Hullavington T 101 ST 8982
Hullbridge T 106 TQ 8194
Hulme End T 138 SK 1059
Hulme Walfield T 137 SJ 8465
Hulne Park 159 NU 1615
Hulne Priory A 159 NU 1615
Hulver Street T 123 TM 4786
Humber (lightship) 143 TA 5813
Humber Bridge Q 142 TA 0224
Humber Court T 113 SO 5356
Humberside Airport 143 TA 0910
Humberston T 143 TA 3005
Humbie T 164 NT 4562
Humbleton, Humbs T 143 TA 2234
Humbleton, Northum T 165 NT 9728
Hume T 164 NT 7041
Humla 179 NG 2000
Humphrey Head Point 145 SD 3973
Humshaugh T 158 NY 9271
Huna T 199 ND 3673
Huncoat T 146 SD 7730
Huncote T 129 SP 5197
Hunda 200 ND 4396
Hundalee T 158 NT 6418
Hunderthwaite T 152 NY 9821
Hunderthwaite Moor 152 NY 9319
Hundleby T 141 TF 3866
Hundleshope Heights H 163 NT 2534
Hundleton T 110 SM 9600
Hundon T 122 TL 7348
Hundred Acres T 95 SU 5911
Hundred End T 145 SD 4122
Hundred Foot Drain or New Bedford River W 121 TL 4987
Hundred Foot Washes, The 121 TL 4988
Hundred House T 112 SO 1154
Hundred Stream W 133 TG 4521
Hundred, The T 116 SO 5264
Huney 205 HP 6506
Hungarton T 129 SK 6907
Hungerford P 102 SU 3368
Hungerford Newtown T 102 SU 3571
Hungry Law, Border H 158 NT 7406
Hungry Law, Northum H 158 NT 7406
Hunmanby T 149 TA 0977
Hunningham T 118 SP 3768
Hunsdon T 105 TL 4114
Hunsingore T 147 SE 4253
Hunsonby T 151 NY 5835
Hunspow T 199 ND 2172
Hunstanton T 132 TF 6741
Hunstanworth T 152 NY 9449
Hunston, Suff T 122 TL 9768
Hunston, W. Susx T 95 SU 8601
Hunstrete T 101 ST 6462
Hunt End T 118 SP 0364
Hunter's Quay T 168 NS 1879
Hunterston House 161 NS 1851
Hunthill Lodge 177 NO 4771
Hunt House 148 SE 8198
Hunthwaite T 139 SK 4659
Huntingdon P 121 TL 2371
Huntingfield T 123 TM 3473
Huntington, H. & W T 113 SO 2553
Huntington, Lothn T 171 NT 4874
Huntington, N. Yks T 147 SE 6256
Huntington, Staffs T 128 SJ 9713
Huntingtower T 170 NO 0625
Hunt Law H 164 NT 5758
Huntley T 114 SO 7219
Huntly T 184 NJ 5340
Hunton, Kent T 97 TQ 7149
Hunton, N. Yks T 152 SE 1892
Hunt's Cross T 136 SJ 4385
Huntsham T 91 ST 0020
Huntspill T 100 ST 3045
Huntspill Level 100 ST 3245
Huntworth T 92 ST 3134
Hunwick T 152 NZ 1832
Hunworth T 132 TG 0735
Hurdsfield T 137 SJ 9274
Hurgin H 116 SO 2379
Hurlers, The A 87 SX 2571
Hurley, Berks T 104 SU 8283
Hurley, Warw T 128 SP 2496
Hurlford T 161 NS 4536
Hurliness T 200 ND 2789
Hurn T 94 SZ 1297
Hursley T 94 SU 4225
Hurst, Berks T 104 SU 7973
Hurst, G. Man T 137 SD 9400
Hurst, N. Yks T 152 NZ 0402
Hurstbourne Priors T 102 SU 4346
Hurstbourne Tarrant T 102 SU 3853
Hurst Castle A 94 SZ 3189
Hurst Green, E. Susx T 97 TQ 7327
Hurst Green, Lancs T 145 SD 6838
Hurst Green, Surrey T 97 TQ 3951
Hurst Moor 152 NZ 0403
Hurstpierpoint T 97 TQ 2816
Hurstwood Resr W 146 SD 8931
Hurt Wood F 96 TQ 0843
Hurworth Burn Reservoir W 153 NZ 4033
Hurworth-on-Tees T 152 NZ 3010
Hury T 152 NY 9519
Hury Resr W 152 NY 9618
Husbands Bosworth T 119 SP 6484
Husborne Crawley T 120 SP 9535
Hushinish T 194 NA 9812
Hushinish Bay W 196 NB 9911
Hushinish Point 194 NA 9811
Husival Mòr H 194 NB 0211
Huskeiran 188 NF 5764
Husthwaite T 147 SE 5174
Hutcherleigh T 89 SX 7850
Huttoft T 141 TF 5176
Hutton, Avon T 100 ST 3558
Hutton, Border T 165 NT 9053
Hutton, Cumbr T 151 NY 4326
Hutton, Essex T 106 TQ 6394
Hutton, Lancs T 145 SD 4926
Hutton, N. Yks T 148 SE 7568
Hutton Bonville T 152 NZ 3300
Hutton Buscel T 149 SE 9784
Hutton Conyers T 147 SE 3273
Hutton Cranswick T 149 TA 0252
Hutton End T 151 NY 4538
Hutton Henry T 153 NZ 4236
Hutton-le-Hole T 148 SE 7090
Hutton Magna T 152 NZ 1212
Hutton Roof, Cumbr T 151 NY 3734
Hutton Roof, Cumbr T 145 SD 5678
Hutton Rudby T 153 NZ 4606
Hutton Sessay T 147 SE 4776
Hutton Wandesley T 147 SE 5050
Huxley T 137 SJ 5161
Huxter, Shetld 202 HU 1757
Huxter, Shetld 203 HU 3950
Huxter, Shetld 203 HU 5662
Huyton-with-Roby T 136 SJ 4391
Hycemoor T 150 SD 0989
Hyde, Glos T 114 SO 8801
Hyde, G. Man T 137 SJ 9494
Hyde, Hants T 94 SU 1612
Hyde Heath T 104 SP 9300
Hyde Park 105 TQ 2780
Hydestile T 96 SU 9740
Hynish T 172 NL 9839
Hynish Bay W 172 NM 0042
Hyssington T 126 SO 3194
Hythe, Hants T 94 SU 4208
Hythe, Kent T 99 TR 1634
Hythe End T 104 TQ 0172
Hythie T 185 NK 0051

I

Iarlshot A 203 HU 3909
Ibberton T 93 ST 7807
Ible T 139 SK 2557
Ibsley T 94 SU 1509
Ibstock T 128 SK 4010
Ibstone T 104 SU 7593
Ibthorpe T 102 SU 3753
Ibworth T 103 SU 5654
Ickburgh T 132 TL 8194
Ickenham T 104 TQ 0786
Ickford T 104 SP 6407
Ickham T 99 TR 2258
Ickleford T 120 TL 1831
Icklesham T 98 TQ 8716
Ickleton T 121 TL 4943
Icklingham T 122 TL 7772
Icknield Way A 121 TL 2836
Ickwell Green T 120 TL 1545
Ickworth House 122 TL 8161
Icomb T 115 SP 2122
Idbury T 115 SP 2320
Iddesleigh T 91 SS 5608
Ide T 89 SX 8990
Ideford T 89 SX 8977
Ide Hill T 97 TQ 4851
Iden T 98 TQ 9123
Iden Green T 98 TQ 8031
Idlicote T 118 SP 2844
Idmiston T 94 SU 2037
Idridgehay T 128 SK 2849
Idrigill T 186 NG 3863
Idrigill Point 186 NG 2536
Idstone T 102 SU 2584
Idvie 177 NO 5347
Ifield T 96 TQ 2537
Ifold T 96 TQ 0231
Iford T 97 TQ 4007
Ifton Heath T 126 SJ 3236
Ightfield T 127 SJ 5938
Ightham T 97 TQ 5956
Iken T 123 TM 4155
Ilam T 128 SK 1350
Ilchester T 93 ST 5222
Ilderton T 165 NU 0121
Ilford T 105 TQ 4586
Ilfracombe T 90 SS 5147
Ilkeston T 129 SK 4642
Ilketshall St Andrew T 123 TM 3787
Ilketshall St Lawrence T 123 TM 3883
Ilketshall St Margaret T 123 TM 3585
Ilkley T 146 SE 1147
Ilkley Moor 146 SE 1146
Illey T 118 SO 9881
Illingworth T 146 SE 0728
Illogan T 86 SW 6643
Illston on the Hill T 129 SP 7099
Ilmer T 104 SP 7605
Ilmington T 118 SP 2143
Ilminster T 92 ST 3514
Ilsington T 89 SX 7876
Ilston T 108 SS 5590
Ilton, N. Yks T 146 SE 1978
Ilton, Somer T 92 ST 3517
Imachar 160 NR 8640
Imber 102 ST 9648
Immingham T 143 TA 1814
Impington T 121 TL 4463
Inbirchworth Reservoir W 138 SE 2105
Ince T 136 SJ 4576
Ince Banks 136 SJ 4578
Ince Blundell T 136 SD 3203
Ince-in-Makerfield T 137 SD 5904
Inchbae Forest 191 NH 3776
Inchbae Lodge 182 NH 4069
Inchbare T 177 NO 6065
Inchberry T 184 NJ 3155
Inchcailloch 169 NS 4190
Inchcolm 170 NT 1882
Incheril T 190 NH 0362
Inchfad 169 NS 4091
Inch Garvie 170 NT 1379
Inchgrundle 176 NO 4179
Inchina T 190 NG 9690
Inchinnan T 169 NS 4769
Inchkeith 171 NT 2982
Inch Kenneth 173 NM 4335
Inchlaggan T 174 NH 1701
Inchlonaig 169 NS 3893
Inchmarnock 160 NS 0259
Inchmickery 171 NT 2080
Inchmore T 182 NH 3940
Inchmurrin 169 NS 3887
Inchnacardoch Forest 182 NH 3309
Inchnadamph T 196 NC 2521
Inchnadamph Forest 196 NC 2821
Inchnadamph National Nature Reserve 196 NC 2619
Inchture T 171 NO 2828
Inchyra 170 NO 1820
Indian Queens T 87 SW 9159
Inerval 166 NR 3242
Ingale Skerry 201 HY 6719
Inga Ness 200 HY 4143
Inganess Bay W 200 HY 4810
Ingatestone T 106 TQ 6499
Ingbirchworth T 139 SE 2206
Ingestre T 128 SJ 9724
Ingham, Lincs T 140 SK 9483
Ingham, Norf T 133 TG 3925
Ingham, Suff T 122 TL 8570
Ingleborough H 145 SD 7474
Ingleby Arncliffe T 153 NZ 4400
Ingleby Greenhow T 153 NZ 5806
Inglesbatch T 101 ST 7061
Inglesham T 115 SU 2098
Ingleton, Durham T 152 NZ 1720
Ingleton, N. Yks T 145 SD 6973
Inglewhite T 145 SD 5440
Inglewood Forest 151 NY 4639
Ingliston T 170 NT 1472
Ingmire Hall 151 SD 6391
Ingoe T 159 NZ 0374
Ingoldisthorpe T 132 TF 6832
Ingoldmells T 141 TF 5668
Ingoldmells Point 141 TF 5768
Ingoldsby T 130 TF 0130
Ingram T 159 NU 0116
Ingrave T 106 TQ 6292
Ings T 151 SD 4498
Ingst T 101 ST 5887
Ingtham Mote A 97 TQ 5853
Ingworth T 133 TG 1929
Inishail 168 NN 1024
Inkberrow T 118 SP 0157
Inkhorn T 185 NJ 9239
Inkpen T 102 SU 3764
Inkstack T 199 ND 2570
Innellan T 168 NS 1470
Innerdouny Hill H 170 NO 0307
Innerhadden 175 NN 6757
Innerhadden Burn W 175 NN 6756
Inner Hebrides, Highld 179 NM 1288
Inner Hebrides, Strath 179 NM 1288
Innerleithen T 164 NT 3336
Innerleven T 171 NO 3700
Innermessan T 154 NX 0863
Inner Sound W 190 NG 6443
Inner Sound W 165 NU 2035
Innerwell Port W 155 NX 4849
Innerwick, Lothn T 164 NT 7274
Innerwick, Tays T 175 NN 5847
Inninmore Bay W 173 NM 7241
Innis Chonain 168 NN 1025
Inns Holm 203 HU 3620
Innsworth T 114 SO 8621
Insch T 184 NJ 6328
Insh T 175 NH 8101
Insh Island 173 NM 7319
Inshore 196 NC 3262
Inshriach Forest F 175 NH 8302
Inskip T 145 SD 4638
Instow T 90 SS 4730
Inver, Grampn T 176 NO 2393
Inver, Highld T 193 NH 8682
Inver, Tays 176 NO 0142
Inverailort T 180 NM 7681
Inveralligin T 190 NG 8457
Inverallochy T 185 NK 0465
Inveramsay T 185 NJ 7424
Inveran T 192 NH 5797
Inveraray T 168 NN 0908
Inverarish T 180 NG 5535
Inverarity T 176 NO 4544
Inverarnan T 168 NN 3118
Inverasdale T 190 NG 8286
Inverbervie T 177 NO 8272
Inverbroom Lodge 191 NH 1883
Inverbrough T 183 NH 8130
Invercauld House 176 NO 1792
Inverchaolain Glen 168 NS 1076
Invercharnan 174 NN 1448
Invercharron House 192 NH 5991
Inverchoran T 182 NH 2650
Inver Cottage 166 NR 4471
Invercreran T 174 NN 0147
Inver Dalavil W 180 NG 5705
Inverdruie T 183 NH 9011
Inverebrie T 185 NJ 9233
Invererman House 184 NJ 3211
Invereshie House 183 NH 8405
Inveresk T 171 NT 3472
Inverey T 176 NO 0889
Inverfarigaig T 182 NH 5224
Invergarry T 174 NH 3001
Invergeldie 169 NN 7427
Invergeldie Burn W 169 NN 7529
Inverghiusachan Point 174 NN 0940
Invergloy House 174 NN 2288
Invergordon T 183 NH 7068
Invergowrie T 171 NO 3430
Inverguhomery T 185 NK 0246
Inverguseran T 180 NG 7407
Inverharroch T 184 NJ 3831
Inverie T 180 NM 7699
Inverie Bay W 180 NM 7699
Inverinan 168 NM 9917
Inverinate T 180 NG 9122
Inverinate Forest 180 NG 9825
Inverkeilor T 177 NO 6649
Inverkeithing T 170 NT 1383
Inverkeithing Bay W 170 NT 1481
Inverkeithny T 184 NJ 6247
Inverkip T 168 NS 2072
Inverkirkaig T 196 NC 0819
Inverlael 191 NH 1885
Inverlael Forest 191 NH 2286
Inverliever Forest F 168 NM 9404
Inverliever Lodge 168 NM 8905
Inverlochlarig 169 NN 4318
Inverlochy Castle 174 NN 1476
Inver Mallie 174 NN 1388
Invermark Lodge 176 NO 4380
Invermoidart T 173 NM 6673
Invermoriston T 182 NH 4216
Invernaver T 197 NC 7060
Inverneill 167 NR 8481
Inverness (Dalcross) Airport 183 NH 7752
Inverness P 183 NH 6645
Invernoaden 168 NS 1297
Inveroran Hotel 174 NN 2741
Inverpattack Lodge 175 NN 5590
Inverpolly Forest 196 NC 1111
Inverpolly Lodge 196 NC 0714
Inverpolly National Nature Reserve 196 NC 1412
Inverquharity 176 NO 4057
Inverroy T 174 NN 2581
Inversanda Bay W 174 NM 9459
Inverscaddle Bay W 174 NN 0268
Invershin T 192 NH 5796
Inversnaid Hotel 168 NN 3308
Inverugie T 185 NK 1048
Inveruglas T 168 NN 3109
Inveruglas Water W 168 NN 2910
Inverurie T 185 NJ 7721
Invervar T 175 NN 6648
Inverwick Forest 182 NH 3413
Inwardleigh T 89 SX 5699
Inworth T 106 TL 8817
Inzie Head 185 NK 0662
Iona 172 NM 2724
Iorcail 179 NG 2606
Iping T 95 SU 8522
Ipplepen T 89 SX 8366
Ipsden T 104 SU 6385
Ipstones T 128 SK 0250
Ipswich P 123 TM 1644
Irby T 136 SJ 2584
Irby in the Marsh T 141 TF 4763
Irby upon Humber T 143 TA 1904
Irchester T 120 SP 9265
Ireby, Cumbr T 150 NY 2339
Ireby, Lancs T 145 SD 6575
Ireland, Orkney T 200 HY 3009
Ireland, Shetld T 203 HU 3722
Ireleth T 144 SD 2277
Ireshopeburn T 152 NY 8638
Ireshope Moor 151 NY 8436
Irfon W 112 SN 9649
Irish Law H 161 NS 2659
Irlam T 137 SJ 7294
Irnham T 130 TF 0226
Iron Acton T 101 ST 6883
Iron-Bridge T 127 SJ 6703
Iron Cross T 118 SP 0652
Ironmacannie T 156 NX 6675
Ironside T 185 NJ 8852
Ironville T 128 SK 4351
Irstead T 133 TG 3620
Irthington T 157 NY 4961
Irthlingborough T 120 SP 9470
Irton T 149 TA 0084
Irvine P 161 NS 3238
Irvine Bay W 161 NS 3038
Isauld T 198 NC 9765
Isay, Highld 186 NG 2157
Isay, W. Isles 189 NB 1002
Isbister, Orkney T 200 HY 2623
Isbister, Orkney T 200 HY 3918
Isbister, Shetld 205 HU 3791
Isbister, Shetld T 203 HU 5764
Isca R 89 SX 9292
Isca Roman Fort R 100 ST 3391
Isfield T 97 TQ 4517
Isham T 120 SP 8874
Islan Davaar 160 NR 7620
Island Macaskin 167 NR 7899
Island of Arran 160 NR 9536
Island of Bute 160 NS 0664
Island of Danna 167 NR 6978
Island of Mull 173 NM 6235
Island of Raasay W 190 NG 6257
Island of Rona W 190 NG 6257
Island of Skye 187 NG 4333
Island of Stroma 199 ND 3577
Islands of Fleet 155 NX 5749
Islawr-dref 125 SH 6815
Islay (Port Ellen) Airport 166 NR 3251
Islay 166 NR 3964
Islay House 166 NR 3362
Isle Abbotts T 92 ST 3520
Isle Brewers T 92 ST 3621
Isleham T 122 TL 6474
Isleham Fen 122 TL 6276
Isle Martin 191 NH 0999
Isle of Axholme 142 SE 7806
Isle of Dogs 105 TQ 3778
Isle of Ewe 190 NG 8588
Isle of Fethaland 205 HU 3794
Isle of Grain 98 TQ 8776
Isle of Harty 99 TR 0267
Isle of Lewis 195 NB 3138
Isle of Man (Ronaldsway) Airport 144 SC 2868
Isle of Man 144 SC 3281
Isle of May 171 NT 6599
Isle of Nibon 204 HU 3073
Isle of Noss 203 HU 5440
Isle of Oxney 98 TQ 9127
Isle of Portland 93 SY 6971
Isle of Purbeck 93 SY 9581
Isle of Sheppey 99 TQ 9769
Isle of Stenness 204 HU 2076
Isle of Thanet 99 TR 3267
Isle of Walney 144 SD 1768
Isle of West Burrafirth 202 HU 2558
Isle of Whithorn T 155 NX 4736
Isle of Wight 95 SZ 4985
Isleornsay or Eilean Iarmain T 180 NG 6912
Isle Ristol 196 NB 9711
Islesburgh T 204 HU 3369
Isles of Scilly 86 SV 8912
Isleworth T 105 TQ 1675
Isley Watton T 128 SK 4225
Islington T 105 TQ 3085
Islip, Northnts T 120 SP 9878
Islip, Oxon T 115 SP 5214
Islivig T 194 NA 9927
Istead Rise T 98 TQ 6369
Isurium A 147 SE 4066
Isycoed T 126 SJ 4050
Itchen Abbas T 95 SU 5333
Itchen Stoke T 95 SU 5632
Itchingfield T 96 TQ 1328
Itchington T 101 ST 6587
Itteringham T 133 TG 1430
Itton T 89 SX 6899
Itton Common T 113 ST 4896
Ivegill T 151 NY 4143
Ivelet T 152 SD 9398
Iver T 104 TQ 0381
Iver Heath T 104 TQ 0282
Iveston T 152 NZ 1350
Ivinghoe T 104 SP 9416
Ivinghoe Aston T 104 SP 9518
Ivington T 113 SO 4756
Ivington Green T 113 SO 4656
Ivybridge T 89 SX 6356
Ivychurch T 99 TR 0227
Ivy Hatch T 97 TQ 5854
Iwade T 98 TQ 8967
Iwerne Courtney or Shroton T 93 ST 8512
Iwerne Minster T 93 ST 8614
Ixworth T 122 TL 9370
Ixworth Thorpe T 122 TL 9172

J

Jack Hill T 146 SE 2051
Jackstown T 185 NJ 7531
Jackton T 162 NS 5953
Jacobstow T 88 SX 1995
Jacobstowe T 91 SS 5801
Jameston T 110 SS 0599
Jamestown, D. & G T 157 NY 2996
Jamestown, Highld T 182 NH 4756
Jamestown, Strath T 169 NS 3981
Jamieson's Point 154 NX 0371
Jarlshof A 203 HU 4039
Jarrow T 159 NZ 3265
Jawcraig T 170 NS 8575
Jaw Reservoir W 169 NS 4975
Jayes Park T 96 TQ 1440
Jaywick T 107 TM 1513
Jedburgh P 158 NT 6520
Jed Water W 158 NT 6710
Jeffreyston T 110 SN 0806
Jemimaville T 183 NH 7265
Jervaulx Abbey A 146 SE 1785
Jevington T 97 TQ 5601
Johnby T 151 NY 4333
John o' Groats T 199 ND 3872
Johnshaven T 177 NO 7967
Johnston T 110 SM 9310
Johnstone T 161 NS 4363
Johnstonebridge T 157 NY 1092
Johnston's Point 160 NR 7613
Jordans T 104 SU 9791
Jordanston T 110 SM 9132
Jumbles Reservoir W 136 SD 2314
Jump T 139 SE 3801
Juniper Green T 163 NT 1968
Jura 166 NR 5683
Jura Forest 166 NR 5072
Jura House 166 NR 4863
Jurby East T 144 SC 3899
Jurby Head 144 SC 3498
Jurby West T 144 SC 3598

K

Kaber T 151 NY 7911
Kaim Dam W 161 NS 3462
Kaimes T 163 NT 2768
Kaim Hill H 161 NS 2253
Kale Water W 164 NT 7326
Kalnakill T 190 NG 6954
Kame of Corrigall H 200 HY 3320
Kame of Flouravoug 205 HP 5916
Kame of Hoy 200 HY 1904
Kame of Sandwick H 205 HU 4787
Kames, Strath T 168 NR 9771
Kames, Strath T 162 NS 6926
Kames Bay W 160 NS 0767
Kame, The 202 HT 9340
Kea T 87 SW 8142
Keadby T 142 SE 8311
Keal T 141 TF 3763
Keal Cotes T 141 TF 3661
Kearsley T 137 SD 7505
Kearstay 194 NA 9617
Kearstwick T 145 SD 6080
Kearton T 152 SD 9999
Kearvaig 196 NC 2972
Kearvaig River W 196 NC 2970
Keasden T 145 SD 7266
Keava 195 NB 1935
Kebister Ness 203 HU 4746
Kebock Head 195 NB 4214
Keddington T 141 TF 3488
Kedington T 122 TL 7046
Kedleston T 128 SK 3041
Keelby T 143 TA 1609
Keele T 127 SJ 8045
Keeley Green T 120 TL 0046
Keelylang Hill H 200 HY 3710
Keen, The 203 HU 5057
Keeston T 110 SM 9019
Keevil T 101 ST 9258
Kegworth T 129 SK 4826
Kehelland T 86 SW 6241
Keig T 184 NJ 6119
Keighley T 146 SE 0540
Keighley Moor 146 SE 0039
Keilarsbrae T 170 NS 8993
Keilhill T 185 NJ 7159
Keillmore T 167 NR 6880
Keillor T 176 NO 2640
Keillour 170 NN 9725
Keillour Forest 170 NN 9623
Keills T 166 NR 4168
Keills Cross A 167 NR 6980
Keil Point 160 NR 6707
Keils T 166 NR 5268
Keinton Mandeville T 93 ST 5430
Keir Hills H 156 NX 8491
Keir Mill T 156 NX 8593
Keisby T 130 TF 0328
Keiss T 199 ND 3461
Keith T 184 NJ 4350
Keith Hall A 185 NJ 7821
Keithock T 177 NO 6063
Kelbrook T 146 SD 9044
Kelburn A 161 NS 2156
Kelby T 130 TF 0041
Keld, Cumbr T 151 NY 5514
Keld, N. Yks T 152 NY 8901
Keldholme T 148 SE 7086
Keld, The W 201 HY 6033
Keldy Castle 148 SE 7791
Kelfield T 147 SE 5938
Kelham T 129 SK 7755
Kelk Beck W 149 TA 0957
Kellan T 173 NM 5240
Kellas, Grampn T 184 NJ 1754
Kellas, Tays T 171 NO 4535
Kellaton T 89 SX 8039
Kelleth T 151 NY 6605
Kellie Castle A 177 NO 6040
Kellie Law H 171 NO 5106
Kelling T 133 TG 0942
Kellington T 147 SE 5524
Kelloe T 153 NZ 3436
Kello Water W 156 NS 6708
Kelly T 88 SX 3981
Kelly Bray T 88 SX 3571

Kelmarsh Kirkmichael

Kelmarsh T 119 SP 7379
Kelmscot T 115 SU 2599
Kelsale T 123 TM 3865
Kelsall T 137 SJ 5268
Kelsey Head 86 SW 7660
Kelshall T 121 TL 3435
Kelso T 164 NT 7234
Kelston T 101 ST 7067
Keltie Water W 169 NN 6310
Keltney Burn, Tays W 175 NN 7650
Keltneyburn, Tays T 175 NN 7749
Kelton T 152 NY 9220
Kelton Hill or Rhonehouse T
156 NX 7459
Kelty T 170 NT 1394
Kelty Water W 169 NS 5095
Kelvedon T 106 TL 8618
Kelvedon Hatch T 105 TQ 5798
Kelynack T 86 SW 3729
Kemacott T 91 SS 6647
Kemback T 171 NO 4115
Kemberton T 127 SJ 7304
Kemble T 114 ST 9897
Kemerton T 117 SO 9437
Kemeys Commander T 113 SO 3504
Kemnay T 185 NJ 7316
Kempley T 114 SO 6729
Kempock Point 168 NS 2477
Kempsey T 117 SO 8549
Kempsford T 115 SU 1597
Kempston T 120 TL 0347
Kempston Hardwick T 120 TL 0344
Kempton T 116 SO 3683
Kemp Town T 97 TQ 3203
Kemsing T 105 TQ 5458
Kenardington T 99 TQ 9732
Kenchester T 113 SO 4442
Kencot T 115 SP 2504
Kendal P 151 SD 5192
Kendoon Loch W 156 NX 6190
Kenfig T 109 SS 8081
Kenfig Burrows 109 SS 7982
Kenfig Hill T 109 SS 8483
Kengharair Farm 173 NM 4348
Kenilworth T 118 SP 2972
Kenknock 175 NN 4636
Kenley, G. Lon T 105 TQ 3259
Kenley, Shrops T 127 SJ 5600
Kenmore, Highld T 190 NG 7557
Kenmore, Tays T 175 NN 7745
Kenmure Castle A 156 NX 6376
Kenn, Avon T 100 ST 4169
Kenn, Devon T 89 SX 9285
Kennacraig 160 NR 8262
Kennedy's Pass 154 NX 1593
Kennerleigh T 91 SS 8107
Kennet T 170 NS 9291
Kennet and Avon Canal, Wilts W 101 ST 8761
Kennet and Avon Canal, Wilts W 102 SU 2363
Kennethmont T 184 NJ 5429
Kennett T 122 TL 7068
Kennford T 89 SX 9186
Kennick Reservoir W 89 SX 8084
Kenninghall T 122 TM 0386
Kennington, Kent T 99 TR 0242
Kennington, Oxon T 115 SP 5202
Kennoway T 171 NO 3502
Kenny Hill T 122 TL 6679
Kennythorpe T 148 SE 7865
Kenovdy T 172 NL 9946
Kensaleyre T 187 NG 4251
Kensington T 105 TQ 2579
Kensworth T 104 TL 0218
Kentallen 174 NN 0057
Kentchurch T 113 SO 4125
Kentchurch Court A 113 SO 4225
Kentford T 122 TL 7166
Kentisbeare T 92 ST 0608
Kentisbury T 91 SS 6243
Kentmere T 151 NY 4504
Kentmere Reservoir W 151 NY 4408
Kenton, Devon T 89 SX 9583
Kenton, G. Lon T 105 TQ 1788
Kenton, Suff T 123 TM 1966
Kentra T 173 NM 6569
Kentra Bay W 173 NM 6469
Kents Bank T 145 SD 3976
Kent's Green T 114 SO 7423
Kent's Oak T 94 SU 3224
Kentwell Hall A 122 TL 8647
Kenwick T 126 SJ 4230
Kenwyn T 87 SW 8245
Kenyon T 137 SJ 6295
Keoldale T 196 NC 3866
Keose T 195 NB 3521
Keppanach 174 NN 0262
Keppoch T 180 NG 8924
Kepwick T 153 SE 4690
Keresley T 118 SP 3284
Kerloch H 177 NO 6987
Kerne Bridge T 113 SO 5819
Kerran Hill H 160 NR 7313
Kerrera 173 NM 8128
Kerridge T 137 SJ 9377
Kerris T 86 SW 4427
Kerry T 116 SO 1490
Kerrycroy T 161 NS 1061
Kerry Hill H 116 SO 1385
Kerrysdale T 190 NG 8273
Kerry's Gate T 113 SO 3933
Kersall T 140 SK 7162
Kersey T 122 TM 0044
Kershader T 195 NB 3420
Kershope Burn, Border W
158 NY 5285
Kershope Burn, Cumbr W
158 NY 5285
Kershopefoot T 157 NY 4782
Kershope Forest F 158 NY 5181
Kersoe T 118 SO 9940
Kerswell T 92 ST 0706
Kerswell Green T 117 SO 8646
Kesgrave T 123 TM 2145
Kessingland T 123 TM 5386
Kestle Mill T 87 SW 8459
Keston T 105 TQ 4164
Keswick, Cumbr T 150 NY 2623
Keswick, Norf T 133 TG 2004
Keswick, Norf T 133 TG 3533
Ketligill Head 204 HU 2784
Kettering P 120 SP 8678
Ketteringham T 133 TG 1602
Kettins T 176 NO 2339
Kettla Ness 203 HU 3428
Kettlebaston T 122 TL 9650
Kettlebridge 171 NO 3007
Kettlebrook T 128 SK 2103
Kettleburgh T 123 TM 2660
Kettleness T 153 NZ 8315
Kettleshulme T 138 SJ 9879
Kettlesing Bottom T 147 SE 2257
Kettlestone T 132 TF 9631
Kettlethorpe T 140 SK 8475
Kettletoft T 201 HY 6538
Kettletoft Bay W 201 HY 6638
Kettlewell T 146 SD 9772
Ketton T 130 SK 9804
Kew T 105 TQ 1877
Kewstoke T 100 ST 3363
Kex Beck W 146 SE 0953
Kexbrough T 139 SE 3009
Kexby, Lincs T 140 SK 8785
Kexby, N. Yks T 148 SE 7051
Kexwith Moor 152 NZ 0305
Key Green T 137 SJ 8963
Keyham T 129 SK 6706
Keyhaven T 94 SZ 3090
Keyingham T 143 TA 2425
Keymer T 97 TQ 3115
Keynsham T 101 ST 6568
Keysley Down H 93 ST 8634
Keysoe T 120 TL 0762
Keysoe Row T 120 TL 0861
Keyston T 120 TL 0475
Keyworth T 129 SK 6130
Kibblesworth T 152 NZ 2456
Kibworth Beauchamp T 129 SP 6893
Kibworth Harcourt T 129 SP 6894
Kidbrooke T 105 TQ 4076
Kiddemore Green T 127 SJ 8508
Kidderminster P 117 SO 8376
Kiddington T 115 SP 4122
Kidlington T 115 SP 4913
Kidmore End T 104 SU 6979
Kidsgrove T 127 SJ 8354
Kidstones T 146 SD 9581
Kidwelly T 111 SN 4106
Kielder T 158 NY 6293
Kielder Burn W 158 NY 6596
Kielder Castle 158 NY 6393
Kielder Forest F 158 NY 6691
Kielderhead Moor 158 NT 6800
Kielder Water W 158 NY 6788
Kiells T 166 NR 4168
Kierfea Hill H 200 HY 4232
Kierfield House 200 HY 2418
Kiessimul Castle A 178 NL 6697
Kilbarchan T 161 NS 4063
Kilbeg T 180 NG 6406
Kilberry T 160 NR 7164
Kilberry Head 160 NR 7064
Kilbirnie T 161 NS 3154
Kilbirnie Loch W 161 NS 3354
Kilblaan Burn W 168 NN 1513
Kilbrannan Sound W 160 NR 8340
Kilbraur Hill H 193 NC 8208
Kilbride, Highld T 180 NG 5820
Kilbride, Strath T 168 NM 8525
Kilbride, W. Isles T 178 NF 7614
Kilbride Bay W 160 NR 9666
Kilbride Point 186 NG 3766
Kilbryde Castle 169 NN 7503
Kilburn, Derby T 128 SK 3845
Kilburn, N. Yks T 147 SE 5179
Kilby T 129 SP 6295
Kilchamaig 160 NR 8061
Kilchattan, Strath T 166 NR 3695
Kilchattan, Strath T 161 NS 1054
Kilchattan Bay W 161 NS 1055
Kilchenzie T 160 NR 6725
Kilcheran 173 NM 8238
Kilchiaran T 166 NR 2060
Kilchiaran Bay W 166 NR 1960
Kilchoan T 173 NM 4863
Kilchoan Bay W 173 NM 4863
Kilchoman T 166 NR 2163
Kilchrenan T 168 NN 0322
Kilchurn Castle A 168 NN 1327
Kilconquhar Loch W 171 NO 4801
Kilconquhar T 171 NO 4802
Kilcot T 114 SO 6925
Kilcoy T 182 NH 5751
Kilcreggon T 168 NS 2380
Kildale T 153 NZ 6009
Kildalloig T 160 NR 7518
Kildalton Cross A 166 NR 4550
Kildalton House 166 NR 4347
Kildary T 193 NH 7675
Kildavanan 160 NS 0266
Kildermorie Forest 192 NH 4678
Kildermorie Lodge 192 NH 5078
Kildonan T 160 NS 0321
Kildonan Burn W 198 NC 9224
Kildonan Lodge 193 NC 9022
Kildonnan T 179 NM 4885
Kildrummy T 184 NJ 4717
Kildwick T 146 SE 0146
Kilennan River W 166 NR 3858
Kilfinan T 168 NR 9378
Kilfinan Bay W 168 NR 9178
Kilfinichen Bay W 173 NM 4928
Kilfinnan T 174 NN 2795
Kilgetty T 110 SN 1207
Kilgwrrwg Common T 113 ST 4798
Kilham, Humbs T 149 TA 0664
Kilham, Northum T 165 NT 8832
Kili Holm 200 HY 4732
Kilkenneth T 172 NL 9444
Kilkerran 161 NS 3002
Kilkhampton T 90 SS 2511
Killamarsh T 139 SK 4580
Killay T 108 SS 6093
Killchianaig T 167 NR 6486
Killean T 160 NR 6944
Killearn T 169 NS 5286
Killegray 188 NF 9783
Killen T 183 NH 6758
Killerby T 152 NZ 1919
Killichonan T 175 NN 5458
Killichonan Burn W 175 NN 5660
Killiechonate T 174 NN 2481
Killiechonate Forest 174 NN 2173
Killiechronan T 173 NM 5441
Killiecrankie T 175 NN 9162
Killiemor T 173 NM 4839
Killilan T 180 NG 9430
Killilan Forest 180 NH 0231
Killimster T 199 ND 3156
Killin T 169 NN 5732
Killinallan 166 NR 3171
Killinghall T 147 SE 2858
Killingholme T 143 TA 1416
Killington T 145 SD 6188
Killington Reservoir W 151 SD 5991
Killin Lodge 182 NH 5209
Killochan Castle A 154 NS 2200
Killochyett T 164 NT 4545
Killocraw 160 NR 6628
Killundine T 173 NM 5849
Kilmacolm T 161 NS 3865
Kilmahumaig T 167 NR 7893
Kilmalieu 173 NM 8955
Kilmaluag T 187 NG 4274
Kilmaluag Bay W 187 NG 4475
Kilmannan Reservoir, Central W 169 NS 4978
Kilmannan Reservoir, Strath W 169 NS 4978
Kilmany T 171 NO 3821
Kilmarie T 187 NG 5417
Kilmarnock P 161 NS 4238
Kilmaron Castle 171 NO 3516
Kilmartin T 167 NR 8398
Kilmar Tor 87 SX 2574
Kilmaurs T 161 NS 4141
Kilmein Hill H 161 NS 4511
Kilmelford T 173 NM 8413
Kilmeny T 166 NR 3965
Kilmersdon T 101 ST 6952
Kilmeston T 95 SU 5926
Kilmichael Glassary T 168 NR 8593
Kilmichael of Inverlussa T
167 NR 7785
Kilmington, Devon T 92 SY 2798
Kilmington, Wilts T 93 ST 7736
Kilmonivaig T 174 NN 1783
Kilmorack T 182 NH 4944
Kilmore, Highld T 180 NG 6507
Kilmore, Strath 168 NM 8824
Kilmory, Highld 179 NG 3503
Kilmory, Highld T 173 NM 5270
Kilmory, Strath T 167 NR 7075
Kilmory, Strath T 160 NR 9621
Kilmory Bay W 167 NR 6974
Kilmory Castle 168 NR 8786
Kilmory Glen 179 NG 3602
Kilmory Lodge 167 NM 7105
Kilmory Water W 160 NR 9723
Kilmuir, Highld T 186 NG 2547
Kilmuir, Highld T 186 NG 3870
Kilmuir, Highld T 183 NH 6749
Kilmuir, Highld T 193 NH 7573
Kilnave T 166 NR 2871
Kilncadzow T 163 NS 8848
Kilndown T 97 TQ 7035
Kilnhurst T 139 SK 4597
Kilninian T 172 NM 4046
Kilninver T 173 NM 8221
Kiln Pit Hill T 152 NZ 0355
Kilnsea T 143 TA 4015
Kilnsey T 146 SD 9767
Kilnwick T 149 SE 9949
Kiloran T 166 NR 3996
Kiloran Bay W 166 NR 4098
Kilpatrick T 160 NR 9027
Kilpatrick Hills H 169 NS 4776
Kilpeck T 113 SO 4430
Kilpheder T 178 NF 7419
Kilphedir T 193 NC 9818
Kilpin T 142 SE 7727
Kilravock Castle 183 NH 8149
Kilrenny T 171 NO 5704
Kilsby T 119 SP 5671
Kilspindie T 171 NO 2225
Kilstay Bay W 154 NX 1338
Kilsyth T 169 NS 7177
Kilsyth Hills H 169 NS 6980
Kiltarlity T 182 NH 5041
Kilton T 100 ST 1643
Kilt Rock 187 NG 5066
Kilvaxter T 186 NG 3869
Kilve T 100 ST 1442
Kilvington T 129 SK 8043
Kilwinning T 161 NS 3043
Kimberley, Norf T 132 TG 0704
Kimberley, Notts T 129 SK 5044
Kimberley House 133 TG 0904
Kimble T 104 SP 8206
Kimblesworth T 152 NZ 2547
Kimble Wick T 104 SP 8007
Kimbolton, Cambs T 120 TL 0967
Kimbolton, H. & W T 116 SO 5261
Kimcote T 119 SP 5586
Kimmeridge T 93 SY 9179
Kimmerston T 165 NT 9535
Kimpton, Herts T 105 TL 1718
Kimpton, Wilts T 102 SU 2846
Kinbrace T 198 NC 8631
Kinbrace Burn W 198 NC 9029
Kinbuck T 169 NN 7905
Kincaple T 171 NO 4618
Kincardine, Fife T 170 NS 9387
Kincardine, Highld T 192 NH 6089
Kincardine Castle 170 NN 9411
Kincardine O'Neil T 177 NO 5999
Kinclaven 176 NO 1538
Kincorth T 185 NJ 9303
Kincorth House 183 NJ 0161
Kincraig T 183 NH 8305
Kincraigie 176 NN 9849
Kindallachan 176 NN 9949
Kinder Reservoir W 138 SK 0588
Kinder Scout H 138 SK 0988
Kineton, Glos T 114 SP 0926
Kineton, Warw T 118 SP 3351
Kinfauns T 170 NO 1622
Kingairloch 173 NM 8352
Kingairloch House 173 NM 8353
Kingarth T 161 NS 0956
Kingcoed T 113 SO 4305
Kingerby T 142 TA 0319
Kingham T 115 SP 2624
Kingholm Quay T 156 NX 9773
Kinghorn T 171 NT 2787
Kinglassie T 171 NT 2398
Kingoodie T 171 NO 3329
King Orry's Grave A 144 SC 4484
King's Acre T 113 SO 4741
Kingsand T 88 SX 4350
Kingsbarns T 171 NO 5912
Kingsbridge, Devon T 89 SX 7344
Kingsbridge, Somer T 91 SS 9837
King's Bromley T 128 SK 1216
Kingsburgh T 187 NG 3955
Kingsbury, G. Lon T 105 TQ 1989
Kingsbury, Warw T 128 SP 2196
Kingsbury Episcopi T 93 ST 4321
King's Caple T 113 SO 5629
King's Cave 160 NR 8371
Kingsclere T 103 SU 5258
King's Cliffe T 130 TL 0097
Kingscote T 101 ST 8190
Kingscott T 91 SS 5318
King's Coughton T 118 SP 0859
Kingscross T 160 NS 0428
Kingscross Point 160 NS 0528
King's Cross Station 105 TQ 3083
King's Delph 131 TL 2495
Kingsdon T 93 ST 5126
Kingsdown T 99 TR 3748
Kingseat T 170 NT 1290
Kingsey T 104 SP 7406
Kingsfold T 96 TQ 1636
Kingsford T 117 SO 8281
King's Forest of Geltsdale
151 NY 6053
Kingshall Street T 122 TL 9161
King's Heath T 118 SP 0781
Kingshouse 169 NN 5620
Kingskerswell T 89 SX 8868
Kingskettle T 171 NO 3008
Kingsland T 116 SO 4461
Kings Langley T 104 TL 0702
Kingsley, Ches T 137 SJ 5574
Kingsley, Hants T 103 SU 7838
Kingsley, Staffs T 128 SK 0147
Kingsley Green T 95 SU 8930
King's Lynn P 132 TF 6119
King's Meaburn T 151 NY 6221
Kings Muir, Border T 163 NT 2539
Kingsmuir, Tays T 177 NO 4749
Kingsnorth, Kent T 98 TQ 8072
Kingsnorth, Kent T 99 TR 0039
King's Norton, Leic T 129 SK 6800
King's Norton, W. Mids T
118 SP 0579
King's Nympton T 91 SS 6819
King's Nympton Station 91 SS 6616
King's Pyon T 113 SO 4450
Kings Ripton T 121 TL 2676
King's Seat H 171 NO 2333
King's Seat Hill H 170 NS 9399
King's Sedge Moor 92 ST 4133
King's Somborne T 94 SU 3631
King's Stag T 93 ST 7210
King's Stanley T 114 SO 8103
Kings Sutton T 119 SP 4936
Kingstanding T 128 SP 0794
Kingsteignton T 89 SX 8773
King Sterndale T 138 SK 0972
Kingsthorne T 113 SO 4932
Kingsthorpe T 119 SP 7563
Kingston, Cambs T 121 TL 3455
Kingston, Devon T 89 SX 6347
Kingston, Dorset T 93 ST 7509
Kingston, Grampn T 184 NJ 3365
Kingston, Hants T 94 SU 1402
Kingston, I. of W T 95 SZ 4781
Kingston, Kent T 99 TR 1951
Kingston, Lothn T 171 NT 5482
Kingston Bagpuize T 115 SU 4098
Kingston Blount T 104 SU 7399
Kingston by Sea T 96 TQ 2305
Kingston Deverill T 93 ST 8437
Kingstone, H. & W T 113 SO 4235
Kingstone, Somer T 92 ST 3713
Kingstone, Staffs T 128 SK 0629
Kingston Lisle T 102 SU 3287
Kingston near Lewes T 97 TQ 3908
Kingston on Soar T 129 SK 5027
Kingston Seymour T 100 ST 4067
Kingston St Mary T 92 ST 2229
Kingston upon Hull P 143 TA 0928
Kingston upon Thames P
105 TQ 1869
Kingstown T 157 NY 3959
King Street, Cambs R 130 TF 1108
King Street, Ches R 137 SJ 6969
King Street, Lincs R 130 TF 1108
King's Walden T 105 TL 1623
Kingswear T 89 SX 8851
Kingswells T 185 NJ 8606
Kingswinford T 117 SO 8888
Kingswood, Avon T 101 ST 6573
Kingswood, Bucks T 104 SP 6819
Kingswood, Glos T 101 ST 7492
Kingswood, H. & W T 113 SO 2954
Kingswood, Kent T 98 TQ 8450
Kingswood, Powys T 126 SJ 2402
Kingswood, Surrey T 96 TQ 2456
Kingswood, Warw T 118 SP 1871
Kings Worthy T 95 SU 4933
Kington, Dorset T 94 SY 9579
Kington, H. & W T 118 SO 9955
Kington, Powys T 113 SO 3056
Kington Langley T 101 ST 9277
Kington Magna T 93 ST 7623
Kington St Michael T 101 ST 9077
Kingussie T 175 NH 7500
King Water W 158 NY 5466
Kingweston T 93 ST 5231
Kinharrachie T 185 NJ 9231
Kininvie House 184 NJ 3144
Kinkell Bridge 170 NN 9316
Kinkell Church A 185 NJ 7819
Kinkell Ness 171 NO 5315
Kinknockie T 185 NK 0041
Kinlet T 117 SO 7280
Kinloch, Fife 171 NO 2812
Kinloch, Highld T 196 NC 3434
Kinloch, Highld T 180 NG 6917
Kinloch, Highld T 179 NM 4099
Kinloch, Tays T 176 NO 1444
Kinloch, Tays 176 NO 2644
Kinlochard T 169 NN 4502
Kinlochbervie T 196 NC 2256
Kinlocheil T 174 NM 9779
Kinlochewe T 190 NH 0261
Kinlochewe Forest 191 NH 0666
Kinloch Glen 179 NG 3800
Kinloch Hourn T 180 NG 9507
Kinloch Laggan T 175 NN 5489
Kinlochleven T 174 NN 1861
Kinloch Lodge 197 NC 5552
Kinlochluichart Forest 182 NH 2769
Kinlochmore T 174 NN 1962
Kinlochourn Forest 180 NG 9409
Kinloch Rannoch T 175 NN 6658
Kinloch River W 197 NC 5451
Kinlochspelve T 173 NM 6526
Kinloss T 183 NJ 0661
Kinmel Bay T 135 SH 9880
Kinmount House 157 NY 1468
Kinmuck T 185 NJ 8119
Kinmundy T 185 NJ 8918
Kinnadie T 185 NJ 9743
Kinnaird T 171 NO 2428
Kinnaird Castle 177 NO 6357
Kinnaird Head 185 NJ 9967
Kinneff 177 NO 8574
Kinneil House A 170 NS 9880
Kinnelhead 157 NT 0301
Kinnell T 177 NO 6050
Kinnel Water W 157 NY 0692
Kinnerley T 126 SJ 3321
Kinnersley, H. & W T 113 SO 3449
Kinnersley, H. & W T 117 SO 8743
Kinnerton, Clwyd T 136 SJ 3361
Kinnerton, Powys T 116 SO 2463
Kinnesswood T 170 NO 1703
Kinninvie T 152 NZ 0521
Kinnordy 176 NO 3655
Kinnoull Hill H 170 NO 1322
Kinoulton T 129 SK 6730
Kinpurney Hill H 176 NO 3241
Kinrive Hill H 192 NH 6875
Kinross T 170 NO 1102
Kinrossie T 170 NO 1832
Kinsham T 116 SO 3664
Kinsley T 139 SE 4114
Kintail Forest 180 NG 9917
Kintarvie T 195 NB 2317
Kintbury T 102 SU 3866
Kintessack T 183 NJ 0060
Kintillo T 170 NO 1317
Kintocher T 184 NJ 5709
Kintore T 185 NJ 7916
Kintour T 166 NR 4551
Kintra 166 NR 3248
Kintra River W 166 NR 3349
Kintyre 160 NR 7439
Kinuachdrachd T 167 NR 7098
Kinuachdrachd Harbour W
167 NR 7098
Kinveachy T 183 NH 9118
Kinver T 117 SO 8484
Kippax T 147 SE 4130
Kippen T 169 NS 6594
Kippenross House 169 NS 7899
Kippford or Scaur T 155 NX 8354
Kirbister, Orkney T 200 HY 3507
Kirbister, Orkney 201 HY 6823
Kirbuster T 200 HY 2825
Kirby Bedon T 133 TG 2805
Kirby Bellars T 129 SK 7117
Kirby Cane T 133 TM 3794
Kirby Cross T 107 TM 2220
Kirby Grindalythe T 149 SE 9067
Kirby Hall A 120 SP 9292
Kirby Hill, N. Yks T 152 NZ 1306
Kirby Hill, N. Yks T 147 SE 3968
Kirby Knowle T 147 SE 4787
Kirby-le-Soken T 107 TM 2221
Kirby Mills T 148 SE 7085
Kirby Misperton T 148 SE 7779
Kirby Muxloe T 129 SK 5204
Kirby Row T 123 TM 3792
Kirby Sigston T 153 SE 4194
Kirby Underdale T 148 SE 8058
Kirby Wiske T 147 SE 3784
Kirdford T 96 TQ 0126
Kiribost Island 188 NF 7564
Kirivick T 195 NB 1941
Kirk T 199 ND 2858
Kirkabister 203 HU 4938
Kirkaig Point 196 NC 0621
Kirkandrews-on-Eden T 157 NY 3558
Kirkbampton T 150 NY 3056
Kirkbean T 156 NX 9759
Kirk Bramwith T 139 SE 6211
Kirkbride T 150 NY 2356
Kirkbuddo T 177 NO 5043
Kirk Burn, Highld W 199 ND 3164
Kirkburn, Humbs T 149 SE 9855
Kirkburton T 138 SE 1912
Kirkby, Lincs T 140 TF 0692
Kirkby, Mers T 136 SJ 4198
Kirkby, N. Yks T 153 NZ 5305
Kirkby Fell 146 SD 8763
Kirkby Fleetham T 152 SE 2894
Kirkby Green T 140 TF 0857
Kirkby in Ashfield T 129 SK 5056
Kirkby Industrial Estate 136 SJ 4398
Kirkby-in-Furness T 144 SD 2282
Kirkby la Thorpe T 130 TF 0945
Kirkby Lonsdale P 145 SD 6178
Kirkby Malham T 146 SD 8961
Kirkby Mallory T 129 SK 4500
Kirkby Malzeard T 147 SE 2374
Kirkby Mills T 148 SE 7085
Kirkbymoorside T 148 SE 6986
Kirkby on Bain T 141 TF 2462
Kirkby Overblow T 147 SE 3249
Kirkby Stephen T 151 NY 7708
Kirkby Thore T 151 NY 6325
Kirkby Underwood T 130 TF 0727
Kirkcaldy P 171 NT 2791
Kirkcambeck T 158 NY 5368
Kirkcarswell T 155 NX 7549
Kirkcolm T 154 NX 0368
Kirkconnel, D. & G T 156 NS 7312
Kirkconnel, D. & G A 157 NY 2575
Kirkconnell 156 NX 9868
Kirkcowan T 154 NX 3260
Kirkcudbright T 155 NX 6851
Kirkcudbright Bay W 155 NX 6645
Kirk Deighton T 147 SE 3950
Kirk Ella T 142 TA 0229
Kirk Fell H 150 NY 1910
Kirkfieldbank T 163 NS 8643
Kirkgunzeon T 156 NX 8666
Kirkham, Lancs T 145 SD 4232
Kirkham, N. Yks T 148 SE 7365
Kirkhamgate T 147 SE 2922
Kirk Hammerton T 147 SE 4655
Kirkharle T 159 NZ 0182
Kirkheaton, Northum T 159 NZ 0177
Kirkheaton, W. Yks T 138 SE 1818
Kirkhill, Highld T 182 NH 5545
Kirkhill, Tays T 177 NO 6860
Kirkhope, Border T 164 NT 3823
Kirk Hope, Orkney W 200 ND 3389
Kirkhouse T 164 NT 3233
Kirkhouse Point 200 ND 4790
Kirkibost, Highld T 180 NG 5517
Kirkibost, W. Isles T 195 NB 1834
Kirkibost Island 188 NF 7564
Kirkinch 176 NO 3144
Kirkinner T 155 NX 4251
Kirkintilloch T 169 NS 6573
Kirk Ireton T 128 SK 2650
Kirkland, Cumbr T 150 NY 0717
Kirkland, Cumbr T 151 NY 6432
Kirkland, D. & G T 156 NS 7214
Kirkland, D. & G T 156 NX 8190
Kirkland Hill H 156 NS 7216
Kirk Langley T 128 SK 2838
Kirkleatham T 153 NZ 5921
Kirklevington T 153 NZ 4209
Kirkley T 123 TM 5391
Kirklington, Notts T 139 SK 6757
Kirklington, N. Yks T 147 SE 3181
Kirklinton T 157 NY 4367
Kirkliston T 170 NT 1274
Kirkmaiden T 154 NX 1236
Kirk Merrington T 152 NZ 2631
Kirk Michael, I. of M T 144 SC 3190
Kirkmichael, Strath T 161 NS 3408

L

Llandinabo Loch Etive

Llandinabo *T* 113 SO 5128
Llandinam *T* 125 SO 0288
Llandissilio *T* 110 SN 1221
Llandogo *T* 113 SO 5204
Llandough, S. Glam *T* 109 SS 9973
Llandough, S. Glam *T* 109 ST 1773
Llandovery *P* 109 SN 7634
Llandow *T* 109 SS 9473
Llandre, Dyfed *T* 125 SN 6287
Llandre, Dyfed *T* 112 SN 6742
Llandrillo *T* 135 SJ 0337
Llandrillo-yn-Rhôs *T* 135 SH 8480
Llandrindod Wells *P* 125 SO 0661
Llandrinio *T* 126 SJ 2917
Llandudno *P* 135 SH 7882
Llandudno Junction *T* 135 SH 8078
Llandudwen *T* 134 SH 2736
Llandwrog *T* 134 SH 4556
Llandybie *T* 111 SN 6115
Llandyfalle Hill *H* 112 SO 0737
Llandyfan *T* 111 SN 6417
Llandyfriog *T* 111 SN 3341
Llandyfrydog *T* 134 SH 4485
Llandygwydd *T* 111 SN 2443
Llandyrnog *T* 135 SJ 1065
Llandyssil *T* 126 SO 1995
Llandysul *T* 111 SN 4141
Llanegryn *T* 124 SH 6005
Llanegwad *T* 111 SN 5221
Llanelian-yn-Rhôs *T* 135 SH 8676
Llanelidan *T* 135 SJ 1050
Llanelieu *T* 109 SO 1834
Llanellen *T* 113 SO 3010
Llanelli *P* 108 SN 5100
Llanelltyd *T* 125 SH 7119
Llanelly *T* 113 SO 2314
Llanelly Hill *T* 109 SO 2212
Llanelwedd *T* 112 SO 0552
Llanelwy or St Asaph *T* 135 SJ 0374
Llanenddwyn *T* 124 SH 5823
Llanengan *T* 124 SH 2927
Llanerchymedd *T* 134 SH 4184
Llanerfyl *T* 125 SJ 0309
Llanfachraeth *T* 134 SH 3182
Llanfachreth *T* 125 SH 7522
Llanfaelog *T* 134 SH 3373
Llanfaes *T* 134 SH 6077
Llanfaethlu *T* 134 SH 3187
Llanfaglan *T* 134 SH 4760
Llanfair *T* 134 SH 5729
Llanfair Caereinion *T* 125 SJ 1006
Llanfair Clydogau *T* 111 SN 6251
Llanfair Dyffryn Clwyd *T* 126 SJ 1355
Llanfairfechan *T* 135 SH 6874
Llanfair Kilgeddin *T* 113 SO 3407
Llanfair-Nant-Gwyn *T* 110 SN 1637
Llanfairpwllgwyngyll *T* 134 SH 5372
Llanfair Talhaiarn *T* 135 SH 9270
Llanfair Waterdine *T* 116 SO 2476
Llanfairyneubwll *T* 134 SH 3076
Llanfairynghornwy *T* 134 SH 3291
Llanfallteg *T* 110 SN 1519
Llanfaredd *T* 112 SO 0750
Llanfarian *T* 124 SN 5977
Llanfechain *T* 126 SJ 1820
Llanfechan *T* 112 SN 9750
Llanfechell *T* 134 SH 3691
Llanfendigaid *T* 124 SH 5605
Llanferres *T* 136 SJ 1860
Llanfflewyn *T* 134 SH 3589
Llanfihangel-ar-arth *T* 111 SN 4539
Llanfihangel Crucorney *T* 113 SO 3220
Llanfihangel Glyn Myfyr *T* 135 SH 9949
Llanfihangel Nant Bran *T* 109 SN 9434
Llanfihangel-nant-Melan *T* 113 SO 1858
Llanfihangel Rhydithon *T* 116 SO 1566
Llanfihangel Rogiet *T* 101 ST 4587
Llanfihangel Tal-y-llyn *T* 109 SO 1128
Llanfihangel-uwch-Gwili *T* 111 SN 4922
Llanfihangel-y-Creuddyn *T* 125 SN 6676
Llanfihangel-yng-Ngwynfa *T* 125 SJ 0816
Llanfihangel yn Nhowyn *T* 134 SH 3277
Llanfihangel-y-pennant, Gwyn *T* 134 SH 5244
Llanfihangel-y-pennant, Gwyn *T* 125 SH 6708
Llanfihangel Ystum Llwern *T* 113 SO 4313
Llanfihangel-y-traethau *T* 134 SH 5935
Llanfilo *T* 109 SO 1233
Llanfoist *T* 113 SO 2913
Llanfor *T* 135 SH 9336
Llanfrechfa *T* 113 ST 3193
Llanfrothen *T* 135 SH 6241
Llanfrynach *T* 109 SO 0725
Llanfwrog, Clwyd *T* 136 SJ 1157
Llanfwrog, Gwyn *T* 134 SH 3084
Llanfyllin *T* 126 SJ 1419
Llanfynydd, Clwyd *T* 126 SJ 2856
Llanfynydd, Dyfed *T* 111 SN 5527
Llanfyrnach *T* 111 SN 2231
Llangadfan *T* 125 SJ 0110
Llangadog *T* 108 SN 7028
Llangadwaladr, Clwyd *T* 126 SJ 1830
Llangadwaladr, Gwyn *T* 134 SH 3869
Llangaffo *T* 134 SH 4468
Llangain *T* 111 SN 3816
Llangammarch Wells *T* 112 SN 9347
Llangan *T* 109 SS 9577
Llangarron *T* 113 SO 5321
Llangasty-Talyllin *T* 109 SO 1326
Llangathen *T* 111 SN 5822
Llangattock *T* 109 SO 2117
Llangattock Lingoed *T* 113 SO 3620
Llangattock-Vibon-Avel *T* 113 SO 4515
Llangedwyn *T* 126 SJ 1824
Llangefni *T* 134 SH 4675
Llangeinor *T* 109 SS 9187
Llangeitho *T* 111 SN 6259
Llangeler *T* 111 SN 3739
Llangelynnin *T* 124 SH 5707
Llangendeirne *T* 111 SN 4514
Llangennech *T* 108 SN 5601
Llangennith *T* 108 SS 4291
Llangenny *T* 113 SO 2418
Llangernyw *T* 135 SH 8767
Llangian *T* 134 SH 2929
Llangiwg *T* 108 SN 7205
Llanglydwen *T* 111 SN 1826
Llangoed *T* 134 SH 6179
Llangoedmor *T* 111 SN 2046
Llangollen *P* 126 SJ 2142
Llangollen Canal, Ches *W* 127 SJ 5747
Llangollen Canal, Clwyd *W* 126 SJ 2342
Llangolman *T* 110 SN 1127
Llangorse *T* 109 SO 1327
Llangorse Lake *W* 109 SO 1326
Llangorwen *T* 124 SN 6083
Llangovan *T* 113 SO 4505
Llangower *T* 135 SH 9032
Llangranog *T* 111 SN 3154
Llangristiolus *T* 134 SH 4373
Llangrove *T* 113 SO 5219
Llangua *T* 113 SO 3925
Llangunllo *T* 116 SO 2171
Llangunnor *T* 111 SN 4320
Llangurig *P* 125 SN 9180
Llangwm, Clwyd *T* 135 SH 9644
Llangwm, Dyfed *T* 110 SM 9909
Llangwm, Gwent *T* 113 SO 4200
Llangwnnadl *T* 134 SH 2033
Llangwyfan *T* 136 SJ 1266
Llangwyllog *T* 134 SH 4379
Llangwyryfon *T* 124 SN 6070
Llangybi, Dyfed *T* 111 SN 6153
Llangybi, Gwent *T* 113 ST 3796
Llangybi, Gwyn *T* 134 SH 4241
Llangyfelach *T* 108 SS 6499
Llangynhafal *T* 136 SJ 1263
Llangynidr *T* 109 SO 1519
Llangynin *T* 111 SN 2519
Llangynog, Dyfed *T* 111 SN 3416
Llangynog, Powys *T* 125 SJ 0526
Llangynwyd *T* 109 SS 8588
Llanhamlach *T* 109 SO 0926
Llanharan *T* 109 ST 0083
Llanharry *T* 109 ST 0180
Llanhennock *T* 100 ST 3592
Llanhilleth *T* 109 SO 2200
Llanidloes *T* 125 SN 9584
Llaniestyn *T* 134 SH 2733
Llanigon *T* 113 SO 2140
Llanilar *T* 125 SN 6275
Llanild *T* 109 SS 9881
Llanishen, Gwent *T* 113 SO 4703
Llanishen, S. Glam *T* 109 ST 1782
Llaniwared *H* 125 SN 8977
Llanllechid *T* 135 SH 6268
Llanlleonfel *T* 112 SN 9449
Llanllowell *T* 113 ST 3998
Llanllugan *T* 125 SJ 0502
Llanllwch *T* 111 SN 3818
Llanllwchaiarn *T* 116 SO 1292
Llanllwni *T* 111 SN 4940
Llanllyfni *T* 134 SH 4752
Llanmadoc *T* 108 SS 4493
Llanmaes *T* 109 SS 9869
Llanmartin *T* 100 ST 3989
Llanmerewig *T* 126 SO 1693
Llanmihangel *T* 109 SS 9872
Llanmiloe *T* 111 SN 2508
Llanmorlais *T* 108 SS 5394
Llannefydd *T* 135 SH 9870
Llannerch Hall 135 SJ 0572
Llannon *T* 111 SN 5408
Llannor *T* 134 SH 3537
Llanon *T* 124 SN 5166
Llanover *T* 113 SO 3108
Llanpumsaint *T* 111 SN 4129
Llanrhaeadr *T* 135 SJ 0863
Llanrhaeadr-ym-Mochnant *T* 126 SJ 1226
Llanrhian *T* 110 SM 8231
Llanrhidian *T* 108 SS 4992
Llanrhidian Sands 108 SS 4995
Llanrhos *T* 135 SH 7980
Llanrhyddlad *T* 134 SH 3389
Llanrhystud *T* 124 SN 5469
Llanrothal *T* 113 SO 4718
Llanrug *T* 134 SH 5363
Llanrwst *T* 135 SH 8062
Llansadurnen *T* 111 SN 2810
Llansadwrn, Dyfed *T* 108 SN 6931
Llansadwrn, Gwyn *T* 134 SH 5676
Llansaint *T* 111 SN 3808
Llansamlet *T* 108 SS 6897
Llansannan *T* 135 SH 9365
Llansannor *T* 109 SS 9977
Llansantffraed, Dyfed *T* 124 SN 5167
Llansantffraed, Powys *T* 109 SO 1223
Llansantffraed-Cwmdeuddwr *T* 125 SN 9667
Llansantffraed-in-Elwel *T* 112 SO 0954
Llansantffraid Glan Conwy *T* 135 SH 8076
Llansantffraid-ym-Mechain *T* 126 SJ 2220
Llansawel *T* 111 SN 6236
Llansilin *T* 126 SJ 2128
Llansoy *T* 113 SO 4402
Llanspyddid *T* 109 SO 0128
Llanstadwell *T* 110 SM 9505
Llanstephan, Dyfed *T* 111 SN 3510
Llanstephan, Powys *T* 112 SO 1142
Llanthony *T* 113 SO 2827
Llantilio Crossenny *T* 113 SO 3914
Llantilio Pertholey *T* 113 SO 3116
Llantrisant, Gwent *T* 113 ST 3997
Llantrisant, Gwyn *T* 134 SH 3683
Llantrisant, M. Glam *T* 109 ST 0483
Llantrithyd *T* 109 ST 0473
Llantwit Fardre *T* 109 ST 0785
Llantwit Major *T* 109 SS 9768
Llantysilio Hall 126 SJ 1943
Llantysilio Mountain *H* 126 SJ 1545
Llanuwchllyn *T* 135 SH 8730
Llanvaches *T* 101 ST 4391
Llanvair Discoed *T* 101 ST 4492
Llanvapley *T* 113 SO 3614
Llanvetherine *T* 113 SO 3617
Llanveynoe *T* 113 SO 3031
Llanvihangel Crucorney *T* 113 SO 3220
Llanvihangel Gobion *T* 113 SO 3409
Llanvihangel-Ystern-Llewern *T* 113 SO 4313
Llanwarne *T* 113 SO 5028
Llanwddyn *T* 125 SJ 0219
Llan-wen Hill *H* 116 SO 2969
Llanwenog *T* 111 SN 4945
Llanwern *T* 100 ST 3688
Llanwinio *T* 111 SN 2626
Llanwnda, Dyfed *T* 110 SM 9339
Llanwnda, Gwyn *T* 134 SH 4758
Llanwnnen *T* 111 SN 5347
Llanwnog *T* 125 SO 0293
Llanwrda *T* 108 SN 7131
Llanwrin *T* 125 SH 7803
Llanwrthwl *T* 125 SN 9763
Llanwrtyd *T* 112 SN 8647
Llanwrtyd-Wells *T* 112 SN 8846
Llanwyddelan *T* 125 SJ 0801
Llanyblodwel *T* 126 SJ 2423
Llanybri *T* 111 SN 3312
Llanybydder *T* 111 SN 5244
Llanycefn *T* 110 SN 0923
Llanychaer *T* 110 SM 9835
Llanycil 135 SH 9134
Llanycrwys *T* 111 SN 6445
Llanymawddwy *T* 125 SH 9019
Llanymynech, Powys *T* 126 SJ 2620
Llanymynech, Shrops *T* 126 SJ 2620
Llanynghenedl *T* 134 SH 3181
Llanynys *T* 135 SJ 1062
Llan-y-pwll *T* 126 SJ 3651
Llanyre *T* 125 SO 0462
Llanystumdwy *T* 134 SH 4738
Llanywern *T* 109 SO 1028
Llawhaden *T* 110 SN 0717
Llawlech *H* 125 SH 6321
Llawnt *T* 126 SJ 2531
Llawr Dref *T* 124 SH 2828
Llawryglyn *T* 125 SN 9391
Llay *T* 126 SJ 3355
Llechcynfarwy *T* 134 SH 3881
Llechfaen *T* 109 SO 0828
Llechryd, Dyfed *T* 111 SN 2143
Llechryd, M. Glam *T* 109 SO 1009
Llechrydau 126 SJ 2234
Lledrod *T* 125 SN 6470
Lleyn Peninsula 134 SH 3035
Llidiad-Nenog *T* 111 SN 5437
Llithfaen *T* 134 SH 3543
Lliw Resrs *W* 111 SN 6505
Llong *T* 136 SJ 2662
Llowes *T* 113 SO 1941
Llwchmynydd *T* 124 SH 1526
Llwn-y-groes *T* 111 SN 5956
Llwydcoed *T* 109 SN 9904
Llwyn *T* 116 SO 2880
Llwyncelyn *T* 111 SN 4459
Llwyndafydd *T* 111 SN 3755
Llwynderw *T* 126 SJ 2003
Llwyndyrys *T* 134 SH 3741
Llwyngwril *T* 124 SH 5909
Llwynhendy *T* 108 SS 5499
Llwynmawr *T* 126 SJ 2237
Llŵyn-on Reservoir *W* 109 SO 0012
Llwynypia *T* 109 SS 9993
Llyn Alaw *W* 134 SH 3986
Llyn Aled *W* 135 SH 9157
Llyn Alwen *W* 135 SH 9056
Llyn Arenig-Fawr *W* 135 SH 8438
Llyn Berwyn *W* 112 SN 7457
Llyn Bodlyn *W* 125 SH 6424
Llyn Brân *W* 135 SH 9659
Llyn Brenig *W* 135 SH 9755
Llyn Brianne Reservoir, Dyfed *W* 112 SN 8050
Llyn Brianne Reservoir, Powys *W* 112 SN 8050
Llyn Celyn *W* 135 SH 8640
Llynclys *T* 126 SJ 2824
Llyn Clywedog *W* 125 SN 9088
Llyn Coch-hwyad *W* 125 SH 9211
Llyn Conwy *W* 135 SH 7846
Llyn Coron *W* 134 SH 3870
Llyn Cowlyd Reservoir *W* 135 SH 7262
Llyn Crafnant Reservoir *W* 135 SH 7561
Llyn Cwellyn *W* 134 SH 5655
Llyn Cwm Dulyn *W* 134 SH 4949
Llyn Cwmystradllyn *W* 134 SH 5644
Llyn Dinas *W* 134 SH 6149
Llyn Efyrnwy *W* 125 SH 9921
Llyn Eigiau Reservoir *W* 135 SH 7265
Llyn Elsi Reservoir *W* 135 SH 7855
Llynfaes *T* 134 SH 4178
Llyn Gwyddior *W* 125 SH 9307
Llyn Gwynant *W* 135 SH 6452
Llyn Gynon *W* 125 SN 8064
Llyn Helyg *W* 136 SJ 1177
Llyn Hywel *W* 124 SH 6626
Llyn Llydaw *W* 135 SH 6254
Llyn Llywenan *W* 134 SH 3481
Llyn Mawr *W* 125 SO 0097
Llyn Nantlle Uchaf *W* 134 SH 5153
Llyn Ogwen *W* 135 SH 6660
Llyn Padarn *W* 134 SH 5761
Llyn Peris *W* 134 SH 5959
Llyn Syfydrin *W* 125 SN 7284
Llyn Tegid or Bala Lake *W* 135 SH 9133
Llyn Teifi *W* 125 SN 7867
Llyn Trawsfynydd *W* 135 SH 6936
Llyn y Fan Fach *W* 109 SN 8021
Llyn y Fan Fawr *W* 109 SN 8321
Llyn y Tarw *W* 125 SO 0297
Llysfaen *T* 135 SH 8977
Llyswen *T* 112 SO 1338
Llysworney *T* 109 SS 9674
Llys-y-frân *T* 110 SN 0424
Llys-y-frân Reservoir *W* 110 SN 0325
Llywel *T* 109 SN 8730
Loadpot Hill *H* 151 NY 4518
Loan 170 NS 9575
Loanend *T* 165 NT 9450
Loanhead *T* 163 NT 2765
Loans *T* 161 NS 3431
Lòba Sgeir 194 HW 8031
Lochaber *T* 174 NN 1492
Lochaber Loch *W* 156 NX 9270
Loch a' Bhaid-luachraich *W* 190 NG 8986
Loch a' Bhealaich, Highld *W* 197 NC 6027
Loch a' Bhealaich, Highld *W* 190 NG 8664
Loch a' Bhealaich, Highld *W* 180 NH 0221
Loch a' Bhealaich Bheithe *W* 175 NN 5172
Loch a' Bhràige *W* 190 NG 6260
Loch a' Bhraoin *W* 191 NH 1374
Loch a Bhùrra *W* 167 NR 6696
Loch a' Chàirn Bhàin *W* 196 NC 2034
Loch Achall *W* 191 NH 1795
Loch Achanalt *W* 182 NH 2761
Loch a' Chaorainn *W* 192 NH 4678
Loch a' Chaoruinn *W* 160 NR 7866
Loch Achilty *W* 182 NH 4356
Loch Achnamoine *W* 198 NC 8132
Loch a' Chnuic Bhric *W* 166 NR 4473
Loch a' Choire *W* 173 NM 8552
Loch a' Choire Mhóir *W* 191 NH 3088
Loch Achonachie *W* 182 NH 4354
Loch a' Chracaich *W* 190 NG 7657
Loch a' Chrathaich *W* 182 NH 3621
Loch Achray *W* 169 NN 5106
Loch Affric *W* 181 NH 1622
Loch a' Garbh-bhaid Mór *W* 196 NC 2748
Loch a' Gheoidh *W* 167 NR 6695
Loch a' Ghlinne *W* 194 NB 0212
Loch a' Ghorm-choire *W* 197 NC 4432
Loch a' Ghriama *W* 196 NC 3926
Loch Ailort, Highld *W* 180 NM 7379
Lochailort, Highld *T* 180 NM 7682
Loch Ailsh *W* 196 NC 3111
Loch Ainort *W* 180 NG 5528
Loch Airdeglais *W* 173 NM 6228
Loch Airigh na Beinne *W* 196 NC 3266
Loch Airigh na h-Airde *W* 195 NB 2123
Loch Akran *W* 198 NC 9260
Loch a' Laip *W* 188 NF 8647
Lochaline, Strath *T* 173 NM 6744
Loch Aline, Strath *W* 173 NM 6946
Loch Alsh *W* 180 NG 8025
Loch Alvie *W* 183 NH 8609
Loch a' Mhuilinn *W* 199 ND 0142
Loch a' Mhuillidh *W* 182 NH 2738
Lochan a' Chairn *W* 192 NH 5184
Loch an Aircill *W* 166 NR 5077
Loch an Alltan Fheàrna *W* 198 NC 7533
Lochan Breaclaich *W* 169 NN 6231
Lochan Burn *W* 157 NT 0300
Loch an Daimh, Highld *W* 191 NH 2794
Loch an Daimh, Tays *W* 175 NN 4846
Loch an Dherue *W* 197 NC 5448
Loch an Doire Dhuibh *W* 196 NC 1310
Loch an Draing *W* 190 NG 7790
Lochan Dubh nan Geodh *W* 199 ND 0647
Loch an Dùin, Highld *W* 175 NN 7280
Loch an Dùin, Tays *W* 175 NN 7280
Loch an Easain Uaine *W* 196 NC 3246
Loch an Eion *W* 190 NG 9251
Loch an Eircill *W* 196 NC 3027
Lochan Fada *W* 190 NH 0271
Lochan Gaineamhach *W* 174 NN 3053
Loch an Iasaich *W* 180 NG 9535
Loch an Laoigh *W* 190 NH 0241
Loch an Leathaid Bhuain *W* 196 NC 2736
Loch an Leothaid *W* 196 NC 1729
Lochan na Bi *W* 168 NN 3031
Lochan na h-Achlaise *W* 174 NN 3148
Lochan na h-Earba *W* 175 NN 4883
Lochan na Lairige *W* 175 NN 5940
Loch an Ruathair *W* 198 NC 8637
Lochans *T* 154 NX 0656
Lochan Shira *W* 168 NN 1720
Lochan Sron Mór *W* 168 NN 1519
Loch an Tachdaidh *W* 181 NH 0938
Lochan Thulachan *W* 199 ND 1041
Loch an t-Seilich *W* 175 NN 7586
Loch Arail *W* 167 NR 8079
Locharbriggs *T* 156 NX 9980
Loch Ard *W* 169 NN 4601
Loch Ard Forest *F* 169 NS 4898
Loch Arichlinie *W* 198 NC 8435
Loch Arienas *W* 173 NM 6851
Loch Arkaig *W* 174 NM 0791
Loch Arklet *W* 169 NN 3709
Lochar Moss 157 NY 0371
Loch Arnish *W* 190 NG 5948
Loch Arthur *W* 156 NX 9068
Lochar Water *W* 156 NY 0272
Loch Ascaig *W* 198 NC 8525
Loch a' Sguirr *W* 190 NG 6052
Loch Ashie *W* 182 NH 6335
Loch Assapol *W* 172 NM 4020
Loch Assynt *W* 196 NC 2124
Lochassynt Lodge 196 NC 1726
Loch a Tuath or Broad Bay *W* 195 NB 5036
Loch Aulasary *W* 188 NF 9473
Loch Avich *W* 168 NM 9314
Loch Avon *W* 176 NJ 0102
Loch Awe, Highld *W* 196 NC 2415
Loch Awe, Strath *W* 168 NM 9914
Lochawe, Strath *T* 168 NN 1227
Loch Bà, Highld *W* 174 NN 3149
Loch Bà, Strath *W* 173 NM 5737
Loch Bad a' Chreamh *W* 190 NG 8180
Loch Bad a' Ghaill *W* 196 NC 0710
Loch Badanloch *W* 198 NC 7734
Loch Bad an Sgalaig *W* 190 NG 8571
Loch Baligill *W* 198 NC 8562
Loch Ballygrant *W* 166 NR 4066
Loch Bay *W* 186 NG 2655
Loch Beanacharan *W* 182 NH 3039
Loch Beanie *W* 176 NO 1668
Loch Beannach, Highld *W* 196 NC 1326
Loch Beannach, Highld *W* 197 NC 6814
Loch Beannacharain *W* 182 NH 2351
Loch Bee *W* 188 NF 7743
Loch Beinn a' Mheadhoin *W* 182 NH 2324
Loch Beinn Uraraidh *W* 166 NR 4053
Loch Benachally *W* 176 NO 0750
Loch Beoraid *W* 180 NM 8285
Loch Bhac *W* 175 NN 8262
Loch Bharcasaig *W* 186 NG 2542
Loch Bhrodainn *W* 175 NN 7483
Loch Bhrollum *W* 189 NB 3103
Loch Blàir *W* 174 NN 0594
Loch Bodavat *W* 194 NB 0619
Lochboisdale, W. Isles *T* 178 NF 7919
Loch Boisdale, W. Isles *W* 178 NF 8018
Loch Boltachan *W* 169 NN 6926
Loch Borralan *W* 196 NC 2610
Loch Borralie *W* 196 NC 3867
Loch Bracadale *W* 186 NG 2838
Loch Bradan Reservoir *W* 155 NX 4297
Loch Bràigh an Achaidh *W* 180 NG 7440
Loch Brandy *W* 176 NO 3475
Loch Breac *W* 199 ND 0637
Loch Breachacha *W* 172 NM 1653
Loch Breivat *W* 195 NB 3345
Loch Brittle *W* 187 NG 4019
Loch Broom, Highld *W* 191 NH 1392
Loch Broom, Tays *W* 176 NO 0158
Loch Brora *W* 193 NC 8508
Loch Bruicheach *W* 182 NH 4536
Loch Buidhe *W* 192 NH 6698
Loch Buidhe Mór *W* 198 NC 7758
Loch Buie, Strath *W* 173 NM 6023
Lochbuie, Strath *T* 173 NM 6125
Loch Builg *W* 184 NJ 1803
Loch Calavie *W* 181 NH 0538
Loch Calder *W* 199 ND 0760
Loch Callater *W* 176 NO 1884
Loch Caluim *W* 199 ND 0252
Loch Càm *W* 166 NR 3466
Loch Caoldair *W* 175 NN 6189
Loch Caolisport *W* 167 NR 7374
Loch Caravat *W* 188 NF 8461
Loch Carloway *W* 195 NB 1842
Lochcarnan, W. Isles *T* 188 NF 8044
Loch Càrnan, W. Isles *W* 188 NF 8243
Loch Caroy *W* 186 NG 3042
Loch Carron, Highld *W* 180 NG 8735
Lochcarron, Highld *T* 180 NG 8939
Loch Ceann Dibig *W* 189 NG 1597
Loch Chaolartan *W* 194 NB 0624
Loch Chaorunn Reservoir *W* 167 NR 8371
Loch Choire *W* 197 NC 6328
Loch Choire Forest 197 NC 6329
Loch Choire Lodge 197 NC 6530
Loch Chon *W* 169 NN 4205
Loch Ciaran *W* 160 NR 7754
Loch Claidh *W* 189 NB 2603
Loch Clàir, Highld *W* 190 NG 7771
Loch Clair, Highld *W* 190 NG 9957
Loch Clash *W* 196 NC 2156
Loch Cliad *W* 172 NM 2058
Loch Cluanie *W* 181 NH 1309
Loch Coire na Saidhe Duibhe *W* 197 NC 4536
Loch Coirigerod *W* 195 NB 1721
Loch Con *W* 175 NN 6867
Loch Connan *W* 186 NG 3843
Loch Connell *W* 154 NX 0168
Loch Coruisk *W* 187 NG 4820
Lochcote Reservoir *W* 170 NS 9773
Loch Coulin *W* 190 NH 0155
Loch Coulside *W* 197 NC 5843
Loch Coulter Reservoir *W* 169 NS 7686
Loch Coultrie *W* 190 NG 8545
Loch Cracail Mór *W* 192 NC 6202
Loch Craggie, Highld *W* 191 NC 3205
Loch Craggie, Highld *W* 197 NC 6152
Loch Craggie, Highld *W* 192 NC 6207
Lochcraig Head *H* 157 NT 1617
Loch Craignish *W* 167 NM 7901
Lochcraig Reservoir *W* 161 NS 5351
Loch Cravadale *W* 194 NB 0212
Loch Creran *W* 174 NM 9442
Loch Crinan *W* 167 NR 7995
Loch Cròcach, Highld *W* 196 NC 1027
Loch Cròcach, Highld *W* 196 NC 1939
Loch Cròcach, Highld *W* 197 NC 4249
Loch Cròcach, Highld *W* 198 NC 8043
Loch Crò Criosdaig *W* 195 NB 0820
Loch Crunachdan *W* 175 NN 5493
Loch Cruoshie *W* 181 NH 0536
Loch Cuaich *W* 175 NN 6987
Loch Culag *W* 196 NC 0921
Loch Dallas *W* 183 NJ 0947
Loch Damh *W* 190 NG 8650
Loch Davan *W* 176 NJ 4400
Loch Dee *W* 155 NX 4779
Loch Derculich *W* 175 NN 8654
Loch Derry *W* 154 NX 2573
Lochdhu Hotel 199 ND 0144
Loch Diabaigas Airde *W* 190 NG 8159
Loch Dionard *W* 196 NC 3549
Loch Dochard *W* 174 NN 2142
Loch Dochart *W* 169 NN 4025
Lochdochart House 169 NN 4327
Loch Doilet *W* 173 NM 8067
Loch Doine *W* 169 NN 4719
Lochdon, Strath *T* 173 NM 7333
Loch Don, Strath *W* 173 NM 7431
Loch Doon, D. & G *W* 155 NX 4998
Loch Doon, Strath *W* 155 NX 4998
Loch Dornal, D. & G *W* 154 NX 2976
Loch Dornal, Strath *W* 154 NX 2976
Loch Droma *W* 191 NH 2675
Loch Druidibeg *W* 178 NF 7937
Loch Druim a' Chliabhain *W* 198 NC 8141
Loch Drunkie *W* 169 NN 5404
Loch Duagrich *W* 187 NG 4040
Loch Dubh *W* 199 ND 0537
Loch Dubh a' Chuail *W* 196 NC 3428
Loch Dùghaill, Highld *W* 196 NC 1952
Loch Dughaill, Highld *W* 190 NG 9947
Loch Duich *W* 180 NG 9021
Loch Dungeon *W* 155 NX 5284
Loch Duntelchaig *W* 182 NH 6231
Loch Dunvegan *W* 186 NG 2153
Lochead 167 NR 7778
Loch Earn, Central *W* 169 NN 6423
Loch Earn, Tays *W* 169 NN 6423
Lochearnhead *T* 169 NN 5823
Loch Eatharna *W* 172 NM 2256
Loch Eck *W* 168 NS 1392
Loch Eck Forest 168 NS 1493
Lochee *T* 171 NO 3631
Loch Eigheach *W* 175 NN 4557
Loch Eil *W* 174 NN 0277
Loch Eilde Beag *W* 174 NN 2565
Loch Eilde Mór *W* 174 NN 2464
Loch Eileanach, Highld *W* 197 NC 5940
Loch Eileanach, Highld *W* 199 ND 0747
Locheil Forest 174 NM 0888
Locheilside Station 174 NM 9978
Loch Eilt *W* 180 NM 8182
Loch Einich *W* 175 NN 9199
Loch Eishort *W* 180 NG 6114
Lochenbreck Loch *W* 156 NX 6465
Lochend, Highld *T* 199 ND 2668
Lochend, Highld *T* 182 NH 5937
Loch Enoch *W* 155 NX 4485
Locheport, W. Isles *T* 188 NF 8563
Loch Eport, W. Isles *W* 188 NF 8863
Locherben *T* 156 NX 9597
Loch Eriboll *W* 197 NC 4460
Loch Ericht, Highld *W* 175 NN 5676
Loch Ericht, Tays *W* 175 NN 5676
Loch Ericht Forest *F* 175 NN 5981
Loch Erisort *W* 195 NB 3420
Loch Errochty *W* 175 NN 6865
Locher Water *W* 161 NS 3763
Loch Esk *W* 176 NO 2379
Loch Etchachan *W* 176 NJ 0000
Loch Etive *W* 168 NN 0535

Maryburgh
Milton Ernest

Maryburgh *T* 182 NH 5456
Marygold *T* 165 NT 8160
Maryhill *T* 185 NJ 8245
Marykirk *T* 177 NO 6865
Marylebone, G. Lon *T* 105 TQ 2881
Marylebone, G. Man *T* 137 SD 5807
Marypark *T* 184 NJ 1938
Maryport, Cumbr *T* 150 NY 0336
Maryport, D. & G *T* 154 NX 1434
Maryport Bay *W* 154 NX 1434
Marystow *T* 88 SX 4382
Mary Tavy *T* 88 SX 5079
Maryton *T* 177 NO 6856
Marywell, Grampn *T* 177 NO 5895
Marywell, Tays *T* 177 NO 6544
Masham *T* 147 SE 2280
Masham Moor 146 SE 1079
Mashbury *T* 106 TL 6511
Masongill *T* 145 SD 6675
Massacamber 188 NF 9382
Massingham Heath 132 TF 7721
Mastrick *T* 185 NJ 9007
Matching *T* 105 TL 5211
Matching Green *T* 105 TL 5311
Matching Tye *T* 105 TL 5111
Matfen *T* 159 NZ 0371
Matfield *T* 97 TQ 6541
Mathern *T* 101 ST 5291
Mathon *T* 117 SO 7345
Mathry *T* 110 SM 8832
Matlaske *T* 133 TG 1534
Matlock *P* 139 SK 3060
Matlock Bath *T* 139 SK 2958
Matson *T* 114 SO 8515
Matterdale End *T* 151 NY 3923
Mattersey *T* 140 SK 6989
Matthew's Port *W* 161 NS 1903
Mattingley *T* 103 SU 7357
Mattishall *T* 132 TG 0511
Mattishall Burgh *T* 132 TG 0511
Mauchline *T* 161 NS 4927
Maud *T* 185 NJ 9248
Maugersbury *T* 115 SP 2025
Maughold *T* 144 SC 4991
Maughold Head 144 SC 4891
Maulden *T* 120 TL 0538
Maulds Meaburn *T* 151 NY 6216
Maunby *T* 147 SE 3586
Maund Bryan *T* 113 SO 5650
Mautby *T* 133 TG 4812
Mavesyn Ridware *T* 128 SK 0717
Mavis Enderby *T* 141 TF 3666
Mavis Grind 204 HU 3468
Mawbray *T* 150 NY 0846
Mawdesley *T* 137 SD 4914
Mawgan *T* 86 SW 7025
Mawla *T* 86 SW 7045
Mawnan *T* 87 SW 7827
Mawnan Smith *T* 86 SW 7728
Maxey *T* 130 TF 1208
Maxstoke *T* 118 SP 2386
Maxton *T* 164 NT 6130
Maxwellheugh *T* 164 NT 7233
Maxwellston 154 NS 2600
Mayar *H* 176 NO 2473
Maybole *T* 161 NS 2909
Mayfield, E. Susx *T* 97 TQ 5826
Mayfield, Lothn *T* 164 NT 3564
Mayfield, Staffs *T* 128 SK 1545
Mayfield, Surrey *T* 96 TQ 0056
Mayford *T* 96 SU 9956
May Hill *H* 114 SO 6921
Mayland *T* 106 TL 9101
Maypole *T* 113 SO 4716
Maypole Green *T* 133 TM 4195
Maywick *T* 203 HU 3724
McArthur's Head 166 NR 4659
McFarlane's Rock 186 NG 3031
McFarquhar's Cave 183 NH 7965
Meadie Burn *W* 197 NC 5137
Meadle *T* 104 SP 8005
Meadowtown *T* 126 SJ 3101
Meal a' Chaorainn *H* 191 NH 1360
Mealasta 194 NB 0022
Mealasta Island 194 NA 9721
Meal Bank *T* 151 SD 5495
Mealdarroch Point 160 NR 8868
Mealista *T* 194 NA 9924
Mealisval *H* 194 NB 0226
Meall a' Bhata *H* 197 NC 6326
Meall a' Bhreacraibh *H* 183 NH 7935
Meall a' Bhuachaille *H* 183 NH 9911
Meall a' Chàise *H* 173 NM 7517
Meall a' Chaorainn *H* 191 NH 1360
Meallach Mhór *H* 175 NN 7790
Meall a' Choire Bhuidhe *H* 176 NO 0671
Meall a' Chrasgaidh *H* 191 NH 1873
Meall a' Chràthaich *H* 182 NH 3622
Meall a' Churain *H* 169 NN 4632
Meall a' Ghrianain *H* 191 NH 3677
Meall a' Mhadaidh *H* 169 NN 5925
Meall a' Mhuic *W* 175 NN 5750
Meall an Aonaich *H* 196 NC 3316
Meall an Arbhair 166 NR 3890
Meallan Buidhe, Highld *H* 181 NH 1337
Meallan Buidhe, Highld *H* 182 NH 3344
Meall an Damhain *H* 173 NM 7259
Meall an Doirein *H* 190 NG 8575
Meall an Fhuarain, Highld *H* 191 NC 2802
Meall an Fhuarain, Highld *H* 197 NC 5130
Meall an Fhuarain, Highld *H* 187 NG 4535
Meall an Inbhire *H* 173 NM 4656
Meallan Liath *H* 197 NC 5150
Meallan Liath Beag *H* 193 NC 8815
Meallan Liath Coire Mhic Dhughaill *H* 196 NC 3539
Meallan Liath Mór *H* 197 NC 6517
Meall an t-Seallaidh *H* 169 NN 5423
Meall an t-Sithe *H* 191 NH 1476
Meall an Tuirc *H* 192 NH 5372
Meall a' Phiobaire *H* 197 NC 6915
Meall a'Phubuill *H* 174 NN 0285
Meall Bhenneit *H* 192 NH 5483
Meall Blair *H* 174 NN 0795
Meall Buidhe, Highld *H* 180 NM 8498
Meall Buidhe, Highld *H* 175 NN 8095
Meall Buidhe, Strath *H* 174 NN 4244
Meall Buidhe, Strath *H* 160 NR 7332
Meall Buidhe, Tays *H* 174 NN 4244
Meall Buidhe, Tays *H* 175 NN 4949
Meall Cala *H* 169 NN 5012
Meall Cruaidh *H* 175 NN 5780
Meall Cruinn *H* 175 NN 4547
Meall Dearg *H* 175 NN 8841
Meall Dheirgidh *H* 192 NH 4794
Meall Dubh, Highld *H* 191 NH 2089
Meall Dubh, Highld *H* 192 NH 2407
Meall Dubh, Strath *H* 168 NS 0789
Meall Fuar-mhonaidh *H* 182 NH 4522
Meall Gainmheich *H* 169 NN 5009
Meall Garbh, Strath *H* 174 NN 1636
Meall Garbh, Tays *H* 175 NN 6443
Meall Geal 195 NB 5660
Meall Ghaordaidh *H* 175 NN 5139
Meall Ghaordaidh *H* 175 NN 5139
Meall Ghiubhais *H* 190 NG 9763
Meall Gorm, Grampn *H* 176 NO 1894
Meall Gorm, Highld *H* 180 NG 7740
Meall Gorm, Highld *H* 182 NH 2269
Meall Leacachain *H* 191 NH 2477
Meall Liath Choire *H* 191 NH 2296
Meall Loch Airigh Alasdair *H* 180 NG 7436
Meall Luaidhe *H* 175 NN 5843
Meall Luidh Mór *H* 174 NN 4179
Meall Meadhonach *H* 196 NC 4162
Meall Mhic Lomhair *H* 182 NH 3167
Meall Mór, Highld *H* 196 NC 1237
Meall Mór, Highld *H* 192 NH 5174
Meall Mór, Highld *H* 183 NH 7335
Meall Mór, Highld *H* 174 NN 1055
Meall Moraig *H* 192 NH 6694
Meall na Caorach *H* 199 ND 1027
Meall na Drochaide *H* 182 NH 5069
Meall na h-Aisre *H* 175 NH 5100
Meall na h-Eilrig *H* 182 NH 5332
Meall na h-Uamha *H* 190 NG 7765
Meall na Leitreach *H* 175 NN 6370
Meall nam Bràdhan *H* 191 NH 2690
Meall na Mèine *H* 190 NG 9081
Meall nam Fuaran *H* 175 NN 8236
Meall nan Caorach, Highld *H* 182 NH 4735
Meall nan Caorach, Tays *H* 170 NN 9233
Meall nan Con, Highld *H* 197 NC 5829
Meall nan Con, Highld *H* 173 NM 5068
Meall nan Creag Leac *H* 173 NM 8674
Meall nan Damh *H* 160 NR 9146
Meall nan Each *H* 173 NM 6364
Meall nan Ruadhag *H* 174 NN 2957
Meall nan Tarmachan *H* 175 NN 5839
Meall nan Tighearn, Central *H* 168 NN 2323
Meall nan Tighearn, Strath *H* 168 NN 2323
Meall na Speireig *H* 182 NH 4966
Meall na Suiramach *H* 187 NG 4469
Meall Odhar, Central *H* 169 NN 6414
Meall Odhar, Strath *H* 168 NM 9416
Meall Odhar, Tays *H* 169 NN 6414
Meall Odhar, Tays *H* 175 NN 6639
Meall Reamhar, Strath *H* 167 NR 8369
Meall Reamhar, Tays *H* 169 NN 6621
Meall Reamhar, Tays *H* 175 NN 8670
Meall Reamhar, Tays *H* 170 NN 8732
Meall Reamhar, Tays *H* 176 NO 0356
Meall Tairneachan *H* 175 NN 8054
Meall Tarsuinn *H* 170 NN 8729
Meall Taurnie, Central *H* 175 NN 4838
Meall Taurnie, Tays *H* 175 NN 4838
Meall Uaine *H* 176 NO 1167
Mealna Letter or Duchray Hill *H* 176 NO 1667
Meal nan Damh *H* 160 NR 9146
Mealsgate *T* 150 NY 2042
Mearbeck *T* 146 SD 8260
Mearbrook *T* 146 SD 8160
Meare *T* 101 ST 4541
Meare Green *T* 92 ST 3326
Mears Ashby *T* 120 SP 8366
Measham *T* 128 SK 3312
Meathop *T* 145 SD 4380
Meaul *H* 155 NX 5091
Meaux *T* 143 TA 0939
Meavag *T* 189 NG 1596
Meavaig *T* 189 NB 0905
Meavaig River *W* 189 NB 1007
Meavy *T* 89 SX 5467
Medbourne *T* 129 SP 8093
Medburn *T* 159 NZ 1370
Meddon *T* 90 SS 2717
Meden Vale *T* 139 SK 5769
Medmenham *T* 104 SU 8084
Medstead *T* 95 SU 6537
Meerbrook *T* 138 SJ 9960
Meer End *T* 118 SP 2474
Meesden *T* 121 TL 4232
Meeth *T* 91 SS 5408
Meggat Water *W* 157 NY 2996
Meggernie Castle 175 NN 5546
Meggethead *T* 163 NT 1621
Megget Reservoir *W* 163 NT 1922
Meg's Craig 177 NO 6844
Meidrim *T* 111 SN 2921
Meifod *T* 126 SJ 1513
Meigle 176 NO 2844
Meigle Hill *H* 164 NT 4636
Meikle Black Law *H* 165 NT 8268
Meikle Carewe Hill *H* 177 NO 8292
Meikle Conval *H* 184 NJ 2937
Meikle Craigs 161 NS 3228
Meikle Earnock *T* 162 NS 7153
Meikle Float 154 NX 0648
Meikle Hard Hill *H* 156 NX 9362
Meikle Hill *H* 183 NJ 1450
Meikleour *T* 176 NO 1539
Meikle Says Law *H* 164 NT 5861
Meikle Strath 177 NO 6471
Meikle Tarty *T* 185 NJ 9928
Meikle Wartle *T* 185 NJ 7230
Meinciau *T* 111 SN 4610
Meir *T* 127 SJ 9342
Meir Heath *T* 127 SJ 9340
Meith Bheinn *H* 180 NM 8287
Melbecks Moor 152 NY 9400
Melbost *T* 195 NB 4632
Melbost Borve *T* 195 NB 4157
Melbost Sands 195 NB 4535
Melbourn *T* 121 TL 3844
Melbourne, Derby *T* 128 SK 3825
Melbourne, Humbs *T* 142 SE 7544
Melbury 90 SS 3719
Melbury Abbas *T* 93 ST 8820
Melbury Bubb *T* 93 ST 5906
Melbury Osmond *T* 93 ST 5707
Melbury Sampford 93 ST 5706
Melby *T* 202 HU 1857
Melchbourne *T* 120 TL 0265
Melchet Court 94 SU 2722
Melcombe Bingham *T* 93 ST 7602
Meldon, Devon *T* 89 SX 5592
Meldon, Northum *T* 159 NZ 1183
Meldon Reservoir *W* 89 SX 5691
Meldreth *T* 121 TL 3746
Meldrum House 185 NJ 8129
Melfort *T* 173 NM 8314
Melgarve *T* 175 NN 4695
Meliden *T* 135 SJ 0681
Melincourt *T* 109 SN 8201
Melin-y-coed *T* 135 SH 8160
Melin-y-ddôl *T* 125 SJ 0907
Melin-y-grug *T* 125 SJ 0507
Melin-y-Wig *T* 135 SJ 0448
Melkinthorpe *T* 151 NY 5525
Melkridge *T* 158 NY 7363
Melksham *T* 101 ST 9063
Melldalloch *T* 168 NR 9374
Mellerstain House 164 NT 6439
Mell Head 199 ND 3476
Melling, Lancs *T* 145 SD 6071
Melling, Mers *T* 136 SD 3900
Mellis *T* 123 TM 1074
Mellon Charles *T* 190 NG 8491
Mellon Udrigle *T* 190 NG 8895
Mellor, G. Man *T* 138 SJ 9888
Mellor, Lancs *T* 145 SD 6530
Mellor Brook *T* 145 SD 6430
Mells, Somer *T* 101 ST 7249
Mells, Suff *T* 123 TM 4076
Melmerby, Cumbr *T* 151 NY 6137
Melmerby, N. Yks *T* 146 SE 0785
Melmerby, N. Yks *T* 147 SE 3376
Melmerby Fell 151 NY 6538
Melowther Hill *H* 162 NS 5648
Melplash *T* 93 SY 4898
Melrose *T* 164 NT 5434
Melsetter 200 ND 2689
Melsonby *T* 152 NZ 1908
Meltham *T* 138 SE 0910
Melton *T* 123 TM 2850
Meltonby *T* 148 SE 7952
Melton Constable *T* 132 TG 0433
Melton Mowbray *P* 129 SK 7519
Melton Ross *T* 142 TA 0710
Meluncart *H* 177 NO 6382
Melvaig *T* 190 NG 7486
Melverley *T* 126 SJ 3316
Melvich *T* 198 NC 8864
Melvich Bay *W* 198 NC 8865
Membury *T* 92 ST 2703
Memsie *T* 185 NJ 9762
Memus 176 NO 4258
Menabilly 87 SX 0951
Menai Bridge *T* 134 SH 5572
Menai Strait *W* 134 SH 5270
Mendham *T* 123 TM 2782
Mendick Hill *H* 163 NT 1250
Mendip Forest 101 ST 5054
Mendip Hills *H* 101 ST 5255
Mendlesham *T* 123 TM 1065
Mendlesham Green *T* 123 TM 0963
Menheniot *T* 88 SX 2862
Mennock *T* 156 NS 8008
Men of Mey 199 ND 3175
Menston *T* 146 SE 1744
Menstrie *T* 169 NS 8496
Menteith Hills *H* 169 NN 5502
Mentmore *T* 104 SP 9019
Meòir Langwell *W* 192 NH 4298
Meole Brace *T* 127 SJ 4810
Meon Hill *H* 118 SP 1745
Meonstoke *T* 95 SU 6119
Meon Valley 95 SU 6016
Meopham *T* 98 TQ 6466
Meopham Station *T* 98 TQ 6467
Mepal *T* 121 TL 4480
Meppershall *T* 120 TL 1436
Merbach *T* 113 SO 3045
Mere, Ches *T* 137 SJ 7281
Mere, Wilts *T* 93 ST 8132
Mere Brow *T* 136 SD 4118
Mereclough *T* 146 SD 8730
Mere Green *T* 128 SP 1299
Mere, The *W* 126 SJ 4035
Mereworth *T* 97 TQ 6553
Mereworth Castle 97 TQ 6653
Mergie *T* 177 NO 7988
Meriden *T* 118 SP 2482
Merkadale *T* 186 NG 3831
Merkland 154 NX 2491
Merkland Lodge 196 NC 4029
Merkland Point 160 NS 0233
Merlin's Bridge *T* 110 SM 9414
Merrick 154 NX 4185
Merrington *T* 127 SJ 4720
Merriott *T* 93 ST 4412
Merrivale *T* 89 SX 5475
Merrymeet *T* 88 SX 2766
Merse 165 NT 8146
Mersea Flats 107 TM 0513
Mersea Island 107 TM 0314
Mersehead Sands 150 NX 9254
Mersham *T* 99 TR 0539
Merstham *T* 97 TQ 2953
Merston *T* 95 SU 8903
Merstone *T* 95 SZ 5284
Merther *T* 87 SW 8644
Merthyr *T* 111 SN 3521
Merthyr Cynog *T* 112 SN 9837
Merthyr Dyfan *T* 109 ST 1170
Merthyr Mawr *T* 109 SS 8877
Merthyr Tydfil *P* 109 SO 0506
Merthyr Vale *T* 109 ST 0799
Merton, Devon *T* 91 SS 5212
Merton, G. Lon *T* 105 TQ 2569
Merton, Norf *T* 132 TL 9098
Merton, Oxon *T* 115 SP 5717
Mervinslaw *T* 158 NT 6713
Meshaw *T* 91 SS 7519
Messing *T* 106 TL 8918
Messingham *T* 142 SE 8904
Metfield *T* 123 TM 2980
Metheringham *T* 140 TF 0761
Methil *T* 171 NT 3699
Methley *T* 147 SE 3926
Methlick *T* 185 NJ 8537
Methven *T* 170 NO 0226
Methwold *T* 132 TL 7394
Methwold Fens 132 TL 6593
Methwold Hythe *T* 132 TL 7194
Mettingham *T* 123 TM 3689
Mevagissey *T* 87 SX 0144
Mevagissey Bay *W* 87 SX 0246
Mew Stone 89 SX 9149
Mexborough *T* 139 SE 4700
Mey *T* 199 ND 2872
Meysey Hampton *T* 115 SP 1200
Miavaig *T* 195 NB 0834
Michael *T* 144 SC 3290
Michaelchurch *T* 113 SO 5225
Michaelchurch Escley *T* 113 SO 3134
Michaelchurch-on-Arrow *T* 113 SO 2450
Michaelstone-y-Fedw *T* 100 ST 2484
Michaelston-le-Pit *T* 109 ST 1573
Michaelstow *T* 87 SX 0878
Micheldever *T* 103 SU 5139
Micheldever Station 103 SU 5142
Micheldever Wood *F* 95 SU 5337
Michelmersh *T* 94 SU 3426
Mickfield *T* 123 TM 1361
Mickleby *T* 153 NZ 8013
Mickle Fell 151 NY 8124
Micklefield *T* 147 SE 4433
Mickleham *T* 96 TQ 1753
Mickleover *T* 128 SK 3135
Mickleton, Durham *T* 152 NY 9623
Mickleton, Glos *T* 118 SP 1643
Mickle Trafford *T* 136 SJ 4469
Mickley *T* 147 SE 2577
Mickley Square *T* 159 NZ 0762
Mid Ardlaw *T* 185 NJ 9463
Midbarrow (lightship) 107 TR 1992
Midbea *T* 200 HY 4444
Mid Beltie *T* 177 NJ 6200
Midberg 205 HU 5988
Middle Assendon *T* 104 SU 7485
Middle Aston *T* 115 SP 4726
Middle Barton *T* 115 SP 4325
Middlebie *T* 157 NY 2176
Middle Claydon *T* 119 SP 7125
Middle Drums 177 NO 5957
Middle Fell *H* 151 NY 7444
Middle Fen 121 TL 5779
Middlefield Law *H* 162 NS 6830
Middle Grounds 100 ST 3576
Middleham *T* 146 SE 1287
Middlehope *T* 116 SO 4988
Middlehope Moor 152 NY 8841
Middle Level Main Drain *W* 131 TF 5405
Middle Littleton *T* 118 SP 0747
Middle Maes-coed *T* 113 SO 3333
Middlemarsh *T* 93 ST 6707
Middle Mill *T* 110 SM 8026
Middle Moor, Cambs 121 TL 2789
Middle Moor, Northum 165 NU 1423
Middle Mouse 134 SH 3895
Middle Muir 163 NS 8525
Middlemuir Farm 185 NJ 9420
Middle Rasen *T* 140 TF 0889
Middle Rigg 170 NO 0608
Middlesbrough *P* 153 NZ 4920
Middle Shield Park 158 NY 6070
Middlesmoor *T* 146 SE 0974
Middleston Moor *T* 152 NZ 2533
Middlestown *T* 139 SE 2617
Middleton, Cumbr *T* 145 SD 6286
Middleton, Derby *T* 138 SK 1963
Middleton, Derby *T* 128 SK 2756
Middleton, Essex *T* 122 TL 8739
Middleton, G. Man *T* 137 SD 8606
Middleton, Grampn 185 NJ 8419
Middleton, Hants *T* 102 SU 4244
Middleton, H. & W *T* 116 SO 5469
Middleton, Lancs *T* 145 SD 4258
Middleton, Lothn *T* 164 NT 3658
Middleton, Norf *T* 132 TF 6615
Middleton, Northnts *T* 120 SP 8490
Middleton, Northum *T* 165 NU 0023
Middleton, Northum *T* 165 NU 1035
Middleton, Northum *T* 159 NZ 0685
Middleton, N. Yks *T* 146 SE 1249
Middleton, N. Yks *T* 148 SE 7885
Middleton, Shrops *T* 126 SJ 3129
Middleton, Shrops *T* 126 SO 2999
Middleton, Shrops *T* 116 SO 5477
Middleton, Strath *T* 172 NL 9443
Middleton, Suff *T* 123 TM 4367
Middleton, Tays 170 NO 1206
Middleton, Tays 176 NO 1447
Middleton, Warw *T* 128 SP 1798
Middleton, W. Yks *T* 147 SE 3028
Middleton Cheney *T* 119 SP 4942
Middleton Common 152 NY 9531
Middleton Green *T* 128 SJ 9935
Middleton Tongue 146 SD 9181
Middleton Hall *T* 165 NT 9825
Middleton-in-Teesdale *T* 152 NY 9425
Middleton-on-Sea *T* 96 SZ 9799
Middleton on the Hill *T* 116 SO 5464
Middleton-on-the-Wolds *T* 149 SE 9449
Middleton Priors *T* 117 SO 6290
Middleton Scriven *T* 117 SO 6887
Middleton St George *T* 153 NZ 3413
Middleton Stoney *T* 115 SP 5323
Middleton Tyas *T* 152 NZ 2205
Middletown *T* 126 SJ 3012
Middle Tysoe *T* 118 SP 3444
Middle Wallop *T* 94 SU 2937
Middlewich *T* 137 SJ 7066
Middle Winterslow *T* 94 SU 2432
Middle Witchyburn *T* 184 NJ 6356
Middle Woodford *T* 94 SU 1136
Middlewood Green *T* 123 TM 0961
Middlewood Station 137 SJ 9484
Middlezoy *T* 92 ST 3732
Middridge *T* 152 NZ 2526
Midfield *T* 197 NC 5865
Midge Hall *T* 145 SD 5123
Midgeholme *T* 158 NY 6358
Midgham *T* 103 SU 5567
Midgley *T* 146 SE 0326
Mid Hill, D. & G *H* 156 NS 6907
Mid Hill, Orkney *H* 200 HY 3324
Mid Hill, Strath *H* 154 NX 2889
Midhope Moors 138 SK 1998
Midhopestones *T* 139 SK 2399
Midhurst *P* 95 SU 8821
Mid Kame *H* 203 HU 4158
Midland Ness 200 HY 3203
Midlem *T* 164 NT 5227
Midmar Forest *F* 185 NJ 7004
Mid Moile *H* 154 NX 0971
Mid Sannox *T* 160 NS 0145
Midsomer Norton *T* 101 ST 6654
Mid Thundergay 160 NR 8846
Midtown *T* 190 NG 8285
Midtown of Buchromb *T* 184 NJ 3143
Mid Urchany 183 NH 8849
Midville *T* 141 TF 3857
Mid Walls *T* 202 HU 2050
Mid Yell *T* 205 HU 5090
Mid Yell Voe *W* 205 HU 5191
Migneint 135 SH 7842
Migvie *T* 184 NJ 4306
Milborne Port *T* 93 ST 6718
Milborne St Andrew *T* 93 SY 8097
Milborne Wick *T* 93 ST 6620
Milbourne *T* 159 NZ 1175
Milburn *T* 151 NY 6529
Milburn Forest *F* 151 NY 7232
Milburn Geo 203 HU 4012
Milbury Heath *T* 101 ST 6690
Milcombe *T* 115 SP 4134
Milden *T* 122 TL 9546
Mildenhall, Suff *T* 122 TL 7174
Mildenhall, Wilts *T* 102 SU 2169
Mildenhall Fen 122 TL 6678
Milebrooke *T* 116 SO 3172
Milebush *T* 97 TQ 7545
Mile Elm *T* 102 ST 9969
Mile End, Essex *T* 122 TL 9927
Mile End, Glos *T* 113 SO 5911
Mileham *T* 132 TF 9119
Mile Hill *H* 176 NO 3157
Milesmark *T* 170 NT 0788
Milfield *T* 165 NT 9333
Milford, Derby *T* 128 SK 3545
Milford, Devon *T* 90 SS 2322
Milford, Staffs *T* 128 SJ 9721
Milford, Surrey *T* 96 SU 9442
Milford Haven, Dyfed *W* 110 SM 8504
Milford Haven, Dyfed *P* 110 SM 9006
Milford on Sea *T* 94 SZ 2892
Milk Hill *H* 102 SU 1064
Milkieston Rings 163 NT 2445
Milkwall *T* 113 SO 5809
Milland *T* 95 SU 8327
Mill Bank *T* 146 SE 0321
Mill Bay, Orkney *W* 200 HY 5736
Mill Bay, Orkney *W* 201 HY 6626
Mill Bay, Orkney *W* 200 ND 3095
Millbounds *T* 200 HY 5635
Millbreck *T* 185 NK 0045
Millbridge *T* 103 SU 8442
Millbrook, Beds *T* 120 TL 0138
Millbrook, Corn *T* 88 SX 4252
Millbrook, Hants *T* 94 SU 3813
Millbrook Station 120 TL 0040
Mill Buie, Grampn *H* 183 NJ 0950
Millbuie, Highld 182 NH 6459
Millburn *T* 161 NS 4429
Millburn Geo, Shetld 203 HU 4012
Millburn Geo, Shetld 203 HU 5239
Mill Corner *T* 98 TQ 8223
Millden Lodge 177 NO 5479
Milldens 177 NO 5450
Milldoe *H* 200 HY 3520
Mill End, Bucks *T* 104 SU 7885
Mill End, Herts *T* 121 TL 3032
Millerhill *T* 171 NT 3269
Miller's Bay *W* 160 NR 7067
Miller's Dale *T* 138 SK 1473
Milleur Point 154 NX 0273
Millfire *H* 155 NX 5084
Mill Green, Essex *T* 106 TL 6401
Mill Green, Shrops *T* 127 SJ 6828
Millheugh *T* 162 NS 7551
Mill Hill *T* 105 TQ 2292
Millholme *T* 151 SD 5690
Millhouse, Cumbr *T* 150 NY 3637
Millhouse, Strath *T* 168 NR 9570
Millikenpark *T* 161 NS 4162
Millington *T* 148 SE 8351
Milljoan Hill *H* 154 NX 1177
Mill Lane *T* 103 SU 7850
Millmeece *T* 127 SJ 8333
Mill of Kingoodie 185 NJ 8325
Millom *T* 144 SD 1780
Millport *T* 161 NS 1655
Mill Rig *H* 162 NS 6334
Mill Side *T* 145 SD 4484
Millstone Edge *H* 157 NT 4300
Millstone Hill, Grampn *H* 184 NJ 4257
Millstone Hill, Grampn *H* 184 NJ 6720
Millstone Point 160 NR 9950
Mill Street *T* 132 TG 0118
Millthrop *T* 151 SD 6691
Milltimber *T* 177 NJ 8501
Millton of Corsindale *T* 185 NJ 6809
Millton of Murtle *T* 177 NJ 8702
Milltown, Derby *T* 139 SK 3561
Milltown, Devon *T* 91 SS 5538
Milltown, D. & G *T* 157 NY 3375
Milltown, Grampn *T* 184 NJ 4716
Milltown, Grampn *T* 184 NJ 5448
Milltown of Aberdalgie *T* 170 NO 0720
Milltown of Auchindoun *T* 184 NJ 3540
Milltown of Campfield *T* 177 NJ 6400
Milltown of Craigston *T* 185 NJ 7655
Milltown of Edinvillie *T* 184 NJ 2640
Milltown of Towie *T* 184 NJ 4612
Milnathort *T* 170 NO 1204
Milne Height *H* 157 NY 1597
Milngavie *T* 169 NS 5574
Milnrow *T* 137 SD 9212
Milnthorpe *T* 145 SD 4981
Milovaig *T* 186 NG 1450
Milray Hill *H* 156 NS 5905
Milson *T* 117 SO 6473
Milstead *T* 98 TQ 9058
Milston *T* 102 SU 1645
Milton, Cambs *T* 121 TL 4762
Milton, Central *T* 169 NN 5001
Milton, Cumbr *T* 158 NY 5560
Milton, D. & G *T* 154 NX 2154
Milton, D. & G *T* 156 NX 8470
Milton, Dyfed *T* 110 SN 0403
Milton, Grampn 184 NJ 1719
Milton, Grampn *T* 184 NJ 5163
Milton, Highld *T* 199 ND 3451
Milton, Highld *T* 182 NH 3055
Milton, Highld *T* 182 NH 4930
Milton, Highld *T* 182 NH 5749
Milton, Highld *T* 193 NH 7674
Milton, Highld *T* 183 NH 9553
Milton, Oxon *T* 115 SP 4535
Milton, Oxon *T* 103 SU 4891
Milton, Staffs *T* 127 SJ 9050
Milton, Strath *T* 169 NS 4274
Milton, Tays 175 NN 9138
Milton, Tays 176 NO 3843
Milton Abbas *T* 93 ST 8001
Milton Abbot *T* 88 SX 4079
Milton Bridge *T* 163 NT 2462
Milton Bryan *T* 120 SP 9730
Milton Burn *W* 170 NN 9532
Milton Clevedon *T* 93 ST 6637
Milton Coldwells *T* 185 NJ 9538
Milton Combe *T* 88 SX 4865
Milton Damerel *T* 90 SS 3810
Miltonduff *T* 184 NJ 1860
Milton Ernest *T* 120 TL 0156

Milton Green Mynydd Rhiw-Saeson

Milton Green *T* 136 SJ 4658
Milton Hill *T* 103 SU 4790
Miltonise 154 NX 2174
Milton Keynes *P* 120 SP 8733
Milton Keynes Village *T* 120 SP 8839
Milton Libourne *T* 102 SU 1960
Milton Loch *W* 156 NX 8471
Milton Malsor *T* 119 SP 7355
Milton Morenish 169 NN 6135
Milton Ness 177 NO 7764
Milton of Auchinhove *T* 184 NJ 5503
Milton of Balgonie *T* 171 NO 3200
Milton of Buchanan *T* 169 NS 4490
Milton of Campsie *T* 169 NS 6576
Milton of Corsindae *T* 185 NJ 6809
Milton of Cushnie *T* 184 NJ 5211
Milton of Edradour 176 NN 9558
Milton of Gollanfield 183 NH 7952
Milton of Lesmore *T* 184 NJ 4628
Milton of Murtle *T* 177 NJ 8702
Milton of Noth 184 NJ 5028
Milton of Tullich *T* 176 NO 3897
Milton on Stour *T* 93 ST 8028
Milton Point 154 NX 3146
Milton Regis *T* 98 TQ 9064
Milton-under-Wychwood *T* 115 SP 2618
Milverton *T* 92 ST 1225
Milwich *T* 128 SJ 9732
Milwr *T* 136 SJ 1974
Minard *T* 168 NR 9796
Minard Castle 168 NR 9794
Minard Point 173 NM 8123
Minchinhampton *T* 114 SO 8700
Minch Moor 164 NT 3533
Mindrum *T* 165 NT 8432
Minehead *T* 91 SS 9746
Minera *T* 126 SJ 2751
Minety *T* 102 SU 0390
Minffordd *T* 134 SH 5938
Mingary *T* 178 NF 7426
Mingay 186 NG 2257
Minginish 187 NG 4224
Mingulay 178 NL 5683
Mingulay Bay *W* 178 NL 5783
Miningsby *T* 141 TF 3264
Minions *T* 88 SX 2671
Minishant *T* 161 NS 3314
Minley Manor 104 SU 8258
Minllyn *T* 125 SH 8514
Minnes *T* 185 NJ 9423
Minnigaff *T* 154 NX 4166
Minnonie 185 NJ 7760
Minnygap Height *H* 156 NY 0296
Minskip *T* 147 SE 3864
Minstead *T* 94 SU 2811
Minster, Kent *T* 98 TQ 9573
Minster, Kent *T* 99 TR 3164
Minsteracres *T* 152 NZ 0255
Minsterley *T* 126 SJ 3705
Minster Lovell *T* 115 SP 3111
Minsterworth *T* 114 SO 7717
Minterne Magna *T* 93 ST 6504
Minting *T* 141 TF 1873
Mintlaw *T* 185 NK 0048
Minto *T* 158 NT 5620
Minto Hills *H* 158 NT 5520
Minton *T* 116 SO 4390
Minwear *T* 110 SN 0413
Minworth *T* 118 SP 1592
Mio Ness, Shetld 205 HU 4279
Mio Ness, Shetld 205 HU 6670
Mirbister *T* 200 HY 3119
Mireland *T* 199 ND 3160
Mirfield *T* 138 SE 2019
Mirkady Point 200 HY 5306
Misbister Geo 199 ND 3388
Miserden *T* 114 SO 9308
Mishnish 173 NM 4656
Miskin *T* 109 ST 0481
Misson *T* 140 SK 6995
Misterton, Leic *T* 119 SP 5583
Misterton, Notts *T* 140 SK 7694
Misterton, Somer *T* 93 ST 4508
Mistley *T* 123 TM 1231
Mistylaw Muir 161 NS 3061
Mitcham *T* 105 TQ 2868
Mitcheldean *T* 114 SO 6618
Mitchell *T* 87 SW 8654
Mitchel Troy *T* 113 SO 4910
Mitford *T* 159 NZ 1786
Mithian *T* 86 SW 7450
Mitton *T* 127 SJ 8815
Mixbury *T* 115 SP 6033
Mixon *T* 138 SK 0457
Mobberley *T* 137 SJ 7879
Moccas *T* 113 SO 3542
Mochdre, Clwyd *T* 135 SH 8278
Mochdre, Powys *T* 125 SO 0788
Mochrum *T* 154 NX 3446
Mochrum Fell *H* 154 NX 3050
Mochrum Loch *W* 154 NX 3053
Mockbeggar Wharf 136 SJ 2591
Mockerkin *T* 150 NY 0923
Modbury *T* 89 SX 6551
Moddershall *T* 127 SJ 9236
Moel-ddu *H* 134 SH 5844
Moel Eilio *H* 134 SH 5557
Moel Fammau *H* 136 SJ 1662
Moel Feity *H* 109 SN 8423
Moel Fferna *H* 126 SJ 1139
Moelfre, Clwyd *T* 126 SJ 1828
Moelfre, Dyfed *H* 111 SN 3236
Moelfre, Gwyn *T* 134 SH 5186
Moelfre, Gwyn *H* 125 SH 6224
Moelfre, Powys *H* 125 SN 8598
Moelfre Isaf *H* 135 SH 9573
Moelfre Uchaf *H* 135 SH 8971
Moel Garegog *H* 126 SJ 2152
Moel Hebog *H* 134 SH 5646
Moel Hiraddug *A* 135 SJ 0678
Moel Hywel *H* 125 SO 0071
Moel Llyfnant *H* 135 SH 8035
Moel Llyn *H* 135 SH 8957
Moel Llys-y-coed *H* 136 SJ 1565
Moel Morfydd *H* 126 SJ 1645
Moel Penamnen *H* 135 SH 7148
Moel Seisiog *H* 135 SH 8657
Moel Ton-mawr *H* 109 SS 8387
Moel Tryfan *H* 134 SH 5156
Moel Wnion *H* 135 SH 6569
Moelwyn Mawr *H* 135 SH 6544
Moel y Feidiog *H* 135 SH 7832
Moel y Gaer *A* 136 SJ 1461
Moel-y-Llyn, Dyfed *H* 125 SN 7191
Moel-y-llyn, Powys *H* 125 SH 9415
Moel y Mor *H* 111 SN 4146
Moel Ysgyfarnogod *H* 135 SH 6534
Moffat *T* 157 NT 0805
Moffat Water *W* 157 NT 1307
Mogerhanger *T* 120 TL 1449
Moidart 173 NM 7673
Moine House 197 NC 5160
Mòine Mhór 167 NR 8293
Moira *T* 128 SK 3115
Mol a' Tuath *W* 178 NF 8535
Mol-chlach *T* 187 NG 4513
Mold *P* 136 SJ 2464
Molehill Green *T* 105 TL 5624
Molescroft *T* 142 TA 0240
Molesworth *T* 120 TL 0775
Molland *T* 91 SS 8028
Molland Common 91 SS 8130
Mollington, Ches *T* 136 SJ 3870
Mollington, Oxon *T* 119 SP 4447
Mollinsburn *T* 169 NS 7171
Mol Truisg *W* 189 NB 3505
Monach Islands or Heisker 188 NF 6262
Monachyle 169 NN 4719
Monachty *T* 124 SN 5062
Monachyle Glen 169 NN 4722
Monadhliath Mountains *H* 183 NH 6610
Monadh Mór, Grampn *H* 175 NN 9394
Monadh Mór, Highld *H* 175 NN 9394
Monamenach *H* 176 NO 1770
Monar Lodge 182 NH 2040
Monaughty Forest *F* 183 NJ 1358
Monawee *H* 176 NO 4080
Monboddo 177 NO 7478
Moncreiffe Hill *H* 170 NO 1319
Mondynes *T* 177 NO 7779
Monewden *T* 123 TM 2458
Moneydie 170 NO 0629
Money Head 154 NX 0448
Mongour *H* 177 NO 7590
Moniaive *T* 156 NX 7791
Monifieth *T* 171 NO 4932
Monikie *T* 171 NO 4938
Monikie Burn *W* 177 NO 5437
Monikie Reservoir *W* 171 NO 5038
Monimail *T* 171 NO 2914
Monington *T* 110 SN 1343
Monivey *W* 200 HY 4048
Monken Hadley *T* 105 TQ 2497
Monk Fryston *T* 147 SE 5029
Monkhopton *T* 127 SO 6293
Monkland *T* 113 SO 4657
Monkleigh *T* 90 SS 4520
Monknash *T* 109 SS 9270
Monkokehampton *T* 91 SS 5805
Monks Eleigh *T* 122 TL 9647
Monk's Heath *T* 137 SJ 8474
Monk Sherborne *T* 103 SU 6056
Monkshill *T* 185 NJ 7941
Monks House Rocks 165 NU 2033
Monkside *H* 158 NY 6894
Monksilver *T* 92 ST 0737
Monks Kirby *T* 119 SP 4683
Monk Soham *T* 123 TM 2165
Monks Risbbrough *T* 104 SP 8004
Monkstone Point 110 SN 1503
Monkswood *T* 113 SO 3402
Monkton, Devon *T* 92 ST 1803
Monkton, Kent *T* 99 TR 2865
Monkton, Strath *T* 161 NS 3527
Monkton, T. & W *T* 159 NZ 3263
Monkton Combe *T* 101 ST 7762
Monkton Deverill *T* 93 ST 8537
Monkton Farleigh *T* 101 ST 8065
Monkton Heathfield *T* 92 ST 2526
Monkton Up Wimborne *T* 94 SU 0113
Monkwood *T* 95 SU 6731
Monmouth *P* 113 SO 5113
Monmouthshire & Brecon Canal *W* 109 SO 1122
Monnington on Wye *T* 113 SO 3743
Monreith *T* 154 NX 3641
Monreith Bay *W* 154 NX 3540
Monreith Mains *T* 154 NX 3643
Montacute *T* 93 ST 4916
Montacute House *A* 93 ST 4917
Montcoffer House 185 NJ 6861
Montford *T* 126 SJ 4114
Montgarrie *T* 184 NJ 5717
Montgomery *T* 126 SO 2296
Montgreenan *T* 161 NS 3444
Montrave 171 NO 3706
Montreathmont Forest *F* 177 NO 5654
Montreathmont Moor 177 NO 5954
Montrose *T* 177 NO 7157
Montrose Basin *W* 177 NO 6957
Montsale *T* 107 TR 0097
Monxton *T* 102 SU 3144
Monyash *T* 138 SK 1566
Monymusk *T* 185 NJ 6815
Monynut Edge *H* 164 NT 7068
Monynut Water *W* 164 NT 6966
Monzie *T* 170 NN 8725
Moonen Bay *W* 186 NG 1446
Moonzie 171 NO 3417
Moorby *T* 141 TF 2964
Moorcot *T* 113 SO 3555
Moor Crichel *T* 94 ST 9908
Moordown *T* 94 SZ 0994
Moore *T* 137 SJ 5884
Moorends *T* 142 SE 6915
Moor Fea *H* 200 ND 1999
Moorfoot Hills, Border *H* 164 NT 3251
Moorfoot Hills, Lothn *H* 164 NT 3251
Moorhall *T* 139 SK 3174
Moorhampton *T* 113 SO 3947
Moorhouse, Cumbr *T* 150 NY 3356
Moorhouse, Notts *T* 140 SK 7566
Moorland or Northmoor Green *T* 92 ST 3332
Moorlinch *T* 92 ST 3936
Moor Loch *W* 170 NS 9488
Moor Monkton *T* 147 SE 5056
Moor of Balvack *T* 184 NJ 6613
Moor Park 169 NS 4792
Moorsholm *T* 153 NZ 6814
Moorside *T* 138 SD 9507
Moors River *W* 94 SZ 1099
Moor, The *T* 97 TQ 7629
Moortown, I. of W *T* 94 SZ 4283
Moortown, Lincs *T* 142 TF 0799
Moota Hill *H* 150 NY 1436
Morangie *T* 193 NH 7683
Morangie Forest *F* 193 NH 7480
Morar *T* 180 NM 6793
Moray Firth *W* 183 NH 9458
Morborne *T* 120 TL 1391
Morchard Bishop *T* 91 SS 7607
Morchard Road Station 91 SS 7505
Morcombelake *T* 92 SY 4094
Morcott *T* 130 SK 9200
Morda *T* 126 SJ 2827
Morden, Dorset *T* 93 SY 9195
Morden, G. Lon *T* 105 TQ 2567
Mordiford *T* 113 SO 5737
Mordon *T* 152 NZ 3226
More *T* 116 SO 3491
Morebath *T* 91 SS 9524
Morebattle *T* 164 NT 7724
Morecambe *P* 145 SD 4364
Morecambe Bay *W* 145 SD 3567
Morefield *T* 191 NH 1195
Moreleigh *T* 89 SX 7652
Morenish 169 NN 5935
Moresby *T* 150 NX 9921
Moresby Parks *T* 150 NX 9919
Morestead *T* 95 SU 5025
Moreton, Dorset *T* 93 SY 8089
Moreton, Essex *T* 105 TL 5307
Moreton, Mers *T* 136 SJ 2690
Moreton, Oxon *T* 104 SP 6904
Moreton, Staffs *T* 127 SJ 7917
Moreton Corbet *T* 127 SJ 5623
Moretonhampstead *T* 89 SX 7586
Moreton-in-Marsh *T* 115 SP 2032
Moreton Jeffries *T* 113 SO 6048
Moreton Morrell *T* 118 SP 3156
Moreton on Lugg *T* 113 SO 5045
Moreton Pinkney *T* 119 SP 5749
Moreton Say *T* 127 SJ 6334
Moreton's Leam *A* 131 TL 3099
Moreton Valence *T* 114 SO 7809
Morfa Bychan *T* 134 SH 5437
Morfa Dyffryn 124 SH 5624
Morfa Glas *T* 109 SN 8706
Morfa Harlech 134 SH 5833
Morfa Nefyn *T* 134 SH 2840
Morgan's Hill *H* 102 SU 0367
Morgan's Vale *T* 94 SU 1921
Morland *T* 151 NY 5922
Morley, Derby *T* 128 SK 3941
Morley, Durham *T* 152 NZ 1227
Morley, W. Yks *T* 147 SE 2627
Morley Green *T* 137 SJ 8282
Morley St Botolph *T* 132 TM 0799
Mormond Hill *H* 185 NJ 9757
Morningside *T* 171 NT 2471
Morningthorpe *T* 123 TM 2192
Mornish 172 NM 3853
Morpeth *P* 159 NZ 1986
Morphie 177 NO 7164
Morrey *T* 128 SK 1318
Morris Fen 131 TF 2907
Morriston *T* 108 SS 6698
Morsgail Forest 195 NB 1217
Morston *T* 132 TG 0048
Mort Bank 145 SD 3067
Morte Bay *W* 90 SS 4343
Morte Point 90 SS 4445
Morthoe *T* 90 SS 4545
Mortimer *T* 104 SU 6564
Mortimer Cross *T* 116 SO 4263
Mortimer's Deep *W* 170 NT 1883
Mortimer West End *T* 104 SU 6363
Mortlake *T* 105 TQ 2075
Mortlich *H* 177 NJ 5301
Morton, Avon *T* 101 ST 6490
Morton, Derby *T* 139 SK 4060
Morton, Lincs *T* 140 SK 8091
Morton, Lincs *T* 130 TF 0924
Morton, Norf *T* 133 TG 1217
Morton, Shrops *T* 126 SJ 2924
Morton Bagot *T* 118 SP 1164
Morton Castle *A* 156 NX 8999
Morton-on-Swale *T* 152 SE 3291
Morton Reservoir *W* 163 NT 0763
Morton's Leam *A* 131 TL 2999
Moruisg *H* 191 NH 1049
Morvah *T* 86 SW 4035
Morval *T* 88 SX 2656
Morven, Grampn *H* 184 NJ 3704
Morven, Highld *H* 198 ND 0028
Morvern 173 NM 6754
Morvich, Highld *T* 193 NC 7500
Morvich, Highld *T* 180 NG 9621
Morville *T* 127 SO 6794
Morwenstow *T* 90 SS 2015
Morwick Hall 159 NU 2303
Mosborough *T* 139 SK 4280
Moscow *T* 161 NS 4840
Mossedale *T* 150 NY 3532
Moseley, H. & W *T* 117 SO 8159
Moseley, W. Mids *T* 118 SP 0883
Moss, Clwyd *T* 126 SJ 3053
Moss, Highld 173 NM 6868
Moss, Strath *T* 172 NL 9644
Moss, S. Yks *T* 139 SE 5914
Mossat *T* 184 NJ 4719
Moss Bank, Mers *T* 137 SJ 5197
Mossbank, Shetld *T* 205 HU 4575
Moss Bay *W* 150 NX 9826
Mossblown *T* 161 NS 4024
Mossburnford *T* 158 NT 6616
Mossdale *T* 156 NX 6670
Mossdale Moor 151 SD 8090
Mossend *T* 162 NS 7360
Mossgiel *T* 161 NS 4828
Moss Hill *H* 184 NJ 3117
Mosside 176 NO 4252
Mossley *T* 138 SD 9701
Moss Moor 138 SE 0014
Moss of Barmuckity *T* 184 NJ 2461
Moss of Cruden 185 NK 0440
Mosspaul Hotel 157 NY 4099
Moss Side *T* 145 SD 3830
Mosstodloch *T* 184 NJ 3360
Mosston 177 NO 5444
Mosterton *T* 93 ST 4505
Mostyn *T* 136 SJ 1580
Mostyn Bank 136 SJ 1482
Motcombe *T* 93 ST 8425
Mote House 98 TQ 7855
Mote of Druchtag *A* 154 NX 3547
Mote of Mark *A* 155 NX 8454
Mote of Urr *A* 156 NX 8164
Motherwell *T* 162 NS 7557
Motte of Dinning *A* 156 NX 8990
Mottingham *T* 105 TQ 4272
Mottisfont *T* 94 SU 3226
Mottistone *T* 94 SZ 4083
Mottram in Longdendale *T* 138 SJ 9995
Mottram St Andrew *T* 137 SJ 8778
Moudy Mea *H* 152 NY 8711
Moughton 146 SD 7971
Mouldsworth *T* 137 SJ 5171
Moulin *T* 175 NN 9459
Moul of Eswick 203 HU 5053
Moulsecoomb *T* 97 TQ 3307
Moulsford *T* 103 SU 5983
Moulsoe *T* 120 SP 9041
Moulton, Ches *T* 137 SJ 6569
Moulton, Lincs *T* 131 TF 3024
Moulton, Northnts *T* 119 SP 7868
Moulton, N. Yks *T* 152 NZ 2303
Moulton, Suff *T* 122 TL 6964
Moulton Chapel *T* 131 TF 2918
Moulton Seas End *T* 131 TF 3227
Mound Rock 193 NH 7898
Mounie Castle 185 NJ 7628
Mount, Corn *T* 87 SW 7856
Mount, Corn *T* 87 SX 1467
Mountain Ash *T* 109 ST 0499
Mountain Cross *T* 163 NT 1446
Mount Battock, Grampn *H* 177 NO 5584
Mount Battock, Tays *H* 177 NO 5584
Mountbenger *T* 164 NT 3125
Mount Blair *H* 176 NO 1662
Mount Bures *T* 122 TL 9032
Mount Caburn *A* 97 TQ 4408
Mount Eagle *H* 182 NH 6459
Mount Edgecumbe 88 SX 4353
Mountfield *T* 97 TQ 7420
Mountgerald *T* 182 NH 5761
Mount Grace Priory *A* 153 SE 4498
Mount Harry *H* 97 TQ 3812
Mount Hawke *T* 86 SW 7147
Mount Hill *H* 171 NO 3316
Mountjoy *T* 87 SW 8760
Mount Keen, Grampn *H* 176 NO 4086
Mount Keen, Tays *H* 176 NO 4086
Mountnessing *T* 106 TQ 6297
Mount of Haddoch *H* 184 NJ 4128
Mounton *T* 113 ST 5193
Mount's Bay *W* 86 SW 5525
Mount Shade *H* 177 NO 6287
Mountsorrel *T* 129 SK 5814
Mountstuart, Strath 161 NS 1059
Mount Stuart, Strath *H* 156 NS 7519
Mount, The *H* 163 NT 1457
Mousa 203 HU 4624
Mousa Sound *W* 203 HU 4424
Mousehole *T* 86 SW 4626
Mousen *T* 165 NU 1232
Mouse Water *W* 163 NS 9145
Mouswald *T* 157 NY 0672
Mouth of the Humber *W* 143 TA 3808
Mouth of the Severn *W* 100 ST 3476
Mow Cop, Ches *T* 137 SJ 8557
Mow Cop, Staffs *T* 137 SJ 8557
Mowhaugh *T* 158 NT 8120
Mowsley *T* 119 SP 6489
Moy *T* 174 NN 4282
Moy Burn *W* 183 NH 7836
Moy Forest 174 NN 4385
Moy Hall 183 NH 7635
Moy House 183 NJ 0159
Moyles Court *T* 94 SU 1608
Moylgrove *T* 110 SN 1144
Moy Lodge 175 NN 4483
Mozie Law, Border *H* 158 NT 8215
Mozie Law, Northum *H* 158 NT 8215
Muasdale *T* 160 NR 6840
Muchalls *T* 177 NO 9092
Much Birch *T* 113 SO 5030
Much Cowarne *T* 113 SO 6247
Much Dewchurch *T* 113 SO 4831
Muchelney *T* 93 ST 4224
Much Hadham *T* 105 TL 4422
Much Hoole *T* 145 SD 4723
Muchlarnick *T* 87 SX 2156
Much Marcle *T* 114 SO 6633
Muchrachd 182 NH 2833
Much Wenlock *T* 127 SO 6299
Muck *H* 179 NM 4179
Muckfoot 154 NX 2186
Mucking *T* 106 TQ 6881
Muckle Burn, Central *W* 169 NN 7807
Muckle Burn, Highld *W* 183 NH 9451
Muckle Burn, Tays *W* 169 NN 7807
Muckle Cairn *H* 176 NO 3776
Muckle Flugga 205 HP 6019
Muckle Green Holm 200 HY 5227
Muckle Holm 205 HU 4088
Muckle Ossa 204 HU 2285
Muckle Roe 203 HU 3165
Muckle Skerry, Orkney 199 ND 4678
Muckle Skerry, Shetld 205 HU 6273
Mucklestone *T* 127 SJ 7237
Muckleton *T* 127 SJ 5921
Muckletown *T* 184 NJ 5721
Muckle Water *W* 200 HY 3930
Muckton *T* 141 TF 3781
Mudale *T* 197 NC 5336
Muddiford *T* 91 SS 5638
Mudeford *T* 94 SZ 1892
Mudford *T* 93 ST 5719
Mudgley *T* 101 ST 4445
Mudlee Bracks, Grampn *H* 177 NO 5185
Mudlee Bracks, Tays *H* 177 NO 5185
Mugdock *T* 169 NS 5576
Mugdock Reservoir *W* 169 NS 5575
Mugeary *T* 187 NG 4439
Mugginton *T* 128 SK 2843
Muggleswick *T* 152 NZ 0450
Muggleswick Common 152 NZ 0146
Muie *T* 192 NC 6704
Muir *T* 176 NO 0689
Muirden *T* 185 NJ 7053
Muirdrum *T* 177 NO 5637
Muirhead, Fife 171 NO 2805
Muirhead, Strath *T* 169 NS 6869
Muirhead, Tays *T* 171 NO 3434
Muirhead Reservoir *W* 161 NS 2556
Muirhouses *T* 170 NT 0280
Muirkirk *T* 162 NS 6927
Muirneag *H* 195 NB 4748
Muir of Dinnet 176 NO 4397
Muir of Fairburn *T* 182 NH 4853
Muir of Fowlis *T* 184 NJ 5612
Muir of Orchil 170 NN 8612
Muir of Ord *T* 182 NH 5250
Muir of the Clans 183 NH 8352
Muir of Thorn 176 NO 0837
Muir Park Reservoir *W* 169 NS 4892
Muirshearlich *T* 174 NN 1380
Muirskie 177 NO 8396
Muirtack, Grampn *T* 185 NJ 8146
Muirtack, Grampn *T* 185 NJ 9937
Muirton, Highld *T* 183 NH 7463
Muirton, Tays *T* 170 NN 9211
Muirton of Ardblair *T* 176 NO 1743
Muirton of Ballochy *T* 177 NO 6462
Muiryfold 185 NJ 7651
Muker *T* 152 SD 9097
Mulbarton *T* 133 TG 1900
Mulben *T* 184 NJ 3550
Muldoanich 178 NL 6994
Mulgrave Castle 153 NZ 8412
Mulindry 166 NR 3559
Mullach Clach a' Bhlàir *H* 175 NN 8892
Mullach Coire a' Chuir *H* 168 NN 1703
Mullach Coire Mhic Fhearchair *H* 191 NH 0573
Mullach Fraoch-choire *H* 181 NH 0917
Mullach Mór *H* 179 NG 3801
Mullach na Càrn *H* 180 NG 6029
Mullach nan Coirean *H* 174 NN 1266
Mullach na Reidheachd *H* 195 NB 0914
Mullardoch House 182 NH 2331
Mull Head, Orkney 200 HY 5055
Mull Head, Orkney 201 HY 5909
Mullion *T* 86 SW 6719
Mullion Cove *T* 86 SW 6617
Mullion Island 86 SW 6617
Mull of Cara 160 NR 6343
Mull of Galloway 154 NX 1530
Mull of Kintyre 160 NR 6006
Mull of Logan 154 NX 0741
Mull of Miljoan *H* 154 NX 2796
Mull of Oa 166 NR 2641
Mullwharchar *H* 155 NX 4586
Mumbles Head 108 SS 6387
Mumbles, The *T* 108 SS 6187
Mumby *T* 141 TF 5174
Muncaster Castle *A* 150 SD 1096
Munderfield Row *T* 117 SO 6551
Munderfield Stocks *T* 117 SO 6550
Mundesley *T* 133 TG 3136
Mundford *T* 132 TL 8093
Mundham, Norf *T* 133 TM 3397
Mundham, W. Susx *T* 95 SU 8701
Mundon *T* 106 TL 8602
Mundurno 185 NJ 9413
Munerigie *T* 174 NH 2702
Mu Ness, Shetld 205 HP 6301
Mu Ness, Shetld 202 HU 1652
Muness Castle *A* 205 HP 6201
Mungasdale *T* 190 NG 9693
Mungrisdale *T* 150 NY 3630
Munlochy *T* 182 NH 6453
Munlochy Bay *W* 183 NH 6753
Munnoch Reservoir *W* 161 NS 2547
Munsley *T* 117 SO 6640
Munslow *T* 116 SO 5287
Murbie Stacks 203 HU 3062
Murch *T* 109 ST 1671
Murcott *T* 115 SP 5815
Murkle *T* 199 ND 1668
Murlaggan, Highld *T* 174 NN 0192
Murlaggan, Highld *T* 174 NN 3181
Murra 200 HY 2104
Murrow *T* 131 TF 3707
Mursley *T* 120 SP 8128
Murthill 177 NO 4657
Murthly *T* 176 NO 0938
Murton, Cumbr *T* 151 NY 7221
Murton, Durham *T* 153 NZ 3947
Murton, Northum *T* 165 NT 9648
Murton, N. Yks *T* 147 SE 6552
Murton Fell, Cumbr 150 NY 0918
Murton Fell, Cumbr 151 NY 7524
Musbury *T* 92 SY 2794
Muscoates *T* 148 SE 6880
Musdale *T* 168 NM 9322
Muskna Field *H* 203 HU 4032
Musselburgh *T* 171 NT 3472
Muston, Leic *T* 130 SK 8237
Muston, N. Yks *T* 149 TA 0979
Mustow Green *T* 117 SO 8774
Muthford *T* 123 TM 4888
Muthill *T* 170 NN 8616
Mutterton *T* 92 ST 0205
Mwdwl Eithin *H* 135 SH 8268
Mybster *T* 199 ND 1652
Myddfai *T* 109 SN 7730
Myddle *T* 126 SJ 4623
Mydroilyn *T* 111 SN 4555
Mylor Bridge *T* 87 SW 8036
Mynachlog-ddu *T* 110 SN 1430
Myndd Bwlch-y-groes *H* 109 SN 8635
Myndtown *T* 116 SO 3989
Mynydd Aberysgir *H* 109 SN 9932
Mynydd Allt-y-grug *H* 109 SN 7507
Mynydd Bach, Dyfed *H* 124 SN 6166
Mynydd Bach, Dyfed *H* 125 SN 7170
Mynydd-bach, Gwent *T* 113 ST 4894
Mynydd Bach, Gwyn *H* 135 SH 7431
Mynydd Baedon *H* 109 SS 8785
Mynydd Bodrochwyn *H* 135 SH 9472
Mynydd Bryn-llech *H* 135 SH 8031
Mynydd Bwlch-y-Groes *H* 109 SN 8635
Mynydd Caerau *H* 109 SS 8994
Mynydd Carningli *H* 110 SN 0637
Mynydd Ceiswyn *H* 125 SH 7713
Mynydd Cerrig *H* 111 SN 5013
Mynydd Clogau *H* 125 SO 0499
Mynydd Cribau *H* 135 SH 7555
Mynydd Dinas *H* 109 SS 7691
Mynydd Dolgoed *H* 125 SH 7913
Mynydd Eglwysilan *H* 109 ST 1292
Mynydd Eppynt *H* 112 SN 9543
Mynydd Figyn *H* 111 SN 5930
Mynydd Garnclochdy *H* 113 SO 2805
Mynydd Garn-fach *H* 111 SN 6506
Mynydd Hiraethog *H* 135 SH 9556
Mynydd Illtyd *H* 109 SN 9726
Mynydd Isa *T* 136 SJ 2564
Mynydd Llanbyther *H* 111 SN 5339
Mynydd Llandegai *T* 134 SH 6065
Mynydd Llangatwg *H* 109 SO 1814
Mynydd Llangorse *H* 109 SO 1626
Mynydd Llangynidr *H* 109 SO 1215
Mynydd Llanllwni *H* 111 SN 5038
Mynydd Llanwenarth *H* 113 SO 2717
Mynydd Llysiau *H* 109 SO 2028
Mynydd Maen *H* 113 ST 2697
Mynydd Maes-teg *H* 109 SS 9790
Mynydd Mallaen *H* 112 SN 7344
Mynydd Marchywel *H* 109 SN 7705
Mynydd Margam *H* 109 SS 8289
Mynydd Mawr, Clwyd *H* 126 SJ 1328
Mynydd Mawr, Gwyn *H* 134 SH 5454
Mynydd Mechell *T* 134 SH 3690
Mynydd Melyn *H* 110 SN 0236
Mynydd Merddin *H* 113 SO 3428
Mynydd Merthyr *H* 109 SO 0501
Mynydd Myddfai *H* 109 SN 8029
Mynydd Pen-bre *H* 111 SN 4503
Mynydd Pencarreg *H* 111 SN 5743
Mynydd Pennant *H* 125 SH 6610
Mynydd Pen-y-fâl *H* 113 SO 2619
Mynydd Perfedd *H* 135 SH 6262
Mynydd Preseli *H* 110 SN 1032
Mynydd Resolfen *H* 109 SN 8603
Mynydd Rhiw-Saeson *H* 125 SH 9006

Norbury Osgathorpe

Norbury, Shrops T 126 SO 3693
Norbury, Staffs T 127 SJ 7823
Nordelph T 131 TF 5500
Norden, Dorset T 94 SY 9483
Norden, G. Man T 137 SD 8514
Nordley T 127 SO 6996
Norham T 165 NT 9047
Norley T 137 SJ 5772
Norleywood T 94 SZ 3597
Normanby, Humbs T 142 SE 8816
Normanby, N. Yks T 148 SE 7381
Normanby-by-Spital T 140 TF 0088
Normanby le Wold T 141 TF 1295
Norman Cross T 120 TL 1690
Normandy T 96 SU 9351
Norman's Green T 92 ST 0503
Norman's Law H 171 NO 3020
Normanton, Derby T 128 SK 3433
Normanton, Lincs T 130 SK 9446
Normanton, Notts T 129 SK 7054
Normanton, W. Yks T 147 SE 3822
Normanton le Heath T 128 SK 3712
Normanton on Soar T 129 SK 5123
Normanton-on-the-Wolds T 129 SK 6233
Normanton on Trent T 140 SK 7968
Normoss T 145 SD 3337
Norrington Common T 101 ST 8864
Norris Hill T 128 SK 3216
Northallerton T 153 SE 3694
Northam, Devon T 90 SS 4429
Northam, Hants T 94 SU 4312
Northampton P 119 SP 7560
North Ascot T 104 SU 9069
North Aston T 115 SP 4728
Northaw T 105 TL 2802
North Baddesley T 94 SU 3919
North Ballachulish T 174 NN 0560
North Barrow T 93 ST 6029
North Barrule H 144 SC 4490
North Barsham T 132 TF 9134
North Bay, Orkney W 201 HY 6542
North Bay, Orkney W 200 ND 2990
North Bay, W. Isles W 178 NF 7302
North Benfleet T 106 TQ 7589
North Berwick T 171 NT 5585
North Berwick Law H 171 NT 5584
North Birny Fell H 157 NY 4791
North Boarhunt T 95 SU 6010
Northborough T 130 TF 1508
Northbourne T 99 TR 3352
North Bovey T 89 SX 7483
North Bradley T 101 ST 8555
North Brentor T 88 SX 4881
North Buckland T 90 SS 4740
North Burlingham T 133 TG 3610
North Burnt Hill H 161 NS 2566
North Cadbury T 93 ST 6327
North Cairn T 154 NW 9770
North Carlton T 140 SK 9477
North Carr (lightship) 171 NO 6714
North Cave T 142 SE 8932
North Cerney T 114 SP 0208
Northchapel T 96 SU 9529
North Charford T 94 SU 1919
North Charlton T 165 NU 1622
North Cheek or Ness Point 149 NZ 9606
North Cheriton T 93 ST 6925
North Chideock T 93 SY 4294
Northchurch T 104 SP 9709
North Cliffe T 142 SE 8737
North Clifton T 140 SK 8272
Northcote Manor 91 SS 6218
North Cotes T 143 TA 3500
Northcott T 88 SX 3392
North Cove T 123 TM 4689
North Cowton T 152 NZ 2803
North Crawley T 120 SP 9244
North Cray T 105 TQ 4972
North Creake T 132 TF 8538
North Curry T 92 ST 3125
North Dalton T 142 SE 9352
North Dawn 200 HY 4703
North Deep W 171 NO 2219
North Deighton T 147 SE 3951
North Downs, Kent H 98 TQ 6762
North Downs, Surrey H 103 SU 8147
North Drove Drain W 130 TF 1817
North Duffield T 142 SE 6837
Northdyke T 200 HY 2320
North Elkington T 141 TF 2890
North Elmham T 132 TF 9820
North End, Avon T 100 ST 4167
Northend, Avon T 101 ST 7768
Northend, Bucks T 104 SU 7392
North End, Hants T 102 SU 4163
North End, Hants T 95 SU 6502
Northend, Warw T 118 SP 3952
North End, W. Susx T 96 TQ 1209
North Erradale T 190 NG 7481
North Esk Reservoir, Border W 163 NT 1558
North Esk Reservoir, Lothn W 163 NT 1558
Northey Island 104 TL 0806
North Fearns T 180 NG 5935
North Fen, Cambs 131 TF 3009
North Fen, Cambs 121 TL 5169
North Ferriby T 142 SE 9825
Northfield, Border T 165 NT 9167
Northfield, Grampn T 185 NJ 9008
Northfield, W. Mids T 118 SP 0279
Northfleet T 98 TQ 6274
North Foreland 99 TR 4069
North Frodingham T 149 TA 0953
North Glen Sannox 160 NR 9947
North Gorley T 94 SU 1611
North Green T 123 TM 2288
North Greetwell T 140 TF 0173
North Grimston T 148 SE 8467
North Harris 189 NB 1307
North Haven, Grampn W 185 NK 1138
North Haven, Shetld W 201 HZ 2272
North Havra 203 HU 3642
North Hayling T 95 SU 7303
North Head, Highld 199 ND 3850
North Head, Orkney 199 ND 3985
North Heasley T 91 SS 7333
North Heath T 96 TQ 0621
North Hill, Cambs T 121 TL 4476
North Hill, Corn T 88 SX 2776
North Hill, Orkney H 200 HY 4048
North Hill, Orkney H 200 HY 4954
North Hill, Somer H 91 SS 9447
North Hinksey Village T 115 SP 4905
North Holms 205 HP 5611
North Holmwood T 96 TQ 1647
North Huish T 89 SX 7156
North Hykeham T 140 SK 9466
Northiam T 98 TQ 8225
Northill T 120 TL 1546
Northington T 95 SU 5737
North Kelsey T 142 TA 0401
North Kelsey Beck, Humbs W 142 TA 0302
North Kelsey Beck, Lincs W 142 TA 0302
North Kessock T 182 NH 6548
North Kilvington T 147 SE 4285
North Kilworth T 119 SP 6183
North Kyme T 130 TF 1552
North Lancing T 96 TQ 1804
Northlands T 131 TF 3453
Northleach T 114 SP 1114
North Lee, Bucks T 104 SP 8309
North Lee, W. Isles H 188 NF 9366
Northleigh, Devon T 92 SY 1995
North Leigh, Oxon T 115 SP 3812
North Leverton with Habblesthorpe T 140 SK 7882
Northlew T 88 SX 5099
North Littleton T 118 SP 0847
North Loch W 201 HY 7545
North Lopham T 122 TM 0383
North Luffenham T 130 SK 9303
North Marden T 95 SU 8016
North Marston T 104 SP 7722
North Medwin W 163 NT 0150
North Middleton T 164 NT 3559
North Molton T 91 SS 7329
Northmoor T 115 SP 4203
Northmoor Green or Moorland T 92 ST 3332
North Morar 180 NM 7892
North Moreton T 103 SU 5689
Northmuir T 176 NO 3855
North Muskham T 140 SK 7959
North Neaps 205 HP 4905
North Ness 202 HU 1861
North Nesting 203 HU 4558
North Nevi 201 HY 6101
North Newbald T 142 SE 9136
North Newington T 118 SP 4239
North Newnton T 102 SU 1257
North Newton T 92 ST 2930
North Nibley T 114 ST 7495
North Oakley T 103 SU 5354
North Ockendon T 106 TQ 5984
Northolt T 105 TQ 1285
Northop T 136 SJ 2468
Northop Hall T 136 SJ 2767
North Ormsby T 141 TF 2893
Northorpe, Lincs T 140 SK 8997
Northorpe, Lincs T 130 TF 0917
North Otterington T 153 SE 3689
North Owersby T 140 TF 0694
Northowram T 146 SE 1126
North Perrott T 93 ST 4709
North Petherton T 92 ST 2933
North Petherwin T 88 SX 2889
North Pickenham T 132 TF 8606
North Piddle T 118 SO 9654
Northpunds T 203 HU 4022
North Queensferry T 170 NT 1380
North Radworthy 91 SS 7534
Northrepps T 133 TG 2439
North Rigton T 147 SE 2849
North Rode T 137 SJ 8966
North Roe, Shetld T 204 HU 3487
North Roe, Shetld T 204 HU 3689
North Ronaldsay 201 HY 7654
North Ronaldsay Firth W 201 HY 7549
North Runcton T 132 TF 6415
North Sandwick T 205 HU 5497
North Scale T 144 SD 1870
North Scarle T 140 SK 8466
North Seaton T 159 NZ 2986
North Shian 173 NM 9143
North Shields T 159 NZ 3568
North Shoebury T 106 TQ 9386
North Shore T 145 SD 3038
North Side T 131 TL 2799
North Somercotes T 141 TF 4296
North Sound, The W 200 HY 5745
North Stack 134 SH 2184
North Stainley T 147 SE 2877
North Stainmore T 151 NY 8315
North Stane 205 HP 6613
North Stifford T 106 TQ 6080
North Stoke, Avon T 101 ST 7069
North Stoke, Oxon T 104 SU 6186
North Stoke, W. Susx T 96 TQ 0210
North Street T 95 SU 6433
North Sunderland T 165 NU 2131
North Sutor 183 NH 8168
North Taing, Orkney 201 HY 6225
North Taing, Orkney 201 HY 6716
North Tamerton T 88 SX 3197
North Tawton T 91 SS 6601
North Third Reservoir W 169 NS 7588
North Thoresby T 143 TF 2998
North Tidworth T 102 SU 2349
North Tolsta T 195 NB 5347
Northton T 188 NF 9889
Northtown T 200 ND 4797
North Tuddenham T 132 TG 0414
North Ugie Water W 185 NJ 9753
North Uist 188 NF 8370
Northwall T 201 HY 7544
North Walsham T 133 TG 2830
North Waltham T 103 SU 5646
North Warnborough T 103 SU 7351
North Water Bridge T 177 NO 6566
North Watten T 199 ND 2458
Northway T 114 SO 9233
North Weald Bassett T 105 TL 4904
North West Passage W 86 SV 8411
North West Point 90 SS 1348
North Wharf 145 SD 3249
North Wheatley T 140 SK 7585
North Whilborough T 89 SX 8766
Northwich P 137 SJ 6573
Northwick, Avon T 101 ST 5686
North Wick, Avon T 101 ST 5865
North Widcombe T 101 ST 5758
North Willingham T 141 TF 1688
North Wingfield T 139 SK 4165
North Witham T 130 SK 9221
Northwold T 132 TL 7597
Northwood, Derby T 139 SK 2664
Northwood, G. Lon T 104 TQ 0991
Northwood, I. of W T 95 SZ 4894
Northwood, Shrops T 126 SJ 4633
Northwood Green T 114 SO 7216
North Wootton, Dorset T 93 ST 6514
North Wootton, Norf T 132 TF 6424
North Wootton, Somer T 101 ST 5641
North Wraxall T 101 ST 8175
North Yardhope 158 NT 9201
North York Moors 148 SE 7398
North Yorkshire Moors Railway 148 SE 8497
Norton, Ches T 137 SJ 5582
Norton, Cleve T 153 NZ 4421
Norton, Glos T 114 SO 8524
Norton, Herts T 121 TL 2334
Norton, H. & W T 117 SO 8851
Norton, H. & W T 118 SP 0447
Norton, I. of W T 94 SZ 3489
Norton, Northnts T 119 SP 6063
Norton, Notts T 139 SK 5772
Norton, N. Yks T 148 SE 7971
Norton, Powys T 116 SO 3067
Norton, Shrops T 127 SJ 5609
Norton, Shrops T 127 SJ 7200
Norton, Shrops T 116 SO 4681
Norton, Suff T 122 TL 9565
Norton, S. Yks T 139 SE 5415
Norton, S. Yks T 139 SK 3682
Norton, Wilts T 101 ST 8884
Norton, W. Susx T 96 SU 9206
Norton Bavant T 101 ST 9043
Norton Bridge T 127 SJ 8730
Norton Canes T 128 SK 0108
Norton Canon T 113 SO 3847
Norton Disney T 140 SK 8959
Norton East T 128 SK 0208
Norton Ferris T 93 ST 7936
Norton Fitzwarren T 92 ST 1925
Norton Green T 94 SZ 3488
Norton Hawkfield T 101 ST 5964
Norton Heath T 106 TL 6004
Norton in Hales T 127 SJ 7038
Norton-in-the-Moors T 127 SJ 8951
Norton-Juxta-Twycross T 128 SK 3207
Norton-le-Clay T 147 SE 4071
Norton Lindsey T 118 SP 2263
Norton Malreward T 101 ST 6065
Norton Mandeville T 105 TL 5804
Norton Marshes 133 TG 4100
Norton St Philip T 101 ST 7755
Norton Subcourse T 133 TM 4198
Norton sub Hamdon T 93 ST 4615
Norwell T 140 SK 7761
Norwell Woodhouse T 140 SK 7462
Norwich P 133 TG 2308
Norwich Airport 133 TG 2113
Norwick, Shetld T 205 HP 6514
Nor Wick, Shetld W 205 HP 6514
Norwood Green T 105 TQ 1378
Norwood Hill T 96 TQ 2443
Noseley T 129 SP 7398
Noss Head 199 ND 3855
Noss Mayo T 89 SX 5447
Nosterfield T 147 SE 2780
Nostie T 180 NG 8527
Notgrove T 114 SP 1120
Nottage T 109 SS 8278
Nottingham P 129 SK 5741
Nottington T 93 SY 6682
Notton, Wilts T 101 ST 9169
Notton, W. Yks T 139 SE 3413
Nounsley T 106 TL 7910
Noup Head 200 HY 3950
Noup of Noss 203 HU 5539
Noup, The 205 HP 6318
Noutard's Green T 117 SO 7966
Novar House 182 NH 6168
Nox T 126 SJ 4110
Nuffield T 104 SU 6787
Nunburnholme T 148 SE 8548
Nuneaton P 118 SP 3691
Nuneham Courtenay T 115 SU 5599
Nun Monkton T 147 SE 5057
Nunney T 101 ST 7345
Nunnington T 147 SE 6679
Nunnykirk T 159 NZ 0892
Nunthorpe T 153 NZ 5314
Nunton, Wilts T 94 SU 1526
Nunton, W. Isles T 188 NF 7653
Nunwick 158 NY 8774
Nursling T 94 SU 3716
Nursted T 95 SU 7621
Nutberry Hill H 162 NS 7433
Nutbourne T 96 TQ 0718
Nutfield T 97 TQ 3049
Nuthall T 129 SK 5144
Nuthampstead T 121 TL 4034
Nuthurst T 96 TQ 1926
Nutley T 97 TQ 4427
Nutwell T 139 SE 6304
Nybster T 199 ND 3663
Nyetimber T 95 SZ 8998
Nyewood T 95 SU 8021
Nyland Hill H 101 ST 4550
Nymet Rowland T 91 SS 7108
Nymet Tracey T 89 SS 7200
Nympsfield T 114 SO 8000
Nynehead T 92 ST 1422
Nyton T 96 SU 9305

O

Oadby T 129 SK 6200
Oad Street T 98 TQ 8662
Oakamoor T 128 SK 0544
Oakbank T 163 NT 0766
Oakdale T 109 ST 1898
Oake T 92 ST 1525
Oaken T 127 SJ 8502
Oakenclough T 145 SD 5447
Oakengates T 127 SJ 7010
Oakenshaw, Durham T 152 NZ 2037
Oakenshaw, W. Yks T 146 SE 1727
Oakford, Devon T 91 SS 9021
Oakford, Dyfed T 111 SN 4558
Oakgrove T 137 SJ 9169
Oakham T 130 SK 8508
Oakhanger T 95 SU 7735
Oakhill T 101 ST 6347
Oakington T 121 TL 4164
Oaklands, Gwyn 135 SH 8158
Oaklands, Herts T 105 TL 2417
Oakle Street T 114 SO 7517
Oakley, Beds T 120 TL 0153
Oakley, Bucks T 104 SP 6312
Oakley, Fife T 170 NT 0289
Oakley, Hants T 103 SU 5650
Oakley, Suff T 123 TM 1677
Oakley Green T 104 SU 9276
Oakley Park T 125 SN 9887
Oakridge T 114 SO 9103
Oaks T 126 SJ 4204
Oaksey T 114 ST 9993
Oakthorpe T 128 SK 3213
Oakwoodhill T 96 TQ 1337
Oakworth T 146 SE 0338
Oare, Kent T 99 TR 0062
Oare, Wilts T 102 SU 1563
Oasby T 130 TF 0039
Oa, The 166 NR 3144
Oathlaw T 177 NO 4756
Oban P 168 NM 8530
Oban Bay W 168 NM 8530
Obney 176 NO 0336
Obney Hills H 176 NO 0238
Oborne T 93 ST 6518
Occlestone Green T 137 SJ 6962
Occold T 123 TM 1570
Ochil Hills H 170 NO 0610
Ochiltree T 161 NS 5021
Ochtermuthill 169 NN 8316
Ochtertyre 169 NN 8323
Ockbrook T 128 SK 4236
Ockham T 96 TQ 0756
Ockle T 173 NM 5570
Ockle Point 173 NM 5471
Ockley T 96 TQ 1440
Ockran Head 204 HU 2484
Ocle Pychard T 113 SO 5946
Odcombe T 93 ST 5015
Odda's Chapel A 114 SO 8729
Odd Down T 101 ST 7362
Oddendale T 151 NY 5913
Oddingley T 117 SO 9159
Oddington, Glos T 115 SP 2225
Oddington, Oxon T 115 SP 5515
Odell T 120 SP 9657
Odie 201 HY 6229
Odiham T 103 SU 7451
Odin Bay W 201 HY 6924
Odness 201 HY 6926
Odstock T 94 SU 1426
Odstock Down H 94 SU 1324
Odstone T 128 SK 3907
Offa's Dyke, Clwyd A 135 SJ 1079
Offa's Dyke, Clwyd A 126 SJ 2948
Offa's Dyke, Glos A 113 SO 5407
Offa's Dyke, H. & W A 113 SO 2959
Offa's Dyke, Powys A 126 SJ 2507
Offa's Dyke, Shrops A 116 SO 2678
Offchurch T 118 SP 3565
Offenham T 118 SP 0546
Offham, E. Susx T 97 TQ 4012
Offham, Kent T 97 TQ 6557
Offord Cluny T 121 TL 2267
Offord D'Arcy T 121 TL 2266
Offton T 122 TM 0649
Offwell T 92 SY 1999
Ogbourne Maizey T 102 SU 1871
Ogbourne St Andrew T 102 SU 1972
Ogbourne St George T 102 SU 2074
Ogden Reservoir W 146 SD 8039
Ogil 176 NO 4561
Ogle T 159 NZ 1378
Ogmore T 109 SS 8876
Ogmore-by-Sea T 109 SS 8675
Ogmore Forest F 109 SS 9489
Ogmore Vale T 109 SS 9390
Ogston Reservoir W 139 SK 3760
Oh Me Edge H 158 NY 7099
Oigh-sgeir 179 NM 1596
Oisgill Bay W 186 NG 1349
Oitir Fhiadhaich 188 NF 7465
Oitir Mhòr, W. Isles W 178 NF 7306
Oitir Mhòr, W. Isles 188 NF 8157
Okeford Fitzpaine T 93 ST 8010
Okehampton P 89 SX 5895
Okehampton Camp T 89 SX 5893
Okehampton Common 89 SX 5790
Okraquoy 203 HU 4331
Olantigh 99 TR 0548
Old T 119 SP 7873
Old Aberdeen T 185 NJ 9408
Old Alresford T 95 SU 5834
Oldany Island 196 NC 0934
Old Basing T 103 SU 6752
Old Bedford River W 131 TL 5496
Oldberrow T 118 SP 1266
Old Bewick T 165 NU 0621
Old Bolingbroke T 141 TF 3565
Oldborough T 91 SS 7706
Old Brampton T 139 SK 3371
Old Bridge of Urr T 156 NX 7767
Old Buckenham T 122 TM 0691
Old Burghclere T 103 SU 4657
Oldbury, Shrops T 117 SO 7192
Oldbury, Warw T 128 SP 3194
Oldbury, Wilts A 102 SU 0569
Oldbury, W. Mids T 118 SO 9889
Oldbury Castle A 102 SU 0469
Oldbury-on-Severn T 101 ST 6192
Oldbury on the Hill T 101 ST 8188
Oldbury Sands 113 ST 5893
Old Byland T 147 SE 5585
Oldcastle T 113 SO 3224
Old Castle Head 110 SS 0796
Old Castleton 158 NY 5190
Oldchapel Hill H 125 SN 9780
Old Cleeve T 100 ST 0341
Old Clipstone T 139 SK 6064
Old Colwyn T 135 SH 8678
Oldcotes T 139 SK 5988
Old Croft River, Cambs W 131 TL 5098
Old Croft River, Norf W 131 TL 5098
Old Dailly T 154 NX 2299
Old Dalby T 129 SK 6723
Old Deer T 185 NJ 9747
Old Denaby T 139 SK 4899
Old Ellerby T 143 TA 1636
Old Felixstowe T 123 TM 3135
Oldfield T 117 SO 8465
Oldford T 101 ST 7850
Old Hall A 136 SJ 4616
Old Hall, The T 143 TA 2717
Oldham P 137 SJ 9204
Oldhamstocks T 164 NT 7370
Old Head 199 ND 4783
Old Heath T 107 TM 0123
Old Howe W 149 TA 1156
Oldhurst T 121 TL 3077
Old Hutton T 145 SD 5688
Old Kea T 87 SW 8441
Old Kilpatrick T 169 NS 4673
Old Kinnernie T 185 NJ 7209
Old Knebworth T 105 TL 2320
Oldland T 101 ST 6771
Old Leake T 131 TF 4050
Old Lynn Channel W 131 TF 5233
Old Malton T 148 SE 7972
Old Man of Coniston, The H 150 SD 2797
Old Man of Hoy 200 HY 1700
Old Man of Storr H 187 NG 5053
Oldmeldrum T 185 NJ 8127
Old Milverton T 118 SP 3067
Old Monkland T 162 NS 7163
Old Newton T 122 TM 0562
Old Oswestry A 126 SJ 2931
Oldpark T 127 SJ 6909
Old Peak or South Cheek 149 NZ 9802
Old Philpstoun T 170 NT 0577
Old Radnor T 113 SO 2559
Old Rayne T 184 NJ 6728
Old River Ancholme W 142 SE 9715
Old Romney T 99 TR 0325
Old Sarum A 94 SU 1332
Old Scone 170 NO 1126
Oldshore Beg T 196 NC 1959
Oldshoremore T 196 NC 2058
Old Soar Manor A 97 TQ 6154
Old Sodbury T 101 ST 7581
Old Somerby T 130 SK 9633
Old South 131 TF 4735
Oldstead T 147 SE 5380
Old Swarland T 159 NU 1601
Old Town, Cumbr T 145 SD 5983
Old Town, Northum T 158 NY 8891
Oldtown of Ord T 184 NJ 6259
Old Warden T 120 TL 1343
Oldways End T 91 SS 8624
Old Weston T 120 TL 1077
Oldwhat T 185 NJ 8651
Old Winchester Hill A 95 SU 6420
Old Windsor T 104 SU 9874
Old Wives Lees T 99 TR 0754
Olenacum Roman Fort R 150 NY 2646
Olgrinmore T 199 ND 0955
Oliver's Battery T 95 SU 4527
Ollaberry T 204 HU 3680
Ollach T 187 NG 5136
Ollerton, Ches T 137 SJ 7776
Ollerton, Notts T 139 SK 6567
Ollerton, Shrops T 127 SJ 6525
Ollinsgarth 203 HU 4430
Ollisdal Geo 186 NG 2138
Olna Firth W 203 HU 3864
Olney T 120 SP 8851
Olrig House 199 ND 1866
Olton T 118 SP 1382
Olveston T 101 ST 6087
Ombersley T 117 SO 8464
Ompton T 140 SK 6865
Onchan T 144 SC 4078
Onchan Head 144 SC 4077
Onecote T 128 SK 0555
Ongar Hill T 131 TF 5824
Ongar Street T 116 SO 3967
Onibury T 116 SO 4579
Onich T 174 NN 0261
Onllwyn T 109 SN 8410
Onneley T 127 SJ 7543
Onslow Village T 96 SU 9949
Opinan, Highld T 190 NG 7472
Opinan, Highld T 190 NG 8796
Opsay 188 NF 9876
Orbost 186 NG 2543
Orby T 141 TF 4967
Orby Marsh 141 TF 5167
Orchard T 93 ST 8215
Orchard Portman T 92 ST 2421
Orcheston T 102 SU 0545
Orcheston Down H 102 SU 0748
Orcop T 113 SO 4726
Orcop Hill T 113 SO 4828
Ord T 180 NG 6113
Ordhead T 184 NJ 6610
Ordie T 176 NJ 4501
Ordie Burn W 170 NO 0733
Ordiequish T 184 NJ 3357
Ord Point 193 ND 0617
Ord River W 180 NG 6212
Ords, The H 203 HU 3413
Ord, The 203 HU 4936
Ore T 98 TQ 8311
Ore Bay W 200 ND 3094
Oreton T 117 SO 6580
Oreval H 195 NB 0810
Orfasay 205 HU 4977
Orford, Ches T 137 SJ 6190
Orford, Suff T 123 TM 4250
Orford Ness 123 TM 4549
Orgreave T 128 SK 1516
Orinsay T 195 NB 3612
Orka Voe W 205 HU 4077
Orknagable 205 HP 5713
Orkney Islands 200 HY 4821
Orleton, H. & W T 116 SO 4967
Orleton, H. & W T 117 SO 6967
Orlingbury T 120 SP 8672
Ormesby T 153 NZ 5317
Ormesby St Margaret T 133 TG 4915
Ormesby St Michael T 133 TG 4814
Ormiclate Castle 178 NF 7331
Ormiscaig T 190 NG 8590
Ormiston T 171 NT 4169
Ormsaigmore T 173 NM 4763
Ormsary House 167 NR 7472
Ormskirk T 136 SD 4108
Ornish Island 178 NF 8538
Oronsay 180 NG 7012
Oronsay, Highld 186 NG 3136
Oronsay, Highld 173 NM 5859
Oronsay, Strath 166 NR 3588
Oronsay, W. Isles 188 NF 8476
Orosay, W. Isles 178 NF 7106
Orosay, W. Isles 178 NF 7217
Orphir 200 HY 3406
Orpington P 105 TQ 4665
Orrell T 137 SD 5305
Orrin Falls W 182 NH 4751
Orrin Reservoir W 182 NH 3749
Orrisdale Head 144 SC 3192
Orroland T 155 NX 7746
Orsay 166 NR 1651
Orsett T 106 TQ 6481
Orslow T 127 SJ 8015
Orston T 129 SK 7741
Orton, Cumbr T 151 NY 6208
Orton, Northnts T 119 SP 8079
Orton Longueville T 130 TL 1796
Orton-on-the-Hill T 128 SK 3003
Orval H 179 NM 3399
Orwell T 121 TL 3650
Osbaldeston T 145 SD 6431
Osbaston T 128 SK 4204
Osborne Bay W 95 SZ 5395
Osborne House 95 SZ 5194
Osbournby T 130 TF 0638
Oscroft T 137 SJ 5067
Ose T 186 NG 3141
Osea Island 105 TL 1106
Osgathorpe T 128 SK 4319

Purton River Arun

Purton, Wilts *T* 102 SU 0987
Purton Stoke *T* 102 SU 0990
Pury End *T* 119 SP 7045
Pusey *T* 115 SU 3596
Putley *T* 117 SO 6437
Putney *T* 105 TQ 2274
Puttenham, Herts *T* 104 SP 8814
Puttenham, Surrey *T* 96 SU 9348
Puxton *T* 100 ST 4063
Pwll *T* 108 SN 4700
Pwllcrochan *T* 110 SM 9202
Pwlldu Head 108 SS 5786
Pwllheli *T* 134 SH 3735
Pwllmeyric *T* 101 ST 5292
Pwll-y-glaw *T* 109 SS 7993
Pwllygranant 110 SN 1247
Pyecombe *T* 97 TQ 2813
Pye Corner *T* 100 ST 3485
Pykestone Hill *H* 163 NT 1731
Pyle, I. of W *T* 95 SZ 4778
Pyle, M. Glam *T* 109 SS 8282
Pylle *T* 101 ST 6038
Pymore *T* 121 TL 4986
Pyrford *T* 104 TQ 0359
Pyrton *T* 104 SU 6895
Pytchley *T* 120 SP 8574
Pyworthy *T* 90 SS 3103

Q

Quabbs *T* 116 SO 2180
Quadring *T* 131 TF 2233
Quainton *T* 104 SP 7420
Quandale 200 HY 3732
Quanter Ness 200 HY 4114
Quantock Hills *H* 92 ST 1537
Quarley *T* 102 SU 2743
Quarndon *T* 128 SK 3341
Quarrier's Homes *T* 161 NS 3666
Quarrington *T* 130 TF 0544
Quarrington Hill *T* 152 NZ 3337
Quarrybank, Ches *T* 137 SJ 5465
Quarry Bank, W. Mids *T* 117 SO 9386
Quarry Head 185 NJ 9066
Quarryhill 193 NH 7481
Quarry, The *T* 114 ST 7399
Quarrywood *T* 184 NJ 1864
Quarter *T* 162 NS 7251
Quarter Fell *H* 154 NX 2070
Quatford *T* 117 SO 7490
Quatt *T* 117 SO 7588
Quebec *T* 152 NZ 1743
Quedgeley *T* 114 SO 8013
Queen Adelaide *T* 121 TL 5681
Queenborough *T* 98 TQ 9172
Queen Camel *T* 93 ST 5924
Queen Charlton *T* 101 ST 6367
Queensberry *H* 156 NX 9899
Queensbury *T* 146 SE 1030
Queen's Carn *H* 192 NH 4672
Queensferry, Clwyd *P* 136 SJ 3168
Queensferry, Lothn *T* 170 NT 1378
Queen's Forest, The *F* 183 NH 9710
Queen's Ground 132 TL 6893
Queenside Muir 161 NS 2864
Queen's View 175 NN 8659
Queenzieburn *T* 169 NS 6977
Quenby Hall *A* 129 SK 7006
Quendale *T* 203 HU 3713
Quendon *T* 121 TL 5130
Queniborough *T* 129 SK 6412
Quenington *T* 115 SP 1404
Quernmore *T* 145 SD 5160
Quethiock *T* 88 SX 3164
Quey Firth *W* 204 HU 3682
Quholm *T* 200 HY 2412
Quidenham *T* 122 TM 0287
Quidhampton, Hants *T* 103 SU 5150
Quidhampton, Wilts *T* 94 SU 1130
Quidnish *T* 189 NG 0987
Quien Hill *H* 160 NS 0559
Quies 87 SW 8376
Quilquox *T* 185 NJ 9038
Quilva Taing 202 HU 1757
Quinag *H* 196 NC 2028
Quindry *T* 200 ND 4392
Quine's Hill *T* 144 SC 3473
Quinish, Strath 173 NM 4254
Quinish, W. Isles 188 NF 8886
Quinish Point 172 NM 4057
Quintin Knowe *H* 156 NS 6507
Quinton *T* 119 SP 7754
Quoditch *T* 88 SX 4097
Quoig 169 NN 8222
Quorndon or Quorn *T* 129 SK 5616
Quorn or Quorndon *T* 129 SK 5616
Quothquan *T* 163 NS 9939
Quoyloo *T* 200 HY 2420
Quoy Ness 201 HY 6236
Quoys *T* 205 HP 6112

R

Raasay House 187 NG 5436
Rabbit Islands 197 NC 6063
Raby *T* 136 SJ 3180
Raby Castle *A* 152 NZ 1221
Rachub *T* 135 SH 6268
Rackenford *T* 91 SS 8518
Rackham *T* 96 TQ 0513
Rackheath *T* 133 TG 2715
Racks *T* 157 NY 0374
Rackwick, Orkney *T* 200 HY 4449
Rack Wick, Orkney *W* 200 HY 4450
Rack Wick, Orkney *W* 200 HY 5042
Rack Wick, Orkney *W* 200 ND 2098
Rackwick, Orkney *T* 200 ND 2099
Radcliffe, G. Man *T* 137 SD 7807
Radcliffe, Northum *T* 159 NU 2602
Radcliffe on Trent *T* 129 SK 6439
Radclive *T* 119 SP 6733
Radcot *T* 115 SU 2899
Raddery *T* 183 NH 7159
Radernie *T* 171 NO 4609
Radford Semele *T* 118 SP 3464
Radlett *T* 105 TQ 1699
Radley *T* 115 SU 5299
Radnage *T* 104 SU 7897
Radnor Forest *F* 116 SO 2064
Radstock *T* 101 ST 6854
Radstone *T* 119 SP 5840
Radway *T* 118 SP 3748
Radway Green *T* 127 SJ 7754
Radwell *T* 121 TL 2335
Radwinter *T* 122 TL 6037
Radyr *T* 109 ST 1080
Raera 173 NM 8320
Raerinish Point 195 NB 4324
Raes Knowes *H* 157 NY 2983
Rafford *T* 183 NJ 0656
Ragdale *T* 129 SK 6619
Raglan *T* 113 SO 4107
Ragnall *T* 140 SK 8073
Rainberg Mór *H* 166 NR 5687
Rainford *T* 137 SD 4801
Rainham, G. Lon *T* 105 TQ 5282
Rainham, Kent *T* 98 TQ 8165
Rainhill *T* 137 SJ 4991
Rainow *T* 138 SJ 9576
Rainton *T* 147 SE 3775
Rainworth *T* 139 SK 5958
Raisbeck *T* 151 NY 6407
Rait *T* 171 NO 2226
Raithby, Lincs *T* 141 TF 3184
Raithby, Lincs *T* 141 TF 3767
Raitts Burn *W* 183 NH 7704
Rake *T* 95 SU 8027
Rake Law *H* 156 NS 8717
Ralfland Forest *F* 151 NY 5413
Ramasaig 186 NG 1644
Rame, Corn *T* 86 SW 7233
Rame, Corn *T* 88 SX 4249
Rame Head 88 SX 4148
Ram Lane *T* 99 TQ 9646
Ramna Stacks 205 HU 3797
Rampisham *T* 93 ST 5602
Rampside *T* 144 SD 2466
Rampton, Cambs *T* 121 TL 4268
Rampton, Notts *T* 140 SK 7978
Ramsbottom *T* 137 SD 7816
Ramsbury *T* 102 SU 2771
Ramscraigs *T* 199 ND 1427
Ramsdean *T* 95 SU 7022
Ramsdell *T* 103 SU 5857
Ramsden *T* 115 SP 3515
Ramsden Bellhouse *T* 106 TQ 7194
Ramsden Heath *T* 106 TQ 7195
Ramsey, Cambs *T* 121 TL 2885
Ramsey, Essex *T* 123 TM 2130
Ramsey, I. of M *T* 144 SC 4594
Ramsey Bay *W* 144 SC 4695
Ramseycleuch *T* 157 NT 2714
Ramsey Forty Foot *T* 121 TL 3087
Ramsey Hollow 121 TL 3286
Ramsey Island, Dyfed 110 SM 7023
Ramsey Island, Essex *T* 106 TL 9505
Ramsey Knowe *H* 157 NT 2516
Ramsey Mereside *T* 121 TL 2889
Ramsey Sound *W* 110 SM 7124
Ramsey St Mary's *T* 121 TL 2588
Ramsgate *P* 99 TR 3765
Ramsgill *T* 146 SE 1171
Ramshorn *T* 128 SK 0845
Rams Ne 205 HU 6087
Ranachan Hill *H* 160 NR 6825
Ranby *T* 139 SK 6581
Rand *T* 141 TF 1078
Randwick *T* 114 SO 8306
Ranfurly *T* 168 NS 3569
Rangemore *T* 128 SK 1823
Rangeworthy *T* 101 ST 6986
Ranish *T* 195 NB 4024
Rankinston *T* 161 NS 4514
Rannoch Forest 175 NN 4565
Rannoch Moor, Highld 174 NN 3852
Rannoch Moor, Tays 174 NN 3852
Rannoch River *W* 173 NM 7147
Rannoch Station 174 NN 4257
Ranskill *T* 139 SK 6587
Ranson Moor 131 TL 3993
Ranton *T* 127 SJ 8524
Ranworth *T* 133 TG 3514
Rapness *T* 200 HY 5141
Rapness Sound *W* 200 HY 5138
Rappach 191 NC 2401
Rappach Water *W* 191 NH 2998
Rascarrel *T* 155 NX 7948
Rascarrel Bay *W* 155 NX 8148
Raskelf *T* 147 SE 4971
Rassau *T* 109 SO 1512
Rastrick *T* 146 SE 1321
Ratae *R* 129 SK 5804
Ratagan *T* 180 NG 9119
Ratagan Forest *F* 180 NG 9020
Ratby *T* 129 SK 5105
Ratcliffe Culey *T* 128 SP 3299
Ratcliffe on the Wreake *T* 129 SK 6314
Rathen *T* 185 NK 0060
Rathillet *T* 171 NO 3620
Rathmell *T* 146 SD 8059
Ratho *T* 170 NT 1370
Ratho Station *T* 170 NT 1372
Rathven *T* 184 NJ 4465
Rat Island 90 SS 1443
Ratley *T* 118 SP 3847
Ratlinghope *T* 126 SO 4097
Rattar *T* 199 ND 2673
Ratten Row *T* 145 SD 4241
Rattery *T* 89 SX 7461
Rattlesden *T* 122 TL 9759
Rattray *T* 176 NO 1845
Rattray Head 185 NK 1058
Rauceby *T* 130 TF 0245
Rauceby Station 130 TF 0344
Raughton Head *T* 151 NY 3845
Raunds *T* 120 SP 9972
Ravenfield *T* 139 SK 4895
Ravenglass *T* 150 SD 0896
Raveningham *T* 133 TM 3996
Ravenscar *T* 149 NZ 9801
Ravensdale *T* 144 SC 3591
Ravensden *T* 120 TL 0754
Ravenseat *T* 152 NY 8603
Ravenshall Point 155 NX 5252
Ravenshead *T* 129 SK 5654
Ravens Knowe *H* 158 NT 7806
Ravensmoor *T* 127 SJ 6250
Ravensthorpe, Northnts *T* 119 SP 6670
Ravensthorpe, W. Yks *T* 139 SE 2220
Ravensthorpe Reservoir *W* 119 SP 6770
Ravenstone *T* 120 SP 8550
Ravenstonedale *T* 151 NY 7204
Ravenstonedale Common 151 NY 6900
Ravenstown *T* 145 SD 3675
Ravenstruther *T* 163 NS 9245
Ravensworth *T* 152 NZ 1407
Raw *T* 149 NZ 9405
Rawcliffe, Humbs *T* 142 SE 6822
Rawcliffe, N. Yks *T* 147 SE 5855
Rawcliffe Bridge *T* 142 SE 7021
Rawdon *T* 146 SE 2139
Rawmarsh *T* 139 SK 4496
Rawreth *T* 106 TQ 7893
Rawridge *T* 92 ST 2006
Rawtenstall *T* 146 SD 8123
Rayburn Lake *W* 159 NZ 1192
Raydon *T* 122 TM 0538
Raylees *T* 158 NY 9291
Rayleigh *T* 106 TQ 8090
Rayne *T* 106 TL 7222
Ray Sand 107 TM 0400
Rea Brook *W* 117 SO 6586
Reach *T* 121 TL 5666
Read *T* 146 SD 7634
Reading *P* 104 SU 7173
Reading Street *T* 98 TQ 9230
Read's Island 142 SE 9622
Reagill *T* 151 NY 6017
Rearquhar *T* 193 NH 7492
Rearsby *T* 129 SK 6514
Rease Heath *T* 127 SJ 6454
Reaster *T* 199 ND 2565
Reawick *T* 203 HU 3244
Reay *T* 198 NC 9664
Reay Forest 196 NC 2939
Rechullin *T* 190 NG 8557
Reculver *T* 99 TR 2269
Redberth *T* 110 SN 0804
Redbourn *T* 105 TL 1012
Redbourne *T* 142 SE 9700
Redbrook *T* 113 SO 5310
Redburn, Highld 182 NH 5767
Redburn, Highld *T* 183 NH 9447
Redcar *T* 153 NZ 6024
Redcastle, Highld *T* 182 NH 5849
Redcastle, Tays 177 NO 6850
Redcleuch Edge *H* 157 NT 3410
Redcliff Bay *T* 101 ST 4475
Red Dial *T* 150 NY 2546
Redding *T* 170 NS 9278
Reddingmuirhead *T* 170 NS 9177
Reddish *T* 137 SJ 8998
Redditch *P* 118 SP 0467
Red Down 88 SX 2685
Rede *T* 122 TL 8055
Redenhall *T* 123 TM 2684
Redesdale *F* 158 NY 8396
Redesdale Camp *T* 158 NY 8298
Redesdale Forest *F* 158 NT 7501
Redesmouth *T* 158 NY 8682
Redford, Durham *T* 152 NZ 0730
Redford, Tays *T* 177 NO 5644
Redfordgreen *T* 157 NT 3616
Redgrave *T* 122 TM 0477
Red Head, Highld 199 ND 3477
Red Head, Orkney 200 HY 5640
Red Head, Tays 177 NO 7047
Redheugh 176 NO 4463
Redhill, Avon *T* 101 ST 4963
Redhill, Grampn *T* 185 NJ 6836
Redhill, Grampn *T* 185 NJ 7704
Red Hill, Powys *H* 112 SO 1550
Redhill, Surrey *P* 97 TQ 2850
Redhythe Point 184 NJ 5767
Redisham *T* 123 TM 4084
Redland, Avon *T* 101 ST 5875
Redland, Orkney *T* 200 HY 3724
Redlingfield *T* 123 TM 1870
Red Lion Hill *H* 125 SO 0577
Redlynch, Somer *T* 93 ST 7033
Redlynch, Wilts *T* 94 SU 2021
Redmarley D'Abitot *T* 114 SO 7531
Redmarshall *T* 153 NZ 3821
Redmile *T* 129 SK 7935
Redmire *T* 152 SE 0491
Redmire Moor 152 SE 0493
Redmires Reservoirs *W* 139 SK 2685
Redmoor *T* 87 SX 0861
Redmyre Loch *W* 171 NO 2833
Rednal *T* 126 SJ 3628
Red Nev 200 HY 4145
Redpath *T* 164 NT 5835
Red Pike *H* 150 NY 1615
Red Point, Highld 198 NC 9365
Redpoint, Highld *T* 190 NG 7369
Red Rock *T* 137 SD 5809
Red Roses *T* 111 SN 2011
Red Row *T* 159 NZ 2599
Redruth *P* 86 SW 7042
Redshin Cove *W* 165 NU 0150
Red Street *T* 127 SJ 8351
Red Wharf Bay, Gwyn *T* 134 SH 5381
Red Wharf Bay, Gwyn *W* 134 SH 5481
Redwick, Avon *T* 101 ST 5486
Redwick, Gwent *T* 100 ST 4184
Redworth *T* 152 NZ 2423
Reed *T* 121 TL 3636
Reedham *T* 133 TG 4101
Reedness *T* 142 SE 7923
Reed Point 165 NT 7872
Reef *T* 195 NB 1134
Reeker Pike *H* 158 NY 6682
Reepham, Lincs *T* 140 TF 0373
Reepham, Norf *T* 133 TG 1023
Reeth *T* 152 SE 0399
Regaby *T* 144 SC 4397
Regent's Park 105 TQ 2882
Regoul *T* 183 NH 8851
Regulbium *R* 99 TR 2169
Réidh Eilean 172 NM 2426
Reiff *T* 196 NB 9614
Reigate *P* 96 TQ 2750
Reighton *T* 149 TA 1375
Reighton Sands 149 TA 1476
Rèisa an t-Sruith 167 NR 7399
Rèisa Mhic Phaidean 167 NM 7501
Reisgill Burn *W* 199 ND 2337
Reiss *T* 199 ND 3354
Rejerrah *T* 87 SW 8056
Relubbus *T* 86 SW 5631
Relugas *T* 183 NH 9948
Remenham *T* 104 SU 7784
Remenham Hill *T* 104 SU 7882
Remony 175 NN 7644
Rempstone *T* 129 SK 5724
Remuil Hill *H* 160 NR 6212
Rendall 200 HY 3819
Rendcomb *T* 114 SP 0209
Rendham *T* 123 TM 3564
Rendlesham *T* 123 TM 3253
Rendlesham Forest *F* 123 TM 3449
Renfrew *T* 161 NS 5067
Renhold *T* 120 TL 0852
Renishaw *T* 139 SK 4477
Renish Point 188 NG 0481
Rennington *T* 159 NU 2118
Renton *T* 169 NS 3878
Renwick *T* 151 NY 5943
Repps *T* 133 TG 4117
Repton *T* 128 SK 3027
Rerwick Head 200 HY 5411
Rescobie 177 NO 5052
Resipole 173 NM 7264
Resolis *T* 183 NH 6765
Resolven *T* 109 SN 8302
Rest and be thankful 168 NN 2307
Reston *T* 165 NT 8862
Reswallie 177 NO 5051
Retew *T* 87 SW 9257
Rettendon *T* 106 TQ 7796
Rettendon Place *T* 106 TQ 7796
Revesby *T* 141 TF 2961
Rewe *T* 89 SX 9499
Reydon *T* 123 TM 4977
Reymerston *T* 132 TG 0206
Reynalton *T* 110 SN 0908
Reynoldston *T* 108 SS 4890
Rhadmad *T* 124 SN 5974
Rhaeadr Cynfal *W* 135 SH 7041
Rhandirmwyn *T* 112 SN 7843
Rhayader *P* 125 SN 9768
Rhedyn *T* 134 SH 2932
Rheindown *T* 182 NH 5247
Rhemore 173 NM 5750
Rhenigidale 189 NB 2201
Rhes-y-cae *T* 136 SJ 1971
Rhewl, Clwyd *T* 135 SJ 1060
Rhewl, Clwyd *T* 126 SJ 1844
Rhian 197 NC 5616
Rhicarn 196 NC 0825
Rhiconich *T* 196 NC 2552
Rhicullen *T* 192 NH 6971
Rhidorroch Forest 191 NH 2398
Rhidorroch House 191 NH 1795
Rhidorroch River *W* 191 NH 2194
Rhifail 198 NC 7349
Rhigos *T* 109 SN 9205
Rhilean Burn *W* 183 NH 8937
Rhilochan *T* 193 NC 7407
Rhinns of Islay 166 NR 2157
Rhinns of Kells 155 NX 5083
Rhinns Point 166 NR 1851
Rhinog Fawr *H* 135 SH 6529
Rhins, The 154 NX 0653
Rhiroy *T* 191 NH 1589
Rhiw *T* 124 SH 2228
Rhiwbryfdir *T* 135 SH 6946
Rhiwderin *T* 100 ST 2687
Rhiwlas, Clwyd *T* 126 SJ 1932
Rhiwlas, Gwyn *T* 134 SH 5766
Rhiwlas, Gwyn *T* 135 SH 9237
Rhobell Fawr *H* 125 SH 7825
Rhodesia *T* 139 SK 5680
Rhodes Minnis *T* 99 TR 1542
Rhondda *T* 109 SS 9896
Rhondda Fach 109 ST 0096
Rhondda Fawr 109 SS 9994
Rhonehouse or Kelton Hill *T* 156 NX 7459
Rhoose *T* 109 ST 0666
Rhos, Dyfed *T* 111 SN 3835
Rhos, W. Glam *T* 108 SN 7303
Rhoscefnhir *T* 134 SH 5276
Rhoscolyn *T* 134 SH 2775
Rhoscrowther *T* 110 SM 9002
Rhos Dirion *H* 109 SO 2133
Rhosesmor *T* 136 SJ 2168
Rhos-fawr *T* 134 SH 3839
Rhosgadfan *T* 134 SH 5057
Rhosgoch, Gwyn *T* 134 SH 4189
Rhos-goch, Powys *T* 113 SO 1847
Rhoshirwaun *T* 134 SH 1929
Rhoslan *T* 134 SH 4841
Rhoslefain *T* 124 SH 5705
Rhosllanerchrugog *T* 126 SJ 2946
Rhosmeirch *T* 134 SH 4677
Rhosneigr *T* 134 SH 3273
Rhosnesni *T* 126 SJ 3551
Rhôs-on-Sea *T* 135 SH 8481
Rhossili *T* 108 SS 4188
Rhossili Bay *W* 108 SS 4089
Rhosson *T* 110 SM 7325
Rhostrehwfa *T* 134 SH 4474
Rhostryfan *T* 134 SH 4957
Rhostyllen *T* 126 SJ 3148
Rhosybol *T* 134 SH 4288
Rhos-y-brithdir *T* 126 SJ 1323
Rhos-y-gwaliau *T* 135 SH 9434
Rhos-y-llan *T* 134 SH 2337
Rhos-y-mawn 135 SH 8566
Rhu, Strath 160 NR 8364
Rhu, Strath *T* 168 NS 2684
Rhuallt *T* 135 SJ 0775
Rhuddlan *T* 135 SJ 0278
Rhue *T* 191 NH 0997
Rhulen *T* 112 SO 1349
Rhum 179 NM 3697
Rhunahaorine *T* 160 NR 7048
Rhu Nòa 190 NH 0064
Rhyd, Gwyn *T* 135 SH 6341
Rhyd, Powys *T* 125 SH 9700
Rhydargaeau *T* 111 SN 4326
Rhydcymerau *T* 111 SN 5839
Rhydd *T* 117 SO 8345
Rhyd-Ddu *T* 134 SH 5753
Rhydding *T* 109 SS 7598
Rhŷd-foel *T* 135 SH 9176
Rhydlewis *T* 111 SN 3447
Rhydlios *T* 134 SH 1830
Rhydlydan *T* 135 SH 8950
Rhydowen *T* 111 SN 4445
Rhyd-Rosser *T* 124 SN 5667
Rhydtalog *T* 126 SJ 2355
Rhydwyn *T* 134 SH 3189
Rhyd-y-clafdy *T* 134 SH 3235
Rhydycroesau *T* 126 SJ 2430
Rhydyfelin, Dyfed *T* 124 SN 5979
Rhydyfelin, M. Glam *T* 109 ST 0988
Rhyd-y-fro *T* 108 SN 7105
Rhydymain *T* 125 SH 8022
Rhydymwyn *T* 136 SJ 2066
Rhyd-yr-onen *T* 124 SH 6102
Rhyl *T* 135 SJ 0181
Rhymney *T* 109 SO 1107
Rhymney River, M. Glam *W* 109 ST 1888
Rhymney River, S. Glam *W* 109 ST 2180
Rhymney Valley 109 ST 1592
Rhynd *T* 170 NO 1520
Rhynie, Grampn *T* 184 NJ 4927
Rhynie, Highld 193 NH 8479
Ribbesford *T* 117 SO 7874
Ribble Head *T* 146 SD 7779
Ribblesdale *H* 146 SD 8158
Ribbleton *T* 145 SD 5630
Ribchester *T* 145 SD 6535
Ribigill 197 NC 5854
Riby *T* 143 TA 1807
Riccall *T* 147 SE 6237
Riccarton *T* 161 NS 4235
Richards Castle *T* 116 SO 4969
Richmond, G. Lon *P* 105 TQ 1874
Richmond, N. Yks *T* 152 NZ 1701
Richmond Park 105 TQ 1972
Rickarton *T* 177 NO 8189
Rickets Head 110 SM 8519
Rickinghall *T* 122 TM 0475
Rickling *T* 121 TL 4931
Rickmansworth *T* 104 TQ 0494
Riddell *T* 164 NT 5124
Riddlecombe *T* 91 SS 6113
Riddlesden *T* 146 SE 0842
Ridge, Dorset *T* 94 SY 9386
Ridge, Herts *T* 105 TL 2100
Ridge, Wilts *T* 94 ST 9532
Ridgehill, Avon *T* 101 ST 5362
Ridge Hill, H. & W *H* 113 SO 5035
Ridge Lane *T* 128 SP 2995
Ridge Way, Berks *A* 103 SU 5481
Ridge Way, Oxon *A* 102 SU 3683
Ridge Way, Wilts *A* 102 SU 0151
Ridge Way, Wilts *A* 102 SU 1168
Ridge Way, Wilts *A* 102 SU 1677
Ridgeway Cross *T* 117 SO 7147
Ridgewell *T* 122 TL 7340
Ridgewood *T* 97 TQ 4719
Ridgmont *T* 120 SP 9736
Riding Mill *T* 159 NZ 0161
Ridlees Cairn *H* 158 NT 8404
Ridlington, Leic *T* 130 SK 8402
Ridlington, Norf *T* 133 TG 3430
Ridsdale *T* 158 NY 9084
Riechip 176 NO 0647
Riemore Lodge 176 NO 0449
Rienachait *T* 196 NC 0430
Riereach Burn *W* 183 NH 8445
Rievaulx *T* 147 SE 5785
Rigg *T* 157 NY 2966
Riggend *T* 169 NS 7670
Riggs Moor 146 SE 0373
Rigg, The *H* 158 NY 6483
Rigmaden Park 145 SD 6184
Rig of the Shalloch *H* 154 NX 3891
Rigside *T* 163 NS 8735
Rileyhill *T* 128 SK 1115
Rilla Mill *T* 88 SX 2973
Rillington *T* 148 SE 8574
Rimington *T* 146 SD 8045
Rimpton *T* 93 ST 6021
Rimsdale Burn *W* 198 NC 7440
Rimswell *T* 143 TA 3128
Rinaston *T* 110 SM 9825
Ringasta *T* 203 HU 3714
Ringford *T* 155 NX 6857
Ringland *T* 133 TG 1313
Ringmer *T* 97 TQ 4412
Ringmore *T* 89 SX 6545
Ringorm *T* 184 NJ 2644
Ring's End *T* 131 TF 3902
Ringsfield *T* 123 TM 4088
Ringshall, Herts *T* 104 SP 9814
Ringshall, Suff *T* 122 TM 0452
Ringshall Stocks *T* 122 TM 0551
Ringstead, Norf *T* 132 TF 7040
Ringstead, Northnts *T* 120 SP 9875
Ringstead Bay *W* 93 SY 7581
Ringwood *P* 94 SU 1405
Ringwood Forest *F* 94 SU 1108
Ringwould *T* 99 TR 3648
Rinmore *T* 184 NJ 4117
Rinn Druim Tallig 195 NB 3150
Rinnigill *T* 200 ND 3193
Rinn Thorbhais 172 NL 9340
Rinsey *T* 86 SW 5927
Ripe *T* 97 TQ 5110
Ripley, Derby *T* 128 SK 4050
Ripley, Hants *T* 94 SZ 1698
Ripley, N. Yks *T* 147 SE 2860
Ripley, Surrey *T* 96 TQ 0456
Riplingham *T* 142 SE 9631
Ripon *P* 147 SE 3171
Rippingale *T* 130 TF 0928
Ripple, H. & W *T* 117 SO 8737
Ripple, Kent *T* 99 TR 3450
Ripponden *T* 138 SE 0319
Rippon Tor *H* 89 SX 7475
Rireavach *T* 190 NH 0295
Risabus *T* 166 NR 3143
Risbury *T* 113 SO 5556
Risby, Humbs *T* 142 SE 9214
Risby, Suff *T* 122 TL 8066
Risca *T* 100 ST 2491
Rise *T* 143 TA 1542
Risegate *T* 130 TF 2129
Rise Hill *H* 145 SD 7388
Riseley, Beds *T* 120 TL 0462
Riseley, Berks *T* 104 SU 7263
Risga 173 NM 6160
Rishangles *T* 123 TM 1668
Rishton *T* 145 SD 7230
Rishworth *T* 138 SE 0318
Rishworth Moor 138 SE 0017
Rising Bridge *T* 146 SD 7825
Risley, Ches *T* 137 SJ 6592
Risley, Derby *T* 129 SK 4635
Risplith *T* 147 SE 2468
Rispond 197 NC 4565
Rivar *T* 102 SU 3161
Rivenhall End *T* 106 TL 8316
River Add *W* 167 NR 8293
River Adur *W* 96 TQ 2118
River Affric *W* 181 NH 0920
River Aire, Humbs *W* 147 SE 6723
River Aire, N. Yks *W* 147 SE 6723
River Aire, W. Yks *W* 147 SE 3630
River Alde *W* 123 TM 2967
River Allen, Corn *W* 87 SX 0678
River Allen, Dorset *W* 94 ST 9906
River Allen, Northum *W* 158 NY 7961
River Almond, Lothn *W* 163 NT 0266
River Almond, Tays *W* 169 NN 7733
River Almond, Tays *W* 170 NO 0228
River Aln *W* 159 NU 1314
River Alne *W* 118 SP 1562
River Alport *W* 138 SK 1292
River Alt, Lancs *W* 136 SD 3403
River Alt, Mers *W* 136 SD 3403
River Alun *W* 110 SM 7627
River Alwin *W* 158 NT 9208
River Alyn or Afon Alun *W* 126 SJ 3756
River Amber *W* 139 SK 4363
River Anker *W* 128 SK 2305
River Annan *W* 157 NY 1373
River Ant *W* 133 TG 3618
River Applecross *W* 190 NG 7347
River Ardle *W* 176 NO 0761
River Arnol *W* 195 NB 3045
River Arrow, H. & W *W* 113 SO 4058
River Arrow, Warw *W* 118 SP 0861
River Arun *W* 96 TQ 0422

River Ash Roadside

River Ash *W* 105 TL 4216
River Ashop *W* 138 SK 1389
River Attadale *W* 180 NG 9337
River Averon *W* 192 NH 6372
River Avon, Avon *W* 101 ST 6966
River Avon, Central *W* 170 NS 8773
River Avon, Devon *W* 89 SX 7557
River Avon, Dorset *W* 94 SZ 1496
River Avon, Grampn *W* 184 NJ 1612
River Avon, H. & W *W* 117 SO 9238
River Avon, Warw *W* 118 SP 2659
River Avon, Wilts *W* 101 ST 9171
River Avon, Wilts *W* 102 SU 1349
River Awe *W* 168 NN 0329
River Axe, Devon *W* 92 ST 3100
River Axe, Somer *W* 101 ST 4647
River Ayr *W* 162 NS 6226
River Bà *W* 174 NN 2648
River Bain *W* 141 TF 2472
River Bank *T* 121 TL 5368
River Barle *W* 91 SS 8534
River Barrisdale *W* 180 NG 9003
River Beauly *W* 182 NH 4743
River Bellart *W* 173 NM 4647
River Beult *W* 98 TQ 7747
River Blackwater *W* 106 TL 8322
River Bladnoch *W* 154 NX 3657
River Bleng *W* 150 NY 1008
River Blithe *W* 128 SK 0822
River Blyth *W* 123 TM 4475
River Blythe, Northum *W* 159 NZ 1877
River Blythe, Warw *W* 118 SP 2185
River Bogie *W* 184 NJ 5234
River Borgie *W* 197 NC 6657
River Bourne *W* 102 SU 2038
River Bovey *W* 89 SX 7583
River Braan *W* 175 NN 9338
River Brain *W* 106 TL 7918
River Bran *W* 182 NH 2160
River Brant *W* 140 SK 9457
River Brathay *W* 150 NY 3203
River Bray *W* 91 SS 6932
River Breamish *W* 158 NT 9215
River Brede *W* 98 TQ 8217
River Brett *W* 122 TM 0145
River Brit *W* 93 SY 4795
River Brittle *W* 187 NG 4023
River Brock *W* 145 SD 5140
River Broom *W* 191 NH 1981
River Brora *W* 197 NC 7010
River Brue *W* 101 ST 4243
River Bure, Norf *W* 133 TG 2521
River Bure, Norf *W* 133 TG 4709
River Calder, Highld *W* 175 NN 6899
River Calder, Lancs *W* 145 SD 5346
River Calder, Lancs *W* 146 SD 7833
River Calder, Strath *W* 161 NS 3262
River Calder, W. Yks *W* 139 SE 2620
River Cale *W* 93 ST 7126
River Cam *W* 121 TL 5268
River Camel *W* 87 SX 0168
River Cam or Granta *W* 121 TL 5231
River Cam or Rhee *W* 121 TL 3648
River Can *W* 106 TL 6907
River Cannich *W* 182 NH 3132
River Carey *W* 88 SX 3687
River Carron, Central *W* 169 NS 6684
River Carron, Highld *W* 190 NG 9644
River Carron, Highld *W* 192 NH 4891
River Cary *W* 93 ST 4530
River Cassley *W* 196 NC 4111
River Ceiriog *W* 126 SJ 2438
River Char *W* 92 SY 3894
River Chater *W* 130 SK 8503
River Chelmer, Essex *W* 106 TL 6520
River Chelmer, Essex *W* 106 TL 7709
River Cherwell, Northnts *W* 119 SP 4947
River Cherwell, Oxon *W* 115 SP 5212
River Chess *W* 104 TQ 0695
River Chet *W* 133 TM 3799
River Churn *W* 114 SP 0108
River Churnet *W* 128 SK 0345
River Claw *W* 88 SX 3498
River Clwyd or Afon Clwyd *W* 135 SJ 0376
River Clyde *W* 162 NS 7753
River Clyst *W* 89 SY 0098
River Cocker *W* 150 NY 1523
River Coiltie *W* 182 NH 4526
River Cole, Oxon *W* 115 SU 2294
River Cole, Wilts *W* 115 SU 2294
River Cole, W. Mids *W* 118 SP 1787
River Coll *W* 195 NB 4540
River Coln *W* 115 SP 1305
River Colne *W* 122 TL 9327
River Conder *W* 145 SD 5158
River Conon, Highld *W* 187 NG 4163
River Conon, Highld *W* 182 NH 4654
River Cononish *W* 168 NN 3128
River Coquet *W* 159 NZ 1699
River Corve *W* 116 SO 5083
River Coulin *W* 190 NH 0254
River Coupall *W* 174 NN 2054
River Cover *W* 146 SE 1186
River Cree, D. & G *W* 154 NX 3184
River Cree, D. & G *W* 155 NX 4462
River Cree, Strath *W* 154 NX 3184
River Crouch *W* 106 TQ 8095
River Culm *W* 92 ST 0105
River Cur *W* 168 NN 1101
River Dalch *W* 91 SS 8011
River Dane, Ches *W* 137 SJ 6868
River Dane, Ches *W* 138 SJ 9664
River Dane, Staffs *W* 138 SJ 9664
River Dart *W* 89 SX 7565
River Darwen *W* 145 SD 6129
River Dean, Ches *W* 137 SJ 8881
River Dean, G. Man *W* 137 SJ 8881
River Dearne *W* 139 SE 3408
River Deben *W* 123 TM 2061
River Dee, D. & G *W* 155 NX 7157
River Dee, Grampn *W* 177 NO 5597
River Dee or Afon Dyfrdwy, Ches *W* 126 SJ 4056
River Dee or Afon Dyfrdwy, Clwyd *W* 136 SJ 2380
River Dee or Afon Dyfrdwy, Clwyd *W* 126 SJ 3743
River Dee or Afon Dyfrdwy, Mers *W* 136 SJ 2380
River Dee or Black Water of Dee *W* 156 NX 5973
River Deer *W* 88 SS 3200
River Delph *W* 131 TL 5596
River Derwent, Cumbr *W* 150 NY 2514
River Derwent, Derby *W* 138 SK 1596
River Derwent, Derby *W* 139 SK 2664
River Derwent, Derby *W* 128 SK 4233
River Derwent, Humbs *W* 142 SE 7035
River Derwent, N. Yks *W* 142 SE 7035
River Derwent, N. Yks *W* 148 SE 8578
River Derwent, S. Yks *W* 138 SK 1596
River Dessarry *W* 174 NM 9592
River Deveron *W* 184 NJ 6247
River Devon, Central *W* 170 NS 9497
River Devon, Notts *W* 129 SK 7847
River Dibb *W* 146 SE 0563
River Dionard *W* 196 NC 3255
River Divie *W* 183 NJ 0344
River Dochart *W* 169 NN 5531
River Doe *W* 182 NH 2013
River Don, Grampn *W* 184 NJ 6619
River Don, S. Yks *W* 139 SK 4696
River Doon *W* 161 NS 4308
River Dorn *W* 115 SP 4420
River Douchary *W* 191 NH 2588
River Douglas *W* 137 SD 4812
River Dove, Derby *W* 128 SK 1431
River Dove, N. Yks *W* 153 SE 6793
River Dove, Staffs *W* 128 SK 1431
River Dove, Suff *W* 123 TM 1370
River Dovey or Afon Dyfi *W* 125 SN 6696
River Drolsay *W* 166 NR 3465
River Druie *W* 183 NH 9011
River Drynoch *W* 187 NG 4330
River Duddon *W* 150 SD 2398
River Dudwell *W* 97 TQ 6824
River Dulnain *W* 183 NH 8419
River Dyke *W* 198 NC 8548
River E *W* 182 NH 5414
River Eamont *W* 151 NY 4725
River Earn *W* 170 NN 9817
River East Allen *W* 151 NY 8354
River Eau *W* 142 SK 9098
River Ebble *W* 94 SU 1126
River Eden, Cumbr *W* 151 NY 5830
River Eden, Fife *W* 171 NO 2709
River Eden, Kent *W* 97 TQ 4645
River Ehen *W* 150 NY 0112
River Eidart *W* 175 NN 9192
River Einig *W* 191 NH 3699
River Elchaig *W* 180 NG 9827
River Ellen *W* 150 NY 1641
River Elwy *W* 135 SJ 0071
River Enrick *W* 182 NH 4629
River Erewash, Derby *W* 129 SK 4743
River Erewash, Notts *W* 129 SK 4743
River Ericht *W* 175 NN 5061
River Erme *W* 89 SX 6355
River Erradale *W* 190 NG 7570
River Esk, Cumbr *W* 150 SD 1297
River Esk, D. & G *W* 157 NY 3666
River Esk, Lothn *W* 171 NT 3470
River Esk, N. Yks *W* 148 NZ 7207
River Esk, N. Yks *W* 149 NZ 8708
River Eskin *W* 182 NH 6311
River Esragan *W* 174 NM 9937
River Etherow, Derby *W* 138 SJ 9791
River Etherow, G. Man *W* 138 SJ 9791
River Evelix *W* 193 NH 7392
River Evenlode *W* 115 SP 3220
River Ewe *W* 190 NG 8679
River Exe, Devon *W* 91 SS 9409
River Exe, Somer *W* 91 SS 8040
River Eye *W* 129 SK 8018
River Fal *W* 87 SW 9246
River Falloch *W* 169 NN 3722
River Farigaig *W* 182 NH 5626
River Farrar *W* 182 NH 3439
River Feshie *W* 175 NN 8596
River Fiag *W* 197 NC 4524
River Fiddich *W* 184 NJ 3232
River Findhorn, Grampn *W* 183 NJ 0155
River Findhorn, Highld *W* 183 NH 8940
River Finnan *W* 180 NM 9183
River Fleet *W* 193 NC 7301
River Forsa *W* 173 NM 6040
River Forth *W* 169 NS 6496
River Foulness *W* 142 SE 7839
River Fowey *W* 87 SX 0962
River Foyers *W* 182 NH 4918
River Freshney *W* 143 TA 2308
River Frome, Avon *W* 101 ST 6377
River Frome, Dorset *W* 93 SY 8089
River Frome, H. & W *W* 117 SO 6544
River Frome, Somer *W* 101 ST 7743
River Fyne *W* 168 NN 2318
River Gairn *W* 176 NJ 2501
River Garnock *W* 161 NS 3051
River Garry, Highld *W* 174 NH 1500
River Garry, Tays *W* 175 NN 8365
River Gaur *W* 175 NN 4856
River Gele *W* 135 SH 9476
River Gelt *W* 151 NY 5654
River Gilpin *W* 145 SD 4687
River Gipping *W* 123 TM 1152
River Glass, Highld *W* 182 NH 3532
River Glass, Highld *W* 182 NH 5766
River Glass, I. of M *W* 144 SC 3680
River Glaven *W* 132 TG 0540
River Glen, Lincs *W* 131 TF 2427
River Glen, Northum *W* 165 NT 9430
River Gloy *W* 174 NN 2689
River Glyme *W* 115 SP 4418
River Gour *W* 174 NM 9464
River Gowy *W* 137 SJ 4765
River Granta *W* 121 TL 5051
River Granta or Cam *W* 121 TL 5231
River Great Ouse, Bucks *W* 119 SP 5936
River Great Ouse, Bucks *W* 120 SP 8646
River Great Ouse, Cambs *W* 122 TL 5990
River Great Ouse, Norf *W* 132 TF 5916
River Greta, Lancs *W* 145 SD 6271
River Greta, N. Yks *W* 145 SD 6271
River Grudie, Highld *W* 190 NG 9566
River Grudie, Highld *W* 182 NH 2864
River Gryfe *W* 161 NS 3766
River Gwash *W* 130 SK 8306
River Hamble *W* 95 SU 5214
River Hart *W* 104 SU 7659
River Haultin *W* 187 NG 4451
River Hayle *W* 86 SW 5632
Riverhead *T* 97 TQ 5055
River Helmsdale *W* 193 NC 9319
River Hepste *W* 109 SN 9512
River Hertford *W* 149 TA 0780
River Hindburn *W* 145 SD 6366
River Hinnisdal *W* 187 NG 4258
River Hiz *W* 120 TL 1833
River Hodder *W* 145 SD 7050
River Hope *W* 197 NC 4760
River Hull *W* 142 TA 0646
River Humber *W* 143 TA 2117
River Hurich *W* 173 NM 8368
River Idle, Humbs *W* 140 SK 7497
River Idle, Notts *W* 140 SK 7497
River Inny *W* 88 SX 2383
River Inver *W* 196 NC 1224
River Irt *W* 150 NY 0900
River Irthing, Cumbr *W* 158 NY 6670
River Irthing, Northum *W* 158 NY 6670
River Irvine *W* 161 NS 4737
River Isbourne *W* 114 SP 0334
River Ise *W* 120 SP 8875
River Isis or Thames, Glos *W* 109 ST 1796
River Isis or Thames, Oxon *W* 115 SP 4302
River Isis or Thames, Wilts *W* 115 SU 1796
River Isla, Grampn *W* 184 NJ 4046
River Isla, Tays *W* 176 NO 2358
River Isle *W* 92 ST 4023
River Itchen, Hants *W* 95 SU 4616
River Itchen, Warw *W* 118 SP 4062
River Ithon *W* 112 SO 0460
River Ivel *W* 120 TL 1938
River Kanaird *W* 191 NC 1702
River Keekle *W* 150 NY 0120
River Keer *W* 145 SD 5472
River Kelvin *W* 169 NS 6875
River Kenn, Avon *W* 101 ST 4269
River Kenn, Devon *W* 89 SX 9385
River Kennet, Berks *W* 103 SU 5355
River Kennet, Wilts *W* 102 SU 2369
River Kennett *W* 122 TL 6969
River Kent *W* 151 NY 4502
River Kerry *W* 190 NG 8272
River Kiachnish *W* 174 NN 0967
River Killin *W* 182 NH 5307
River Kingie *W* 174 NN 0297
River Kirkaig *W* 196 NC 1018
River Knaik *W* 169 NN 8112
River Kym *W* 120 TL 1066
River Lael *W* 191 NH 2284
River Laggan *W* 166 NR 3256
River Làir *W* 190 NG 9949
River Lambourn *W* 102 SU 4370
River Lark *W* 122 TL 6476
River Lave *W* 146 SE 2072
River Laxay *W* 195 NB 3122
River Laxdale *W* 195 NB 4035
River Laxford *W* 196 NC 2545
River Leach *W* 115 SP 1707
River Leadon *W* 114 SO 7628
River Leam *W* 119 SP 4568
River Lea or Lee, G. Lon *W* 105 TQ 3695
River Lea or Lee, Herts *W* 105 TL 2609
River Lednock *W* 169 NN 7625
River Leen *W* 129 SK 5450
River Lee or Lea, G. Lon *W* 105 TQ 3695
River Lee or Lea, Herts *W* 105 TL 2609
River Len *W* 98 TQ 8054
River Leven, Highld *W* 174 NN 2160
River Leven, N. Yks *W* 153 NZ 4906
River Leven, Strath *W* 169 NS 3977
River Lew *W* 91 SS 5301
River Liever *W* 168 NM 9007
River Ling *W* 180 NG 9835
River Livet *W* 184 NJ 2523
River Liza *W* 150 NY 1313
River Loanan *W* 196 NC 2418
River Lochay *W* 175 NN 5136
River Lochy, Highld *W* 174 NN 1581
River Lochy, Strath *W* 168 NN 2529
River Loddon *W* 104 SU 7568
River Lodon *W* 113 SO 6152
River Lossie, Grampn *W* 183 NJ 1045
River Lossie, Grampn *W* 184 NJ 2466
River Loughor *W* 111 SN 6108
River Loughor or Afon Llwchwr *W* 108 SS 4897
River Lovat or Ouzel *W* 120 SP 8831
River Lowther *W* 151 NY 5120
River Loxley *W* 139 SK 2989
River Loy *W* 174 NN 1084
River Loyne *W* 181 NH 0805
River Lugg, H. & W *W* 113 SO 5251
River Lugg, Powys *W* 116 SO 3364
River Luineag *W* 183 NH 9410
River Lune, Cumbr *W* 151 NY 6205
River Lune, Durham *W* 152 NY 8820
River Lune, Lancs *W* 145 SD 6075
River Lydden *W* 93 ST 7208
River Lyne *W* 157 NY 4972
River Lynher *W* 88 SX 3663
River Lyon, Tays *W* 175 NN 4641
River Lyon, Tays *W* 175 NN 6547
River Lyvennet *W* 151 NY 6120
River Mallie *W* 174 NN 0887
River Manifold *W* 128 SK 1152
River Mashie *W* 175 NN 5787
River Maun *W* 139 SK 6166
River Mease, Derby *W* 128 SK 2711
River Mease, Leic *W* 128 SK 2711
River Mease, Staffs *W* 128 SK 2711
River Meden *W* 139 SK 5565
River Medina *W* 95 SZ 5094
River Medway, Kent *W* 97 TQ 6446
River Medway, Kent *W* 98 TQ 8673
River Meig, Highld *W* 191 NH 1648
River Meig, Highld *W* 182 NH 3355
River Meoble *W* 180 NM 7987
River Meon *W* 95 SU 5407
River Mersey *W* 136 SJ 4081
River Misbourne *W* 104 SU 9696
River Mite *W* 150 SD 0998
River Moidart *W* 173 NM 7574
River Mole, Devon *W* 91 SS 7327
River Mole, Surrey *W* 105 TQ 1263
River Mole, Surrey *W* 96 TQ 2347
River Monnow or Afon Mynwy, Gwent *W* 113 SO 4717
River Monnow or Afon Mynwy, H. & W *W* 113 SO 4717
River Moriston *W* 182 NH 3314
River Mudale *W* 197 NC 5435
River Muick *W* 176 NO 3288
River Nadder *W* 94 SU 0130
River Nairn *W* 183 NH 7846
River Nar *W* 132 TF 6812
River Naver *W* 198 NC 7250
River Neath *W* 108 SS 7292
River Nene (old course) *W* 121 TL 3291
River Nene, Cambs *W* 131 TL 2398
River Nene, Lincs *W* 131 TF 4617
River Nene, Norf *W* 131 TF 4617
River Nene, Northnts *W* 119 SP 5959
River Nene, Northnts *W* 120 TL 0385
River Ness *W* 182 NH 6442
River Nethan *W* 162 NS 7835
River Nethy *W* 183 NJ 0213
River Nevis *W* 174 NN 1371
River Nidd *W* 147 SE 3357
River Nith *W* 156 NS 5612
River Noe *W* 138 SK 1385
River North Esk, Grampn *W* 177 NO 6266
River North Esk, Lothn *W* 163 NT 2158
River North Esk, Tays *W* 177 NO 6266
River North Tyne *W* 158 NY 8974
River Ock *W* 115 SU 4095
River Oich *W* 182 NH 3405
River Okement *W* 91 SS 5901
River Orchy *W* 168 NN 2028
River Ore, Fife *W* 171 NT 2896
River Ore, Suff *W* 123 TM 3845
River Orrin *W* 182 NH 4050
River Orwell *W* 123 TM 2138
River Ose *W* 186 NG 3442
River Ossian *W* 174 NN 4171
River Otter *W* 92 SY 0996
River Ottery *W* 88 SX 2788
River Oude *W* 173 NM 8416
River Ouse, E. Susx *W* 97 TQ 4208
River Ouse, N. Yks *W* 147 SE 4959
River Ouzel or Lovat *W* 120 SP 8831
River Oykel *W* 191 NC 3503
River Pang *W* 103 SU 5971
River Pant *W* 122 TL 6631
River Parrett *W* 92 ST 3927
River Pattack *W* 175 NN 5484
River Pean *W* 174 NM 9490
River Penk *W* 127 SJ 9005
River Perry *W* 126 SJ 3926
River Petteril *W* 151 NY 4543
River Piddle or Trent *W* 93 SY 8591
River Plym *W* 89 SX 5464
River Polly *W* 196 NC 0713
River Pont *W* 159 NZ 1676
River Poulter *W* 139 SK 6475
River Quaich *W* 175 NN 7939
River Quin *W* 121 TL 3927
River Ray, Oxon *W* 115 SP 5917
River Ray, Wilts *W* 102 SU 1191
River Rea, H. & W *W* 117 SO 6773
River Rea, Shrops *W* 117 SO 6773
River Rede *W* 158 NY 8298
River Rha *W* 187 NG 4065
River Rhee or Cam *W* 121 TL 3648
River Rhiw *W* 126 SJ 1302
River Rib *W* 105 TL 3818
River Ribble *W* 145 SD 6434
River Riccal *W* 147 SE 6382
River Roach, Essex *W* 107 TQ 9692
River Roach, G. Man *W* 137 SD 8712
River Roden *W* 127 SJ 5915
River Romesdal *W* 187 NG 4354
River Rother, E. Susx *W* 97 TQ 6125
River Rother, E. Susx *W* 98 TQ 9423
River Rother, Hants *W* 95 SU 7625
River Rother, W. Susx *W* 96 SU 9420
River Roy *W* 174 NN 3088
River Ruel, Strath *W* 168 NS 0289
River Ruel, Strath *W* 168 NS 0289
River Runie *W* 191 NC 1403
River Rye *W* 147 SE 5784
River Ryton *W* 139 SK 6384
River Sand *W* 190 NG 7679
River Sark *W* 157 NY 3372
River Scaddle *W* 174 NM 9768
River Seaton *W* 88 SX 3059
River Sence, Leic *W* 128 SK 3604
River Sence, Leic *W* 129 SP 6096
River Seph *W* 153 SE 5691
River Seven *W* 148 SE 7380
River Severn, Glos *W* 114 SO 6905
River Severn, H. & W *W* 117 SO 8551
River Severn, Powys *W* 125 SO 0289
River Severn, Shrops *W* 127 SJ 6902
River Sgitheach *W* 182 NH 5765
River Sheaf *W* 139 SK 3484
River Shiel *W* 180 NG 9913
River Shin *W* 192 NH 5798
River Shira *W* 168 NN 1518
River Skerne *W* 152 NZ 3026
River Skinsdale *W* 193 NC 7620
River Skirfare *W* 146 SD 8875
River Slea *W* 130 TF 0948
River Sligachan *W* 187 NG 4927
River Snizort *W* 187 NG 4244
River Soar, Leic *W* 129 SK 5600
River Soar, Notts *W* 129 SK 5123
River Solva *W* 110 SM 8327
River Sorn *W* 166 NR 3664
River South Esk, Lothn *W* 164 NT 3157
River South Esk, Tays *W* 176 NO 3372
River South Tyne *W* 151 NY 6854
River Sow *W* 127 SJ 8528
River Sowe *W* 118 SP 3777
River Spean *W* 174 NN 2680
River Spey, Grampn *W* 184 NJ 3253
River Spey, Highld *W* 183 NH 9315
River Sprint *W* 151 SD 5297
River Stiffkey *W* 132 TF 9332
River Stinchar *W* 154 NX 2291
River Stort *W* 121 TL 4829
River Stour, Dorset *W* 93 ST 7617
River Stour, Dorset *W* 94 SZ 1096
River Stour, Essex *W* 122 TL 9233
River Stour, H. & W *W* 117 SO 8083
River Stour, Kent *W* 99 TR 2763
River Stour, Warw *W* 118 SP 2248
River Strae *W* 168 NN 1833
River Strathy *W* 198 NC 8256
River Swale *W* 152 SE 2796
River Swere *W* 115 SP 4733
River Swift *W* 119 SP 5283
River Taff *W* 109 ST 1777
River Tale *W* 92 ST 0702
River Tamar, Corn *W* 88 SX 3682
River Tamar, Devon *W* 88 SX 3682
River Tame, G. Man *W* 137 SJ 9092
River Tame, Staffs *W* 128 SK 1807
River Tame, Warw *W* 118 SP 2091
River Tarbert *W* 173 NM 9159
River Tarff *W* 174 NH 3902
River Tavy *W* 88 SX 4765
River Taw *W* 91 SS 6614
River Tawe *W* 108 SS 6798
River Tay *W* 176 NO 1339
River Tees, Cumbr *W* 151 NY 7733
River Tees, Durham *W* 151 NY 7733
River Tees, Durham *W* 152 NZ 2711
River Tees, N. Yks *W* 152 NZ 2711
River Teign *W* 89 SX 7689
River Teith *W* 169 NN 6407
River Teme, H. & W *W* 117 SO 7166
River Teme, Powys *W* 116 SO 3273
River Teme, Shrops *W* 116 SO 3273
River Ter *W* 106 TL 7714
River Tern, Shrops *W* 127 SJ 7037
River Tern, Staffs *W* 127 SJ 7037
River Test *W* 94 SU 3637
River Teviot *W* 164 NT 6424
River Thame *W* 104 SP 7713
River Thames, Essex *W* 105 TQ 5576
River Thames, Kent *W* 105 TQ 5576
River Thames or Isis, Glos *W* 109 ST 1796
River Thames or Isis, Oxon *W* 115 SP 4302
River Thames or Isis, Wilts *W* 115 SU 1796
River Thet *W* 122 TL 9584
River Thrushel *W* 88 SX 4789
River Thurne *W* 133 TG 4017
River Thurso *W* 199 ND 1154
River Tiddy *W* 88 SX 3064
River Til *W* 120 TL 0268
River Till, Lincs *W* 140 SK 9078
River Till, Northum *W* 165 NT 9732
River Tillingham *W* 98 TQ 8720
River Tilt, Tays *W* 175 NN 9374
River Tilt, Tays *W* 176 NN 9576
River Tirry *W* 197 NC 5418
River Tone *W* 92 ST 3127
River Torne *W* 139 SE 6502
River Torridge *W* 91 SS 5509
River Torridon *W* 190 NG 9256
River Toscaig *W* 180 NG 7337
River Tove *W* 119 SP 7746
River Traligill *W* 196 NC 2720
River Trent, Derby *W* 128 SK 2826
River Trent, Humbs *W* 142 SE 8619
River Trent, Notts *W* 129 SK 6541
River Trent, Staffs *W* 127 SJ 9330
River Trent or Piddle *W* 93 SY 8591
River Tromie *W* 175 NN 7795
River Trothy or Afon Troddi *W* 113 SO 4512
River Truim *W* 175 NN 6485
River Tud *W* 133 TG 0912
River Tummel, Tays *W* 175 NN 7459
River Tummel, Tays *W* 176 NN 9654
River Turret *W* 174 NN 3393
River Tweed, Border *W* 164 NT 7737
River Tweed, Northum *W* 165 NT 9452
River Tyne, Lothn *W* 171 NT 5575
River Tyne, Northum *W* 159 NZ 0261
River Ugie *W* 185 NK 0849
River Ure *W* 146 SE 2085
River Urie *W* 185 NJ 6927
River Usk, Gwent *W* 113 SO 2615
River Usk, Powys *W* 109 SN 9329
River Ver *W* 105 TL 1209
River Vyrnwy or Afon Efyrnwy *W* 126 SJ 1714
River Waldon *W* 90 SS 3610
River Wampool *W* 150 NY 2553
River Wansbeck *W* 159 NZ 1185
River Washburn *W* 146 SE 1261
River Waveney, Norf *W* 123 TM 4691
River Waveney, Suff *W* 123 TM 2381
River Waveney, Suff *W* 123 TM 4691
River Waver *W* 150 NY 1950
River Wear *W* 152 NZ 1134
River Weaver *W* 137 SJ 5477
River Welland, Leic *W* 130 SP 8995
River Welland, Lincs *W* 131 TF 2727
River Welland, Northnts *W* 130 SP 8995
River Wenning *W* 145 SD 7167
River Wensum *W* 132 TG 0518
River Went, N. Yks *W* 139 SE 6117
River Went, S. Yks *W* 139 SE 6117
River West Allen *W* 151 NY 7856
River Wey, Hants *W* 103 SU 7742
River Wey, Surrey *W* 96 TQ 0557
River Wharfe *W* 146 SE 0262
River Wheelock *W* 137 SJ 7062
River Windrush *W* 115 SP 1816
River Winster *W* 145 SD 4185
River Wiske, N. Yks *W* 153 NZ 4300
River Wiske, N. Yks *W* 153 SE 3497
River Wissey, Norf *W* 132 TF 8502
River Wissey, Norf *W* 132 TL 6797
River Witham, Lincs *W* 140 SK 9363
River Witham, Lincs *W* 131 TF 2548
River Wolf *W* 88 SX 4290
River Worfe *W* 127 SO 7696
River Worth *W* 146 SE 0137
River Wreake *W* 129 SK 6616
River Wye, Derby *W* 138 SK 2169
River Wye, H. & W *W* 113 SO 4341
River Wye or Afon Gwy, Glos *W* 127 SO 5398
River Wye or Afon Gwy, Gwent *W* 127 SO 5398
River Wye or Afon Gwy, Powys *W* 112 SO 0153
River Wylye *W* 94 SU 0536
River Wyre, Lancs *W* 145 SD 4440
River Wyre, Lancs *W* 145 SD 5454
River Yar *W* 95 SZ 6186
River Yare, Norf *W* 133 TG 1108
River Yare, Norf *W* 133 TG 3604
River Yarrow *W* 137 SD 5117
River Yarty *W* 92 ST 2505
River Yealm *W* 89 SX 6056
River Yeo, Devon *W* 91 SS 7306
River Yeo, Devon *W* 91 SS 7726
River Yeo, Dorset *W* 93 ST 6214
River Yeo, Somer *W* 93 ST 4723
River Ythan *W* 185 NJ 8339
Rivington *T* 137 SD 6214
Riv, The 201 HY 6847
Rivvalee 205 HP 4805
Roachill *T* 91 SS 8422
Roade *T* 119 SP 7551
Roadmeetings *T* 163 NS 8649
Roadside *T* 199 ND 1560

Roadside of Catterline St Ann's Head

Roadside of Catterline *T* 177 NO 8579
Roadside of Kinneff *T* 177 NO 8476
Road, The *W* 86 SV 8912
Roadwater *T* 100 ST 0338
Roag *T* 186 NG 2744
Roa Island 144 SD 2365
Roana Bay *W* 201 HY 5905
Roan Fell, Border *H* 157 NY 4593
Roan Fell, D. & G *H* 157 NY 4593
Roan Head 200 ND 3896
Roath *T* 109 ST 1977
Robbingworth *T* 105 TL 5305
Roberton, Border *T* 157 NT 4314
Roberton, Strath *T* 163 NS 9428
Roberton Law *H* 163 NS 9129
Robertsbridge *T* 97 TQ 7323
Roberttown *T* 146 SE 1922
Robeston Cross *T* 110 SM 8909
Robeston Wathen *T* 110 SN 0815
Robin Hood's Bay *T* 149 NZ 9505
Roborough *T* 91 SS 5717
Rob Roy's Cave 168 NN 3310
Rob Roy's House 168 NN 1516
Roby Mill *T* 137 SD 5107
Rocester *T* 128 SK 1139
Roch *T* 110 SM 8821
Rochdale *P* 137 SD 8913
Rochdale Canal, G. Man *W* 137 SD 9420
Rochdale Canal, W. Yks *W* 137 SD 9420
Roche *T* 87 SW 9860
Roche Abbey *A* 139 SK 5489
Rochester, Kent *T* 98 TQ 7369
Rochester, Northum *T* 158 NY 8398
Rochford, Essex *T* 106 TQ 8790
Rochford, H. & W *T* 117 SO 6368
Rock, Corn *T* 87 SW 9475
Rock, H. & W *T* 117 SO 7371
Rock, Northum *T* 159 NU 2020
Rockbeare *T* 92 SY 0295
Rockbourne *T* 94 SU 1118
Rockbourne Down *H* 94 SU 1021
Rockcliffe, Cumbr *T* 157 NY 3561
Rockcliffe, D. & G *T* 155 NX 8454
Rocken End 95 SZ 4975
Rock Ferry *T* 136 SJ 3386
Rockfield, Gwent *T* 113 SO 4814
Rockfield, Highld *T* 193 NH 9283
Rockham Bay *W* 90 SS 4546
Rockhampton *T* 114 ST 6593
Rockingham *T* 120 SP 8691
Rockingham Forest *F* 120 SP 9791
Rockland All Saints *T* 132 TL 9996
Rockland St Mary *T* 133 TG 3104
Rockland St Peter *T* 132 TL 9997
Rockley *T* 102 SU 1671
Rockwell End *T* 104 SU 7988
Rodbourne *T* 102 ST 9383
Rodd *T* 116 SO 3262
Roddam *T* 159 NU 0220
Rodden *T* 93 SY 6184
Rode *T* 101 ST 8053
Rode Heath, Ches *T* 137 SJ 8057
Rodeheath, Ches *T* 137 SJ 8766
Rodel *T* 188 NG 0483
Roden *T* 127 SJ 5716
Rodhuish *T* 100 ST 0139
Rodings, The 105 TL 5814
Rodington *T* 127 SJ 5814
Rodley *T* 114 SO 7411
Rodmarton *T* 114 ST 9498
Rodmell *T* 97 TQ 4106
Rodmersham *T* 98 TQ 9261
Rodney Stoke *T* 101 ST 4850
Rodono Hotel 163 NT 2321
Rodsley *T* 128 SK 2040
Roecliffe *T* 147 SE 3765
Roehampton *T* 105 TQ 2373
Roe Ness 203 HU 3242
Roer Water *W* 204 HU 3386
Roesound 203 HU 3465
Roewen *T* 135 SH 7572
Roffey *T* 96 TQ 1932
Rogan's Seat *H* 152 NY 9103
Rogart *T* 193 NC 7303
Rogart Station 193 NC 7202
Rogate *T* 95 SU 8023
Roger Sand 131 TF 4841
Rogerstone *T* 100 ST 2788
Rogerton *T* 162 NS 6256
Rogiet *T* 101 ST 4687
Roineabhal *H* 188 NG 0486
Roineval, Highld *H* 187 NG 4135
Roineval, W. Isles *H* 195 NB 2321
Roinn a' Bhuic 195 NB 4057
Rois-Bheinn *H* 180 NM 7577
Roker *T* 159 NZ 4059
Rollesby *T* 133 TG 4415
Rolleston, Leic *T* 129 SK 7300
Rolleston, Notts *T* 129 SK 7452
Rolleston, Staffs *T* 128 SK 2327
Rollright Stones *A* 115 SP 2831
Rolston *T* 143 TA 2145
Rolvenden *T* 98 TQ 8431
Rolvenden Layne *T* 98 TQ 8530
Romaldkirk *T* 152 NY 9922
Romanby *T* 153 SE 3693
Romannobridge *T* 163 NT 1648
Roman River *W* 107 TL 9920
Romansleigh *T* 91 SS 7220
Roman Steps 135 SH 6530
Rombalds Moor 146 SE 0945
Romford *T* 105 TQ 5188
Romiley *T* 137 SJ 9491
Romney Marsh 99 TR 0529
Romney Sands 99 TR 0823
Romsey *T* 94 SU 3521
Romsley, H. & W *T* 118 SO 9680
Romsley, Shrops *T* 117 SO 7882
Rona 194 HW 8132
Ronachan House 160 NR 7455
Ronachan Point 160 NR 7455
Ronague *T* 144 SC 2472
Ronas Hill *H* 204 HU 3083
Ronas Voe *W* 204 HU 2882
Rona, The *W* 203 HU 3260
Ronay 188 NF 8955
Roneval *H* 178 NF 8114
Rookby *T* 151 NY 8010
Rooken Edge *H* 158 NY 7896
Rookhope *T* 152 NY 9342
Rookley *T* 95 SZ 5084
Rooks Bridge *T* 100 ST 3652
Roos *T* 143 TA 2930
Roosebeck *T* 144 SD 2567
Roos Wick *W* 201 HY 6545
Rootpark *T* 163 NS 9554
Ropley *T* 95 SU 6431
Ropley Deane *T* 95 SU 6331
Ropsley *T* 130 SK 9934
Rora *T* 185 NK 0650
Rora Head 200 ND 1799
Rora Moss 185 NK 0451
Rorandle 184 NJ 6518
Rorrington *T* 126 SJ 3000
Rosarie Forest 184 NJ 3547
Rose *T* 86 SW 7754
Roseacre *T* 145 SD 4336
Rose Ash *T* 91 SS 7821
Rosebank *T* 163 NS 8049
Rosebery Reservoir *W* 164 NT 3056
Rosebush *T* 110 SN 0729
Rosedale 148 SE 7196
Rosedale Abbey *T* 148 SE 7295
Rosedale Moor 148 SE 7299
Roseden *T* 165 NU 0321
Rosefield 183 NH 8552
Rosehall *T* 192 NC 4702
Rosehaugh Mains 183 NH 6855
Rosehearty *T* 185 NJ 9367
Rosehill *T* 127 SJ 6630
Roseisle *T* 183 NJ 1467
Roseisle Forest *F* 183 NJ 1267
Rosemarket *T* 110 SM 9508
Rosemarkie *T* 183 NH 7357
Rosemarkie Bay *W* 183 NH 7457
Rosemary Lane *T* 92 ST 1514
Rosemount, Strath *T* 161 NS 3729
Rosemount, Tays *T* 176 NO 1843
Rosemullion Head 87 SW 7928
Rosenannon *T* 87 SW 9566
Rose Ness 200 ND 5298
Rosewell *T* 163 NT 2862
Roseworthy *T* 86 SW 6139
Rosgill *T* 151 NY 5316
Roshven *T* 180 NM 7078
Rosinish 178 NL 6187
Roskhill *T* 186 NG 2745
Rosley *T* 150 NY 3245
Roslin *T* 163 NT 2663
Rosliston *T* 128 SK 2416
Rosneath *T* 168 NS 2583
Rosneath Point 168 NS 2780
Ross, D. & G *T* 155 NX 6444
Ross, Northum *T* 165 NU 1337
Ross, Tays 169 NN 7621
Rossall Point 145 SD 3147
Rossdhu House 169 NS 3689
Rossett *T* 136 SJ 3757
Rossie Moor 177 NO 6554
Rossie Ochill 170 NO 0813
Rossie Priory 171 NO 2830
Rossington *T* 139 SK 6298
Rossinish 188 NF 8653
Rosskeen 183 NH 6869
Rossland *T* 169 NS 4470
Ross of Mull 172 NM 4021
Ross-on-Wye *P* 113 SO 6024
Ross Priory 169 NS 4187
Roster *T* 199 ND 2639
Rostherne *T* 137 SJ 7483
Rosthwaite *T* 150 NY 2514
Roston *T* 128 SK 1341
Rosyth *T* 170 NT 1183
Rothbury *T* 159 NU 0501
Rothbury Forest *F* 159 NZ 0599
Rotherby *T* 129 SK 6716
Rotherfield *T* 97 TQ 5529
Rotherfield Greys *T* 104 SU 7282
Rotherfield Peppard *T* 104 SU 7181
Rotherham *P* 139 SK 4492
Rother Levels 98 TQ 9025
Rothersthorpe *T* 119 SP 7156
Rotherwick *T* 103 SU 7156
Rothes *T* 184 NJ 2749
Rothesay *T* 161 NS 0864
Rothesay Bay *W* 161 NS 0865
Rothiebrisbane *T* 185 NJ 7437
Rothiemurchus 183 NH 9308
Rothienorman *T* 185 NJ 7235
Rothiesholm *T* 201 HY 6223
Rothiesholm Head 201 HY 6020
Rothley *T* 129 SK 5812
Rothley Lakes *W* 159 NZ 0490
Rothmaise *T* 185 NJ 6832
Rothwell, Lincs *T* 143 TF 1599
Rothwell, Northnts *T* 120 SP 8181
Rothwell, W. Yks *T* 147 SE 3428
Rothwell Loch *W* 176 NO 0247
Rotsea *T* 149 TA 0651
Rottal *T* 176 NO 3769
Rottingdean *T* 97 TQ 3702
Rottington *T* 150 NX 9613
Roud *T* 95 SZ 5180
Rougham *T* 132 TF 8320
Rougham Green *T* 122 TL 9061
Roughburn *T* 174 NN 3781
Rough Close *T* 127 SJ 9239
Rough Common *T* 99 TR 1259
Rough Hill *H* 161 NS 5445
Rough Island 155 NX 8453
Roughlee *T* 146 SD 8440
Roughley *T* 128 SP 1299
Rough Pike *H* 158 NY 6286
Roughrigg Reservoir *W* 163 NS 8164
Roughsike *T* 158 NY 5275
Roughton, Lincs *T* 141 TF 2464
Roughton, Norf *T* 133 TG 2136
Roughton, Shrops *T* 127 SO 7594
Rough Tor, Corn *H* 87 SX 1480
Rough Tor, Devon *H* 89 SX 6079
Rough Tower 123 TM 3927
Round Fell *H* 155 NX 5372
Roundhay *T* 147 SE 3337
Round Hill, Cumbr *H* 151 NY 7436
Round Hill, Grampn *H* 184 NJ 3427
Round Hill, N. Yks *H* 146 SE 1253
Roundhill Resr *W* 146 SE 1577
Round Island 86 SV 9017
Round Loch of the Dungeon *W* 155 NX 4684
Roundstreet Common *T* 96 TQ 0528
Roundway *T* 102 SU 0163
Rounton *T* 153 NZ 4103
Rousay 200 HY 4030
Rousay Sound *W* 200 HY 4529
Rousdon *T* 92 SY 2991
Rous Lench *T* 118 SP 0153
Routenburn 161 NS 1961
Routh *T* 143 TA 0942
Row, Corn *T* 87 SX 0976
Row, Cumbr *T* 151 SD 4589
Rowallan Castle *A* 161 NS 4342
Rowanburn *T* 157 NY 4077
Rowardennan Forest *F* 169 NS 3996
Rowardennan Lodge 168 NS 3599
Rowde *T* 102 ST 9862
Rowe Ditch *A* 113 SO 3859
Rowfoot *T* 158 NY 6860
Row Head 200 HY 2218
Rowhedge *T* 107 TM 0221
Rowhook *T* 96 TQ 1234
Rowington *T* 118 SP 2069
Rowland *T* 138 SK 2172
Rowland's Castle *T* 95 SU 7310
Rowlands Gill *T* 159 NZ 1658
Rowledge *T* 103 SU 8243
Rowlestone *T* 113 SO 3727
Rowley *T* 126 SJ 3006
Rowley Regis *T* 118 SO 9687
Rowly *T* 96 TQ 0440
Rowney Green *T* 118 SP 0471
Rownhams *T* 94 SU 3817
Rowsham *T* 104 SP 8518
Rowsley *T* 139 SK 2566
Rowston *T* 130 TF 0856
Rowton, Ches *T* 136 SJ 4464
Rowton, Shrops *T* 127 SJ 6119
Rowton Castle 126 SJ 3712
Roxburgh *T* 164 NT 6930
Roxby, Humbs *T* 142 SE 9217
Roxby, N. Yks *T* 153 NZ 7616
Roxby High Moor 153 NZ 7511
Roxton *T* 120 TL 1554
Roxwell *T* 106 TL 6408
Royal British Legion Village *T* 97 TQ 7257
Royal Forest 174 NN 2153
Royal Greenwich Observatory 97 TQ 6410
Royal Leamington Spa *P* 118 SP 3265
Royal Military Academy 104 SU 8661
Royal Military Canal *W* 99 TR 0133
Royal Sovereign (lightship) 97 TV 7194
Royal Tunbridge Wells *T* 97 TQ 5839
Roybridge *T* 174 NN 2781
Roydon, Essex *T* 105 TL 4010
Roydon, Norf *T* 132 TF 7022
Roydon, Norf *T* 123 TM 0980
Royl Field *H* 203 HU 3928
Royston, Herts *T* 121 TL 3540
Royston, S. Yks *T* 139 SE 3511
Royton *T* 137 SD 9107
Ruabon *T* 126 SJ 3043
Ruabon Mountain *H* 126 SJ 2446
Ruadh Sgeir 167 NR 7292
Ruadh-stac Mór *H* 190 NG 9561
Ruaig *T* 172 NM 0647
Ruan Lanihorne *T* 87 SW 8942
Ruan Minor *T* 86 SW 7215
Ruardean *T* 113 SO 6217
Ruardean Woodside *T* 113 SO 6216
Rubers Law *H* 158 NT 5815
Rubery *T* 118 SO 9977
Rubha a' Ghraineig 172 NM 1555
Rubha Aird Druimnich 173 NM 5772
Rubha Airigh Bheirg 160 NR 8847
Rubha a' Mhail 166 NR 4279
Rubha' a' Mharaiche 160 NR 5812
Rubha an Aird 172 NM 3855
Rubha an Daraich 180 NG 7909
Rubha an Dùine 188 NF 9771
Rubha an Fhasaidh 179 NM 4387
Rubha an Ridire 173 NM 7340
Rubha' Ard na Bà 190 NG 8584
Rubha Ard Slisneach 180 NG 7409
Rubha Ardvule 178 NF 7029
Rubha Bàn 190 NG 7379
Rubha Beag 190 NG 8997
Rubh' a' Bhacain 167 NR 7096
Rubh' a' Bhaid Bheithe 174 NN 0259
Rubh' a' Bhàigh Uaine 195 NB 4228
Rubh' a' Bhaile Fo Thuath 188 NF 9087
Rubh' a' Bhaird 189 NB 3101
Rubha Bhilidh 178 NF 8632
Rubh' a' Bhinnein 172 NM 2263
Rubh' a' Bhiogair 195 NB 3452
Rubha Bhlanisgaidh 195 NB 3755
Rubha Bhocaig *T* 189 NG 1891
Rubha Bhoisnis 188 NF 8880
Rubha Bholsa 166 NR 3878
Rubha Bhrollum 189 NB 3202
Rubha Bolum 178 NF 8328
Rubha Buidhe 180 NG 7811
Rubha Cam nan Gall *T* 188 NF 8847
Rubha Caol 195 NB 2447
Rubha Caolard 168 NR 8783
Rubha Carrach 173 NM 4670
Rubh' a' Chàirn Bhàin 160 NR 6754
Rubh' a' Chamais 166 NR 5978
Rubh' a' Chaoil 172 NM 3346
Rubha Charn nan Cearc 180 NG 5503
Rubha Chlachan 160 NR 6105
Rubh' a' Choin 196 NC 0315
Rubha Chràiginis 172 NL 9245
Rubh' a' Chrois-aoinidh 166 NR 5080
Rubha Chuaig 190 NG 6959
Rubha Coigeach 196 NB 9818
Rubha Crago *T* 189 NG 2397
Rubha Creagan Dubha 160 NR 9352
Rubha Dubh, Strath 172 NM 0948
Rubha Dubh, Strath 173 NM 5621
Rubha Dubh, Strath 166 NR 3991
Rubha Dubh Tighary 188 NF 7072
Rubha Dùin Bhàin 160 NR 5914
Rubha Fàsachd 172 NM 1653
Rubha Fiart 173 NM 7835
Rubha Garbh-àird 173 NM 8736
Rubha Garbh-ard 167 NR 7896
Rubh' a' Geogha 166 NR 4399
Rubha Ghlamraidh 166 NR 1758
Rubha Hellisdale 178 NF 8430
Rubha Hogh 172 NM 1759
Rubha Hunish 189 NG 4077
Rubha Iosal 195 NB 4216
Rubh' Aird an Fhedh 180 NM 6375
Rubh' Aird an t-Sionnaich 196 NC 1443
Rubh' Aird-mhicheil *T* 178 NF 7333
Rubh' Aird na Sgitheich 166 NR 4779
Rubha Lamanais 166 NR 2068
Rubha Langanes 179 NG 2306
Rubha Leacach 188 NB 0107
Rubha Leathan 160 NR 9261
Rubha Leathann 195 NB 3654
Rubha Leumair 196 NC 0426
Rubha Màs a' Chnuie 188 NF 9795
Rubha Meall na Hoe 178 NF 8217
Rubh' a' Mhàil 166 NR 4379
Rubha Mhic 188 NF 9363
Rubh' a' Mhill Dheirg 196 NC 0228
Rubh' a' Mhucard 196 NC 1638
Rubha Mór, Highld 196 NB 9814
Rubha Mór, Highld 190 NG 8696
Rubha Mór, Highld 174 NM 9655
Rubha Mór, Strath 172 NM 2464
Rubha Mór, Strath 173 NM 5743
Rubha Mór, Strath 166 NR 2948
Rubha Mór, W. Isles 178 NL 6997
Rubha na Brèige 196 NC 0519
Rubha na Crannaig 179 NM 4984
Rubha na Creige Mòire, W. Isles 195 NB 4218
Rubha na Creige Mòire, W. Isles 178 NF 8320
Rubha na Faing 166 NR 1553
Rubha na Faing Mòire 180 NM 6477
Rubha na Fearn 190 NG 7261
Rubha na Gainmhich 166 NR 4346
Rubha na Greine 195 NB 5633
Rubha na h-Airde 167 NR 7083
Rubha na h-Airde Glaise 187 NG 5145
Rubha na h-Airde Uinnsinn 173 NM 8752
Rubha na h-Aiseig 187 NG 4476
Rubha na h-Easgainne 187 NG 5211
Rubha na h-Uamha 172 NM 4028
Rubha na h-Uamha-sàile 166 NR 6094
Rubha na' Leac *W* 180 NG 5938
Rubha na Leacaig 196 NC 2056
Rubha nam Bàirneach 195 NB 5531
Rubha nam Bàrr 167 NR 7491
Rubha nam Bràithrean 173 NM 4317
Rubha nam Brathairean 187 NG 5262
Rubha na Mèise Bàine 166 NR 3341
Rubha nam Faoilean 167 NR 6704
Rubha nam Maol Mòra 172 NM 3316
Rubha nam Meirleach 179 NM 3691
Rubha nam Plèac 188 NF 9467
Rubha nan Cearc 172 NM 3225
Rubha nan Clach 186 NG 3033
Rubha nan Còsan 196 NC 0734
Rubha nan Crann 166 NR 6181
Rubha nan Eun 178 NF 7307
Rubha nan Gall, Strath 172 NM 4141
Rubha nan Gall, Strath 173 NM 5057
Rubha nan Leacan 166 NR 3140
Rubha nan Oirean 172 NM 3551
Rubha nan Sasan 190 NG 8192
Rubha nan Sgarbh, Highld 193 NH 7088
Rubha nan Sgarbh, Strath 160 NR 7934
Rubha nan Totag 188 NB 0303
Rubha nan Tri Chlach 179 NM 4988
Rubha na-Ordaig 178 NF 8414
Rubha na Rodagrich 188 NF 8954
Rubha na Roinne 179 NG 4200
Rubha na Seann Charraige 172 NM 0545
Rubha na Sròine 172 NM 3642
Rubha na Tràille 166 NR 5162
Rubh' an Dùnain, Highld 186 NG 3816
Rubh' an Dùnain, W. Isles 195 NB 2448
Rubha Nead a' Gheòidh 172 NM 0947
Rubh' an Fhir Léithe 196 NC 1863
Rubh' an Teampuill 188 NF 9791
Rubh' an Tòrra Mhòir 187 NG 5232
Rubh' an t-Sàilein 166 NR 5082
Rubh' an t-Suibhein 172 NM 3645
Rubh' Aoineadh Mhéinis 172 NM 6521
Rubha Port Bhiosd 172 NL 9648
Rubha Port na Caranean 179 NM 4298
Rubha Port Scolpaig 188 NF 7068
Rubha Quidnish 189 NG 1086
Rubha Raonuill 180 NM 7399
Rubha Raouill 188 NF 7166
Rubh' Ardalanish 172 NM 3516
Rubha Reidh 190 NG 7391
Rubha Righinn 167 NM 7002
Rubh' Arisaig 180 NM 6184
Rubha Rodha 196 NC 0523
Rubha Romagi 188 NG 0396
Rubha Rossel 178 NF 8734
Rubha Ruadh, Highld 196 NC 1651
Rubha Ruadh, Highld 180 NG 8208
Rubha Seanach 173 NM 8025
Rubha Sgeirigin 188 NF 9998
Rubha Sgorr an t-Snidhe 179 NM 3493
Rubha Shamhnan Insir 179 NG 3704
Rubha Suisnish 180 NG 5815
Rubha Thormaid 197 NC 5468
Rubha Tràigh an Dùin 172 NM 0443
Rubh' Dubh 195 NB 5229
Ru Chorachan 186 NG 3761
Ruckcroft *T* 151 NY 5344
Ruckinge *T* 99 TR 0233
Ruckland *T* 141 TF 3378
Ruckley *T* 127 SJ 5300
Ruddington *T* 129 SK 5733
Ruddons Point 171 NO 4500
Rudge *T* 101 ST 8251
Rudgeway *T* 101 ST 6286
Rudgwick *T* 96 TQ 0833
Rudhall *T* 113 SO 6225
Rudland Rigg *H* 153 SE 6595
Rudloe *T* 101 ST 8469
Rudry *T* 109 ST 1986
Rudston *T* 149 TA 0967
Rudyard *T* 138 SJ 9557
Rudyard Reservoir *W* 137 SJ 9459
Rue Point 144 NX 4003
Rueval *H* 188 NF 8253
Rufford *T* 136 SD 4515
Rufforth *T* 147 SE 5351
Rufus Stone *A* 94 SU 2712
Rugby *T* 119 SP 5075
Rugeley *T* 128 SK 0417
Ruilick *T* 182 NH 5146
Ruinsival *H* 179 NM 3594
Ruisgarry *T* 188 NF 9282
Ruishton *T* 92 ST 2624
Ruislip *T* 104 TQ 0987
Ruislip Common *T* 104 TQ 0889
Rumble 203 HU 6060
Rumbling Bridge *T* 170 NT 0199
Rumblings 205 HP 6019
Rumburgh *T* 123 TM 3481
Rumford *T* 87 SW 8970
Rumley Point 200 ND 4894
Rumney *T* 109 ST 2279
Rumps Point 87 SW 9381
Rumsdale Water *W* 198 NC 9840
Rumster Forest *F* 199 ND 2138
Runcorn *P* 137 SJ 5182
Runcton *T* 95 SU 8802
Runcton Holme *T* 132 TF 6109
Runfold *T* 103 SU 8747
Runhall *T* 132 TG 0507
Runham *T* 133 TG 4611
Runnel Stone 86 SW 3620
Runnington *T* 92 ST 1121
Runswick Bay *T* 153 NZ 8016
Runtaleave 176 NO 2868
Runwell *T* 106 TQ 7494
Ruperra Castle *A* 109 ST 2286
Ruscombe *T* 104 SU 7976
Rushall, H. & W *T* 114 SO 6435
Rushall, Norf *T* 123 TM 1982
Rushall, Wilts *T* 102 SU 1255
Rushall, W. Mids *T* 128 SK 0301
Rushbrooke *T* 122 TL 8961
Rushbury *T* 116 SO 5192
Rushden, Herts *T* 121 TL 3031
Rushden, Northnts *T* 120 SP 9566
Rushford *T* 122 TL 9281
Rush Green *T* 105 TQ 5187
Rushlake Green *T* 97 TQ 6218
Rushmere *T* 123 TM 4987
Rushmere St Andrew *T* 123 TM 2046
Rushmoor *T* 103 SU 8740
Rushmore House 94 ST 9518
Rushock *T* 117 SO 8871
Rusholme *T* 137 SJ 8695
Rushton, Ches *T* 137 SJ 5864
Rushton, Northnts *T* 120 SP 8482
Rushton, Shrops *T* 127 SJ 6008
Rushton Spencer *T* 137 SJ 9462
Rushwick *T* 117 SO 8253
Rushyford *T* 152 NZ 2828
Rushy Knowe *H* 158 NY 9299
Rusk Holm 200 HY 5135
Ruskie *T* 169 NN 6200
Ruskington *T* 130 TF 0851
Rusland *T* 145 SD 3488
Rusper *T* 96 TQ 2037
Ruspidge *T* 114 SO 6512
Russaness Hill *H* 203 HU 3749
Russell's Water *T* 104 SU 7189
Rustington *T* 96 TQ 0401
Ruston Parva *T* 149 TA 0661
Ruswarp *T* 149 NZ 8809
Rutherford *T* 164 NT 6430
Rutherglen *T* 162 NS 5961
Ruthernbridge *T* 87 SX 0166
Ruthin *P* 136 SJ 1258
Ruthrieston *T* 185 NJ 9204
Ruthven, Grampn *T* 184 NJ 5047
Ruthven, Highld *T* 183 NH 8133
Ruthven, Tays *T* 176 NO 2848
Ruthven Barracks 175 NN 7699
Ruthven House 176 NO 3048
Ruthvoes *T* 87 SW 9260
Ruthwell *T* 157 NY 1067
Rutland Water *W* 130 SK 9207
Rutupiae *R* 99 TR 3260
Ruyton-XI-Towns *T* 126 SJ 3922
Ryal *T* 159 NZ 0174
Ryal Fold *T* 145 SD 6621
Ryall *T* 92 SY 4094
Ryarsh *T* 98 TQ 6759
Rydal *T* 150 NY 3606
Rydal Fell 150 NY 3609
Rydal Water *W* 150 NY 3505
Ryde *T* 95 SZ 5992
Ryde Roads *W* 95 SZ 5893
Ryder's Hill *H* 89 SX 6569
Rye *T* 98 TQ 9120
Rye Bay *W* 99 TQ 9617
Rye Dale 147 SE 5982
Rye Foreign *T* 98 TQ 9022
Rye Harbour *T* 98 TQ 9419
Rye Water *W* 161 NS 2752
Ryhall *T* 130 TF 0310
Ryhill *T* 139 SE 3914
Ryhope *T* 153 NZ 4152
Ryknild Street, Derby *R* 128 SK 2930
Ryknild Street, H. & W *R* 118 SP 1148
Ryknild Street, Staffs *R* 128 SK 1512
Ryknild Street, Warw *R* 118 SP 0862
Ryknild Street, W. Mids *R* 128 SP 0897
Rylstone *T* 146 SD 9758
Ryme Intrinseca *T* 93 ST 5810
Rysa Little 200 ND 3197
Ryther *T* 147 SE 5539
Ryton, Glos *T* 114 SO 7332
Ryton, N. Yks *T* 148 SE 7975
Ryton, Shrops *T* 127 SJ 7602
Ryton, T. & W *T* 159 NZ 1564
Ryton-on-Dunsmore *T* 118 SP 3874

S

Saasaig *T* 180 NG 6608
Sabden *T* 146 SD 7837
Sabden Brook *W* 146 SD 7535
Sàbhal Beag *H* 196 NC 3742
Sacombe *T* 105 TL 3319
Sacquoy Head 200 HY 3835
Sacriston *T* 152 NZ 2447
Sadberge *T* 153 NZ 3416
Saddell *T* 160 NR 7832
Saddell Bay *W* 160 NR 7931
Saddell Glen 160 NR 7733
Saddington *T* 119 SP 6591
Saddington Reservoir *W* 119 SP 6691
Saddleback or Blencathra *H* 150 NY 3127
Saddle Bow *T* 132 TF 6015
Saddle Hill *H* 183 NH 7843
Saddle, The, Highld *H* 180 NG 9312
Saddle, The, Strath *H* 168 NS 2296
Saddlethorpe *T* 142 SE 8329
Saddleworth Moor 138 SE 0305
Saddle Yoke *H* 157 NT 1412
Sadgill *T* 151 NY 4805
Sae Breck *H* 204 HU 2178
Saffron Walden *T* 121 TL 5438
Saham Toney *T* 132 TF 9002
Saighton *T* 136 SJ 4462
Sail Chalmadale *H* 160 NR 9140
Sàil Mhór *H* 190 NH 0388
St Abbs *T* 165 NT 9167
St Abb's Head 165 NT 9169
St Agnes, Corn *T* 86 SW 7150
St Agnes, I. Scilly 86 SV 8807
St Agnes Head 86 SW 6951
St Alban's or St Aldhelm's Head 94 SY 9675
St Aldhelm's or St Alban's Head 94 SY 9675
St Allen *T* 87 SW 8250
St Andrews *P* 171 NO 5016
St Andrews Bay *W* 171 NO 5218
St Andrews Major *T* 109 ST 1371
St Annes *T* 145 SD 3128
St Ann's *T* 157 NY 0793
St Ann's Chapel, Corn *T* 88 SX 4170
St Ann's Chapel, Devon *T* 89 SX 6647
St Ann's Head 110 SM 8002

St Anthony-in-Meneage
Seaton Burn

St Anthony-in-Meneage T 87 SW 7825
St Arvans T 113 ST 5196
St Asaph or Llanelwy T 135 SJ 0374
St Athan T 109 ST 0168
St Austell P 87 SX 0152
St Austell Bay W 87 SX 0650
St Baldred's Boat 171 NT 6185
St Baldred's Cradle 171 NT 6381
St Bees T 150 NX 9711
St Bees Head 150 NX 9413
St Blazey T 87 SX 0654
St Boswells T 164 NT 5930
St Breock T 87 SW 9771
St Breock Downs H 87 SW 9668
St Breward T 87 SX 0976
St Briavels T 113 SO 5604
St Brides T 110 SM 7910
St Brides Bay W 110 SM 8017
St Bride's Major T 109 SS 8975
St Bride's-super-Ely T 109 ST 0977
St Brides Wentlooge T 100 ST 2982
St Budeaux T 88 SX 4558
Saintbury T 118 SP 1139
St Buryan T 86 SW 4025
St Catherine T 101 ST 7770
St Catherines T 168 NN 1207
St Catherine's Bay W 201 HY 6326
St Catherine's Dub 185 NK 0428
St Catherine's Point 95 SZ 4975
St Clears P 111 SN 2816
St Cleer T 87 SX 2468
St Clement T 87 SW 8543
St Clement's Isle 86 SW 4726
St Clether T 88 SX 2084
St Colmac T 160 NS 0467
St Colme House 170 NT 1884
St Columb Major T 87 SW 9163
St Columb Minor T 87 SW 8462
St Columb Road T 87 SW 9159
St Combs T 185 NK 0563
St Cross South Elmham T 123 TM 2984
St Cyrus T 177 NO 7464
St David's, Dyfed T 110 SM 7525
St Davids, Fife T 170 NT 1482
St David's, Tays T 170 NN 9520
St David's Head 110 SM 7228
St Day T 86 SW 7342
St Dennis T 87 SW 9557
St Dogmaels T 110 SN 1646
St Dominick T 88 SX 4067
St Donats T 109 SS 9368
St Endellion T 87 SW 9978
St Enoder T 87 SW 8956
St Erme T 87 SW 8449
St Erth T 86 SW 5535
St Erth Praze T 86 SW 5736
St Ervan T 87 SW 8970
St Eval T 87 SW 8769
St Ewe T 87 SW 9746
St Fagans T 109 ST 1277
St Fergus T 185 NK 0952
St Fergus Moss 185 NK 0553
St Fillans T 169 NN 6924
St Florence T 110 SN 0801
St Gennys T 88 SX 1497
St George T 135 SH 9775
St Georges, Avon T 100 ST 3762
St George's, S. Glam T 109 ST 1076
St George's or Looe Island 87 SX 2551
St Germans T 88 SX 3657
St Giles in the Wood T 91 SS 5318
St Giles on the Heath T 88 SX 3690
St Govan's Head 110 SR 9792
St Gwynno Forest F 109 ST 0396
St Harmon T 125 SN 9972
St Helen Auckland T 152 NZ 1927
St Helens, I. of W T 95 SZ 6288
St Helen's, I. Scilly 86 SV 9017
St Helens, Mers P 137 SJ 5095
St Hilary, Corn T 86 SW 5531
St Hilary, S. Glam T 109 ST 0173
Saint Hill T 97 TQ 3835
St Illtyd T 109 SO 2202
St Ishmael's T 110 SM 8307
St Issey T 87 SW 9271
St Ive T 88 SX 3067
St Ives, Cambs T 121 TL 3172
St Ives, Corn T 86 SW 5140
St Ives, Dorset T 94 SU 1204
St Ives Bay W 86 SW 5441
St James South Elmham T 123 TM 3281
St John T 88 SX 4053
St Johns, H. & W T 117 SO 8454
St John's, I. of M T 144 SC 2781
St John's Beck W 150 NY 3121
St John's Chapel T 152 NY 8838
St John's Fen End T 131 TF 5311
St John's Hall 152 NZ 0634
St John's Head 200 HY 1803
St John's Highway T 131 TF 5214
St John's Loch W 199 ND 2272
St John's Point 199 ND 3175
St John's Town of Dalry T 156 NX 6281
St Judes T 144 SC 3996
St Just T 86 SW 3631
St Just in Roseland T 87 SW 8535
St Katherines T 185 NJ 7834
St Keverne T 87 SW 7921
St Kew T 87 SX 0276
St Kew Highway T 87 SX 0375
St Keyne T 87 SX 2461
St Kilda or Hirta 188 NF 0999
St Lawrence, Corn T 87 SX 0466
St Lawrence, Essex T 107 TL 9604
St Lawrence, I. of W T 95 SZ 5376
St Leonards, Bucks T 104 SP 9107
St Leonards, Dorset T 94 SU 1002
St Leonards, E. Susx T 98 TQ 7909
St Leonard's Forest F 96 TQ 2231
St Leven T 86 SW 3822
St Lppollitts T 120 TL 1927
St Lythans T 109 ST 1173
St Mabyn T 87 SX 0473
St Magnus's Church A 200 HY 4630
St Manus Bay W 204 HU 2668
St Margarets T 113 SO 3533
St Margaret's at Cliffe T 99 TR 3644
St Margaret's Bay W 99 TR 3744
St Margaret's Hope, Fife W 170 NT 1081
St Margaret's Hope, Orkney T 200 ND 4493
St Margaret South Elmham T 123 TM 3183
St Mark's T 144 SC 2974
St Martin, Corn T 86 SW 7323
St Martin, Corn T 88 SX 2655
St Martin's, I. Scilly 86 SV 9215
St Martin's, Shrops T 126 SJ 3236
St Martins, Tays T 170 NO 1530
St Mary Bourne T 102 SU 4250
St Mary Church T 109 ST 0071
St Mary Cray T 105 TQ 4767
St Mary Hill T 109 SS 9678
St Mary Hoo T 98 TQ 8076
St Mary in the Marsh T 99 TR 0627
St Mary's, I. Scilly 86 SV 9111
St Mary's, Orkney T 200 HY 4701
St Mary's Bay T 99 TR 0927
St Mary's Isle 155 NX 6749
St Mary's Loch W 163 NT 2422
St Mary's Marshes 106 TQ 8078
St Mary's or Bait Island 159 NZ 3575
St Mary's or Newton Haven W 165 NU 2424
St Mary's Sound W 86 SV 8909
St Mawes T 87 SW 8433
St Mawgan T 87 SW 8765
St Mellion T 88 SX 3865
St Mellons T 100 ST 2381
St Merryn T 87 SW 8873
St Mewan T 87 SW 9951
St Michael Caerhays T 87 SW 9642
St Michael Penkevil T 87 SW 8542
St Michaels, H. & W T 116 SO 5865
St Michaels, Kent T 98 TQ 8835
St Michael's Island 144 SC 2967
St Michael's Mount A 86 SW 5129
St Michael's on Wyre T 145 SD 4641
St Michael South Elmham T 123 TM 3483
St Minver T 87 SW 9677
St Monance T 171 NO 5201
St Neot T 87 SX 1867
St Neots T 120 TL 1860
St Newlyn East T 87 SW 8256
St Nicholas, Dyfed T 110 SM 9035
St Nicholas, S. Glam T 109 ST 0974
St Nicholas at Wade T 99 TR 2666
St Ninians T 169 NS 7991
St Ninian's Cave A 155 NX 4236
St Ninian's Chapel A 155 NX 4836
St Ninian's Isle 203 HU 3620
St Ninian's Point 160 NS 0361
St Osyth T 107 TM 1215
St Osyth Marsh 107 TM 1113
St Owen's Cross T 113 SO 5424
St Pancras Station 105 TQ 3082
St Patrick's Isle 144 SC 2484
St Paul's Cray T 105 TQ 4768
St Paul's Walden T 105 TL 1922
St Peter's T 99 TR 3868
St Peter's Flat 107 TM 0408
St Petrox T 110 SR 9797
St Pinnock T 87 SX 2063
St Quivox T 161 NS 3724
St Radegund's Abbey A 99 TR 2741
St Serf's Island 170 NO 1500
St Stephen T 87 SW 9453
St Stephens, Corn T 88 SX 3285
St Stephens, Corn T 88 SX 4158
St Teath T 87 SX 0680
St Tudwal's Islands 124 SH 3325
St Tudwal's Road W 124 SH 3328
St Tudy T 87 SX 0676
St Twynnells T 110 SR 9597
St Vigeans T 177 NO 6342
St Wenn T 87 SW 9664
St Weonards T 113 SO 4924
St Winnow T 87 SX 1156
's Airde Beinn H 173 NM 4754
Salachan Glen 174 NM 9951
Salcey Forest F 119 SP 8051
Salcombe T 89 SX 7338
Salcombe Regis T 92 SY 1488
Salcott T 106 TL 9413
Sale T 137 SJ 7891
Saleby T 141 TF 4578
Sale Green T 117 SO 9358
Salehurst T 97 TQ 7424
Salem, Dyfed T 111 SN 6226
Salem, Dyfed T 125 SN 6684
Salem, Gwyn T 134 SH 5456
Salen, Highld T 173 NM 6864
Salen, Strath T 173 NM 5743
Salen Forest F 173 NM 5147
Salesbury T 145 SD 6732
Sales Point 107 TM 0309
Salford, Beds T 120 SP 9339
Salford, G. Man P 137 SJ 8098
Salford, Oxon T 115 SP 2828
Salford Priors T 118 SP 0751
Salfords T 97 TQ 2846
Salhouse T 133 TG 2913
Saligo Bay W 166 NR 2066
Saline T 170 NT 0292
Salisbury P 94 SU 1429
Salisbury Plain 102 SU 0645
Sallachan Point 174 NM 9961
Sallachy, Highld 192 NC 5508
Sallachy, Highld T 180 NG 9130
Salle T 133 TG 1025
Salmonby T 141 TF 3273
Salmonds Muir 177 NO 5837
Salperton T 114 SP 0720
Salph End T 120 TL 0752
Salsburgh T 163 NS 8262
Salt T 128 SJ 9527
Saltash T 88 SX 4259
Saltburn T 183 NH 7269
Saltburn-by-the-Sea T 153 NZ 6621
Saltby T 130 SK 8526
Saltcoats T 161 NS 2441
Saltdean T 97 TQ 3802
Salter T 145 SD 6062
Salterforth T 146 SD 8845
Saltergate 148 SE 8594
Salter's Bank 145 SD 3028
Salter's Brook Bridge, Derby 138 SE 1300
Salter's Brook Bridge, S. Yks 138 SE 1300
Salterswall T 137 SJ 6267
Saltfleet T 141 TF 4593
Saltfleetby All Saints T 141 TF 4590
Saltfleetby St Clement T 141 TF 4591
Saltfleetby St Peter T 141 TF 4389
Saltford T 101 ST 6867
Salthaugh Grange T 143 TA 2321
Salthouse T 132 TG 0743
Salt Island 134 SH 2583
Saltmarshe T 142 SE 7924
Saltom Bay W 150 NX 9515
Salton T 148 SE 7180
Salt Scar 153 NZ 6126
Saltwick 159 NZ 1779
Saltwick Bay W 149 NZ 9211
Saltwood T 99 TR 1535
Salum T 172 NM 0648
Salwarpe T 117 SO 8762
Salwayash T 93 SY 4596
Salwick Sta 145 SD 4632
Samala T 188 NF 7962
Samalaman Island 180 NM 6678
Samalan Island 173 NM 4536
Sambourne T 118 SP 0662
Sambrook T 127 SJ 7124
Samlesbury T 145 SD 5930
Samlesbury Bottoms T 145 SD 6128
Sampford Arundel T 92 ST 1018
Sampford Brett T 100 ST 0840
Sampford Courtenay T 91 SS 6301
Sampford Peverell T 92 ST 0314
Sampford Spiney T 89 SX 5372
Samphrey 205 HU 4676
Samson 86 SV 8712
Samuelston T 171 NT 4871
Sanachan T 180 NG 8340
Sanaigmore 166 NR 2370
Sancreed T 86 SW 4229
Sand, Highld T 190 NG 9091
Sand, Shetld T 203 HU 3447
Sandaig T 180 NG 7102
Sandaig Bay W 180 NG 7101
Sandaig Islands 180 NG 7614
Sanda Island 160 NR 7204
Sanda Stour 203 HU 3441
Sanday, Highld 179 NG 2704
Sanday, Orkney 201 HY 6841
Sanday Airport 201 HY 6740
Sanday Sound W 201 HY 6634
Sandbach T 137 SJ 7560
Sandbank T 168 NS 1680
Sandbanks T 94 SZ 0487
Sand Bay W 100 ST 3264
Sandend T 184 NJ 5566
Sandend Bay W 184 NJ 5666
Sanderstead T 105 TQ 3461
Sandford, Avon T 101 ST 4259
Sandford, Cumbr T 151 NY 7216
Sandford, Devon T 91 SS 8202
Sandford, Dorset T 94 SY 9389
Sandford, Strath T 162 NS 7143
Sandford Bay W 185 NK 1243
Sandfordhill T 185 NK 1142
Sandford-on-Thames T 115 SP 5301
Sandford Orcas T 93 ST 6220
Sandford St Martin T 115 SP 4226
Sandgate T 99 TR 2035
Sandgreen T 155 NX 5752
Sandhaven T 185 NJ 9667
Sandhead T 154 NX 0950
Sandhoe T 159 NY 9766
Sandholme, Humbs T 142 SE 8230
Sandholme, Lincs T 131 TF 3337
Sandhurst, Berks T 104 SU 8361
Sandhurst, Glos T 114 SO 8323
Sandhurst, Kent T 98 TQ 7928
Sandhutton, N. Yks T 147 SE 3882
Sand Hutton, N. Yks T 148 SE 6958
Sandiacre T 129 SK 4736
Sandilands T 141 TF 5280
Sandiway T 137 SJ 6071
Sandleheath T 94 SU 1214
Sandleigh T 115 SP 4701
Sandling T 98 TQ 7558
Sandness T 202 HU 1956
Sandness Hill H 202 HU 1955
Sandon, Essex T 106 TL 7404
Sandon, Herts T 121 TL 3234
Sandon, Staffs T 127 SJ 9429
Sandown T 95 SZ 5984
Sandown Bay W 95 SZ 6183
Sandplace T 87 SX 2457
Sand Point 100 ST 3165
Sandray 178 NL 6491
Sandridge T 105 TL 1710
Sandringham T 132 TF 6928
Sandsend T 153 NZ 8612
Sandside Bay, Highld W 198 NC 9665
Sandside Bay, Orkney W 201 HY 5906
Sandside Burn W 198 NC 9660
Sandside House 198 NC 9565
Sands of Forvie 185 NK 0227
Sands of Nigg 193 NH 7771
Sandsound T 203 HU 3548
Sandsound Voe W 203 HU 3548
Sandtoft T 142 SE 7408
Sand Water, Shetld W 203 HU 4154
Sand Water, Shetld W 205 HU 4274
Sandwich T 99 TR 3358
Sandwich Bay W 99 TR 3759
Sandwich Flats 99 TR 3561
Sandwick, Cumbr T 151 NY 4219
Sandwick, Orkney 200 HY 2519
Sand Wick, Orkney W 200 ND 4389
Sandwick, Orkney T 199 ND 4488
Sand Wick, Shetld W 205 HP 6202
Sandwick, Shetld H 203 HU 3924
Sandwick, Shetld T 203 HU 4323
Sand Wick, Shetld W 203 HU 4323
Sandwick, W. Isles T 195 NB 4432
Sandwick, W. Isles T 188 NF 8243
Sandwith T 150 NX 9614
Sandwood Loch W 196 NC 2364
Sandy T 120 TL 1649
Sandycroft T 136 SJ 3367
Sandy Edge H 158 NT 5201
Sandygate T 144 SC 3797
Sandy Lane T 102 ST 9668
Sangobeg T 197 NC 4266
Sanna 173 NM 4469
Sanna Bay W 173 NM 4368
Sanna Point 173 NM 4370
Sannox Bay W 160 NS 0145
Sanquhar T 156 NS 7809
Santon T 142 SE 9039
Santon Bridge T 150 NY 1101
Santon Downham T 122 TL 8187
Santon Head 144 SC 3370
Sapcote T 129 SP 4893
Sapey Common T 117 SO 7064
Sapiston T 122 TL 9175
Sapperton, Glos T 114 SO 9403
Sapperton, Lincs T 130 TF 0133
Saracen's Head T 131 TF 3427
Sarclet T 199 ND 3443
Sarclet Head 199 ND 3543
Sarisbury T 95 SU 5008
Sarkfoot Point 157 NY 3265
Sarn, M. Glam T 109 SS 9083
Sarn, Powys T 116 SO 2091
Sarnau, Dyfed T 111 SN 3151
Sarnau, Dyfed T 111 SN 3318
Sarnau, Gwyn T 135 SH 9739
Sarnau, Powys T 126 SJ 2315
Sarn Bach T 124 SH 3026
Sarnesfield T 113 SO 3751
Sarn Helen, Dyfed R 111 SN 6449
Sarn Helen, Gwyn R 125 SH 7228
Sarn Helen, Powys R 109 SN 9216
Sarn Helen, W. Glam R 109 SN 8205
Sarn Meyllteyrn T 134 SH 2332
Saron, Dyfed T 111 SN 3737
Saron, Dyfed T 111 SN 6012
Sarratt T 104 TQ 0499
Sarre T 99 TR 2565
Sarsden T 115 SP 2823
Sarsgrum 196 NC 3864
Satley T 152 NZ 1143
Satterleigh T 91 SS 6622
Satterthwaite T 150 SD 3392
Sauchar Point 171 NT 4999
Sauchen T 185 NJ 7011
Saucher T 171 NO 1933
Sauchieburn T 177 NO 6669
Sauchie Law H 157 NT 2910
Sauchrie T 161 NS 3014
Saughall T 136 SJ 3670
Saugh Hill H 154 NX 2197
Saughtree T 158 NY 5696
Saughtree Fell H 158 NY 5699
Saul T 114 SO 7409
Saundby T 140 SK 7986
Saundersfoot T 110 SN 1304
Saundersfoot Station 110 SN 1206
Saunderton T 104 SP 7901
Saunderton Station 104 SU 8198
Saunton T 90 SS 4537
Sausthorpe T 141 TF 3869
Saval T 192 NC 5908
Savary 173 NM 6346
Savernake Forest F 102 SU 2266
Saviskaill W 200 HY 4233
Saviskaill Head 200 HY 4034
Savon Street T 122 TL 6759
Sawbridgeworth T 105 TL 4814
Sawdon T 149 SE 9484
Sawley, Derby T 129 SK 4732
Sawley, Lancs T 146 SD 7746
Sawley, N. Yks T 147 SE 2467
Sawrey T 151 SD 3795
Sawston T 121 TL 4849
Sawtry T 120 TL 1783
Saxa Vord H 205 HP 6316
Saxby, Leic T 130 SK 8220
Saxby, Lincs T 140 TF 0086
Saxby All Saints T 142 SE 9916
Saxelbye T 129 SK 7020
Saxilby T 140 SK 8975
Saxlingham T 132 TG 0239
Saxlingham Nethergate T 133 TM 2297
Saxmundham T 123 TM 3863
Saxondale T 129 SK 6839
Saxtead T 123 TM 2565
Saxtead Green T 123 TM 2564
Saxthorpe T 133 TG 1130
Saxton T 147 SE 4736
Sayers Common T 96 TQ 2618
Scabbacombe Head 89 SX 9251
Scabra Head 200 HY 3631
Scackleton T 147 SE 6472
Scadabay T 189 NG 1792
Scad Head 200 HY 2900
Sca Fell 150 NY 2006
Scafell Pike H 150 NY 2107
Scaftworth T 139 SK 6691
Scagglethorpe T 148 SE 8372
Scaladale River W 195 NB 1709
Scalasaig T 166 NR 3994
Scalby T 149 TA 0190
Scalby Ness Rocks 149 TA 0391
Scald Law H 163 NT 1961
Scaldwell T 119 SP 7672
Scaleby T 157 NY 4463
Scaleby Hill T 157 NY 4363
Scale Houses T 151 NY 5845
Scales, Cumbr T 150 NY 3426
Scales, Cumbr T 144 SD 2672
Scales Moor 145 SD 7177
Scalford T 129 SK 7624
Scaling T 153 NZ 7413
Scaling Reservoir, Cleve W 153 NZ 7412
Scaling Reservoir, N. Yks W 153 NZ 7412
Scalla Field H 203 HU 3857
Scallastle 173 NM 6938
Scallastle Bay W 173 NM 6939
Scalloway T 203 HU 4039
Scalpay, Highld 180 NG 6030
Scalpay, W. Isles 189 NG 2395
Scalpay House 180 NG 6328
Scalpsie Bay W 160 NS 0558
Scalp, The H 184 NJ 3637
Scamblesby T 141 TF 2778
Scammonden Water W 138 SE 0516
Scamodale 173 NM 8373
Scampston T 148 SE 8675
Scampton T 140 SK 9479
Scapa 200 HY 4409
Scapa Bay W 200 HY 4307
Scapa Flow W 200 HY 3800
Scar 201 HY 6645
Scaraben H 199 ND 0626
Scarastavore T 188 NG 0092
Scaravay 188 NG 0178
Scarba 167 NM 7004
Scarborough P 149 TA 0488
Scarcliffe T 139 SK 4968
Scarcroft T 147 SE 3641
Scardroy T 182 NH 2151
Scares 154 NX 2634
Scarff 204 HU 2480
Scarfskerry T 199 ND 2674
Scarfskerry Point 199 ND 2674
Scargill T 152 NZ 0510
Scargill High Moor 152 NY 9909
Scargill Reservoir W 147 SE 2353
Scar Hill H 177 NJ 4801
Scar House Reservoir W 146 SE 0577
Scarinish T 172 NM 0444
Scarisbrick T 136 SD 3713
Scarning T 132 TF 9512
Scarp 194 NA 9615
Scarrington T 129 SK 7341
Scars, The 159 NZ 2993
Scarth Gap Pass 150 NY 1813
Scarth Hill T 136 SD 4206
Scartho T 143 TA 2606
Scarva Taing 200 HY 5708
Scar Water W 156 NX 8195
Scarweather (lightship) 108 SS 6574
Scat Ness 203 HU 3809
Scatsta 205 HU 3972
Scaur Hill H 163 NS 8830
Scaur or Kippford T 155 NX 8354
Scawby T 142 SE 9705
Scawton T 147 SE 5483
Scayne's Hill T 97 TQ 3623
Scethrog T 109 SO 1025
Schiehallion H 175 NN 7154
Schil, The, Border H 165 NT 8622
Schil, The, Northum H 165 NT 8622
Scholar Green T 137 SJ 8357
Scholes, W. Yks T 138 SE 1607
Scholes, W. Yks T 147 SE 3737
Schooner Point 179 NM 3098
Scilly Isles (St Mary's) Airport 86 SV 9210
Scleddau T 110 SM 9434
Scoat Fell H 150 NY 1511
Scole T 123 TM 1579
Scolpaig T 188 NF 7275
Scolton T 110 SM 9922
Scolty H 177 NO 6793
Sconce Point 94 SZ 3389
Scone Palace 170 NO 1126
Sconser T 187 NG 5131
Scoor T 172 NM 4119
Scootmore Forest F 184 NJ 1638
Scopwick T 140 TF 0758
Scoraig T 190 NH 0096
Scorborough T 142 TA 0145
Score Head 203 HU 5145
Score Horan 186 NG 2859
Scorrier T 86 SW 7244
Scorton, Lancs T 145 SD 5048
Scorton, N. Yks T 152 NZ 2500
Sco Ruston T 133 TG 2821
Scotasay T 189 NG 1897
Scotby T 151 NY 4454
Scotch Corner O 152 NZ 2105
Scotforth T 145 SD 4859
Scothern T 140 TF 0377
Scotland Gate T 159 NZ 2584
Scotlandwell T 170 NO 1801
Scotney Castle 97 TQ 6835
Scotsburn T 193 NH 7276
Scotscalder Station 199 ND 0955
Scotscraig 171 NO 4428
Scots' Gap T 159 NZ 0486
Scots Hole T 141 TF 1264
Scotston 175 NN 9042
Scotston Hill H 168 NR 9090
Scotstown T 173 NM 8263
Scotstown Head 185 NK 1251
Scottarie Burn W 193 NC 8008
Scottas T 180 NG 7400
Scotter T 142 SE 8800
Scotterthorpe T 142 SE 8702
Scotton, Lincs T 142 SK 8899
Scotton, N. Yks T 152 SE 1896
Scotton, N. Yks T 147 SE 3259
Scottow T 133 TG 2723
Scoughall T 171 NT 6183
Scoulag 161 NS 1059
Scoulag Point 161 NS 1160
Scoulton T 132 TF 9800
Scoured Rig 164 NT 5851
Scourie T 196 NC 1544
Scourie Bay W 196 NC 1445
Scousburgh T 203 HU 3717
Scout Hill H 145 SD 5682
Scraada 204 HU 2179
Scrabster T 199 ND 0970
Scrainwood T 159 NT 9909
Scrane End T 131 TF 3841
Scraptoft T 129 SK 6405
Scratby T 133 TG 5115
Scratchbury A 101 ST 9144
Scrayingham T 148 SE 7360
Screapadal T 190 NG 5844
Scredington T 130 TF 0940
Screel Hill H 155 NX 7855
Screes, The 150 NY 1504
Scremby T 141 TF 4467
Scremerston T 165 NU 0049
Scriven T 147 SE 3458
Scrooby T 139 SK 6590
Scropton T 128 SK 1930
Scrub Hill T 131 TF 2355
Scruton T 152 SE 3092
Sculthorpe T 132 TF 8930
Scunthorpe P 142 SE 8910
Scurdie Ness 177 NO 7356
Scurrival Point 178 NF 6909
Scuthvie Bay W 201 HY 7744
Seaborough T 93 ST 4306
Seacombe T 136 SJ 3290
Seacombe Cliff 94 SY 9876
Seacroft T 141 TF 5660
Seafield 161 NT 0066
Seafield Bay W 123 TM 1232
Seafield Tower A 171 NT 2788
Seaford T 97 TV 4899
Seaforth T 136 SJ 3297
Seaforth Head T 195 NB 2916
Seaforth Island 195 NB 2010
Sea Geo 200 ND 4995
Seagrave T 129 SK 6117
Seaham T 153 NZ 4249
Seahouses T 165 NU 2131
Seal T 97 TQ 5556
Sealand T 136 SJ 3568
Sealky Head 199 ND 3852
Seal Sand 131 TF 5633
Seal Skerry, Orkney 200 HY 5331
Seal Skerry, Orkney 201 HY 7856
Seamer, N. Yks T 153 NZ 4910
Seamer, N. Yks T 149 TA 0183
Seamill T 161 NS 2047
Seana Bhraigh H 191 NH 2887
Seana Chamas W 190 NG 7484
Sea of the Hebrides W 178 NF 9209
Sea Palling T 133 TG 4226
Searby T 142 TA 0705
Seasalter T 99 TR 0965
Seascale T 150 NY 0301
Seatallan H 150 NY 1308
Seathorne T 141 TF 5765
Seathwaite, Cumbr T 150 NY 2312
Seathwaite, Cumbr T 150 SD 2296
Seathwaite Tarn W 150 SD 2598
Seaton, Corn T 88 SX 3054
Seaton, Cumbr T 150 NY 0130
Seaton, Devon T 92 SY 2490
Seaton, Durham T 153 NZ 3949
Seaton, Humbs T 143 TA 1646
Seaton, Leic T 130 SP 9098
Seaton, Northum T 159 NZ 3276
Seaton Bay W 92 SY 2489
Seaton Burn T 159 NZ 2373

Skelfhill Pen Staffin Island

Skelfhill Pen *H* 157 NT 4403
Skellingthorpe *T* 140 SK 9271
Skellister *T* 203 HU 4654
Skellow *T* 139 SE 5210
Skelmanthorpe *T* 139 SE 2310
Skelmersdale *P* 136 SD 4605
Skelmonae 185 NJ 8839
Skelmorlie *T* 161 NS 1967
Skelmuir 185 NJ 9842
Skelpick *T* 198 NC 7256
Skelpick Burn *W* 198 NC 7355
Skelton, Cleve *T* 153 NZ 6518
Skelton, Cumbr *T* 151 NY 4335
Skelton, N. Yks *T* 152 NZ 0900
Skelton, N. Yks *T* 147 SE 3668
Skelton, N. Yks *T* 147 SE 5756
Skelwick, Orkney *T* 200 HY 4844
Skel Wick, Orkney *W* 200 HY 4945
Skelwith Bridge *T* 150 NY 3403
Skendleby *T* 141 TF 4369
Skene House 185 NJ 7709
Skenfrith *T* 113 SO 4520
Skerne *T* 149 TA 0455
Skeroblingarry 160 NR 7026
Skerray *T* 197 NC 6563
Skerries 134 SH 2794
Skerry of Eshaness 204 HU 2076
Skervuile Lighthouse 166 NR 6071
Sketty *T* 108 SS 6293
Skewen *T* 108 SS 7297
Skewsby *T* 147 SE 6271
Skeyton *T* 133 TG 2425
Skiag Bridge 196 NC 2324
Skibo Castle 193 NH 7389
Skidbrooke *T* 141 TF 4492
Skidby *T* 142 TA 0133
Skiddaw *H* 150 NY 2529
Skiddaw Forest *F* 150 NY 2729
Skigersta *T* 195 NB 5461
Skilgate *T* 91 SS 9827
Skillington *T* 130 SK 8925
Skinburness *T* 150 NY 1255
Skinflats *T* 170 NS 9083
Skinidin *T* 186 NG 2247
Skinningrove *T* 153 NZ 7119
Skipness *T* 160 NR 9057
Skipness Bay *W* 160 NR 9057
Skipness Point 160 NR 9157
Skipsea *T* 149 TA 1655
Skipton *T* 146 SD 9951
Skipton-on-Swale *T* 147 SE 3679
Skipwith *T* 147 SE 6638
Skirling *T* 163 NT 0739
Skirmett *T* 104 SU 7790
Skirpenbeck *T* 148 SE 7457
Skirwith *T* 151 NY 6132
Skirza *T* 199 ND 3868
Skirza Head 199 ND 3968
Skokholm Island 110 SM 7305
Skomer Island 110 SM 7209
Skroo 201 HZ 2274
Skuda Sound *W* 205 HU 6099
Skulamus *T* 180 NG 6622
Skullomie *T* 197 NC 6161
Skye (Broadford) Airport 180 NG 6924
Skye of Curr *T* 183 NH 9924
Slack *T* 146 SD 9728
Slackhall *T* 138 SK 0781
Slackhead *T* 184 NJ 4063
Slacks of Cairnbanno *T* 185 NJ 8446
Slad *T* 114 SO 8707
Slade *T* 90 SS 5146
Slade Green *T* 105 TQ 5276
Slaggan Bay *W* 190 NG 8394
Slaggyford *T* 151 NY 6752
Slaidburn *T* 145 SD 7152
Slaithwaite *T* 138 SE 0814
Slaley *T* 152 NY 9757
Slaley Forest *F* 152 NY 9555
Slamannan *T* 170 NS 8573
Slapton, Bucks *T* 104 SP 9320
Slapton, Devon *T* 89 SX 8245
Slapton, Northnts *T* 119 SP 6446
Slate, The *H* 160 NR 6316
Slaugham *T* 96 TQ 2527
Slawston *T* 129 SP 7794
Sleach Water *W* 199 ND 0344
Sleaford, Hants *T* 103 SU 8038
Sleaford, Lincs *P* 130 TF 0645
Sleagill *T* 151 NY 5919
Sleapford *T* 127 SJ 6315
Sledge Green *T* 114 SO 8134
Sledmere *T* 149 SE 9364
Sleightholme *T* 152 NY 9510
Sleightholme Moor 152 NY 9207
Sleights *T* 148 NZ 8607
Slepe *T* 93 SY 9293
Sletill Hill *H* 198 NC 9346
Sliabh Gaoil *H* 167 NR 8174
Slickly *T* 199 ND 3066
Sliddery *T* 160 NR 9322
Sliddery Water *W* 160 NR 9527
Slidderywater Foot 160 NR 9321
Slieau Dhoo *H* 144 SC 3589
Slieau Ruy *H* 144 SC 3282
Sliemore 183 NJ 0320
Sligachan Hotel 187 NG 4829
Slimbridge *T* 114 SO 7403
Slindon, Staffs *T* 127 SJ 8232
Slindon, W. Susx *T* 96 SU 9608
Slinfold *T* 96 TQ 1131
Slingsby *T* 148 SE 6974
Slioch, Grampn *T* 184 NJ 5638
Slioch, Highld *H* 190 NH 0069
Slios Garbh *H* 180 NM 8384
Slip End *T* 104 TL 0818
Slipton *T* 120 SP 9579
Slitrig Water *W* 158 NT 5107
Slochd *T* 183 NH 8424
Slockavullin *T* 167 NR 8297
Sloc nam Feàrna 168 NR 8673
Sloley *T* 133 TG 2924
Sloothby *T* 141 TF 4970
Slouchnawen Bay *W* 154 NW 9563
Slough, Berks *P* 104 SU 9780
Slough, Powys *T* 116 SO 3063
Slugaide Glas *W* 166 NR 2846
Slymaback, Central *H* 169 NN 7510
Slymaback, Tays *H* 169 NN 7510
Slyne *T* 145 SD 4765
Sma' Glen 170 NN 9030
Smailholm *T* 164 NT 6436
Smallbridge *T* 137 SD 9115
Smallburgh *T* 133 TG 3324
Smallburn, Grampn *T* 185 NK 0141
Smallburn, Strath *T* 162 NS 6826
Small Dole *T* 96 TQ 2112
Small Downs *W* 99 TR 3955
Smalley *T* 128 SK 4044
Smallfield *T* 97 TQ 3143
Small Hythe *T* 98 TQ 8930
Small Isles 166 NR 5468
Smallridge *T* 92 ST 3000
Smardale *T* 151 NY 7308
Smarden *T* 98 TQ 8842
Smasha Hill *H* 157 NT 4416
Smeatharpe *T* 92 ST 1910
Smeeth *T* 99 TR 0739
Smeeton Westerby *T* 119 SP 6792
Smerclate *T* 178 NF 7515
Smerral *T* 199 ND 1733
Smethwick *T* 118 SP 0288
Smiddy Shaw Reservoir *W* 152 NZ 0446
Smigel Burn *W* 198 NC 9257
Smirisary *T* 180 NM 6477
Smisby *T* 128 SK 3419
Smithey Fen 121 TL 4570
Smithfield *T* 157 NY 4465
Smithincott *T* 92 ST 0611
Smith Sound *W* 86 SV 8706
Smithton *T* 183 NH 7146
Snaefell *H* 144 SC 3988
Snaigow House 176 NO 0843
Snailbeach *T* 126 SJ 3702
Snailwell *T* 122 TL 6467
Snainton *T* 149 SE 9282
Snaip Hill *H* 163 NT 0232
Snaith *T* 147 SE 6422
Snape, N. Yks *T* 147 SE 2684
Snape, Suff *T* 123 TM 3958
Snap, The 205 HU 6587
Snarestone *T* 128 SK 3409
Snarford *T* 140 TF 0582
Snargate *T* 99 TQ 9828
Snarravoe 205 HP 5601
Snave *T* 99 TR 0129
Snead *T* 116 SO 3192
Sneaton *T* 149 NZ 8907
Sneatonthorpe *T* 149 NZ 9006
Snelland *T* 140 TF 0780
Snelston *T* 128 SK 1543
Snettisham *T* 132 TF 6834
Sneug, The *H* 202 HT 9439
Sneuk Head 200 ND 2095
Snilesworth Moor 153 SE 5296
Snishival *T* 178 NF 7634
Snitter *T* 159 NU 0203
Snitterby *T* 140 SK 9894
Snitterfield *T* 118 SP 2160
Snitton *T* 116 SO 5575
Snodhill *T* 113 SO 3240
Snodland *T* 98 TQ 7061
Snook Point 165 NU 2426
Snowdon *H* 134 SH 6154
Snowhope Hill *H* 152 NY 9434
Snowshill *T* 114 SP 0933
Soa, Strath 172 NM 0746
Soa, Strath 172 NM 1551
Soa Island 172 NM 2419
Soa Mòr 189 NB 0605
Soay, Highld 187 NG 4413
Soay, W. Isles 188 NA 0601
Soay Sound *W* 187 NG 4416
Soberton *T* 95 SU 6116
Soberton Heath *T* 95 SU 6014
Socach Burn *W* 168 NR 8999
Socach, The *H* 184 NJ 2714
Soham *T* 122 TL 5973
Soham Mere 121 TL 5773
Soldon Cross *T* 90 SS 3210
Soldridge *T* 95 SU 6535
Solent *W* 95 SZ 4797
Sole Street, Kent *T* 98 TQ 6567
Sole Street, Kent *T* 99 TR 0949
Solihull *P* 118 SP 1579
Sollas *T* 188 NF 8174
Sollers Dilwyn *T* 113 SO 4255
Sollers Hope *T* 113 SO 6033
Sollom *T* 136 SD 4518
Solva *T* 110 SM 8024
Solway Firth *W* 150 NX 9845
Solway Moss 157 NY 3469
Somerby *T* 129 SK 7710
Somercotes *T* 128 SK 4253
Somerford Keynes *T* 114 SU 0295
Somerley *T* 95 SZ 8198
Somerleyton *T* 133 TM 4796
Somersal Herbert *T* 128 SK 1335
Somersby *T* 141 TF 3472
Somersham, Cambs *T* 121 TL 3678
Somersham, Suff *T* 123 TM 0848
Somersham High North Fen 121 TL 3681
Somerton, Norf *T* 133 TG 4719
Somerton, Oxon *T* 115 SP 4928
Somerton, Somer *T* 93 ST 4828
Sompting *T* 96 TQ 1704
Sonachan Hotel 173 NM 4566
Sonning *T* 104 SU 7575
Sonning Common *T* 104 SU 7080
Soonhope Burn *W* 164 NT 5356
Sopley *T* 94 SZ 1697
Sopworth *T* 101 ST 8286
Sorbie *T* 155 NX 4346
Sor Brook *W* 119 SP 4437
Sordale *T* 199 ND 1561
Sorisdale *T* 172 NM 2763
Sorn *T* 161 NS 5526
Sornhill 161 NS 5134
Soroba Hill *H* 167 NM 7905
Sortat *T* 199 ND 2863
Sotby *T* 141 TF 2078
Sots Hole *T* 141 TF 1164
Sotterley *T* 123 TM 4584
Soudley *T* 127 SJ 7229
Soughton or Sychdyn *T* 136 SJ 2466
Soulbury *T* 120 SP 8827
Soulby *T* 151 NY 7410
Souldern *T* 115 SP 5231
Souldrop *T* 120 SP 9861
Soulseat Loch *W* 154 NX 1058
Sound, Shetld *T* 203 HU 3850
Sound, Shetld *T* 203 HU 4640
Sound Gruney 205 HU 5896
Sound of Arisaig *W* 180 NM 6580
Sound of Barra *W* 178 NF 7509
Sound of Berneray, W. Isles *W* 188 NF 9079
Sound of Berneray, W. Isles *W* 178 NL 5581
Sound of Bute *W* 160 NS 0155
Sound of Canna *W* 179 NG 3002
Sound of Eigg *W* 179 NM 4382
Sound of Eriskay *W* 178 NF 7913
Sound of Faray *W* 200 HY 5437
Sound of Fiaray *W* 178 NF 7009
Sound of Fuday *W* 178 NF 7208
Sound of Gigha *W* 160 NR 6749
Sound of Handa *W* 196 NC 1547
Sound of Harris *W* 188 NF 9681
Sound of Hellisay *W* 178 NF 7503
Sound of Hoxa *W* 200 ND 3993
Sound of Insh *W* 173 NM 7419
Sound of Iona *W* 172 NM 2923
Sound of Islay *W* 166 NR 4369
Sound of Jura *W* 167 NR 6580
Sound of Kerrera *W* 173 NM 8228
Sound of Luing *W* 173 NM 7209
Sound of Mingulay *W* 178 NL 5885
Sound of Monach *W* 188 NF 7063
Sound of Mull *W* 173 NM 6145
Sound of Pabbay, W. Isles *W* 188 NF 9085
Sound of Pabbay, W. Isles *W* 178 NL 6288
Sound of Papa *W* 202 HU 1758
Sound of Pladda *W* 160 NS 0320
Sound of Raasay *W* 190 NG 5654
Sound of Rhum *W* 179 NM 4390
Sound of Sandray *W* 178 NL 6493
Sound of Shiant *W* 189 NB 3701
Sound of Shillay *W* 188 NF 8890
Sound of Shuna *W* 173 NM 9249
Sound of Sleat *W* 180 NG 6806
Sound of Spuir *W* 188 NF 8685
Sound of Taransay *W* 188 NG 0599
Sound of Ulva *W* 173 NM 4439
Sound of Vatersay *W* 178 NL 6297
Sound, The *W* 88 SX 4752
Soundwell *T* 101 ST 6575
Sourhope *T* 158 NT 8420
Sourin *T* 200 HY 4331
Sourton *T* 89 SX 5390
Soutergate *T* 144 SD 2281
Souter Head 177 NJ 9601
South Acre *T* 132 TF 8114
Southall *T* 105 TQ 1280
South Allington *T* 89 SX 7938
South Alloa *T* 170 NS 8791
Southam, Glos *T* 114 SO 9725
Southam, Warw *T* 118 SP 4161
South Ambersham *T* 96 SU 9120
Southampton (Eastleigh) Airport 95 SU 4517
Southampton *P* 94 SU 4112
Southampton Water *W* 95 SU 4506
South Bank *T* 153 NZ 5320
South Barrow *T* 93 ST 6027
South Barrule *H* 144 SC 2575
South Bay *W* 201 HY 7551
South Benfleet *T* 106 TQ 7785
Southborough *T* 97 TQ 5842
Southbourne, Dorset *T* 94 SZ 1491
Southbourne, W. Susx *T* 95 SU 7705
South Brent *T* 89 SX 6960
Southburgh *T* 132 TF 9904
South Burlingham *T* 133 TG 3707
South Burn *W* 200 ND 2299
South Cadbury *T* 93 ST 6325
South Cairn 154 NW 9769
South Carlton *T* 140 SK 9576
South Cave *T* 142 SE 9231
South Cerney *T* 114 SU 0597
South Channel *W* 99 TR 3272
South Channel *W* 142 SE 9621
South Chard *T* 92 ST 3205
South Charlton *T* 159 NU 1620
South Cheek or Old Peak 149 NZ 9802
South Cheriton *T* 93 ST 6925
Southchurch *T* 106 TQ 9085
South Cliffe *T* 142 SE 8736
South Clifton *T* 140 SK 8270
South Cove *T* 123 TM 4980
South Creake *T* 132 TF 8536
South Croxton *T* 129 SK 6810
South Dalton *T* 142 SE 9645
South Darenth *T* 105 TQ 5669
South Deep *W* 171 NO 2218
South District 131 TL 5298
South Downs, E. Susx *H* 97 TQ 3707
South Downs, W. Susx *H* 96 SU 9214
South Drove Drain *W* 130 TF 2114
South Duffield *T* 142 SE 6833
Southease *T* 97 TQ 4205
South Elkington *T* 141 TF 2988
South Elmsall *T* 139 SE 4711
Southend, Berks *T* 103 SU 5970
South End, Cumbr *T* 144 SD 2063
Southend, Strath *T* 160 NR 6908
Southend Airport 106 TQ 8789
Southend-on-Sea *P* 106 TQ 8785
Southerndown *T* 109 SS 8874
Southerness *T* 150 NX 9754
Southerness Point 150 NX 9754
South Erradale *T* 190 NG 7471
Southery *T* 132 TL 6294
Southery Fens 132 TL 6193
South Fambridge *T* 106 TQ 8595
South Fawley *T* 102 SU 3980
South Ferriby *T* 142 SE 9820
Southfield Reservoir *W* 139 SE 6519
Southfleet *T* 98 TQ 6171
South Foreland 99 TR 3643
South Forty Foot Drain *W* 130 TF 1633
South Galson River *W* 195 NB 4557
South Garth 205 HU 5499
South Garvan *T* 174 NM 9977
Southgate, G. Lon *T* 105 TQ 3094
Southgate, Norf *T* 132 TF 6833
Southgate, Norf *T* 133 TG 1424
Southgate, W. Glam *T* 108 SS 5588
South Godstone *T* 97 TQ 3648
South Goodwin (lightship) 99 TR 4342
South Gorley *T* 94 SU 1610
South Green *T* 106 TQ 6893
South Hanningfield *T* 106 TQ 7497
South Harbour *W* 201 HZ 2069
South Harris 189 NG 0993
South Harris Forest 189 NG 1098
South Harting *T* 95 SU 7819
South Havra 203 HU 3627
South Hayling *T* 95 SZ 7299
South Head, Highld 199 ND 3749
South Head, Shetld 204 HU 2382
South Heath *T* 104 SP 9102
South Heighton *T* 97 TQ 4503
South Hetton *T* 153 NZ 3745
South Hiendley *T* 139 SE 3912
South Hill *T* 88 SX 3372
South Hole *T* 90 SS 2219
South Holland Main Drain *W* 131 TF 3718
South Holms 205 HP 5710
South Holmwood *T* 96 TQ 1745
South Hornchurch *T* 105 TQ 5283
South Hylton *T* 153 NZ 3556
Southill *T* 120 TL 1542
South Isle of Gletness 203 HU 4750
South Kelsey *T* 142 TF 0498
South Kilvington *T* 147 SE 4284
South Kilworth *T* 119 SP 6881
South Kirkby *T* 139 SE 4510
South Kirkton *T* 185 NJ 7405
South Kyme *T* 130 TF 1749
South Kyme Fen 130 TF 1848
South Laggan Forest *F* 174 NN 2794
South Lancing *T* 96 TQ 1803
South Lee *H* 188 NF 9165
Southleigh, Devon *T* 92 SY 2093
South Leigh, Oxon *T* 115 SP 3908
South Level 122 TL 5985
South Leverton *T* 140 SK 7881
South Littleton *T* 118 SP 0746
South Lochboisdale *T* 178 NF 7717
South Lopham *T* 122 TM 0481
South Luffenham *T* 130 SK 9401
South Malling *T* 97 TQ 4111
South Marston *T* 102 SU 1988
South Medwin *W* 163 NT 0244
South Milford *T* 147 SE 4931
South Milton *T* 89 SX 6942
South Mimms *T* 105 TL 2201
Southminster *T* 106 TQ 9599
South Molton *T* 91 SS 7125
South Moor, Durham *T* 152 NZ 1851
Southmoor, Oxon *T* 115 SU 4098
South Morar 180 NM 7588
South Moreton *T* 103 SU 5688
South Mundam *T* 95 SU 8700
South Muskham *T* 140 SK 7957
South Ness 202 HT 9636
South Nesting 203 HU 4554
South Nesting Bay *W* 203 HU 4856
South Nevi 201 HY 6000
South Newington *T* 115 SP 4033
South Newton *T* 94 SU 0834
South Normanton *T* 129 SK 4456
South Norwood *T* 105 TQ 3468
South Nuffield *T* 97 TQ 3049
South Ockendon *T* 106 TQ 5982
Southoe *T* 120 TL 1860
Southolt *T* 123 TM 1968
South Ormsby *T* 141 TF 3775
Southorpe *T* 130 TF 0803
South Otterington *T* 147 SE 3787
Southowram *T* 146 SE 1123
South Oxhey *T* 105 TQ 1193
South Perrott *T* 93 ST 4706
South Petherton *T* 93 ST 4316
South Petherwin *T* 88 SX 3182
South Pickenham *T* 132 TF 8504
South Pool *T* 89 SX 7740
Southport *P* 136 SD 3316
South Queich *W* 170 NO 0303
South Radworthy 91 SS 7432
South Raynham *T* 132 TF 8724
Southrepps *T* 133 TG 2536
South Reston *T* 141 TF 4083
Southrey *T* 141 TF 1366
South Ronaldsay 200 ND 4490
Southrop *T* 115 SP 2003
Southrope *T* 103 SU 6744
South Runcton *T* 132 TF 6308
South Scarle *T* 140 SK 8463
Southsea *T* 95 SZ 6498
South Shian 173 NM 9042
South Shields *P* 159 NZ 3666
South Shore *T* 145 SD 3033
South Skirlaugh *T* 143 TA 1439
South Somercotes *T* 141 TF 4193
South Sound *W* 205 HU 5390
South Stack 134 SH 2082
South Stainley *T* 147 SE 3063
South Stainmore *T* 151 NY 8413
Southstoke, Avon *T* 101 ST 7461
South Stoke, Oxon *T* 103 SU 5983
South Stoke, W. Susx *T* 96 TQ 0210
South Street *T* 97 TQ 3917
South Tawton *T* 89 SX 6594
South Thoresby *T* 141 TF 4076
South Tidworth *T* 102 SU 2448
South Town, Hants *T* 95 SU 6536
Southtown, Orkney *T* 200 ND 4895
South Ugie Water *W* 185 NK 0046
South Uist 178 NF 7829
South View 203 HU 3842
Southwaite *T* 151 NY 4545
South Walls 200 ND 3189
South Walsham *T* 133 TG 3613
South Ward *H* 203 HU 3264
South Warnborough *T* 103 SU 7247
Southwater *T* 96 TQ 1525
Southway *T* 101 ST 5142
South Weald *T* 105 TQ 5793
Southwell, Dorset *T* 93 SY 6870
Southwell, Notts *T* 129 SK 7054
South Weston *T* 104 SU 7098
South West Point 90 SS 1343
South Wheatley *T* 88 SX 2492
Southwick, Hants *T* 95 SU 6208
Southwick, Northnts *T* 120 TL 0292
South Wick, Shetld *W* 204 HU 3191
Southwick, T. & W *T* 159 NZ 3758
Southwick, Wilts *T* 101 ST 8355
Southwick, W. Susx *T* 96 TQ 2405
South Widcombe *T* 101 ST 5856
South Wigston *T* 129 SP 5898
South Willingham *T* 141 TF 1983
South Wingfield *T* 128 SK 3755
South Witham *T* 130 SK 9219
Southwold *T* 123 TM 5076
South Wonston *T* 95 SU 4635
Southwood, Norf *T* 133 TG 3905
Southwood, Somer 93 ST 5533
South Woodham Ferrers *T* 106 TQ 8097
South Wootton *T* 132 TF 6422
South Zeal *T* 89 SX 6593
Soutra Mains *T* 164 NT 4553
Soval Lodge 195 NB 3424
Sowerby, N. Yks *T* 147 SE 4381
Sowerby, W. Yks *T* 146 SE 0423
Sowerby Bridge *T* 146 SE 0623
Sowerby Row *T* 151 NY 3940
Sow of Atholl, The *H* 175 NN 6274
Sow, The 200 HY 1802
Sowton *T* 89 SX 9791
Soyea Island 196 NC 0422
Soyland Moor 138 SD 9819
Spa Common *T* 133 TG 2930
Spadeadam Fm 158 NY 5870
Spadeadam Forest *F* 158 NY 6373
Spade Mill Reservoirs *W* 145 SD 6237
Spalding *P* 131 TF 2422
Spaldington *T* 142 SE 7633
Spaldwick *T* 120 TL 1272
Spalford *T* 140 SK 8369
Spango Hill *H* 156 NS 8118
Spanish Head 144 SC 1865
Sparham *T* 132 TG 0719
Spark Bridge *T* 145 SD 3084
Sparkford *T* 93 ST 6026
Sparkwell *T* 89 SX 5857
Sparrowpit *T* 138 SK 0980
Sparsholt, Hants *T* 94 SU 4331
Sparsholt, Oxon *T* 102 SU 3487
Spartleton Edge *H* 164 NT 6565
Spaunton *T* 148 SE 7289
Spaunton Moor 148 SE 7293
Spaxton *T* 92 ST 2237
Spean Bridge *T* 174 NN 2281
Spear Head 199 ND 0971
Speen, Berks *T* 103 SU 4668
Speen, Bucks *T* 104 SU 8499
Speeton *T* 149 TA 1574
Speinne Mór *H* 173 NM 4949
Speke *T* 136 SJ 4483
Speldhurst *T* 97 TQ 5541
Spellbrook *T* 105 TL 4817
Spelsbury *T* 115 SP 3521
Spencers Wood *T* 104 SU 7166
Spennithorne *T* 146 SE 1388
Spennymoor *T* 152 NZ 2534
Spetchley *T* 117 SO 8954
Spetisbury *T* 93 ST 9102
Spexhall *T* 123 TM 3780
Spey Bay, Grampn *T* 184 NJ 3565
Spey Bay, Grampn *W* 184 NJ 3767
Speybridge *T* 183 NJ 0326
Speymouth Forest 184 NJ 3557
Spilsby *T* 141 TF 4066
Spindlestone *T* 165 NU 1533
Spinningdale *T* 192 NH 6789
Spirthill *T* 102 ST 9975
Spital Burn *W* 177 NO 6583
Spithead *W* 95 SZ 6396
Spithurst *T* 97 TQ 4217
Spittal, Dyfed *T* 110 SM 9723
Spittal, Highld *T* 199 ND 1654
Spittal, Lothn *T* 171 NT 4677
Spittal, Northum *T* 165 NU 0051
Spittalfield *T* 176 NO 1040
Spittal of Glenmuick *T* 176 NO 3085
Spittal of Glenshee *T* 176 NO 1070
Spixworth *T* 133 TG 2415
Spofforth *T* 147 SE 3651
Spondon *T* 128 SK 4035
Spo Ness 200 HY 4846
Spooner Row *T* 133 TM 0997
Spoo Ness 205 HP 5607
Sporle *T* 132 TF 8411
Spott *T* 171 NT 6775
Spratton *T* 119 SP 7170
Spreakley *T* 103 SU 8341
Spreyton *T* 89 SX 6996
Spridlington *T* 140 TF 0084
Springburn *T* 162 NS 6068
Springcorrie *T* 195 NB 2332
Springfield, Fife *T* 171 NO 3411
Springfield, Grampn *T* 183 NJ 0560
Springfield, W. Mids *T* 118 SP 0981
Springfield Reservoir *W* 163 NS 9052
Springholm *T* 156 NX 8069
Springkell 157 NY 2575
Spring Mill Reservoir *W* 137 SD 8717
Springside *T* 161 NS 3738
Springthorpe *T* 140 SK 8789
Sproatley *T* 143 TA 1934
Sproston Green *T* 137 SJ 7366
Sprotbrough *T* 139 SE 5402
Sproughton *T* 120 TL 1244
Sprouston *T* 164 NT 7535
Sprowston *T* 133 TG 2411
Sproxton, Leic *T* 130 SK 8524
Sproxton, N. Yks *T* 147 SE 6181
Spuir 188 NF 8584
Spurn (lightship) 143 TA 4809
Spur Ness 151 NY 6033
Spurness Sound *W* 201 HY 6232
Spurn Head 143 TA 3910
Spurstow *T* 137 SJ 5557
Spur, The 199 ND 1769
Spùt Rollà *W* 169 NN 7228
Square and Compass *T* 110 SM 8531
Srath a' Chràisg 197 NC 5324
Srath Beag 196 NC 3853
Srath Dionard 196 NC 3453
Srath Lungard 190 NG 9164
Srath nan Lòn 191 NC 2401
Srath na Seilge 197 NC 7019
Srianach 195 NB 4010
Sròn Ach' a' Bhacaidh *H* 192 NH 6198
Sròn a' Chleirich *H* 175 NN 7876
Sròn a' Choire Ghairbh *H* 174 NN 2294
Sron a' Gheodha Dhuibh 190 NG 7792
Sròn Bheag, Highld 173 NM 4662
Sròn Bheag, Tays *H* 175 NN 5262
Sròn Mhór *H* 169 NN 6526
Sròn na Carra 190 NG 7473
Sròn na Clèite 190 NG 7389
Sròn na h-Iolaire 179 NM 3891
Sronphadruig Lodge 175 NN 7178
Sròn Romul *H* 194 NA 9615
Sròn Ruadh 195 NB 4636
Sron Rubha na Gaoithe 193 NC 9911
Stab Hill *H* 154 NX 1471
Staca Leathann 194 NA 9828
Stac a' Mheadais 186 NG 3325
Stac an Aoineidh 172 NM 2522
Stac an Tuill 186 NG 3521
Stack Clò Kearvaig 196 NC 2973
Stackhouse *T* 146 SD 8165
Stack Islands 178 NF 7807
Stack o' da Noup 203 HU 3516
Stack of Billyageo 203 HU 4421
Stack of Birrier 205 HU 6494
Stack of the Brough 203 HU 4015
Stackpole *T* 110 SR 9896
Stackpole Head 110 SR 9994
Stack Rocks 110 SM 8113
Stacks of Duncansby 199 ND 4071
Stacksteads *T* 146 SD 8421
Stac na Cathaig *H* 182 NH 6430
Stac na h-Iolaire *H* 183 NJ 0109
Stac Pollaidh *H* 196 NC 1010
Stac Shuardail 195 NB 4830
Staddiscombe *T* 88 SX 5151
Staddlethorpe *T* 142 SE 8428
Stadhampton *T* 115 SU 6098
Staffa 172 NM 3235
Staffield *T* 151 NY 5442
Staffin *T* 187 NG 4867
Staffin Bay *W* 187 NG 4869
Staffin Island 187 NG 4969

Thelwall Treforest Industrial Estate

Thelwall T 137 SJ 6487
Themelthorpe T 132 TG 0523
Thenford T 119 SP 5241
Therfield T 121 TL 3377
Thetford P 122 TL 8783
Thetford Warren 122 TL 8383
Theydon Bois T 105 TQ 4598
Thickwood T 101 ST 8272
Thieves Holm 200 HY 4614
Thimbleby, Lincs T 141 TF 2369
Thimbleby, N. Yks T 153 SE 4595
Thirkleby T 147 SE 4778
Thirlby T 147 SE 4884
Thirlestane T 164 NT 5647
Thirlestane Castle A 164 NT 5347
Thirlmere W 150 NY 3116
Thirl, The 199 ND 1872
Thirlwall Castle A 158 NY 6666
Thirlwall Common 158 NY 6769
Thirn T 146 SE 2186
Thirsk P 147 SE 4382
Thirstane Hill H 156 NS 8709
Thistleton T 130 SK 9117
Thistley Green T 122 TL 6676
Thixendale T 148 SE 8461
Thockrington 158 NY 9579
Tholomas Drove T 131 TF 4006
Tholthorpe T 147 SE 4766
Thomas Chapel T 110 SN 1008
Thomastown T 184 NJ 5736
Thompson T 132 TL 9296
Thomshill T 184 NJ 2157
Thong T 98 TQ 6770
Thoralby T 146 SE 0086
Thoresby Hall A 139 SK 6371
Thoresway T 141 TF 1696
Thorganby, Lincs T 141 TF 2197
Thorganby, N. Yks T 142 SE 6942
Thorgill 148 SE 7096
Thorington T 123 TM 4274
Thorington Street T 122 TM 0135
Thorlby T 146 SD 9652
Thorley T 105 TL 4718
Thormanby T 147 SE 4974
Thornaby-on-Tees T 153 NZ 4516
Thornage T 132 TG 0536
Thornborough, Bucks T 119 SP 7433
Thornborough, N. Yks T 147 SE 2979
Thornbury, Avon T 101 ST 6490
Thornbury, Devon T 90 SS 4008
Thornbury, H. & W T 113 SO 6259
Thornby T 119 SP 6775
Thorncliffe T 138 SK 0158
Thorncombe T 92 ST 3703
Thorncombe Street T 96 TQ 0042
Thorndon T 123 TM 1369
Thorndon Cross T 89 SX 5393
Thorne T 142 SE 6913
Thorne Moors or Waste 142 SE 7315
Thorner T 147 SE 3840
Thorness Bay W 95 SZ 4594
Thorne St Margaret T 92 ST 0921
Thorne Waste or Moors 142 SE 7315
Thorney, Cambs T 131 TF 2804
Thorney, Notts T 140 SK 8573
Thorney Hill T 94 SZ 2099
Thorney Island 95 SU 7503
Thornfalcon T 92 ST 2823
Thornford T 93 ST 6013
Thorngumbald T 143 TA 2026
Thornham T 132 TF 7343
Thornham Magna T 123 TM 1071
Thornham Parva T 123 TM 1172
Thornhaugh T 130 TF 0600
Thornhill, Central T 169 NS 6699
Thornhill, Derby T 138 SK 1983
Thornhill, D. & G T 156 NX 8795
Thornhill, Hants T 95 SU 4712
Thornhill, M. Glam T 109 ST 1584
Thornhill Edge T 139 SE 2518
Thornicombe T 93 ST 8703
Thornley, Durham T 152 NZ 1137
Thornley, Durham T 153 NZ 3639
Thornliebank T 161 NS 5559
Thorns T 122 TL 7455
Thornthwaite, Cumbr T 150 NY 2225
Thornthwaite, N. Yks T 146 SE 1758
Thornton, Bucks T 119 SP 7535
Thornton, Fife T 171 NT 2897
Thornton, Humbs T 142 SE 7645
Thornton, Humbs T 142 TA 0817
Thornton, Lancs T 145 SD 3442
Thornton, Lincs T 141 TF 2467
Thornton, Mers T 136 SD 3300
Thornton, Northum T 165 NT 9547
Thornton, Tays 176 NO 3946
Thornton Beck W 148 SE 8381
Thornton Castle 177 NO 6871
Thornton Dale T 148 SE 8382
Thorntonhall T 162 NS 5955
Thornton Hough T 136 SJ 3081
Thornton-in-Craven T 146 SD 9048
Thornton-le-Beans T 153 SE 3990
Thornton-le-Clay T 148 SE 6865
Thornton le Moor, Lincs T 140 TF 0596
Thornton-le-Moor, N. Yks T 147 SE 3988
Thornton-le-Moors T 136 SJ 4474
Thorntonloch T 164 NT 7574
Thornton Moor Reservoir W 146 SE 0533
Thornton Reservoir, Leic W 129 SK 4707
Thornton Reservoir, N. Yks W 146 SE 1888
Thornton Rust T 146 SD 9788
Thornton Steward T 146 SE 1787
Thornton Watlass T 147 SE 2385
Thornwood Common T 105 TL 4704
Thorny Hill H 155 NX 5388
Thornyhive Bay W 177 NO 8882
Thoroton T 129 SK 7642
Thorp Arch T 147 SE 4345
Thorpe, Cumbr T 151 NY 4926
Thorpe, Derby T 128 SK 1550
Thorpe, Lincs T 141 TF 4982
Thorpe, Norf T 133 TM 4398
Thorpe, Notts T 129 SK 7649
Thorpe, N. Yks T 146 SE 0161
Thorpe, Surrey T 104 TQ 0268
Thorpe Abbotts T 123 TM 1979
Thorpe Acre T 129 SK 5120
Thorpe Arnold T 129 SK 7720
Thorpe Audlin T 139 SE 4716
Thorpe Bassett T 148 SE 8673
Thorpe Bay T 106 TQ 9185
Thorpe by Water T 130 SP 8996
Thorpe Constantine T 128 SK 2609
Thorpe End T 133 TG 2811
Thorpe Fendykes T 141 TF 4560
Thorpe Green T 122 TL 9354
Thorpe Hall 147 SE 5776
Thorpe Hesley T 139 SK 3796
Thorpe in Balne T 139 SE 5910
Thorpe Langton T 119 SP 7492
Thorpe Larches T 153 NZ 3826
Thorpe le Fallows T 140 SK 9180
Thorpe-le-Soken T 107 TM 1822
Thorpe Malsor T 120 SP 8379
Thorpe Mandeville T 119 SP 5344
Thorpe Market T 133 TG 2435
Thorpe Morieux T 122 TL 9453
Thorpeness T 123 TM 4759
Thorpe on the Hill T 140 SK 9065
Thorpe Salvin T 139 SK 5281
Thorpe Satchville T 129 SK 7311
Thorpe St Andrew T 133 TG 2609
Thorpe Thewles T 153 NZ 4023
Thorpe Underwood T 147 SE 4659
Thorpe Waterville T 120 TL 0281
Thorpe Willoughby T 147 SE 5730
Thorp St Peter T 141 TF 4860
Thorrington T 107 TM 0920
Thorverton T 91 SS 9202
Thrandeston T 123 TM 1176
Thrapston T 120 SP 9978
Threapwood T 126 SJ 4445
Threave Castle A 156 NX 7362
Three Bridges T 97 TQ 2837
Three Cocks T 113 SO 1737
Three Crosses T 108 SS 5794
Three Holes T 131 TF 5000
Three Hundreds of Aylesbury, The 104 SP 8607
Threekingham T 130 TF 0836
Three Leg Cross T 97 TQ 6831
Three Legged Cross T 94 SU 0506
Three Mile Cross T 104 SU 7167
Threemilestone T 87 SW 7844
Three Pikes H 151 NY 8334
Three Sisters, The H 174 NN 1656
Threipmuir Reservoir W 163 NT 1763
Threlkeld T 150 NY 3125
Threshfield T 146 SD 9863
Thrigby T 133 TG 4612
Thringarth T 152 NY 9322
Thringstone T 128 SK 4217
Thrintoft T 152 SE 3293
Thriplow T 121 TL 4346
Throcking T 121 TL 3330
Throckley T 159 NZ 1566
Throckmorton T 118 SO 9849
Throphill T 159 NZ 1385
Thropton T 159 NU 0202
Throsk 170 NS 8591
Throwleigh T 89 SX 6690
Throwley T 99 TQ 9955
Throwley Forestal T 99 TQ 9854
Thrumpton T 129 SK 5031
Thrumster T 199 ND 3345
Thrunton T 159 NU 0810
Thrunton Wood F 159 NU 0709
Thrupp, Glos T 114 SO 8603
Thrupp, Oxon T 115 SP 4815
Thruscross Reservoir W 146 SE 1558
Thrushelton T 88 SX 4487
Thrushgill T 145 SD 6562
Thruxton, Hants T 102 SU 2945
Thruxton, H. & W T 113 SO 4334
Thrybergh T 139 SK 4695
Thundersley T 106 TQ 7988
Thurcaston T 129 SK 5610
Thurcroft T 139 SK 4988
Thurgarton, Norf T 133 TG 1834
Thurgarton, Notts T 129 SK 6949
Thurgoland T 139 SE 2901
Thurlaston, Leic T 129 SP 5099
Thurlaston, Warw T 119 SP 4670
Thurlby, Lincs T 140 SK 9061
Thurlby, Lincs T 130 TF 0916
Thurleigh T 120 TL 0558
Thurlestone T 89 SX 6742
Thurloxton T 92 ST 2730
Thurlstone T 139 SE 2303
Thurlton T 133 TM 4198
Thurmaston T 129 SK 6109
Thurnham, Kent T 98 TQ 8057
Thurnham, Lancs T 145 SD 4554
Thurning, Norf T 133 TG 0829
Thurning, Northnts T 120 TL 0883
Thurnscoe T 139 SE 4505
Thursby T 150 NY 3250
Thursford T 132 TF 9833
Thursley T 103 SU 9039
Thurso P 199 ND 1168
Thurso Bay W 199 ND 1170
Thurstaston T 136 SJ 2484
Thurston T 122 TL 9265
Thurstonfield T 150 NY 3156
Thurstonland T 138 SE 1610
Thurton T 133 TG 3200
Thurvaston T 128 SK 2437
Thuxton T 132 TG 0307
Thwaite, N. Yks T 152 SD 8998
Thwaite, Suff T 123 TM 1168
Thwaite St Mary T 133 TM 3395
Thwing T 149 TA 0570
Tianavaig Bay W 187 NG 5138
Tibbermore T 170 NO 0523
Tibber's Castle A 156 NX 8698
Tibberton, Glos T 114 SO 7622
Tibberton, H. & W T 117 SO 9057
Tibberton, Shrops T 127 SJ 6820
Tibbie Sheils Inn 157 NT 2420
Tibshelf T 139 SK 4360
Tibthorpe T 149 SE 9655
Ticehurst T 97 TQ 6930
Tichborne T 95 SU 5730
Tickencote T 130 SK 9809
Tickenham T 101 ST 4471
Tick Fen 121 TL 3484
Tickhill T 139 SK 5893
Ticklerton T 116 SO 4890
Ticknall T 128 SK 3523
Tickton T 142 TA 0641
Tidcombe T 102 SU 2958
Tiddington, Oxon T 104 SP 6504
Tiddington, Warw T 118 SP 2255
Tidebrook T 97 TQ 6129
Tideford T 88 SX 3459
Tidenham T 113 ST 5596
Tidenham Chase 113 ST 5598
Tideswell T 138 SK 1575
Tidmarsh T 104 SU 6374
Tidmington T 118 SP 2638
Tidpit T 94 SU 0719
Tiers Cross T 110 SM 9010
Tiffield T 119 SP 6951
Tifty T 185 NJ 7740
Tigerton T 177 NO 5464
Tigharry T 188 NF 7172
Tigh-na-Blair 169 NN 7716
Tighnabruaich T 168 NR 9772
Tighnafiline T 190 NG 8789
Tighvein H 160 NR 9927
Tigley T 89 SX 7560
Tilbrook T 120 TL 0869
Tilbury P 98 TQ 6376
Tile Cross T 118 SP 1686
Tile Hill T 118 SP 2878
Tilehurst T 104 SU 6673
Tilford T 103 SU 8743
Tillathrowie T 184 NJ 4735
Tillicoultry T 170 NS 9196
Tillingham T 107 TL 9903
Tillington, H. & W T 113 SO 4645
Tillington, W. Susx T 96 SU 9621
Tillington Common T 113 SO 4546
Tillyarblet 177 NO 5267
Tillycorthie T 185 NJ 9023
Tillydrine T 177 NO 6098
Tillyfourie T 184 NJ 6412
Tillygarmond 177 NO 6393
Tillygreig T 185 NJ 8823
Tillykerrie 185 NJ 8321
Tilly Whim Caves 94 SZ 0376
Tilmanstone T 99 TR 3051
Tilney All Saints T 131 TF 5617
Tilney High End T 131 TF 5617
Tilney St Lawrence T 131 TF 5413
Tilshead T 102 SU 0347
Tilstock T 127 SJ 5437
Tilston T 126 SJ 4651
Tilstone Fearnall T 137 SJ 5660
Tilsworth T 104 SP 9724
Tilton on the Hill T 129 SK 7405
Timberland T 141 TF 1258
Timberland Delph W 141 TF 1560
Timbersbrook T 137 SJ 8962
Timberscombe T 91 SS 9542
Timble T 146 SE 1853
Timperley T 137 SJ 7888
Timsbury, Avon T 101 ST 6658
Timsbury, Hants T 94 SU 3424
Timsgarry T 194 NB 0534
Timworth Green T 122 TL 8669
Tincleton T 93 SY 7791
Tindale T 158 NY 6159
Tindale Tarn, Cumbr W 158 NY 6058
Tindale Tarn, Northum W 158 NY 6058
Tind, The 205 HU 6790
Tingewick T 119 SP 6532
Tingley T 147 SE 2826
Tingrith T 120 TL 0032
Tingwall 200 HY 4023
Tinhay T 88 SX 3985
Tinnis Castle A 163 NT 1434
Tinnis Hill H 157 NY 4385
Tinshill T 147 SE 2539
Tinsley T 139 SK 4090
Tintagel T 88 SX 0588
Tintagel Head 88 SX 0489
Tintern Abbey A 113 SO 5300
Tintern Parva T 113 SO 5301
Tintinhull T 93 ST 4919
Tinto H 163 NS 9534
Tinto Hills H 163 NS 9434
Tintwistle T 138 SK 0297
Tinwald T 156 NY 0081
Tinwell T 130 TF 0006
Tipperty T 185 NJ 9627
Tipperweir H 177 NO 6885
Tipton T 118 SO 9592
Tipton St John T 92 SY 0991
Tiptree T 106 TL 8916
Tirabad T 112 SN 8841
Tiree 172 NM 0045
Tiree Airport 172 NM 0045
Tirfergus Hill H 160 NR 6617
Tirga Mòr H 194 NB 0511
Tirley T 114 SO 8328
Tirphil T 109 SO 1303
Tir Rhiwiog H 125 SH 9316
Tirymynach 125 SH 9201
Tisbury T 94 ST 9429
Tissington T 128 SK 1752
Titchberry T 90 SS 2427
Titchfield T 95 SU 5305
Titchmarsh T 120 TL 0279
Titchwell T 132 TF 7643
Titley T 113 SO 3360
Titlington T 159 NU 0915
Tittensor T 127 SJ 8738
Titterstone Clee Hill H 117 SO 5978
Tittesworth Reservoir W 138 SJ 9959
Tittleshall T 132 TF 8921
Tiumpan Head 195 NB 5737
Tiverton, Ches T 137 SJ 5560
Tiverton, Devon T 91 SS 9512
Tiverton Junction Station 92 ST 0311
Tivetshall St Margaret T 123 TM 1686
Tivetshall St Mary T 123 TM 1686
Tixall T 128 SJ 9722
Tixover T 130 SK 9700
Toab, Orkney T 200 HY 5106
Toab, Shetld T 203 HU 3811
Toa Galson 195 NB 4560
Tobermory T 173 NM 5055
Toberonochy T 173 NM 7408
Tobson T 195 NB 1338
Tocher T 185 NJ 6932
Tockenham T 102 SU 0479
Tockenham Wick T 102 SU 0381
Tockholes T 145 SD 6623
Tockington T 101 ST 6086
Tockwith T 147 SE 4752
Todber T 93 ST 7920
Toddington, Beds T 120 TL 0028
Toddington, Glos T 114 SP 0332
Toddun H 189 NB 2102
Todenham T 118 SP 2436
Todhead Point 177 NO 8777
Tod Hill H 160 NR 7211
Todhills T 157 NY 3663
Tod Law H 162 NS 7735
Todmorden T 146 SD 9324
Todwick T 139 SK 4984
Toes 110 SR 8994
Toft, Cambs T 121 TL 3656
Toft, Lincs T 130 TF 0617
Toft Hill T 152 NZ 1528
Toft Monks T 133 TM 4294
Toft next Newton T 140 TF 0488
Toftrees T 132 TF 8927
Toft Sand 131 TF 4440
Tofts Voe W 205 HU 4375
Toftwood T 132 TF 9911
Togston T 159 NU 2401
Tokavaig T 180 NG 6011
Tokers Green T 104 SU 6977
Tolland T 92 ST 1032
Tollard Royal T 94 ST 9417
Toll Bar T 139 SE 5508
Toll Creagach H 181 NH 1928
Toller Fratrum T 93 SY 5797
Toller Porcorum T 93 SY 5697
Tollerton, Notts T 129 SK 6034
Tollerton, N. Yks T 147 SE 5164
Tollesbury T 106 TL 9510
Tolleshunt D'Arcy T 106 TL 9211
Tolleshunt Major T 106 TL 9011
Toll of Birness 185 NK 0034
Tollomuick Forest 191 NH 3380
Tolmount, Grampn H 176 NO 2180
Tolmount, Tays H 176 NO 2180
Tolpuddle T 93 SY 7994
Tolquhon Castle A 185 NJ 8728
Tolsta Chaolais T 195 NB 1937
Tolsta Head 195 NB 5647
Tolworth T 105 TQ 1965
Tom a' Chòinich H 181 NH 1627
Tom an t-Saighdeir H 168 NM 9715
Tom an t-Suidhe Mhòir H 183 NJ 1118
Tomatin T 183 NH 8029
Tom Bailgeann H 182 NH 5829
Tombane Burn W 175 NN 9341
Tombreck T 183 NH 6934
Tomchrasky T 182 NH 2512
Tomdoun T 174 NH 1501
Tomich, Highld T 182 NH 3027
Tomich, Highld T 193 NH 7071
Tomich House 182 NH 5347
Tomintoul, Grampn T 184 NJ 1618
Tomintoul, Grampn T 176 NO 1490
Tomlachlan Burn W 183 NH 9337
Tom na h-Iolaire H 168 NR 9484
Tomnaven 184 NJ 4033
Tomnavoulin T 184 NJ 2126
Tomont End 161 NS 1859
Tom's Cairn H 177 NO 6194
Tomsléibhe 173 NM 6137
Tom Soilleir H 173 NM 8409
Tomtain H 169 NS 7281
Tonbridge T 97 TQ 5947
Tondu T 109 SS 8984
Tong, Shrops T 127 SJ 7907
Tong, W. Isles T 195 NB 4436
Tonga 205 HP 5815
Tonge T 128 SK 4123
Tongham T 103 SU 8849
Tongland T 155 NX 6953
Tongue (lightship) 107 TR 3485
Tongue T 197 NC 5956
Tongue Bay W 197 NC 6061
Tongue House 197 NC 5958
Tongwynlais T 109 ST 1382
Tòn Mhòr H 166 NR 2371
Tonna T 109 SS 7799
Ton-teg T 109 ST 0986
Tòn Tire 173 NM 6020
Tonwell T 105 TL 3317
Tonypandy T 109 SS 9992
Tonyrefail T 109 ST 0188
Toot Baldon T 115 SP 5600
Toot Hill, Essex T 105 TL 5102
Toothill, Hants T 94 SU 3818
Topcliffe T 147 SE 4026
Topcroft T 123 TM 2692
Topcroft Street T 123 TM 2691
Toppesfield T 122 TL 7337
Toppings T 137 SD 7213
Topsham T 89 SX 9688
Torbay, Devon P 89 SX 8962
Tor Bay, Devon W 89 SX 9259
Torbeg T 160 NR 9029
Torboll Farm 193 NH 7599
Torbreck Burn W 193 NC 7006
Torbryan T 89 SX 8166
Torcastle 174 NN 1378
Torcross T 89 SX 8242
Tore T 182 NH 6052
Tore Hill H 183 NH 9917
Torfichen Hill, Border H 164 NT 3353
Torfichen Hill, Lothn H 164 NT 3353
Torhousemuir 154 NX 3957
Torksey T 140 SK 8378
Torlum, Tays H 169 NN 8119
Torlum, W. Isles T 188 NF 7851
Torlum Wood F 169 NN 8218
Torlundy T 174 NN 1477
Tormarton T 101 ST 7778
Tormisdale 166 NR 1958
Tormitchell T 154 NX 2394
Tormore T 160 NR 8932
Tornagrain T 183 NH 7649
Tornahaish T 184 NJ 2908
Tornashean Forest F 184 NJ 3710
Tornaveen T 184 NJ 6106
Torness, Highld T 182 NH 5827
Tor Ness, Orkney 200 HY 4219
Tor Ness, Orkney 201 HY 6520
Tor Ness, Orkney 201 HY 7555
Tor Ness, Orkney 199 ND 2588
Torogay 188 NF 9178
Torosay Castle 173 NM 7235
Torpantau H 109 SO 0418
Torpenhow T 150 NY 2039
Torphichen T 170 NS 9672
Torphins T 177 NJ 6202
Torpoint T 88 SX 4355
Torquay T 89 SX 9164
Torquhan T 164 NT 4447
Torrachilty Wood F 182 NH 4355
Torran, Highld T 190 NG 5948
Torran, Strath 168 NM 8704
Torrance T 169 NS 6274
Torran Rocks 172 NM 2814
Torrans 173 NM 4825
Torran Tùrach H 168 NS 0070
Torran Water W 199 ND 0553
Torrent Walk 125 SH 7518
Torridon T 190 NG 8956
Torridon Forest 190 NG 9058
Torridon House 190 NG 8657
Torrin T 180 NG 5720
Torrisdale, Highld T 197 NC 6761
Torris Dale, Strath 160 NR 7837
Torrisdale Bay W 197 NC 6962
Torrisdale Castle 160 NR 7936
Torrish 193 NC 9718
Torrisholme T 145 SD 4564
Torr Meadhonach H 160 NR 9551
Tòrr Mòr H 161 NS 1052
Torr Nead an Eoin H 160 NR 9549
Torroble T 192 NC 5904
Torrs Warren 154 NX 1454
Torr, The H 160 NR 9125
Torry, Grampn T 184 NJ 4340
Torry, Grampn T 185 NJ 9505
Torry Bay W 170 NT 0185
Torryburn 170 NT 0286
Torrylin T 160 NR 9521
Torrylinwater Foot 160 NR 9520
Torsa 173 NM 7613
Torside Reservoir W 138 SK 0698
Torterston T 185 NK 0747
Torthorwald T 157 NY 0378
Tortington T 96 TQ 0005
Tortworth T 114 ST 7093
Torvaig T 187 NG 4944
Torver T 150 SD 2894
Torwood T 169 NS 8485
Torworth T 139 SK 6586
Toscaig T 180 NG 7138
Toseland T 121 TL 2362
Tosside T 146 SD 7756
Tosside Beck, Lancs W 146 SD 7853
Tosside Beck, N. Yks W 146 SD 7853
Tosson Hill H 159 NZ 0098
Tostock T 122 TL 9563
Totaig T 186 NG 2050
Totarol T 195 NB 1834
Tote, Highld T 187 NG 4149
Tote, Highld T 187 NG 5159
Totegan T 198 NC 8268
Totland T 94 SZ 3287
Totland Bay W 94 SZ 3186
Totley T 139 SK 3079
Totnes T 89 SX 8060
Totronald 172 NM 1656
Totscore T 186 NG 3866
Tottenham T 105 TQ 3390
Tottenhill T 132 TF 6410
Totteridge, Bucks T 104 SU 8793
Totteridge, G. Lon T 105 TQ 2494
Totternhoe T 104 SP 9821
Tottiford Reservoir W 89 SX 8183
Tottington T 137 SD 7712
Totton T 94 SU 3613
Touch Hills H 169 NS 7291
Tournaig T 190 NG 8783
Toux, Grampn T 184 NJ 5459
Toux, Grampn T 185 NJ 9850
Tovil T 97 TQ 7554
Towan Head 87 SW 7962
Toward T 156 NS 6812
Toward Point 161 NS 1367
Towcester T 119 SP 6948
Towednack T 86 SW 4838
Tower Point 110 SM 7910
Towersey T 104 SP 7305
Towie T 184 NJ 4412
Towiemore T 184 NJ 3945
Tow Law T 152 NZ 1139
Towneley Hall A 146 SD 8530
Town End T 131 TL 4195
Townhead, Cumbr T 151 NY 6334
Townhead, D. & G T 155 NX 6946
Townhead of Greenlaw T 156 NX 7464
Townhill T 170 NT 1089
Townshend T 86 SW 5932
Town Yetholm T 165 NT 8228
Towthorpe T 147 SE 6258
Towton T 147 SE 4839
Towyn T 135 SH 9779
Toynton All Saints T 141 TF 3964
Toynton Fen Side T 141 TF 3962
Toynton St Peter T 141 TF 4063
Toy's Hill T 97 TQ 4651
Trabboch T 161 NS 4321
Trabbochburn T 161 NS 4621
Traboe T 86 SW 7421
Tradespark, Highld T 183 NH 8656
Tradespark, Orkney T 200 HY 4508
Traeth Bach 134 SH 5836
Traeth Lafan or Lavan Sands 135 SH 6375
Trafford Park T 137 SJ 7896
Trahenna Hill H 163 NT 1337
Traigh House 180 NM 6590
Tràigh Mhòr 178 NF 7005
Trallong T 109 SN 9629
Trallwng or Welshpool P 126 SJ 2207
Tranent T 171 NT 4072
Trannon H 125 SN 9196
Trantlemore T 198 NC 8953
Tranwell T 159 NZ 1883
Trapp T 111 SN 6519
Traprain T 171 NT 5975
Traprain Law A 171 NT 5874
Traquair T 164 NT 3334
Traquair House A 164 NT 3335
Trawden T 146 SD 9138
Trawsallt H 125 SN 7870
Trawsfynydd T 135 SH 7035
Trealaval H 195 NB 2623
Trealaw T 109 ST 0092
Treales T 145 SD 4433
Trearddur T 134 SH 2579
Treaslane T 187 NG 3953
Trebartha T 88 SX 2677
Trebetherick T 87 SW 9377
Treborough T 92 ST 0136
Trebudannon T 87 SW 8961
Treburley T 88 SX 3477
Trecastle T 109 SN 8829
Trecwn T 110 SM 9632
Trecynon T 109 SN 9903
Tredavoe T 86 SW 4528
Tredegar T 109 SO 1409
Tredegar Park A 100 ST 2885
Tredington T 118 SP 2543
Tredinnick T 87 SW 9270
Tredomen T 109 SO 1231
Tredrizzick T 87 SW 9576
Tredunnock T 113 ST 3894
Treen T 86 SW 3923
Treeton T 139 SK 4387
Trefdraeth T 134 SH 4070
Trefeca T 109 SO 1432
Trefeglwys T 125 SN 9790
Trefenter T 124 SN 6068
Treffgarne T 110 SM 9523
Treffynnon T 110 SM 8428
Trefil T 109 SO 1212
Trefilan T 111 SN 5557
Trefnanney T 126 SJ 2015
Trefnant T 135 SJ 0570
Trefonen T 126 SJ 2527
Trefor T 134 SH 3780
Treforest T 109 ST 0889
Treforest Industrial Estate 109 ST 1186

Vale of Gloucester West Bradley

Vale of Gloucester 114 SO 8320
Vale of Mawgan or Lanherne 87 SW 8964
Vale of Neath 109 SN 8303
Vale of Pewsey 102 SU 1158
Vale of Taunton Deane 92 ST 1727
Vale of White Horse, Oxon 102 SU 2689
Vale of White Horse, Wilts 102 SU 2689
Valla Field 205 HP 5807
Vallay, W. Isles 188 NF 7776
Vallay, W. Isles 188 NG 0582
Vallay Strand 188 NF 7875
Valle Crucis Abbey *A* 126 SJ 2044
Valley Airport 134 SH 3075
Valleyfield *T* 170 NT 0086
Valsgarth *T* 205 HP 6413
Valtos, Highld *T* 187 NG 5163
Valtos, W. Isles *T* 195 NB 0937
Vange *T* 106 TQ 7287
Varne (lightship) 99 TR 3830
Varragill River *W* 187 NG 4738
Varteg *T* 113 SO 2606
Vatersay, W. Isles 178 NL 6296
Vatersay, W. Isles *T* 178 NL 6394
Vatersay Bay *W* 178 NL 6495
Vatisker Point 195 NB 4939
Vatten *T* 186 NG 2843
Vaul 172 NM 0448
Vaul Bay *W* 172 NM 0548
Vauld, The *T* 113 SO 5349
Vaynol Hall 134 SH 5369
Vaynor *T* 109 SO 0510
Vaynor Park *T* 126 SJ 1700
Veantrow Bay *W* 200 HY 5020
Veensgarth *T* 203 HU 4244
Veilish Point 188 NF 8178
Velindre *T* 113 SO 1836
Vell 205 HU 4890
Vellan Head 86 SW 6614
Vementry 202 HU 2860
Ve Ness, Orkney 200 HY 3705
Veness, Orkney *T* 200 HY 5729
Venford Reservoir *W* 89 SX 6870
Vennington *T* 126 SJ 3409
Venn Ottery *T* 92 SY 0791
Venta, Gwent *R* 101 ST 4790
Venta, Hants *R* 95 SU 4729
Ventnor *T* 95 SZ 5677
Vercovicium *R* 158 NY 7968
Vere, The 205 HP 6403
Vernham Dean *T* 102 SU 3456
Vernham Street *T* 102 SU 3557
Vernolds Common *T* 116 SO 4780
Verran Island *T* 178 NF 7234
Verulamium *R* 105 TL 1307
Verwig *T* 111 SN 1849
Verwood *T* 94 SU 0908
Veryan *T* 87 SW 9139
Veryan Bay *W* 87 SW 9640
Ve Skerries 202 HU 1065
Vestra Fiold *H* 200 HY 2322
Vicarage *T* 92 SY 2088
Vickerstown *T* 144 SD 1868
Victoria *T* 87 SW 9861
Victoria Station 105 TQ 2979
Vidlin *T* 203 HU 4765
Vidlin Voe *W* 203 HU 4866
Viewing Hill *H* 151 NY 7833
Viewpark *T* 162 NS 7161
Village Abberley, The *T* 117 SO 7567
Village, The *T* 117 SO 8989
Vinehall Street *T* 97 TQ 7520
Vines Cross *T* 97 TQ 5917
Vinessan 178 NL 6695
Virda Field *H* 202 HU 1561
Virginia Water *T* 104 SU 9967
Virginstow *T* 88 SX 3792
Virley Channel *W* 107 TM 0011
Viroconium *R* 127 SJ 5608
Vobster *T* 101 ST 7049
Voe, Shetld 204 HU 3381
Voe, Shetld *W* 203 HU 4015
Voe, Shetld *T* 203 HU 4062
Voe of Cullingsburgh *W* 203 HU 5142
Voe of Dale *W* 202 HU 1751
Voe of Snarraness *W* 202 HU 2356
Vord Hill *H* 205 HU 6293
Voreda *R* 151 NY 4938
Vorogay 188 NF 7864
Vowchurch *T* 113 SO 3636
Voxter 205 HU 3770
Voy 200 HY 2514
Vuia Beag 195 NB 1233
Vuia Mór 195 NB 1234
Vyne, The *A* 103 SU 6357

W

Waberthwaite *T* 150 SD 1093
Wackerfield *T* 152 NZ 1522
Wacton *T* 123 TM 1791
Wadbister Voe *W* 203 HU 4450
Wadborough *T* 117 SO 9047
Waddesdon *T* 104 SP 7416
Waddingham *T* 140 SK 9896
Waddington, Lancs *T* 145 SD 7243
Waddington, Lincs *T* 140 SK 9764
Wadebridge *P* 87 SW 9872
Wadeford *T* 92 ST 3110
Wadenhoe *T* 120 TL 0183
Wadesmill *T* 105 TL 3517
Wadhurst *T* 97 TQ 6332
Wadshelf *T* 139 SK 3171
Wadsworth Moor 146 SD 9833
Wadworth *T* 139 SK 5797
Waen-fâch *T* 126 SJ 2017
Wag 199 ND 0126
Wainfleet All Saints *T* 141 TF 4958
Wainfleet Bank *T* 141 TF 4759
Wainfleet Sand 131 TF 5455
Wainhope 158 NY 6790
Wainhouse Corner *T* 88 SX 1895
Wainscott *T* 98 TQ 7471
Wainstalls *T* 146 SE 0428
Waitby *T* 151 NY 7508
Wakefield *P* 139 SE 3320
Wakerley *T* 130 SP 9599
Wakes Colne *T* 122 TL 8928
Walberswick *T* 123 TM 4974
Walberton *T* 96 SU 9705
Walbury Hill *H* 102 SU 3761
Walcot, Lincs *T* 130 TF 0635
Walcot, Shrops *T* 127 SJ 5912
Walcot, Shrops *T* 116 SO 3485
Walcot, Warw *T* 118 SP 1258
Walcote *T* 119 SP 5683
Walcott, Lincs *T* 130 TF 1356
Walcott, Norf *T* 133 TG 3632
Walden *T* 146 SE 0083
Walden Head *T* 146 SD 9880
Walden Stubbs *T* 139 SE 5516
Waldersey 131 TF 4204
Waldershare House 99 TR 2848
Walderslade *T* 98 TQ 7663
Walderton *T* 95 SU 7810
Walditch *T* 93 SY 4892
Waldridge *T* 152 NZ 2550
Waldringfield *T* 123 TM 2844
Waldron *T* 97 TQ 5419
Wales *T* 139 SK 4882
Walesby, Lincs *T* 141 TF 1392
Walesby, Notts *T* 140 SK 6870
Walford, H. & W *T* 116 SO 3972
Walford, H. & W *T* 113 SO 5820
Walford, Shrops *T* 126 SJ 4320
Walgherton *T* 127 SJ 6949
Walgrave *T* 119 SP 8072
Walkden *T* 137 SD 7403
Walker *T* 159 NZ 2964
Walkerburn *T* 164 NT 3637
Walker Fold *T* 145 SD 6741
Walkeringham *T* 140 SK 7692
Walkerith *T* 140 SK 7893
Walkern *T* 121 TL 2826
Walker's Green *T* 113 SO 5247
Walkerwood Reservoir *W* 138 SJ 9898
Walkhampton *T* 89 SX 5369
Walkington *T* 142 SE 9937
Walk Mill *T* 146 SD 8630
Wall, Northum *T* 158 NY 9169
Wall, Staffs *T* 128 SK 1006
Wallace's Hill *H* 164 NT 3036
Wallacetown *T* 161 NS 3522
Walland Marsh 99 TQ 9923
Wallasey *P* 136 SJ 2992
Wallbury *A* 105 TL 4917
Waller's Haven *W* 97 TQ 6607
Wall Hill *H* 155 NX 7344
Wall Hills *A* 113 SO 6359
Walling Fen 142 SE 8829
Wallingford *T* 103 SU 6089
Wallington, G. Lon *T* 105 TQ 2863
Wallington, Hants *T* 95 SU 5806
Wallington, Herts *T* 121 TL 2933
Wallington Hall *A* 132 TF 6211
Wallis *T* 110 SN 0125
Walliswood *T* 96 TQ 1238
Walls *T* 202 HU 2449
Wallsend *T* 159 NZ 2966
Walls, The *A* 127 SO 7896
Wall under Heywood *T* 116 SO 5092
Wallyford *T* 171 NT 3672
Walmer *T* 99 TR 3750
Walmer Bridge *T* 145 SD 4824
Walmersley *T* 137 SD 8013
Walmley *T* 128 SP 1393
Walpole *T* 123 TM 3674
Walpole Highway *T* 131 TF 5113
Walpole St Andrew *T* 131 TF 5017
Walpole St Peter *T* 131 TF 5016
Walsall *P* 128 SP 0198
Walsall Wood *T* 128 SK 0503
Walsden *T* 146 SD 9322
Walsgrave on Sowe *T* 118 SP 3881
Walsham le Willows *T* 122 TM 0071
Walshaw Dean Reservoir *W* 146 SD 9633
Walsoken *T* 131 TF 4710
Walston *T* 163 NT 0545
Walter's Ash *T* 130 SP 8398
Walterstone *T* 113 SO 3425
Waltham, Humbs *T* 143 TA 2603
Waltham, Kent *T* 99 TR 1048
Waltham Abbey *T* 105 TL 3300
Waltham Chase *T* 95 SU 5615
Waltham Cross *T* 105 TL 3601
Waltham on the Wolds *T* 129 SK 8025
Waltham St Lawrence *T* 104 SU 8276
Walthamstow *T* 105 TQ 3788
Walton, Bucks *T* 120 SP 8836
Walton, Cumbr *T* 158 NY 5264
Walton, Derby *T* 139 SK 3569
Walton, Leic *T* 119 SP 5986
Walton, Powys *T* 113 SO 2559
Walton, Shrops *T* 127 SJ 5918
Walton, Somer *T* 93 ST 4636
Walton, Suff *T* 123 TM 2935
Walton, Warw *T* 118 SP 2853
Walton, W. Yks *T* 139 SE 3517
Walton, W. Yks *T* 147 SE 4447
Walton Cardiff *T* 114 SO 9032
Walton East *T* 110 SN 0223
Walton Highway *T* 131 TF 4912
Walton-in-Gordano *T* 101 ST 4273
Walton-le-Dale *T* 145 SD 5527
Walton-on-Thames *T* 105 TQ 1066
Walton-on-the-Hill, Staffs *T* 128 SJ 9521
Walton on the Hill, Surrey *T* 96 TQ 2254
Walton-on-the-Naze *T* 107 TM 2521
Walton on the Wolds *T* 129 SK 5919
Walton-on-Trent *T* 128 SK 2118
Walton West *T* 110 SM 8612
Walworth *T* 152 NZ 2318
Walwyn's Castle *T* 110 SM 8711
Wambrook *T* 92 ST 2908
Wamphray Water *W* 157 NT 1400
Wanborough *T* 102 SU 2183
Wandlebury *A* 121 TL 4953
Wandsworth *T* 105 TQ 2673
Wangford *T* 123 TM 4679
Wangford Fen 122 TL 7484
Wangford Warren 122 TL 7782
Wanlip *T* 129 SK 5910
Wanlockhead *T* 156 NS 8712
Wansdyke, Avon *A* 101 ST 6763
Wansdyke, Wilts *A* 102 SU 1264
Wansford, Cambs *T* 130 TL 0799
Wansford, Humbs *T* 149 TA 0656
Wanstead *T* 105 TQ 4087
Wanstrow *T* 101 ST 7141
Wanswell *T* 114 SO 6801
Wantage *T* 102 SU 4088
Wantyn's Dyke *A* 116 SO 1990
Wapley *T* 101 ST 7179
Wappenbury *T* 118 SP 3769
Wappenham *T* 119 SP 6245
Warbleton *T* 97 TQ 6018
Warborough *T* 115 SU 5993
Warboys *T* 121 TL 3080
Warbstow *T* 88 SX 2090
Warburton *T* 137 SJ 7089
Warcop *T* 151 NY 7415
Warcop Fell 151 NY 7820
Warden *T* 99 TR 0271
Warden Point 99 TR 0272
Ward Green *T* 122 TM 0463
Ward Hill, Orkney *H* 200 HY 2202
Ward Hill, Orkney *H* 200 HY 3307
Ward Hill, Orkney *H* 200 HY 5530
Ward Hill, Orkney *H* 199 ND 4588
Wardington *T* 119 SP 4946
Wardlaw Hill *H* 162 NS 6822
Wardle, Ches *T* 137 SJ 6157
Wardle, G. Man *T* 137 SD 9116
Wardley *T* 130 SK 8300
Wardlow *T* 138 SK 1874
Ward of Bressay *H* 203 HU 5038
Ward of Culswick *H* 202 HU 2645
Ward of Redland *H* 200 HY 3617
Ward of Scousburgh *H* 203 HU 3818
Ward of Veester *H* 203 HU 4126
War Down *H* 95 SU 7219
Ward's Stone 145 SD 5858
Wardy Hill *T* 121 TL 4782
Ware *T* 105 TL 3514
Wareham *T* 93 SY 9287
Wareham Forest *F* 93 SY 8792
Warehorne *T* 99 TQ 9832
Warenford *T* 165 NU 1328
Waren Mill *T* 165 NU 1434
Warenton *T* 165 NU 1030
Wareside *T* 105 TL 3915
Waresley *T* 121 TL 2554
Warfield *T* 104 SU 8872
Wargrave *T* 104 SU 7878
Warham *T* 132 TF 9441
Wark, Northum *T* 165 NT 8238
Wark, Northum *T* 158 NY 8677
Wark Forest *F* 158 NY 7377
Warkleigh *T* 91 SS 6422
Warks Burn *W* 158 NY 8176
Warkton *T* 120 SP 8979
Warkworth *T* 159 NU 2406
Warlaby *T* 153 SE 3591
Warland *T* 137 SD 9420
Warland Reservoir *W* 138 SD 9620
Warleggan *T* 87 SX 1569
Warley Moor Reservoir *W* 146 SE 0331
Warlingham *T* 105 TQ 3458
Warmfield *T* 139 SE 3720
Warmingham *T* 137 SJ 7161
Warmington, Northnts *T* 120 TL 0791
Warmington, Warw *T* 118 SP 4147
Warminster *P* 101 ST 8644
Warmsworth *T* 139 SE 5400
Warmwell *T* 93 SY 7585
Warndon *T* 117 SO 8857
War Ness 200 HY 5528
Warnford *T* 95 SU 6223
Warnham *T* 96 TQ 1533
Warninglid *T* 96 TQ 2526
Warren, Ches *T* 137 SJ 8970
Warren, Dyfed *T* 110 SR 9397
Warren Row *T* 104 SU 8180
Warren Street *T* 98 TQ 9253
Warrington, Bucks *T* 120 SP 8953
Warrington, Ches *P* 137 SJ 6088
Warsash *T* 95 SU 4906
Warslow *T* 138 SK 0858
Warsop *T* 139 SK 5667
Warter *T* 149 SE 8750
Warth Hill, Cumbr *H* 145 SD 5684
Warth Hill, Highld *H* 199 ND 3769
Warthill *T* 147 SE 6755
Wart Holm 200 HY 4838
Wartling *T* 97 TQ 6509
Wartnaby *T* 129 SK 7123
Warton, Lancs *T* 145 SD 4028
Warton, Lancs *T* 145 SD 5072
Warton, Northum *T* 159 NU 0002
Warton, Warw *T* 128 SK 2803
Warton Sands 145 SD 4472
Wart, The, Orkney *H* 201 HY 6337
Wart, The, Orkney *H* 200 ND 4393
Warwick, Cumbr *T* 151 NY 4656
Warwick, Warw *P* 118 SP 2865
Warwick Bridge *T* 151 NY 4756
Wasbister *T* 200 HY 3932
Wasdale Head *T* 150 NY 1808
Washaway *T* 87 SX 0369
Washbourne *T* 89 SX 7954
Washfield *T* 91 SS 9315
Washford *T* 100 ST 0441
Washford Pyne *T* 91 SS 8111
Washingborough *T* 140 TF 0270
Washington, T. & W *T* 152 NZ 3056
Washington, W. Susx *T* 96 TQ 1212
Wash *W* 131 TF 5342
Wash, The *W* 110 SR 9294
Wasing *T* 103 SU 5764
Waskerley, Durham *W* 152 NZ 0244
Waskerley, Durham *T* 152 NZ 0545
Wasperton *T* 118 SP 2658
Wass *T* 147 SE 5579
Wass Wick *W* 200 HY 4122
Wast Water *W* 150 NY 1606
Watchet *T* 100 ST 0743
Watchfield, Oxon *T* 102 SU 2590
Watchfield, Somer *T* 100 ST 3446
Watchgate *T* 151 SD 5299
Watch Hill, Border *H* 157 NY 4390
Watch Hill, Cumbr *H* 151 NY 6246
Watch Hill, D. & G *H* 157 NY 4390
Watch Water Reservoir *W* 164 NT 6656
Watendlath *T* 150 NY 2716
Water *T* 146 SD 8425
Waterbeach *T* 121 TL 4965
Waterbeck *T* 157 NY 2477
Waterden *T* 132 TF 8836
Water End, Herts *T* 104 TL 0310
Water End, Herts *T* 105 TL 2204
Waterfall *T* 128 SK 0851
Waterfoot, Lancs *T* 146 SD 8321
Waterfoot, Strath *T* 162 NS 5655
Waterford *T* 105 TL 3114
Watergate Bay *W* 87 SW 8264
Watergrove Resr *W* 137 SD 9017
Waterhead, Cumbr *T* 151 NY 3703
Waterhead, Strath *T* 161 NS 5411
Waterhead Hill *H* 156 NS 5700
Waterhead Moor 161 NS 2662
Waterheads 163 NT 2450
Waterhouses, Durham *T* 152 NZ 1841
Waterhouses, Staffs *T* 128 SK 0850
Wateringbury *T* 97 TQ 6853
Waterlip *T* 101 ST 6544
Waterloo, Dorset *T* 94 SZ 0094
Waterloo, Mers *T* 136 SJ 3198
Waterloo, Norf *T* 133 TG 2219
Waterloo, Strath *T* 163 NS 8054
Waterloo, Tays *T* 176 NO 0536
Waterloo Station 105 TQ 3179
Waterlooville *T* 95 SU 6809
Watermeetings *T* 156 NS 9512
Watermillock *T* 151 NY 4422
Water Newton *T* 130 TL 1097
Waternish 186 NG 2757
Waternish Point 186 NG 2367
Water of Ae *W* 157 NY 0485
Water of Ailnack, Grampn *W* 183 NJ 1313
Water of Ailnack, Highld *W* 183 NJ 1313
Water of App *W* 154 NX 0774
Water of Aven *W* 177 NO 6088
Water of Buchat *W* 184 NJ 3716
Water of Caiplich, Grampn *W* 183 NJ 0910
Water of Caiplich, Highld *W* 183 NJ 0910
Water of Charr *W* 177 NO 6180
Water of Coyle *W* 161 NS 4713
Water of Dye *W* 177 NO 6587
Water of Feugh *W* 177 NO 6792
Water of Girvan *W* 161 NS 3004
Water of Ken *W* 156 NX 6394
Water of Leith *W* 163 NT 1364
Water of Luce *W* 154 NX 1761
Water of Mark *W* 176 NO 3883
Water of May *W* 170 NO 0611
Water of Milk *W* 157 NY 1781
Water of Minnoch *W* 154 NX 3782
Water of Nevis *W* 174 NN 1868
Water of Nochty *W* 184 NJ 3215
Water of Ruchill *W* 169 NN 7418
Water of Saughs *W* 176 NO 4373
Water of Tanar *W* 176 NO 4594
Water of Tarf *W* 177 NO 4883
Water of Tig *W* 154 NX 1482
Water of Tulla *W* 174 NN 3647
Water of Unich *W* 176 NO 3679
Water Orton *T* 118 SP 1891
Waterperry *T* 104 SP 6206
Waterrow *T* 92 ST 0525
Watersfield *T* 96 TQ 0115
Waterside, Strath *T* 161 NS 4308
Waterside, Strath *T* 161 NS 4843
Waterside, Strath *T* 161 NS 5160
Waterside, Strath *T* 169 NS 6773
Water Sound *W* 200 ND 4695
Waterstein Head 186 NG 1547
Waterstock *T* 104 SP 6305
Waterston *T* 110 SM 9306
Water Stratford *T* 119 SP 6534
Waters Upton *T* 127 SJ 6319
Waterthorpe *T* 139 SK 4382
Water Yeat *T* 150 SD 2889
Watford, Herts *P* 105 TQ 1097
Watford, Northnts *T* 119 SP 6068
Wath, N. Yks *T* 146 SE 1467
Wath, N. Yks *T* 147 SE 3276
Wath upon Dearne *T* 139 SE 4300
Watling Street, G. Lon *R* 105 TQ 1792
Watling Street, Herts *R* 105 TL 1110
Watling Street, Leic *R* 119 SP 4490
Watling Street, Staffs *R* 127 SJ 8310
Watling Street, Warw *R* 128 SK 2500
Watlington, Norf *T* 132 TF 6110
Watlington, Oxon *T* 104 SU 6894
Watnall *T* 129 SK 5045
Wat's Dyke *A* 136 SJ 2762
Wats Ness 202 HU 1650
Watten *T* 199 ND 2454
Watterow *T* 92 ST 0525
Wattisfield *T* 122 TM 0174
Wattisham *T* 122 TM 0151
Watton, Humbs *T* 149 TA 0150
Watton, Norf *T* 132 TF 9100
Watton at Stone *T* 105 TL 3019
Watton Beck *W* 149 TA 0448
Wattston *T* 169 NS 7769
Wattstown *T* 109 ST 0294
Wattsville *T* 109 ST 2091
Watty Bell's Cairn *H* 158 NT 8901
Wauchope Forest *F* 158 NT 6104
Waulkmill Bay *W* 200 HY 3806
Waunarlwydd *T* 108 SS 6095
Waun Fâch *H* 109 SO 2130
Waunfawr *T* 134 SH 5259
Waun Lysiog 109 SO 0216
Waun-oer *H* 125 SH 7814
Wavendon *T* 120 SP 9037
Waverley Abbey *A* 103 SU 8645
Waverton, Ches *T* 136 SJ 4564
Waverton, Cumbr *T* 150 NY 2247
Wawne *T* 143 TA 0937
Waxham *T* 133 TG 4326
Waxholme *T* 143 TA 3229
Wayford *T* 92 ST 4006
Wayland's Smithy *A* 102 SU 2885
Way Village *T* 91 SS 8810
Wealdstone *T* 105 TQ 1689
Weald, The 97 TQ 6035
Weare *T* 100 ST 4152
Weare Giffard *T* 90 SS 4721
Wearhead *T* 151 NY 8539
Weasdale *T* 151 NY 6903
Weasenham All Saints *T* 132 TF 8421
Weasenham St Peter *T* 132 TF 8522
Weather Ness 200 HY 5240
Weaverham *T* 137 SJ 6174
Weaver Hills *H* 128 SK 0946
Weaver's Point 188 NF 9568
Weaverthorpe *T* 149 SE 9670
Webheath *T* 118 SP 0266
Weddel Sound *W* 200 ND 3394
Wedder Dod *H* 156 NS 8215
Wedder Holm 205 HU 6197
Wedderlairs *T* 185 NJ 8532
Wedder Law *H* 156 NS 9302
Weddington *T* 128 SP 3693
Wedhampton *T* 102 SU 0657
Wedholme Flow 150 NY 2253
Wedmore *T* 101 ST 4347
Wednesbury *T* 128 SO 9995
Wednesfield *T* 128 SJ 9500
Weedon *T* 104 SP 8118
Weedon Bec *T* 119 SP 6359
Weedon Lois *T* 119 SP 6047
Weeford *T* 128 SK 1404
Week *T* 91 SS 7316
Weekley *T* 120 SP 8880
Week St Mary *T* 88 SX 2397
Weeley *T* 107 TM 1422
Weeley Heath *T* 107 TM 1520
Weem *T* 175 NN 8449
Weem Hill *H* 175 NN 8351
Weeping Cross *T* 127 SJ 9421
Wee Queensberry *H* 156 NX 9897
Weeting *T* 122 TL 7788
Weeton, Lancs *T* 145 SD 3834
Weeton, N. Yks *T* 147 SE 2847
Weeton Station 147 SE 2747
Weets Hill *H* 146 SD 8544
Weetwood Hall 165 NU 0129
Weir *T* 146 SD 8725
Weir Dike *W* 142 SE 9714
Weir Wood Reservoir *W* 97 TQ 3934
Weisdale 203 HU 3953
Weisdale Voe *W* 203 HU 3747
Welbeck Abbey *T* 139 SK 5574
Welborne *T* 132 TG 0609
Welbourn *T* 130 SK 9654
Welburn *T* 148 SE 7268
Welbury *T* 153 NZ 3902
Welby *T* 130 SK 9738
Welches Dam *T* 121 TL 4686
Welcombe *T* 90 SS 2218
Weldon *T* 120 SP 9289
Weldrake *T* 142 SE 6845
Welford, Berks *T* 102 SU 4173
Welford, Northnts *T* 119 SP 6480
Welford-on-Avon *T* 118 SP 1552
Welham *T* 119 SP 7692
Welham Green *T* 105 TL 2305
Well, Hants *T* 103 SU 7646
Well, Lincs *T* 141 TF 4473
Well, N. Yks *T* 147 SE 2681
Welland *T* 117 SO 7940
Wellbank *T* 177 NO 4736
Wellesbourne *T* 118 SP 2855
Wellgrain Dod *H* 156 NS 9017
Well Hill, D. & G *H* 156 NS 9106
Well Hill, Kent *T* 105 TQ 4963
Welling *T* 105 TQ 4775
Wellingborough *T* 120 SP 8967
Wellingham *T* 132 TF 8722
Wellingore *T* 130 SK 9856
Wellington, H. & W *T* 113 SO 4948
Wellington, Shrops *T* 127 SJ 6511
Wellington, Somer *T* 92 ST 1320
Wellington Heath *T* 117 SO 7140
Welloe 86 SW 5825
Well of Kildinguie 201 HY 6527
Wellow, Avon *T* 101 ST 7358
Wellow, I. of W *T* 94 SZ 3888
Wellow, Notts *T* 139 SK 6766
Wells *P* 101 ST 5445
Wellsborough *T* 128 SK 3602
Wells-next-the-Sea *T* 132 TF 9143
Wellwood *T* 170 NT 0989
Welney *T* 131 TL 5293
Welshampton *T* 126 SJ 4335
Welsh Bicknor *T* 113 SO 5917
Welsh Channel *W* 135 SJ 1086
Welsh End *T* 127 SJ 5136
Welsh Frankton *T* 126 SJ 3633
Welsh Grounds 101 ST 4381
Welsh Hook *T* 110 SM 9327
Welsh Newton *T* 113 SO 5018
Welshpool or Trallwng *P* 126 SJ 2207
Welsh St Donats *T* 109 ST 0276
Welton, Cumbr *T* 150 NY 3544
Welton, Humbs *T* 142 SE 9527
Welton, Lincs *T* 140 TF 0179
Welton, Northnts *T* 119 SP 5866
Welton le Marsh *T* 141 TF 4768
Welton le Wold *T* 141 TF 2787
Welwick *T* 143 TA 3421
Welwyn *T* 105 TL 2316
Welwyn Garden City *T* 105 TL 2313
Wem *T* 127 SJ 5129
Wembdon *T* 92 ST 2837
Wembley *T* 105 TQ 1985
Wembury *T* 88 SX 5148
Wembury Bay *W* 88 SX 5147
Wembworthy *T* 91 SS 6609
Wemyss Bay *T* 168 NS 1969
Wenallt 135 SH 9842
Wendens Ambo *T* 121 TL 5135
Wendlebury *T* 115 SP 5619
Wendling *T* 132 TF 9312
Wendover *T* 104 SP 8607
Wendron *T* 86 SW 6731
Wendy *T* 121 TL 3247
Wenhaston *T* 123 TM 4275
Wenlock Edge *H* 116 SO 5190
Wennington, Cambs *T* 121 TL 2379
Wennington, G. Lon *T* 105 TQ 5381
Wennington, Lancs *T* 145 SD 6170
Wensley, Derby *T* 139 SK 2661
Wensley, N. Yks *T* 152 SE 0989
Wensleydale 146 SD 9988
Wentbridge *T* 139 SE 4817
Wentnor *T* 116 SO 3892
Wentwood *F* 113 ST 4294
Wentworth, Cambs *T* 121 TL 4878
Wentworth, S. Yks *T* 139 SK 3898
Wentworth Castle 139 SE 3203
Wenvoe *T* 109 ST 1273
Weobley *T* 113 SO 4051
Weobley Marsh *T* 113 SO 4151
Wereham *T* 132 TF 6801
Wergs *T* 127 SJ 8701
Wernrheolydd *T* 113 SO 3912
Werrington, Cambs *T* 130 TF 1603
Werrington, Corn *T* 88 SX 3287
Werrington, Staffs *T* 127 SJ 9447
Wervin *T* 136 SJ 4272
Wesham *T* 145 SD 4232
Wessington *T* 139 SK 3757
West Acre *T* 132 TF 7815
West Allerdean *T* 165 NT 9646
West Alvington *T* 89 SX 7243
West Anstey *T* 91 SS 8527
West Ashby *T* 141 TF 2672
West Ashling *T* 95 SU 8107
West Ashton *T* 101 ST 8755
West Auckland *T* 152 NZ 1726
West Bagborough *T* 92 ST 1633
West Barns *T* 171 NT 6578
West Barsham *T* 132 TF 9033
West Baugh Fell 151 SD 7394
West Bay, Dorset *T* 93 SY 4690
West Bay, Dorset *W* 93 SY 6773
West Beckham *T* 133 TG 1339
West Benula Forest 181 NH 0827
Westbere *T* 99 TR 1961
West Bergholt *T* 122 TL 9627
West Bexington *T* 93 SY 5386
West Bilney *T* 132 TF 7115
West Blatchington *T* 97 TQ 2806
Westborough *T* 130 SK 8544
Westbourne, Dorset *T* 94 SZ 0791
Westbourne, W. Susx *T* 95 SU 7507
West Bradford *T* 145 SD 7444
West Bradley *T* 93 ST 5536

West Bretton Whyle

West Bretton T 139 SE 2813
West Bridgford T 129 SK 5837
West Bromwich P 118 SP 0092
West Buckland, Devon T 91 SS 6531
West Buckland, Somer T 92 ST 1720
West Burra 203 HU 3632
West Burrafirth T 202 HU 2657
West Burton, Lancs T 146 SD 9961
West Burton, N. Yks T 146 SE 0186
West Burton, W. Susx T 96 SU 9913
Westbury, Bucks T 119 SP 6235
Westbury, Shrops T 126 SJ 3509
Westbury, Wilts T 101 ST 8751
Westbury Leigh T 101 ST 8650
Westbury-on-Severn T 114 SO 7214
Westbury-sub-Mendip T 101 ST 5048
Westby T 145 SD 3831
West Caister T 133 TG 5111
West Calder T 163 NT 0163
West Camel T 93 ST 5724
West Challow T 102 SU 3688
West Charleton T 89 SX 7542
West Chelborough T 93 ST 5405
West Chevington T 159 NZ 2297
West Chiltington T 96 TQ 0918
West Chinnock T 93 ST 4613
West Clandon T 96 TQ 0452
West Cliffe T 99 TR 3544
Westcliff-on-Sea T 106 TQ 8685
West Clyne T 193 NC 8805
West Coker T 93 ST 5113
Westcombe T 101 ST 6739
West Compton, Dorset T 93 SY 5694
West Compton, Somer T 101 ST 5942
Westcote T 115 SP 2220
Westcott, Bucks T 104 SP 7117
Westcott, Devon T 92 ST 0204
Westcott, Surrey T 96 TQ 1448
Westcott Barton T 115 SP 4225
West Cross T 108 SS 6189
West Cullerley T 185 NJ 7603
West Curry 88 SX 2893
West Curthwaite T 150 NY 3248
West Dart River W 89 SX 6373
Westdean, E. Susx T 97 TV 5299
West Dean, Hants T 94 SU 2527
West Dean, W. Susx T 95 SU 8612
West Deeping T 130 TF 1008
West Derby T 136 SJ 3993
West Dereham T 132 TF 6500
West Ditchburn T 159 NU 1320
West Down, Devon T 90 SS 5142
West Down, Wilts H 102 SU 0548
West Drayton, G. Lon T 104 TQ 0679
West Drayton, Notts T 140 SK 7074
West End, Avon T 101 ST 4469
West End, Beds T 120 SP 9853
West End, Hants T 95 SU 4614
West End, Humbs T 142 SE 9130
West End, Norf T 133 TG 4911
West End, N. Yks T 146 SE 1457
West End, Oxon T 115 SP 4204
West End, Surrey T 104 SU 9460
West End Green T 104 SU 6661
Wester Culbeuchly Crofts T 184 NJ 6562
Westerdale, Highld T 199 ND 1251
Westerdale, N. Yks T 153 NZ 6605
Westerdale Moor 153 NZ 6602
Wester Denoon 176 NO 3443
Wester Fearn Burn W 192 NH 6086
Westerfield, Shetld T 202 HU 3551
Westerfield, Suff T 123 TM 1747
Wester Fintray T 185 NJ 8116
Westergate T 96 SU 9305
Wester Gruinards T 192 NH 5192
Westerham T 97 TQ 4454
Wester Hoevdi 202 HT 9338
Wester Lealty 192 NH 6073
Westerleigh T 101 ST 7079
Western Cleddau W 110 SM 9521
Wester Newburn 171 NO 4405
Westernhope Moor 152 NY 9133
Western Isles or Hebrides, Highld 178 NG 0239
Western Isles or Hebrides, Strath 178 NG 0239
Western Isles or Hebrides, W. Isles 178 NG 0239
Western Rocks 86 SV 8306
Wester Quarff T 203 HU 4135
Wester Ross 191 NH 0562
Wester Skeld T 202 HU 2943
Westerton T 177 NO 6654
Westerwick, Shetld T 202 HU 2842
Wester Wick, Shetld W 202 HU 2842
West Farleigh T 97 TQ 7152
West Fell H 151 NY 6601
West Felton T 126 SJ 3425
West Fen, Cambs 131 TL 3799
West Fen, Cambs 121 TL 5182
West Fen, Lincs 131 TF 3154
Westfield, E. Susx T 98 TQ 8115
Westfield, Highld T 199 ND 0664
Westfield, Lothn T 170 NS 9472
Westfield, Norf T 132 TF 9909
West Firle T 97 TQ 4707
West Fleetham T 165 NU 1928
Westgate, Durham T 152 NY 9038
Westgate, Humbs T 142 SE 7707
Westgate, Norf T 132 TF 9740
Westgates on Sea T 99 TR 3270
West Gerinish T 188 NF 7741
West Ginge T 103 SU 4486
West Glen River W 130 TF 0022
West Grafton T 102 SU 2460
West Green T 103 SU 7456
West Grimstead T 94 SU 2126
West Grinstead T 96 TQ 1720
West Haddlesey T 147 SE 5626
West Haddon T 119 SP 6371
West Hagbourne T 103 SU 5187
West Hall, Cumbr T 158 NY 5667
Westhall, Grampn 184 NJ 6726
Westhall, Suff T 123 TM 4181
West Hallam T 128 SK 4341
West Halton T 142 SE 9021
Westham, E. Susx T 97 TQ 6304
West Ham, G. Lon T 105 TQ 4083
Westham, Somer T 100 ST 4046
Westhampnett T 95 SU 8806
West Handley T 139 SK 3977
West Hanney T 102 SU 4092
West Hanningfield T 106 TQ 7399
West Hardwick T 139 SE 4118
West Harptree T 101 ST 5656
West Hatch T 92 ST 2820
Westhay T 101 ST 4342
Westhead T 136 SD 4307
West Heath T 103 SU 8556
West Helmsdale T 193 ND 0115
West Hendred T 103 SU 4488
West Heslerton T 149 SE 9175
Westhide T 113 SO 5844
West Hill, Devon T 92 SY 0693
Westhill, Grampn T 185 NJ 8307
West Hoathly T 97 TQ 3632
West Holme T 93 SY 8885
Westhope, H. & W T 113 SO 4651
Westhope, Shrops T 116 SO 4786
West Horndon T 106 TQ 6288
Westhorpe, Lincs T 130 TF 2131
Westhorpe, Suff T 122 TM 0569
West Horrington T 101 ST 5747
West Horsley T 96 TQ 0752
West Hougham T 99 TR 2640
Westhoughton T 137 SD 6505
Westhouse T 145 SD 6774
Westhouses T 139 SK 4258
West Hoyle Bank 135 SJ 1087
Westhumble T 96 TQ 1651
West Hyde T 104 TQ 0391
West Ilsley T 103 SU 4782
Westing T 205 HP 5705
West Itchenor T 95 SU 7901
West Kame H 203 HU 3959
West Kennett T 102 SU 1168
West Kilbride T 161 NS 2147
West Kingsdown T 105 TQ 5762
West Kington T 101 ST 8177
West Kirby T 136 SJ 2186
West Knighton T 93 SY 7387
West Knock H 177 NO 4775
West Knoyle T 93 ST 8532
Westlake T 89 SX 6253
West Langdon T 99 TR 3247
West Langwell T 197 NC 6909
West Lavington, Wilts T 102 SU 0053
West Lavington, W. Susx T 95 SU 8920
West Lavington Down H 102 ST 9949
West Layton T 152 NZ 1409
West Leake T 129 SK 5226
Westleigh, Devon T 90 SS 4728
Westleigh, Devon T 92 ST 0616
Westleton T 123 TM 4469
West Lexham T 132 TF 8417
Westley, Shrops T 126 SJ 3607
Westley, Suff T 122 TL 8264
Westley Waterless T 122 TL 6156
West Lilling T 147 SE 6465
West Linga 203 HU 5364
Westlington T 104 SP 7610
West Linton, Border T 163 NT 1551
Westlinton, Cumbr T 157 NY 3964
West Littleton T 101 ST 7675
West Loch Tarbert, Strath W 160 NR 8163
West Loch Tarbert, W. Isles W 189 NB 0903
West Lomond H 171 NO 1906
West Lulworth T 93 SY 8280
West Lutton T 149 SE 9369
West Mains 163 NS 8549
West Malling T 97 TQ 6757
West Malvern T 117 SO 7646
West Marden T 95 SU 7713
West Markham T 140 SK 7272
Westmarsh T 99 TR 2761
West Marton T 146 SD 8950
West Meon T 95 SU 6423
West Mersea T 107 TM 0112
Westmeston T 97 TQ 3313
Westmill T 121 TL 3627
West Milton T 93 SY 5096
Westminster P 105 TQ 2979
West Monar Forest 191 NH 0842
West Monkton T 92 ST 2628
West Moors T 94 SU 0802
West Moulie Geo 202 HU 2940
West Mouse 134 SH 3094
Westmuir, Tays T 176 NO 3652
West Muir, Tays T 177 NO 5661
West Ness, Fife 171 NO 6106
Westness, Orkney 200 HY 3829
Westnewton, Cumbr T 150 NY 1344
West Newton, Humbs T 143 TA 1937
West Newton, Norf T 132 TF 6927
West Norwood T 105 TQ 3171
West Ogwell T 89 SX 8270
Weston, Avon T 101 ST 7266
Weston, Berks T 102 SU 4073
Weston, Ches T 137 SJ 5080
Weston, Ches T 127 SJ 7352
Weston, Dorset T 93 SY 6871
Weston, Hants T 95 SU 7221
Weston, Herts T 121 TL 2630
Weston, Lincs T 131 TF 2925
Weston, Northnts T 119 SP 5847
Weston, Notts T 140 SK 7767
Weston, N. Yks T 146 SE 1747
Weston, N. Yks T 148 SE 7565
Weston, Shrops T 127 SJ 5629
Weston, Shrops T 127 SO 5993
Weston, Staffs T 128 SJ 9727
Weston Bampfylde T 93 ST 6124
Weston Bay W 100 ST 3060
Weston Beggard T 113 SO 5841
Westonbirt T 101 ST 8589
Weston by Welland T 119 SP 7791
Weston Colville T 122 TL 6153
Weston Green T 122 TL 6252
Weston Heath T 127 SJ 7713
Weston Hill H 116 SO 5582
Weston Hills T 131 TF 2720
Westoning T 120 TL 0332
Weston-in-Gordano T 101 ST 4474
Weston Jones T 127 SJ 7624
Weston Longville T 133 TG 1115
Weston Lullingfields T 126 SJ 4224
Weston-on-the-Green T 115 SP 5318
Weston-on-Trent T 128 SK 4028
Weston Patrick T 103 SU 6946
Weston Rhyn T 126 SJ 2835
Weston-sub-Edge T 118 SP 1241
Weston-super-Mare P 100 ST 3261
Weston Turville T 104 SP 8511
Weston-under-Lizard T 127 SJ 8010
Weston under Penyard T 113 SO 6323
Weston under Wetherley T 118 SP 3669
Weston Underwood, Bucks T 120 SP 8650
Weston Underwood, Derby T 128 SK 2942
Westonzoyland T 92 ST 3534
West Overton T 102 SU 1367
West Parley T 94 SZ 0898
West Peckham T 97 TQ 6452
West Pennard T 101 ST 5438
West Pentire T 86 SW 7760
West Perry T 120 TL 1466
Westport T 92 ST 3820
West Putford T 90 SS 3515
West Quantoxhead T 100 ST 1141
West Rainton T 152 NZ 3146
West Rasen T 140 TF 0689
Westray 200 HY 4446
Westray Airport 200 HY 4552
Westray Firth W 200 HY 4735
West Raynham T 132 TF 8725
West Reef 172 NM 2414
Westrigg T 163 NS 9067
West Road W 99 TR 0015
West Row T 122 TL 6775
West Rudham T 132 TF 8127
West Runton T 133 TG 1842
Westruther T 164 NT 6350
Westry T 131 TL 3998
West Saltoun T 164 NT 4667
West Sandwick T 205 HU 4588
West Scar 153 NZ 6026
West Scrafton T 146 SE 0783
West Sedge Moor 92 ST 3625
Westside 200 HY 3729
West Somerset Railway 92 ST 1334
West Stafford T 93 SY 7289
West Stockwith T 140 SK 7994
West Stoke T 95 SU 8308
West Stonesdale T 152 NY 8802
West Stoughton T 100 ST 4148
West Stour T 93 ST 7822
West Stourmouth T 99 TR 2562
West Stow T 122 TL 8170
West Stowell T 102 SU 1362
West Street T 98 TQ 9054
West Tanfield T 147 SE 2678
West Tarbert T 160 NR 8467
West Tarbert Bay W 160 NR 6553
West Thorney T 95 SU 7602
West Thurrock T 105 TQ 5877
West Tilbury T 98 TQ 6677
West Tisted T 95 SU 6529
West Tofts T 170 NO 1034
West Torrington T 141 TF 1382
West Town T 101 ST 4868
West Tytherley T 94 SU 2729
West Tytherton T 102 ST 9574
West Voe W 203 HU 3730
West Voe of Sumburgh W 203 HU 3909
West Walton T 131 TF 4713
Westward T 150 NY 2744
Westward Ho! T 90 SS 4329
West Water W 177 NO 5367
West Water Reservoir W 163 NT 1152
Westwell, Kent T 99 TQ 9947
Westwell, Oxon T 115 SP 2210
Westwell Leacon T 99 TQ 9647
West Wellow T 94 SU 2919
West Wemyss T 171 NT 3294
West Wick, Avon T 100 ST 3661
Westwick, Cambs T 121 TL 4265
Westwick, Norf T 133 TG 2726
West Wickham, Cambs T 122 TL 6149
West Wickham, G. Lon T 105 TQ 3866
West Winch T 132 TF 6315
West Winterslow T 94 SU 2332
West Wittering T 95 SZ 7898
West Witton T 146 SE 0688
Westwood, Devon T 92 SY 0198
Westwood, Wilts T 101 ST 8059
West Woodburn T 158 NY 8986
West Woodhay T 102 SU 3963
West Woodlands T 101 ST 7743
Westwoodside T 142 SK 7499
West Worldham T 95 SU 7436
West Wratting T 122 TL 6051
West Wycombe T 104 SU 8394
West Yell T 205 HU 4583
Wetheral T 151 NY 4654
Wetherby T 147 SE 4048
Wether Cairn H 158 NT 9411
Wetherden T 122 TM 0062
Wether Fell 146 SD 8787
Wether Hill, D. & G H 156 NX 7087
Wether Hill, D. & G H 156 NX 7094
Wether Hill, Tays H 170 NN 9205
Wetheringsett T 123 TM 1266
Wether Lair H 158 NY 7096
Wether Law H 163 NT 1948
Wethersfield T 122 TL 7131
Wethersta T 203 HU 3665
Wetherup Street T 123 TM 1464
Wetley Rocks T 128 SJ 9649
Wet Sleddale Reservoir W 151 NY 5411
Wettenhall T 137 SJ 6261
Wetton T 128 SK 1155
Wetwang T 149 SE 9359
Wetwood T 127 SJ 7733
Wexcombe T 102 SU 2759
Weybourne T 133 TG 1143
Weybread T 123 TM 2480
Weybridge T 104 TQ 0764
Weydale T 199 ND 1564
Weyhill T 102 SU 3146
Weymouth P 93 SY 6779
Weymouth Bay W 93 SY 6980
Whaddon, Bucks T 119 SP 8034
Whaddon, Cambs T 121 TL 3546
Whaddon, Glos T 114 SO 8313
Whaddon, Wilts T 94 SU 1926
Whaddon Chase 119 SP 8032
Whale T 151 NY 5221
Whale Chine 95 SZ 4678
Whale Firth W 205 HU 4694
Whale Geo 205 HU 4493
Whale Island 95 SU 6302
Whaley T 139 SK 5171
Whaley Bridge T 138 SK 0181
Whaley Thorns T 139 SK 5371
Whaligoe 199 ND 3240
Whalley T 145 SD 7336
Whalsay 203 HU 5563
Whalsay Airport 203 HU 5966
Whalton T 159 NZ 1381
Whalwick Taing 204 HU 2381
Wham T 146 SD 7762
Whaness T 200 HY 2502
Whaplode T 131 TF 3224
Whaplode Drove T 131 TF 3113
Whaplode Fen 131 TF 3320
Whaplode River W 131 TF 3429
Wharfe T 146 SD 7869
Wharfedale 147 SE 2646
Wharles T 145 SD 4435
Wharncliffe Side T 139 SK 2994
Wharram le Street T 148 SE 8666
Wharton, Ches T 137 SJ 6666
Wharton, H. & W T 113 SO 5055
Whashton T 152 NZ 1406
Whatcombe T 93 ST 8301
Whatcote T 118 SP 3044
Whatfield T 122 TM 0246
Whatley T 101 ST 7347
Whatlington T 97 TQ 7518
Whatstandwell T 128 SK 3354
Whatton T 129 SK 7439
Whauphill T 154 NX 4049
Whaw 152 NY 9804
Wheatacre T 133 TM 4693
Wheathampstead T 105 TL 1713
Wheathill T 117 SO 6282
Wheatley, Hants T 103 SU 7840
Wheatley, Oxon T 115 SP 5905
Wheatley Hill T 153 NZ 3738
Wheatley Lane T 146 SD 8338
Wheaton Aston T 127 SJ 8512
Wheat Stack 165 NT 8671
Wheddon Cross T 91 SS 9238
Wheedlemont T 184 NJ 4726
Wheeldale Moor 148 SE 7898
Wheelerstreet T 96 SU 9440
Wheelock T 137 SJ 7559
Wheelton T 145 SD 6021
Wheen 176 NO 3671
Whelford T 115 SU 1799
Whelpley Hill T 104 SP 9904
Whenby T 147 SE 6369
Whepstead T 122 TL 8358
Whernside 145 SD 7382
Wherstead T 123 TM 1540
Wherwell T 102 SU 3840
Wheston T 138 SK 1376
Whetsted T 97 TQ 6545
Whetstone T 129 SP 5597
Whicham T 144 SD 1382
Whichford T 115 SP 3134
Whickham T 159 NZ 2061
Whiddon Down T 89 SX 6992
Whigstreet T 177 NO 4844
Whillan Beck W 150 NY 1802
Whilton T 119 SP 6364
Whimple T 92 SY 0497
Whimpwell Green T 133 TG 3829
Whinburgh T 132 TG 0009
Whinfell Beacon H 151 NY 5700
Whinlatter Pass 150 NY 1924
Whinnyfold T 185 NK 0833
Whins Brow H 145 SD 6353
Whippingham T 95 SZ 5193
Whipsnade T 104 TL 0118
Whipsnade Park Zoo 104 TL 0017
Whipton T 89 SX 9493
Whissendine T 130 SK 8214
Whissonsett T 132 TF 9123
Whistley Green T 104 SU 7974
Whiston, Mers T 137 SJ 4791
Whiston, Northnts T 120 SP 8460
Whiston, Staffs T 127 SJ 8914
Whiston, Staffs T 128 SK 0347
Whiston, S. Yks T 139 SK 4590
Whitaloo Point 200 HY 2628
Whitbeck T 144 SD 1184
Whitbourne T 117 SO 7256
Whitburn, Lothn T 163 NS 9464
Whitburn, T. & W T 159 NZ 4062
Whitby, Ches T 136 SJ 3975
Whitby, N. Yks P 149 NZ 8910
Whitchurch, Avon T 101 ST 6167
Whitchurch, Bucks T 104 SP 8020
Whitchurch, Devon T 88 SX 4972
Whitchurch, Dyfed T 110 SM 8025
Whitchurch, Hants T 103 SU 4648
Whitchurch, H. & W T 113 SO 5517
Whitchurch, Oxon T 104 SU 6377
Whitchurch, S. Glam T 109 ST 1580
Whitchurch, Shrops P 127 SJ 5441
Whitchurch Canonicorum T 92 SY 3995
Whitchurch Hill T 104 SU 6478
Whitcott Keysett T 116 SO 2782
Whiteacen 184 NJ 2545
Whiteadder Reservoir W 164 NT 6563
Whiteadder Water, Border W 165 NT 9154
Whiteadder Water, Lothn W 164 NT 6366
Whiteash Hill Wood F 184 NJ 3758
Whitebridge T 182 NH 4815
Whitebrook T 113 SO 5306
Whitecairns T 185 NJ 9218
White Cart Water W 161 NS 5263
White Castle A 113 SO 3716
White Caterthun 177 NO 5466
Whitechapel T 145 SD 5541
Whitecliff Bay W 95 SZ 6486
White Coomb H 157 NT 1615
White Coppice T 137 SD 6119
Whitecraig, Lothn T 171 NT 3570
White Craig, Strath H 163 NT 0753
Whitecroft T 113 SO 6206
White Esk W 157 NY 2598
Whiteface T 193 NH 7089
Whitefarland Point 160 NR 8642
Whitefauld Hill H 156 NY 0293
White Fen 121 TL 3492
Whitefield, G. Man T 137 SD 8105
Whitefield, Tays 170 NO 1734
Whitefield Loch W 154 NX 2355
Whiteford T 185 NJ 7226
Whiteford Point 108 SS 4496
Whitegate T 137 SJ 6369
Whitehall T 201 HY 6528
Whitehaugh Forest F 184 NJ 5723
Whitehaven T 150 NX 9717
White Hill, Border H 158 NT 5212
White Hill, Grampn H 177 NO 5388
Whitehill, Hants T 95 SU 7934
White Hill, Lancs H 145 SD 6758
White Hill, Strath H 156 NS 8820
White Hill, Tays H 176 NO 4073
Whitehills T 184 NJ 6565
White Hope Edge H 157 NY 3397
Whitehope Law H 164 NT 3344
White Horse A 93 SY 7184
Whitehouse, Grampn T 184 NJ 6115
Whitehouse, Strath T 160 NR 8161
White Island 86 SV 9217
Whitekirk T 171 NT 5981
White Kirkley T 152 NZ 0235
White Knowes H 156 NS 6104
White Lackington T 93 SY 7198
White Ladies Aston T 117 SO 9252
Whitelake W 101 ST 5240
White Law, Border H 165 NT 8526
White Law, Northum H 165 NT 8526
Whitelaw Hill, Border H 163 NT 1935
Whitelaw Hill, Lothn H 171 NT 5771
Whitelee Forest F 161 NS 5443
Whiteley Village T 104 TQ 0962
White Loch W 154 NX 1060
White Lyne W 158 NY 5473
Whitemans Green T 97 TQ 3025
White Meldon H 163 NT 2142
Whitemill Bay W 201 HY 6946
Whitemill Point 201 HY 7046
Whitemire T 183 NH 9754
Whitemoor T 87 SW 9757
Whitemoor Reservoir W 146 SD 8743
White Mounth H 176 NO 2383
White Ness, Kent 99 TR 3971
White Ness, Shetld 203 HU 3844
Whiteness, Shetld 203 HU 4147
Whiteness Head 183 NH 8058
Whiteness Sands 183 NH 8386
Whiteness Voe W 203 HU 3943
Whiten Head or An Ceann Geal 197 NC 5068
White Notley T 106 TL 7818
Whiteparish T 94 SU 2423
White Preston H 158 NY 5977
Whiterashes T 185 NJ 8523
White Rocks T 113 SO 4424
White Roding or White Roothing T 105 TL 5613
White Roothing or White Roding T 105 TL 5613
Whiterow T 199 ND 3548
Whitesand Bay W 86 SW 3527
Whitesand Bay or Porth-mawr W 110 SM 7227
White Sands 136 SJ 2772
White Shank H 157 NT 2006
White Sheet Hill, Wilts H 93 ST 8034
Whitesheet Hill, Wilts H 94 ST 9524
Whiteshill T 114 SO 8407
Whiteshoot Hill H 94 SU 2833
Whiteside, Lothn T 163 NS 9668
Whiteside, Northum 158 NY 7069
Whitesmith T 97 TQ 5214
Whitestaunton T 92 ST 2810
Whitestone T 89 SX 8693
Whitestone Hill H 158 NT 7915
White Top of Culreoch H 156 NX 6063
White Waltham T 104 SU 8577
Whiteway T 114 SO 9210
Whiteway House 89 SX 8782
Whitewell T 145 SD 6547
Whiteworks 89 SX 6071
Whitewreath T 184 NJ 2357
Whitfell H 150 SD 1593
Whitfield, Avon T 101 ST 6791
Whitfield, Bucks T 119 SP 6039
Whitfield, Kent T 99 TR 3045
Whitfield, Northum T 158 NY 7858
Whitfield Moor 151 NY 7453
Whitford, Clwyd T 136 SJ 1478
Whitford, Devon T 92 SY 2595
Whitgift T 142 SE 8122
Whitgreave T 127 SJ 8928
Whithorn T 155 NX 4440
Whithorse Hill H 102 SU 3086
Whiting Bay, Strath T 160 NS 0425
Whiting Bay, Strath W 160 NS 0526
Whitland T 111 SN 2016
Whitletts T 161 NS 3622
Whitley, Berks T 104 SU 7170
Whitley, Ches T 137 SJ 6179
Whitley, N. Yks T 147 SE 5621
Whitley, Wilts T 101 ST 8866
Whitley Bay T 159 NZ 3572
Whitley Chapel T 152 NY 9257
Whitley Row T 97 TQ 4952
Whitlock's End T 118 SP 1077
Whitminster T 114 SO 7708
Whit Moor 145 SD 5964
Whitmore T 127 SJ 8141
Whitnage T 92 ST 0215
Whitnash T 118 SP 3263
Whitney-on-Wye, H. & W T 113 SO 2747
Whitney-on-Wye, H. & W T 113 SO 2747
Whitrigg, Cumbr T 150 NY 2038
Whitrigg, Cumbr 150 NY 2257
Whitsand Bay W 88 SX 3751
Whitsbury T 94 SU 1219
Whitsome T 165 NT 8650
Whitson T 100 ST 3883
Whitstable T 99 TR 1166
Whitstone T 88 SX 2698
Whittingham T 159 NU 0611
Whittingslow T 116 SO 4389
Whittington, Derby T 139 SK 3874
Whittington, Glos T 114 SP 0121
Whittington, H. & W T 117 SO 8752
Whittington, Lancs T 145 SD 6076
Whittington, Norf T 132 TL 7199
Whittington, Shrops T 126 SJ 3231
Whittington, Staffs T 128 SK 1608
Whittington, Staffs T 117 SO 8682
Whittlebury T 119 SP 6943
Whittle-le-Woods T 145 SD 5821
Whittlesey T 131 TL 2797
Whittlesey Mere 131 TL 2290
Whittlesford T 121 TL 4748
Whittlewood Forest F 119 SP 7242
Whitton, Border T 164 NT 7622
Whitton, Cleve T 153 NZ 3822
Whitton, Humbs T 142 SE 9024
Whitton, Northum T 159 NU 0501
Whitton, Powys T 116 SO 2767
Whitton, Shrops T 116 SO 5772
Whitton, Suff T 123 TM 1447
Whittonditch T 102 SU 2972
Whittonstall T 152 NZ 0757
Whitwell, Derby T 139 SK 5276
Whitwell, Herts T 105 TL 1820
Whitwell, I. of W T 95 SZ 5278
Whitwell, Leic T 130 SK 9208
Whitwell, N. Yks T 152 SE 2899
Whitwell-on-the-Hill T 148 SE 7265
Whitwick T 128 SK 4316
Whitwood T 147 SE 4024
Whitworth T 137 SD 8818
Whixall T 127 SJ 5134
Whixley T 147 SE 4458
Whorlton, Durham T 152 NZ 1014
Whorlton, N. Yks T 153 NZ 4802
Whorlton Moor 153 SE 5098
Whygate 158 NY 7776
Whyle T 116 SO 5661

Whyteleafe

Wreningham

Whyteleafe T 105 TQ 3458
Wiay, Highld 186 NG 2936
Wiay, W. Isles 188 NF 8746
Wibdon T 113 ST 5697
Wibtoft T 119 SP 4787
Wichenford T 117 SO 7860
Wichling T 98 TQ 9256
Wick, Avon T 101 ST 7073
Wick, Dorset T 94 SZ 1591
Wick, Highld P 199 ND 3650
Wick, H. & W T 118 SO 9645
Wick, M. Glam T 109 SS 9272
Wick, Shetld 203 HU 4439
Wick, Wilts T 94 SU 1621
Wick, W. Susx T 96 TQ 0203
Wick Airport 199 ND 3652
Wickam Street T 122 TL 7554
Wick Bay W 199 ND 3750
Wick Down H 94 SU 1321
Wicken, Cambs T 121 TL 5771
Wicken, Northnts T 119 SP 7439
Wicken Bonhunt T 121 TL 5033
Wickenby T 140 TF 0881
Wickersley T 139 SK 4891
Wickford T 106 TQ 7493
Wickham, Berks T 102 SU 3971
Wickham, Hants T 95 SU 5711
Wickham Bishops T 106 TL 8412
Wickhambreaux T 99 TR 2259
Wickhambrook T 122 TL 7554
Wickhamford T 118 SP 0641
Wickham Market T 123 TM 3055
Wickhampton T 133 TG 4205
Wickham Skeith T 123 TM 0969
Wickham St Paul T 122 TL 8336
Wickham Street T 123 TM 0969
Wick Hill H 104 SU 8064
Wicklewood T 132 TG 0702
Wickmere T 133 TG 1733
Wick of Breakon W 205 HP 5205
Wick of Gruting W 205 HU 6592
Wick of Macklabrek W 202 HT 9438
Wick of Sandsayre W 203 HU 4325
Wick of Shunni W 203 HU 3515
Wick of Tresta W 205 HU 6389
Wick River W 199 ND 3052
Wick St Lawrence T 100 ST 3665
Wickwar T 101 ST 7288
Widdale Fell 146 SD 8088
Widdington T 121 TL 5331
Widdop Resr W 146 SD 9333
Widdrington T 159 NZ 2595
Widdrington Station 159 NZ 2494
Widdybank Fell 151 NY 8330
Widecombe in the Moor T 89 SX 7176
Wide Firth W 200 HY 4315
Wideford Hill H 200 HY 4111
Widegates T 88 SX 2857
Widemouth Bay T 90 SS 2002
Wide Open T 159 NZ 2372
Widewall T 200 ND 4390
Widewall Bay W 200 ND 4292
Widford, Essex T 106 TL 6905
Widford, Herts T 105 TL 4215
Widmerpool T 129 SK 6328
Widnes P 137 SJ 5185
Wife Geo 199 ND 3969
Wigan P 137 SD 5805
Wiggaton T 92 SY 1093
Wiggenhall St Germans T 132 TF 5914
Wiggenhall St Mary Magdalen T 132 TF 5911
Wiggenhall St Mary the Virgin T 131 TF 5813
Wiggington T 147 SE 5958
Wigginton, Herts T 104 SP 9310
Wigginton, Oxon T 115 SP 3833
Wigginton, Staffs T 128 SK 2106
Wigglesworth T 146 SD 8157
Wiggonby T 150 NY 3053
Wiggonholt 96 TQ 0616
Wighill T 147 SE 4746
Wighton T 132 TF 9439
Wightown Bay W 155 NX 5348
Wigmore, H. & W T 116 SO 4169
Wigmore, Kent T 98 TQ 8064
Wigsley T 140 SK 8670
Wigsthorpe T 120 TL 0482
Wigston T 129 SP 6099
Wig, The W 154 NX 0367
Wigtoft T 131 TF 2636
Wigton T 150 NY 2548
Wigtown T 155 NX 4355
Wigtown Bay W 155 NX 5447
Wigtown Sands 155 NX 4556
Wilbarston T 120 SP 8188
Wilberfoss T 148 SE 7351
Wilburton T 121 TL 4874
Wilby, Norf T 122 TM 0389
Wilby, Northnts T 120 SP 8666
Wilby, Suff T 123 TM 2471
Wilcot T 102 SU 1460
Wildboarclough T 138 SJ 9868
Wilden, Beds T 120 TL 0955
Wilden, H. & W T 117 SO 8272
Wildhern T 102 SU 3550
Wildmore Fen 131 TF 2552
Wildsworth T 140 SK 8097
Wiley Sike H 158 NY 6470
Wilford T 129 SK 5637
Wilkesley T 127 SJ 6241
Wilkhaven T 193 NH 9487
Wilkieston T 163 NT 1268
Willand T 92 ST 0310
Willaston, Ches T 136 SJ 3377
Willaston, Ches T 127 SJ 6752
Willen T 120 SP 8741
Willenhall, W. Mids T 128 SO 9799
Willenhall, W. Mids T 118 SP 3676
Willerby, Humbs T 142 TA 0230
Willerby, N. Yks T 149 TA 0079
Willersey T 118 SP 1039
Willersley T 113 SO 3147
Willesborough Lees T 99 TR 0342
Willesden T 105 TQ 2284
Willett T 92 ST 1033
Willey, Shrops T 127 SO 6799
Willey, Warw T 119 SP 4984
William Law H 164 NT 4739
Williamscot T 119 SP 4745
Willian T 121 TL 2230
Willimontswick 158 NY 7763
Willingale T 106 TL 5907
Willingdon T 97 TQ 5802
Willingdon Hill H 97 TQ 5700
Willingham T 121 TL 4070
Willingham by Stow T 140 SK 8784
Willington, Beds T 120 TL 1149
Willington, Derby T 128 SK 2928
Willington, Durham T 152 NZ 1935
Willington, T. & W T 159 NZ 3167
Willington, Warw T 118 SP 2639
Willington Corner T 137 SJ 5367
Willitoft T 142 SE 7435
Williton T 100 ST 0741
Willoughby, Lincs T 141 TF 4771
Willoughby, Warw T 119 SP 5167
Willoughby-on-the-Wolds T 129 SK 6325
Willoughby Waterleys T 119 SP 5792
Willoughton T 140 SK 9393
Willy Howe A 149 TA 0672
Wilmcote T 118 SP 1658
Wilmington, Devon T 92 SY 2199
Wilmington, E. Susx T 97 TQ 5405
Wilmington, Kent T 105 TQ 5372
Wilmslow T 137 SJ 8481
Wilnecote T 128 SK 2201
Wilpshire T 145 SD 6832
Wilsden T 146 SE 0936
Wilsford, Lincs T 130 TF 0043
Wilsford, Wilts T 102 SU 1057
Wilsford, Wilts T 102 SU 1339
Wilsill T 146 SE 1864
Wilson T 128 SK 4024
Wilson's Pike H 158 NY 5589
Wilstead T 120 TL 0643
Wilsthorpe T 130 TF 0913
Wilstone T 104 SP 9014
Wilstone Reservoir W 104 SP 9013
Wilton, Cleve T 153 NZ 5819
Wilton, N. Yks T 148 SE 8682
Wilton, Wilts T 94 SU 0931
Wilton, Wilts T 102 SU 2661
Wilton Dean T 157 NT 4914
Wilton House A 94 SU 0931
Wimbish T 122 TL 5936
Wimbish Green T 122 TL 6035
Wimbleball Lake W 91 SS 9730
Wimbledon T 105 TQ 2470
Wimbledon Park 105 TQ 2472
Wimblington T 121 TL 4192
Wimblington Fen 121 TL 4489
Wimborne Minster P 94 SU 0100
Wimbotsham T 132 TF 6205
Wimpole Hall A 121 TL 3351
Wimpstone T 118 SP 2149
Wincanton T 93 ST 7128
Wincham T 137 SJ 6775
Winchburgh T 170 NT 0874
Winchcombe T 114 SP 0228
Winchelsea T 98 TQ 9017
Winchelsea Beach T 98 TQ 9116
Winchester P 95 SU 4729
Winchfield T 103 SU 7654
Winchmore Hill, Bucks T 104 SU 9395
Winchmore Hill, G. Lon T 105 TQ 3194
Wincle T 138 SJ 9666
Windbury Point 90 SS 2826
Windermere, Cumbr W 151 SD 3995
Windermere, Cumbr P 151 SD 4198
Winderton T 118 SP 3240
Windlesham T 104 SU 9363
Windlestraw Law H 164 NT 3743
Windley T 128 SK 3045
Windmill Hill, E. Susx T 97 TQ 6412
Windmill Hill, Somer T 92 ST 3116
Windrush T 115 SP 1913
Windsor T 104 SU 9676
Windsor Forest F 104 SU 9373
Windsor Great Park 104 SU 9572
Wind Wick W 199 ND 4687
Windy Crag H 158 NT 7705
Windygates T 171 NO 3400
Windy Gyle, Border H 158 NT 8515
Windy Gyle, Northum H 158 NT 8515
Windyheads Hill H 185 NJ 8561
Windy Hill H 168 NS 0469
Windy Standard, D. & G H 156 NS 6201
Windy Standard, Strath H 161 NS 5204
Wineham T 96 TQ 2320
Winestead T 143 TA 3024
Winfarthing T 123 TM 1086
Winford T 101 ST 5465
Winforton T 113 SO 2947
Winfrith Newburgh T 93 SY 8084
Wing, Bucks T 104 SP 8822
Wing, Leic T 130 SK 8903
Wingate T 153 NZ 4037
Wingates, G. Man T 137 SD 6507
Wingates, Northum T 159 NZ 0995
Wingerworth T 139 SK 3767
Wingfield, Beds T 120 TL 0026
Wingfield, Suff T 123 TM 2376
Wingfield, Wilts T 101 ST 8256
Wingham T 99 TR 2457
Wingrave T 104 SP 8619
Win Green H 93 ST 9220
Winkburn T 140 SK 7158
Winkelbury A 94 ST 9521
Winkfield T 104 SU 9072
Winkfield Row T 104 SU 8970
Winkhill T 128 SK 0651
Winkleigh T 91 SS 6308
Winksley T 147 SE 2571
Winless T 199 ND 3054
Winmarleigh T 145 SD 4647
Winna Ness 205 HU 6098
Winnersh T 104 SU 7870
Winscales T 150 NY 0226
Winscar Reservoir W 138 SE 1502
Winscombe T 101 ST 4257
Winsford, Ches T 137 SJ 6566
Winsford, Somer T 91 SS 9034
Winsford Hill H 91 SS 8734
Winsham T 92 ST 3706
Winshill T 128 SK 2623
Winskill T 151 NY 5835
Winslade T 103 SU 6548
Winsley T 101 ST 8061
Winslow T 119 SP 7627
Winson T 114 SP 0908
Winster, Cumbr T 151 SD 4193
Winster, Derby T 139 SK 2460
Winston, Durham T 152 NZ 1416
Winston, Suff T 123 TM 1861
Winstone T 114 SO 9609
Winswell T 90 SS 4913
Winterborne Clenston T 93 ST 8303
Winterborne Herringston T 93 SY 6888
Winterborne Houghton T 93 ST 8104
Winterborne Kingston T 93 SY 8697
Winterborne Monkton T 93 SY 6787
Winterborne Stickland T 93 ST 8304
Winterborne Whitechurch T 93 ST 8300
Winterborne Zelston T 93 SY 8997
Winterbourne, Avon T 101 ST 6580
Winterbourne, Berks T 103 SU 4572
Winterbourne Abbas T 93 SY 6190
Winterbourne Bassett T 102 SU 1075
Winterbourne Dauntsey T 94 SU 1734
Winterbourne Earls T 94 SU 1734
Winterbourne Gunner T 94 SU 1834
Winterbourne Monkton T 102 SU 1072
Winterbourne Steepleton T 93 SY 6289
Winterbourne Stoke T 102 SU 0740
Winterburn T 146 SD 9358
Winterburn Reservoir W 146 SD 9460
Wintercleuch Fell H 156 NS 9910
Winter Hill H 137 SD 6615
Winterhope Reservoir W 157 NY 2782
Winteringham T 142 SE 9222
Winterley T 137 SJ 7457
Wintersett T 139 SE 3815
Wintershill T 95 SU 5217
Winterton T 142 SE 9218
Winterton-on-Sea T 133 TG 4919
Winthorpe, Lincs T 141 TF 5665
Winthorpe, Notts T 130 SK 8156
Winton, Cumbr T 151 NY 7810
Winton, Dorset T 94 SZ 0893
Winton Fell 151 NY 8307
Wintringham T 149 SE 8873
Winwick, Cambs T 120 TL 1080
Winwick, Northnts T 119 SP 6273
Winyates T 118 SP 0767
Wirksworth T 128 SK 2854
Wirral, Ches 136 SJ 3181
Wirral, Mers 136 SJ 3181
Wirswall T 127 SJ 5444
Wisbech P 131 TF 4609
Wisbech St Mary T 131 TF 4208
Wisborough Green T 96 TQ 0426
Wiseton T 140 SK 7189
Wishaw, Strath T 162 NS 7955
Wishaw, Warw T 128 SP 1794
Wisp Hill, Border H 157 NY 3899
Wisp Hill, D. & G H 157 NY 3899
Wispington T 141 TF 2071
Wissett T 123 TM 3679
Wiss, The H 157 NT 2620
Wistanstow T 116 SO 4385
Wistanswick T 127 SJ 6629
Wistaston T 127 SJ 6853
Wistlandpound Reservoir W 91 SS 6441
Wiston, Dyfed T 110 SN 0218
Wiston, Strath T 163 NS 9531
Wiston, W. Susx T 96 TQ 1413
Wiston Park 96 TQ 1512
Wistow, Cambs T 121 TL 2780
Wistow, N. Yks T 147 SE 5935
Wiswell T 145 SD 7437
Witcham T 121 TL 4679
Witchampton T 94 ST 9806
Witchford T 121 TL 5078
Witham T 106 TL 8115
Witham Friary T 101 ST 7440
Witham on the Hill T 130 TF 0516
Withens Clough Reservoir W 146 SD 9823
Witherenden Hill T 97 TQ 6426
Witheridge T 91 SS 8014
Witherley T 128 SP 3297
Withern T 141 TF 4382
Withernsea T 143 TA 3427
Withernwick T 143 TA 1940
Withersdale Street T 123 TM 2681
Withersfield T 122 TL 6547
Witherslack T 145 SD 4383
Witherslack Hall 145 SD 4386
Withiel T 87 SW 9965
Withiel Florey T 91 SS 9833
Withi Gill H 200 ND 2496
Withington, Ches T 137 SJ 8169
Withington, Glos T 114 SP 0315
Withington, G. Man T 137 SJ 8592
Withington, H. & W T 113 SO 5643
Withington, Shrops T 127 SJ 5713
Withington Green T 137 SJ 8071
Withleigh T 91 SS 9012
Withnell T 145 SD 6422
Withybrook T 118 SP 4384
Withycombe T 100 ST 0141
Withyham T 97 TQ 4935
Withypool T 91 SS 8435
Withypool Common 91 SS 8234
Witley T 96 SU 9440
Witnesham T 123 TM 1850
Witney T 115 SP 3509
Wittering T 130 TF 0502
Wittersham T 98 TQ 8927
Witton Bridge T 133 TG 3431
Witton Gilbert T 152 NZ 2345
Witton-le-Wear T 152 NZ 1431
Witton Park T 152 NZ 1730
Wiveliscombe T 92 ST 0827
Wivelsfield T 97 TQ 3420
Wivelsfield Green T 97 TQ 3519
Wivelsfield Station 97 TQ 3219
Wivenhoe T 107 TM 0322
Wiveton T 132 TG 0443
Wix T 123 TM 1628
Wixford T 118 SP 0954
Wixoe T 122 TL 7142
Woburn T 120 SP 9433
Woburn Abbey 120 SP 9632
Woburn Sands T 120 SP 9235
Woden Law H 158 NT 7612
Wokefield Park T 104 SU 6765
Woking T 104 TQ 0058
Wokingham T 104 SU 8068
Wold Fell 146 SD 7885
Woldingham T 97 TQ 3756
Wold Newton, Humbs T 149 TA 0473
Wold Newton, Humbs T 143 TF 2498
Wolds, The, Humbs H 149 SE 9763
Wolds, The, Lincs H 141 TF 2583
Wolferlow T 117 SO 6761
Wolferton T 132 TF 6528
Wolf Fell H 145 SD 6045
Wolfhill T 170 NO 1533
Wolfhole Crag 145 SD 6357
Wolf Rock 86 SW 2711
Wolf's Castle T 110 SM 9526
Wolfsdale T 110 SM 9321
Woll T 164 NT 4622
Wollaston, Northnts T 120 SP 9063
Wollaston, Shrops T 126 SJ 3312
Wollerton T 127 SJ 6230
Wolsingham T 152 NZ 0737
Wolsingham Park Moor 152 NZ 3040
Wolston T 118 SP 4175
Wolvercote T 115 SP 4909
Wolverhampton P 127 SO 9198
Wolverley, H. & W T 117 SO 8379
Wolverley, Shrops T 127 SJ 4731
Wolverton, Bucks T 120 SP 8140
Wolverton, Warw T 118 SP 2062
Wolveshewton T 113 ST 4599
Wolverton T 103 SU 5558
Wolvey T 118 SP 4387
Wolviston T 153 NZ 4525
Wombleton T 147 SE 6683
Wombourne T 127 SO 8793
Wombwell T 139 SE 3902
Womenswold T 99 TR 2250
Wonastow T 113 SO 4811
Wonersh T 96 TQ 0245
Wonson T 89 SX 6789
Wonston, Dorset T 93 ST 7408
Wonston, Hants T 103 SU 4739
Wooburn T 104 SU 9087
Wooburn Green T 104 SU 9189
Woodale T 146 SE 0279
Woodbastwick T 133 TG 3315
Woodbeck T 140 SK 7777
Woodborough, Notts T 129 SK 6347
Woodborough, Wilts T 102 SU 1159
Woodbridge T 123 TM 2747
Woodbury T 92 SY 0187
Woodbury Hill A 117 SO 7564
Woodbury Salterton T 92 SY 0188
Woodchester T 114 SO 8402
Woodchurch T 98 TQ 9434
Woodcote, Oxon T 104 SU 6481
Woodcote, Shrops 127 SJ 7615
Woodcroft T 113 ST 5495
Wood Dalling T 133 TG 0827
Woodeaton T 115 SP 5312
Woodend, Cumbr T 150 SD 1696
Wood End, Herts T 121 TL 3225
Woodend, Northnts T 119 SP 6149
Wood End, Warw T 118 SP 1071
Wood End, Warw T 128 SP 2498
Woodend, W. Susx 95 SU 8108
Wood Enderby T 141 TF 2763
Woodfalls T 94 SU 1920
Woodford, Corn T 90 SS 2113
Woodford, Devon T 89 SX 7950
Woodford, G. Lon T 105 TQ 4090
Woodford, G. Man T 137 SJ 8982
Woodford, Northnts T 120 SP 9677
Woodford Bridge T 105 TQ 4291
Woodford Green T 105 TQ 4192
Woodford Halse T 119 SP 5452
Woodgate, H. & W T 118 SO 9766
Woodgate, Norf T 132 TG 0216
Woodgate, W. Mids T 118 SO 9982
Woodgate, W. Susx T 96 SU 9304
Wood Green, G. Lon T 105 TQ 3090
Woodgreen, Hants T 94 SU 1717
Woodhall T 152 SD 9790
Woodhall Loch W 156 NX 6767
Woodhall Spa T 141 TF 1963
Woodham T 104 TQ 0362
Woodham Ferrers T 106 TQ 7999
Woodham Mortimer T 106 TL 8104
Woodham Walter T 106 TL 8007
Woodhaven T 171 NO 4026
Woodhead, Grampn T 185 NJ 7938
Woodhead, Grampn 185 NJ 8961
Woodhenge A 102 SU 1543
Woodhill T 117 SO 7384
Woodhorn T 159 NZ 2989
Woodhouse, Leic T 129 SK 5415
Woodhouse, S. Yks T 139 SK 4185
Woodhouse Eaves T 129 SK 5314
Woodhouselee T 163 NT 2464
Woodhurst T 121 TL 3176
Woodingdean T 97 TQ 3605
Woodditton T 122 TL 6558
Woodland, Devon T 89 SX 7968
Woodland, Durham T 152 NZ 0726
Woodland Bay W 154 NX 1795
Woodland Fell, Cumbr 150 SD 2689
Woodland Fell, Durham 152 NZ 0325
Woodlands, Dorset T 94 SU 0509
Woodlands, Grampn T 177 NO 7895
Woodlands, Hants T 94 SU 3211
Woodlands Park T 104 SU 8578
Woodlands St Mary T 102 SU 3474
Wood Lanes T 137 SJ 9381
Woodleigh T 89 SX 7348
Woodlesford T 147 SE 3629
Woodley T 104 SU 7673
Woodmancote, Glos T 114 SP 0009
Woodmancote, W. Susx T 95 SU 7707
Woodmancote, W. Susx T 96 TQ 2314
Woodmancott T 103 SU 5642
Woodmansey T 142 TA 0537
Woodmansterne T 105 TQ 2760
Woodminton T 94 SU 0022
Woodnesborough T 99 TR 3056
Woodnewton T 130 TL 0394
Wood Norton T 132 TG 0127
Wood of Ordiequish F 184 NJ 3655
Woodplumpton T 145 SD 5034
Woodrising T 132 TF 9803
Woodseaves, Shrops T 127 SJ 6830
Woodseaves, Staffs T 127 SJ 8025
Woodsend T 102 SU 2276
Woodsetts T 139 SK 5583
Woodsford T 93 SY 7690
Woodside, Berks T 104 SU 9371
Woodside, Herts T 105 TL 2506
Woodside, Tays T 176 NO 2037
Woodstock T 115 SP 4416
Wood Street T 96 SU 9551
Woodthorpe, Derby T 139 SK 4574
Woodthorpe, Leic T 129 SK 5417
Woodton T 133 TM 2993
Woodtown T 90 SS 4925
Woodville T 128 SK 3119
Woodwalton T 121 TL 2180
Wood Wick W 200 HY 3923
Woodyates T 94 SU 0219
Woody Bay W 91 SS 6849
Woofferton T 116 SO 5268
Wookey T 101 ST 5145
Wookey Hole T 101 ST 5347
Wool T 93 SY 8486
Woolacombe T 90 SS 4543
Woolage Green T 99 TR 2349
Woolaston T 113 ST 5899
Woolavington T 100 ST 3441
Woolbeding T 95 SU 8722
Wooler T 165 NT 9928
Wooley House 102 SU 4179
Woolfardisworthy, Devon T 90 SS 3124
Woolfardisworthy, Devon T 91 SS 8208
Woolfords Cottages T 163 NT 0057
Woolhampton T 103 SU 5766
Woolhope T 113 SO 6135
Woolland T 93 ST 7707
Woolley, Cambs T 120 TL 1574
Woolley, W. Yks T 139 SE 3213
Woolmer Green T 105 TL 2518
Woolpit T 122 TL 9762
Woolscott T 119 SP 4967
Woolsington T 159 NZ 1970
Woolstaston T 126 SO 4598
Woolsthorpe T 130 SK 8333
Woolston, Ches T 137 SJ 6489
Woolston, Devon T 89 SX 7141
Woolston, Hants T 94 SU 4310
Woolston, Shrops T 126 SJ 3224
Woolston, Shrops T 116 SO 4287
Woolstone, Bucks T 120 SP 8638
Woolstone, Oxon T 102 SU 2987
Woolston Green T 89 SX 7766
Wooltack Point 110 SM 7509
Woolton T 136 SJ 4286
Woolton Hill T 102 SU 4361
Woolverstone T 123 TM 1838
Woolverton T 101 ST 7953
Woolwich T 105 TQ 4478
Woore T 127 SJ 7342
Woorton T 115 SP 4319
Wooton, Northnts T 119 SP 7656
Wooton, Oxon T 115 SP 4702
Wooton, Staffs T 128 SK 1045
Wooton Rivers T 102 SU 1963
Wooton St Lawrence T 103 SU 5953
Wootton, Beds T 120 TL 0045
Wootton, Hants T 94 SZ 2498
Wootton, Humbs T 143 TA 0916
Wootton, Kent T 99 TR 2246
Wootton, Oxon T 115 SP 4702
Wootton, Staffs T 127 SJ 8227
Wootton Bassett T 102 SU 0783
Wootton Bridge T 95 SZ 5491
Wootton Common T 95 SZ 5391
Wootton Courtenay T 91 SS 9343
Wootton Fitzpaine T 92 SY 3695
Wootton Wawen T 118 SP 1563
Worbarrow Bay W 93 SY 8679
Worcester P 117 SO 8555
Worcester and Birmingham Canal W 117 SO 9465
Worcester Park T 105 TQ 2266
Wordsley T 117 SO 8987
Worfield T 127 SO 7595
Work 200 HY 4713
Workington P 150 NX 9928
Worksop P 139 SK 5879
Worlaby T 142 TA 0113
World's End, Berks T 103 SU 4876
World's End, Clwyd 126 SJ 2347
Worle T 100 ST 3562
Worlebury A 100 ST 3162
Worleston T 127 SJ 6556
Worlingham T 123 TM 4489
Worlington, Cambs T 122 TL 6973
Worlington, Devon T 91 SS 7713
Worlingworth T 123 TM 2268
Wormbridge T 113 SO 4331
Wormegay T 132 TF 6611
Wormelow Tump T 113 SO 4930
Wormersley T 139 SE 5319
Wormhill T 138 SK 1274
Wormiehills T 177 NO 6139
Wormingford T 122 TL 9331
Worminghall T 104 SP 6408
Wormington T 118 SP 0436
Worminster T 101 ST 5742
Wormit T 171 NO 3926
Wormleighton T 119 SP 4453
Wormley T 105 TL 3605
Wormley West End T 105 TL 3305
Worms Head or Penryn-gwyr 108 SS 3887
Wormshill T 98 TQ 8857
Wormsley T 113 SO 4247
Worplesdon T 96 SU 9753
Worrall T 139 SK 3092
Worsbrough T 139 SE 3503
Worsley T 137 SD 7501
Worstead T 133 TG 3026
Worsthorne T 146 SD 8732
Worston T 146 SD 7642
Worth, Kent T 99 TR 3356
Worth, W. Susx T 97 TQ 2936
Worth Abbey 97 TQ 3134
Wortham T 123 TM 0877
Worthen T 126 SJ 3204
Worthenbury T 126 SJ 4246
Worthing, Norf T 132 TF 9919
Worthing, W. Susx P 96 TQ 1402
Worthington T 128 SK 4020
Worth Matravers T 94 SY 9777
Worthy Down H 95 SU 4534
Wortley T 139 SK 3099
Worton T 102 ST 9757
Wortwell T 123 TM 2784
Wotherton T 126 SJ 2800
Wotter T 89 SX 5561
Wotton T 96 TQ 1247
Wotton-under-Edge T 114 ST 7593
Wotton Underwood T 104 SP 6816
Woughton on the Green T 120 SP 8737
Wouldham T 98 TQ 7164
Wrabness T 123 TM 1731
Wrafton T 90 SS 4935
Wragby T 141 TF 1378
Wrakendike R 159 NZ 3262
Wramplingham T 133 TG 1106
Wrangham T 184 NJ 6331
Wrangle T 131 TF 4250
Wrangway T 92 ST 1217
Wrantage T 92 ST 3022
Wrawby T 142 TA 0108
Wraxall, Avon T 101 ST 4972
Wraxall, Somer T 93 ST 6036
Wraxall, Wilts T 101 ST 8364
Wray T 145 SD 6067
Wray Castle 151 NY 3701
Wraysbury T 104 TQ 0073
Wrea Green T 145 SD 3931
Wreay, Cumbr T 151 NY 4349
Wreay, Cumbr T 151 NY 4423
Wrekenton T 159 NZ 2759
Wrekin, The H 127 SJ 6308
Wrelton T 148 SE 7686
Wrenbury T 127 SJ 5947
Wreningham T 133 TM 1698

Y

Z

ORDNANCE SURVEY PRODUCTS

Ordnance Survey produces and publishes maps in a variety of forms and scales described below, beginning with large-scale maps from which the wide range of small-scale maps are derived.

LARGE SCALE MAPS
Highly detailed maps of Great Britain for people that need accurate large-scale information.

1:1250 scale maps (1 cm to 12·5 metres or 50 inches to 1 mile)
These are the largest scale maps published by the Ordnance Survey and are available for cities and other significant urban areas throughout Britain. There are over 50,000 maps in this series. Each map represents an area of 500 m by 500 m and carries Natioanl Grid lines at 100 metre intervals. Every building, road and most other features are shown, even post boxes. Street names, house names or numbers are included as well as administrative amd parliamentary boundaries. Height information and some survey control points are also shown.

1:2500 scale maps (1 cm to 25 metres or 25 inches to 1 mile)
These maps cover all parts of the country other than significant urban areas (1:1250) and mountain and moorland areas (1:10 000 scale). Normally each plan covers an area of 2 km east to west by 1 km north to south. National Grid lines are shown at 100 metre intervals. Areas of land parcels are given in acres and hectares as well as features shown on 1:1250 scale maps.

1:10 000 scale maps (1 cm to 100 metres or about 6 inches to 1 mile)
These maps cover the whole country. They are also the largest scale of mapping to cover mountain and moorland and to show contours. Some maps are at 1:10 560 scale with contours at 25 feet intervals, but they are being replaced by 1:10 000 scale maps with contours at 10 metre intervals in mountainous areas and 5 metre intervals elsewhere.

Updated Survey Information
Two services are provided to make the latest 1:1250 and 1:2500 scales survey information available before a new edition map is printed.

SUSI (Supply of Updated Survey Information) provides the most up-to-date large-scale information available. Anyone can call at their local Ordnance Survey office (listed in the Telephone Directory) and order a copy of the surveyor's working document known as Master Survey Drawings (MSD's) on paper or film.

SIM (Survey Information on Microfilm) provides copies of MSD's after a fixed amount of survey change has been recorded. These copies at original map scale are available through Ordnance Survey Agents either on paper or film. Copies of current edition 1:1250 and 1:2500 maps are also provided through the SIM service.

DIGITAL MAPPING
A growing number of 1:1250 and 1:2500 scale maps are available on magnetic tape in the form of numerical co-ordinates suitable for computer manipulation. Data on the tape can be recalled to produce an exact scale map copy or a larger or smaller scale copy as required. Furthermore selected detail can be recalled rather than the whole map.

A digital topographic database from maps at 1:625 000 scale (10 miles to 1 inch) has also been developed by Ordnance Survey and is now available. The structure of the data allows feature selection by location, type or name, the extraction of information for a named area, and the analysis of road or river networks.

SMALL SCALE MAPS
Pathfinder Maps 1:25 000 scale (4 cm to 1 km or 2½ inches to 1 mile)
These coloured maps are ideal for the walker or rambler showing the countryside in great detail with footpaths, rights of way in England and Wales and field boundaries. The maps normally cover an area 20 km (12½ miles) east to west by 10 km (6¼ miles) north to south. Coverage of the country by Pathfinder mapping will be complete by 1990.

Outdoor Leisure Maps 1:25 000 scale (4 cm to 1 km or 2½ inches to 1 mile)
This series covers selected popular leisure and recreation areas of the country. Packed with detail they are invaluable to the serious walker or climber. A wealth of tourist information makes them equally popular with the less dedicated outdoor enthusiast. The area covered by the map varies but is much larger than the Pathfinder.

Landranger Maps 1:50 000 scale (2 cm to 1 km or about 1¼ inches to 1 mile)
Landranger maps are suitable for motoring, walking, educational and business purposes. The series covers the whole of the country in 204 sheets. Each map covers an area of 40 km by 40 km (25 miles by 25 miles). All show tourist information, and sheets covering England and Wales include public rights of way. Like other Ordnance Survey maps National Grid squares are provided so that any feature can be given a unique reference number.

Tourist Maps 1:63 360 scale (1 inch to 1 mile) and 1:50 000 scale
These maps cover popular touring and holiday areas and are designed to help visitors explore the countryside in detail. The mapping is enhanced with additional tourist information and some include a useful guide to the area. Public rights of way are also shown.

Routemaster Maps 1:250 000 scale (1 cm to 2·5 km or 1 inch to 4 miles)
Nine Routemaster maps cover Great Britain. They are designed for the motorist to help find the shortest or most scenic route. The maps are regularly revised and show motorways, trunk main and secondary routes prominently depicted to ease map reading. Colour shading and contours are used to depict relief. Road distances and tourist information are also included.

Great Britain Routeplanner 1:625 000 scale (1 cm to 6·25 km or approximately 1 inch to 10 miles)
This map covers the whole of Great Britain on one sheet. Southern England and Wales appear on one side with Northern England and Scotland on the other. Frequently updated, the map also features inset diagrams of major towns, and National Parks, Forest Parks and areas of outstanding natural beauty. A mileage chart and gazetteer of towns and cities is also included.

OTHER PRODUCTS AND FURTHER INFORMATION
Further information on Ordnance Survey products and services can be obtained from Information and Enquiries, Ordnance Survey, Romsey Road, Maybush, Southampton, SO9 4DH.

Key to 1:250 000 Maps, atlas pages 86-205

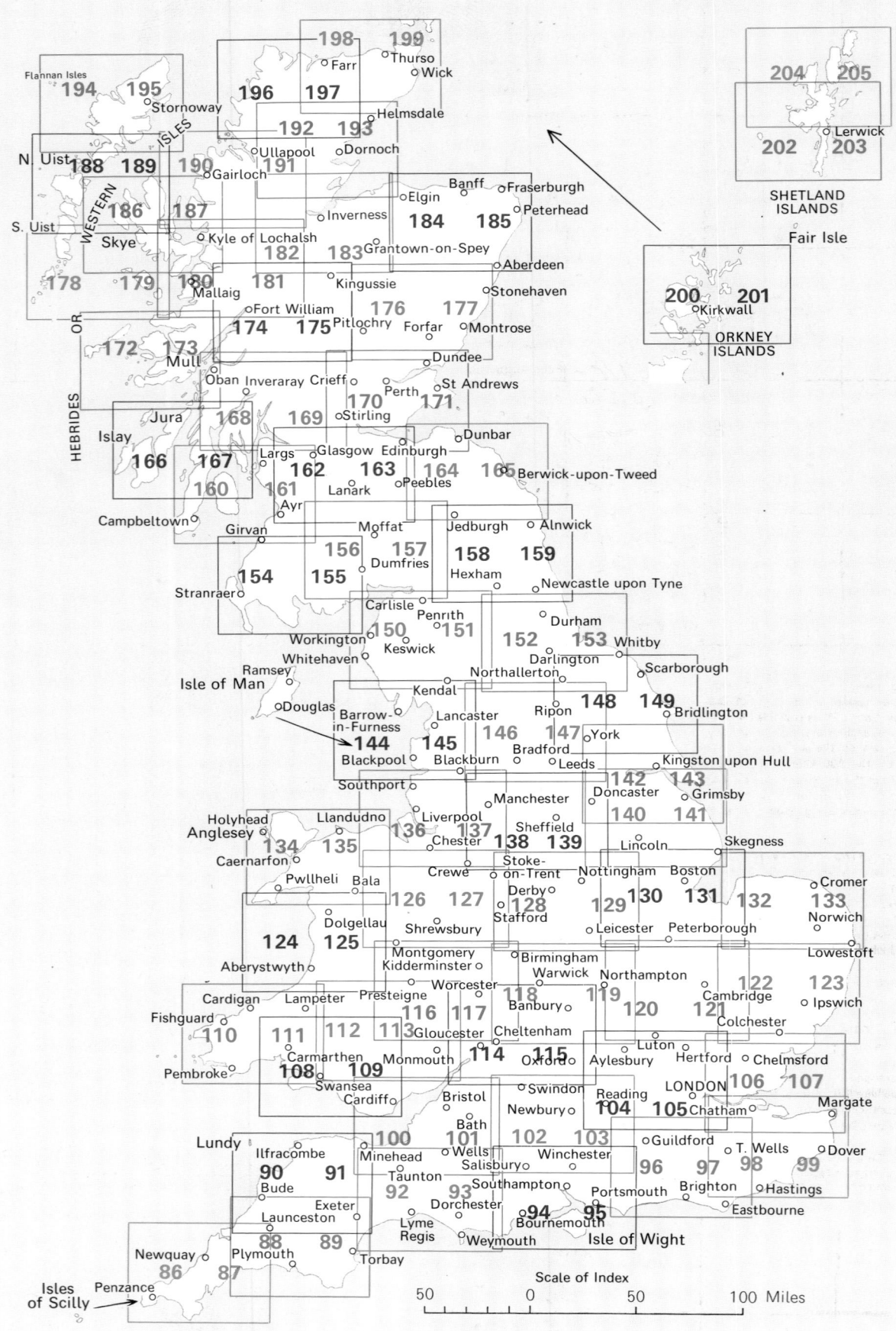

Flannan Isles
194 195
Stornoway
ISLES
198 199
Farr
Thurso
Wick
196 197
Helmsdale
192 193
Ullapool
Dornoch
N. Uist 188 189 190
Gairloch
191
WESTERN
186 187
S. Uist
Skye
Kyle of Lochalsh
182 183
Grantown-on-Spey
178 179 180
Mallaig
181
Kingussie
174 175
Fort William
Pitlochry Forfar
176 177
172 173
Mull
Oban Inveraray Crieff
170 171
Perth St Andrews
168 169
Stirling
Jura
Islay
166 167
160
161
154 155
Stranraer

Elgin Banff Fraserburgh
Inverness
184 185
Peterhead
Aberdeen
Stonehaven
Montrose
Dundee
Dunbar
Largs Glasgow Edinburgh
162 163 164 165 Berwick-upon-Tweed
Lanark Peebles
Ayr
Moffat Jedburgh Alnwick
156 157 158 159
Dumfries Hexham Newcastle upon Tyne
Carlisle Penrith Durham
Workington 150 151 152 153 Whitby
Keswick Darlington Scarborough
Whitehaven Northallerton
Ramsey
Isle of Man Kendal 148 149 Bridlington
Douglas Lancaster Ripon
Barrow-in-Furness 146 147 York
144 145 Bradford Leeds Kingston upon Hull
Blackpool Blackburn
Southport 142 143 Grimsby
Manchester Doncaster
Llandudno 140 141
Holyhead Liverpool
Anglesey 136 137 Sheffield Lincoln Skegness
Caernarfon Chester 138 139 Cromer
Pwllheli Bala Crewe Stoke-on-Trent Nottingham Boston
Derby 129 130 131 132 133 Norwich
126 127 128 Leicester Peterborough Lowestoft
124 125 Shrewsbury Stafford
Dolgellau Birmingham 122 123
Aberystwyth Montgomery Warwick Northampton Ipswich
Kidderminster 118 119 Cambridge
Cardigan Lampeter Presteigne Worcester 120 121 Colchester
110 111 112 113 Gloucester Banbury Luton
Fishguard Carmarthen Monmouth 114 115 Chelmsford
Pembroke 108 109 Oxford Aylesbury Hertford
Swansea Cheltenham LONDON 106 107
Cardiff Bristol Swindon Reading Margate
Bath Newbury 104 105 Chatham
Lundy 100 101 102 103 Guildford T. Wells Dover
Ilfracombe Minehead Wells Winchester 96 97 98 99
90 91 Taunton Salisbury Southampton Brighton Hastings
Bude 92 93 Portsmouth Eastbourne
Exeter Dorchester 94 95
Newquay Launceston 88 89 Lyme Bournemouth Isle of Wight
86 Plymouth Torbay Weymouth
Penzance 87
Isles of Scilly

Fair Isle

204 205
202 203
SHETLAND ISLANDS

200 201
Kirkwall
ORKNEY ISLANDS

Scale of Index
50   0   50   100 Miles